MW01640229

Handbook of Research on Civic Engagement in Youth

Editors

Lonnie R. Sherrod

Judith Torney-Purta

Constance A. Flanagan

John Wiley & Sons, Inc.

This book is printed on acid-free paper. ♾

Copyright © 2010 by John Wiley & Sons, Inc. All rights reserved.

Published by John Wiley & Sons, Inc., Hoboken, New Jersey.
Published simultaneously in Canada.

No part of this publication may be reproduced, stored in a retrieval system, or transmitted in any form or by any means, electronic, mechanical, photocopying, recording, scanning, or otherwise, except as permitted under Section 107 or 108 of the 1976 United States Copyright Act, without either the prior written permission of the Publisher, or authorization through payment of the appropriate per-copy fee to the Copyright Clearance Center, Inc., 222 Rosewood Drive, Danvers, MA 01923, (978) 750-8400, fax (978) 646-8600, or on the web at www.copyright.com. Requests to the Publisher for permission should be addressed to the Permissions Department, John Wiley & Sons, Inc., 111 River Street, Hoboken, NJ 07030, (201) 748-6011, fax (201) 748-6008.

Limit of Liability/Disclaimer of Warranty: While the publisher and author have used their best efforts in preparing this book, they make no representations or warranties with respect to the accuracy or completeness of the contents of this book and specifically disclaim any implied warranties of merchantability or fitness for a particular purpose. No warranty may be created or extended by sales representatives or written sales materials. The advice and strategies contained herein may not be suitable for your situation. You should consult with a professional where appropriate. Neither the publisher nor author shall be liable for any loss of profit or any other commercial damages, including but not limited to special, incidental, consequential, or other damages.

This publication is designed to provide accurate and authoritative information in regard to the subject matter covered. It is sold with the understanding that the publisher is not engaged in rendering professional services. If legal, accounting, medical, psychological or any other expert assistance is required, the services of a competent professional person should be sought.

Designations used by companies to distinguish their products are often claimed as trademarks. In all instances where John Wiley & Sons, Inc. is aware of a claim, the product names appear in initial capital or all capital letters. Readers, however, should contact the appropriate companies for more complete information regarding trademarks and registration.

For general information on our other products and services please contact our Customer Care Department within the U.S. at (800) 762-2974, outside the United States at (317) 572-3993 or fax (317) 572-4002.

Wiley also publishes its books in a variety of electronic formats. Some content that appears in print may not be available in electronic books. For more information about Wiley products, visit our web site at www.wiley.com.

Library of Congress Cataloging-in-Publication Data Handbook of research on civic engagement in youth / editors, Lonnie R. Sherrod, Judith Torney-Purta, Constance A. Flanagan.
p. cm.
Includes index.
ISBN 978-0-470-52274-5 (cloth); 9780470636787 (ePDF); 9780470636794 (eMobi); 9780470636800 (ePub); 9780470767603 (O-Bk).
1. Youth—Political aspects—Handbooks, manuals, etc. 2. Political participation—Handbooks, manuals, etc. 3. Social action—Handbooks, manuals, etc. I. Sherrod, Lonnie R. II. Torney-Purta, Judith, 1937–. III. Flanagan, Constance A.
HQ799.2.P6H36 2010
323′.0420835—dc22

2009054054

Printed in the United States of America

10 9 8 7 6 5 4 3 2 1

Contents

Contributors

Jo-Ann Amadeo
University of Maryland
College Park, MD

Erik Amnå
Örebro University
Örebro, Sweden

Molly Andolina
DePaul University
Chicago, IL

Jennifer Astuto
New York University
New York, NY

Elizabeth Beaumont
University of Minnesota
Minneapolis, MN

W. Lance Bennett
University of Washington
Seattle, WA

Charmagne Campbell-Patton
World Savvy
Minneapolis, MN

Sergio Cardenas
Col. Lomas de Santa Fe
México, D.F.

Jason Lee Crockett
University of Arizona
Tucson, AZ

Michelle Fine
The Graduate Center, City
University of New York
New York, NY

Andrea Finlay
The Pennsylvania State University
University Park, PA

Constance Flanagan
The Pennsylvania State University
University Park, PA, and
University of Wisconsin
Madison, WI

Madeline Fox
The Graduate Center
City University of New York
New York, NY

Deen Freelon
University of Washington
Seattle, WA

Rebecca Lakin Gullan
The Children's Hospital of
Pennsylvania and
Gwynedd-Mercy College
Gwynedd Valley, PA

Daniel Hart
Rutgers University
Camden, NJ

Helen Haste
Harvard University
Cambridge, MA, and
University of Bath
Bath, United Kingdom

Diana Hess
University of Wisconsin-Madison
Madison, WI

Ann Higgins-D'Alessandro
Fordham University
Bronx, NY

Lene Arnett Jensen
Clark University
Worcester, MA

Ronald Kassimir
The New School
New York, NY

Janet Kwok
Harvard University
Cambridge, MA

Carolyn Laub
Gay-Straight Alliance Network
San Francisco, CA

James Lauckhardt
Fordham University
Bronx, NY

Nam-Jin Lee
University of Wisconsin-Madison
Madison, WI

Peter Levine
Tufts University
Medford, MA

Meira Levinson
Harvard University
Cambridge, MA

Hugh McIntosh
Consultant
Oakton, VA

Jack McLeod
University of Wisconsin
Madison, WI

Kavitha Mediratta
Brown University
New York, NY

Aaron Metzger
West Virginia University
Morgantown, WV

Michael Quinn Patton
Utilization-Focused Evaluation
Saint Paul, MN

Fernando Reimers
Harvard University
Cambridge, MA

Martin D. Ruck
The Graduate Center, City University of New York
New York, NY

Jessica Ruglis
Johns Hopkins Bloomberg School of Public Health
Baltimore, MD

Stephen T. Russell
University of Arizona
Tucson, AZ

Hinda Seif
University of Illinois at Springfield
Springfield, IL

Robert L. Selman
Harvard University
Cambridge, MA

Dhavan Shah
University of Wisconsin-Madison
Madison, WI

Seema Shah
International Baccalaureate
New York, NY

Lonnie R Sherrod
Society for Research in Child Development
Ann Arbor, MI and
Fordham University
Bronx, NY

Judith G. Smetana
University of Rochester
Rochester, NY

Tara M. Stoppa
Eastern University
St. Davids, PA

Brett Stoudt
John Jay College
City University of New York
New York, NY

Michael Stout
Missouri State University
Springfield, MO

Amy K. Syvertsen
The Pennsylvania State University
University Park, PA
Search Institute
Minneapolis, MN

Russell B. Toomey
University of Arizona
Tucson, AZ

Judith Torney-Purta
University of Maryland
College Park, MD

Chris Wells
University of Washington
Seattle, WA

Britt Wilkenfeld
University of Maryland
College Park, MD

Laura Wray-Lake
The Pennsylvania State University
University Park, PA
Claremont Graduate University
Claremont, CA

James Youniss
The Catholic University of America
Washington, DC

Pär Zetterberg
Uppsala University
Uppsala, Sweden

Preface: Promoting Research on Youth Civic Engagement

This Handbook is the final product of a consortium of researchers from multiple disciplines who focused on youth political development. This Consortium funded by the William T. Grant Foundation was formed in fall 2000, as the first editor of this Handbook left the vice presidency of the Foundation. The Foundation devoted funds to this effort, because of its recognition that citizenship is as important to adult functioning as work or family. Yet the topic of citizenship has received far less attention from researchers. The Consortium had five aims: (1) to promote research on youth civic development, (2) to identify the areas where research is needed, (3) to explore research strategies and methods, (4) to serve as a clearinghouse for research in the area and to develop networks as a means of fostering collaborations, and (5) to promote consideration of research/practice interactions in the area. This Handbook, although not specifically addressing each of these goals, represents the culmination of the Consortium's almost 10-year history. The authors of this Handbook were asked to summarize research and especially to consider multidisciplinary work, international perspectives, and implications for policy, each of which relates to the Consortium's goals.

Core members of the Consortium in addition to the founder and organizer Lonnie Sherrod include: LaRue Allen, New York University; William Damon, Stanford University; Constance Flanagan, Pennsylvania State University and now the University of Wisconsin-Madison; Alan Gitelson, Loyola University, Chicago; Daniel Hart, Rutgers University; Ron Kassimir, Social Science Research Council (SSRC) and now The New School; Jack McLeod, University of Wisconsin; Steven Russell, Arizona State University; Alex Stepick, Florida International University; Judith Torney-Purta, University of Maryland; and James Youniss, Catholic University. Guests at Consortium meetings included: Michael Delli Carpini, Pew Charitable Trusts and now the Annenberg School at the University of Pennsylvania; Cynthia Gibson, Carnegie Corporation of New York; Lisa Sullivan, LISTEN; Harry Boyte, University of Minnesota; as well as graduate students from Fordham and Grant Foundation staff. The Consortium's first goal, which was to promote research on youth civic engagement, was of most importance to the group, and we believe we have been successful in this regard.

Eight meetings were held. Practitioners and staff from interested foundations, for example, were invited or informed of meetings and their results. Many of these individuals participated in publications including authoring chapters in this Handbook. Within a few years of the establishment of the group, two major publications emerged: a special issue of *Applied Developmental Science,* October 2002, edited by Lonnie Sherrod, Constance Flanagan, and James Youniss; and an *Encyclopedia of Youth Activism*, edited by Lonnie Sherrod, Constance Flanagan, Ron Kassimir, and Amy Syvertsen, published by Greenwood Press in 2005.

One of the Consortium's major accomplishments was the publication of the special issue of the journal *Applied Developmental Science* on youth civic development in fall 2002. It contained summary articles and empirical research articles in a variety of relevant areas. This issue was one of the first efforts to examine civic development in minority youth, including sexual minority youth, and it is now cited widely. Furthermore, additional copies of this journal were purchased and mailed to a list of nearly 500 policy-makers, foundation executives, program directors, and other researchers. The Foundation's mailing list was a basic source for identifying these opinion leaders in this field.

It is of course impossible to say that these publications were the direct cause of the developments we describe for the field. Nonetheless, we believe that research on civic engagement has grown in both popularity and perceived importance during this period. When the Consortium began in 2000, the only sessions on related topics at meetings such as the Society for Research in Child Development or the Society for Research on Adolescence were those organized by Consortium members. Now sessions are numerous, there have been preconferences, and *citizenship* and *civic engagement* have become established as keywords in the submission process. Both the Annenberg and Spencer Foundations are considering or are launching initiatives in the area. Consortium members routinely receive applications from graduate students interested in the topic. Relevant items have been added to studies such as Add Health and there already have been multiple publications based on these data. Interdisciplinary and comparative studies have begun in several European nations. Several senior researchers in social development more generally have added the topic to their repertoire of research interests. In fact, we believe the field has matured to the point where this Handbook is needed.

Our publications have explicitly addressed our second goal, which is to identify areas where research is needed. Each chapter in the Handbook, for example, addresses research needs and policy implications. The project's goal was field development, not generation of new knowledge per se. However, we have been successful in promoting research on the topic of urban disadvantaged and minority youth, immigrant youth, and sexual minority young people.

In fulfilling its third goal the Consortium has explored methods of research on youth civic engagement and has formulated a list of available datasets to support research on civic engagement; one example is the National Longitudinal Survey of Youth (NLSY), with which member Daniel Hart has worked. Member Constance Flanagan worked with the Add Health study to add a module on civic engagement in the last round of data collection. Since the mid-1990s Judith Torney-Purta had been leading the International Association for the Evaluation of Educational Achievement (IEA) Civic Education Study, which surveyed 140,000 adolescents in 28 countries on several dimensions of civic engagement. These data are available for use by researchers. Working with schools to conduct new data collection is proving to be difficult for researchers in all parts of the country, and the Consortium has explored vehicles for doing research with youth other than the usual survey approach. For example, Lonnie Sherrod held focus groups of youth in the Bronx in order to obtain youth input into the research agenda.

The Consortium has established lasting contacts with other relevant organizations such as the SSRC Committee on Youth Development, CIRCLE (Center for Information and Research on Civic Learning and Engagement), the Carnegie Corporation of New York, the Spencer Foundation, the Pew Charitable Trusts, and others. Representatives from these organizations have attended Consortium meetings.

We believe the Consortium has been successful, and this Handbook, the first in this area, is a major reflection of that success. The purpose of this resource volume is to present the state of the field. With sections on conceptualization and definition (including international and multidisciplinary perspectives), development and developmental influences, and measurement and methods of research, the volume aims to be comprehensive. Each author was invited to address both research needs and implications for policy. A number of early career scholars who were not members of the Consortium were invited to contribute chapters. The extension of the grant allowed a meeting in New York City in May 2008 of contributors, at which summaries of chapters were presented. This meeting contributed greatly to the overall quality of the volume.

The fourth and fifth aims of the Consortium have been dealt with as we have discussed other aspects of the collaborative work. In fact, it is impossible to list all the publications of all consortium members influenced by their participation because for many it would involve listing all of their publications during the past 10 years. However, the following publications were produced by the Consortium:

Sherrod, L. R., Flanagan, C., Kassimir, R., & Bertelsen, A. (Edss.). (2005). *Youth activism: An international encyclopedia*. New York: Greenwood Publishing Group.

Sherrod, L. R., Flanagan, C., & Youniss, J. (Eds.). (2002). Growing into citizenship: Multiple pathways and diverse influences. A special issue of *Applied Developmental Science*, 6(4).

Sherrod, L. R., Torney-Purta, J., & Flanagan, C. (2010). *Handbook of research on civic engagement in youth*. Hoboken, NJ: John Wiley & Sons, Inc.

PRODUCTION PROCESS

The idea for the Handbook was hatched and a skeleton outline created at a meeting of the Consortium about midpoint in its history. Authors then met at a meeting in May 2008, and presented preliminary drafts of the papers; and the current editorship trio was formed. Subsequently, a number of chapters were added to round out the coverage. Not every member of the Consortium was able to contribute a chapter but no one dropped out after their initial commitment. Quite the contrary, almost everyone we contacted to contribute a chapter willingly agreed to do so.

When chapter drafts were received, the first and third editors read each one and offered comments to the authors. This review particularly addressed the extent to which the chapter addressed multidisciplinary, international, or policy issues. These same two editors then read revisions and if no further substantive change was merited, the chapter was read by the second editor who reviewed at a more fine-grained level, checking for style, overlap across chapters, and so forth.

ACKNOWLEDGMENTS

There are numerous folks to thank. Patricia (Tisha) Rossi at Wiley was tremendously patient and understanding, and offered a wealth of information and advice. Anne Perdue on the Society for Research in Child Development (SRCD) staff provided absolutely invaluable administrative support helping us keep track of different versions of each chapter and generally staying on task. Robert Granger and Ed Seidman at the William T. Grant Foundation were heroic in allowing us to extend the Consortium grant to probably the longest in Foundation history, and Sharon Brewster deserves a big thank-you for dealing with the administrative headaches this inevitably created. Finally, we thank each author for tolerating our obsessive and constant requests for more work.

INTRODUCTION

Research on the Development of Citizenship: A Field Comes of Age

LONNIE R. SHERROD
Society for Research in Child Development and Fordham University

JUDITH TORNEY-PURTA
University of Maryland

CONSTANCE FLANAGAN
The Pennsylvania State University and University of Wisconsin-Madison

THE PUBLICATION OF a handbook signals that a field has come of age, that there is a sufficient body of research and a large enough cohort of researchers to merit a substantial summary of the field. We believe that the field of youth civic engagement has come of age. There are now numerous scholars across many disciplines and throughout the world working in this area. There have been a number of important publications. Most meetings of professional associations in psychology, education, political science, and sociology include sessions on the topic of civic engagement. Many peer-reviewed journals now have both theoretical and empirical research articles and there is a new generation of scholars from different disciplines committed to this topic. Policy-makers and practitioners are increasingly looking for research to guide their efforts because they recognize the importance to democracies of investing in the development of citizenship. In summary, audiences ranging from senior professors to graduate students, from those with policy-making responsibilities to advocates for changes in youth or education policy, from school or program administrators to teachers and youth workers, from journalists to publishers of educational materials need a handbook such as this. The fact that individuals in one discipline who study this field are often unaware of the work done by those in other disciplines is a compelling argument for this as an interdisciplinary volume.

While the field has come of age, it is still young. This is its first handbook. The senior editor of this publication used to begin every paper with a call for research on civic engagement: Functioning as a citizen is as important an adult behavior as working or raising a family, yet developmental science has until recently ignored civic engagement, focusing overwhelmingly on cognitive and social development leading to work or family formation.

There were surges of research on civic engagement or political socialization, as it has often been called, in the 1960s and early 1970s (reviewed by Flanagan & Sherrod, 1998). The second editor of this Handbook has been studying the topic since 1960, as a number of these *waves of attention* crested and then receded (Torney-Purta, 2009). The historical perspective is an explicit part of the chapters by Astuto and Ruck; Torney-Purta, Amadeo, and Andolina; and Higgins-D'Alessandro, while the contested nature of the meaning of citizenship and of civic education in the current globalizing era is discussed by Haste and by Kassimir and Flanagan.

It was a new wave of attention in the 1990s that resulted in the field coming of age. Many of the chapter authors comment on the worldwide upsurge in interest at this time in citizenship education and concerns about the engagement of youth as citizens. Concerns for the rights of children in international accords such as the United Nations Declaration on the Rights of the Child demand attention to participation opportunities for children and youth (Ruck, Abramovitch, & Keating, 1998), and many governments have placed these rights high on their agendas (Torney-Purta, Wilkenfeld, & Barber, 2008).

Many scholars have argued that the current wave of attention to this area was prompted in part by Robert Putnam's landmark declaration that many countries in the developed world, especially the United States, face a crisis in terms of declining levels of civic involvement of younger generations (1996, 2000). The fall of the Berlin Wall followed by monumental political and educational changes in Eastern Europe set the stage for attention to this area. Research increased markedly during the 1990s, and now almost two decades later, the field has come of age and this Handbook can serve to further develop the research area.

The field of youth civic engagement has been enriched by interdisciplinary work linking political science and developmental psychology. This has resulted in a broadened conceptualization of civic participation that goes beyond voting and electoral politics. In addition, the field has benefited from two theoretical perspectives in the broader field of human development: a life-span or life-course approach is one, and positive youth development is the other. We briefly review each of these issues before describing the goals and nature of this Handbook.

THEORETICAL PERSPECTIVES

A life-span perspective has not been well used in research on child and adolescent development, although it has been important to studies of adult development. We argue that it has also been important to research on youth civic development. A positive youth development (PYD) perspective is on the other hand an increasingly important force in research on adolescent and youth development. Although PYD acknowledges the importance of the development of citizenship, research on civic engagement has not been explicit about the role played by a focus on positive development.

A Life-Span or Life-Course Perspective

Ideas and methods from life-span research arose in the 1970s and have become increasingly popular across the succeeding decades. The life-span perspective (so-called by psychologists) or life-course perspective (so-called by sociologists) promotes a view of lifelong plasticity. In other words, growth and change continues throughout life. This perspective emphasizes a plurality of developmental paths and outcomes rather than a single model, and the interaction of person and environment. Both stand in contrast to the classic theories of development offered by theorists such as Freud and Piaget, who argue that development has a single path and is complete by early adolescence. It also recognizes multiple influences on development, for example, the importance of social-political context and the role of historical factors as well as the more typically studied age-graded or maturational factors. Because of this focus on multiple influences, the life-span view also advocated for the importance of longitudinal, and especially for cohort-sequential, research using multiple methods (Baltes, Reese, & Lipsitt, 1980; Hetherington, Lerner, & Perlmutter, 1988). Generally, it supports genuine developmental research throughout the life span. Additionally, theories such as those of Bronfenbrenner (1989), Bandura (2001), and Lave and Wenger (1991), though they are not strictly speaking life-span developmental theories, can be applied to individuals of all ages, as illustrated in chapters in this volume by Wilkenfeld, Lauckhardt, and Torney-Purta; Beaumont; and McIntosh and Youniss.

Questions of plasticity and the life course also have figured in the field of political science in studies of political socialization. With respect to plasticity, political scientists have debated the extent to which political ideas and opinions crystallize early in life or are malleable into mid- or later life (Sears & Levy, 2003). Life-course arguments also have been invoked to explain lower levels of youth engagement in electoral politics vis-à-vis that of their elders. The chapters by Amnå and Zetterberg; Finlay, Wray-Lake, and Flanagan;

McLeod, Shah, Hess, and Lee; and Reimers and Cardenas consider these issues.

Since civic engagement usually reaches fruition in adulthood, the life-span approach points to the need for research on citizenship that crosses several developmental periods and continues throughout life. As we describe in the next section, it also considers multiple influences such as sociopolitical context and history graded influence. Finally, research in this volume clearly demonstrates that there are multiple pathways to diverse outcomes. These life-span conceptualizations provided tools for the research on civic engagement that began to emerge in the mid-1990s, adding further impetus to its growth (Sherrod & Lauckhardt, 2008a).

Positive Youth Development

This new wave of research on youth civic engagement and political socialization also benefited from a new approach to research and policy in youth development, which arose in the 1990s: Positive Youth Development (PYD). Generally, PYD is an approach, not an actual construct or theory as is a life-span approach to developmental research (Sherrod, Busch, & Fisher, 2004). It is particularly relevant here because political or civic participation can be seen as both a contributor to and an outcome of positive youth development (Sherrod & Lauckhardt, 2008b).

PYD argues that development is promoted by assets, both internal and external. There is variability in the assets individuals bring to each of their contexts for growth; furthermore, there are numerous contexts including families, schools, communities, and societies or nations that convey and promote the further development of these assets. These contexts vary in the assets they offer that promote development, especially across individual youth (Benson, Leffert, Scales, & Blyth, 1998; Larsen, 2000). PYD arose in part because of decades of largely unsuccessful research and policy oriented to preventing negative outcomes by reducing risk. PYD examines the strengths youth possess—rather than focusing on their risks—and designs policies and programs that are oriented to promoting positive outcomes rather than preventing negative ones (Lerner, 2004; Sherrod, 2006). Recent research has continued to examine and define the specific nature of assets (Theokas, Almerigi, Lerner, Dowling, Benson, Scales, & Von Eye, 2005). Nonetheless, the PYD approach clearly highlights the need for youth policy to promote development based on the resources available to them in their families, schools, and communities, and this need is especially critical in regard to the encouragement of civic engagement. It emphasizes empowerment as an important ingredient to engaging youth successfully in their communities (Sherrod, 2007). The PYD approach offers tools for the conceptualization of civic engagement that can lead to better measurement and also to arguments for policy change that are convincing to the general public as well as specialists (Sherrod & Lauckhardt, 2008a).

The PYD perspective articulates six Cs: Character, Competence, Confidence, Connection, Caring, and Contribution. The sixth, Contribution, emerges from the first five. Youth who exemplify the first 5 Cs are likely to be productive members of their community (Damon, Menon, & Bronk, 2003), that is, they are likely to be civically engaged. Contribution, which is the sixth C, most directly relates to civic participation (Lerner, 2004). A young person who is involved in civic service or political action represents an instance of positive development, and the activity contributes to further positive development. The two aspects reinforce one another, which is why this approach is so important to research on civic engagement (Sherrod, 2007). At the same time, the field of positive youth development can benefit from greater attention to the social class and racial or ethnic divides in civic opportunities noted in the field of youth civic engagement (Flanagan, Syvertsen, & Wray-Lake, 2007; Kahne & Middaugh, 2009; Torney-Purta, Barber, & Wilkenfeld, 2007). Unequal opportunities for asset building and for civic skill development is a critical issue in need of policy attention and is a major focus of the chapters by Levinson; Finlay and collaborators; Fox and collaborators; Hart and Gullan; and Haste, Jensen, and Seif.

Together, a life-span perspective and the positive youth development approach provide frameworks for research on youth civic engagement. The firm establishment and enhancement of these approaches contributed to the maturation of the youth civic engagement field.

THE NATURE OF RESEARCH ON YOUTH CIVIC ENGAGEMENT

Research on civic engagement shows several qualities that may explain its appeal across a wide range of scholars, and thereby also contribute to the growth of the field. These same qualities also present challenges to research, especially in regard to methods and measures and connections to policy and programs.

MULTIFACETED CONCEPTUALIZATION

Civic engagement is certainly a multifaceted and complex phenomenon.

While this quality generates scholarly interest, it also creates challenges. The fact that research on civic engagement is both international and multidisciplinary complicates the problem of conceptualization. Political socialization has been, for example, the favored term in sociology and political science. If you ask youth the question, "What is a good citizen?" they most frequently report that citizenship is simply good behavior such as obeying laws or perhaps voting, and they will rarely offer more than one such quality (Sherrod, 2003). Few scholars would be comfortable with such a definition.

The American Heritage Dictionary defines citizenship as "the status of a citizen with its duties, rights and privileges." The political theorist Michael Walzer (1989) defines a citizen as "most simply, a member of a political community, entitled to whatever prerogatives and encumbered with whatever responsibilities are attached to membership." The emphasis on membership, rights, and responsibilities is useful for a developmental perspective because it helps the field conceptualize critical features to look for in formative environments (Flanagan, 2004). That is, to develop democratic competencies and dispositions, youth need opportunities to experience what it means to be a member of community organizations and institutions (schools and cultural, ethnic, faith-based, or environmental groups). And they need opportunities in those groups to exercise voice, deliberate and negotiate with fellow members of the organization, and assume responsibility for group projects and the integrity of the organization. Astuto and Ruck make the point that school is one of the first institutions to offer these opportunities to children.

Walzer also emphasizes that the words *civic* and *political* have common roots with the Latin *civis* and the Greek *polites*, referring to the political community. However, as Flanagan and Faison (2001) note, today the word *political* has come to mean affairs of the state, the business of government, or actions in the electoral or partisan arena. The term *civic* has a broader meaning associated with being a member of the polity, community, or civil society. Hence, Flanagan and Faison chose to use civic as the broader version. They then differentiate civic literacy as knowledge of community affairs and political issues, civic skills as competencies in achieving group goals, and civic attachment as a feeling or belief that the individual matters. They present evidence that social relations, opportunities for practice, and the values and behaviors communicated by adults and social institutions determine youth's civic development in these three areas.

This is a very useful approach to definition, but Walzer's idea of citizenship also includes membership, which is similar to but not isomorphic with the idea of civic attachment. Membership involves both rights and responsibilities. Nation is the typical body of membership, at least for those interested in politics or citizenship. Responsibilities of citizenship include generally taking an interest in and being involved in one's country by obeying laws, voting, following current events, and taking a stand against unjust policies or laws. By virtue of their membership in the polity, individual citizens enjoy certain rights such as freedom of speech and certain benefits such as public education—although the conceptualization of prerogatives and obligations and the very meaning of citizenship vary, especially across nations

(Flanagan, Martinez, & Cumsille, 2009). This is the reason that the international IEA Civic Education Study began with a series of case studies delineating conceptualization of civic education and their specific instantiations in 24 nations (Steiner-Khamsi, Torney-Purta, & Schwille, 2002; Torney-Purta, Schwille, & Amadeo, 1999). It is through the civic engagement of succeeding generations, through their exercise of rights and responsibilities, that democratic polities and the rights of citizens are sustained.

Adolescents do have opinions about the duties and rights they will acquire as adult citizens and these views map onto the differentiation of civic and political described above. High-school students in the United States see citizen responsibilities consisting of both civic ones, such as support for social justice, and political ones, such as voting (Bogard & Sherrod, 2008). They see citizen rights consisting of freedoms that relate to political participation and entitlements, which relate to supports from their community (Sherrod, 2008). Certainly membership including rights and obligations is one characteristic across most conceptualizations of civic engagement (Sherrod & Lauckhardt, 2008b).

Membership is the dimension of civic engagement that raises the most complexities in defining the *citizen*; one can be a member of institutions, or attached to institutions, other than the nation state or the government of the country in which one resides. Such memberships also carry both benefits and duties. As a result, the individual can express some of those same behaviors that constitute citizenship through membership in or allegiance to other institutions. Examples of other allegiances or memberships include one's community or fellow members of one's organization (Kirshner, 2009), family (Fuligni, Tseng, & Lam, 1999), religion (Sherrod & Spiewak, 2008), or race/ethnic group (Hughes & Chen, 1997; Torney-Purta, Barber, & Wilkenfeld, 2007), and research has shown that these other allegiances relate to adolescents' views of citizenship (Bogard & Sherrod, 2008). But the controversy in regard to the definition of citizenship is to what extent the behaviors associated with allegiances to community or family should be viewed as important to citizenship and to political behaviors such as voting. Certainly these other allegiances relate to the accrual of social capital, which is important to the civic health of the nation (Hyman, 2002). The civic side of citizenship would also relate to some of these other allegiances.

Another important issue for the definition of citizenship is whether tolerance, concern for others, and altruism should be viewed as a component of citizenship. Working for one's community by doing service is, for example, usually seen as altruistic, and research shows a correlation between community service in youth and later civic engagement (Youniss, McLellan, & Yates, 1997; Youniss & Levine, 2009). Research also shows that experiences of community service vary a great deal. Qualities such as type of service (tutoring versus working in a soup kitchen, for example), being mandatory or volunteer, providing an opportunity for reflection, and the characteristics of organizing groups affect its relation to civic engagement (Reinders & Youniss, 2006; Youniss, McLellan, & Yates, 1997; Torney-Purta, Amadeo, & Richardson, 2007). However, altruism cannot be the only motivation underlying political action. Politics also reflects working for one's group interests and contesting for power. Whether the motivation is contesting for power or acting on behalf of the common good, taking political action implies that an individual sees his or her life and goals connected with those of others, although the definition of others can be more or less expansive and heterogeneous.

Some consider a concern for social justice to be a critical aspect of civic engagement and view activism as an important form of participation (Ginwright & Watts, 2006); in this volume, Hart and Gullan address the importance of activism to youth in disadvantaged communities. Russell, Toomey, Crockett, and Laub describe how concern for the rights of sexual minority youth get some young people politically involved. Haste and also Metzger and Smetana discuss activism originating in concern about a political or social issue such as human rights. Reimers and Cardenas deal extensively with tolerance of diverse groups among Mexican youth. But concern for others, participation in community service, and activism for social justice are not universally acknowledged as forms of civic engagement.

The clarity and appropriateness of research questions and the value of multimethod approaches are important considerations in research on this topic, and are dealt with at length in the chapter by Torney-Purta, Amadeo, and Andolina. A research approach employing young people themselves as the researchers is found in the chapter by Fox and associates. Measures and their meaningfulness and validity are considered in relation to several theories by Wilkenfeld, Lauckhardt, and Torney and with reference to the concept of political efficacy by Beaumont.

Sherrod & Lauckhardt (2008a), in an attempt to articulate a comprehensive view of civic engagement, proposed a model involving three components: political involvement or civic activities; concern for others and tolerance; and allegiance, attachment, or membership. Their conceptualization is similar to that of Flanagan and Faison (2001). The point is that citizenship is certainly a complex domain of adult behavior (Sherrod, Flanagan, & Youniss, 2002), and this complexity may account for its increasing popularity as a research topic (Youniss, Bales, Christmas-Best, Diversi, McLaughlin, & Silbereisen, 2002). It is likely that there are multiple developmental paths to different types of civic outcomes, as advocated by life-span theorists. And civic engagement clearly exemplifies positive youth development. As a research topic, it therefore appeals to a diverse group of scholars.

These qualities also mean it is important to examine the topic carefully across the diverse population of youth in the world, and research has begun to do this across ethnicity, immigrant status, and social class (Flanagan, Cumsille, Gill, & Gallay, 2007; Flanagan, Syvertsen, Gill, & Gallay, 2009; Flanagan & Tucker, 1999; Hart, Atkins, & Ford, 1998; Sanchez-Jankowski, 1992; Jensen & Flanagan, 2008; Stepick, Stepick, & Labissiere, 2008; Torney-Purta, Barber, & Wilkenfeld, 2007). This theme is threaded throughout the chapters in this Handbook.

This Handbook, especially the chapters in the first section, addresses the nature of civic engagement from the perspective of different disciplines and from international viewpoints. There has been variability in the definitions that have framed the research. McIntosh and Youniss offer a multidisciplinary theory of political socialization. Haste describes the critical approach of European psychology in her examination of previous research and its manifestations in civic education. Levine and Higgins D'Alessandro consider explicitly how different fields, especially philosophy and psychology, address normative issues that serve as the basis for different approaches to civic education and engagement programs. Kassimir and Flanagan focus on different framings of civic engagement for youth in the developing world. Amnå and Zetterberg and Reimers focus on Swedish and Mexican youth, respectively. Throughout the book, international themes are addressed, however, by the presentation of findings from the IEA Civic Education Study (summarized in Torney-Purta, 2002) and from the study by Flanagan and her colleagues (1998).

This complexity of conceptualization also creates challenges for research. How civic engagement is defined, of course, determines what is examined in regard to development. Clarity of the research question becomes critical. Is the researcher interested in explicitly political participation, concerns for social justice and activism, or civic attachment or identity, for example? Is the researcher looking for age or gender differences or trying to examine the process of learning and development? Research questions then determine what is measured. Controversy around definition is healthy as long as the conceptualization of civic engagement and its relation to research questions and to measurement is clear. It is our hope that this Handbook will contribute to some clarification of conceptualizations and their relation to measurement.

Developmental Discontinuity

Developmental discontinuity means that either the behavior or the construct underlying that behavior changes in important ways across age or developmental period. Attachment, for example, is a construct that is interesting in this respect; a healthy person is typically able to show some attachment to significant others in their lives and therefore the construct of attachment shows some stability across development. The behaviors indexing attachment, however, change dramatically with age. Proximity seeking is one key indicator of attachment in infants; not needing proximity and being able to tolerate separations is an indicator at older ages. Stability in both behavior and construct is called homotypic continuity; when the behavior indexing a particular construct changes developmentally, heterotypic continuity or discontinuity is shown (Kagan, 1980). Civic engagement shows heterotypic developmental discontinuity, which enhances its appeal to developmental scientists.

One does not typically engage in behaviors that we define as active citizenship until adulthood. Eighteen years is the legal voting age in most democracies, although there is a trend toward lowering the voting age. Several chapters in this Handbook address the issue of age appropriateness for other aspects of citizenship.

Young persons (under 18 years) can and should be informed about political events. And some adolescents do work in political campaigns, become active in student government, or participate in some kind of consumer advocacy, for example. Nonetheless, most people consider these behaviors to be childhood and adolescent precursors of adult citizenship. That is, the developmental progression toward the behaviors explicitly defined as citizenship may involve earlier dispositions and behaviors that are only loosely related to civic and political engagement in adulthood. In this regard, civic engagement clearly shows heterotypic continuity or developmental discontinuity.

Because of the complexity of the developmental process, this topic forms a substantial part of the Handbook. The chapter by Astuto and Ruck asks what might be the early childhood precursors of civic engagement; they make the interesting point that schools, including preschools, are the first contact children have with a societal context that introduces them to rights and responsibilities. And they further argue that some of the cognitive and prosocial competencies expressed in play form the basis for later civic engagement. The chapter by Metzger and Smetana reviews how some of the basic theories of development underlie the growth of civic engagement, and the chapter by Wilkenfeld, Lauckhardt, and Torney-Purta considers the implications for measurement of several theories of development. Finlay, Wray-Lake, and Flanagan examine the emergence of adult or mature forms of civic engagement as youth make the transition to adulthood and explore how changing social institutions provide different opportunities for different groups of youth at this developmental juncture. Beaumont also deals with the period of late adolescence and early adulthood in her chapter on students operating within varying college or university contexts, integrating

Bandura's psychological theory with views about efficacy developed by political scientists.

The point is that civic engagement clearly shows developmental discontinuity and this greatly increases its appeal to researchers and may therefore partly account for increased research attention, at least by developmental scientists. As was true for the complexity of definition, developmental discontinuity also raises serious problems for measurement across age. Several chapters addressing development deal with this measurement challenge.

Multiple Developmental Influences

A complex conceptualization and developmental discontinuity both imply the existence of multiple influences. Civic engagement does not develop as part of the natural growth of the organism in interaction with a proximal environment as does cognition, for example. Instead, civic engagement results from the person's interaction with her society and its institutions, relying on underlying basic or natural development in cognition, emotion, or social competencies. Civic engagement is a set of behaviors that results from a process that is often called socialization, and research has identified numerous agents who facilitate this process. Research has shown earlier influences to include civic education, school activities, youth programs, community service, and service-learning programs (Eccles & Barber, 1999; McFarland & Thomas, 2006; Youniss & Levine, 2009). And, of course, parents and families are important. The process of developing political understanding has been called the social construction of knowledge (Haste & Torney-Purta, 1992). We intentionally chose to cover in this Handbook those influences with the strongest research basis. We do not have specific chapters on the influences of families or community-based organizations. Rather, family influences and youth programs are covered within existing chapters. The Fox, Mediratta, Ruglis, Stoudt, Shah, and Fine chapter covers community programs as part of its overall topic, while Selman and Kwok examine how one program, Facing History and Ourselves, contributes to the development of reflective social and civic engagement.

Additionally, although there is a great deal of research examining civic education in school (e.g., Niemi & Junn, 1998), we do not devote a separate chapter to it. Instead, we attempt to cover several perspectives that have been brought to research on education. For example, Flanagan, Stoppa, Syvertsen, and Stout examine how relationships and practices in schools contribute to the development of social trust, a disposition that is positively related to civic engagement and tolerance. Levinson addresses the achievement gap across different ethnic groups and social classes, while Beaumont deals with higher education institutions. Education is one topic for which there has been a lot of international and cross-national research. The IEA Civic Education Study, led by the second editor of this Handbook, is one example; results from this study are covered in several of the chapters.

Most societies formally introduce programs specifically targeted at enhancing civic knowledge to students during early adolescence. In addition, in recent years there have been many programs aimed at shaping the values and attitudes, even of younger students. There are now a few programs in the United States oriented to promoting civic engagement with associated evaluations (McDevitt & Chaffee, 2000), and there has been some research connected to other programs. For example, Higgins-D'Alessandro reviews civic engagement and character education programs as she considers the importance and nature of evaluation research in this field.

In recent years, scholars have addressed the power of the media, especially the new media, in influencing the development of civic engagement (McLeod, 2000; Meyrowitz, 1985). We have two chapters in the Handbook addressing this issue: Bennett, Freelon, and Wells; and also McLeod, Shah, Hess, and Lee. The Obama 2008 Presidential Campaign demonstrated the power of new media and technology in attracting young people to politics. And there are now several programs, such as Student Voices, oriented to influencing young people's use of the media for political purposes.

The array of independent variables that one might explore in examining the development of civic engagement means that most scholars can find something of interest, increasing the appeal of the topic. As a result, the field has attracted a number of new scholars, and this in turn has contributed to the growth in research on the topic.

ORGANIZATION OF THIS HANDBOOK

The organization of this Handbook reflects the field of research and policy on youth civic engagement. It is organized into three sections: global and multidisciplinary perspectives; development, socialization, and diversity; and methods and measures. We have already addressed part of our rationale in regard to the coverage of specific topics. Here, we wish to explain this overarching organizational framework.

Global and Multidisciplinary Perspectives

Research on civic engagement is inherently multidisciplinary. Certainly the complex conceptualization and the multiple influences on development underlie this multidisciplinarity. Understandably, political science is the discipline with the most longstanding interest. However, psychologists have long been interested in attitudes and behavior, and developmental psychologists have focused on the development of civic engagement. Sociologists study the role of social institutions, and anthropologists, the role of culture, though the boundaries of these disciplines have changed in the recent past. Each discipline brings its own set of lenses to bear on research on civic engagement, and the fact that the different disciplines operate at different levels of analysis means the topic is more thoroughly explored. Few other research topics can make this claim. The first seven chapters of the Handbook illustrate the multidisciplinary nature of research on civic engagement.

The field is also inherently international. Every democratic nation is dependent on an informed and active citizenry. For no other topic in research on children and youth are transnational comparisons more important. One of the most ambitious international undertakings is the IEA study examining the civic education and engagement of 90,000 14-year-olds, who were representative samples of 28 countries tested in 1999 (Torney-Purta, 2002; Torney-Purta, Lehmann, Oswald, & Schulz, 2001). The instruments in this study asked about the young people's understanding of democratic processes, their acceptance of their rights and responsibilities as citizens, and their attitudes toward social justice and minorities. This study demonstrated that having an open classroom climate for discussion and giving students real power in their schools were among the most important correlates of both civic knowledge and of civic engagement (Torney-Purta & Wilkenfeld, 2009; Torney-Purta, Wilkenfeld, & Barber, 2008). A parallel study of upper secondary students was also conducted in 16 countries in 2000.

Another ambitious international study examined adolescents' civic commitments in seven countries: three stable democracies and four that were in the midst of social change. Overall, this study demonstrated that differences in adolescents' civic beliefs and behaviors reflected differences in the social contracts in differentiations and in how the terms of the social contract applied to subgroups within a nation. The study also found that, across all nations, personal values and civic commitments were consistently linked (Bowes, Flanagan, & Taylor, 2001; Flanagan, Bowes, Jonsson, Csapo, & Sheblanova, 1998; Flanagan & Campbell, 2003; Macek et al., 1998). These two international studies demonstrate the power of an international approach, as will a new IEA effort called the International Civics and Citizenship Study, whose results will appear beginning in 2010.

The chapters in this Handbook explore the dimensions of international comparisons that are important to contemporary research on youth civic engagement. For example, the Hart chapter describes how the proportion of youth in a society, which shows considerable cross-national variability, affects young people's civic involvement. Kassimir and Flanagan deal with youth in the developing world, where they form a large proportion of the population and where there are constraints on many of the types of civic engagement taken for granted in the rest of the world. The Reimers and Cardenas chapter is the only one that describes civic engagement in a specific country as an illustration of a country-specific approach. However, the Amnå chapter describes research with a Scandinavian sample. Campbell-Patton and Patton developed many of their evaluation methodologies in international contexts. Finally, Wilkenfeld, Lauckhardt, and Torney-Purta illustrate how theory development has framed international studies of civic and political engagement.

Because being multidisciplinary and international is a natural characteristic of research on civic engagement, in addition to having it be the focus of the first section, we asked each chapter to address these issues.

DEVELOPMENT, SOCIALIZATION, AND DIVERSITY

Civic engagement has developmental influences, benefits from multiple socialization influences, and varies across the various demographic characteristics that characterize the world's population of young people. These three qualities of the field are captured in the second and longest section of the Handbook. Each of these approaches to research on civic engagement among youth is also pursued by multiple disciplines and covered differently across different areas of the world. Youth development is the overarching rubric that captures all of this work. However, in this Handbook, for the first time in more than two decades, we attempt to capture development from early childhood through young adulthood. Attention to socialization and diversity should be an aspect of any good developmental research, and these characteristics have been well represented in research on youth engagement. Attention to diversity and the role of culture and context is more recent in research on civic engagement but, as this Handbook documents, is now as robust as in any other field. The Jensen and Seif chapters on immigrant youth and the Russell, Crocket, Toomey, and Laub chapter on sexual minority youth are important inclusions.

METHODS AND MEASURES

Any field is only as good as its measures and methods, and research on youth civic engagement is no exception. However, this Handbook is one of the first publications in the field to attend directly to the methods of research, to the need for developing and refining measures, and to the challenge of improving research questions to better address processes and contexts of development. The third section offers numerous ideas and directions for the field in regard to methods and measures, and we hope that it makes an important contribution to improving research and evaluation in this regard. In fact, the chapters deal with a wide range of potential methodologies in addition to the usual surveys; these methods include focus groups, hypothetical dilemmas, content analysis of youth media, interviews, program evaluation assessment strategies, and the use of young people themselves as researchers.

GOALS FOR THE HANDBOOK

Authors were asked to review the state of research and policy on the topic of their chapter, as is standard for a handbook chapter. Although we did not disallow presentation of empirical data, we were clear that this should not be the central focus of any chapter. Data should be used to support points made in the review of the topic.

Each author was also asked to touch on international and multidisciplinary perspectives and on implications for policy, to the extent possible and appropriate. Of course, the extent to which the author could do this varied by topic. In few cases was it possible to address all three. Most were, however, able to address at least one.

CONCLUSION

The editors of this volume frequently make the point that an active, engaged citizenry is essential to the survival of a democracy. Since most countries in the world today are democratic, most governments appreciate the merit of this statement. The impact of Putnam's work on policy-makers as well as scholars is a testament to this point. As a result, the development of citizenship is of worldwide importance. The authors whose work is included in this Handbook recognize this fact and have devoted at least a portion of their research careers to understanding the development of citizenship.

We as editors also believe that any effort undertaken to influence human development, to help children and families, or even to help nations, must be based on empirical data. And research is the main vehicle we have for acquiring reliable and valid information. Hence, research on the development of citizenship is essential to local, national, and worldwide efforts to promote an active, engaged citizenship. While this Handbook focuses mainly on research, most authors did address some implications for policy. The research reported in each chapter should be made available to those who are responsible for promoting the development of citizenship in their countries. These groups include practitioners in youth organizations and schools or universities, those responsible for policy and the allocation of resources, and those who influence public opinion through the media.

We as editors hope that this first Handbook in the field furthers research on civic engagement in youth and, in so doing, also contributes to the worldwide promotion of the development of democratic citizenship.

REFERENCES

Baltes, P., Reese, H., & Lipsitt, L. (1980). Life span developmental psychology. *Annual Review of Psychology, 31,* 65–100.

Bandura, A. (2001). Social cognitive theory: An agentic perspective. *Annual Review of Psychology, 52,* 1–26.

Benson, P., Leffert, N., Scales, P., & Blyth, D. (1998). Beyond the village rhetoric: Creating healthy communities for children and adolescents. *Applied Developmental Science, 2,* 138–159.

Bogard, K., & Sherrod, L. (2008). Citizenship attitudes and allegiances in diverse youth. *Cultural Diversity and Ethnic Minority Psychology, 14(4),* 286–296.

Bowes, J. M., Flanagan, C., & Taylor, A. J. (2001). Adolescents' ideas about individual and social responsibility in relation to children's household work: Some international comparisons. *International Journal of Behavioral Development, 25,* 60–68.

Bronfenbrenner, U. (1989). Ecological systems theory. In R. Vasta (Ed.), *Annals of child development: Vol. 6. Six theories of child development: Revised formulations and current issues* (pp. 187–249). Greenwich, CT: JAI Press.

Damon, W., Menon, J., & Bronk, K. C. (2003). The development of purpose during adolescence. *Applied Developmental Science, 7,* 119–128.

Eccles, J., & Barber, B. (1999). Student council, volunteering, basketball, or marching band: What kind of extracurricular involvement matters? *Journal of Adolescent Research, 12,* 287–315.

Flanagan, C. A. (2004). Volunteerism, leadership, political socialization, and civic engagement. In R. M. Lerner & L. Steinberg (Eds.), *Handbook of adolescent psychology* (pp. 721–746). Hoboken, NJ: John Wiley & Sons.

Flanagan, C., Bowes, J., Jonsson, B., Csapo, B., & Sheblanova, E. (1998). Ties that bind: Correlates of male and female adolescents' civic commitments in seven countries. *Journal of Social Issues, 54,* 457–476.

Flanagan, C. A., & Campbell, B. with L. Botcheva, J. Bowes, B. Csapo, P. Macek, & Sheblanova, E. (2003). Social class and adolescents' beliefs about justice in different social orders. *Journal of Social Issues, 59(4),* 711–732.

Flanagan, C., Cumsille, P., Gill, S., & Gallay, L. (2007). School and community climates and civic commitments: Processes for ethnic minority and majority students. *Journal of Educational Psychology, 99(2),* 421–431.

Flanagan, C., & Faison, N. (2001). Youth civic development: Implications of research for social policy and programs. *Social Policy Reports,* No. 1.

Flanagan, C., Martinez, M. L., & Cumsille, P. (2009). Civil societies as developmental and cultural contexts for civic identity formation. In L. Arnett Jensen (Ed.), *Bridging cultural and developmental psychology: New syntheses in theory, research and policy.* New York: Oxford University Press.

Flanagan, C., & Sherrod, L. R. (1998). Youth political development: An introduction. Political development: Growing up in a global community. *Journal of Social Issues, 54,* 447–456.

Flanagan, C. A., Syvertsen, A. K., Gill, S., & Gallay, L. S. (2009). Ethnic awareness, prejudice, and civic commitments in four ethnic groups of American adolescents. *Journal of Youth and Adolescence, 38(4),* 500–518.

Flanagan, C., Syvertsen, A. B., & Wray-Lake, L. (2007). Youth political activism: Sources of public hope in the context of globalization. In R. K. Silbereisen & R. M. Lerner (Eds.), *Approaches to positive youth development* (pp. 243–256). Thousand Oaks, CA: Sage Publications.

Flanagan, C .A., & Tucker, C. J. (1999). Adolescents' explanations for political issues: Concordance with their views of self and society. *Developmental Psychology, 35(5),* 1198–1209.

Fuligni, A. J., Tseng, V., & Lam, M. (1999). Attitudes toward family obligations among American adolescents from Asian, Latin American, and European backgrounds. *Child Development, 70,* 1030–1044.

Ginwright, S., & Watts, R. (Eds.). (2006). *Beyond resistance! Youth activism and community change: New democratic possibilities for practice and policy for America's children.* New York: Routledge.

Hart, D., Atkins, R., & Ford, D. (1998). Urban America as a context for the development of moral identity in adolescence. *Journal of Social Issues, 54,* 513–530.

Haste, H., & Torney-Purta, J. (1992). Social construction and individual construction in the development of political understanding: An introduction. In H. Haste & J. Torney-Purta (Eds.), *The development of political understanding: A new perspective* (pp. 11–25). San Francisco: Jossey-Bass.

Hetherington, E., Lerner, R., & Perlmutter, M. (1988). *Child development in life span perspective.* Hillsdale, NJ: Erlbaum.

Hughes, D., & Chen, L. (1997). When and what parents tell children about race: An examination of race related socialization among African-American families. *Applied Developmental Science, 1,* 200–214.

Hyman, J. B. (2002). Exploring social capital and civic engagement to create a framework for community building. *Applied Developmental Science, 6,* 196–202.

Jensen, L. A., & Flanagan, C. (Eds.). (2008). Special issue on civic engagement among immigrant youth. *Applied Developmental Science, 12,* 55–56.

Kagan, J. (1980). Perspectives on continuity. In O. G. Brim, Jr., & J. Kagan (Eds.), *Constancy and change in human development* (pp. 26–74). Cambridge, MA: Harvard University Press.

Kahne, J., & Middaugh, E. (2009). Democracy for some: The civic opportunity gap in high school. In J. Youniss & P. Levine (Eds.), *Engaging young people in civic life* (pp. 29–58). Nashville, TN: Vanderbilt University Press.

Kirshner, B. (2009). "Power in numbers": Youth organizing as a context for exploring civic identity. *Journal of Research on Adolescence, 19(3),* 414–440.

Larsen, R. (2000). Toward a psychology of positive youth development. *American Psychologist, 55,* 170–183.

Lave, J., & Wenger, E. (1991). *Situated learning: Legitimate peripheral participation.* Cambridge: Cambridge University Press.

Lerner, R. (2004). Liberty: Thriving and civic engagement among America's youth. Thousand Oaks, CA: Sage Publications.

Macek, P., Flanagan, C., Gallay, L., Kostron, L., Botcheva, L., & Csapo, B. (1998). Post-communist societies in times of transition: Perceptions of change among adolescents in Central and Eastern Europe. *Journal of Social Issues, 54(3),* 547–560.

McDevitt, M., & Chaffee, S. (2000). Closing gaps in political communication and knowledge: Effects of a school intervention. *Communication Research, 27(3),* 259–292.

McFarland, D. A., & Thomas, R. J. (2006). Bowling young: How youth voluntary associations influence adult political participation. *American Sociological Review, 71,* 401–425.

McLeod, J. (2000). Media and civic socialization of youth. *Journal of Adolescent Health, 27,* 45–51.

Meyrowitz, J. (1985). *No sense of place: The impact of electronic media on social behavior.* New York: Oxford University Press.

Neimi, R., & Junn, J. (1998). *Civic education: What makes students learn.* New Haven, CT: Yale University Press.

Putnam, R. (1996). The strange disappearance of civic America. *The American Prospect,* 34–48.

Putnam, R. (2000). *Bowling alone: The collapse and revival of American community.* New York: Simon and Schuster.

Reinders, H., & Youniss, J. (2006). School-based required community service and civic development in adolescents. *Applied Developmental Science, 10(1),* 2–12.

Ruck, M., Abramovitch, R., & Keating, D. (1998). Children and adolescents' understanding of rights: Balancing nurturance and self-determination. *Child Development, 64,* 404–417.

Sanchez-Jankowski, M. (1992). Ethnic identity and political consciousness in different social orders. *New Directions for Child Development, 56,* 79–93.

Sears, D. O., & Levy, S. (2003). Childhood and adult political development. In D. O. Sears, L. Huddy, & R. Jerevis (Eds.), *Oxford handbook of political psychology* (pp. 60–109). New York: Oxford University Press.

Sherrod, L. R. (2003). Promoting the development of citizenship in diverse youth. *PS: Political Science and Politics, 36(2),* 287–292.

Sherrod, L. R. (2006). Promoting citizenship and activism in today's youth. In S. Ginwright & R. Watts, (Eds.), *Beyond resistance! Youth activism and community change: New democratic possibilities for practice and policy for America's children* (pp. 287–300). New York: Routledge.

Sherrod, L. R. (2007). Civic engagement as an expression of positive youth development. In R. K. Silbereisen & R. M. Lerner (Eds.), *Approaches to positive youth development*. Thousand Oaks, CA: Sage Publications.

Sherrod, L. R. (2008). Youth's perceptions rights as reflected in their views of citizenship. In M. Ruck, & S. Horn (Eds.), Young people's perspectives on the rights of the child. *Journal of Social Issues, 64(4),* 771–790.

Sherrod, L. R., Busch, N., & Fisher, C. (2004). Applying developmental science: Methods, visions, and values. In R. Lerner & L. Steinberg (Eds.), *Handbook of adolescent psychology* (pp. 747–780). Hoboken, NJ: John Wiley & Sons.

Sherrod, L., Flanagan, C., & Youniss, J. (2002). Dimensions of citizenship and opportunities for youth development: The what, why, when, where, and who of citizenship development. *Applied Developmental Science, 6(4),* 264–272.

Sherrod, L., & Lauckhardt, J. (2008a). The development of citizenship. In R. Lerner & L. Steinberg (Eds.), *Handbook of adolescent psychology* (Volume 2, 3rd ed., pp. 372–408). Hoboken, NJ: John Wiley & Sons.

Sherrod, L., & Lauckhardt, J. (2008b). Cultivating civic engagement. In J. Rettew (Ed.), *Positive psychology: Pursuing human flourishing,* Vol. 4. Westport, CT: Greenwood Publishing Group.

Sherrod, L. R., & Spiewak, G. (2008). Assessing spiritual development in relation to civic and moral development during adolescence. In R. Roeser, R. Lerner, & E. Phelps (Eds.), *On the study of spirituality and development during adolescence* (pp. 322–338). West Conshohocken, PA: Templeton Press.

Stepick, A., Stepick, C., & Labissiere, Y. (2008). South Florida's immigrant youth and civic engagement: Major engagement: Minor differences. *Applied Developmental Science, 12(2),* 57–65.

Steiner-Khamsi, G., Torney-Purta, J., & Schwille, J. (Eds.). (2002). *New paradigms and recurring paradoxes in education for citizenship.* Amsterdam: Elsevier Science.

Stoneman, D. (2002). The role of youth programming in the development of civic engagement. *Applied Developmental Science, 6(4),* 221–226.

Theokas, C., Almerigi, J., Lerner, R., Dowling, E., Benson, P., Scales, P., & Von Eye, A. (2005). Conceptualizing and modeling individual and ecological asset components of thriving in early adolescence. *Journal of Early Adolescence, 25(1),* 113–143.

Torney-Purta, J. (2002). The school's role in developing civic engagement: A study of adolescents in twenty-eight countries. *Applied Developmental Science, 6(4),* 202–211.

Torney-Purta, J. (2009). Award for distinguished contributions to the international advancement of psychology and international psychological research that matters for policy and practice. *American Psychologist, 64(8),* 822–837.

Torney-Purta, J., Amadeo, J., & Richardson, W. (2007). Civic service among youth in Chile, Denmark, England and the United States: A psychological perspective. In A. McBride & M. Sherraden (Eds.), *Civic service worldwide: Impact and inquiries* (pp. 95–132). Armonk, NY: M. E. Sharpe.

Torney-Purta, J., Barber, C., & Wilkenfeld, B. (2007). Latino adolescents' civic development in the United States: Research results from the IEA Civic Education Study. *Journal of Youth and Adolescence, 36,* 111–125.

Torney-Purta, J., Lehmann, R., Oswald, H., & Schulz, W. (2001). *Citizenship and education in twenty-eight countries: Civic knowledge and engagement at age fourteen.* Amsterdam: IEA.

Torney-Purta, J., Schwille, J., & Amadeo, J. (Eds.). (1999). *Civic education across countries: Twenty-four national case studies from the IEA Civic Education Project.* Amsterdam, NL: International Association for the Evaluation of Educational Achievement (IEA).

Torney-Purta, J., & Wilkenfeld, B. (2009). *Paths to 21st century competencies through civic education classrooms: An analysis of survey results from ninth graders.* Chicago, IL: American Bar Association Division for Public Education. Retrieved from http://www.civicyouth.org

Torney-Purta, J., Wilkenfeld, B., & Barber, C. (2008). How adolescents in 27 countries understand, support and practice human rights. *Journal of Social Issues, 64(4),* 857–880.

Walzer, M. (1989). *Citizenship.* New York: Cambridge University Press.

Youniss, J., McLellan, D., & Yates, M. (1997). What we know about engendering civic identity. *American Behavioral Scientist, 40,* 620–631.

Youniss, J., & Levine, P. (2009). *Engaging young people in civic life.* Nashville, TN: Vanderbilt University Press.

Youniss, J., Bales, S., Christmas-Best, V., Diversi, M., McLaughlin, M., & Silbereisen, R. (2002). Youth civic engagement in the twenty-first century. *Journal of Research on Adolescence, 12,* 121–148.

SECTION I

MULTIDISCIPLINARY RESEARCH: CONCEPTUAL AND INTERNATIONAL PERSPECTIVES

THE STUDY OF youth civic engagement is a topic that, by its nature and from its history, requires multidisciplinary attention and raises issues concerning appropriate conceptual frameworks and definitions. In addition, increasing global connections result in cross-national dimensions becoming important in all research, and this is especially true for this topic. These chapters describe how several disciplines have explored civic engagement among youth, bring an international perspective to the topic, and consider the need for further cross-national and interdisciplinary research collaboration. The chapters in this first section also describe the major conceptual issues facing the field of research on youth civic engagement and offer suggestions for policy-related studies.

The chapter by McIntosh and Youniss develops a theory of political socialization based on the particular characteristics of political and civic engagement, especially its public, voluntary, and collaborative character and the frequency of conflict. This approach is derived largely from theories on situated cognition, scaffolding of learning, and perspective taking. The chapter concludes with a discussion of policy implications and mechanisms of political socialization (e.g., families, schools, community-based organizations).

The chapter by Amnå and Zetterberg develops four hypotheses that might account for cross-national differences in attitudes toward civic engagement among youth: the civic hypothesis, the social capital hypothesis, the public-institutional hypothesis, and the modernization hypothesis. The explanatory power of each hypothesis is tested by reviewing political socialization research as well as analyses of the IEA Civic Education data on 14-year-olds in 24 European and North American countries. The specific situation of Scandinavian young people and adults is discussed.

The chapter by Hart and Gullan reviews research on youth activism and includes survey data collected from adolescents both within the United States and internationally in the IEA Civic Education Study. Excerpts from interviews with minority adolescents living in an inner-city, impoverished neighborhood are also presented. They conclude that political activism comprises of a set of overlapping activities and motivations and that political activism is deeply embedded in psychological, social, and political contexts.

The chapter by Kassimir and Flanagan reviews two reports on youth citizenship in the developing world issued by major global institutions and reflects on their inclusion of citizenship as a key component of adolescent transitions to adulthood. Youth are not merely citizens in the making but active civic agents in the present. Given the deficits of public institutions in much of the developing world, young people are often thrust into active political and civic roles; this can remove obstacles that stand in their way of making a transition to adult status.

The chapter by Levine and Higgins-D'Alessandro argues that educating young people for citizenship is an intrinsically normative task that involves choosing and transmitting values to citizens so that they will build and sustain societies embodying particular forms of justice and virtue. This chapter reviews several contemporary moral theories and identifies the criteria that each would expect to find in a good program or policy relating to civic education. It then examines several leading programs and asks what moral theories they rest on or assume.

The chapter by Reimers and Cardenas examines the civic engagement of youth in Mexico, summarizing data from National Surveys about Political Culture (ENCUP), and a survey about youth demographic characteristics and perceptions (ENJUVE). Changes in political institutions making electoral politics more competitive do not appear to have resulted in changes in people's perceptions of democracy in their daily lives. If reforms are not accompanied by educational programs, the institutionalization of democracy is placed at risk.

The chapter by Haste surveys the contemporary state of civic education and argues that it is vital both for scholarship and good policy-making to avoid U.S.-centric parochialism as well as unchallenged assumptions about political systems and about the development of civic engagement. It focuses on social and developmental psychology approaches that attend to social and cultural context and that recognize the individual as an active agent in making sense of experience rather than a passive product of socialization.

Together these seven chapters demonstrate how essential cross-disciplinary and cross-national perspectives are to research on youth civic engagement.

CHAPTER 1

Toward a Political Theory of Political Socialization of Youth

HUGH McINTOSH
Consultant, Oakton, Virginia

JAMES YOUNISS
The Catholic University of America

THE THEME OF this chapter is expressed well by a quotation from the philosopher John Stuart Mill regarding how democracy is acquired and sustained: "We do not learn to read or write, to ride or swim, by merely being told how to do it, but by doing it, so it is only in practicing popular government on a limited scale, that people will ever learn how to exercise it on a larger [scale]" (Alperovitz, 2005, p. 44). This statement applies to developmental theories of political socialization, which, in general, have treated the acquisition of political acumen as an extension of social or cognitive development. Although there is likely some connection between these psychological functions and political development, the difference is as large as the difference between *being told* and *doing*. Acquisition of skills and attitudes that constitute the elements of citizenship occurs in the doing within a political context. If this thesis is correct, then we need a developmental theory directed to the acquisition of civic and political capacities and identities. The aim of this chapter is to outline the rationale for and the elements of such a theory.

Our intention is to integrate insights from developmental psychology and political science in a way that moves us toward an understanding of how youth become citizens within a democratic polity. We consciously seek to overcome the tendency to think in categories originally designed to account for psychological development, as if they translated directly into political prowess. Again, there is probably a connection between these domains. But the person who is considered well-integrated psychologically is not quite the same as the person who is a well-functioning citizen. The politically able person operates in public, recognizes his or her own interests, can promote them in the face of competing interests, knows his or her place within a larger sphere of ideologies, and identifies with the democratic political system, which allows diverse views to interact according to agreed-upon rules. This citizen differs in makeup from the private individual whose internal workings are designed to maintain coherence, sustain logical reasoning, achieve emotional balance, and keep the self intact in an ever-changing and pluralistic world.

BACKGROUND

For half a century, political scientists have drawn ideas from developmental theory as they sought to understand the roots of citizenship in childhood and adolescent experiences. This interdisciplinary relationship has taken several forms over the years, whether it has used Freudian theory to explain naive faith in authority figures, learning theory to explain parents' influence on children's attitudes, or cognitive theory to account for the ability of youth to construct new ideas in opposition to existing political institutions (Cook, 1985; Merelman, 1971).

Circumstances have contrived to keep this interdisciplinary relationship alive even though no definitive integration has ever taken hold. Cognitive theory, for example, replaced Freudian thinking in the 1970s when it was recognized that young children's loyalty to political authorities, such as police or the president, was transformed into youthful baby boomers' mistrust of any authority embodied in persons older than age 30. Cognitive theory was convenient for accounting for the intergenerational shift that occurred during the uproarious days of student protests when the expected transmission of viewpoints from parents to offspring faltered. Instead, youth collectively reasoned toward independent and anti-traditional conclusions about military service, civil rights, and equality of opportunity. But the same cognitive theory hardly explains why recent cohorts of youth score poorly on tests of basic civic knowledge (e.g., Niemi & Junn, 1998), show little investment in community well-being (Pryor, Hurtado, Saenz, Santos, & Korn, 2007), and avoid electoral duties at alarming rates (Donovan, Lopez, & Sagoff, 2005).

The recurring pattern for developmental theory to appear promising, but then not to predict the next youth cohort's behavior, suggests to us that a problem might lie in the asymmetric relationship whereby researchers of political socialization have looked to developmental theory for guidance. Easton and Dennis (1969) seem to have anticipated this problem four decades ago in their classic book on the diffuse nature of children's relationship to the political system. They reasoned that developmental theory is designed to account for the acquisition of individual characteristics such as personality features, moral orientations, and emotional attachments. Although there is no consensus definition of what constitutes a mature citizen, it is something different than personality characteristics and involves something explicit about functioning successfully in political processes. Thus, Easton and Dennis proposed, developmental theory was helpful for explaining "diffuse support" of the political system but lacked the capacity to deal with political behavior itself. What was needed for that was a "political theory of political socialization" (p. 18).

The distinction between diffuse support and the ability to function politically is readily illustrated by what Easton and Dennis (1969) term the *allocative* function of political systems. Mature political functioning entails taking public positions having to do with one's political, social, moral, and economic interests. Taking a public stance, however, necessarily involves meeting and dealing with contending positions taken by other persons. The public nature of political thought expressed in action sets in motion a new dynamic that has no parallel in private ideas. For example, people may find allies who support their position and provide resources by way of group experiences, strategies, or rationales. Alliances with like-minded others allow the establishment of a power bloc that enhances subsequent negotiation with opposing views. In the main, developmental theories emphasize the achievement of order, resolution of conflict, drive for coherence, and ability to fend off intruding forces from the outside. Such versions of the individual are inadequate to advance understanding of the engaged democratic citizen.

Political Implies Public

As was noted previously, there was excitement in the 1970s when cognitive theory offered a fresh model of the active, constructing individual. This person was able to go beyond empirical input to analyze and organize information in an effort to create stable relationships with the outside world. This insight should not be minimized, because it freed the individual from having to replicate the world as given and permitted the individual to deal with ambiguity and to project ideals that might never be realized but that have logical bases.

One of the limits of cognitive theory in its application to political life, however, is its focus on private mental activity and the ability to stand on one's own by taking recourse to logic when challenged by outside forces. This seeming advantage has a downside in that thought is separated from action. Furthermore, one individual is divided from another in independent units. The result can be seen in the way some theorists have applied cognitive theory to the political realm with an emphasis on critical thinking (see Haste & Torney-Purta, 1992, for a review). Surely the ability to analyze political phenomena is important. But in itself, it does not address the fullness of the political life, which at its roots, entails efforts to affect government or direct public policy (Verba, Schlozman, & Brady, 1995).

It might be argued that the private and isolated individual, no matter how mature his or her reasoning, often falls short of being able to participate in the political domain. This is because that domain is, by definition, public and social, or collective. It might be argued that having thoughts about political events is not actually political because it is internally directed rather than being designed to meet and interact with the thoughts of other people. Once ideas enter the public realm, they become open to unanticipated and uncontrolled forms of feedback with which the individual must contend. In dealing with this unexpected and often unwanted intrusion, individuals are forced into a new form of reflection, which is driven from the outside and ultimately may alter what the self understands, as has been proposed by researchers such as Piaget (1970) and Vygotsky (Mahn, 2003; Tudge & Scrimsher, 2003).

Eliasoph (1998) offers an interesting view on the relationship between political and public thinking. She studied ways people tend to avoid the contentiousness of politics in their everyday lives. She was a participant observer in a variety of voluntary groups ranging in type from recreational to advocacy, and from this insider position was able to note the kind of conversations group members had. She observed how common it was for members to talk about concerns openly until they reached a point where the concerns might be construed as contentious and political or sided. At that point, they often withheld views and reverted to silence and the safety of privacy.

Going beyond this analysis of avoidance, we can look closer at the dynamics of this avoidance, which suggest that only in making views public do people enter the political realm. Once views are expressed publicly, they become signs that identify a person's interests and invite responses from others to offer their views. Eliasoph's analysis suggests that once views enter the public sphere, they become open to processes of honing via argument, justification, mutual reflection, and the like.

Gamson (1992) offered a similar analysis after observing how people make sense of political information conveyed via newspapers, television, and other media. He observed that adults honed their views by discussing them with others. For example, when approaching contentious issues such as warring factions in the Middle East, adults did not simply take in information, say, from newscasts and turn it into private thoughts. Rather, the information was mulled over by being voiced back to others so that in the process of discussion, it was turned into something much different from what it was at the point of reception. For example, issues were often organized into a *we versus they* framework, which allowed individuals to sharpen their identities by aligning with friendly arguments and contrasting themselves from opposing views (e.g., Barabas, 2004; Harwood Group, 1993).

It is in the give-and-take of such discussions that ideas become political. They both affect and are affected by the ideas of others, and this very process is political. The political realm involves persuasion, argument, debate, defense, compromise, and the like. Without being touched by these processes, ideas remain private and have no impact on society or the polity. Although this process has a parallel in private reflection, the public version forces rethinking as new ideas cannot be discarded when the opposing position is represented by a visible other. Understanding that *political* connotes "public" is essential to constructing a theory of political development. Outside the public sphere, thought remains private and individualistic. Once that thought enters the social arena, it may be strengthened through public interaction, and the process itself defines the political.

In the remainder of this chapter we explore how youth develop the capabilities of mature political functioning. We begin by considering the defining elements of political engagement. We then propose theory that explains how individuals can develop the capacity for political engagement while accounting for the peculiarities of political engagement. Finally, we explore mechanisms that could bring youth from political naiveté to full membership in the political community.

THE NATURE OF POLITICAL ENGAGEMENT

In addition to being *public,* political engagement has at least three more characteristics that distinguish it from other types of human activities. Political engagement requires *collaboration* with others having similar interests in order to develop the collective power to influence the political system. When groups of similarly minded people do take public action, they find that politics frequently involves *conflict* with the interests and ideologies of other groups of citizens. Finally, political engagement is *voluntary.* People don't have to—and many don't want to—enter the rough and tumble of the public arena. In fact, rational choice theory proposes that in most cases, payoff is higher for nonparticipation than for participation (see explanations and counter-arguments in Ostrom, 1990, and Verba et al., 1995). This suggests that unless citizens find relevance in political engagement, they simply won't participate. At a minimum, a useful theory of political socialization must take into account these defining characteristics of political engagement.

COLLABORATION

A single voice speaking out for change seldom has much impact on political structures. An essential part of political engagement, therefore, involves learning to join into a collectivity of like-minded people who, together, generate sufficient resources to change public policy or practice. The civil rights marches of the early 1960s and the massive demonstrations against the Vietnam War in the late 1960s attest to the power and importance of cooperative action for political change on the national level (e.g., Klandermans, 1997). At the state and local levels, petition drives to put initiatives on the ballot, political campaigns to put individuals into or out of political office, and joining community organizations dedicated to social or political change demonstrate the use and effectiveness of cooperative activity. While some political activity, such as voting or writing a check to support a political candidate, is essentially solitary behavior, political change more commonly occurs through collective, cooperative action (Gibson, 2006).

CONFLICT

Political engagement in a democracy such as the United States, where political decisions are made by citizens or their representatives, almost always involves some level of conflict. Rarely are decisions made by unanimous consent or decree. Rather, decisions more commonly emerge from discussion, debate, or heated political battle among majorities, minorities, factions, interests, and ideologies. "Political participants almost always engage in conflict with other persons in their society," writes Merelman (1985). "No matter how they rationalize their efforts under the guise of public service or contribution to the common good, participants must still struggle against others of different partisan hue" (p. 43).

In stable, uncontested democracies such as the United States, however, adolescents tend to avoid major conflict (Merelman, 1990). A study of political conflict and power, for instance, found that only 10% to 20% of the more than 900 sixth and eighth graders questioned felt that partisan conflict in government was desirable, although most felt it was inevitable (Sears, 1972). In many of the countries participating in the IEA Civic Education Study, students thought it "bad" or "very bad" for democracy when political parties expressed conflicting opinions on political issues (Torney-Purta, Lehmann, Oswald, & Schulz, 2001, p. 74). Such conflict-avoidant attitudes may derive from several sources, including parents. Children often rely on parents (and other familiar adults) to help them interpret political events (Connell, 1971), and many American adults prefer to avoid political controversy (Eliasoph, 1998). A nationally representative survey of nearly 1,300 adults found that

26% agreed that political argument made them feel uneasy, and 86% felt that political argument is unnecessary (Hibbing & Theiss-Morse, 2002). Another contributor to conflict-avoidant attitudes in youth may be the lack of opportunity to learn how to deal positively with political controversy. A study of democracy education in Chicago Public Schools, for example, revealed that only 8% of the 135 middle- and high-school classes evaluated included the study of controversial social problems (Kahne, Rodriguez, Smith, & Thiede, 2000). In addition, Berman (1997) reported that students who do explore controversial social issues in their classes sometimes disengage from the study because of despair over the possibility of ever resolving such difficult problems. Whatever the reasons for shunning political involvement, if youth are going to become politically engaged, they need to be able to deal with the many conflicts, small and large, that political activity entails.

Voluntary

Political engagement is voluntary in the United States. No law says citizens must vote or participate in the political process. Citizens, therefore, need to be persuaded that participation in the political system is in some way relevant to their lives. For example, emerging adults (ages 18 to 24) reported in one national survey that they would be more willing to vote if issues directly related to their lives were addressed by politicians (National Association of Secretaries of State, 1999). Relevance means different things to different people. For slightly less than 30% of voters, going to the polls is motivated by their sense of duty or responsibility (Center for Information and Research on Civic Learning and Engagement, 2002; National Association of Secretaries of State, 1999). Many citizens need to see that their participation can make a difference in political outcomes before they will get involved. Thus, contested elections stimulate higher levels of voting and political participation than do uncontested, lopsided ones (Gimpel, Lay, & Schukneckt, 2003). For some, political participation is linked to self-interest (Delli Carpini & Keeter, 1996; Galston, 2001). Others get involved because they find political or governmental systems unresponsive to their concerns (e.g., Larson & Hansen, 2005). No matter whether citizens are motivated through self-interest, feelings that they can make a difference, a desire for change, or a sense of duty, they need to find some measure of personal relevance in political engagement or they simply won't get involved (Gimpel et al., 2003; see also Fox et al., this volume).

In summary, the nature of political engagement calls for a socialization process that involves developing reasons to become involved, joining with like-minded others to work toward collective goals, and learning to interact with competing interest groups to achieve mutually agreeable solutions to political problems. In the next section, we explore how that might happen.

THEORY OF POLITICAL SOCIALIZATION

In order to outline essential elements of a theory of political development, we turn to theoretical and empirical research on situated learning, adult scaffolding, and perspective taking for leads. Together, these theories provide the prerequisites of a political-developmental framework for understanding the political socialization of youth. Although many of our ideas and data are drawn from research on North American school-age adolescents, the findings may also contribute to understanding the political socialization of young persons in other parts of the world.

Situated Learning

Situated learning theory proposes that people learn best by actually doing what they are trying to learn within a coherent context. This concept was illustrated in our opening paragraph with a quote from John Stuart Mill regarding the acquisition of democratic practices through doing. Situated learning, however, implies more than simply learning by doing (Lave & Wenger, 1991; Rogoff, 1991). It is based on the idea that individuals acquire habits and identities when they become meaningfully involved in a community of practice. Such communities involve people engaging over time in shared activities such as playing football, supporting the local school, or helping to elect a political candidate. These activities define membership in a community because they demonstrate, in effect, what membership entails. Newcomers to a group initially perform simpler tasks in cooperation with expert members in an apprentice-like relationship. Over time, as newcomers master more complex activities, they move into full participation in the community (see Torney-Purta, Amadeo, & Andolina, this volume). For example, newcomers to a homeowners association might initially work with the membership director to build and maintain a strong membership base, and with more experience, plan and chair the organization's membership meetings and other activities.

Boyte (2004) offers an argument regarding political development that meshes neatly with this concept. He proposes that the best training for democratic citizenship occurs through what he calls *public work*. This is defined as activity that is designed to promote the community and affect public policy. When people engage in public work, they acquire a sense of ownership that cannot be easily obtained indirectly. Politics becomes not something "out there" in the province of elected officials, but activity that is part of everyday life.

For our purposes, the key tenet of situated learning is that learning is a social enterprise. It takes place through cooperation with more expert members on the meaningful work of the group. Collaboration becomes the critical process for participating in the group and reaping the developmental benefits of group participation. One of the most important of these benefits is relevance. In making meaningful contributions to the goals of the organization, the newcomer appropriates the ideology of the organization and links him- or herself to that rationale through personal contributions to the work of the organization. Although the newcomer may derive personal meaning from participation, it is the organization's ideology or reason for existence that provides a relevant system of meaning that sustains the newcomer's motivation to participate over the long term, even when personal meaning flags. Thus, participation helps to build further interest in the goals of the organization, and the rationale of the organization, in turn, helps to sustain the individual's participation.

In addition, research documents links between participation in prosocial groups and some long-term developmental benefits. Traditionally, youth have learned cooperation through organized youth activity. A rich body of evidence demonstrates that such involvement during adolescence is associated with participation in political organizations, as well as religious and other community institutions, in adulthood (Beane, Turner, Jones, & Lipka, 1981; Hanks & Eckland, 1978; Ladewig & Thomas, 1987; Otto, 1976; Verba et al., 1995; for a review, see Youniss, McLellan, & Yates, 1997). In the political realm, studies suggest that interventions that situate youth in real-life political arenas help youth develop political knowledge and skills. For example, evaluation of the Kids Voting USA program found that the most effective program component was involving youth in community get-out-the-vote campaigns, which was linked to increased levels of volunteering, campus activism, political discussion, and information integration (i.e., integrating new information with existing knowledge), as well as other civic measures two years after the intervention (McDevitt & Kiousis, 2006).

Participation in political discussion is an important type of situated learning activity (e.g., Hess, 2009). Adolescents who frequently talk about political and other current events with their parents score higher on measures of political knowledge, news monitoring, and other civic outcomes and, when they enter young adulthood, vote, volunteer, and engage in other civic activities more frequently than do youth who seldom discuss politics with their parents (Andolina, Jenkins, Zukin, & Keeter, 2003; McIntosh, Hart, & Youniss, 2007). Similarly, youth whose teachers discuss politics and current events with them, orchestrate youth discussions of controversial topics, and create "open classrooms" where diverse student opinions are heard and respected score higher than other students on measures of political knowledge and other civic outcomes (Andolina et al., 2003; Torney-Purta et al., 2001; McLeod, Shah, Hess, & Lee, this volume). And when teachers and peers engage youth in open political discussion, youth are more able to envision themselves as political actors who can effect change by looking toward informed policy (Youniss & Yates, 1997). In brief, political discussion and other activities that enable youth to participate in meaningful, cooperative activities toward political ends constitute a potent means of political socialization and the incorporation of youth into civic life.

SCAFFOLDING

So far, we have proposed that political socialization occurs in real-life settings where youth cooperate with others in meaningful work toward common ends and deliberate with competing interests. However, youth are generally not prepared to do this on their own. Therefore support, or *scaffolding*, by the community's adults—via schools, youth programs, and other social institutions—is critical for helping youth participate in the real-life arena of political contention (Youniss & Hart, 2005). Research indicates that when such adults are involved, youth achieve higher civic engagement outcomes. Simply having a relatively high ratio of adults to children in a neighborhood is associated with higher levels of political knowledge among youth (Hart, Atkins, Markey, & Youniss, 2004). Larson and Hansen (2005) describe how with adult support, adolescents in a civic activism program in Chicago were able to organize a youth summit, work to get a college preparation program introduced into local schools, and lobby the city school board on a range of issues. Youth participation in political discussions with adults is associated with a variety of positive civic outcomes (Andolina et al., 2003; McIntosh et al., 2007; Torney-Purta & Richardson, 2004).

Research suggests that scaffolding involves at least three major components: training, access to a real political system, and support while participating in that system. Training aims at providing youth with the knowledge needed for newcomer participation in a political system. The youth activist program studied by Larson and Hansen (2005), for example, conducted training that involved both learning about social movements and practice (role playing a political confrontation). This training prepared youth for their real-life efforts at political change. Access to a political system is provided through participation with a group that is engaged in that system. In addition, support for youth participation is provided by the group, its resources, and, in particular, its adult members who counsel the youth as they become more-expert participants in the political process. In brief, given the complexity of political engagement, it is difficult to imagine youth becoming involved to a large degree without the guidance and support of knowledgeable adults at home, school, and other places in the community.

An overlooked aspect of political development is the role that organizations play in the lives of youth who are entering the political system. The United States is rich in offering youth access to and membership in recreational groups, civic associations, advocacy organizations, church groups, and the like. Many of these organizations have political and civic purposes and, therefore, serve as socializing agents in the clearest sense of the term. When youth associate with such a group, they are able to share in the history of the organization and the experiences of the adult members, a process that shortcuts the task of youth having to acquire this learning on their own. Developmental theory has generally neglected the positive role these organizations play in youth's political development (Youniss, 2009). Religious organization, 4-H clubs, political parties, and environmental coalitions offer to youth opportunities to participate in well-honed civic enterprises (Youniss et al., 1997). It is a strange conceit that each individual adolescent or youth must construct a political ideology on his or her own. Our society is replete with organizations that have articulated political stances and that offer youth opportunities to incorporate them.

Perspective Taking

Joining a group or organization with political goals nearly always puts one in conflict with other groups having different interests and needs. Although expanding the number of one's allies to achieve political goals by majority force sometimes works, that approach is often not possible nor even desirable in democratic societies. Rather, practical necessity, as well as the principles of democratic participation, requires interest groups to deliberate, or to present their own interests, listen to others' interests, and negotiate a mutually agreeable decision. A crucial skill in such political discussions is the ability to see and understand an issue from a perspective different from one's own. Such perspective taking is at the center of strong democracy (Barber, 2003). Indeed, the abilities of understanding another's point of view and understanding one's own are considered the two core competencies of social development (Selman, 2003).

How citizens use perspective-taking skill depends on their purpose. Political candidates, for instance, may use an opponent's perspective to understand his or her weaknesses and then exploit those weaknesses in a formal political debate. Participants in political discussions try to understand other perspectives in order to arrive at a new and clearer understanding of an issue. Similarly, persons with differing views on a problem try to appreciate others' points of view when deliberating collective decisions and actions. Thus, perspective taking is an important skill in several types of political situation.

MECHANISMS OF POLITICAL SOCIALIZATION

We have described major elements of political engagement and suggested the rudiments of a theory to explain how youth can develop the capacity to function politically. Theoretically, any mechanism that involves adults scaffolding youth in real political activity should work. Families are one example (Andolina et al., 2003; Lake Snell Perry and Associates, 2002; McIntosh et al., 2007). Parents can build their children's interest in political and social issues through family discussions, which also teach perspective-taking skills. Families can also act as collectives of like-minded individuals working for political or social change.

Schools are another place rich in the processes that serve to enhance political socialization and civic engagement (Andolina et al., 2003; Kahn & Westheimer, 2003; Levinson, 2005; Niemi & Junn, 1998). Public schools have long been charged with the civic education of youth generally (Carnegie Corporation of New York & Center for Information and Research on Civic Learning and Engagement, 2003). Schools can provide students with opportunities to discuss current political issues and social controversies, to participate in the governance of schools, to address political issues in the community, or to participate in other forms of learning experiences that are situated in real life and scaffolded by adults.

Community-based organizations are yet another possible mechanism for political socialization. Many of these involve youth programs designed to foster youth political engagement and leadership (e.g., Larson & Hansen, 2005; Sherman, 2002). Others are "adult" political organizations that aim to bring young persons into the activities and membership of the group. During the Freedom Summer campaign to register African-American voters in 1964, civil rights groups recruited and trained youthful volunteers to participate in the political work and goals of the organizations (McAdam, 1988). More recently, Checkoway & Guitierrez (2006) described how community organizers in several cities brought youth into their organizations and helped them develop the skills to work with residents and government officials to address neighborhood problems.

Each of these social mechanisms has the potential to nurture youth into political engagement. Experience suggests, however, that neither families, schools, nor community organizations are sufficient, by themselves, to shoulder the responsibility of drawing the community's youth into sustained political activity. Unless a family engages, rather than avoids, competing interests and ideas, its efforts remain private and don't enter the political arena. Public schools are frequently prohibited by school boards from engaging in political action and from encouraging their students to take political action. And although community organizations have the freedom to take political action, they generally do not have a mandate to civically educate all youth. Thus, each of these mechanisms, though potentially useful for political socialization, has important limitations.

Context

The model of political socialization outlined in this chapter is a general model that should be useful in describing the process of youth political development in a wide range of circumstances. Because political socialization is embedded in institutions and adult relationships, context matters. The process of political socialization will vary in response to the presence or absence of opportunities for youth to participate in situated-learning political activities or, simply, public life (Boyte, 2004). For example, Larson and Hansen (2005) documented how a youth activism program in a low-income Chicago neighborhood helped high-school students develop the political competence to effect positive changes in their school district. Similarly, Sherman (2002) described how a youth empowerment program in San Francisco enabled students to investigate sexual harassment issues in classes and to propose remedial policy to the school board (see also Kirshner, 2007; Ginwright & James, 2002). Based on these and other examples cited in their review of research on social institutions and civic development, Youniss and Hart (2005) concluded, "Adolescents can, with provision of adequate resources, be thoughtful and effective participants in the continuous renewal of democratic society" (p. 79). See also Fox et al., this volume.

The nature of social institutions that engage youth in politics also matters. Our viewpoint stipulates how youth political engagement can be fostered, but it says nothing about the aims of that participation. Many politically active organizations, such as the youth empowerment groups mentioned above, do strive for prosocial ends, but others do not. History provides examples of both types of organization. The civil rights movement in the South was fueled by a coalition of churches, civic groups, private foundations, unions, and the like, which allowed thousands of youthful volunteers to participate in political actions on behalf of social justice (McAdam, 1988; Fendrich, 1993; Morris, 1984). However, youth can also be enlisted for malevolent ends, as illustrated by the Hitler Youth in Germany during the 1930s, which sought to prepare teenage boys to fight for the Third Reich while indoctrinating them with anti-Semitism (Laqueur, 1962). A more recent example of misdirecting young people is the ZANU-PF party in Zimbabwe, which in 2008 used its youth members to break up opposition rallies and intimidate citizens in an effort to win the re-election of President Robert Mugabe (Banya, 2008). There seems to be no limit on ways youth have been recruited as soldiers and terrorists in the name of negative political causes (Barber, 2008).

Policy Implications

The nature of political engagement, the varied mechanisms of engaging youth in political activity, and the importance of context suggest several policy implications. First, we need to bring youth into the public arena of political action, whether by participating in politically oriented activities or by engaging in discussion or debate about real political issues. Youth cannot learn to become citizens solely through textbooks or other indirect means. Schools have roles to play through civics classes and related activities (Levine, 2007). Communities also have roles, whether they include youth in agencies of government (Sirianni & Schor, 2009) or invite them to serve on boards of volunteer civic organizations (Zeldin & Camino, 1999). As Boyte (2004) proposes and as situated learning suggests, effective citizenship begins with meaningful participation in the politics that touches everyday life.

Second, it is important to bring youth into organizations and adult relationships that can scaffold young people during their political development. During the student demonstrations of the 1960s, Erikson (1968) bemoaned the failure of value-bearing institutions to offer youth compelling visions of a just society. Adults took offense at youth protest when they might have presented them with the kinds of intellectual resources youth were striving to create on their own. The value of intergenerational exchange remains central to political socialization. Although it is youth's obligation to adapt value systems to the historical circumstances they confront, it is adults' duty to support youth in this effort.

Finally, we must provide sufficient prosocial scaffolding opportunities to youth who don't have access to them. Much has been made of recent efforts to mobilize youth voters, who from 1972 to 2000 showed persistent declines in rates of voting (Donovan et al., 2005). The reversal of this trend in recent elections has sparked optimism about youth and the future of our democracy. But a closer look at the data reveals a problem that is only beginning to be recognized. To wit, the youth vote is not distributed evenly across all demographic categories, but is tilted heavily toward more educated youth, especially those heading for or graduated from college. For example, whereas 60% of 18- to 24-year-old college students voted in the 2004 presidential election, only one-third of non-college youth voted (Marcelo & Kirby, 2008). The challenge, then, is not simply to mobilize youth, but to include all youth in the business of public life, especially those who do not have the opportunity to enroll in college (Zaff, Youniss, & Gibson, 2009).

Conclusions

In this chapter we have described elements that we believe are useful for a theory of political development. We argued that such a theory needs to take account of the peculiar nature of political engagement and cannot simply rely on an extension of what we know about cognitive, social, or emotional development in other settings. Our approach starts with the elements of what it means to be political in a democracy that encourages active citizen involvement.

In her creative analysis of the recent history of theories of political socialization, Sapiro (2004) proposes that older models of political socialization need to be revised in light of new political realities. The fall of the Berlin Wall woke scholars up to the challenges of making democratic citizens. For example, the people of East Germany did not suddenly take on democratic practices the day they were unified with their West German cousins. So too, our children and youth do not suddenly become engaged citizens at age 18 when they acquire the right to vote. We can assume that they are cognitively able, emotionally intact, and socially oriented. But all of these things do not ensure that they will participate in sustaining democracy by taking an active hand in the political process. What is needed for this assurance is something more—their inclusion in these processes, not as distant observers, but as co-participants. If politics is only something in Washington, then political development will be stalled before it ever begins. But if politics becomes part of youth's everyday life and they are given opportunities to participate, then democracy will likely endure in the next generation of well-practiced citizens.

REFERENCES

Alperovitz, G. (2005). *America beyond capitalism: Reclaiming our wealth, our liberty, and our democracy*. Hoboken, NJ: John Wiley & Sons.

Andolina, M. W., Jenkins, K., Zukin, C., & Keeter, S. (2003). Habits from home, lessons from school: Influences on youth civic development. *PS: Political Science and Politics, 36*, 275–280.

Banya, N. (2008). *Mugabe's rival Tsvangirai pulls out of election*. Retrieved October 31, 2008, from http://www.reuters.com/article/homepageCrisis/idUSL22697262._CH_.2400

Barabas, J. (2004). How deliberation affects policy opinions. *American Political Science Review, 98*, 687–701.

Barber, B. K. (2008). *Adolescents and war: How youth deal with violence*. New York: Oxford University Press.

Barber, B. R. (2003). *Strong democracy: Participatory politics for a new age*. Berkeley: University of California Press.

Beane, J., Turner, J., Jones, D., & Lipka, R. (1981). Long-term effects of community service programs. *Curriculum Inquiry, 11(2),* 143–155.

Berman, S. (1997). *Children's social consciousness and the development of social responsibility*. Albany: State University of New York Press.

Boyte, H. C. (2004). *Everyday politics: Reconnecting citizens and public life*. Philadelphia: University of Pennsylvania Press.

Carnegie Corporation of New York & Center for Information and Research on Civic Learning and Engagement. (2003, February). *The civic mission of schools*. New York: Authors.

Center for Information and Research on Civic Learning and Engagement. (2002). *National Youth Survey, 2002* (questionnaire and toplines). Retrieved January 14, 2009, from http://www.civicyouth.org/PopUps/nys02toplines.pdf

Checkoway, B. N., & Guitierrez, L. M. (Eds.). (2006). Youth participation and community change. *Journal of Community Practice*, 14, Nos. 1 & 2.

Connell, R. W. (1971). *The child's construction of politics*. Melbourne, Australia: Melbourne University Press.

Cook, T. E. (1985). The bear market in political socialization and the costs of misunderstood psychological theories. *American Political Science Review, 79,* 1079–1093.

Delli Carpini, M. X., & Keeter, S. (1996). *What Americans know about politics and why it matters*. New Haven, CT: Yale University Press.

Donovan, C., Lopez, M. H., & Sagoff, J. (2005). *Youth voter turnout during the 2004 presidential and 2002 midterm elections*. Center for Information and Research on Civic Learning and Engagement Fact Sheet. Retrieved January 14, 2009, from http://www.civicyouth.org/PopUps/FactSheets/FS_04_state_vote.pdf

Easton, D., & Dennis, J. (1969). *Children in the political system: Origins of political legitimacy*. New York: McGraw-Hill.

Eliasoph, N. (1998). *Avoiding politics: How Americans produce apathy in everyday life*. New York: Cambridge University Press.

Erikson, E. (1968). *Identity: Youth and crisis*. New York: W. W. Norton & Company, Inc.

Fendrich, J. M. (1993). *Ideal citizens: The legacy of the civil rights movement*. Albany: State University of New York Press.

Galston, W. A. (2001). Political knowledge, political engagement, and civic education. *Annual Review of Political Science, 4,* 217–234.

Gamson, W. A. (1992). *Talking politics*. New York: Cambridge University Press.

Gibson, C. M. (2006). *Citizens at the center: A new approach to civic engagement*. Retrieved April 17, 2008, from http://www.casefoundation.org/spotlight/civic_engagement/gibson

Gimpel, J. G., Lay, J. C., & Schukneckt, J. E. (2003). *Cultivating democracy: Civic environments and political socialization in America*. Washington, DC: Brookings Institution.

Ginwright, S., & James, T. (2002). From assets to agents: Social justice, organizing, and youth development. *Youth Participation: Improving Institutions and Communities: New Directions in Youth Development, 96,* 27–46.

Hanks, M., & Eckland, B. K. (1978). Adult voluntary associations and adolescent socialization. *Sociological Quarterly, 19,* 481–490.

Hart, D., Atkins, R., Markey, P., & Youniss, J. (2004). Youth bulges in communities: The effects of age structure on adolescent civic knowledge and civic participation. *Psychological Science, 15,* 591–597.

Harwood Group. (1993). *Meaningful chaos: How people form relationships with public concerns.* Dayton, OH: Kettering Foundation.

Haste, H. E., & Torney-Purta, J. (1992). *The development of political understanding.* San Francisco: Jossey-Bass.

Hess, D. (2009). Principles that promote discussion of controversial political issues in the curriculum. In J. Youniss & P. Levine (Eds.), *Engaging young people in civic life* (pp. 59–77). Nashville, TN: Vanderbilt University Press.

Hibbing, J. R., & Theiss-Morse, E. (2002). *Stealth democracy: Americans' beliefs about how government should work.* Cambridge, UK: Cambridge University Press.

Kahne, J., Rodriguez, M., Smith, B. A., & Thiede, K. (2000). Developing citizens for democracy? Assessing opportunities to learn in Chicago's social studies classrooms. *Theory and Research in Social Education, 28,* 311–338.

Kahne, J., & Westheimer, J. (2003). Teaching democracy: What schools need to do. *Phi Delta Kappan, 85(1),* 34–40, 47–66.

Kirshner, B. (Ed.). (2007). Youth activism as a context for learning and development. *American Behavioral Scientist, 51(3),* 403–418.

Klandermans, B. (1997). *The social psychology of protest.* Cambridge, MA: Blackwell Publishing.

Ladewig, H., & Thomas, J. K. (1987). *Assessing the impact of 4-H on former members.* College Station: Texas A&M University.

Lake Snell Perry and Associates. (2002). *Short-term impacts, long-term opportunities: The political and civic engagement of young adults in America.* Summary report for Center for Information and Research on Civic Learning and Engagement. Retrieved May 22, 2006, from http://www.civicyouth.org/research/products/national_youth_survey.htm

Laqueur, W. Z. (1962). *Young Germany: A history of the German youth movement.* New York: Basic Books.

Larson, R., & Hansen, D. (2005). The development of strategic thinking: Learning to impact human systems in a youth activist program. *Human Development, 48,* 327–349.

Lave, J., & Wenger, E. (1991). *Situated learning: Legitimate peripheral participation.* Cambridge, UK: Cambridge University Press.

Levine, P. (2007). *The future of democracy: Developing the next generation of American citizens.* Medford, MA: Tufts University Press.

Levinson, M. (2005). Solving the civic achievement gap in de facto segregated schools. *Philosophy & Public Policy Quarterly, 25(1/2),* 2–10.

Mahn, H. (2003). Periods in child development: Vygotsky's perspective. In A. Kozulin & B. Gindis (Eds.), *Vygotsky's educational theory in cultural context* (pp. 119–137). New York: Cambridge University Press.

Marcelo, K. B., & Kirby, E. H. (2008). *The youth vote in the 2008 Super Tuesday states.* Center for Information and Research on Civic Learning and Engagement Fact Sheet. Retrieved January 14, 2009, from http://www.civicyouth.org/PopUps/FactSheets/FS08_supertuesday_exitpolls.pdf

McAdam, D. (1988). *Freedom summer*. New York: Oxford University Press.

McDevitt, M., & Kiousis, S. (2006). *Experiments in political socialization: Kids Voting USA as a model for civic education reform* (CIRCLE Working Paper 49). Medford, MA: CIRCLE. Retrieved May 26, 2009, from http://www.civicyouth.org/PopUps/WorkingPapers/WP49McDevitt.pdf

McIntosh, H., Hart, D., & Youniss, J. (2007). The influence of family political discussion on youth civic development: Which parent qualities matter? *PS: Political Science and Politics, 40,* 495–499.

Merelman, R. M. (1971). The development of political thinking in adolescence. *American Political Science Review, 65,* 1033–1047.

Merelman, R. M. (1985). Role and personality among adolescent political activists. *Youth & Society, 17,* 37–68.

Merelman, R. M. (1990). The role of conflict in children's political learning. In O. Ichilov (Ed.), *Political socialization, citizenship education, and democracy* (pp. 47–65). New York: Teachers College Press.

Morris, A. (1984). *The origins of the civil rights movement: Black communities organizing for change*. New York: Free Press.

National Association of Secretaries of State (1999). *New Millennium Project—Part I: American youth attitudes on politics, citizenship, government, and voting*. Washington, DC: Author.

Niemi, R. G., & Junn, J. (1998). *Civic education: What makes students learn*. New Haven, CT: Yale University Press.

Ostrom, E. (1990). *Governing the commons: The evolution of institutions for collective action*. Cambridge, UK: Cambridge University Press.

Otto, L. B. (1976). Social integration and status-attainment process. *American Journal of Sociology, 81,* 1360–1383.

Piaget, J. (1970). Piaget's theory. In P. H. Mussen (Ed.), *Carmichael's manual of child psychology* (3rd ed., Vol. 1, pp. 703–732), New York: John Wiley & Sons.

Pryor, J. H., Hurtado, S., Saenz, V. B., Santos, J. L., & Korn, W. S. (2007). *The American freshman: Forty year trends*. Los Angeles: Higher Education Research Institute.

Rogoff, B. (1991). *Apprenticeship in thinking: Cognitive development in social context*. New York, NY: Oxford University Press.

Sapiro, V. (2004). Not your parents' political socialization: Introduction for a new generation. *Annual Review of Political Science, 7,* 1– 23.

Sears, D. O. (1972). *Development of concepts of political conflict and power by 5th and 8th graders*. Final report. Retrieved May 28, 2009, from http://eric.ed.gov/ERICWebPortal/contentdelivery/servlet/ERICServlet?accno=ED071959

Selman, R. L. (2003). *The promotion of social awareness: Powerful lessons from the partnership of developmental theory and classroom practice*. New York: Russell Sage Foundation.

Sherman, R. (2002). Building young people's public lives: One foundation's strategy. *New Directions for Youth Development, 96,* 65–82.

Sirianni, C., & Schor, D. M. (2009). City government as enabler of youth civic engagement. In J. Youniss & P. Levine (Eds.), *Engaging young people in civic life*. Nashville, TN: Vanderbilt University Press.

Torney-Purta, J., Lehmann, R., Oswald, H., & Schulz, W. (2001). *Citizenship and education in twenty-eight countries: Civic knowledge and engagement at age fourteen*. Retrieved July 7, 2006, from http://www.wam.umd.edu/~jtpurta/interreport.htm

Torney-Purta, J., & Richardson, W. (2004). Anticipated political engagement among adolescents in Australia, England, Norway, and the United States. In J. Demaine (Ed.), *Citizenship and political education today* (pp. 41–58). London: Palgrave/MacMillan.

Tudge, J. R. H., & Scrimsher, S. (2003). Lev S. Vygotsky on education. In B. J. Zimmerman & D. H. Schunk (Eds.), *Educational Psychology*. Mahwah, NJ: Erlbaum.

Verba, S., Schlozman, K. L., & Brady, H. E. (1995). *Voice and equality: Civic voluntarism in American politics*. Cambridge, MA: Harvard University Press.

Youniss, J. (2009). When morality meets politics in development. *Journal of Moral Education, 38,* 129–144.

Youniss, J., & Hart, D. (2005). Intersection of social institutions with civic development. *New Directions for Child and Adolescent Development, 109,* 73–81.

Youniss, J., McLellan, J. A., & Yates, M. (1997). What we know about engendering civic identity. *American Behavioral Scientist, 40,* 620–631.

Youniss, J., & Yates, M. (1997). *Community service and social responsibility in youth*. Chicago: University of Chicago Press.

Zaff, J. F., Youniss, J., & Gibson, C. M. (2009). *An inequitable invitation to citizenship: Non-college-bound youth and civic engagement.* Retrieved from Philanthropy for Active Civic Engagement web site: http://www.pacefunders.org/publications/NCBY.pdf.

Zeldin, S., & Camino, L. (1999). Youth leadership: Linking research and program theory to exemplary practice. *New Designs for Youth Development, 15,* 10–15.

CHAPTER 2

A Political Science Perspective on Socialization Research: Young Nordic Citizens in a Comparative Light

ERIK AMNÅ
Örebro University, Sweden

PÄR ZETTERBERG
Uppsala University, Sweden

POLITICAL SCIENTISTS ARE generally interested in the study of political participation, often in contrast to scholars from psychology, sociology, or educational studies, who focus more on formation of orientation and identities.[1] Cross-national research indeed has shown substantial variation in political activism. In many respects, citizens of the Nordic countries show the highest levels of political participation (Teorell, Torcal, & Montero, 2007).[2] For instance, Nordic adults are relatively active citizens in voting and party membership and also in associational involvement. Political scientists have put forward various explanations for this pattern. Nordic citizens are said to be more politically motivated, have more political resources, and have stronger participatory norms than others, partly depending on a long tradition of democracy (Andersen & Hoff, 2006). Some scholars put the relatively participatory democracy of the Nordic countries in relation to cultural

1 A very early draft of this chapter was presented at the 2004 ECPR Joint Sessions of Workshops (Uppsala, Sweden). We benefited from the comments of workshop participants. Professor Ingrid Munck provided constructive advice at different stages during the writing of the chapter. The invaluable feedback of the editors of this volume was very helpful in the completion of the chapter. We equally share the responsibility for any remaining errors and omissions.

2 We ascribe to a commonly used definition of political participation, including "deliberate acts by ordinary citizens to influence political outcomes" (Teorell, Torcal, & Montero, 2007, p. 355; see also Brady, 1999).

factors, such as strong emancipative and tolerant values resulting from socio-economic development and Protestantism (Inglehart, 1997; Welzel, Inglehart, & Klingemann, 2003). Others focus on the quality of public institutions, not least the importance of having a fairly uncorrupted public sector (Rothstein & Stolle, 2008), or a long tradition of strong civic information and education, especially for adults (Milner, 2002). Still others point at North Europeans' substantial amount of social capital, assumed to be gained from activities in civic organizations or from networks promoting interpersonal trust (Putnam, 2002). Finally, this relatively extensive participation could simply reflect, at least until recently, absence of ethnic diversity. Heterogeneity has been held to be harmful for a factor close to participation, namely interpersonal trust (Stolle, Soroka, & Johnston, 2008).

Taking a political science perspective on socialization, it is an intriguing challenge to reveal the roots and trajectories that shape discernible participatory patterns across political systems. Hitherto, however, comparative empirical analyses of pre-adults' political attitudes and behavior are scarce (Jennings, 2007). Until recently, the discipline has not had the data needed to explore the answers to questions about why attitudes toward political involvement differ across young people around the world. For this reason, political scientists have made relatively few theoretical contributions to comparative political socialization research. Because of the lack of comparative data, most analyses have therefore paid attention to a single societal context (see, however, Percheron & Jennings, 1981; Niemi & Westholm, 1992; see Jennings, 2007, for a review that crosses contexts).

Cross-national data from the IEA Civic Education Study (1999/2000) on adolescents in more than 20 countries has opened up new possibilities for comparative socialization research (Torney-Purta, Lehmann, Oswald, & Schulz, 2001; Torney-Purta & Amadeo, 2003; Torney-Purta, Barber, & Richardson, 2004). Using IEA data on 14-year-olds in 24 countries, this chapter aims to contribute new theoretical and empirical insights about the trajectories of political involvement as well as about the impact of contextual and individual factors on young people's attitudes toward political participation. Since our point of departure is the map of participation among adults, which illuminates a distinguished Nordic civic activism, our first task is to examine whether a similar pattern is found among adolescents' attitudes toward political participation. In other words, are Nordic youth more inclined to expect to engage in extensive political activism when becoming adults than youth in other societies? Secondly, how appropriate are the theories that account for country variance in political behavior among adults in understanding differences in adolescents' participatory anticipations? As for the first question, our focus is on anticipated political behavior with regard to four modes of political participation—voting, representing (joining a political party or running for local office), legal protesting, and illegal protesting. To answer the second question, we elaborate hypotheses by drawing on political science theories that address cross-national differences in adult political behavior. These theories are partly competing and partly complementary, and incorporate various relevant macro, meso, and micro characteristics of the countries (Norris, 2002).

ANTICIPATED POLITICAL BEHAVIOR AMONG YOUNG ADOLESCENTS: TURNING THE EUROPEAN PARTICIPATORY MAP UPSIDE DOWN

For a long time political participation was seen as unidimensional; citizens were considered as being either active or not. During the last few decades, the concept has been substantially nuanced. It has been shown that a citizen might be positive toward some modes of activities but reluctant toward others. For instance, non-voting does not necessarily imply that a citizen is politically apathetic.

Consequently, modes of political participation could be divided along at least two different dimensions. The first is about the mechanisms through which citizens can exert influence. A distinction is usually made between *exit* and *voice* (Hirschman, 1970). In this analysis, voting is the only exit-based mechanism for political influence; if people are not satisfied with the government, they might choose not to turn out, or alternatively to vote for a party or candidate in opposition (see also Teorell, Torcal, & Montero, 2007). In contrast, the other three participatory modes analyzed here—representing, protesting, and illegal protesting—are referred to as voice-based mechanisms of influence; citizens act by raising their voices in various ways (see Haste, this volume). The second dimension deals with channels of expression. A distinction could be made between representational and extra-representational channels (Teorell, Torcal, & Montero, 2007). Voting and representing refer to the former channel; they focus on the electoral decision-making process. The two modes of protesting, on the other hand, are extra-representational channels of expression; these voice-based activities might be directed not only toward government personnel (cf. Verba & Nie, 1972) but also toward market actors, media, or a wider general public in order to call for political responses and changes.

Analyzing the anticipated political action of 14-year-olds in the 24 countries, Figure 2.1 shows that Southern European youth demonstrates the widest range of expected participatory modes. Regardless of participatory mode, adolescents in Southern Europe claim that they, when becoming adults, will participate to a greater extent than young people

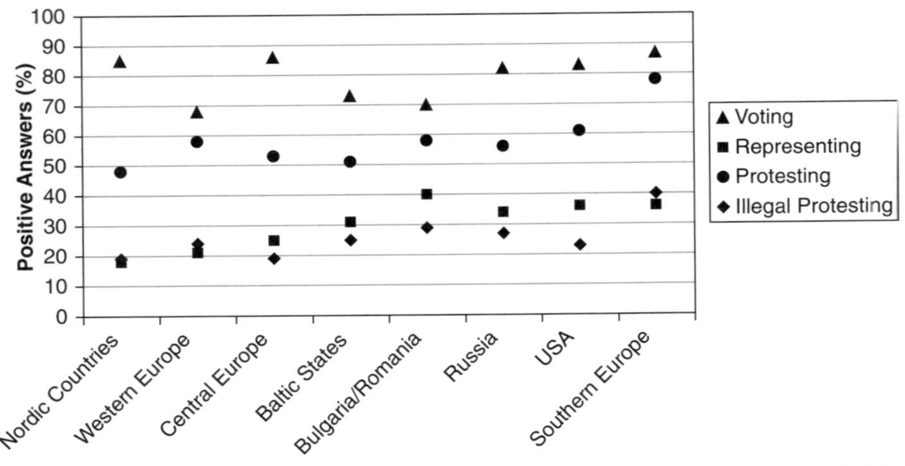

Figure 2.1 Regional Differences for Anticipated Political Participation as an Adult

in other countries. Nordic youth, on the other hand, represents the other extreme. In contrast to political behavior among adults, young people of the Nordic countries anticipate less political action than young people in other countries. An exception is voting, for which the Nordic youth is most inclined to participate, together with Southern European teenagers. In sum, the map of participation might in most respects be turned upside down; the region in the world with the most politically active adult population appears to have offspring who foresee a relatively politically passive adulthood.

FOUR HYPOTHESES ON CROSS-NATIONAL DIFFERENCES IN ADOLESCENTS' PARTICIPATORY INTENTIONS

In order to understand the country pattern of self-prognosticated participatory modes, we turn to the literature on comparative adult political behavior. Some researchers consider cross-national differences to be mainly due to the countries' differing economic or institutional qualities, while others emphasize social and cultural characteristics. Norris (2002) has categorized these theories into four types. The first, modernization theories, stresses the importance of socio-economic development—and subsequent cultural changes—at a macro level. At the meso level, Norris identifies two theories: institutional accounts claim that opportunities for political participation are defined by the structure of the state; agency theories focus on the role of mediating organizations in mobilization and engagement (see also Krishna, 2002). Finally, a micro level theory—the civic voluntarism model—pinpoints the importance of resources, motivational factors, and recruitment options for the willingness to act politically (Norris, 2002). Inspired by Norris's categorization, and applying it to a cross-national analysis of youth's attitudes toward political behavior, we develop four hypotheses at various analytical levels: the modernization hypothesis, the public institutional hypothesis, the social capital hypothesis, and the civic volunteerism hypothesis.

The Modernization Hypothesis

The modernization hypothesis puts emphasis on the socio-economic development of a country. We identify two different strands in the literature delineating the process by which socio-economic development may promote political behavior. The first strand emphasizes the positive impact that strong economic performance has on citizens' resources, and subsequently, on citizens' political action. Higher per capita income enables more people to gain access to education, and consequently, to political information. Moreover, macroeconomic progress facilitates the element of leisure time that is necessary for political participation (Fornos, Power, & Garand, 2004; see also Filer, Kenny, & Morton, 1993).

A second branch of modernization theories underlines the cultural shift and the value changes that are claimed to take place among a society's population, following macroeconomic progress. The argument puts forward that better living conditions (education, income, etc.) and higher levels of existential security erode the impact of all kinds of authority. As a result, citizens tend to question traditional leaderships (whether religious or political). Instead, citizens appear to develop values that are oriented toward self-realization and self-fulfillment. These changes in belief systems have been claimed to have a number of long-term consequences; for instance, more critical attitudes toward authorities are claimed to lead people "from elite-directed participation toward increasing rates of elite-challenging participation" (Inglehart & Catterberg, 2003, p. 303). Thus, citizens are more inclined to participate in politics, but only through specific modes of participation. It is mainly the more loosely coordinated activities that are likely to increase; these activities neither mandate membership nor presuppose a more long-term involvement. On the other hand, it is suggested that activities attached to the representative-democratic institutions such as political party activities will decline.

Transforming this discussion to an analysis on adolescents' participatory intentions, these two variations of modernization theory generate somewhat different hypotheses. Following the line of argument of the first strand, we put forward that the more socioeconomically developed a country, the more positive a young person's attitudes toward all four modes of participation. Given the second strand, our hypothesis is twofold: Firstly, the more modernized a country, the more positive a young person is in that country toward participating in extra-representational (elite-challenging) activities (protesting and illegal protesting). Secondly, the more modernized a country, the more negative a young person is in that country toward participating in representational (elite-driven) activities (voting and representing).

The Public Institutional Hypothesis

The public institutional hypothesis stresses the importance of political institutions in shaping citizens' political attitudes and activities. Institutional approaches focus on a broad range of issues, such as on the ways in which the design and regulation of political institutions and public policies affect civic capacities, incentives, and opportunities to participate. We are synthesizing the approaches into two broad categories: literature on institutional design and literature on institutional performance. The former body of literature emphasizes formal rules and constitutional and electoral regulations. Research has shown that the electoral system plays a key role in explaining differences in voter turnout. For instance, systems with proportional representation (PR) appear to be associated with a larger turnout than plurality systems (Jackman 1987; Blais & Carty, 2006). Since a wider spectrum of ideas is likely to be represented in a PR system (e.g., Duverger, 1954), more people tend to be motivated to vote. The electoral system also impacts the opportunity structures for citizens. For instance, if elections are held on a weekday, fewer people are likely to vote. In addition, more recent work has analyzed the impact of specific institutional or electoral arrangements not only on voting, but also on other modes of action (e.g., Zetterberg, 2009). There are reasons to assume that different institutional designs, by shaping citizen involvement in politics, also affect the formation of adolescents' political attitudes. For instance, the better the political system reflects a myriad of political opinions, the more probable that young people grow up in a civic culture in which their parents' political values are represented somewhere in that political system. As a consequence, both parents' and children's political engagement may be promoted.

As regards literature on institutional performances, an analytical distinction should be made between different strands. Roughly speaking, there are those having a macro-political perspective; they emphasize the quality of the delivery of public goods. Others pay attention to citizens' perceptions of political institutions and public representatives. The former group usually examines the effectiveness of government performance and how it relates to citizens' willingness to be politically engaged. For instance, suggestions have been made that as a government becomes more efficient in delivering public goods, more issues are politicized and thus addressed in the public debate. An increased politicization of issues is hypothesized to increase citizens' attention to politics, and consequently their political interest (van Deth & Elff, 2004). Because of the proximity between political interest and political participation (e.g., Verba, Schlozman, & Brady, 1995), effective governments might be argued to generate also more politically active citizens.

Citizens' perceptions about institutional performance have been frequently examined in survey data analyses. Questions have been asked about citizens' confidence in political regime type (democracy), government, parliament, political parties, and individual legislators. A rich body of literature has examined the ways in which attitudes toward political institutions affect citizen involvement. For instance, scholars have disagreed about whether satisfaction or dissatisfaction with democratic institutions foster protest behavior (e.g., Inglehart & Catterberg, 2003; Kriesi & Westholm, 2007). Others suggest the importance of citizens perceiving their political system to be responsive to citizens' demands, and feeling that it is worthwhile to try to influence policy outcomes (so-called external efficacy) (Campbell, Converse, Miller, & Stokes, 1960; Abramson, 1983).

General attitudes toward governments' performance could be the result of impressions based on media reports and news coverage. However, scholars have also paid attention to citizens' direct experiences with public representatives and officials as well as of involvement in publicly organized welfare programs. It has been argued that it is in the interface between citizen and public organization that the mechanism for an "institutionalized citizen empowerment" can be found (Kumlin, 2002, p. 24). To start with citizens' direct experiences of public institutions, it has been claimed that the more consultative public institutions are in their exercise of public authority, the greater the citizens' willingness to engage in politics. More precisely, impartiality—or procedural fairness—has been claimed to be a key issue in building institutional legitimacy (Rothstein & Teorell, 2008; Andersen & Roßteutscher, 2007). When citizens perceive that they have been treated fairly by public officials, their motivation to become involved in politics is suggested to increase. As for involvement in policy programs (e.g., Mettler & Soss, 2004), such activities might also increase citizens' political resources in terms of civic knowledge.

Transforming this discussion to the analysis of youth's political development, it is important to compare the impact of not only the overall political system (or large-scale democracy; see van Deth, Montero, & Westholm, 2007), but also public authorities (or small-scale democracy). In particular, those institutions that one would expect a 14-year-old to have most direct contact with—the schools—deserve attention (Torney-Purta, Barber, & Richardson, 2004; Flanagan, Cumsille, Gill, & Gallay, 2007; Gunnarson, 2008). For instance, recent reports confirm that the choice of teaching methods makes a difference for the development of civic orientations. For instance, a deliberative classroom climate has been found to be of utmost importance, in combination with political self-esteem to explain civic engagement (Ekman, 2007; Almgren, 2006). This includes studies in Sweden and in a broader range of countries (Torney-Purta et al., 2001; McLeod, Shah, Hess, & Lee, this volume). In this chapter, we aim at finding out more about the role of schools. More specifically, we explore the relation between a young person's intended political participation and the level of confidence in schools, feelings of internal efficacy in the schools, the schools' mechanisms for collective action, and the openness of the classroom climate. Similarly, for large-scale democracy, we expect that the more confidence in a country's political parties, the greater the willingness of a young person to participate in politics.

THE SOCIAL CAPITAL HYPOTHESIS

The social capital hypothesis emphasizes the agencies that mobilize interaction between people. More precisely, social capital is commonly defined as "connections among individuals—social networks and the norms of reciprocity and trustworthiness that arise from them" (Putnam, 2000, p. 19). In the growing literature on social capital, several qualifications of the concept have been offered. Usually, a distinction is made between structural social capital (which refers to networks such as memberships in associations) and attitudinal social capital (which refers to interpersonal trust and attitudes of reciprocity, and so forth) (Hooghe & Stolle, 2003; Edwards & Foley, 1998). Regarding structural social capital, it has been assumed that associational activity promotes participatory attitudes as well as knowledge and democratic attitudes. Associations are seen as schools of democracy; they generate positive effects on confidence in public institutions as well as on senses of political efficacy. However, the socialization mechanisms do not seem to operate in the same way regardless of modes of political involvement. For instance, participation in voluntary associations seems to influence voting behavior positively in early adulthood (Frisco, Muller, & Dodson, 2004), while it may have a different effect for demonstrating.

In addition, research has shown that there are reasons to separate types of association. For adolescents, memberships in politically oriented associations seem to be associated with political engagement in some contexts (Amnå, 2007). Regarding adults, it has been argued that affiliation per se, independent of the intensity of participation, is the only thing that matters (Maloney, van Deth, & Roßteutscher, 2007). Furthermore, in analyses of young adolescents in various countries, the same type of associational membership appears to have different effects on political participation in different political contexts (see Amnå, 2007).

However, there are scholars who highlight the attitudinal kind of social capital. They call into question the role of associations in promoting democratic citizenship (Uslaner, 2002; Newton, 2007). More specifically, they raise doubts about the causal link from associational participation to citizen involvement, arguing that many social capital analyses suffer from problems of self-selection bias (Newton, 1997; Stolle, 2003; Armingeon, 2007). Such criticism calls into doubt findings of previous research; early work on the impact of social capital suggested for instance that a mechanism linking associational involvement to political behavior is the interaction with fellow citizens and its spillover effects to self-reliance and confidence in political institutions (Brehm & Rahn, 1997). More recent analyses suggest that the causal link may be reversed: A citizen's confidence in his or her civil servants and public officials spills over into interpersonal trust (Rothstein, 2005).

Putting this discussion into hypotheses about youth's political socialization, the social capital hypothesis asserts that the more social capital a young person possesses, the higher the level of anticipated political participation. More specifically, the hypothesis is split up in two parts, one is more structurally oriented, the other more attitudinal. Firstly, the more involved a young person is in associational life, the more prone he or she is to anticipate extensive political participation. Secondly, the more trusting toward his or her fellow citizens, the more extensive anticipated participation of a young person.

The Civic Volunteerism Hypothesis

The civic volunteerism hypothesis, finally, is rooted in a micro-theory of political participation. A comprehensive model summarizing the micro factors is labeled the Civic Voluntarism Model (Verba et al., 1995). It emphasizes three characteristics that are of crucial importance for political activism. Firstly, and perhaps most investigated, is the impact of a person's civic resources in terms of education, time, skills, and knowledge. Secondly, and less empirically researched (Galston, 2001; Norris, 2002), motivational factors pay attention to individuals' willingness to take part in politics. Such willingness might for instance stem from specific participatory norms (e.g., a sense of duty) or from feelings of being politically empowered. Finally, differences in recruitment options play an important role for an individual's likelihood to take part in civic life. To be asked by others to participate seems to influence a person's decision to activate his or her political citizenship.

From a comparative point of view, it is possible that individuals in some countries are on average more politically motivated than those in other societies. Such differences might relate to diverse macro or meso characteristics. In other words, micro factors such as resources, motivation, and recruitment options might be powerful mechanisms, linking macro or meso processes to citizens' political involvement. For instance, we have previously mentioned the possibility that the level of a society's economic development promotes a citizen's civic reasoning skills, which in turn could impact political behavior.

Putting this discussion in a youth development context, we hypothesize that the more civic resources, motivation, and recruitment options an adolescent has, the more likely he or she is to be inclined to participate in representative arenas (voting and representing) as well as in extra-parliamentarian activities (protesting and illegal protesting).

EXPLAINING THE PARTICIPATORY INTENTIONS: EXPLORING EMPIRICAL RESULTS

To explore the hypotheses empirically, we use data that reflect specific country characteristics as well as personal experiences of the youth. The contextual model that we use illuminates associations between the 14-year-olds' anticipations and country-specific (macro) factors, individuals' relations to political socialization and mobilization arenas (meso factors), and adolescents' own resources and motivations (micro factors).

Our exploration is based on a set of questions from the IEA Civic Education Study relating to political action: "When you are an adult, what do you expect that you will do?" The alternative answers were "I will certainly not do this," "I will probably not do this," "I will probably do this," "I will certainly do this," and "Don't know." There are nine items pertaining to *voting, representing* (joining a political party or running for local office), *protesting* (writing letters to editors, collecting signatures, or protesting peacefully), and *illegal protesting* (spray-painting, blocking traffic, or occupying buildings).

Regarding the explanatory factors, we use a frequently utilized variable to explore the modernization hypothesis (e.g., Norris, 2002; van Deth & Elff, 2004): the level of human development, measured by using an index composed by estimated income, life expectancy at birth, and the level of education (UNDP, 2000). In contrast to meso and micro factors, this macro factor emphasizes the surrounding environment's association with a young person's anticipations of participation.

Meso factors, on the other hand, relate to the 14-year-olds' personal experiences of potential political socialization arenas such as public institutions and social networks (including associational life). We use six measures to explore the public institutional hypothesis: First, individuals' confidence in their country's political parties is used to identify how much the adolescents trust key actors of representative democracy. This item attempts to cover more general perceptions about the political system, or the large-scale democracy. Second, five variables measure the 14-year-olds' daily experiences of a publicly regulated activity, that is, school. These variables are the adolescents' trust in the school system, their confidence in joint action at school, their beliefs about having a personal say in school matters (internal school efficacy), the openness of the classroom climate, and the extent to which they discuss political or societal issues with their teacher(s). The social capital hypothesis, on the other hand, is measured with two variables: participation in 15 types of associations (structural social capital) and the adolescents' trust in their fellow citizens (attitudinal social capital).

Finally, the micro factors of the civic volunteerism hypothesis are explored with four variables. These variables cover key aspects of the civic voluntarism model (Verba et al., 1995), which points at the importance of individuals' sets of resources and motivations: norms about good citizenship (civic norms), motivational factors (frequency of political discussion with parents and friends), and resources (internal efficacy and political knowledge, the latter captured by 38 multiple-choice items in a civic knowledge test). Unfortunately, there were no questions about recruitment to political action in the dataset.

We examined two models, the first showing the associations when we restrict the analysis to macro and meso factors. The restriction was made because micro factors could be mediating factors, linking macro and meso characteristics to participatory intentions. Therefore, if we only presented a model in which micro factors are included, we might erroneously conclude that there is a nonsignificant relationship between macro or meso factors and the youths' participatory intentions. More specifically, we might fail to detect a possible *indirect* relationship. Therefore, we examined a first analysis without taking micro factors into account. A second model also included micro factors.

A general finding, not shown here[3], is that the differences in participatory anticipations appear to be traced to the adolescents' personal experiences; the pure macro-based hypothesis, the modernization hypothesis, gained no empirical support. We have noted previously that the youth of the socioeconomically most developed European countries (i.e., the Nordic countries) anticipate the most limited political participation, while those of Southern Europe have high expectation for participation.

With respect to the other three hypotheses, there is a mixed picture. One mode of action seems to follow one of our models, while others seem to

3 For tables as well as additional details on measurements and the analyses, see our preparation paper, YeS Working paper 2009:1 at http://www.oru.se/English/Research/Research-environments/Research-environment/Youth–Society-YeS/Publications/

follow other models. The public institutional hypothesis appears relatively accurate for two modes of action: voting and protesting. Perceptions about both key actors of representative democracy (political parties) and public institutions that affect the 14-year-olds' daily lives (school) appear related to these anticipations. The youths' beliefs about their possibility to understand school matters appear to be especially important for their anticipations of broader participation. The same could be said about the students' political discussions with their teachers, as well as their confidence in political parties.

The social capital hypothesis gains most support for protest activities. Both structural and attitudinal social capital appears to be positively associated to this mode of action. Voting, on the other hand, is unrelated to both involvement in organizations and trust in fellow citizens. As for representing (joining a political party or running for local office), one of the two aspects of social capital—structural social capital—appears to be of importance, while attitudinal social capital seems to matter for illegal protesting.

Given the proximity between political attitudes and civic resources, motivations and norms, it is perhaps not surprising that our exploration gives the greatest support to the civic volunteerism hypothesis. It appears plausible for every type of action except illegal protest. Interestingly, there is a positive relationship between internal efficacy and each of the four modes of action. In other words, the adolescents' sense of understanding and having a say in politics seems to be of particular importance. This is, however, not necessarily related to the youths' actual knowledge about politics. Political knowledge is positively related only to voting, for example. In addition to internal efficacy, civic norms also appear to be particularly relevant for the participatory intentions.

To sum up, differences in participatory intensions among European and North American youth appears to be attributable to the 14-year-olds' perceived resources and motivations, but to some extent also to the youths' experiences of school and the political system as well as their social networks. A country's level of development, on the other hand, appears not to be related to the participatory intentions of adolescents. Following these lines of reasoning, there appear to be fewer highly motivated young people living in the Nordic countries than in Southern Europe. In addition, Nordic teenagers do not perceive as much as Southern European youth that they could understand and make a difference in politics.

We cannot exclude the possibility that already highly motivated students become involved in voluntary associations and in a broad range of participatory modes. In this case, the participatory anticipations are not a result of a student's involvement in associational life (Finkel, 1985). One of the reasons for this possibility is related to our use of cross-sectional data. Another reason is the fact that the strongest school factor, internal school efficacy (and also social network factors such as participation in organizations), is not necessarily related to the performance of the school. As we go forward with our analysis, we are cautious not to overstate the impact of the meso factors. This also emphasizes the value of having longitudinal data in socialization analyses.

REPORTED POLITICAL ACTIVITY IN LATE ADOLESCENCE AND EARLY ADULTHOOD: RESHAPING THE POLITICAL ENGAGEMENT MAP

The quite surprising pattern among youth, with Nordic youth anticipating the least involvement in politics, highlights an intriguing question for scholars and practitioners who are interested in citizens' political engagement: Do the findings give indications of a revised participatory map among European adults? Or do the results highlight possible fluctuations in the political socialization processes of European and North American youth? To put it differently, the findings raise questions about possible generational or life-cycle effects: Nordic youth's more limited participatory intentions might be heralds of a new participatory pattern distinctively deviating from earlier generations; or their activist behavior is developed later in life (Zukin et al., 2006; see also Amnå, Ekman, & Almgren, 2007). This question relates to a further question—that is, whether there are lasting formative effects of experiences in early childhood; some political scientists (as well as educators) have argued that there are certain factors, mainly from school, that shape an individual's political formation (Verba et al., 1995; see also Easton & Dennis, 1967). Others have questioned the impact of early childhood experiences; they claim that late adolescence represents crucial formative years for political socialization (Watts, 1999; Jennings & Stoker, 2004).

To address these issues and shed light on which of these mechanisms (generational or life-cycle effects) seem to be operating, we compare the adolescents' participatory intentions with reported participation by about the same cohort a few years later. In order to perform the analysis, we use cross-national data from the European Social Survey (ESS) on 16- to 25-year-olds in 15 European (and with the IEA study overlapping) countries (2002 to 2003).[4] The ESS data set includes many overlapping questions with the

4 The countries are Denmark, Finland, Norway, and Sweden (Nordic countries); Belgium, England, Germany, and Switzerland (Western Europe); Czech Republic, Hungary, Poland, and Slovenia (Central Europe); and Greece, Italy, and Portugal (Southern Europe). The major shortcomings of using this dataset are that we are dealing with neither the same individuals nor the full set of countries, and that we have to include some years older than the cohort of interest, due to small-N problems. However, comparative panel data are very rare.

IEA dataset; for instance, it asks questions about all four modes of action. However, because of the very small number (less than 4%) of individuals engaging in party or campaign activities as well as in illegal protests, the analysis is restricted to voting (in the last national election) and protesting (signed a petition during the last 12 months). However, because of its generally manifested proximity to political participation, we supplement the two participatory modes with the degree of political interest (*very, quite, hardly, not at all*). This factor has been held to be particularly important for more time-consuming activities such as party activism (Brady, Verba, & Schlozman, 1995). Political interest could therefore be characterized as a proxy for certain kinds of political activities.

Figure 2.2 compares the participatory intentions among young adolescents with the behavior of young adults. It is shown that for both modes of participation the level of reported behavior is lower than the participatory intentions at an earlier age. In contrast to the findings on the 14-year-olds' participatory intentions, the empirical analysis also indicates that the north-south division is not present in the reported actual behavior among older adolescents and young adults. As shown in Figure 2.2, there are no indications that 16- to 25-year-olds in Southern Europe participate more intensively in politics than Northern Europeans. On the contrary, there is a reversed tendency regarding both voting and protest activities; 16- to 25-year-olds in the Nordic countries participate to a greater extent than others. In other words, already in late adolescence and early adulthood there appears to be a reshaping of the participatory map in Europe. Thus, life-cycle effects seem to be operating; there appears to be no general change in participatory pattern due to generational changes. This study therefore gives support

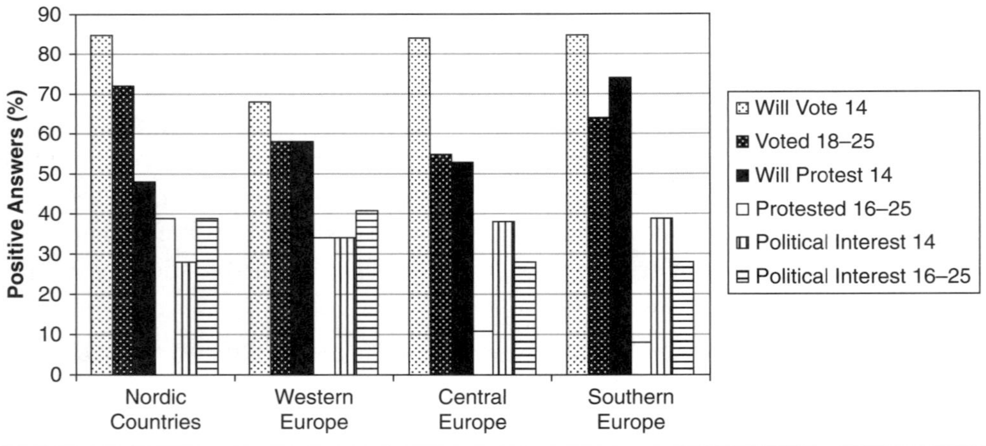

Figure 2.2 Regional Differences in Political Interest and Predicted/Reported Political Participation for Young People Aged 14 and 16–25

to those who have argued that developments during late adolescence and early adulthood seem to be of importance for participatory norms (Watts, 1999; Jennings & Stoker, 2004). The development of political interest also illustrates this pattern. Whereas political interest generally decreases from early to late adolescence in Central and Southern Europe, Nordic youth (as well as western Europeans) becomes on average more interested in politics during this period.

Here we also used a regression analysis in order to try to explore the reasons for a different participatory pattern among older adolescents and young adults than the one apparent among the 14-year-olds. More specifically, we construct an explanatory model that encompasses the same hypotheses as for the younger adolescents. We want to understand if there are similar or different factors accounting for variance in engagement among older adolescents and young adults than in early adolescence. As for the variables, they are in many ways similar to those of the 14-year-olds: The modernization hypothesis is measured through the United Nations Development Programmes (UNDP) human development index; the social capital hypothesis uses an index of associational engagement as well as an index related to trust in fellow citizens; and the civic hypothesis is explored by analyzing civic norms, internal efficacy, and political discussion. The main difference is that the public institutional hypothesis mainly covers aspects related to the large democracy; and everyday life experiences of publicly regulated activities (such as the younger adolescents' school experiences) are not generally included. There is one possible exception, however: Questions about the individuals' confidence in the police and the legal system might perhaps relate to these slightly older citizens' direct contact with public authorities.

The impact of macro and meso factors is in many ways similar, although not identical, for the older adolescents' participation as was the case for the 14-year-olds' participatory anticipations. First, there is still a limited support for the modernization hypothesis.[5] For instance, the level of socioeconomic development appears not to be positively related to the young adults' political interest. This contrasts with findings on European adults (see van Deth & Elff, 2004). However, in one respect the hypothesis gains support: As a country becomes more economically developed, its young citizens tend to be more willing to engage in protest activities (see also Inglehart and Catterberg, 2003). Second, confidence in the political system appears in some respect to foster political engagement also among older adolescents. For instance,

5 Again, for tables as well as additional details on measurements and the analyses, see our preparation paper, YeS Working paper 2009:1 at http://www.oru.se/English/Research/Research-environments/Research-environment/Youth--Society-YeS/Publications/

confidence in politicians as well as in the parliament is positively related to both voting and political interest. However, positive experiences from public officials of the legal system are, on the other hand, negatively related to most political involvement. Thus, the impact of everyday life experiences of publicly regulated activities appears to differ over time; whereas school mostly generates a willingness to engage in politics, the legal system appears not to do so. Third, when examining older adolescents and young adults, the social capital hypothesis gains partial support. However, the pattern is in one respect more clear-cut at this older age: It is associational involvement (or structural social capital) that appears to matter for political participation, not individuals' trust in their fellow citizens. In other words, participation in voluntary associations seems to be a boosting factor for both voting and protest activities, as well as for political interest. For the younger adolescents, there was a more mixed impact of associational involvement.

There is general support for the civic volunteerism hypothesis. Political discussion is positively related to voting and protest activities. So is internal efficacy, which is also positively related to political interest. Civic norms seem to impact political interest and the propensity to vote, however, not the willingness to protest. In other words, the findings related to resources, norms, and motivation are in most respects similar for the older respondent to the ESS as they were for the 14-year-old respondents to the IEA survey.

By comparing the findings of the 14-year-olds with those of the older adolescents and young adults, it appears that the factors accounting for differences in young people's political engagement are similar across the years from 14 through 25. Positive attitudes toward the political system, involvement in civic organizations, as well as resources and motivation appear to have a general positive impact on the willingness to participate in politics. The only factor that has no general association with adolescents' and young adults' political engagement is the level of socioeconomic modernization in the individual's country. In this respect, there is a difference from research on adults' political behavior. A more far-reaching conclusion of the comparative analysis is that there seem to be different general political socialization trajectories across regions. At the age of 14, mainly Southern Europeans seem to have the confidence in the political institutions, social networks, resources, and motivation needed to foresee a large participatory repertoire. However, a few years later in life, such attributes are more common in the Nordic countries. In conclusion, this puts emphasis on the time period of late adolescence and early adulthood. As has been highlighted in political socialization research, these seem to be formative years that greatly affect how people perceive politics. This analysis adds a dimension to this literature: The formative years of late adolescence appear not only to be important for our understanding of diverse political development among individuals in a single context; they also seem to generate different system-specific developments of political orientations among young people in different societies.

FORMATIVE YEARS OF EMERGING *STAND-BY CITIZENS*

In this chapter, perspectives from political science have been introduced in order to contribute to our understanding of political socialization. The point of departure of the analysis has been the participatory pattern among adult citizens in European and North American societies, and the fact that adults of the Nordic countries appear to be relatively politically active. Our aim has been to present and explore patterns of participation envisioned among young people in these parts of the world. First, we addressed the question of at what age civic orientations are developed, by examining if indications of a relatively politically engaged Nordic citizenry are visible in early adolescence (14-year-olds). Second, we drew on political science literature of comparative political behavior to understand cross-national differences in participatory anticipations.

Our main result is that among young adolescents, the participatory map seems to be turned upside down in comparison with the countries' adult citizens: The Nordic youth anticipated the least involvement in politics when becoming adults. However, when comparing these results with reported political action from late adolescence and early adulthood (16- to 25-year-olds), it was shown that the Nordic citizens participate to a greater extent than others. The participatory map well-known from studies of adults was largely restored. When explaining the participatory intentions, positive attitudes toward the political system, involvement in civic organizations, as well as resources and motivation appear to have a general positive impact. In contrast to adults, however, one factor appeared not to be influential, namely the level of socioeconomic modernization.

The absence of strong participatory norms among Nordic 14-year-olds puts emphasis on the possibility that there are certain formative years in late adolescence that appear to be crucial for the development of political values and beliefs (see also Watts, 1999; Jennings & Stoker, 2004; Finlay, Wray-Lake, & Flanagan, this volume; Torney-Purta, Amadeo, & Andolina, this volume). In order to try to understand the changes, we refer to recent governmental *democratic audits* in Denmark (Andersen, 2006), Norway (Selle & Østerud, 2006), and Sweden (Amnå, 2006). Indeed, all Scandinavian democratic audits pointed at emerging modes of more temporary, individually empowered and conditioned attitudes. Similar tendencies, seen as a shift from duty-based to engaged citizenship, have also been discussed elsewhere (Zukin, Ketter, Andolina, Jenkins, & Delli Carpini, 2006; Dalton, 2008; Bennett, Freelon, & Wells, this volume).

In order to theoretically capture these civic orientations, we suggest the concept of the *stand-by citizen* (Amnå, 2008, 2010). It takes not only manifest but also latent civic engagement dimensions of attitudes and behavior into account. Stand-by citizens are characterized by a certain amount of political interest and motivation, which is only occasionally transformed into manifest action, more specifically when citizens perceive that they are needed. They identify a problem as well as a solution that is both effective and meaningful. Due to complex motivational dynamics, citizens seem to stay alert regarding what is going on and what is being done in politics. They keep an eye on the political commons; however, most of the time they cannot be found in any public political action. But over a lifetime, they cannot be seen as passive. Empirically, the concept of a stand-by citizen is in harmony with longitudinal panel data manifesting a continuous and stable level of Swedish citizens' political discussions with their fellow citizens over the last quarter of a century (Amnå, 2008). Furthermore, it supports Andersen's, Hoff's, and others' claims about Scandinavian exceptionalism: A comparatively high level of political interest in this region can not only be explained by a large number of politically involved citizens, but also by a small number of citizens who over their entire lifetime are totally withdrawn from politics (Andersen and Hoff, 2006; van Deth & Elff, 2004).

Transforming the discussion of stand-by citizens to a cross-national analysis of youth's civic development, we suggest that a reason for Nordic young adolescents' relatively low participatory expectations might be because their contributions in politics rest on being asked to become engaged (Amnå, 2008; see also Kriesi & Westholm, 2007; Andersen & Roßteutscher, 2007). At the age of 14, Nordic adolescents rarely experience their involvement being requested, not in politics and not in other forms of collective decision making. However, as they approach the age of 18 (when they are given the right to vote), there is a demand for Nordic, and perhaps also for Western European, young people to get involved in politics. They are encouraged to take part in different kinds of public activities, which are likely to nourish their interest in politics in a wide sense (see also Dalton, Cain, & Scarrow, 2003). In comparison, Southern European adolescents' relatively high political interest appears to decrease when approaching adulthood. It may reflect that the participatory options for small-scale actions are not as wide as in the Nordic countries (Kriesi & Westholm, 2007). Because of the fewer participatory options in Southern Europe, the threshold for stepping into the political process is perceived as higher: "Action is more dependent on capacity and less on subjectively felt needs" (Kriesi & Westholm, 2007, p. 277).

This line of reasoning may be taken a step further into some preliminary policy implications. Our analysis seems to reveal a crucial dynamic between individual resources and institutional responsiveness. A political system that wants to facilitate civic engagement not only has to design general welfare policies that could create various civic resources and capacities; it also has to offer public institutions that are accessible for citizen involvement by being operated transparently, impartially, and accountably. At this early stage, these suggestions are tentative, and more comparative research is required. The intriguing findings of this analysis give us reason to examine political socialization in a longitudinal perspective, also paying attention to the fact that political socialization processes appear to operate differently across countries—a phenomenon that to our knowledge has been previously overlooked. There is a lack of knowledge about the development of political and civic engagement over the entire period of adolescence and emerging adulthood that takes the influence from various contextual settings into account. Longitudinal studies are therefore needed that contain measures that are able to (1) explore a variety of theoretically specified processes and mechanisms of youths' experiences; (2) cover a broad range of political and civic activities; and (3) take into consideration the variety of contexts and everyday life experiences (Amnå, Ekström, Kerr, & Stattin, 2009). In short, a major challenge for research is to include a longitudinal perspective in order to capture variations over time, such as the rise of stand-by citizens in contemporary democracies.

REFERENCES

Abramson, P. R. (1983). *Political attitudes in America: Formation and change*. San Francisco, CA: Freeman.

Almgren, E. (2006). *Att fostra demokrater: Om skolan i demokratin och demokratin i skolan*. Uppsala: Skrifter utgivna av Statsvetenskapliga föreningen.

Amnå, E. (2006). Playing with fire? A Swedish mobilisation for participatory democracy. *Journal of European Public Policy, 13(4)*, 587–606.

Amnå, E. (2007). Associational life, youth, and political capital formation in Sweden: Historical legacies and contemporary trends. In L. Trägårdh (Ed.), *The state and civil society in northern Europe: The Swedish model reconsidered* (pp. 165–204). New York and Oxford: Berghahn Books.

Amnå, E. (2008). *Jourhavande medborgare. Samhällsengagemang i en folkrörelsestat*. Lund: Studentlitteratur.

Amnå, E. (2010). Active, passive, or stand-by citizens: Latent and manifest political participation. In E. Amnå (Ed.), *New forms of citizen participation: Normative implications* (pp. 191–203). Baden Baden: Nomos.

Amnå, E., Ekman, T., & Almgren, E. (2007). The end of a distinctive model of democracy? Country-diverse orientations among young adult Scandinavians. *Scandinavian Political Studies, 30(1)*, 61–86.

Amnå, E., Ekström, M., Kerr, M., & Stattin, H. (2009). Political socialization and human agency. The development of civic engagement from adolescence to adulthood. *Statsvetenskaplig Tidskrift, 111(1),* 27–40.

Andersen, J. G., (2006). Political power and democracy in Denmark: Decline of democracy or change in democracy? *Journal of European Public Policy, 13(4),* 569–586.

Andersen, J. G., & Hoff, J. (2006). *Democracy and citizenship in Scandinavia*. Hampshire: Palgrave.

Andersen, J. G., & Roßteutscher, S. (2007). Small-scale democracy: Citizen power in the domains of everyday life. In J. van Deth, J. R. Montero, & A. Westholm (Eds.), *Citizenship and involvement in European democracies: A comparative analysis* (pp. 221–254). Oxin and New York: Routledge.

Armingeon, K. (2007). Political participation and associational involvement. In J. van Deth, J. R. Montero, & A. Westholm (Eds.), *Citizenship and involvement in European democracies: A comparative analysis* (pp. 358–383). Oxin and New York: Routledge.

Berglund, S., & Aarebrot, S. (1997). *The political history of Eastern Europe in the 20th century: The struggle between democracy and dictatorship*. Cheltenham: Edward Elgar.

Blais, A., & Carty, R. K. (2006). Does proportional representation foster voter turnout? *European Journal of Political Research, 18(2),* 167–181.

Brady, H. E. (1999). Political participation. In J. P. Robinson, P. R. Shaver, & L. S. Wrightman (Eds.), *Measures of political attitudes* (pp. 737–801). San Diego, CA: Academic Press.

Brady, H. E., Verba, S., & Schlozman, K. (1995). Beyond SES: A resource model of political participation. *American Political Science Review, 89,* 271–294.

Brehm, J., & Rahn, W. (1997). Individual-level evidence for the causes and consequences of social capital. *American Journal of Political Science, 41(3),* 999–1023.

Campbell, A., Converse, P. E., Miller, W. E., & Stokes, D. (1960). *The American voter*. New York: John Wiley & Sons.

Dalton, R. J. (2008). Citizenship norms and the expansion of political participation. *Political Studies, 56(1),* 76–98.

Dalton, R. J., Cain, B. E., & Scarrow, S. E. (2003). Democratic publics and democratic institutions. In B. E. Cain, R. J. Dalton, & S. E. Scarrow (Eds.), *Democracy transformed? Expanding political opportunities in advanced industrial democracies* (pp. 250–275). Oxford: Oxford University Press.

Duverger, M. (1954). *Political parties: Their organization and activities in the modern state*. London: Methuen.

Easton, D., & Dennis, J. (1967). The child's acquisition of regime norms: Political efficacy. *American Political Science Review, 61,* 25–38.

Edwards, B., & Foley, M. W. (1998). Civil society and social capital beyond Putnam. *American Behavioral Scientist, 42(1),* 124–139.

Ekman, T. (2007). *Demokratisk kompetens: Om gymnasiet som demokratiskola*. Göteborg: Statsvetenskapliga institutionen.

Filer, J. E., Kenny, L. W., & Morton, R. B. (1993). Redistribution, income, and voting. *American Journal of Political Science, 37,* 63–87.

Finkel, S. E. (1985). Reciprocal effects of participation and political efficacy: A panel analysis. *American Journal of Political Science, 29(4),* 891–913.

Flanagan, C., Cumsille, P., Gill, S., & Gallay, L. (2007). School and community climates and civic commitments: Patterns for ethnic minority and majority students. *Journal of Educational Psychology, 99,* 421–431.

Fornos, C. A., Power, T. J., & Garand, J. C. (2004). Explaining voter turnout in Latin America, 1980 to 2000. *Comparative Political Studies, 37(8),* 909–940.

Frisco, M. L., Muller, C., & Dodson, K. (2004). Participation in voluntary youth-serving associations and early adult voting behavior. *Social Science Quarterly, 85(3),* 660–676.

Galston, W. A. (2001). Political knowledge, political engagement, and civic education. *Annual Review of Political Science, 4,* 217–234.

Gunnarson, C. (2008). *Cultural warfare and trust: Fighting the mafia in Palermo.* Manchester: Manchester University Press.

Hirschman, A. O. (1970). *Exit, voice, and loyalty: Responses to decline in firms, organisations, and states.* Cambridge: Cambridge University Press.

Hooghe, M., & Stolle, D. (2003). Age matters: Life cycle and cohort differences in the socialisation effect of voluntary participation. *European Political Science, 2(3),* 49–56.

Huckfeldt, R., & Sprague, J. (1993). Citizens, contexts, and politics. In A.W. Finifter (Ed.), *Political science: The state of the discipline II* (pp. 281–303). Washington: The American Political Science Association.

Inglehart, R. (1997). *Modernization and postmodernization: Cultural, economic, and political change in 43 societies.* Princeton NJ: Princeton University Press.

Inglehart, R., & Catterberg, G. (2003). Trends in political action: The development trend and the post-honeymoon decline. *International Journal of Comparative Sociology, 43(3-5),* 300–316.

Jackman, R. W. (1987). Political institutions and voter turnout in the industrial democracies. *American Political Science Review, 81,* 405–423.

Jennings, M. K. (2007). Political socialization. In R. J. Dalton & H. D. Klingemann (Eds.), *The Oxford handbook of political behavior* (pp. 29–44). Oxford: Oxford University Press.

Jennings, M. K., & Stoker, L. (2004). Social trust and civic engagement across time and generations. *Acta Politica, 39,* 342–379.

Kriesi, H., & Westholm, A. (2007). Small-scale democracy. The determinants of action. In J. van Deth, J. R. Montero, & A. Westholm (Eds.), *Citizenship and involvement in European democracies. A comparative analysis* (pp. 221–254). Oxin and New York: Routledge.

Krishna, A. (2002). Enhancing political participation in democracies: What is the role of social capital? *Comparative Political Studies, 35(4),* 437–460.

Kumlin, S. (2002). Institutions—experiences—preferences: How welfare state design affects political trust and ideology. In B. Rothstein & S. Steinmo (Eds.), *Restructuring the welfare state: Political institutions and policy change* (pp. 20–50). New York: Palgrave Macmillan.

Maloney, W. A., van Deth, J., & Roßteutscher, S. (2007). Civic orientations: Does associational type matter? *Political Studies, 56(2),* 261–287.

Mettler, S., & Soss, J. (2004). The consequences of public policy for democratic citizenship: Bridging policy studies and mass politics. *Perspectives on Politics, 2(1),* 55–73.

Milner, H. (2002). *Civic literacy. How informed citizens make democracy work.* Hannover, NH: Tufts University.

Newton, K. (2007). Social and political trust. In R. J. Dalton & H. D. Klingemann (Eds.), *The Oxford handbook of political behavior* (pp. 342–361). Oxford: Oxford University Press.

Niemi, R. G. (1999). Editor's introduction. *Political Psychology, 20(3),* 471–476.

Niemi, R. G., & Westholm, A. (1992). Political institutions and political socialization: A cross-national study. *Comparative Politics, 25,* 25–41.

Norris, P. (2002). *Democratic phoenix: Reinventing political activism.* Cambridge: Cambridge University Press.

Percheron, A., & Jennings, M. K. (1981). Political continuities in French families: A new perspective on an old controversy. *Comparative Politics, 13,* 421–436.

Putnam, R. D. (2000). *Bowling alone: The collapse and revival of American community.* New York: Simon & Schuster.

Putnam, R. (Ed.). (2002). *Democracies in flux: The evolution of social capital in contemporary society.* Oxford: Oxford University Press.

Putnam, D. (2007). E pluribus unum: Diversity and community in the twenty-first century. *The Johan Skytte Prize Lecture. Scandinavian Political Studies, 30(2),* 137–174.

Rothstein, B. (2005). *Social traps and the problem of trust.* Cambridge: Cambridge University Press.

Rothstein, B., & Stolle, D. (2008). How political institutions create and destroy social capital: An institutional theory of generalized trust. *Comparative Politics, 40(4).*

Rothstein, B., & Teorell, J. (2008). What is quality of government? A theory of impartial government institutions. *Governance, 21(2),* 165–190.

Sapiro, V. (2004). Not your parents' political socialization: Introduction for a new generation. *Annual Review of Political Science, 7,* 1–23.

Selle, P., & Østerud, Ø. (2006). The eroding of representative democracy in Norway. *Journal of European Public Policy, 13(4),* 551–568.

Stolle, D. (2003). The sources of social capital. In M. Hooghe & D. Stolle (Eds.), *Generating social capital: Civil society and institutions in comparative perspective* (pp. 19–42). New York: Palgrave.

Stolle, D., Soroka, S., & Johnston, R. (2008). When does diversity erode trust? Neighborhood diversity, interpersonal trust and the mediating effect of social interactions. *Political Studies, 56,* 57–74.

Teorell, J. (2003). Linking social capital to political participation: Voluntary associations and networks of recruitment in Sweden. *Scandinavian Political Studies, 26(1),* 49–66.

Teorell, J., Torcal, M., & Montero, J. R. (2007). Political participation: Mapping the terrain. In J. van Deth, J. R. Montero, & A. Westholm (Eds.), *Citizenship and involvement in European democracies. A comparative analysis* (pp. 334–357). Oxin and New York: Routledge.

Torney-Purta, J., Lehmann, R., Oswald, H., & Schulz, W. (2001). *Civic education in twenty-eight countries: Civic knowledge and engagement at age fourteen.* Amsterdam: IEA.

Torney-Purta, J., & Amadeo, A. (2003) A cross-national analysis of political and civic involvement among adolescents. *PS: Political Science and Politics* (April), 269–274.

Torney-Purta, J., Barber, C. H., & Richardson, W. K. (2004). Trust in government-related institutions and political engagement among adolescents in six countries. *Acta Politica, 39,* 380–406.

UNDP. (2000). Human development index. Retrieved from http://hdr.undp.org/en/reports/global/hdr2000/

Uslander, E. (2002). *The moral foundations of trust.* New York: Cambridge University Press.

van Deth, J., & Elff, M. (2004). Politicisation, economic developement and political interest in Europe. *European Journal of Political Research, 43(3),* 477–508.

van Deth, J., Montero, J. R., & Westholm, A. (Eds.). (2007). *Citizenship and involvement in European democracies: A comparative analysis.* Oxin and New York: Routledge.

Verba, S., & Nie, N. H. (1972). *Participation in America: Political democracy and social equality.* New York: Harper & Row.

Verba, S., Schlozman, K. L., & Brady, H. E. (1995). *Voice and equality: Civic voluntarism in American politics.* Cambridge, MA: Harvard University Press.

Watts, M. W. (1999). Are there typical age curves in political behavior? The "Age Invariance" hypothesis and political socialization. *Political Psychology, 20(3),* 477–499.

Welzel, C., Inglehart, R., & Klingemann, H. D. (2003). The theory of human development: A cross-cultural analysis. *European Journal of Political Research, 42,* 341–379.

Zetterberg, P. (2009). Do gender quotas foster women's political engagement? Lessons from Latin America. *Political Research Quarterly, 62(4),* 715–730.

Zukin, C., Ketter, S., Andolina, M., Jenkins, K., & Delli Carpini, M. X. (2006). *A new engagement? Political participation, civic life, and the changing American citizen.* New York: Oxford University Press.

CHAPTER 3

The Sources of Adolescent Activism: Historical and Contemporary Findings

DANIEL HART
Rutgers University

REBECCA LAKIN GULLAN
The Children's Hospital of Philadelphia and Gwynedd-Mercy College

Youth activism refers to behavior performed by adolescents and young adults with a political intent. Young activists are both reviled and revered, viewed as idealists by some and criminal anarchists by others. Activism itself can be seen as an activity through which adolescents gain insight, cognitive skills, and organizational capacity (e.g., Larson & Hansen, 2005), or as indoctrination into lawlessness (Useem, 1998).

Our goals for this chapter include a review of research on youth activism. Much of this research emerged in response to widespread youth activism evident throughout the Western world in the 1960s and 1970s. This work contributes to an understanding of the nature of youth activism and its psychological, political, and social roots. We supplement this review with analyses of survey data collected from adolescents both within the United States and around the world. These data are also used to explore the influence of demographic factors on youth activism. Finally, information from interviews with minority adolescents living in an inner-city, impoverished neighborhood is used to illustrate how the present research can inform policy and practice in youth activism.

We offer three conclusions. The first of these is that political activism is a set of overlapping activities and motivations. Youth activism observed in different historical and cultural contexts bears some similarities to youth activism studied in others. In some respects, then, it is meaningful to discuss youth political activism as a social-psychological phenomenon that is refracted by contexts and individuals into different forms such as demonstrations, riots, social organizations, and so forth. Yet there are meaningful distinctions among types of political activism that can be explored, and we discuss these distinctions as well.

The second conclusion is that political activism is deeply embedded in psychological, social, and political contexts. The consequence is that adolescent activism is relatively common in some historical periods, in some strata of youth, and in some with particular attributes, but rare in other periods, in other cohorts, and in some types of adolescents.

Third, we conclude that efforts to increase youth political activism can benefit from an understanding of the origins and development of activism. In particular, we shall argue that research findings concerning the importance of social capital and trust have implications for effective scaffolding of youth activism.

We begin with a historical overview, and then move through the research on the roots of adolescent political activism.

PROTESTS, RIOTING, AND ORGANIZING

Activism in the 1960s

Freedom Summer. McAdam (1986, 1988) has extensively studied adolescent and young adult participants in the civil rights action that has become known as *Freedom Summer*. In 1964, hundreds of college students were recruited to spend the summer in Mississippi, registering Black Americans to vote, staffing summer schools for Black children, and generally heightening awareness of civil rights issues in an area of the United States where such rights were regularly denied to Black Americans. Participation was costly; the youth were not paid, many were threatened by local White populations hostile to the goals of the program, and some were assaulted.

College students interested in volunteering in Mississippi were accepted following a screening process, one part of which was a written questionnaire. McAdam (1986) coded the responses to the questionnaire for attitudes, organizational affiliations, and social bonds. These codes were then used in a comparison of those who were accepted for and participated in Freedom Summer *(participants)* with those who were accepted but did not participate *(non-participants)*.

Three findings are particularly relevant for this chapter. First, McAdam found that while participants' written responses to the question "Why do you want to work in Mississippi?" were twice as long, on average, as those of the non-participants, there was little difference in the content of the responses. Both groups were opposed to segregation and strongly in favor of civil rights; however, the participants' views on these matters seemed more elaborated than those of non-participants. Second, participants were linked more closely to other participants in Freedom Summer in advance of participation than were non-participants. Third, participants had more extensive histories of organizational participation than did non-participants. Together, these findings led McAdam to conclude that participation in Freedom Summer was as much a social psychological phenomenon reflecting the influence of relationships and social institutions on behavior as it was a reflection of ideological or personality characteristics of the individual.

Riots. If the participants in Freedom Summer are now generally considered altruistic idealists, those who participated in the riots that were so common in the United States in the 1960s are even now often viewed as delinquent, lawless individuals drawn into mindless mobs. Surely this characterization was true of many participants, just as some participants in Freedom Summer were self-absorbed adventurers looking for escape or novelty in a summer in Mississippi. Nonetheless, careful examinations of American riots suggest significant differences between those who did and did not participate.

Paige (1971) interviewed Black adolescents and young adults in Newark six months after the city's infamous 1967 riot, a convulsion of anger and property destruction that largely, but not exclusively, was peopled by young Black males. Paige asked questions tapping trust in government, political knowledge, participation in the 1967 riot, registration as a voter, and attendance at meetings of civil rights organizations. Two findings are relevant. First, political knowledge was positively associated with participation in riots, registration as a voter, and attendance at meetings of civil rights organizations; men who knew little about the political system were unlikely to participate in any of these activities. Second, participation in riots was particularly high among those who were knowledgeable about the political system and deeply distrustful of it. This finding suggests that the combination of an awareness of how the political system works and a sense that it is not working on behalf of oneself potentiates anger, resistance, and rioting. Paige found that high trust and high knowledge contributed to the desire to participate in system-affirming activities. For example, registration as a voter was highest among those knowledgeable about the political system and trusting of it.

Together, these findings suggest that rioting and conventional political behavior, such as voting and attendance at meetings of civil rights organizations, share commonalities not immediately evident from common perceptions of them.

ACTIVISM IN THE TWENTY-FIRST CENTURY

Local focus. Contemporary youth activism in the United States often is focused on local community issues, rather than the broad national ones—the Vietnam war, civil rights—that characterized activism in the 1960s. For example, Kirshner (2008, p. 67) describes three youth activism programs, one intended to "reduce negative portrayals of youth" through presentations to community members, another intended to "persuade high schools to increase student input in school governance" through local rallies and presentations to the local school board, and the third to "persuade politicians to limit military recruitment in public schools" through a conference and resolution. Pearce and Larson (2006, p. 62) describe a social justice program for teenagers in which youth "identify and research problems that directly impact their lives." Hamilton and Flanagan (2007) present a summer youth activism initiative in which the goal was to promote responsibility for peers via the production of a short video. Ginwright (2007, p. 407) studied a youth group with the philosophy that "community change occurs through personal transformation." O'Donoghue and Strobel (2007) report on an initiative called "Youth as Effective Citizens" that focused on local projects such as a community garden, child care center, and youth-run media studio. Based on analyses of focus groups with, and surveys of, college students, Levine and Cureton (1998, p. 145) claimed that activism on college campuses changed in focus from the national issues of Vietnam and civil rights, common in the 1960s, to "student activism [that] focuses largely on local issues and has done so since the late 1970s. As a result, protest activities, in the main, are campus specific and almost invisible."

The change in focus from national issues to local ones is probably the result of the fact that the national issues of the 1960s were directly relevant to the interests of young Americans. Millions of young American men were required to consider the possibility of being drafted into military service to fight in Vietnam, for example. Similarly, racist laws and policies affected the lives of millions of African Americans. While there are surely many motivations for political activism besides self-interest, it is likely that concerns for personal welfare among millions of Americans created an atmosphere in which issues were discussed and wide mobilization was possible. In the absence of such national issues relevant to self-interest, it is possible that youth activism must focus on local issues that are of personal relevance.

Extent of activism. Contemporary American youth are, in general, less likely to be engaged in traditional forms of political activism—demonstrations, rallies, protests, and so on—than were youth of the 1960s (Galston, 2007). Evidence for this claim is based upon the Roper Survey of Political and Social Attitudes dataset, which contains survey responses from representative

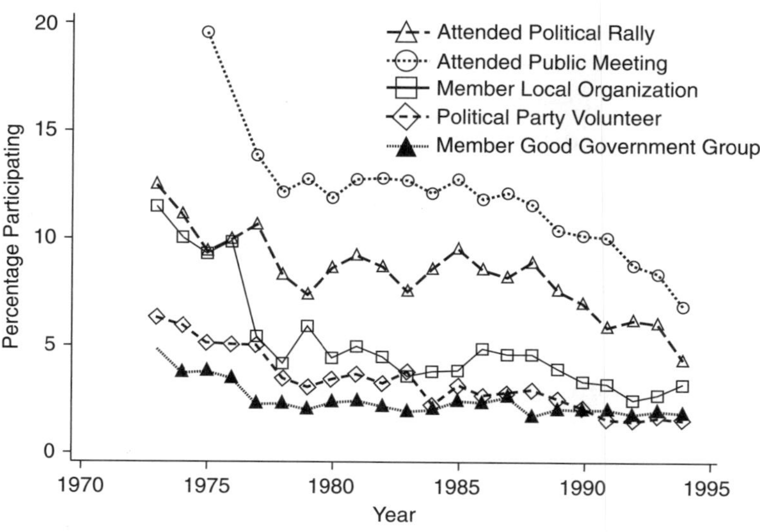

Figure 3.1 Historical Rates of Participation in Different Forms of Political Activity Among Americans 18 to 24 (trends calculated by the authors from the Roper Social and Political Trends data)

samples of Americans questioned each year between 1974 and 1994. Each year, the Roper organization asked Americans whether in the past year they had participated in any of 12 political activities such as "attended a political rally or speech," "served on a committee for some local organization," "attended a public meeting on town or school affairs," "been a member of some group like the League of Women Voters, or some other group interested in better government," "worked for a political party," and so forth. Figure 3.1 presents the percentage of Americans between the ages of 18 and 24 who reported participating in a range of these activities for each year between 1974 and 1994. For each of the activities, the trend is clear: participation declines with historical time. Youth near the close of the century were much less likely to report political participation—50% less likely in some instances—than were youth just 20 years earlier. While data are not available for the 15 years since, there is little reason to imagine that youth political activism as measured in the Roper Survey has increased.

ORIGINS OF YOUTH ACTIVISM

Activism as a General Phenomenon

Not every youth becomes politically active; indeed, Horn and Knott (1971) estimate that only 15% of American youth in the 1960s, which is, by consensus, a historical period of high activism, could be thought of as activists. A great deal of research has been directed toward identifying the reasons that some youth became activists while others did not. Progress toward this goal is complicated by the fact that the various activities in which youth are involved have different foci. McAdam's interviews with and intensive study of participants in Freedom Summer led him to conclude that those who participate in risky activism, or political action that is associated with real potential for harm to the participants, differ substantially from those who are involved in low-risk political action. Similarly, youth activism that affirms the prevailing political and legal structure, or intends to change the political hierarchy through legal means, may have different roots than illegal action intended to promote change in the political system or regime change. For these reasons, McAdam asked rhetorically, "Would anyone really want to argue that the same mix of factors that explains riot participation accounts for the signing of a nuclear freeze petition?" (1986, p. 67). It might be argued, then, that *activism* is a term without clear referent; each form of activism might be unique and incommensurate with other forms.

Yet as we noted above, Paige's (1971) work reveals similarities between rioters in Newark and participants in Freedom Summer. And the various *actions* that are subsumed in everyday notions of political activism are related to each other. For example, the 12 forms of legal political action included in the Roper survey, described earlier, are associated with each other (these analyses are available from the authors). This means that individuals who report attending political rallies are more likely than those who did not attend rallies to be members of committees, to sign petitions, and so forth. Moreover, the various political actions all show the same general historical declines. While McAdam's (1986) caution against assuming all forms of political activism are identical in function and motivation must be noted, the tendency of different types of activist behavior to co-occur, combined with at least broad similarities evident in the psychology of disparate lines of activism such as Freedom Summer participation and rioting, suggest that political activism might be usefully considered as a single phenomenon (while simultaneously recognizing the value of investigations aiming to explicate the unique features of any single incident of youth activism).

Education, Social Class, and Social Capital

One way to enter into an examination of the roots of political activism is through a consideration of its decline in the United States between 1974 and 1994. *Why* did political participation decline? There is no single explanation for this phenomenon. Putnam (2000) has examined the decline closely, and suggested that it reflects the erosion of social capital—the network of social relationships and connections to social institutions upon which an individual can draw—in the United States. Putnam has argued that the rise of television, increasing participation of women in the workforce, and growing geographical separation of work from residence resulting in lengthy commute times, along with other factors, have all contributed to the fraying of relationships among individuals in neighborhoods, which in turn reduces participation in the civic life of the community. The decline in political participation over the last half of the twentieth century is just one reflection of a broader trend toward withdrawal from public life.

We have used the Roper dataset (discussed earlier) to identify both historically contingent and time-invariant factors associated with political activism in American youth in the two decades of the study. Historically contingent factors are those that are predictive of political activism in one historical time but not another, while time-invariant influences are those that are important for political activism across different developmental periods. For example, *educational attainment* might have been important in the 1970s in heightening political activism but not so important in the 1990s. This hypothesis is consistent with many scholars' emphasis on the prominence of college students in the civil rights movement and Vietnam protests in the 1960s and 1970s. There are few accounts in the last two decades that identify colleges and college students as hotbeds for political activism among youth. Familial social class might play a similar role; accounts of the activists in the 1960s and 1970s often highlight their privileged backgrounds and wealthy parents.

As noted earlier, Putnam has argued that declines in political activism reflect the general erosion of social capital over the last half of the twentieth century in the United States. The Roper dataset has two measures of social capital measured regularly between 1974 and 1994: church attendance ("Gone to church or religious service in the past week"), an indicator of institutional affiliation, and number of long-distance phone calls per month to friends and family members living more than 100 miles away, an indicator of relationships.

McAdam (1986) argued that those who had relationships with participants in Freedom Summer were more likely to participate themselves than were those without social connections to the movement. Certainly, then, there are reasons to imagine that social relationships and institutional memberships were important influences in fostering political participation. There are good reasons to imagine that these same factors are time-invariant influences on political participation. For example, Ginwright (2007) has discussed the importance of social capital for political activism among contemporary Black youth.

To examine these various possibilities, using the Roper dataset, we regressed the sum of political activities reported by a youth on the year of the survey, family income (in thousands of dollars, adjusted for inflation), education level (on a four-point scale, from one [no school] to four [college]), and the number of long-distance phone calls made to friends and family in the previous month (top-coded as 10; this is the best index of informal social connection to others available at multiple time periods in the dataset), and the interactions of all these predictors with the year of the study. The details of these regression analyses are available from the authors. In general, political activism in 1974 was more tightly connected to educational attainment and family social class than it was in 1994. Family income was positively correlated with political activity for youth in 1974—as family income increased, so did the number of political activities—but there was virtually no association between family income and political activity in 1994. Similarly, the association of educational attainment with political activism was stronger in 1974 than in 1994. However, social capital—whether in the form of social relationships, measured by the number of long-distance phone calls with friends and family, or in the form of institutional memberships in churches and religious organizations—was associated with political activism no matter the time period.

The importance of institutions and social relationships in contemporary youth activism permeates research reports on the topic. Kirshner (2007, p. 370) noted, "Activism groups typically embody cross-age collaborations in which young adults (usually in their twenties) play critical roles as organizers and advisers." Kirshner (2007) also discussed the development of adolescent activism as a process akin to apprenticing, with adults playing a crucial role in transmitting skills and attitudes. Pearce and Larson (2006) studied intensively a youth activism group and found that the adult leader played a crucial role in maintaining group cohesion and in organizing the group's activities. An important question to which the answer is currently unknown is whether these relationships with older adults are necessary for the activism of adolescents who are out of high school and may have social networks composed largely of peers that serve the same functions of facilitating entry into, and supporting, activism. The fundamental importance of institutions and social relationships for fostering youth activism is also evident in international analyses. In order to explore the importance of institutions and social relationships for understanding political activism, we have re-analyzed data from the International Association for the Evaluation of Educational Achievement (IEA CIVED) assessment of civic attitudes and civic behaviors in 90,000 adolescents from 28 countries, 23 of them in Europe and the other five from four other continents. For a full description of this study, its sample, and its instruments, see Torney-Purta, Lehmann, Oswald, & Schulz (2001). In each country, a representative sample of 14-year-olds completed an in-class questionnaire eliciting endorsement of forms of political behavior, both those potentially enacted in adolescence and those foreseen in adulthood.

Two subscales concerning political behavior were identified by Husfeldt, Barber, and Torney-Purta (2005; psychometric information concerning these scales, which are IRT scales set to an international mean of 10 and SD of 2, is provided there). The measure of *conventional political activity* reflects anticipated membership in a political party, letter-writing about social and political concerns, and willingness to become a political candidate. Second, a measure of *protest* was derived from three items concerning anticipated participation in spray-painting slogans, blocking traffic, and occupying buildings as forms of political protest. Our analyses indicate that these forms of intended political and civic action are weakly correlated with each other.

To investigate the roots of youth activism, we analyzed the relation of social capital to each of the two forms of political activism—traditional and protest. Social capital was assessed with two sets of questions. Adolescents were asked to judge the frequency of their participation in a variety of clubs and organizations (scouts, sports teams, and so forth) and in informal socializing with their friends on a four-point scale ranging from never to daily. Because participants are nested within countries, these analyses use a multi-level approach. In our analyses, we adjusted the results for parental educational attainment and other factors. First, our analyses suggest that adolescents' endorsement of future traditional political participation is related to frequency of participation in institutions (clubs, organizations) but not to informal social participation with peers. In contrast, expected protest participation is associated with informal social participation with peers but not with organized participation in clubs. While predicted participation, which was measured in the IEA CIVED study, is different than actual behavior, the results are consonant with our assertion that social relationships and social institutions are of fundamental importance in fostering political activism. Moreover, the results suggest that protest activities have different social sources than do traditional political activities. Other analyses of subgroups of countries from the CIVED dataset suggest a similar conclusion. Torney-Purta (2009) examined five Western European and five Eastern European countries in a cluster analysis that identified an alienated and peer-group oriented cluster of adolescents in each country who were especially likely to participate in illegal protest, but not in conventional political activities.

Trust and Civic Knowledge

Paige's (1971) study of rioters in Newark and McAdam's (1986) investigation of participants in Freedom Summer both suggest that social trust and civic knowledge are crucial for understanding political activism. Trust in relation to political action includes having confidence in elected officials, institutions, government, the media, and fellow citizens (Flanagan & Gallay, 2008).

Whereas individuals high in civic knowledge tend to engage in a range of political activities (both conventional and protest or high-risk activities), those who are high in civic knowledge and have confidence in institutions, policies, and individuals tend to take part in social actions that differ from those of individuals who are high in civic knowledge but low in trust. As previously discussed in the context of Paige's (1971) investigation of rioting, trust and civic knowledge are key constituents, along with participation, in citizenship (Galston, 2004; Sullivan & Transue, 1999). In large surveys in which political activism is assessed in terms of frequency of participation in conventional, generally lawful actions, research seems to suggest that activists tend to know more about the political system than adults less politically active (Brady, Scholzman, & Verba, 1999). Moreover, those who participate in political activity tend to be higher in trust than those who are removed from political activity (Sullivan & Transue, 1999).

Political and Demographic Contexts

Political tolerance of dissent. In important respects, the focus on the individual and social characteristics of activists, particularly those prominent in the United States during the last half of the twentieth century, distorts our understanding of youth activism. This is so because the very same characteristics that were linked to political activism in youth of this era and in this political context might not result in political activism in a different context. Consider, for example, the long tradition in the United States of encouraging and protecting political expression. The historical record is replete with examples in which political expression has been repressed in the United States; nonetheless, in comparison to other countries in the same time period—for example, China or the U.S.S.R.—the social and legal climate of the United States was relatively supportive of the forms of expression characteristic of political activism. It is unlikely that the wave of activism characteristic of American youth in the 1960s could have occurred in countries with traditions of active repression of political dissent.

Demographic contexts. Youth activism of all sorts occurs in community and societal context. The widespread activism seen across the United States in the 1960s and the 1970s—rioting, protest movements, and so forth—is widely recognized to reflect in some measure broad structural and political conditions of society. For example, McAdam (1988) speculated that the youth activism reflected in Freedom Summer reflected the combination of coming of age in the baby boom combined with the relative affluence of children born in the late 1940s and 1950s. American riots of the 1960s were often viewed as the direct outcomes of poverty and economic hardship characteristic of urban areas with large populations of Black Americans (Kerner,

1968). Racial and ethnic heterogeneity of American cities also was viewed as a possible source of riots (Spilerman, 1971). None of these explanations seems fully satisfactory; poverty was not a good predictor of which cities experienced riots in the 1970s (Olzak, Shanahan, & McEneaney, 1996), and the relation of racial heterogeneity to political behavior is mixed.

One demographic quality of populations that may be associated with youth activism is the percentage of the population that is composed of children or youth (Hart, Atkins, Markey, & Youniss, 2004). The idea that the foundation for activism is an adolescent living in a society with a cohort of adolescents that is large relative to the size of other age cohorts in the society has received some credence from work by political scientists. For example, Moller (1968) has linked youth bulges to the Protestant Reformation, and to revolutions in eighteenth-century France and twentieth-century Indonesia, and Huntington (1996) has suggested that youth are generally more attracted to such movements than are adults. Goldstone (2002) pointed out that youth may be less invested in the existing social and religious structures, given that they are less likely than adults to be married, have children, occupy prestigious positions in their communities and churches, and so forth, and that as a consequence youth may be more open to movements that seek to overthrow or revise existing orthodoxies. There is a great deal of fascinating writing on the relation of youth bulges to the emergence of powerful social and religious movements (Moller, 1968, is particularly thoughtful). However, there is a dearth of systematic research of the type found in the study of youth bulges and welfare.

Why might youth bulges possibly be associated with warfare, revolution, and activism? Two broad answers have been offered. One explanation for activism, revolution, and warfare accompanying the maturation of a youth bulge focuses on the dismal economic conditions that may confront those entering the job market. Young adults in a maturing youth bulge are members of a large cohort seeking jobs, and there are likely to be too few opportunities in the existing workforce to accommodate the unusually large number of young adults. Inevitably, there is a collision between career expectations and the realities of an economy with too few openings for all young adults seeking jobs; many young adults are unable to obtain jobs, and those who do find employment may be paid poorly. The consequence for a young adult of the sharp contrast between expectation and reality is disillusionment in prospects for the future (see Finlay, Flanagan, & Wray-Lake, this volume).

This disillusionment may be the emotional fuel for lines of action that are associated with activism, revolution, and reform. For example, disillusioned youth may join political movements that aim to reform society. Sayre (2003) has analyzed economic and historical data concerning the frequency of Palestinian suicide bombings, and has concluded that these tragic events are most likely to occur when unemployment is high. If economists (e.g., Kahn & Mason, 1987) are correct in concluding that job prospects are poorer for those in youth bulges than for youth in smaller cohorts, then Sayre's research is consistent with claims that the economic conditions associated with youth bulges may lead to extreme forms of political activism. The economic explanation is undoubtedly the most popular, although not all studies find confirming evidence for it (e.g., Urdal, 2006).

Hart, Atkins, Markey, and Youniss (2004) have offered a second explanation for the relation of youth bulges to warfare and activism. These authors suggest that the economic theory neglects the consequences of growing up from birth to adolescence in large cohorts of similarly aged individuals. They further suggest that those who grow up in communities and societies with large cohorts of children (child-saturated contexts) are less likely to be influenced by adults than are children who develop in communities and societies in which adults constitute large majorities (adult-saturated contexts). They hypothesized that growing up in adult-saturated contexts results in the transmission, from adults to children, of the knowledge of and respect for the culture and society. This transmission is possible because in adult-saturated contexts many of a child's interactions will naturally involve adults, who typically possess knowledge about society and culture. In contrast, in child-saturated contexts, children interact frequently with other children, and less transmission of cultural information can take place because children typically have little information about their societies. Hart et al. (2004) demonstrated that children living in child-saturated communities in the United States have less civic knowledge than do children living in adult-saturated communities, and showed as well that children in child-saturated countries possess less civic knowledge than do children in adult-saturated countries. We also suggested, but have not proved, that those who possess little civic knowledge are more likely to become involved in radical political and social activism than are those who possess more civic knowledge. In summary, members of youth bulges have less civic knowledge than youth of the same age who were not socialized in large cohorts of children, and a deficit in civic knowledge can lead to participation in extremist political activities.

We have analyzed the links among trust, civic knowledge, political climate, child saturation, and youth activism using the IEA CIVED data. We chose to use the following scores: trust in governmental institutions (sample item: "How much of the time can you trust . . . the federal government?") and a 38-item civic knowledge test score (sample item: "In a democratic political system, which of the following ought to govern the country? (a) moral or religious leaders, (b) a small group of well-educated people, (c) popularly elected representatives, or (d) experts on government and political affairs") from the IEA CIVED study.

We also used two country-level characteristics. Political climate characterizing each country, specifically tolerance of dissent, is indexed using a measure drawn from work by Kaufmann, Kraay, and Mastruzzi (2008). These researchers combined hundreds of survey scale items, ratings from non-governmental organizations, and other forms of data to create a measure of *voice and accountability*. *Voice and accountability* refers to "the extent to which a country's citizens are able to participate in selecting their government, as well as freedom of expression, freedom of association, and a free media" (Kaufmann, Kray, & Mastruzzi, 2008, p. 7). United Nations data (Fukuda-Parr, 2002) were the source for the measure of child saturation (the percentage of children under the age of 15) for each of the 28 countries in the IEA study. Our prediction was that adolescents were more likely to endorse political activism in countries tolerant of political dissent (high in *voice and accountability)* and in countries with a greater percentage of children under the age of 15.

We used hierarchical models to analyze the data, regressing each of the four political action scores on the linear effects of maternal education, adolescent trust, adolescent civic knowledge, child saturation, political voice, frequency of participation in organizations and informal socializing with friends, and for the interactions among trust, knowledge, child saturation, and political voice. The child saturation and voice measures were at the country level (split at the median), and the remainder were individual variables.

The results of these analyses suggest that political trust was a predictor of both forms of political activity. In the case of illegal protest, the association was negative, with high levels of political trust predictive of low levels of illegal protest. Trust was a positive predictor of conventional political activity. Second, civic knowledge was also predictive of both forms of political activity. Of particular importance for our purposes in this chapter are the interactions among political trust, civic knowledge, child saturation, and the degree to which a country promotes citizens' voice and accountability. In particular, adolescents' endorsement of items in the illegal protest scale suggests that this form of political activism reflects the interplay of individual-level characteristics (political trust, civic knowledge) with the political and demographic qualities of the country. To ease discussion of these interactions, we provide depictions of them in Figures 3.2 to 3.4.

In Figure 3.2, the significant interactions obtained in the prediction of illegal protest are presented. Illegal protest is most likely to be endorsed by adolescents low in political trust; those high in trust are least likely to view illegal protest favorably. Those living in child-saturated countries are particularly unlikely to endorse protest.

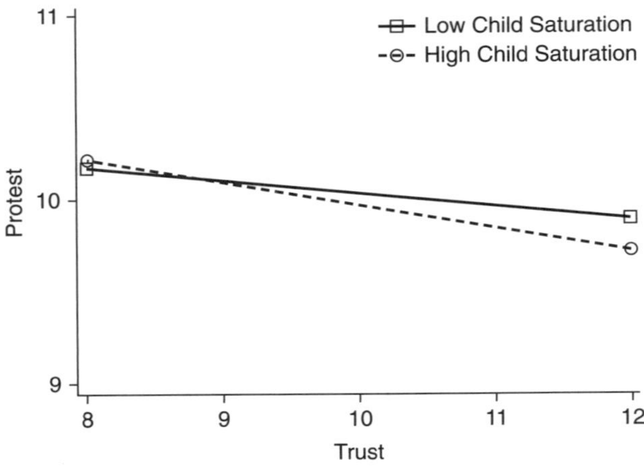

Figure 3.2 Future Protest as a Function of Individuals' Political Trust and the Country's Child Saturation

Figure 3.3 suggests that low levels of political trust are associated with high levels of expectations of illegal protest, particularly in countries high in giving political voice to citizens. High levels of political trust are associated with low levels of expectations of protest in these same countries. Political trust does not seem predictive of illegal protest among adolescents living in countries that are not receptive to political dissent. The implication is that illegal protest is most likely to occur in countries that protect political dissent and among adolescents who are distrustful of political institutions.

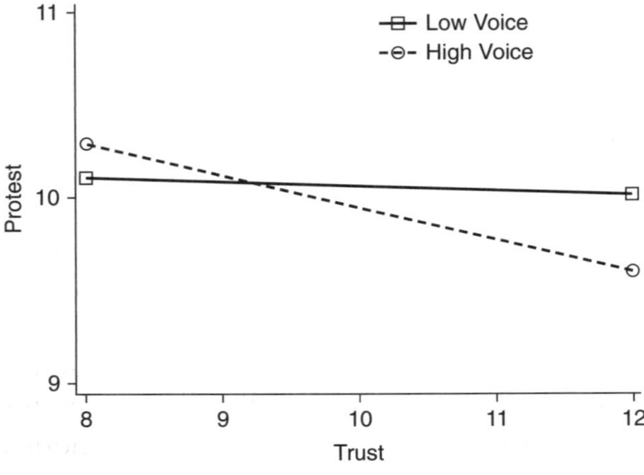

Figure 3.3 Future Protest as a Function of Individuals' Political Trust and the Country's Encouragement of Political Voice

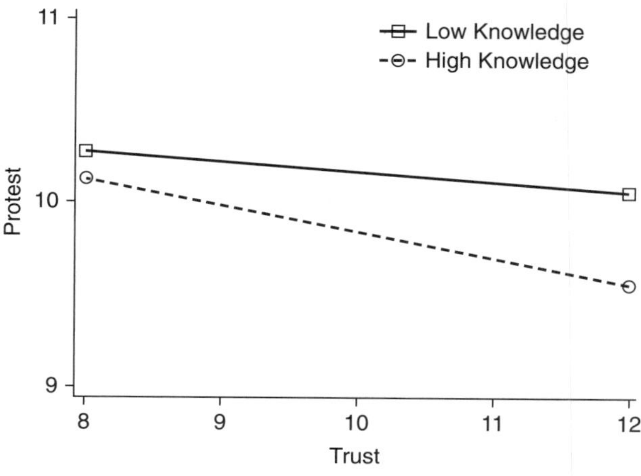

Figure 3.4 Future Protest as a Function of Individuals' Political Trust and Political Knowledge (graphs are based on data from the IEA CIVED Study)

Finally, Figure 3.4 indicates that adolescents who are low in civic knowledge endorse illegal protest, no matter whether they trust the government or not; adolescents knowledgeable about civic matters are less likely to endorse illegal protest as their trust in political institutions increases. This suggests that widespread youth participation in illegal protest is most likely to occur when political trust is low, but that even when political trust is high, those least knowledgeable about political institutions might be mobilized to participate in illegal political actions.

These results are quite similar to those found in a subgroup of six countries from the IEA CIVED dataset (Torney-Purta, Barber, & Richardson, 2004), but here we have the additional advantage of including a measure of protection of political voice and child saturation at the country level.

To summarize, the results in Figures 3.2 to 3.4 show that endorsement of illegal protest is associated with low levels of political trust combined with low levels of civic knowledge, country-level acceptance of political dissent, and high levels of child saturation. Certainly the last two qualities were characteristic of the United States during the 1960s (Moller, 1968).

We also examined interactions obtained in the prediction of conventional political participation. Child saturation is predictive of conventional political activity. Interestingly, and rather unexpectedly, adolescents living in countries low in child saturation and who themselves are relatively knowledgeable about political issues are the least likely to endorse conventional political participation.

In summary, trust in political institutions is positively associated with the forms of political activism societies traditionally aim to foster, and negatively associated with illegal forms of political protest. Also, widespread youth support for illegal protest probably requires a confluence of forces, which include: low trust, high child saturation, and a society accepting of political dissent.

POLICY IMPLICATIONS

The United States and nations around the word have a long history of legislative and fiscal support for engaging young people in civic action (Corporation for National and Community Service, 2007). Not surprisingly, efforts to encourage community involvement have often focused on educating youth about how government and the political process work (Carnegie Corporation of New York & CIRCLE, 2003). Our review indicates that increased civic knowledge does not guarantee youth involvement in political or civic action and that other factors must also be considered when attempting to promote youth engagement. In particular, our review of others' research and our analyses suggest that *social capital* and *trust* in governmental institutions are crucial in fostering traditional political action. This means that youth with connections to social institutions and a high level of trust were more engaged and interested in the political process and less likely to report intent to take part in illegal or risky political activities. These findings suggest that efforts to promote involvement in a range of political activities should not only focus on the transmission of civic knowledge but should also directly address connections to others and to youth trust. This might be particularly imperative in communities where there is a high level of child saturation and fewer opportunities to interact with and learn from adult role models.

INTERVENTIONS

Targeting social capital and trust might be particularly critical for promoting civic engagement in traditionally disenfranchised populations, such as minority youth. Not surprisingly, children from ethnic minority groups often report lower levels of trust than European-American adolescents (Flanagan & Gallay, 2008; Levinson, this volume). Yet effecting change, creating trust, and fostering civic activism in these populations are complicated and difficult enterprises.

Issues of distrust within at-risk populations have been found in research by one of us (RLG) in work with African American youth living in inner-city, high-poverty neighborhoods. A mixed method study using surveys and interviews was adopted (similar to that recommended by Torney-Purta, Amadeo, & Andolina, this volume). For example, on a measure assessing trust in the government, elected officials, the media, and other institutions or people in power, the vast majority of sixth-grade students (N=32) reported "very little" trust or confidence across the board (modal response: one on a four-point scale from "very little" to "a lot"). Indeed, in an interview about ethnicity and civic action, one sixth-grade girl reported that the president of the United States at the time "does not want Black people to achieve. He thinks [we're] stupid."

Given youth distrust in public officials and institutions intended to address community needs, it is not surprising that many are ambivalent or resistant to taking part in either traditional political activities or community action. For example, one student expressed an interest in learning more about politics, "but it might be something bad saying I want to be in politics." Illustrating how attempts to engage in political action often prove ineffective, another student said: "My brother wrote [the government] and all he got was a picture back." Indeed, this experience reflects the potentially *dis*empowering consequence when efforts to create change are unsuccessful (Kahne & Westheimer, 2006). In the words of a seventh-grade student: "The government doesn't read every letter. I don't want to be all sitting there and writing and they be sitting there not reading and I be writing for my health."

Another reason minority, inner-city youth might resist engaging in traditional civic activity is the seemingly intractable nature of problems in their neighborhoods and communities. Thus, a number of youth in the above study reported that community issues were overwhelming and insurmountable:

> "How they gonna stop shooting if little kids tell them?"
>
> "If you try to change people, still gonna be the same stuff. Just gonna stay how it is."
>
> "[People] can't do anything. If they try to stop it, that person might shoot them."
>
> "It's the same. Every day, it's the same."

Youth descriptions of impotence toward community problems raise the question of how they perceive and plan for the future in an atmosphere rife with seemingly insurmountable problems. For many, the answer lies in escape. Thus, one seventh-grade girl stated:

> I feel like some day I will get out of here because of all the stuff that do go on around here. And a lot of people don't take pride or clean up after themselves or they try to plant trees and pick stuff up, but sooner or later it just goes back to the way it was. I am not saying I like white people and I'm not saying I don't like white people because I am not racist, but I would want to live in a white neighborhood because they care what goes on their street and stuff. And I noticed that white people—well, I'm not going to say white people, but people—clean up and keep their stuff clean. It is like a good community because they tight. Around here, we still tight, but it's dirty and all contaminated.

A veteran teacher in the school this girl attended spoke of how the focus on "escape" and association of success with whiteness relates to an increased disconnect between African American youth and their cultural roots. Referring to the parents of present-day youth as the "lost generation," this teacher discussed how one of the unintended consequences of the civil rights era might have been the movement (both literal and figurative) of African Americans away from the community. Thus, as things "got more open, we were less closed," and as a result the solution to community issues became getting out of the neighborhood, rather than attempting to fix problems that can be overwhelming and even life-threatening (e.g., gangs, violence). In other words, once African Americans had the opportunity to access mainstream sources of power, influence, and industry, there was no longer a compelling or logical reason to stay and fight (and potentially risk one's life, family, or livelihood) against seemingly impenetrable problems.

The outflux of primarily middle-class African Americans from tight-knit, predominantly Black communities might have subsequently served to dilute the transition of cultural knowledge and pride through the generations. As such, this inner-city teacher, who was raised in the neighborhood where she taught, noted that the "current generation of parents, unlike twenty years ago, is a group that has no identity. They grew up after the community opened up and they lost the sense of culture." This is reflected in the common reaction of *it's just a color* among youth asked what their race or ethnicity meant to them. Thus, when the civil rights generation grew up, they gave their children freedom, but with freedom might have also come a breakdown in their connection to each other and their cultural grounding. Consequently, the bonds that form the basis for collective civic action might not be as strong as they were in decades past, and youth in these neighborhoods have decreased opportunities to be a part of something larger than themselves.

Even in the face of significant barriers and repeated defeats, a number of youth living in disenfranchised communities continue to express hope and commitment to the future of their neighborhoods. Indeed, some students feel that it is even more important for minorities to participate in politics and social action. For example, one girl stated that with "all the bad stuff that happened in our past, now we have the chance to express our mind. If people don't take it, it saddens my heart. We need to pitch in to make the world a better place." Or in the words of a seventh-grade boy, there are "more Black people on the front lines. [It's] time for Black people to help and protect their community."

As noted above, overcoming barriers to civic and political engagement for youth living in high-risk neighborhoods likely requires efforts beyond simply increasing civic knowledge and providing opportunities for action.

In circumstances where community problems are overwhelming and seemingly insurmountable, organized efforts must be made to directly address distrust in politics and social institutions and to promote successful engagement in community action. One strategy to address youth distrust is to make the political world personally relevant. In other words, when working in communities with a high level of distrust in public officials and institutions, it is critical that youth feel their experiences and influence are an important part of a larger context. Ginwright (2007) discusses this critical need to promote social capital by encouraging Black youth to identify how their personal struggles reflect societal problems that can be collectively addressed. He notes that this can best be accomplished through establishing community-based organizations oriented toward developing a collective cultural identity.

In our intervention to promote civic engagement in inner-city African American youth, we attempt to address issues of trust and cultural identity through teaching the history of African American social action. For example, students explore the historical 1965 march on Selma, Alabama, wherein African Americans (as well as White supporters) peacefully and successfully worked together to change unfair voting laws. In addition, it is critical to engage youth with adult role models from their community who are currently engaged in civic action in order to broaden their understanding of the possibilities for themselves and support their skill development (Kirshner, 2007). Local and national minority politicians can also serve as prominent symbols of the opportunity to gain access to systems of power.

In addition to helping youth identify themselves or people like them in politics and social movements, it is also critical that efforts to engage youth in civic action be done in a way that does not ultimately prove disempowering (Swift, 1992). For example, engagement should be carefully mentored by an adult who can provide training, guidance, and support when obstacles arise, but who does not take on the role of primary decision maker (see Fox et al., this volume). Kirshner (2008) highlights the critical and nuanced role of the adult in his description of three youth activism organizations, pointing out that there is a range in the extent to which organizations were youth-led. Thus, although there is often a theoretical commitment to youth empowerment, the need to balance this with the desire to teach youth critical skills and support their success can be challenging. Ideally, Kirshner (2007) suggests a scaffolding approach in which adults provide opportunities and support for youth to reach increasingly higher in their skill development. In our program, we attempt to do this through teaching youth the mechanisms behind power and how to successfully employ strategies to gain influence. For example, we teach youth the benefits of collective action, how influencing ideology can garner support, and how to interact effectively with those in power. We then support their practice and application of these skills to issues they identify as important to themselves and their communities.

CONCLUSION

Youth activism is probably best understood as a collection of related political pursuits. Participation in political organizations, signing petitions, respecting boycotts, and so forth, are associated with each other. This means that an adolescent involved in a political action group is more likely to sign a petition than is an adolescent without membership in a political action group. Concretely, then, the relations among forms of political behavior make it possible to discuss youth activism as a construct, and to explore its roots. Nonetheless, it is important to remember as well that different forms of political activity are partially independent of each other, and each has its own sources. Our analyses suggested that protest activities may be motivated more by associations with friends than by institutional affiliations, while traditional political activity apparently is energized more by involvement with organizations than by peer relationships. Moreover, political activism is motivated by political goals, and these goals change as well. By reviewing the literature with the overarching *youth activism* as an organizing construct, this chapter sketches the outlines of political activity in youth, the sources of such activity, and how this activity might be promoted. But there remain important lessons to be gained from complementary research that examines specific forms of political activity with the aim of identifying the unique nature and motivations for the youthful political activity under consideration.

Our second conclusion is that youth activism is knit into psychological, social, and political contexts. Unlike some characteristics—for example, language—which characterize all members of the species and consequently are suggestive of deeply ingrained, highly canalized, biologically based tendencies, youth political activism occurs in some intersections of adolescents and environments but not in others. This fact is highlighted by historical and cross-cultural differences. We reviewed research suggesting that youth political activism declined substantially in the United States over the 20 years between 1974 and 1994. Moreover, the focus of youth activism changed as well, from a concern with issues of national scope to community-based problems. There are also important differences in youth activism across countries. The findings we presented in the chapter suggest that a country's political atmosphere and demographic characteristics influence the level and type of political activism among its youth. Context matters enormously in understanding political activism. Indeed, we suggested that some characteristics that facilitated entry into political activism in one context may not do the same in another. Such was the case with social class and educational status, which were associated with youthful activism in the United States in the 1970s but less so in the 1990s.

Youthful activism also has roots in the individual and the immediate social network. Our review suggests that civic knowledge and political trust, which are characteristics of the individual, matter substantially. Generally, our findings suggest that lawful political activism is positively associated with civic knowledge and political trust, although these associations are moderated by demographic and political climate characteristics. Similarly, political activism seems most likely among adolescents with connections to peers and affiliations with neighborhood institutions such as schools, clubs, religious organizations, and so forth.

Finally, our analyses presented in this chapter and experience promoting youth activism (briefly described in the previous section), and the research by others reviewed earlier, together suggest that the promotion of political activism among youth benefits from an understanding of the roots of political activism. Our review suggests that political involvement is best facilitated not only through civic education, but through directly addressing issues of trust (Kahne & Sporte, 2008) and by providing the kinds of social connections to institutions that are associated with constructive political activity. In particular, we must make a coordinated effort to address the needs of traditionally disenfranchised populations, such as minority youth living in high-poverty, inner-city neighborhoods. Specifically, policy and practice must focus on helping youth feel connected, effective, and represented within a range of political and civic activities and institutions (Ginwright, 2007). Ultimately, increasing youth familiarity, connection, and confidence in political processes as well as their individual and collective skill influencing these systems will not promote key developmental assets, but has the potential to produce a new generation of youth and young adults who are actively engaged in their communities. This can be difficult to achieve, particularly among those living in social contexts in which trust in institutions is already frayed. Nonetheless, if we aspire to provide opportunities for youth to become political leaders, and provide these opportunities to all youth living in all social and political niches in the United States, then this work needs to be done.

REFERENCES

Brady, H. E., Schlozman, K. L., & Verba, S. (1999). Prospecting for participants: Rational expectations and the recruitment of political activists. *American Political Science Review, 93(1)*, 153–168.

Carnegie Corporation of New York & The Center for Information and Research on Civic Learning and Engagement (2003). *The civic mission of schools.* New York, NY.

Corporation for National and Community Service (2007). Fiscal year 2008 budget. Retrieved August 25, 2008, from http://www.nationalservice.org/about/budget/2008.asp

Flanagan, C., & Gallay, L. (2008). *Adolescent development of trust (Circle Working Paper 61).* Retrieved February 25, 2010, from http://www.civicyouth.org/?page_id=152.

Fukuda-Parr, S. (2002). *Human Development Report, 2002.* Retrieved February 15, 2003, from United Nations Development Programme Web site: http://www.undp.org/hdr2002/complete.pdf

Galston, W. A. (2004). Civic education and political participation. *PS: Political Science and Politics, 37(02),* 263–266.

Galston, W. A. (2007). Civic knowledge, civic education, and civic engagement: A summary of recent research. *International Journal of Public Administration, 30(6),* 623–642.

Ginwright, S. A. (2007). Black youth activism and the role of critical social capital in Black community organizations. *American Behavioral Scientist, 51(3),* 403–418.

Goldstone, J. A. (2002). Population and security: How demographic change can lead to violent conflict. *Journal of International Affairs, 56(1),* 3–23.

Hamilton, C., & Flanagan, C. (2007). Reframing social responsibility within a technology-based youth activist program. *American Behavioral Scientist, 51(3),* 444.

Hart, D., Atkins, R., Markey, P., & Youniss, J. (2004). Youth bulges in communities. *Psychological Science, 15,* 591–597.

Horn, J. L., & Knott, P. D. (1971). Activist youth of the 1960s. *Science, 171(3975),* 977–985.

Husfeldt, V., Barber, C., & Torney-Purta, J. (2005). Students' social attitudes and expected political participation: New scales in the enhanced database of the IEA Civic Education Study. *College Park, MD: Civic education data and researcher services.* Department of Human Development, University of Maryland College Park. Retrieved July 20, 2006.

Huntington, S. P. (1996). *The clash of civilizations and the remaking of world order.* New York: Simon & Schuster.

Kahn, J. R., & Mason, W. M. (1987). Political alienation, cohort size, and the Easterlin hypothesis. *American Sociological Review, 52(2),* 155–169.

Kahne, J. E., & Sporte, S. E. (2008, June 10). Developing citizens: The impact of civic learning opportunities on students' commitment to civic participation. *American Educational Research Association Journal,* Article10.3102. Retrieved May 1, 2009, from http://aerj.aera.net

Kahne, J., & Westheimer, J. (2006). The limits of efficacy: Educating citizens for a democratic society. *PS: Political Science and Politics, 39(2),* 289–296.

Kaufmann, D., Kraay, A., & Mastruzzi, M. (2008). Governance matters VII: Aggregate and individual governance indicators, 1996–2007. *World.*

Kerner, O. (1968). *Report of the national advisory commission on civil disorders*. New York: New York Times Company.

Kirshner, B. (2007). Introduction: Youth activism as a context for learning and development. *American Behavioral Scientist, 51(3)*, 367–379.

Kirshner, B. (2008). Guided participation in three activism organizations: Facilitation, apprenticeship, and joint work. *The Journal of the Learning Sciences, 17*, 60–101.

Larson, R., & Hansen, D. (2005). The development of strategic thinking: Learning to impact human systems in a youth activism program. *Human Development, 48(6)*, 327–349.

Levine, A., & Cureton, J. S. (1998). Student politics: The new localism. *Review of Higher Education, 21*, 137–150.

McAdam, D. (1986). Recruitment to high-risk activism: The case of Freedom Summer. *American Journal of Sociology, 92(1)*, 64.

McAdam, D. (1988). *Freedom Summer*. New York: Oxford University Press.

Moller, H. (1968). Youth as a force in the modern world. *Comparative Studies in Sociology and History, 10*, 238–260.

O'Donoghue, J. L., & Strobel, K. R. (2007). Directivity and freedom: Adult support of activism among urban youth. *American Behavioral Scientist, 51(3)*, 465.

Olzak, S., Shanahan, S., & McEneaney, E. H. (1996). Poverty, segregation, and race riots: 1960 to 1993. *American Sociological Review, 61(4)*, 590–613.

Paige, J. M. (1971). Political orientation and riot participation. *American Sociological Review, 36(5)*, 810–820.

Pearce, N. J., & Larson, R. W. (2006). How teens become engaged in youth development programs: The process of motivational change in a civic activism organization. *Applied Developmental Science, 10(3)*, 121–131.

Putnam, R. D. (2001). *Bowling alone: The collapse and revival of American community*. New York: Touchstone Books.

Sayre, W. (2003). *The Economics of Palestinian Suicide Bombing*. Working Paper. University of Texas at Austin.

Spilerman, S. (1971). The causes of racial disturbances: Tests of an explanation. *American Sociological Review, 36(3)*, 427–442.

Sullivan, J. L., & Transue, J. E. (1999). The psychological underpinnings of democracy: A selective review of research on political tolerance, interpersonal trust, and social capital. *Annual Review of Psychology, 50*, 625–650.

Swift, C. F. (1992). Empowerment: The greening of prevention. In M. Kessler, S. Goldston, & J. Joffe (Eds.), *The present and future of prevention* (pp. 99–111). Newbury Park: Sage Publications.

Sullivan, J. L., & Transue, J. E. (1999). The psychological underpinnings of democracy: A selective review of research on political tolerance, interpersonal trust, and social capital. *Annual Review of Psychology, 50*, 625–650.

Torney-Purta, J. (2009). International psychological research that matters for policy and practice. *American Psychologist, 64(8)*, 822–837.

Torney-Purta, J., Lehmann, R., Oswald, H., & Schulz, W. (2001). *Citizenship and education in twenty-eight countries*. Amsterdam: International Association for the Evaluation of Educational Achievement.

Torney-Purta, J., Barber, C., & Richardson, W. (2004). Trust in government related institutions and political engagement among adolescents in six countries. *Acta Politica, 39,* 380–406.

Urdal, H. (2006). A clash of generations? Youth bulges and political violence. *International Studies Quarterly, 50(3),* 607–629.

Useem, B. (1998). Breakdown theories of collective action. *Annual Review of Sociology, 24(1),* 215–238.

CHAPTER 4

Youth Civic Engagement in the Developing World: Challenges and Opportunities

RONALD KASSIMIR
The New School

CONSTANCE FLANAGAN
The Pennsylvania State University, and University of Wisconsin—Madison

Citizenship was featured in two prominent international reports on youth in the developing world in 2005 and 2007. Becoming a citizen was presented as one of five life transitions marking the attainment of adult status. Both *Growing Up Global: The Changing Transitions to Adulthood in Developing Countries (GUG),* issued by the National Research Council and Institute of Medicine (2005), and *World Development Report 2007: Development and the Next Generation (WDR),* issued by the World Bank (2007), considered achieving full citizenship as significant a transition as school completion, the attainment of health and work to support an adult livelihood, and family formation, in defining what it means to be a mature and contributing member of society.

The fact that citizenship was listed with these other typical markers is significant in its own right. Such reports are a kind of pulse-taking for developing countries, and they inform the perceptions of and policies toward the developing world among western aid agencies and international organizations. These two important reports, one written primarily by economists and public policy specialists, the other by demographers, economists, and public health experts, saw their task as incomplete without including a chapter on citizenship, social responsibility, and the public good. This is an indication of the extent to which civic engagement as a marker of human development and full incorporation into society has become mainstreamed in research and policy circles. Furthermore, it is noteworthy that youth civic engagement is seen as not only important in itself, but as critical for the economic and social health of local communities and nation-states.

The authors of the two reports framed the discussion of citizenship as connected with other transitions in schooling, work, health, and family formation. Opportunities and constraints in one domain were connected with opportunities and challenges in others. In addition, the concept of a transition was used to capture late adolescence and young adulthood as a time in between the dependent status of children and the greater self-sufficiency of mature adults (Finlay, Wray-Lake, & Flanagan, this volume). For many youth, this period of transition has become protracted in part due to a dearth of opportunities for work sufficiently remunerative to support a family but also due to impoverished school systems, poorly trained and underpaid teachers, and student absenteeism.

By including citizenship, these reports call attention to the political opportunities (or lack thereof) available to young people around the world, as well as to how different societies and cultures conceive of the social compact and thus the benefits and responsibilities conferred by membership in a political community. Furthermore, the reports also contain recommendations for policies to enhance the social inclusion and civic incorporation of youth. For example, the *World Development Report* (WDR) devotes considerable attention to the need for governments to provide second chances for young people whose lives have been diverted by civil war (child soldiers) or by the commission of status offenses (i.e., behaviors designated as criminal because the individual is a young person rather than an adult).

These two reports provide a springboard for our chapter, which has several goals: first, to discuss the context for and meaning of citizenship for youth in developing countries and the particular challenges for young people and for their nations within a global context. Second, to focus on youth not only as citizens in formation, but as citizens in the present—a distinction we will refer to as *being* versus *becoming*. With this in mind, we have intentionally avoided the phrase "transition to citizenship" used in the WDR. Third, to point to the balance between core aspects of the civic domain that are universal with those shaped by local and particular social-economic, political, and cultural circumstances. The universal include the compact of rights and obligations that bind citizens and states. The role of mediating institutions (faith-based organizations, community-based micro-enterprise projects, self-help groups) is central to how these universal aspects are localized and the degree to which they are realized. They are thus key to incorporating younger generations into the polity. Finally, we point to the emphasis in both reports on gender inequalities and the second-class status of females, making the case that policies that empower women and educate girls can alleviate poverty and stabilize democratic governance.

THE CONTEXT FOR YOUTH CITIZENSHIP AND CIVIC ENGAGEMENT IN THE DEVELOPING WORLD

Given the relative lack of attention to young people's civic engagement on a global basis, it is useful to briefly describe the most critical contextual differences in the life situations of most young people in the developing world in relation to those in developed societies. Taking these differences seriously cautions against importing into the global South those analytical frameworks that were generated for understanding and documenting civic engagement for youth in developed countries. For example, certain unarticulated assumptions inform much of the work on youth civic engagement in the developed world. One is what we might call a framework based on Maslow's (1943) hierarchy of human needs and motivations, that is, that people engage in civic affairs only if their basic needs are satisfied. A second is that the state or government and the mediating institutions of civil society are functional and committed to providing for the needs of citizens.

Problems of food security, potable water, sanitation, safety, transportation, and communication are common in developing nations. Poor communication and transportation infrastructures make access to information or having a voice in public affairs a challenge. Further, when compared to nations in the developed world, public institutions and states in general in the developing world have much less capacity to provide services, from education to sanitation to health to security.

Subsistence (collecting water, firewood) claims a large share of the time of individual youth and may preclude attention to civic affairs. At the same time, collective awareness about the lack of basic provisions can motivate political action, which can take different forms. For example, the limited capacity of states to provide services or of public and private institutions to create the conditions in which needs can be met, means that collective action by people themselves often fills the gap. Self-help, charitable, or religious organizations, the non-state, non-governmental institutions, often seen as the components of civil society, play a significant role in filling in for the functions that the state is not providing. We refer to these organizations as mediating institutions because they create social spaces and social relationships that connect citizens of all ages to each other and to the other major sectors of society (i.e., the state and the market).

Mediating institutions not only compensate for the shortcomings of the state and the market in fulfilling people's needs. In Africa, many of these institutions provide services directly (taking on a governance role) and also make claims to other powerful institutions (a representational role) (Kassimir, 2001). In this representational sense, these institutions also provide spaces where citizens can engage in political work that holds the state or market accountable and challenge these institutions to perform their designated functions. Mediating institutions provide the mechanisms whereby citizens exercise their rights and make claims on the political system to provide conditions that enable them to live a complete life (Nussbaum, 1999).

Social exclusion—in the form of poverty, inequality, limited opportunities for social mobility, and various types of discrimination—is the norm for the vast majority of young people in the developing world. Data cited in the two reports make this clear, although they also indicate great differences across and within the nations of the developing world. For example, opportunities for social incorporation (via education and work) vary widely within nations based on a person's gender, class, caste, ethnicity, or language. The two reports see active citizenship as a means for challenging such inequities and incorporating marginalized groups. For example, the WDR points to the work of the Panchayat Raj program in India in informing women and marginalized groups (*dalits*) about their rights as a means for increasing participation in democratic governance.

Likewise, educating elementary and secondary age children, especially those in marginalized communities, about their rights to protection and to self-determination has been a major outgrowth of the United Nations Declaration on the Rights of the Child (Tibbitts, 2002). In fact, education is intertwined with civic engagement in many ways. Aside from the well-documented positive relationship between education and participation, education also can be a means whereby marginalized groups become aware of their exclusion. For example, the WDR cites one 30-year study of *favelados* (urban slum dwellers in Brazil), which found that as each successive generation became more educated, it also became increasingly aware of the group's exclusion from political participation. The knowledge and skills that students gain in civic education programs can even empower them to challenge the state, an outcome that may not have been intended. For example, some of the leaders of the Pinguinos, a Chilean student movement demanding school reforms to promote equity (Domedel, & Peña y Lillo, 2008), had participated in a high-school civic education program. That program, called "Debates," was provided by the Centro de Estudios de la Argumentación y el Razonamiento at the University Diego Portales and was funded by the Ministry of Education. Coincidentally, the Ministry cut the funding for this program after the massive student protests for school reform organized by the Pinguinos (personal communication, Carmen de Silva, November, 2009).

The effects of deprivation on the extent and forms of civic engagement among the young are only slowly being documented. For example, high levels of student absenteeism from school is due to a host of factors including a family's inability to pay school fees, the long distance and lack of transportation between home and school, the family's need for the young person's labor, and teacher absenteeism. Such concrete conditions of educational and work life in the developing world mean that many young adults are not prepared to support themselves by the age of majority. Consequently, in many nations *youth* are officially designated in national youth policy as persons between the ages of 15 and 35 or even 40.

Issues surrounding migration provide a powerful example of the implications for citizenship posed by deprivation in the developing world. And here we mean citizenship in its most formal sense of recognized membership in a political community. Disproportionately, it is the young who migrate, whether from rural to urban centers within their own country or to other countries, typically in search of work. Migration can have both costs and benefits for civic engagement. Those who leave may lose the social supports and networks that provided a sense of belonging and purpose, along with social incorporation and social control in their local community. Even more dramatically, those who leave their nation in search of better opportunities in other countries often have no guarantees or protections as citizens. They are not citizens of their receiving country, and their sending country has little political clout and few resources to represent their interests in the receiving nation.

At the same time, migration can expose young people to new ideas about their rights in contrast to the routine arrangements to which they are accustomed in traditional communities that can be restrictive, especially for women. One straightforward example is that women's access to health care—physical in terms of availability and psychological in terms of women's sense that they have a right to health care—is higher in urban than in rural areas of Ghana (Boateng & Flanagan, 2008). This fact has many consequences for younger women who are more likely to migrate and to have health care access needs associated with child-bearing.

Internationally, diaspora groups often play a role in the national politics of the sending country. And the migration policies of Western governments themselves may have an effect on young people's politics in the developing world. For example, in Cameroon, the tightening of European emigration policies, which placed stricter limits on the numbers of young educated Cameroonians seeking their fortunes outside their home country, coincided with the ruling party's creation of a national youth organization. Jua (2003, p. 30) describes this organization as "a competitive resource in accessing the state" at a time in which job opportunities were scarce and the ability to migrate was limited. Other young people in Cameroon were attracted to opposition and even secessionist movements at this time (Fokwang, 2003).

Documentation of birth or citizenship is an essential record for obtaining many of the rights and access to services associated with citizenship. In other words, proof of citizenship opens doors to other opportunities for social incorporation. Yet many people in developing countries have no such documentation. According to UNICEF, more than half of all births in developing countries are unregistered; lack of documentation is a major reason that children do not enroll in school. In China and Vietnam, migration has resulted in floating populations of young people, often women, who lack local residence cards needed to obtain housing, education, and health care. For many youth in the developing world, obtaining a passport can be financially prohibitive. Thus, policies that would cut the costs of passports and make proof of legal identity more available would incorporate more youth into society, many of whom are marginalized by policies in the current system. Consequently, one policy recommendation in the WDR is that governments subsidize the cost of passports or identity papers as these are crucial for access to services and institutions such as institutions of higher education or workplaces.

Our discussion of migration points to the more general dimensions of globalization and its effects on citizenship. Although the futures of young people in all nations are affected by ideas and forces outside their national borders, the nature and degree of that impact vary greatly. This can matter for citizenship because it means that many of the institutions and forces that shape the lives of developing world youth are beyond their household, county seat, or even national capital.

The World Bank itself has had a powerful role in setting economic policies and political reforms across the globe through its structural adjustment programs. The debate rages on the degree to which these programs have alleviated or exacerbated poverty. Either way, the point is that powerful institutions—from the World Bank, the International Monetary Fund, to the World Trade Organization to western governments, the United Nations, and multinational corporations—affect the everyday conditions of life for people in the developing world. Yet, engaging in civic actions to hold these institutions accountable is beyond the reach of most young people; it is even a challenge for the leaders of the nations in which they live. That absence of accountability may affect how developing world youth calculate the potential efficacy of engaging in civic or political behaviors and the forms their actions might take.

At the same time, one should not reify the differences in the conditions for youth civic engagement in the developing and developed world as if they applied to all young people. In fact, some youth in developing countries grow up in material conditions similar to those of middle and upper class youth in the West. Conversely, some western youth, often members of minority and immigrant groups, are born into and live with forms of social exclusion that resemble the experiences of the majority of young people in the global South. However, even the more privileged youth in developing countries who have opportunities to continue into higher education may face challenges in finding work in their country once they have completed their education. The global economy has been advantageous to educated youth and those with English fluency in some parts of the world, as the call centers of Bangalore illustrate. At the same time, neoliberal economic policies have sharply cut jobs in the civil service where, in the past, those with higher levels of education often found work. These jobs are often not replaced by decent private sector opportunities. This state of economic affairs has constrained the capacities of governments in the developing world to effectively intervene in creating employment opportunities for new generations of educated citizens.

Lastly, salient cultural differences may impact forms of youth civic engagement. Again, it is important not to draw too absolute a distinction between western and non-western cultures, nor to ignore the tremendous cultural differences within the global South. But at a general level, anthropologists and cultural psychologists have provided examples of the difference between a western orientation toward individual self-fashioning as opposed to a more interdependent or communal orientation in much of the South. We elaborate on this theme later in the chapter.

To summarize, in this section we have called attention to key aspects of many if not most developing nations that provide the larger context in which youth's experiences of citizenship take place. This includes widespread deprivation and social exclusion, ineffective state institutions, migration, vulnerable positions in the global political and economic order, and cultural factors.

YOUTH BULGES, HUMAN CAPITAL, AND CITIZENSHIP

We now turn to our assessment of the reasons that these two reports may have focused on citizenship in the context of a larger consideration of youth and the transition to adulthood. According to GUG (National Research Council and Institute of Medicine, 2005), citizenship is a key component of the transition to adulthood:

> The definition of a successful transition to adult citizenship must include the capability to make choices through the acquisition of a sense of self and a sense of personal competence, as well as the acquisition of prosocial values and the ability to contribute to the collective well-being as citizen and community participant. (2005, p. 352)

The WDR adopts a more or less similar definition and goes on to hypothesize the connection between this micro-transition at the level of the individual with macro-socioeconomic development:

> Citizenship affects development outcomes through three channels: by enhancing the human and social capital of individuals, by promoting

> government accountability for basic service delivery, and by enhancing the overall climate for investment. (2007, p. 161)

Both studies, given their foundations in demography and economics, frame the urgency of their focus on young people in developing nations, in large part, on the *youth bulge*, the growing disproportion of young people as a percentage of overall population in the global South. Indeed, this has moved policy-makers to put youth at the center of policy agendas in many parts of the developing world (Fussell & Greene, 2002). One reason for this attention is a claim that the youth bulge is associated with propensities for conflict, violence, and criminality (Reimers & Cardenas, this volume). The WDR is measured on this point, noting that cohort size itself does not increase the propensity for conflict. A large youth cohort can correlate with increased conflict, but only in countries with poor economic performance. However, worries about youth as a politically destabilizing political force are not reserved to developing nations. In places where the age pyramid is reversed (i.e., with an aging adult population), such as Western Europe, concerns about young people are linked closely to debates over immigration in light of the relative youth of many migrants.

According to the WDR, there are roughly 1.5 billion people between the ages of 12 and 24 in the world, with 1.3 billion of them in developing countries. This bulge is, in part, a sign of success in prenatal and childhood immunization campaigns to eradicate infant mortality—evidence of progress related to health, which is seen as one of the key transitions to adulthood. At the same time, the youth bulge has more troubling implications for other transitions to adulthood, including citizenship. Specifically, political stability is undermined when large numbers of young people are unable to get the education and jobs that would enable them to become fully participating members of their society. In many places, more young people mean greater expenses in schooling, and more difficulty in placing them in productive work. A dearth of employment opportunities constrains young adults' capacities to support families. Biology and social opportunity clash: Sexual maturation and reproduction continue apace in some countries, but the formation of autonomous households lags behind.

Even when governments invest in human capital, if their economies are not simultaneously strong, the result can be a well-educated workforce with no work. In fact, this is the case in some countries that have invested heavily in higher education without building strong economies. As Hamilton and Hamilton (2009) point out, the consequence is that in some nations young people postpone marriage to complete their education but then take jobs below their qualification level and further postpone marriage because they cannot support a family on their low wages. Thus, the transition to adulthood (and movement out of the youth phase) is delayed due both to human capital accumulation and to a weak economy.

The effects of such a scenario on citizenship and a sense of political efficacy are substantial. Limited access to meaningful work and to the social markers of adult status (like forming an autonomous household), in a phrase, social exclusion, may lead to anomie, criminality, or political violence (see Torney-Purta, 2009, for evidence of a similar phenomenon in post-Communist countries such as Latvia and Bulgaria). The fear is that the youth bulge will threaten young people's sense of citizenship and lead to apathy or highly uncivil forms of engagement. Neither the GUG nor the WDR is especially alarmist here, at least compared to more apocalyptic treatments. They both talk about the opportunities as well as the threats that the youth bulge brings. The bulge is usually invoked to highlight dangers during the transition to adulthood, associated limits on socioeconomic development, and threats to political stability:

> Too many young people (particularly men) with not enough to do can be a recipe for disaster. Historical data suggest that cycles of rebellion and military or civil conflict tend to coincide with periods when young people comprise an unusually large proportion of the population. (GUG, 2005, p. 45)

The WDR notes that youth unemployment, which the bulge exacerbates, "not only wastes human resources—it also risks misaligned expectations and social unrest that could dampen the investment climate and growth" (2007, p. 4). Elsewhere, in a sidebar on the youth bulge debate, the report argues that the evidence does not support the more extreme causal claims between the youth bulge and collective violence, but that a "large youth cohort can aggravate the tensions caused by poor growth but does not by itself lead to conflict" (p. 166). (Also see the discussion of youth bulge and political activism in Hart and Lakin Gullan's chapter in this volume.)

The WDR's emphasis on investment climate links the social incorporation of youth to issues of political risk and stability that affect the investment decisions of local and foreign capital and the potential for economic growth. Citizenship, then, becomes a way of conceiving of the social incorporation of younger generations, but principally through a lens focused on human capital formation, economic outcomes, and political stability of the nation.

Connecting individual development and transitions to adulthood to socioeconomic development and collective transitions, very much at the center of the WDR, is not new. Indeed, the core of the report is directly in the tradition of development economics through its connection of life-course transitions to the perennial question of the role of human capital formation in economic growth and development. Beyond human capital, with its attendant focus on education and skills, both reports treat youth as a multidimensional social category. And youth citizenship—observed and expressed as values, attitudes, knowledge, identities, and practices—is seen as having a direct impact on human *and* social capital and as creating the political conditions within which socioeconomic development is possible.

In general, though, framing citizenship largely through a human capital lens is, in our view, myopic. Citizenship becomes principally a means to an end, and young people's political claims and the public good are not viewed as ends in themselves. This approach also emphasizes citizenship as a future role rather than one in the present. And it stigmatizes conflict as inherently a problem rather than as a symptom of other problems, some of which are generated by investment decisions of global capital. Witness the revolt, with a great deal of participation by young people, against multinational oil companies in the Niger Delta region of Nigeria as one example (Ukeje, 2006). As generational replacement theorists have argued, the incorporation of younger generations into the polity is a force both for social stability and social change. Both revolutionary activity and cynical passivity can be signs of critical political consciousness.

As we discussed in the previous section, the two reports pay too little attention to some of the contextual factors that are especially consequential to citizenship in the developing world. We would call particular attention to the global political economy and how it is entwined with the limited state capacity in many developing countries, not least through structural adjustment programs promoted by international financial organizations such as the World Bank. In other words, there is a wider global economic and political ecology in which governments in the developing world make fiscal decisions—from investing in a growing young adult population to nationalizing or selling of natural resources. Cultural differences are also of importance, in the sense that even well-meaning international institutions may assume that models of civic education, civic engagement, and empowerment developed in the West will be accepted and productive in developing world contexts (Bunting & Merry, 2007). In short, deep inequities in political power, the clout of multinational corporations and international financial institutions, and even the resources and practices of western aid and advocacy groups, disproportionately shape the civic incorporation of youth citizenship in the developing world, and the ability of governments in the developing world to effectively support the transitions that the two reports highlight. In summary, we contend that structuring citizenship within a human capital framework limits the discourse and the policy possibilities for two reasons: First, it too narrowly connects the development of persons with the development of economies and societies. Second, it focuses on young people as citizens in the making and thus treats them as less capable and consequential political actors in the present.

This is not to say that the two reports ignore the latter. GUG's chapter on citizenship includes a section on "the practice of," as well as "the formation of" citizenship (2005, Chapter 6). The WDR has a section entitled "Youth can be political actors while still in their youth" (2007, p. 167). Both call attention to social institutions from the military to national youth service to voluntary organizations as sites for citizenship practices. They cite survey data and examples of behaviors such as voting, campaigning, and community activism. But the overall focus on transitions to adulthood, the human capital that young people are (or are not) building, and the threatening aspects of the youth bulge tend to overshadow young people as actors in the present and instead give attention to the more negative dimensions of youth politics. In the WDR chapter, there is a far more extensive discussion of youth's participation in gangs and political violence than in youth development and youth action programs. In the case of the WDR, one reason for these anomalies is the importing of what have been called *populist* concepts from grassroots development work and academic approaches that sit uncomfortably alongside the standard economics framework of the WDR (Kassimir, 2007). While entirely laudable, it makes the reconciling of different images of youth as citizens a difficult matter. The two populist terms we call attention to are *agency* and *voice* in relation to young people.

Agency gets heavy emphasis in the parts of the WDR that emphasize capabilities and youth decision making. This concept has a contested history in the social sciences, and typically refers to the degree and kind of autonomy in practice and thinking that social actors have in light of the broader constraints and conditions in which they live (see Beaumont, this volume). But the report has only one citation on agency—a thoughtful but relatively obscure article on women's empowerment (Kabeer, 1999). One would expect that the use of concepts from economics would not be referenced so superficially in a WDR. But more importantly, the term is transformed by its usage. The definition of agency in the article is "the ability to define goals and act upon them" (Kabeer, 1999, p. 438; paraphrased in WDR, 2007, p. 16). But throughout the report, this is translated as young people "having better decision-making capabilities." Thus, it is not enough for young people to have the capacity for agency, but it must be agency that is "resourced, informed, and responsible" in order for that agency to be used to make good and constructive decisions. (Note the similar definition in the GUG cited above.)

Voice has less of a history in social science thinking, both in general and in relation to youth. In economics its best-known treatment is in the economist, Albert Hirschman's classic, *Exit, Voice and Loyalty* (Hirschman, 1970). This is apparently not the source for it in the WDR. Voice is defined and used in two ways in the report. One, consistent with a grassroots and populist usage, is that voice is not just about expression but also about recognition by powerful others and inclusion of that voice in consequential decisions. The other, consistent with a more economic than political approach, sees voice as *client power* and means holding accountable those institutions that provide services to youth. However, it sometimes is used in the report as an example of youth performing those services themselves (i.e., servicing their own needs or those of fellow community members). These two versions of voice are not contradictory, but they use the imagery of youth as citizen and youth as client or consumer and youth as producer in ways that are often in tension.

An additional tension in the WDR is related to what kind of agents young people are. At times youth are portrayed in the way that economics often portrays humankind—as *homo economicus* or autonomous individual agents who know their own interests and have an unambiguous sense of their preferences. As the report says, young people's "decisions indicate their preferences" (2007, p. 81). In discussing health, the report notes, "People engage in risky behavior because it yields benefits," in the sense that the benefits are subjectively defined preferences (2007, p. 132). That you can infer what people want from the decisions and actions they take is the bedrock behavioral assumption of modern microeconomics.

Yet, the ways in which concepts like agency are actually used in the WDR contradict this assumption with respect to young people. For youth agency to be a positive attribute, it must be resourced, informed, and responsible. Otherwise, it is feared that the choices young people make will not be good for them or their families and societies. This is complex because the report also argues in several places that young people are prone to experimentation, irrational behavior, and risk-taking. The WDR section on information technology, for example, argues that young people are not prepared to sort through the morass of information on the Internet. Overall, qualifying agency in this way implies that young people are not (yet) able to know their own interests. There is extensive research and voluminous debate in the field of youth development on these issues, some cited in the WDR. To take this issue seriously is to challenge the behavioral assumptions used in standard economics and to problematize the idea that changing incentive structures, a principal policy strategy implied in rational actor models, will succeed in changing young people's preferences and thus their behavior (see Haste, this volume). Most immediately, neither the assumption of youth as rational actors nor as incomplete adults is especially helpful in engaging the citizenship practices of developing world youth in the local and global contexts of their lives.

THE CIVIC DOMAIN

Considering youth civic engagement in the developing world expands the notion of the civic domain but raises other questions. For example, if forms of engagement differ across nations and groups, are there any universals to this domain? Hatano and Takahashi (2005) answer this question by arguing that some aspects of the civic domain may be privileged knowledge, that is, knowledge that human beings need to survive. They hypothesize that, although the forms of organization in modern societies are relatively recent phenomena in human evolution, there are universal necessities of societal organization including such things as production, resource distribution, division of labor, exchange, and social status, which may be basic to the life of the human species.

Drawing from work by Flanagan, Martinez, and Cumsille (in press), we posit the following universal aspects of youth civic engagement, which are manifest in culturally specific forms and opportunities. First, a social compact or implied bargain between governments and citizens is such a universal, but the specific tenets of this bargain will vary based on the principles that organize a society (e.g., the degree of individual self-determination, the recognition of rights of social citizenship such as health care or social protection, as embodied in the welfare state). Our focus on citizenship in the developing world also has emphasized the government's capacities to deliver on this social compact. For example, although a nation may be a signatory to the United Nations Convention on the Rights of the Child, its capacities as a developing nation to implement the articles ensuring children's rights to nurturance and care may be inadequate.

The second universal is the role of collective identity in citizenship and civic action. To develop that identity, younger citizens need opportunities to bond with others, to work collaboratively toward common ends, to appreciate how their interests are shared with others, and to understand that civic goals are achieved through collective action. At the same time, the collective identity routes that are open to many youth in developing countries are often very local and are practiced within a homogeneous group. Ethnic and religious (collective) identities, both in the developed and developing world, have been used to stir up political divisions and rivalries, often at the expense of democratic governance and the rule of law. A collective identity, then, is a necessary but insufficient condition for citizenship, and there are cultural differences in the traditions and practices that achieve a sense of collective identity.

Third, although liberal models of democracy that prioritize autonomy and self-determination are distinguishing features of citizenship in Western Europe and North America, in many parts of the developing world, community practices are more likely to emphasize the interdependent and relational aspects of civic membership. Durham (2008) provides examples from her fieldwork in Botswana about practices with peers and adults through which younger generations are incorporated into and learn about membership in a political community.

She explains that in a culture where a person's life is organized around increasing interdependencies, youth is a period of building up a wide range of relationships. Building those connections occurs in peer group practices (i.e., joining formal groups such as the Herero Youth Association and in nonformal gatherings such as practicing traditional songs together) and in adult-youth relationships (performing labor for a wide range of households). In formal meetings of the entire community, young people have a chance to speak but also learn that their voice is part of a chorus of other voices and that their identity is part of a larger community with a history and traditions. In community gatherings, each member of the community may speak and everyone is expected to listen, but age and status within the community structure the process. The eldest members, who speak last, are expected to integrate the many voices of the community into a sense of *We*: "These elders listen to the speeches of all the others, and then, when the time is right, they speak, referring to others' points, considering all the angles, and relating these to 'our customs' before forming and presenting their own understanding" (Durham, 2008, p. 171). By participating in these cultural activities, Botswanan youth build relationships and become integral members of their community. As Vygotsky (1978) argued, their ideas about the social and civic domain and their place in it derive from these activities.

At the same time, traditions, cultural practices, and norms in some nations present unique challenges to individual autonomy and democratic citizenship. As the WDR points out, legal rules or customary practices throughout much of Africa ascribe rights such as land ownership, economic opportunities, religions, and family matters to communities and not to individuals. The decisions of the chiefs, who have the authority to make decisions on behalf of the community, may or may not have the effect of distributing resources equally or according to the needs of members of the group. But the power to decide remains in the chiefs' hands. Thus, cultural traditions, practices, and norms structure the forms of civic engagement and the meaning of citizenship in ways that may be empowering or disempowering to those who have to live with the decisions.

A fourth universal aspect of the civic domain is the fact that the social compact and the sense of collective identity as citizens varies for different subgroups within a nation. In earlier parts of this chapter we have discussed the fact of social exclusion based on group membership (gender or caste, for example). Here we make the point that, in developing nations the terms of the social compact also vary for different subgroups, as they do for minorities in the West. Flanagan et al. (in press) have adapted the notion of *selfways* from cultural psychology (Markus, Mullally, & Kitayama, 1997) and invoked the concept of *groupways* to emphasize that young people's lay theories about the political and economic system are refracted through lenses of the social class, caste, racial/ethnic, religious, and gender groups to which they belong. Consequently, their political theories are likely to vary according to the way the tenets of their particular political and economic system play out for people "like them" (Flanagan & Campbell, 2003) and the groupways in which those tenets are enacted. Attention to the developing world brings these groupways into stark relief. Nonetheless, we argue that they are present in all systems and can become a basis for political organizing and challenge. In the next section we will discuss gender differences in political power to illustrate the concept of groupways and how the terms of the social compact advantage some groups of citizens over others.

MEDIATING INSTITUTIONS AND YOUTH CITIZENSHIP

Cutting across these universals is a ubiquitous dimension of social life that takes a variety of forms and has different purposes in various contexts. These are mediating institutions, or the organizations, institutions, and relationships of civil society (for a related discussion, see Youniss and Hart, 2005). As discussed above, these institutions take on a particular salience in contexts of weak states and when public and private institutions provide insufficient avenues for the transition to adulthood or space for civic and political participation. Engaging in activities through these institutions is the means whereby young people typically enact citizenship in ways that may reinforce and stabilize the political status quo or, alternatively, contest and challenge it.

We want to highlight mediating institutions as resources and as sites where young people can enact citizenship in the present, rather than only as citizens-in-the-making. By offering youth opportunities to engage in civic practice, mediating institutions also are enabling young people to develop civic identities and skills that carry over into their adult lives. Scholars have long been interested in the relationship between the two, that is, how people's civic and political experiences in their youth shape their adult citizenship orientations and practices (McAdam, 1988).

As mentioned earlier, the WDR and GUG do not ignore young people as citizens in the present. However, in their focus on transitions to adulthood and on citizenship as one of several transitions, the role that mediating institutions play in preparing young people for citizenship roles in the future is foregrounded. Especially because these transitions to adulthood are troubled and often prolonged in the developing world, as the two reports document in great detail, we call attention to the citizenship practices of young people that make a difference for them and their societies while they are still socially recognized as youth rather than as adults.

In an incisive chapter about youth growing up in poverty in the developing world, Hamilton and Hamilton (2009) use the construct of *structural lag* to describe the mismatch between the competencies and needs of an age group and the lacuna in institutional opportunities and social structures. From this perspective, the youth bulge presents a rare opportunity to think creatively about new institutional forms that could respond both to the assets that youth bring and to the absence of regular employment even for the well-educated in many developing nations. Drawing from their work and others, the remainder of this paper identifies characteristics of promising institutions based on the opportunities they afford for the needs of youth in the developing world at the brink of adulthood: feelings of purpose and agency; human capital; and social capital formation. These are the features of institutions that hold promise for developing youth as assets to their communities.

One illustrative organization discussed by Hamilton and Hamilton is The Community Cleaning Service (CCS), created by young men in partnership with a community-based organization and a multinational corporation that meets a community need while creating jobs and fostering entrepreneurship. Importantly, the CCS is a small business, not a civic engagement project, per se, and so calls attention to the issue of how social entrepreneurship is part of young people's enactment of citizenship. However, the project illustrates two points relevant to youth civic engagement in the developing world. First, mediating institutions are often the means whereby the needs of citizens (especially the poorest citizens) are met when the state is unable or unwilling to meet them. Second, particular kinds of partnerships between grassroots entrepreneurial projects and multinational corporations can be a means whereby uneducated youth develop the social capital, sense of purpose, economic stability, political information and critique, and leadership skills that are the foundations for civic engagement.

With respect to fulfilling citizen needs, the CCS cleans bathrooms in the apartment complexes of Mathare, a slum in Nairobi, Kenya. Importantly, the CCS team of young, uneducated men contract directly with the poor whom they are serving. They are using what Hamilton and Hamilton (2009) refer to as the "Base of the Pyramid" strategy, that is, responding to the needs of massive numbers of the poor at the base of the population pyramid by selling very inexpensive services to large numbers of people. To make their small business sustainable, certain kinds of *civic practices* (our term) are needed. Specifically, Hamilton and Hamilton discuss a *co-creation logic*, a partnering between the youth in the small business and community members in identifying needs. In addition, to sustain the business, new forms of leadership by the young people had to emerge, forms that moved away from the hierarchy within the informal group and turned instead to styles of leadership that were effective in working with community members and selling a service. In a partnership with the SC Johnson Company, the CCS youth became independent owners of their own company. This partnering model means that the youth can develop a sense of collective identity, purpose, and agency in which they are a partner to, not employees of, a large multinational company. Further, the partnership enables the uneducated (some are illiterate) and poor youth who own the business to develop both human and social capital, critical assets for civic participation. Not only do the youth gain access to powerful people, but the youth themselves become mentors for others. The CCS, then, is an innovative example of a mediating institution. In the process of banding together to provide a service that the state is not providing, youth develop their own civic capacities and improve the quality of life of fellow citizens at the bottom of the pyramid.

Under certain conditions, the assets in civic participation accumulated by young people have been put to political use. Diouf (1996) presents a narrative of urban youth in Dakar, Senegal, and the transformations of youth-led community organizations that have taken on a range of public purposes (an example used several times in GUG, 2005, Chapter 6). Again, community organizations are key sites in which young people address the structural lag. Faced with lack of education, or lack of employment opportunities for the educated, these organizations provide a vehicle for youth to create a future for themselves in a hostile environment through both self-help and protest.

In the case of Dakar, local athletic and cultural associations came together with student organizations in the late 1980s and 1990s both to call attention to their plight and to do something about it. They first engaged in massive and sometimes violent protest during an electoral campaign against the return of the ruling party. Having failed to prevent victory for the incumbents, some groups of these youths turned on ethnic minorities in the city. Then, in what Diouf called an act of purification for the recent violence, they set about to clean up and beautify their neighborhoods, providing desperately needed public services and a sense of public space while demonstrating an autonomy from a political system from which they already felt excluded. Diouf characterizes this movement, called Set Setal, as the development of new ways of doing politics by these marginalized young people that "rest principally on a refusal of traditional political action and assesses new forms and practices of citizenship" (p. 247). Mediating institutions of the neighborhood stood alongside student organizations to act, self-assess, and change direction toward self-reliance and more constructive public purposes.

The case of urban Senegalese youth points to a common aspect of much youth organizing to enact citizenship—the interplay of multiple mediating institutions that cross boundaries of locality, class, education, ideology, religion, ethnicity, and gender. Mische's (2008) rich study of Brazilian youth activism in that country's remarkable transformation from dictatorship to democracy traces this interplay over a 20-year period. The activists that Mische follows were often members of five or six organizations simultaneously or in rapid succession. Their social networks included rural organizations devoted to land reform, labor unions, student groups, professional associations, religious communities inspired by liberation theology, and emerging political parties (when the authoritarian government began to liberalize in the 1980s).

Mische accounts for both the tensions that networking and multiple memberships can bring, but also the great potential for innovation by youth leaders who developed the capacity to communicate across very different styles and cultures of protest and political strategizing. At times they served as a bridge between organizations that made collective action more possible. For example, the trajectory of one youth activist includes affiliation with a professionally oriented agronomy student group, church-affiliated rural organizations, a student organization, and the new Worker's Party. In the course of his activism, he brought middle-class students with knowledge of agriculture into alliance with land reform groups in the countryside while also connecting them to student union politics. He further acted as a national youth coordinator for the Worker's Party and tried to balance his work in student and civic organizations with his commitments to the party. Mische writes of this individual: "These intersecting identities contributed to his ability to build relations across groups, while expanding the cultural and organizational resources he brought to the various collectivities to which he belonged" (p. 18).

However, these overlapping networks are not in themselves sufficient for collaboration and innovation in political action to occur, in part because different mediating institutions had different political projects and modes of deliberation. Mische continues: "The activists responded to such challenges by developing particular styles of communication by which they mediated among their multiple involvements. These communicative styles channeled youth in different ways, toward competition versus collaboration, or towards ideas versus actions" (p. 22).

The centrality of mediating institutions for the enactment of youth citizenship plays out in a range of scales and registers. In the CCS in Kenya, youth formed a small business in response to community needs and in the process developed civic skills of collaboration, leadership, and agency as well as accrued social capital. The organizations that came together in the Set Setal cleanup movement in Senegal harnessed the frustrations of marginalized youth to take important aspects of local governance into their own hands, improving the sense of efficacy of their communities. And networks of mediating institutions in Brazil put youth at the forefront of deepening a democratic project committed to social justice by building coalitions across diverse social actors—students, workers, farmers, and political party activists.

The barriers to the full incorporation of younger generations of citizens in the developing world are massive. The few case studies of youth civic engagement that we have discussed point to the political consciousness and creative organizing of young people. Besides the challenges to civic engagement from poverty, lack of government capacity, and multinational corporate policies, certain entrenched traditions and relationships violate basic human rights and the capacities of groups to enact citizenship. As one example of this, we end the chapter with a discussion of gender discrimination and policies to address it.

The reports of the World Bank and the Population Council make the point that policies have to address the lower status of women and girls if developing countries are going to emerge from poverty and political strife. An even stronger argument is put forth by Kristof and WuDunn (2009), who make the case that gender is the moral challenge for the twenty-first century. They refer to Amartya Sen's observation that more than 100 million females in the developing world are "missing" due to various forms of *gendercide*—selective abortions, preferential treatment of male children (in nutrition, vaccinations, medical care, schooling), maternal mortality, and human rights violations such as dowry murders. They point out that policies that educate females and enable women to start their own businesses have large dividends for the social stability and well-being of a society. When women have a say in or control a larger share of family finances, there are greater benefits to the whole family because more money tends to be spent on nutrition, health, and housing. Likewise, investment in girls' education has repeatedly been shown to have a demographic dividend in terms of delayed family formation and ultimately to have a ripple effect on the health, nutrition, and education of other family members. Such evidence leads the authors to specific policy recommendations, many of which address the problems that entrenched patriarchal practices pose for democratic governance in the developing world. For example, they recommend that donor countries encourage poor countries to adjust their laws so that widows (rather than male kin) can inherit the property of their deceased husbands. This is connected to other recommendations related to women's economic security and financial self-sufficiency, which are bolstered by laws that make it easy for women to hold property and bank accounts and by policies that build on the successful practices of micro-financing schemes.

Hamilton and Hamilton (2009) cite a second example of a mediating institution in Kenya that has directly addressed the issue of gender discrimination. The Tap and Reposition Youth (TRY) project was created in the slums of Nairobi, Kenya, by the K-Rep Development Agency and the Population

Council to adapt microfinance strategies to the needs of young women (16- to 22-year-olds) who are vulnerable to sexual exploitation and to the risks of HIV. Like many poor youth in the developing world, these women migrated from rural communities to the city in search of work and live in informal settlements that lack law enforcement and other government services. Without the extended supports of their rural families, they are on their own. Their predicament illustrates very well the concept of groupways, which draws attention to the fact that the social compact between states and citizens varies according to the groups to which an individual citizen belongs (Flanagan, Martinez, & Cumsille, in press).

TRY uses the microfinance principles of the Grameen Bank of Bangladesh developed by Muhammad Yunus. The Grameen model of small loans to women (who typically are formed into groups of women who guarantee one another's debts) has proven to be a very successful model for sustainable microenterprise in the developing world. Not only are the women highly reliable in paying back debt, the fact that they earn money enhances their autonomy and freedom within highly patriarchal families. But the model also has political and consciousness-raising potential. In the regularly scheduled group meetings, feelings of group solidarity develop and the women also are likely to discuss social issues such as family planning, sexuality, or girls' education (Kristof & WuDunn, 2009). And the small loans enable women to be their own bosses rather than dependent recipients of aid. In the TRY project, the women decided as a group which projects were the most viable and thus would receive the first investments of their pooled resources. Hamilton and Hamilton (2009) discuss the evolution of the TRY model in response to the needs of younger versus older women in the group, with mentoring and Young Savers Clubs developed to meet the needs of the younger women.

With respect to youth civic engagement, both TRY and CCS are examples of the critical importance of flexible and creative mediating institutions that fill the lacuna in services from the state, and at the same time, build solidarity and community infrastructure among marginalized groups of young citizens in developing countries. These mediating institutions not only serve their needs, they develop their civic capacities and identities. In so doing, these mediating institutions stabilize governance in fragile democratic societies but also are a space where disenfranchised groups (women or the poor) can make collective decisions and challenge the status quo.

The GUG and WDR reports draw attention to the challenges and opportunities that a large youth demographic portends for the developing world and point to the interconnections between civic engagement and other transitions to adulthood. Despite the challenges, specific policies could facilitate the incorporation of younger generations. These include subsidizing the costs of official papers that document their citizenship such as passports, which young people need in order to apply for schooling or jobs. Investing in the education of young women and providing micro-financing for small businesses owned by women are policies that would help to incorporate a large group who is disenfranchised in many developing countries. Such policies also tend to have a ripple effect in extended family benefits.

Citizenship implies a social compact that binds governments and citizens but, for many reasons outlined in this chapter, governments in the developing world are often unable to deliver on this compact. We have argued that young people often take up the slack by providing services and, in the process, they develop civic competencies and identities. Mediating institutions are a key site where these activities occur. These institutions provide the social spaces where young people collectively can engage in civic actions. Those actions may take the form of claims on the public (government) or the private (market) sectors or they may compensate for the failures of those sectors. In any case, attention to youth as citizens in developing nations expands the meaning of and motivation behind civic action.

REFERENCES

Boateng, J., & Flanagan, C. (2008). Women's access to health care in Ghana: Effects of education, residence, lineage, and self-determination. *Biodemography and Social Biology, 54(1)*, 56–73.

Bunting, A., & Merry, S. E. (2007). Global regulation and local political struggles: Early marriage in Northern Nigeria. In S. A. Venkatesh & R. Kassimir (Eds.), *Youth, globalization, and the law.* Palo Alto, CA: Stanford University Press.

Diouf, M. (1996). Urban youth and Senegalese politics: 1988–1994. *Public Culture, 8(2)*, 225–249.

Domedel, A., & Peña y Lillo, M. (2008). *El mayo de los pinguinos.* Santiago, Chile: Editorial Universidad de Chile.

Durham, D. (2008). Apathy and agency: The romance of agency and youth in Botswana. In J. Cole & D. Durham (Eds.), *Figuring the future: Globalization and the temporalities of children and youth* (pp. 151–178). Santa Fe, NM: School for Advanced Research Press.

Flanagan, C. A., & Campbell, B. (2003), with L. Botcheva, J. Bowes, B. Csapo, P. Macek, & E. Sheblanova. Social class and adolescents' beliefs about justice in different social orders. *Journal of Social Issues, 59 (4)*, 711–732

Flanagan, C., Martinez, M. L., & Cumsille, P. (2009). Civil societies as developmental and cultural contexts for civic identity formation. In L. Arnett Jensen (Ed.), *Bridging cultural and developmental psychology: New syntheses in theory, research and policy.* New York: Oxford University Press.

Fokwang, J. (2003). Ambiguous transitions: mediating citizenship among youths in Cameroon. *Africa Development, 28(1&2)*, 173–201.

Fussell, E., & Greene, M. E. (2002). Demographic trends affecting youth around the world. In B. B. Brown, R. W. Larson, & T. S. Saraswathi (Eds.), *The world's youth: Adolescence in eight regions of the globe* (pp. 21–60). Cambridge: Cambridge University Press.

Hamilton, S. F., & Hamilton, M. A. (2009). The transition to adulthood: Challenges of poverty and structural lag. In R. M. Lerner and L. Steinberg (Eds.), *Handbook of adolescent psychology* (3rd ed.). *Volume 2, Contextual influences on adolescent development* (pp. 492–526). New York: Wiley.

Hatano, G., & Takahashi, K. (2005). The development of societal cognition: A commentary. In M. Barrett & E. Buchanan-Barrow (Eds.), *Children's understanding of society* (pp. 287–303). East Sussex, UK: Psychology Press.

Hirschman, A. O. (1970). *Exit, voice, and loyalty: Responses to decline in firms, organizations, and states*. Cambridge, MA: Harvard University Press.

Jua, N. (2003). Differential responses to disappearing transitional pathways: Redefining possibility among Cameroonian youths. *African Studies Review, 46(2)*, 13–36.

Kabeer, N. (1999). Resources, agency, achievements: Reflections on the measurement of women's empowerment. *Development and Change, 30(3)*, 435–464.

Kassimir, R. (2007, May 16–17). *Banking on the young: Young people and the international development agenda*. Presentation at the African Development: The Next Generation, International Development Centre conference, The Open University, Milton Keynes, UK.

Kassimir, R. (2001). Producing local politics: Governance, representation and non-state organizations in Africa. In T. Callaghy, R. Kassimir, & R. Latham (Eds.), *Intervention and transnationalism in Africa: Global-local networks of power* (pp. 93–112). Cambridge: Cambridge University Press.

Kristof, M. D., & WuDunn, S. (2009). *Half the sky: Turning oppression into opportunity for women worldwide.* New York: Alfred A. Knopf.

Markus, H. R., Mullally, P., & Kitayama, S. (1997). Selfways: Diversity in modes of cultural participation. In U. Neisser & D. Jopling (Eds.), *The conceptual self in context: Culture, experience, self-understanding* (pp. 13–61). Cambridge: Cambridge University Press.

McAdam, D. (1988). *Freedom Summer*. Oxford: Oxford University Press.

Maslow, A. H. (1943). A theory of human motivation. *Psychological Review, 50(4)*, 370–396.

Mische, A. (2008). *Partisan publics: Communication and contention across Brazilian youth activist networks*. Princeton, NJ: Princeton University Press.

National Research Council and Institute of Medicine (2005). *Growing up global (GUG): The changing transitions to adulthood in developing countries*. Washington, DC: National Academies Press.

Nussbaum, M. (1999). *Sex and social justice.* New York: Oxford University Press.

Tibbitts, F. (2002). Understanding what we do: Emerging models of human rights education. *International Review of Education, 48*, 159–171.

Torney-Purta, J. (2009). International psychological research that matters for policy and practice. *American Psychologist, 64(8)*, 825–837.

Ukeje, C. (2006). Youth movements and youth violence in Nigeria's oil delta region. In C. Daiute, Z. Beykont, C. Higson-Smith, & L. Nucci (Eds.), *International Perspectives on Youth Conflict and Development* (pp. 289–304). New York: Oxford University Press.

Vygotsky, L. S. (1978). *Mind in society: The development of higher psychological processes.* Cambridge, MA: Harvard University Press.

The World Bank (2007). *World Development Report 2007: Development and the next generation*. Washington, DC: The World Bank.

Youniss, J., & Hart, D. (2005). Intersection of social institutions with civic development. *New directions for child and adolescent development, 109*, 73–81.

CHAPTER 5

Youth Civic Engagement: Normative Issues

PETER LEVINE
Tufts University

ANN HIGGINS-D'ALESSANDRO
Fordham University

THE RELEVANCE OF NORMATIVE PHILOSOPHY TO YOUTH CIVIC ENGAGEMENT

EDUCATING YOUNG PEOPLE for citizenship is an intrinsically *normative* task.[1] In other words, it is a matter of choosing and transmitting values to citizens so that they will build and sustain societies that embody particular forms of justice and virtue. Adults who teach history, civics, or social studies, who guide adolescents in community service projects, or who recruit youth as activists generally do so for normative reasons—because of values that they hold and wish to transmit. Likewise, most scholars who evaluate and study such work do so because of their own demanding moral principles. They have chosen to examine service-learning or youth organizing—instead of distance-learning or the stock market—because something about youth civic engagement strikes them as deeply valuable. Yet there is relatively little discussion of the precise normative reasons for particular forms of civic education in schools and other institutions or of the values that scholars bring to the work of evaluating such efforts. Higgins-D'Alessandro (this volume) addresses the latter issue.

This lack of explicit attention to normative reasons is unfortunate. Reasonable people have defined "good citizens" in various ways: for example, as dutiful members of communities, as independent critics of public institutions,

[1] We use the word *normative* to encompass what is ethical, just, fair, or moral—not as the antonym of *deviant*, nor as a synonym for *typical* or *average*.

as bearers of rights, and as proponents of social justice (Schudson, 1998; Westheimer & Kahne, 2004). Deciding which of these values to transmit is a public task in which everyone has a stake. Adults who lead or study civic education, or do both, have considerable influence over youth, who are not permitted to choose most of their educational experiences. As a matter of accountability, these adults ought to explain—both to the youth they serve and to other adults—which civic values and habits they are trying to develop, and why. In short, they should be willing to participate in a democratic discussion about their public work.

Second, explicit discussion of values can reveal the tradeoffs that often arise in civic education. One category of tradeoffs (as an example) involves quantity versus equality. Many voluntary programs attract adolescents who already have relatively strong commitments to civic engagement and relatively strong skills for civic and political participation. Student governments, for instance, usually draw students who are already on a leadership track. Those students tend to be successful in school and thus likely to hold privileged social positions as adults. Offering them civic opportunities may enhance their capacity to participate in politics and community affairs. That is a good result if we want to develop more experienced leaders in the next generation. But it is a bad outcome if we are mainly concerned about *equality* of civic participation by social class (McNeal, 1998).

Another type of tradeoff involves freedom versus moral authority. Even if it is desirable for young people to become tolerant, trusting, caring, and committed to the common good, there is a separate question about whether any particular group of adults (e.g., parents, teachers, policy-makers, or taxpayers) has a responsibility or a right to inculcate these values. Depending on one's theory of how power should be exercised in education, one might think that it is the duty of public school teachers to decide which values to inculcate in their students; or that they should teach only the values that elected officials select for public schools; or that they should try to leave value-questions to parents; or that communities of teachers and students should choose values democratically.

Third, we need normative reasons to address a vexing problem. When young people do not engage with a public institution (for example, when they do not vote), that could be because they lack some mental state that we wish they possessed, such as interest, knowledge, concern, confidence, or commitment. Or it could be because the institution is severely flawed and does not deserve to be engaged. (For instance, electoral districts in the United States have been drawn to discourage competition, thereby making most campaigns meaningless.) Whether to change young people's minds or reform institutions—or both—is a crucial issue that cannot be addressed without deciding what constitutes a just society.

Finally, explicit normative argumentation can provide persuasive reasons to invest in civic development—reasons that would otherwise be overlooked. Today, the default justification for any educational investment is its impact on individual students' long-term *human capital*: their value in the labor market, as revealed by their grades and degrees. There is evidence that some civic opportunities increase human capital. For example, mandatory service-learning in high school seems to improve students' grades and increases their likelihood of completing college (Dávila & Mora, 2007). However, many adults who organize such opportunities have defensible motives other than enhancing human capital. By elucidating these alternative reasons, we may be able to increase public support for civic development. We may also reduce our dependence on fragile empirical rationales. For instance, even if service-learning enhances students' grades, it may turn out that other interventions do so more efficiently. Should we therefore give up on service-learning? That would be an appropriate conclusion *if* the only purpose of service-learning were to increase human capital. But there are other plausible reasons for it.

PHILOSOPHICAL PERSPECTIVES

Contemporary moral and political philosophy provides rich and diverse resources for thinking about youth civic development. After several decades of groundbreaking empirical work on civic development—including a paradigm shift to "positive youth development" (Lerner, 2004), it would now be useful to renew the dialogue between psychology and philosophy. One starting point is to ask how each of the main current schools of moral philosophy would assess major forms of civic education. Actual philosophers are often eclectic, drawing from more than one school or tradition. Nevertheless, these main schools provide useful heuristics.

One major stream of modern moral reasoning is consequentialist. It assesses any action or institution by measuring its net outcomes or consequences. The leading subset of consequentialism is utilitarianism, which presumes that the consequences that matter are measures of human *welfare*. Welfare, in turn, can be defined in terms of subjective satisfaction or happiness; objective indicators, such as life expectancy; or the ability to satisfy preferences. Utilitarianism has had an enormous influence on welfare economics and, more generally, the social sciences. It is a demanding ethical doctrine, requiring that we do whatever is possible to maximize aggregate welfare. If taken seriously, it would require deep changes in social policies, including (most probably) massive increases in educational investments.

A utilitarian might favor civic opportunities because they have been found to enhance students' welfare. For instance, an evaluation of the Quantum Opportunities Program (QOP) studied randomly selected students and a control group. For about $2,500 per year over four years, QOP was able to reduce the likelihood of dropping out to 8%, compared to 44% for the control group. QOP's approach included academic programs that were individually paced for each student; mandatory community service; enrichment programs; and pay for each hour of participation (Hahn, Leavitt, & Aaron, 1994; Eccles & Gootman, 2002). For a utilitarian, the cost of this program would be a disadvantage (because having to pay taxes presumably reduces the welfare of the taxpayers); but the social benefits might outweigh the costs. People who complete high school are generally better off, economically and in other ways, than those who do not. They also contribute more to the economy, thereby enhancing other people's welfare. Indeed, the evaluators estimate the social benefits of QOP at $39,037 per student, and the net benefits (i.e., the benefits minus the costs) at $28,427. "This exercise," they conclude, "shows that QOP will pay large dividends." A utilitarian reading this report would conclude that programs like QOP are moral imperatives, unless some other approach turns out to be even more effective (Hahn, Leavitt, & Aaron, 1994, p. 19).

One standard argument against utilitarianism is that it overlooks fairness among individuals by focusing on aggregate welfare (Rawls, 1971/2005, pp. 19–24). There are situations in which making disadvantaged people even worse off can increase aggregate social welfare; in such cases, simple utilitarianism is blind to fairness. However, utilitarians can provide indirect arguments for focusing resources on the most disadvantaged young people. One argument is that the marginal benefits are likely to be greatest when we offer opportunities to adolescents who would otherwise be "at risk" of failure in school. For instance, the QOP program obtained efficient outcomes because it was directed at disadvantaged middle-school students, many of whom were otherwise likely to become pregnant.

The other utilitarian argument for equity is political. Jeremy Bentham, the first utilitarian, asserted that representative democracy was the form of government that would best promote aggregate welfare. Democratic governments were most likely to address genuine public needs and allocate resources efficiently. Our actual democracy, however, is marked by highly *unequal* participation and does not respond equally to everyone's needs (American Political Science Association, 2004). In order to achieve more equitable representation, we need to help young people develop the skills, habits, knowledge, and motivations that will increase their participation.

Utilitarianism does not provide direct reasons to protect individual freedom and choice. Utilitarians would support mandatory civic education programs that enhance social welfare even if youth do not wish to enroll. Most Americans have utilitarian intuitions with respect to adolescents: We are willing to override young people's freedom to promote their welfare.

Unlike utilitarianism, Kantianism puts autonomy at the center. Immanuel Kant is perhaps best known as the proponent of the Categorical Imperative, which says that we must be able to generalize the *maxims* of our actions so that they would apply to everyone in similar circumstances. This principle proves vague in application, and many contemporary Kantians believe that the useful heart of his philosophy lies elsewhere. Kant argued that we had two fundamental duties: to develop our own rational autonomy, and to help others develop and pursue reasonable goals of their own choosing (Baron, 1997). The measure of an action was not its consequences, but the quality of the free human will that lay behind it. To be autonomous, goals had to be freely chosen, but they also had to be rational (i.e., examined, coherent, and capable of public justification).

A Kantian would not be concerned about the impact of civic programs on objective measures of welfare, such as graduation rates. However, a Kantian might be impressed by programs or opportunities that seem to enhance the autonomy of their participants. Programs would seem especially promising to Kantians if they encouraged young people to reflect upon moral issues and choices, form and defend their own opinions, and act accordingly (see Beaumont, this volume). The Just Community (JC) approach to civic and moral education is a good example (Power & Higgins-D'Alessandro, 2008; Higgins-D'Alessandro & Power, 2005; Power, Higgins, & Kohlberg, 1989). Students and teachers create a school community together using principles of fairness and democratic processes (e.g., one person, one vote; open discussion and debate) to govern themselves. Self-governance develops students' (and teachers') autonomy, critical moral reasoning, and leadership as well as a sense of group membership, affectionate ties, and responsibility. The school's aspirational norms and values become embodied in rules and sanctions and the intrinsic valuing of community. In the JC schools, students' moral reasoning is significantly higher after two to three years relative to that of comparison students. Kantians might also value outcomes such as success in school, but only as *indirect* evidence that students were developing autonomy. To continue with the same example, the Just Community's focus on self-governance at the community level leads to self-governance or autonomy on the individual level, which translates into better school attendance, class participation, and academic performance (Power et al., 1989; Higgins-D'Alessandro, 2008). The effects on academic performance would strike a utilitarian as strong arguments for JC; for Kantians, they matter only insofar as success in school implies greater autonomy for students.

Both Kantians and utilitarians have reasons to favor programs such as QOP and the Just Community (assuming that the evaluations cited above are accurate). However, their reasons are quite different, and this difference matters when we confront questions such as whether to mandate service-learning, whether youth should always co-lead their own service projects with teachers, or whether to count economic welfare as a positive outcome of service. These issues are complex, and Kantians need not always take different sides from utilitarians. For instance, although utilitarians are not directly concerned about freedom, they might be dissuaded from imposing service requirements if such obligations usually breed resentment. Kantians care a great deal about freedom, but they might support a service *mandate* if service reliably expands young people's sense of options and possibilities and therefore enhances their autonomy later on. They would be more likely to support a mandate if students recognize and agree with the proposition that mandatory service not only helps others, it also enhances their own future autonomy. This has happened in one JC school, where students have voted to impose service mandates on themselves but have also voted to remove the same mandates when they seemed to lose their meaning. Such cycles reveal the need for human beings—in this case, students—to make meaning of their experiences as discussed under civic republicanism in this chapter. A substantial majority of alumni from the last two decades of this JC school reported that they are currently civically or politically active in their communities whether they participated in mandatory *or* volunteer service as students (Vozzola, Rosen, Higgins-D'Alessandro, & Horan, 2009). Overall, Kantians and utilitarians will seek different evidence and may reach different conclusions in concrete cases. They will also justify the very same program in different ways; and justifications matter in the public debate.

A third relevant stream of modern philosophy is civic republicanism. Its core idea is that civic participation (deliberating, collaborating, volunteering, advocating, and voting) is not a cost. It is not work that we must unfortunately do in order to sustain a just society. Rather, it is a good and an intrinsically dignified and rewarding form of human behavior. Some civic republicans rank various human pursuits and place political activism high on their lists. Aristotle, for example, considered politics the second-highest way of life after philosophy itself (*Nicomachean Ethics*, 1177b). Others are pluralists. They do not believe that there is one universal and objective ranking of human goods, but they consider civic participation to be a good rather than a cost (Galston, 2002).

Civic republicans should view civic opportunities for young people as intrinsically valuable, regardless of their outcomes. For example, a one-time service project is unlikely to boost any long-term outcomes; thus it has weak appeal for utilitarians. But civic republicans could argue that schools and colleges are communities. Good communities offer opportunities for collaboration and service. Therefore, even one-time service projects are valuable.

Civic republicans could argue, further, that young people should be exposed to the satisfactions of participation so that they may choose to be engaged when they are adults. We are barraged by advertising for other goods, such as consumer products. Civic participation is not widely promoted. Civic republicans might see effective forms of civic education as advertisements for participation.

A related argument in favor of civic participation begins with the observation that human beings *make meaning*. That is, they create narratives, images, performances, rituals, and melodies that integrate simple facts or impressions into more ambitious, more significant wholes. Meaning-making can be seen as a source of happiness and satisfaction, as an expression of rational autonomy, or as intrinsically valuable. In other words, it can be linked to utilitarianism, Kantianism, or civic republicanism, albeit in different ways.

In any event, civic engagement is essential for meaning-making. By interacting in groups and trying to persuade peers, we create narratives about ourselves and our communities and develop opinions. Hannah Arendt used *acting* as a specialized term for persuasion and collaboration (in contrast to *work*, which for her meant individual creativity, and *labor*, which meant subsistence). She wrote, "In acting and speaking, men show who they are, reveal actively their unique personal identities and thus make their appearance in the human world" (Arendt, 1958, p. 179). Civic participation rewarded eloquence, and eloquence was a way to make meaning.

People who participate in groups also generate *collective* narratives and build institutions whose buildings, logos, mission statements, and rituals reflect common meanings. This kind of work is a powerful antidote to mass culture. As de Tocqueville observed, members of large democratic societies tend to prefer cultural goods that are popular. Books are advertised as "best sellers," movies as "blockbusters," and songs as "hits" because democratic audiences trust popularity as evidence of quality. In aristocratic cultures, on the other hand, elites have disproportionate consumer power and tend to view popularity as a mark of vulgarity (de Tocqueville, 1954, II, 3, xvii). Therefore, we should expect that mass-produced culture will prevail in a democracy, and then most people will be less able to create meaning. All our narratives, images, and melodies will come out of Hollywood (or its equivalent). However, when people participate actively in communities and associations, they have opportunities to create distinctive cultural goods, and they have audiences for their products. They also have incentives to influence the content of cultural products; and if they lose debates about what meanings to make, they can exit and create new associations. Thus, in a strong civil society, cultural products become diverse; and that diversity is an argument for civic engagement.

Philosophical schools such as utilitarianism, Kantianism, and civic republicanism consistently apply a few abstract principles to all relevant cases. That methodology has itself been criticized, most notably by communitarians.

Drawing on Hume, Hegel, and other classic sources, they argue that our duties are not abstract and general, but derive from our particular and contingent connections to fellow members of our own communities and families, with whom we happen to have common histories. Denying these bonds in the name of autonomy or universality, according to communitarians, leaves us bereft of the basic materials of a good life (Sandel, 1984; Taylor, 1984). Certain kinds of civic opportunities, especially voluntary service, seem to embody communitarian values. Some forms of feminism and critical race theory are communitarian in their emphasis on respecting identity differences. There are Kantian and utilitarian reasons for paying attention to racial and gender equity, but not for valuing ethnic or gender solidarity as intrinsic goods.

Another critic of abstract philosophical principles was John Dewey, a major influence on pragmatist theorists of education ever since. Dewey asserted that no general principles (no "antecedent universal propositions") could distinguish just institutions from unjust ones. The nature of a good society was "something to be critically and experimentally determined" (Dewey, 1927, p. 74). Any effort to identify and apply independent criteria would be naïve, because philosophy is always "intrinsically" connected to "social history" (Dewey, 1931, p. 3). Dewey's skepticism or relativism would seem to invalidate any normative distinctions, but he tried to construct a positive ideal out of a few modest commitments. One commitment was *learning*: A good society continuously revisited and changed its normative commitments. The second was *experience*: The only way to learn was to try things in the real world. And the third was *deliberation*: Learning worked best when people of different backgrounds discussed, planned, and experienced together. Therefore, in Dewey's view, such democratic institutions as "popular voting, majority rule and so on" were valuable *only* because "to some extent they involve a consultation and discussion which uncover social needs and troubles" (Dewey, 1927, p. 206). All groups (even criminal bands) promote some internal discussion, but some groups were better than others. The criterion for assessing a group was not whether it endorsed the right principles (no such things could be identified), but rather whether its membership were diverse and open. The two questions to use in evaluating a group were: "How numerous and varied are the interests which are consciously shared?" and "How full and free is the interplay with other forms of association?" (Dewey, 1916, p. 89).

These criteria can be applied to schools as communities. Deweyan pragmatists understand them as institutions within which people (including youth) make—rather than discover—moral values. We can assess schools morally not by asking whether they have reached the right conclusions about matters like rights and duties, but whether their discussions were diverse, open, and experiential. The Deweyan justification for activities like service-learning is straightforward, as long as the "learning" aspect is strong and participants are diverse. The Just Community is an example of a self-consciously created open, diverse, democratic learning community grounded in this Deweyan ideal. The JC theory of education as development mixes the Kantian emphasis on autonomy and critical moral reasoning with the actual practice of building a self-governing community. As mentioned earlier, many actual philosophers draw on more than one tradition in developing their views. An important and relevant example is the "capabilities approach" as defended by Amartya Sen and Martha Nussbaum (Alkire, 2002, pp. 32–43; Crocker, 1995). Sen and Nussbaum share the Kantian intuition that autonomy is an essential human value. They criticize objective measures of social welfare, because free human beings may reasonably choose *not* to pursue these outcomes. For example, some communities are committed to religion rather than affluence. The fact that monks do not eat well does not mean that they lack welfare (Sen, 1985). Likewise, an individual may choose hardships in order to be closer to nature.

On the other hand, Sen and Nussbaum reject the idea that autonomy is simply a matter of free choice. First of all, some actual choices harm the true interests of the individual: Using addictive narcotics would be an example. Other choices reflect a narrow sense of what is possible, constrained by cultural biases. Moreover, people need goods before they can be truly autonomous: for instance, education, legal rights, and a sense of self-respect.

Therefore, Sen and Nussbaum recommend *capabilities* as the criteria of social justice. In a good society, everyone has certain core capabilities, such as working, playing, raising children, participating in politics, and appreciating nature and art. These capabilities can be expressed in various ways or even forgone, depending on the free choices of individuals. For example, if I have the ability to raise children but choose not to act on it, there is no injustice. In Sen's terminology, I may have the "capability" but not the "functioning" of parenthood. Justice is measured by the objective amount and distribution of capabilities, not functionings.

The capabilities approach would support certain forms of youth civic engagement, for several reasons. The youth themselves would develop one particular capability, namely, political participation. Some of their other capabilities might be strengthened as well; for example, service appears to boost educational success. Finally, Sen and Nussbaum believe that communities must decide democratically how to develop and promote the capabilities of their own members. Civic and democratic education (which may or may not include service) seems relevant here as a means to develop the capability of political participation. Sen and Nussbaum offer lists of human capabilities that are intended to be objective and universal, but many subsidiary choices remain to be made democratically (see Haste, this volume). By developing young people's skills of social analysis and deliberation, we help to promote democratic decision making and thereby optimize society's support for capabilities.

We have not been able to find any scholarly work that connects the capabilities approach (which is influential in development economics and political philosophy) with the theory of "positive youth development" (which arose in developmental psychology and influences youth programming). Positive youth development asserts that young people should be treated as assets to their communities who can contribute distinctively because of their energy, creativity, independence, and fresh thinking. They will "thrive" better, on this view, if they are encouraged to contribute than if they are treated as vulnerable to pathologies and failures, such as crime, suicide, academic failure, or sexually transmitted diseases (Lerner, 2004, pp. 85–107; cf. Nussbaum & Sen, 1993, p. 1). Positive youth development is a critique of the prevailing deficit model, which encourages strategies of monitoring, prevention, remediation, and discipline that, in the aggregate, send an alienating and disempowering message to adolescents. Young people respond better when given opportunities to be actively engaged and to serve. Especially in the work of Richard M. Lerner, a positive relationship between adolescents and their communities is understood as bi-directional; when things go well, youth benefit from serving their communities, and communities improve because of youth service and voice.

This is an empirical thesis for which there is considerable support (Eccles & Gootman, 2002). But one might ask why we *hope* that the evidence supports the theory of positive youth development. Wouldn't it be easier if one could solve adolescent pathologies with efficient programs of monitoring and prevention? The underlying normative reason, we believe, is best articulated in the capabilities approach, which suggests that the first duty of a just regime is not to maximize welfare but to enhance individuals' capacities to play *their choice* of positive roles. We should not specify our goals for adolescents in terms of reducing the high-school dropout rate or cutting teen pregnancy. These are measures of welfare, not of capabilities. A highly capable young person will probably finish high school and avoid early pregnancy *in order* to enhance her ability to pursue challenging ends of her own choice. Thus the measure of our success is her capability, not her success in school or her age when becoming a parent.

This brief sketch of philosophical views toward youth civic engagement has omitted other questions that are equally relevant. For instance: Who deserves citizenship (i.e, full membership in a community)? What rights and obligations should come with citizenship? What civic or political roles should be played by, for instance, elected representatives, voluntary associations, and the clergy? Which public problems should be addressed by the people acting through the state, and which should be addressed in civil society?

Plainly, these are enormous questions, basic to political theory. Even a short list underlines how deeply our views of "civic engagement" depend upon our ideas of justice, fairness, the good life, and the good society.

WHAT NORMATIVE POSITIONS ARE EMBODIED IN ACTUAL PROGRAMS?

Dozens of trademarked programs attempt to teach various aspects of civic engagement to American youth. They range from the federally funded Center for Civic Education and its *We the People . . . The Citizen and the Constitution* curriculum (with a heavy emphasis on constitutional law) to grassroots voluntary associations like *Sistas on the Rise* in the Bronx, NY, which helps "young mothers and women of color raise consciousness, build sisterhood and take action for social change." In addition, many thousands of schoolteachers and staff of youth programs develop and teach their own curricula or combinations of curricula. Each of these interventions has goals and intentions, which, in the case of the trademarked programs, can usually be read in mission statements and on web sites. But interventions may also have undisclosed or inadvertent messages and effects. To make matters even more complicated, the messages and the effects may not coincide, for students may take away unintended lessons. Thus, it is a complex matter to determine what normative positions are embodied in real-life classes and programs.

In order to provide some brief illustrations, we have consulted professional program evaluations of several prominent trademarked programs. In each case, students were assessed using measures that had good psychometric properties and that seemed to fit the intentions of the program's designers, who were involved in various ways in these studies. In each case, the evaluation found positive impacts on the measures tested (notwithstanding some variation in methodology and rigor among the studies). Thus we can say that these programs attempted to—and actually did—enhance the specified outcomes for their enrolled students. Our question is what normative orientation would lead someone to *want* to have these effects.

1. *Facing History and Ourselves* is a nonprofit organization that provides curricula, professional development, and materials related to historical examples of severe intergroup conflict, such as the Holocaust. Students are encouraged to discuss and critically evaluate their own identities and responsibilities. (See Selman & Kwok, this volume, on the program.) In an evaluation by Schultz, Barr, and Selman (2001), participating students and

a comparison group were given questionnaires with scales designed to measure numerous aspects of "interpersonal development," understood as "interpersonal understanding" (knowledge of how groups interrelate), interpersonal skills (strategies that support good relationships), and personal meaning (the ability to reflect on "one's actions and emotional investment in a particular relationship"). For instance, students were given the Multigroup Ethnic Identity Measure instrument developed by Jean Phinney, which includes items such as: "I have a strong sense of belonging to my own ethnic group" (Phinney, 1992). They were also asked about their own "modern racism," as measured by their response to prompts such as: "Over the last few years, racial and ethnic minorities have gained more economically than they deserve" (Schultz et al., 2001, p. 12). And they were given self-reported measures of behavior, such as involvement with social issues and fighting, among others.

The results indicate that students in *Facing History and Ourselves* "showed increased relationship maturity and decreased fighting behavior, racist attitudes, and insular ethnic identity relative to comparison students" (Schultz et al., p. 23). These outcomes are treated as positive, as evidence of the program's *efficacy*. That is not a particularly controversial judgment, although the evaluators' interpretation of "opposition to affirmative action" as evidence of "subtle prejudice" *would be* controversial (Schultz et al., p. 12). There could also be controversy about whether the goals of the program (such as *relationship maturity*) justify allocations of students' time; whether and where the program fits into the broader curriculum; and whether the U.S. government has a right to promote some of these attitudes, such as a lessening of *insular ethnic identity*. A certain image of the good citizen emerges from the evaluation: He or she will be conscious of ethnic identities and capable of working peacefully and respectfully across lines of difference.

Dennis Barr, evaluation director of *Facing History and Ourselves*, writes that the program "integrates the study of history and ethics in order to promote young people's capacity and commitment to be thoughtful and active participants in society who are able to balance self-interest with a genuine concern for the perspectives, rights and welfare of others" (Barr, 2005, p. 156). There is a strong element of Kantian ethics in this summary statement. Being thoughtful and self-critical, seeing matters from others' perspectives, and being concerned about rights are core Kantian values. The themes of positive youth development and building student capacities in *Facing History* align with Sen and Nussbaum's ideas that a just society builds human capabilities.

Facing History is also concerned with ethnic group membership as a form of identity. That goal is in some tension with utilitarianism and Kantianism, both of which classically understand human beings as part of a single, undifferentiated human community. For Lawrence Kohlberg, the highest stage of moral development is a "universal-ethical-principle orientation." This stage (as Kohlberg wrote) has "a distinctively Kantian ring" (1973, p. 632).

In Kant's original terms, the fully developed moral agent is a citizen of one universal and undifferentiated *Kingdom of Ends*. John Rawls (1971/2005, p. 136) operationalized this idea by proposing that we try to reason about justice behind a "veil of ignorance," in which we do not know our own identities. Likewise, in classical utilitiarianism, each human being is to count for one and none for more than one. With its respect for, and interest in, ethnic particularism, *Facing History and Ourselves* seems to depart from classical Kantian and utilitarian thinking. But bridges can be built. For example, a core Kantian principle is respect for others; if ethnic identity is constitutive of selves, then one must understand and appreciate ethnicities to be respectful of others. Likewise, if people's happiness or welfare depends on having healthy attitudes toward their own ethnic groups, then understanding and even celebrating ethnic identity is important from a utilitarian perspective.

Indeed, in Kolhberg's work, the highest stage of moral reasoning, *Stage 6*, gradually developed into a *balance* between abstract and impersonal justice and personalized care or sympathy. Kohlberg, Boyd, and Levine (1986) stated the idea this way:

> ... although these two attitudes (benevolence and justice) are in tension with each other, they are at the same time mutually supportive and coordinated with a Stage 6 conception of respect for persons. This coordination can be summarized thus: benevolence constrains the momentary concern for justice to remain consistent with the promotion of good for all, while justice constrains benevolence not to be inconsistent with promoting respect for the rights of individuals conceived as autonomous agents. (p. 6)

Moreover, Kohlberg argued that the motivator for moral decision making is the feeling of sympathy for others; without that, we would not put ourselves in their place or adopt the view of the impartial spectator to try to reach a fair solution; we would just take what we could get. He said that starting moral decision making with an act of empathy (taking the original position or playing moral musical chairs, as Kohlberg characterized it) leads to a more just decision, one that is more clearly reversible. Sympathy of this sort becomes refined throughout development and transformed at Stage 6 into the moral point of view. Kohlberg's late statements about Stage 6 seem quite consistent with *Facing History*'s approach.

2. *We the People...* is a curriculum with supporting materials and professional development opportunities funded by the U.S. Department of Education through the Center for Civic Education. Its relatively substantial and

stable funding has allowed it to reach more than 26 million students (Hartry & Porter, 2004). Evaluations to date have used less rigorous designs than the evaluations we summarize here for other programs, but it is important to review the outcomes included in the *We the People* evaluations because they reflect an effort to articulate purposes for a publicly funded and authorized program.

In a 1991 evaluation by the Educational Testing Service, participating students and comparison groups were given items from the National Assessment of Education Progress Civics Assessment. Students were asked questions such as: "Prayer periods in public schools are allowed by the Supreme Court..." (Correct answer: "in no instances.") Participants scored higher than comparison students, leading the evaluators to conclude, "The We the People... program had a strong positive impact on high school students' knowledge of the history and principles of the U.S. Constitution" (Educational Testing Service, 1991, p. 2). Again, a concept of good citizenship emerges: Americans are supposed to understand core principles embodied in the U.S. Constitution and other classic texts.

The evaluation by the Educational Testing Service does not explain why public funds should be used to enhance such understanding. However, in a later evaluation by Hartry and Porter (2004), the central goal of *We the People*... is described as "promoting civic competence and responsibility." This goal is operationalized as a long list of outcomes that include positive attitudes toward American political institutions, knowledge of these institutions, and political participation (e.g., working for a political party or candidate; participating in a peaceful protest).

A 2007 evaluation by RMC Research investigated the *Project Citizen* middle-school program from the Center for Civic Education, which involves student research and advocacy on local policy issues. Students were observed to gain "civic knowledge, civic discourse skills, and public problem solving skills." Changes were greater than in comparison classrooms. A methodological limitation, however, is that "Potential classrooms for the study were identified by state or national coordinators of Project Citizen." Teachers in the Project Citizen classrooms suggested the comparison classrooms. This method raises serious questions about generalizing the findings to the program as a whole (Root & Northup, 2007, pp. 5, 35).

Although these evaluations do not advance elaborate normative justifications, it is implicit that the Center for Civic Education values high rates of informed and enthusiastic political participation within the mainstream American political system because that system is beneficial (for utilitarian, Kantian, and/or civic republican reasons). In addition, since it is used in civic education courses required for high school graduation by every state in the United States, it seems the Center for Civic Education relies on the normative justifications of such laws. Civic education is deemed necessary for the continuance of the U.S. system of government.

A different criterion for evaluation would involve the *distribution* of benefits from *We the People* to different groups of students. *We the People* participants are involved in team competitions at the local and national level. There is a risk that academically stronger students would progress further in these competitions and thereby benefit more. Root and Northrup (2007) address this question, finding that gains in participating students' skills were the same regardless of gender or home language. On some measures, non-White students made more progress than White students. However, family socioeconomic status was not controlled in this evaluation, and the population studied was 84% White in grades 6 to 8 and 88% White in grades 9 to 12. This suggests that *Project Citizen* may serve disproportionately advantaged students, which would be problematic from an egalitarian or utilitarian perspective.

3. *KidsVoting USA* is a third nonprofit organization that provides curricula, materials, and professional development. The students' culminating experience is a mock election modeled on the official election in the district where they are enrolled, but there are also intensive discussions and class projects related to government and current issues. In an evaluation by Patrick C. Meirick and Daniel B. Wackman, the program was found to raise students' knowledge of politics (measured by current factual questions, such as "Who is the governor of Texas?"); to reduce gaps in knowledge between the most and least knowledgeable students; and to increase the consistency between students' opinions on issues and their own voting behavior. (Meirick & Wackman, 2004). Other evaluations by Michael McDevitt and colleagues reinforce these conclusions (McDevitt, 2003; McDevitt & Kiousis, 2004; McDevitt & Kiousis, 2006). Evaluations of the value of procedural learning (participating in mock elections) on future voting have not been done to our knowledge, but if they showed effectiveness (increased voting), it would suggest a utilitarian justification.

Here, the normative frame is egalitarian. The evaluators cite evidence that knowledge of current political events is a precursor to voting (Delli Carpini & Keeter, 1996). Voting is a source of power but unequally distributed. *KidsVoting USA* "works" to the extent that it decreases political inequality by increasing usable political knowledge and reducing gaps. Perhaps the most intriguing result is that *parents* were more likely to discuss politics and current events if their children were enrolled in *KidsVoting*—a "trickle-up effect" (McDevitt, Kiousis, Wu, Losch, and Ripley, 2004). The underlying reason for that goal might be utilitarian, since a polity that responds equally to all members should maximize aggregate welfare. As in *We the People*, many of the outcomes are measures of factual knowledge; but *KidsVoting*

USA emphasizes information that is immediately relevant to political action. (For instance, you need to know the identity of the governor of your state in order to vote in a gubernatorial election that features the incumbent.)

Note that these three widely used programs chose sets of evaluation measures that hardly overlapped at all, probably because they chose measures based on each particular program's content. All were successful on their own terms, but each cultivated different kinds of civic engagement. The range would be much greater if we also discussed religious, political, and union-sponsored programs.

4. *The Just Community* is a fourth approach that has taken a more explicit philosophical stance. In contrast to the others discussed here, it is not a product, but rather an approach to education. Kohlberg saw development as the goal of education (Kohlberg & Mayer, 1981) distinguishing between his psychological theory of moral reasoning development and an educational theory that supports children's development. Thus, developmental theories can inform educational theories regarding the developmental capacities and needs of students of different ages but cannot be substituted for them (Kohlberg & Higgins, 1987). The educational theory, the Just Community approach, developed over time from 1974 with an increasing understanding of the developmental processes through which JC schools enhance both individual and group moral decision making, autonomy, valuing of community, and teachers' and students' investment in learning. As noted above, the JC approach is consonant with Dewey's (1916) progressive educational ideas that schools should be communities that sufficiently mirror the larger democratic society if they are to promote effective learning and future citizenship. As the name implies, both justice and community constitute goals and means of the approach. Justice is embodied in the following democratic institutions: one large weekly community meeting, smaller class-size advisory groups to prepare for the community meeting and discuss current issues, and fairness and agenda committees. Justice is a means because these institutions focus on issues of fairness, rights, duties, and equity.

The JC school is democratically governed, one person one vote. Community meetings establish norms and values through open discussion of the importance of rules and rights as well as rule making and enforcement. Community building is, in part, what educators now describe as creating a positive school climate. However, it is more. By taking ownership for the governance of their own group and making decisions about what kind of community they want to form, students and teachers build a community they intrinsically value as well as one that is personally meaningful and instrumentally helpful. Thus, justice and community are the main moral content of JC schools.

In democratic, self-governed programs, concrete understanding the experiences of other members from their viewpoint, rather than from one's own, can lead to decisions to change the community itself. For example, for one JC school, ethnic identity became an explicit issue when Blacks argued that their numerical minority status interfered with their feeling the same strong sense of ownership of the community as did White students. For the next two years, this JC school admitted mostly Black students (reverse discrimination) until all members felt they truly "owned" the school. Different educational means that are used to give students prolonged and varied experiences of deeply sympathetic perspective-taking can modify or, as one of us would say, actualize universalism.

Although in a JC school, teachers and students are formally equal in many respects, teachers continue to have more inherent authority as adults and are recognized as curricular and pedagogical experts. Just Community teachers learn to be advocates for the good of the community, and not only for their own positions. Teacher advocacy does not constitute moral constraint because its effects are open to democratic discussion and decisions (and has been challenged and addressed in some JC schools as *teacher intimidation*).

The Just Community approach is informed by Durkheim (1973) almost as much as it is by the constructivist theories of Piaget (1932) and Kohlberg (Kohlberg & Mayer, 1981), with their focus creating educational conditions to foster development, that is, active and challenging interactions and decision making among peers. Durkheim's socialization theory of moral formation argues that respect for rules arises from a group's authority and thus, that fostering attachment to the group and group solidarity is vital to understanding one's moral duty. A tension with Durkheimian thought is whether the content of moral norms is relative to each group or society. The Just Community approach adapts Durkheim by infusing a Kantian attitude and resting the idea of moral duty not on the group's authority but on the authority of individuals as autonomous and members of a community. The group's power comes from self-conscious sharing of the norms to which all have agreed, norms of respect for each other, for dialogue, and for the community itself. Like Kant, the Just Community does not equate a majority vote with what is morally right; it developed practices to ensure minority voice as in the aforementioned example in which White students listened and acted on the concerns of their Black peers to feel fully enfranchised. Just as Durkheim believed that altruistic morality arose from feelings of attachment and solidarity with the group, the JC approach strives to build communities of trust in which students and teachers alike consciously and spontaneously look after each other's interests. Lastly, following Durkheim's lead, the purpose of discipline is to reintegrate a violator back into the community, not just to sanction him. At the heart of this intervention is civic republicanism, or learning to appreciate the obligations of a democratic society for their own sake and weaving together individual and group narratives that form the basis of symbolic interactionists' theory of the moral self (Higgins-D'Alessandro & Power, 2005; Kohlberg & Higgins, 1987).

In summary, the Just Community approach is one of the few prosocial education interventions to elaborate its philosophical and psychological assumptions and how they inform practice. JC schools aim to foster moral awareness and development as well as ethical engagement with others, with a community, and with broader political and civic issues. The JC pursues these goals by transforming the nature of schooling, by turning a school into a valued community that promotes voice, growing autonomy, and shared experiences of students and teachers as they form a community together using the ideas of justice, rights, duties, and equity.

Research on the secondary-level JC schools shows that students' social and moral thinking develops, and that students working side-by-side with teachers are able to create and sustain self-governing communities with increasingly positive and effective moral cultures. An analysis of community meeting discussions over four years showed more fair, inclusive, and equitable norms developed, sanctions became more constructive, the need for discipline dropped off dramatically, and attachment to school and valuing community increased (Higgins, Power, & Kohlberg, 1989; Higgins-D'Alessandro & Power, 2005; Oser, Althof, & Higgins-D'Alessandro, 2008). In addition, a study of alumni showed that high percentages of respondents continue to be actively engaged in community service and credit not only the service learning program and outreach activities but also the sense of self and community they gained while in a Just Community school (Vozzola, Rosen, Higgins-D'Alessandro, & Horan, 2009). It should also be mentioned that JC teachers' social and moral reasoning develops over time due to the richness of the teaching environment, with almost all reasoning post-conventionally (i.e., reasoning from a prior-to-society perspective that what is right is determined by moral considerations first and by legal and conventional considerations second, Stage 5, after about five or more years). They also report teaching in a democratic community transforms them professionally and personally (Higgins-D'Alessandro, 2002). The major studies of this approach were done within an action research paradigm, meaning that the researchers in the first JC schools were also the interventionists. This may be seen as a limitation because researchers who conduct action research, similar to those involved in participatory evaluations, realize they have taken a value position that they will better understand a program from straddling the line between inside and outside. This means they must carefully monitor their assumptions and inclinations and create methodological procedures that optimize transparency so that others may judge their work.

IMPLICATIONS FOR RESEARCH AND PRACTICE

Good social scientists know that values are important as both explanations and outcomes of human behavior and that values differ between people, communities, and programs. Some social scientists study values (their development, their correlates, and their prevalence in different cultures and times); and some social scientists are capable of seeing the world from different value perspectives than their own (Flanagan, 2003).

Good evaluators know that programs embody values and that different programs embody different values. They are skillful at elucidating the values that each program represents.

That someone holds a particular value is an empirical claim. It is either true or false (or maybe a mix of the two). A normative claim is different. It is a claim that particular values are good or right, or bad or wrong. That kind of claim is rarely published in social science journals and academic program evaluations (although it is the mainstay of academic philosophy and political theory). A social scientist might say that working class urban youth hold a particular value, and that this value is important to them and important for the effectiveness of any programs that engage them. The researcher may quote the youth and even design an evaluation in collaboration with them. But if the researcher asserts that their value is right or wrong, that claim is no longer seen as *science*. In a scientific publication, the author is supposed to reduce the significance of his or her value judgments, which are understood as opinions or even biases, not as facts. And yet nothing is more important than having good values and explaining why they are good.

We still live in a positivist age. Positivism implies a strict distinction between facts (seen as observable and testable) and values (seen as important and interesting, perhaps, but also as arbitrary and subjective). Our controversial claim is that the designers of programs, evaluators, and researchers should adopt values of their own, put them on the table, and defend them, because the debate about values—not who holds which values, but which ones are good—is the most important discussion. The alternative is to submerge the discussion about values into an empirical literature that is actually rife with value judgments. Science should be a public enterprise rather than one that hides behind a cloak of objectivity, which in the end is impossible.

In the studies cited above (as in almost all published evaluations in the field of youth civic engagement), substantial attention is given to the psychometric properties of survey questions and scales.[2] Items should work the same when reused later; different scorers should obtain the same results when they use the same instruments on the same populations; subjects should understand the questions as they were intended; and items that are supposed to measure the same factors should correlate. These are empirical matters that do not directly raise value questions. But the measures that show these good psychometric properties did not come from nowhere. Someone decided to ask about the Constitution rather than the *Communist Manifesto,* and the governor of Texas rather than the Dallas Cowboys' starting quarterback. Scales of questions about Marxism or American football could have high Cronbach alphas (strong internal reliability), but that would not make them good evaluation measures for civics. Many survey and test questions involve subtle judgments about institutions. For example, it is common to ask whether respondents regularly read a newspaper. To treat that as a positive outcome presumes an overall favorable judgment about newspapers today (which is, however, compatible with various criticisms of newspapers). Asking about newspaper use also presumes that it is beneficial for *many* citizens to engage directly with the press. These are controversial assumptions. Their merit will change as institutions change; newspapers are quite different from their predecessors in 1950 or 1850.

Often evaluations cite literature in which the same measures have been used before. But previous use of an item in an empirical study does not prove that it measures valuable outcomes (or even that it measures what it purports to measure). Whether our measures are good depends essentially on whether our values are right. To be guided by values is not a limitation or a bias. If our values are good, following them is a virtue. Unfortunately, our values differ. In our view, it is most important to specify one's normative positions in detail and to defend them with ethical reasons. It is essential to use valid and reliable measures and to find genuine empirical links between interventions and outcomes; that is the role of science. But an exclusive reliance on scientific-sounding criteria can avoid ethical accountability if one fails to disclose *and defend* the real reasons for one's goals.

Disclosure is relatively straightforward; one notes the fact that one holds certain values. Defending such values is harder, especially if one does not resort automatically to utilitarianism. Moral argumentation requires a shift out of a positivist framework, as one gives non-empirical *reasons* for one's positions. Philosophy and normative social theory provide rich resources for such arguments. With a few exceptions, such as Facing History and Just

---

[2] Of the studies cited here, only the evaluations of *We the People...* lack elaborate discussions of psychometrics, but they borrow items from the National Assessment of Education Progress, which is carefully tested and constructed.

Communities, we do not see much explicit moral argumentation in either the justifications or the evaluations of civic programs. Influential and relevant schools of philosophy, such as the Capabilities Approach of Sen and Nussbaum, are entirely missing in the empirical literature on youth civic engagement. In turn, recent academic philosophy has not benefited enough from reflecting on innovative youth programs, a method that Plato, Erasmus, Rousseau, Dewey, and others found generative in earlier times.

REFERENCES

Alkire, S. (2002). *Valuing freedoms: Sen's capability approach and poverty reduction*. Oxford University Press.

American Political Science Association, Task Force on Inequality and American Democracy. (2004). *American democracy in an age of rising inequality*. Washington, DC: American Political Science Association.

Arendt, H. (1958). *The human condition*. Chicago: University of Chicago Press.

Baron, M. (1997). Kantian ethics. In M. Baron, P. Pettit, & M. Slote (Eds.), *Three methods of ethics* (pp. 3–91). Oxford: Blackwell.

Barr, D. J. (2005). Early adolescents' reflections on social justice: Facing history and ourselves in practice and assessment. *Intercultural Education, 16(2)*, 145–60.

Crocker, D. A. (1995). Functioning and capability: The foundations of Sen's and Nussbaum's development ethic. In M. Nussbaum & J. Glover (Eds.), *Women, culture and development: A study in human capabilities* (pp. 153–198). Oxford: Oxford University Press.

Dávila, A., & Mora, M. T. (2007). *Civic engagement and high school academic progress: An analysis using NELS data* (CIRCLE Working Paper 52). Medford, MA: CIRCLE. Retrieved from http://www.civicyouth.org

Delli Carpini, M. X., & Keeter, S. (1996). *What Americans know about politics and why it matters*. New Haven: Yale University Press.

De Tocqueville, A. (1954). *Democracy in America* (H. Reeve & P. Bradley, Trans.). New York: Vintage Books.

Dewey, J. (1916). *Democracy and education*. New York: Macmillan.

Dewey, J. (1927). *The public and its problems*. New York: Henry Holt.

Dewey, J. (1931). *Philosophy and civilization*. New York: Minton, Balch, & Co.

Durkheim, E. (1973). *Moral education*. New York: Free Press.

Eccles, J., & Gootman, J. A. (Eds.) (2002). *Community programs to promote youth development*. A report of the National Research Council and Institute of Medicine, Board on Children, Youth, and Families, Committee on Community-Level Programs for Youth. Washington, DC: The National Academies Press.

Educational Testing Service. (1991). *A comparison of the impact of the We the People . . . curricular materials on high school students compared to university students*. Pasadena, CA: Educational Testing Service.

Flanagan, C. (2003). Developmental roots of political engagement. *PS: Political Science and Politics, 36(2)*, 257–261.

Galston, W. A. (2002). *Liberal pluralism: The implications of value pluralism for political theory and practice*. Cambridge: Cambridge University Press.

Hahn, A., Leavitt, T., and Aaron, P. (1994). *Evaluation of the Quantum Opportunities Program (QOP)*. Boston: Brandeis University Press.

Hartry, A., & Porter, K. (2004). *We the People curriculum: Results of a pilot tes*t. MPR Associates, Inc.

Higgins-D'Alessandro, A. (2008). The judgment-action gap: A modest proposal. In F. K. Oser & W. Veulegers (Eds.), *Getting involved: Global citizenship development and sources of moral values*. Book 1 in moral development and citizenship education series. Rotterdam, The Netherlands: Sense Publishers.

Higgins-D'Alessandro, A. (2002). The necessity of teacher development. In A. Higgins-D'Alessandro & K. Jankowski (Eds.), *Science for society: Informing policy and practice through research in developmental psychology*. New directions for child and adolescent development series. Chicago, IL: Jossey-Bass.

Higgins-D'Alessandro, A., & Power, F. C. (2005). Character, responsibility, and the moral self. In D. Lapsley & F. C. Power (Eds.), *Character psychology and character education* (pp. 101–120). Notre Dame, IN: University of Notre Dame Press.

Kohlberg, L. (1973). Justice as reversibility: The claim to moral adequacy of a highest stage of moral judgment. *The Journal of Philosophy, 70(18)*, 630–46.

Kohlberg, L., & Higgins, A. (1987). School democracy and social interaction. In J. Gewirtz & W. Kurtines (Eds.), *Social development and social interaction*. New York: Wiley Interscience.

Kohlberg, L., & Mayer, R. (1981). Development as the aim of education. In L. Kohlberg (Ed.), *The Philosophy of Moral Judgment*. San Francisco: Harper & Row.

Kohlberg, L., Boyd, D., & Levine, C. (1986). The return of stage 6: Its principle and moral point of view. In W. Edelstein & G. Nunner-Winkler (Eds.), *Zur bestimmung der moral philosophische und socialwissenschaftliche beitrage zur moralforschung* (1985, October). Paper presented at the International Council of Scientific Unions (ICSU) Ringberg Conference, Tegernsee, Germany.

Lerner, R. M. (2004). *Liberty: Thriving and civic engagement among America's youth*. Thousand Oaks, CA: Sage Publications.

McDevitt, M. (2003). *The civic bonding of school and family: How KidsVoting students enliven the domestic sphere* (CIRCLE Working Paper 07). Medford, MA: CIRCLE. Retrieved from http://www.civicyouth.org

McDevitt, M., & Kiousis, S. (2004). *Education for deliberative democracy: The long-term influence of KidsVoting USA* (CIRCLE Working Paper 22). Medford, MA: CIRCLE. Retrieved from http://www.civicyouth.org

McDevitt, M., & Kiousis, S. (2006). *Experiments in political socialization: KidsVoting USA as a model for civic education reform* (CIRCLE Working Paper 49). Medford, MA: CIRCLE. Retrieved from http://www.civicyouth.org

McDevitt, M., Kiousis, S., Wu, X., Losch, M., & Ripley, T. (2004). *The civic bonding of school and family: How KidsVoting students enliven the domestic sphere* (CIRCLE Working Paper 7). Medford, MA: CIRCLE. Retrieved from http://www.civicyouth.org

McNeal, R. B., Jr. (1998). High school extracurricular activities: Closed structures and stratifying patterns of participation. *The Journal of Educational Research, 91(3),* 183–91.

Meirick, P. C. & Wackman, D. B. (2004) Kids Voting and political knowledge: Narrowing gaps, informing votes. *Social Science Quarterly, 85(5),* 1161–1177

Nussbaum, M. C., & Sen, A. (Eds.) (1993). *The quality of life.* Oxford: Oxford University Press.

Oser, F., Althof, W., & Higgins-D'Alessandro, A., (2008) The Just Community approach to moral education: System change or individual change? *Journal of Moral Education, 37(3),* 395–416.

Phinney, J. (1992). The multigroup ethnic identity measure: A new scale for use with adolescents and young adults from diverse groups. *Journal of Adolescent Research,* 7, 156–176.

Piaget, J. (1932). *The moral judgment of the child.* London: Kegan Paul.

Power, F. C., & Higgins-D'Alessandro, A. (2008). The Just Community approach to moral education and the moral atmosphere of the school. In L. P. Nucci & D. Narvaez (Eds.), *Handbook of moral and character education* (pp. 230–247). New York: Routledge.

Power, F. C., Higgins, A., & Kohlberg, L. (1989). *Lawrence Kohlberg's approach to moral education.* New York: Columbia University Press.

Rawls, J. (1971/2005). *A theory of justice: Revised edition.* Cambridge, MA: Harvard University Press.

Root, S., & Northup, J. (2007). *Project citizen evaluation report.* RMC Research for the Center for Civic Education. Available (from the Center): http://www.civiced.org/pdfs/PC/ProjectCitizen%20FullReport%202007.pdf

Sandel, M. J. (1984). Justice and the Good. In M. Sandel (Ed.), *Liberalism and its critics.* New York: New York University Press.

Schudson. M. (1998). *The good citizen: A history of American civic life.* New York: The Free Press.

Schultz, L. H., Barr, D. J., and Selman, R. L. (2001). The value of a developmental approach to evaluating character development programmes: An outcome study of facing history and ourselves. *Journal of Moral Education, 30(1),* 3–27.

Sen, A. (1985.) Well-being, agency, and freedom: The Dewey lectures, 1984. *Journal of Philosophy, 82(4),* 169–221.

Taylor, C. (1984). Hegel: History and politics. In M. Sandel (Ed.), *Liberalism and its critics.* New York: New York University Press.

Vozzola, E., Rosen, J., Higgins-D'Alessandro, A., & Horan, J. (2009). The Scarsdale Alternative School: Perspectives of alumni 5-25 years later on the Just Community experiences. (July 2–5, 2009). Paper presented at the annual conference of the Association for Moral Education, Utrecht, The Netherlands.

Westheimer, J., & Kahne, J. (2004). What kind of citizen? The politics of educating for democracy. *American Educational Research Journal, 41(2),* 237–269.

CHAPTER 6

Youth Civic Engagement in Mexico

FERNANDO REIMERS
Harvard Graduate School of Education

SERGIO CARDENAS
Center for Economic Research and Teaching, Mexico

INTRODUCTION

IN THIS CHAPTER, we examine data about civic engagement in Mexico, describing the main characteristics of civic knowledge and attitudes, as well as civic and electoral behavior of youth.[1] We situate the analysis of Mexico in the context of civic engagement of youth in Latin America, to draw some implications for future research and policy design.

The principal finding of this chapter is that changes in political institutions in the direction of making electoral politics more competitive apparently have not resulted in visible changes in how people experience democracy in their daily lives, at least in the short term. In particular, we find that political knowledge, attitudes, and engagement of youth in Mexico apparently have not changed even as electoral politics became more competitive and the role of political parties increased.

The study of the civic knowledge and engagement of youth in Latin America is relevant for several reasons. First, because during the past three decades, there has been a transition from authoritarian to democratic rule, which makes Latin America a rich context in which to examine how quickly democratic values and practices change in response to the transformation of political institutions. Indeed, comparisons between generations

[1] We examine data from ENCUP, a survey of political culture administered to a nationally representative sample of people over 18 years old that has been administered in 2001, 2003, 2005, and 2008. We also analyze data from the National Survey of Youth (ENJUVE), a nationally representative random sample survey, administered in 2000 and 2005 to nearly 60,000 young people.

before and after democratic transitions provide a unique window into those changes.

Second, most countries in Latin America have been undergoing a demographic transition so that youth represent an increasing substantial share of the population (see Flanagan & Kassimir, this volume, for a discussion of the youth bulge in the global South generally). Thus, the political knowledge and values of the current generation of young people are of critical importance to the prospects for the consolidation of democratic transitions. For instance, in 2010, around 20% of the population in Mexico will be aged between 10 and 19 years old (INEGI, 2005).

Because of their large numbers relative to the total population, these new voters and future parents will determine the extent to which the democratic transition progresses from electoral democracy toward democracy as a way of life. This will be reflected in the development and effective support of institutions that promote citizenship participation and voice in the public sphere, trust toward institutions, tolerance, respect for differences, and non-discrimination.

A third reason it is of interest to examine civic engagement of Latin American youth is to provide a comparative perspective to the studies on youth civic engagement cross-nationally, which generally have documented a lack of engagement in and political apathy about formal political institutions, but more engagement in other forms of participation with community and grassroots associations (Torney-Purta, Lehmann, Oswald, & Schulz, 2001).

Given the low levels of trust in political institutions and leaders exhibited by Mexican youth, which will be one focus of this chapter, exploring their political engagement is also of interest to discern how social context and institutional performance shape political trust.

POLITICAL CONTEXT AND TRANSITIONS IN LATIN AMERICA

During the last 20 years, the countries in Latin America experienced significant political change. The early 1980s marked a return to democratic rule for the majority of Latin American nations, which had experienced periods of military rule prior to this. Increased political participation and representation, in a context in which deep-seated economic and social institutions reproduced high levels of social inequality and poverty, have brought new questions about satisfaction with democratic institutions and new questions about how to deepen democracy—in other words, how to move from electoral democracy to democracy as a widely accepted way of life (UNDP, 2004).

Public opinion polls of adults in the region have revealed high levels of dissatisfaction with democratic institutions and limited support for democracy as a form of government. While the majority of the population in Latin America prefers democracy to another kind of political organization (57% in Latin America, 43% in Mexico), only about 37% of the population in this region, and 23% in Mexico, is actually satisfied with democracy (Latinobarómetro, 2008).

Of particular interest are the tradeoffs that Latin Americans make between freedom and economic security: 53% of the population would not object to an authoritarian government in power if it is able to address the economic needs of the population (61% in Mexico) (Latinobarómetro, 2008). This might reflect the fact that in nearly every country (with the exception of Venezuela), citizens considered economic issues (e.g., unemployment, inflation) as the main problem they face as individuals.

The pinnacle of the most recent political transition in Mexico was the presidential elections of 2000. Unlike the political transitions in other countries of Latin America in the 1980s, it did not involve a transition from a de facto military to a civilian elected government. The presidential transition in 2000 was preceded by a number of changes in political institutions and culture that paved the way for a deepening of democracy. These included the creation of the Federal Electoral Institute in 1990, an autonomous government agency tasked with ensuring the transparency of elections as well as with creating a democratic culture, through formal and non-formal education programs. A cycle of electoral reforms from 1977 to 1996 allowed the incorporation of new political forces and the strengthening of political opposition parties, mainly in local governments and the Federal Congress.

The results of the presidential and congressional elections of July 2, 2000, were part of a political transition started several years earlier (Flores, 2007). The changes that preceded the democratic transition included a series of reforms in the national curriculum of civic education beginning in 1993. Until 1993, civic education in Mexico had focused on fostering national unity and supporting the consolidation of the State by teaching facts about the institutions of government. A curriculum reform in 1993 introduced values education and until 1999, civic education in Mexico was a subject in the secondary school curriculum at grades 7 to 9, emphasizing the study of legal and government institutions in Mexico. The focus of the curriculum was on knowledge (e.g., the organization of government), with relatively limited coverage of concepts related to the functioning of democratic institutions (e.g., the need for independence of the three branches of government, the role of due process under the law). Teaching of history reflected also a limited conception of citizenship, ignoring for instance the study of historical episodes illustrating the right of citizens to demonstrate against the government, such as the student movement of 1968 to which the government responded with brutal repression.

With the 1999 reform, the subject Civic and Ethics Education ("Formación Cívica y Ética") was incorporated into the secondary curriculum with the purpose of developing student democratic competencies and skills, giving more emphasis to the role of school experiences as part of the development of citizenship. This new subject was also incorporated into the primary level in 2002. This new subject was designed in collaboration with the Federal Electoral Institute. This Institute developed and implemented several programs of citizenship education, some of them through schools. For instance, in partnership with the Center for Civic Education in the United States, they prepared an adaptation of the *Project Citizen*. They also prepared a series of self-instructional materials for teachers describing activities that could be incorporated in the curriculum to foster democratic skills. They supported, in cooperation with the Ministry of Education, a program of mock elections in the schools, in which students participated in elections regarding issues affecting the life of the schools.

The new subject of Civic and Ethics Education was described by the Ministry of Education as:

> ... a set of organized experiences that promote development of students as free and responsible for individual actions and decisions made in the relationships they establish with others, as well as their role as active members of a society that demands their committed participation for improvement and enhancement (Secretaria de Educación Pública, 2006, p. 15, our translation).

The programs focused on strengthening students' critical thinking skills, setting the foundation for free and responsible actions in their individual development and to benefit society.

In spite of these changes in the curriculum of civic education in Mexico (with similar changes observed in other Latin American countries over the last decade), there is limited evidence that changes in teacher practice and school culture are taking place in ways that would be supportive of students' experiencing democratic relationships in schools and engaging in democratic practices. For instance, recent surveys of teachers in several countries of the region reveal that many of them hold attitudes that are neither accepting nor appreciative of diversity (Reimers, 2007). The levels of political knowledge of Latin American youth have also been found to be low. For instance, a survey including the publicly released questions of the 1999 IEA Civic Education Study administered in Mexico, in 2002, found that only about 40% understood that in a democracy, popularly elected representatives should govern, rather than elites or experts (Guevara & Tirado, 2006). Equally low was knowledge of the Constitution, the function of civic organizations and of laws, and the ability to identify corruption, as well as the function of regularly held elections, political parties, Congress, and the press. Indeed, barely half of the respondents were able to identify the function of laws, and nearly 60% of respondents believed that women should stay out of politics. In addition, more than half of the respondents agreed with the statement: "If the law is against your interests it is legitimate not to abide by it."

Similarly low levels of civic knowledge and engagement are also found among youth in other countries in Latin America. The 1999 Study of Civic Education, which included samples of youth in Chile and Colombia, established that youth in these countries were at the bottom of the distribution of scores from 28 countries reflecting political knowledge and understanding (Torney-Purta, Lehmann et al., 2001). Chilean and Colombian students obtained particularly low scores in understanding threats to democracy such as nepotism and political control of the judiciary. In addition, the study reported that youth in Colombia and Chile do not trust their government institutions such as the courts, and do not believe that public institutions are able to address or find solutions to their problems (Torney-Purta & Amadeo, 2004).

The lack of political and civic engagement of youth in Latin America has been confirmed in other studies. A recent public opinion survey administered in Latin America showed that youth are not particularly politically engaged or active and they are perceived (by adults and by themselves) to be slightly more violent than the rest of the population (Latinobarómetro, 2008). There is little variability in these indicators among countries in the region, and Mexican youth on average are perceived to exhibit about the same levels of violence, participation, engagement, or generosity as the rest of youth in the region.

Of potential interest to future forms of political engagement in Latin American youth is that in 2008, they were found to be significantly more likely to have used the Internet than the rest of the population. The percentage of those who had used the Internet was 60% for those aged 18 to 25, 39% for those 26 to 40, 2% for those 41 to 60, and 8% for those over 61. The political engagement of youth on e-government and e-politics in Latin America represents one of the areas that will require further study, given the use of Internet as a source of political information (see Bennett, Freelon, & Wells, this volume).

In their low levels of political knowledge and engagement, Latin American youth do not differ very much from adults, according to previous studies. In general, adults in Latin America have only modest levels of knowledge, and only moderate support for and satisfaction with democracy. About three-quarters of the adults in Latin America believe that their country is governed by a few groups who govern to take care of their own interests rather than the interests of the majority of the population (Latinobarómetro, 2008).

In summary, on average, Latin Americans express low levels of trust and satisfaction with democracy. Furthermore, youth, a sizeable percentage of the population, apparently do not differ from adults, even though they have higher levels of education, have been educated at a time when political institutions were more democratic, and in several cases curricula included an explicit focus on the development of democratic citizenship. The following section examines in greater detail the political culture of youth in Mexico.

POLITICAL CULTURE AND YOUTH IN MEXICO: CHANGE IN INSTITUTIONS WITH LITTLE CHANGE IN THE WAY DEMOCRACY IS LIVED

In Mexico, as in the rest of Latin America, the demographic transition has changed the structure of the population, with youth accounting for an increasing proportion. In addition, as a result of decreases in fertility rates, the current group of youth will be the largest cohort in the predictable future. Of special interest to political stability and social development is the fact that one in four youth in Mexico (ages 10 to 29) is neither in school nor working (Oueda y Martinez, 2007), but are instead in a "social limbo" that characterizes a large number of youth in parts of the developing world, where lack of economic opportunity appears to limit the transition of youth to adulthood (see Kassimir & Flanagan, this volume). The sizable share of young people who are not participating in the institutions of education or of work may have potentially serious effects on political stability. This marginalization could alienate these youth from the legal framework and social norms in ways that undermine their future reintegration, and given their large numbers, could also challenge governance and political stability.

Mexico's traditional political culture, the product of 70 years of continuous rule by the same political party (PRI for the initials of *Partido Revolucionario Institucional*), has been usually characterized by a weak culture of legality, mistrust in institutions, persistent authoritarianism, negative perception of the performance of institutions and of the judicial system, weak sense of civic efficacy, presidentialism, and a lack of tradition of accountability (Meixueiro, 2007).

Based on the indicators of governance provided by the World Governance Indicators Project, Mexico is at the midpoint compared with most countries in the world. Mexico is around the 50th percentile with regard to voice and accountability, at the 25th percentile with regard to political stability, at the 61st percentile in government effectiveness, 30th percentile in rule of law, and 50th percentile in control of corruption. Mexico is also in the bottom quarter for most of all of these indicators relative to the rest of Latin America. There was relatively little change in the country's relative standing in these indicators between 1998 and 2008, except for political stability indicators, where

Mexico's relative position improved considerably between 1998 and 2003, to then regress to the previous levels in 2008 (Kaufmann et al., 2009). This stagnation of governance in Mexico corresponds, as will be discussed in the rest of the chapter, to a similar stagnation in political attitudes and engagement, in spite of the institutional changes that made electoral politics more competitive and in spite of increased participation in electoral democracy.

Expansion in Electoral Participation

Over the last 50 years, political participation in Mexico expanded as a result of extending the right to vote to various groups of the population. Women gained the right to vote in 1953, and this change increased the number of registered voters from 3,642,000 in 1952 to 7,472,000 in 1958. In addition, the age to vote was lowered from 21 to 18 in 1970, arguably in response to a student movement, which in 1968 led a number of political demonstrations challenging the very limited political rights of citizens and the authoritarian practices of a State that had been governed by the same political party for 40 years. The state responded to this student movement with brutal repression, which led to large numbers of arrests and "missing" students. This response was considered as one of the factors that deterred and marked political participation among youth for decades.

The lowering of the voting age again increased the number of registered voters significantly, from 9,425,000 in 1964 to 14,063,000 in 1970. These changes, along with the high fertility rates in the 1970s, made youth an increasing percentage of the total number of registered voters in the 1990s.

In the presidential elections of 2000, 67% of youth voted. However, in the congressional elections of 2003 only 33% of youth voted, compared to 50% of older adults. In the presidential elections of 2006, only 50% of those aged 18 to 23 voted, compared to 66% for those aged 20 to 39 and over 60% for other older adults (Fernandez Poncela, 2009). When youth political engagement is compared to that of older adults, they are less interested in politics and in political news and they don't differ in their approval of political institutions (Flores, 2007).

Some authors have interpreted these low levels of political engagement of Mexican youth as reflecting disillusionment with conventional forms of politics (Meixueiro, 2007). For instance, youth in Mexico perceived a lack of rule of law in the country. When asked what is most important to them, about three-quarters of the youth chose a society ruled by law where those laws are enforced (Meixueiro, 2007). But these low levels of political engagement may also reflect low levels of trust in people and institutions. Of particular consequence for the prospects of democracy in Mexico are the low levels of trust youth express for political institutions and politicians in most studies done within the last 10 years. Youth exhibited low levels of trust in the president, members of congress, political parties, police, and social actors. They were significantly unengaged with political parties and unions (less than 3%), and much more engaged in sports associations (30%), with about 10% in cultural or neighborhood associations (Meixueiro, 2007; Calderon, 2008).

To give a more detailed picture, in what follows we present the results of our analysis of the National Survey of Youth (ENJUVE) and of the National Survey of Political Culture (known as ENCUP by its acronym in Spanish). These studies were administered by conducting personal interviews to nationally representative samples between 2001 and 2008. The National Survey of Youth was also nationally representative and administered in 2001 and 2005, conducting personal interviews. We present the results of this analysis in three sections. We will first describe the political engagement of those aged 18 to 24 using ENCUP in comparison to those 25 years and older. Next, we describe the political engagement of those aged 10 to 29 from ENJUVE, analyzing the differences across four age subgroups, those 10 to 14, 15 to 19, 20 to 24, and 25 to 29, in an attempt to understand age differences in youth political understandings and behavior. Finally, to illustrate how political engagement changes over time, we will compare the political engagement of those aged 18 to 24 with those 25 and older in 2001 and in 2008 using ENCUP data.

As we have mentioned, the presidential election of 2000 marked the culmination of a longer process of political transition. The National Survey on Political Culture, administered for the first time in the year 2001, was intended to capture the expectations of youth and adults regarding emerging practices in the political realm derived from the arrival of a government that many considered as the first democratically elected government in decades. The administration of this survey every two or three years (2001, 2003, 2005, and 2008) allows the examination of changes in the views of youth of political institutions, their level of trust in government agencies and autonomous organizations, and their political knowledge and involvement.

In contrast to the first wave of data from this survey collected in 2001, the data collected in ENCUP in 2008 would likely reflect the perception of the first generation of young Mexicans living under a new political regime. The cross-sectional nature of the data examined in this chapter poses limitations to the inferences we can draw regarding how political culture develops as young people grow, making it difficult to attribute those changes to psychological development or to changes in the contextual conditions experienced by youth of different cohorts. Of interest are the responses that are relatively invariant across age groups, showing that, at least after the age of 14, neither developmental processes nor contextual conditions that have accompanied the incremental process of democratization in Mexican political culture seem to have had much effect. In other words, the most remarkable finding from our analysis is the similarity between the younger groups of Mexican youth, those aged 10 to 14 or 15 to 19, and their older peers, those aged 20 to 24 or 25 to 29.

It is important to point out that the older group analyzed in these surveys, those who were 25 to 29 in 2006, went to school under the old programs of studies of civic education, whereas those aged 10 to 19 were schooled under the new programs of civic education, especially in elementary school. In interpreting the data provided in this chapter, it is important to keep in mind the fact that in 2006 there were presidential and congressional elections in Mexico, the very first after the political transition. To some extent, the political culture during the time the survey was administered was atypical and overheated relative to non-election years, thus respondents may have reported an artificially high political participation and mobilization.

National Survey of Political Culture: Little Evidence of a Distinctive Youth Political Culture in Mexico

Using data from the National Survey of Political Culture (ENCUP) administered in 2008, we compared the views of those aged 18 to 24 with respondents aged 25 and older. This section describes the comparison of political views between these groups, identifying a remarkable similarity in the responses of those whose ages range from 18 to 24 to those who are 25 and older in all of the indicators discussed in this section. Unless otherwise noted, there are few apparent differences between youth and those aged 25 and older in the aspects of political culture discussed.

Political Participation, Civic Engagement, and Views of Political Institutions

Political participation in Mexico has been largely limited to voting, which could be a result of the restrictive political environment that was present for decades in this country. Only a small percentage of the population engages in other forms of political action, even when they say that these forms are effective. On average, the respondents manifest very negative views of political institutions, groups, and politicians, and dissatisfaction with democracy, perhaps resulting from the lack of rule of law, reflecting the existence of a "low intensity citizenship" condition, as described by O'Donell (1993). In some indicators the population is divided, suggesting significant cleavages in political culture as analysis of the ENCUP data suggests (Secretaria de Gobernación, 2003).

Most people in Mexico are registered to vote (95%). According to the ENCUP surveys, about 76% of those over 24 in 2003 voted in the presidential elections of 2000, and 79% of those over 24 in 2008 voted in the presidential elections of 2006. For those ages 23 and 24, who would have been of voting age in those elections, reported voting rates were 75% in 2000 and 72% in 2006. In spite of the high levels of voting behavior, only half of the population believed that there is democratic rule in Mexico. Only a third of the population were satisfied with democracy in Mexico or the state of basic rights in the country, or believed that the laws were applied to benefit all. In spite of the widespread perception that political institutions and democracy were ineffective, private practices were reported to be consistent with the rule of law. For example, only 13% agreed with bribing a government official to expedite a bureaucratic process (see Torney-Purta, 2009, for evidence of similar percentages of alienated students in some countries in Eastern Europe).

In addition, there were relatively low levels of knowledge about political institutions: Less than half of those surveyed correctly identified the three branches of government. The large majority knew the political party to which the state governor belongs. However, only about a third knew which party currently had more members of congress, or knew the duration of the term of members of congress.

In spite of the high percentage of citizens voting, there is very limited political engagement. For instance, few people discussed politics with others or had an interest in what the government does. When asked whether people in Mexico met to discuss politics, only a third said that they did much or to some extent, and when asked to what extent people in general were interested to learn what the government does, only a third said much or to some extent.

In addition, only a third of those surveyed in both age groups expressed an interest in politics. Limited engagement with political affairs may reflect the perception that those affairs are too complicated. Half of the respondents thought that politics in general are so complicated that they can't understand them.

In spite of these reported low levels of interest in politics or in seeking information about politics, people had views on the performance of political actors and institutions. Two thirds of the population approved the president's performance on the job, and the performance of their governor. A third approved the performance of members of congress and senators. Only about half of the population agreed that democracy is preferable to any form of government. Two-thirds of those interviewed thought elections in Mexico were corrupt and nearly half believed winners did not deserve to be elected. There were few age differences in these beliefs.

In addition, half of the population thought that their vote was the only way they had to make their views heard. Almost another half thought that the government was not interested in what they thought about political issues. Political discussions generally took place among close friends and relatives, rarely with co-workers, teachers, or priests.

There were remarkably low levels of association and organization of any form of collective action, even though a large percentage of the population thought these were helpful to address community needs. For instance, only about one-fifth had associated with neighbors to address a problem in their community or complained to the authorities about a community problem, even though more than half thought that these activities were likely to be helpful. Also, there were more people who believed that political activities were effective than people who actually engaged in these activities. This included activities such as the following: publishing a letter in a newspaper to bring attention to a problem, requesting support from an organization of civil society, signing or circulating petitions, requesting assistance from elected or appointed officials, and placing posters expressing demands.

In contrast, Mexicans engage in a number of actions that expressed solidarity with others. Most of the surveyed Mexicans had made contributions to the Red Cross. Half had donated clothes, medicine, or food after natural disasters, and a fourth had volunteered in a community activity. These forms of private solidarity contrast, however, with the very limited forms of association for collective action. Only a small percentage of the population had formed part of associations such as political parties, professional organizations, cooperatives, citizens' organizations, or environmental groups. The only organizations to reach 10% of the population were unions and religious organizations, and the only group that reached 20% were parent organizations (with members old enough to have children).

Trust in Institutions and People and Perceptions of Political Power It is possible that the low levels of political engagement reflect low levels of trust in political and social actors, and other institutions. The Catholic Church and teachers are among the most trusted, whereas unions, social and political organizations, or leaders are less trusted. About half of those interviewed trusted the president, their governor of the state, and their mayor. Only a third trusted judges and businessmen. In fact, levels of social trust are also low: The large majority thought that if they were not careful, others would take advantage of them (the issue of trust will be dealt with in more detail later in the chapter).

The emphasis in political participation was on electoral participation. Most people thought that citizens and organizations (including religious) had little power to change anything. They attributed power to the president, political parties, members of congress, and big business.

Tolerance The low levels of association and civic engagement already described may also reflect insufficient ability to establish common ground among people who perceived themselves as different from others on a number of social divides. Intolerance toward multiple forms of differences, including political views, may have hindered the capacity for establishing collective action.

The population was split evenly with regard to thinking that people in Mexico can listen to others who have different political views. Only a third of the interviewed thought people in Mexico respected the rights of other people, or the law. When asked whether there is discrimination in Mexico, about three-quarters reported class-based discrimination and discrimination based on sexual orientation. About half reported discrimination based on skin color, political preferences, and religious beliefs. These attributions of intolerance to others were mirrored, but with less intensity, in their own intolerance as reflected in the responses to a question of whether they would rent a room in their home to people with varied characteristics as shown. In one of the few seemingly systematic age differences in these data, those under 25 were more tolerant of individuals ranging from indigenous persons to persons of different social classes or of different religions or political preferences. However, it is important to observe again the lack of trust toward politics and politicians: those aged 19 to 24 perceived living with someone involved in politics quite negatively (similar to living with those of a different race, or with people who have AIDS).

POLITICAL CULTURE OF YOUTH

This section looks at a more fine-grained set of differences by age using the dataset collected in 2005 in ENJUVE. Consistent with the analysis of youth and adults reported previously, the analysis of the survey of the political culture of those aged 10 to 29 showed that Mexican youth exhibit limited participation and trust in political organizations. There was also very limited participation in other civic organizations, including neighborhood associations. In contrast, sports and student organizations engaged a much greater percentage of youth. Mexican youth also had limited views of political participation, identifying it with voting. A sizable proportion of youth had extremely negative views about political parties and institutions, and most youth thought that political decisions should be based on the personal characteristics of candidates rather than on the political party they represent.

Political and Civic Engagement Mexican youth reported few associational experiences that reflected and fostered civic engagement. Sports were the primary means of association in which Mexican youth engaged with others (the percentage who participated in sports was about half for those aged 10 to 14 and those aged 15 to 19, and about one-quarter for those aged 20 to 24 and for those aged 25 to 29). About 15% of Mexican young people participated in student organizations, except for those aged 25 to 29, where the figure was lower. Participation in political parties, civic organizations including neighborhood organizations, labor organizations, community service, or environmental organizations was less than 5%.

To provide some context, the IEA Civic Education Study asked questions about participation in 28 countries. In the United States, for example, about half of ninth graders in 1999 surveyed in this study reported belonging to an organization conducting volunteer work. Other countries with at least one-third of students reporting volunteering included Australia, Chile, Colombia, Denmark, and England. Countries where one-quarter or more belonged to an environmental organization included Colombia, Greece, Hungary, Portugal, and the United States (Torney-Purta, Lehmann, Oswald, & Schulz, 2001, p. 142). In short, youth in both Chile and Colombia were generally more participative than Mexican youth.

Limited Conceptions of Political Participation Most of the Mexican youth surveyed identified political participation with electoral participation, although interest in voting was modest. When asked how interested they were in politics, only about 10% reported that they were very interested. When asked why they were not interested in politics, a quarter replied that they just did not find it interesting, a similar percentage did not reply, and about one in five provided reasons suggesting lack of trust in politicians or the political process.

In spite of these low levels of interest in politics, most Mexican youth believed that voting makes sense. However, a significant group of Mexican youth was less positive: Youth still associated political participation with electoral participation. Similar results were found with the question "What is the best way to participate in politics?," to which many said they didn't know. For those who provided an answer, most chose voting (about 30% for the 10- to 14-year-olds and 40% or more for those aged from 15 to 29). Negligible numbers of youth selected options like participating in political parties, denouncing corrupt politicians, supporting politicians, speaking up in support of political causes, participating in political campaigns, helping other people, verifying transparency in elections, participating in community meetings, and organizing with other people.

Only about half of the youth preferred democracy to other forms of government (about 40% for the 10- to 14-year-olds and more than 50% for those from 15 through 29 years of age). When asked what they would expect from democracy, the majority of the younger group did not know, and the rest of the respondents were widely distributed on a range of responses, suggesting a lack of shared expectations.

Asked for what reasons they had voted or would vote, about 40% responded, "because it was a legal obligation" (although there is no defined sanction for not voting). Between 40% and 60% said that they did so because it was a requirement for the functioning of democracy (the percentage who said this increased with age). Half said that they voted because they were good citizens, believed in democracy, or so that things would improve, or any combination of the three.

Politics is generally understood by Mexican youth as a highly personal endeavor. Two-thirds of youth agreed that in voting, it is more important to consider the candidate than the political party the candidate represents. This perception was more prevalent among the older groups. More youth disagreed than agreed with the statement "It is better to identify with a political party than not." A relatively small percentage thought that it would be best if political parties did not exist in Mexico. It should be noted that the percentage who answered *don't know* was quite large for many of these questions, especially among the younger groups.

Trust Trust was higher among the younger group and lower in the older group. Consistent with the large percentage of youth who expressed low levels of trust in others, most Mexican youth also thought that with regard to other people it was necessary to be cautious, because most people would try to take advantage of you, and most youth believed that people are only interested in themselves. However, most youth also believed that when people have problems there are other people willing to help them.

Tolerance Many Mexican youth expressed views associated with gender inequality. Forty percent of youth agreed totally or in part with the notion that household chores are for women, with no difference by age group. A similar percentage believed that women act emotionally whereas men act rationally. Half of the youth believed that in homes where women work, children are neglected. Over half of the youth believed that men should be the only ones responsible for financially supporting the household; a similar percentage thought that it was natural that men earn more than women and that unemployment was less important among women than among men.

Mexican youth were more tolerant of family members or friends than of strangers. It is noteworthy that the levels of intolerance are quite invariant across age groups, suggesting that these are deeply entrenched attitudes, not changed by the schooling and life experiences to which they are exposed once those views are formed. It is noteworthy as well that people engaged in politics were the subject of considerable intolerance, quite close to the intolerance youth communicate regarding homosexuals, people living with AIDS, alcoholics, criminals, and drug addicts.

Table 6.1
Tolerance toward Different Groups (I Would Accept as a Neighbor...) (In Percentages)

	Age Group			
Neighbor	10–14	15–19	20–24	25–29
Close relatives	73	71	67	63
Indigenous people	70	72	68	69
Unmarried couples	68	75	71	70
People of a different religion	61	70	66	64
People of another race	57	65	62	58
Foreigners	53	61	58	60
People who are involved in politics	40	43	40	41
Homosexuals	32	47	45	44
People living with AIDS	31	44	39	40
Alcoholics	16	23	25	21
People who have been convicted of a criminal offense	15	26	23	17
Drug addicts	11	20	21	19

Source: Author's calculations based on ENJUVE.

Table 6.1 presents the percentage of youth who said they would accept having neighbors from a range of different groups, an indicator of tolerance. There was greater acceptance of close relatives, indigenous people, and unmarried couples. Acceptance declined for people of a different religion, a different race, and foreigners. Furthermore, only about 40% of youth would accept as a neighbor someone involved in politics. These levels of tolerance were similar by age group: Intolerance is greater with regard to homosexuals, people living with AIDS, alcoholics, criminals, and drug addicts.

Youth were more likely to trust family members, co-workers, and fellow students, as well as those with less money and Mexicans in general. They trusted less people with more money, people who professed another religion, community leaders, and people of a different race. There was more trust in medical doctors, teachers, schools, universities, and religious leaders. There was less trust in police officers, political parties, members of congress, unions, the Supreme Court, the president, and the federal government. In general, the pillars of democracy had relatively low levels of trust among youth.

School as Civic Spaces The political views and practices of Mexican youth are shaped by experiences at home and in school, as well as in other forms of association. As we have discussed, other than sports, Mexican youth had very limited associational experiences. This makes the experiences at home and in school all the more important. Both of these institutions are to be expected to reproduce, to some extent, the political norms and values of society, reflected in this survey. Of the two, however, it is arguably schools that hold the greatest potential for change.

Students described their schools in moderately positive terms: On average, youth gave the school they last attended high marks on a 1 to 10 scale on the following dimensions: preparation of teachers, instructional materials, instructional content, utility of content, preparation for work, area where the school is located, relations with classmates, physical plant, and behavior rules in school. However, about 20% of students described the school they last attended as a place where there was some or much violence among classmates. About 5% reported violence from teachers toward students and a similar percentage reported violence from students toward teachers as well as sales of drugs and drug consumption. Fifteen percent reported violence in the community where the school was located; about 10% report crime in the area where their school was located. Both conditions may reflect the importance of promoting specific interventions at the school level, in order to create conditions for better associational experiences.

How Political Engagement Changed between 2001 and 2008

By comparing the responses of ENCUP 2001 and ENCUP 2008, we concluded that political culture and engagement was relatively stable during this period of political transition to democratic rule. Indeed, there was a decrease in the level of satisfaction with democracy during this period for the group of < 25 years old, a condition that might be associated with the high expectations the newly elected government generated and the lack of effectiveness it had to address severe and complex social problems (Difference = –6.8% among < 25 years old).

In this section, different aspects from two main categories will be analyzed: differences in political participation and satisfaction with democracy, and disparities regarding the level of trust in institutions and political figures. Both categories are central in the consolidation of democratic governance.

Political Participation and Satisfaction with Democracy Over these seven years, electoral participation remained high (e.g., 81.3% for > 25 years old), while participation in other forms of political action remained low. In addition, the level of satisfaction regarding democracy in Mexico declined slightly during this period. Voter registration was also high and growing, and the percentage of citizens who voted in the last election remained stable

Table 6.2
Have You Participated in Any of These Activities? (% Responding "Yes")

Age	2001	2008
Activity: Form groups with people affected by any public problem.		
<25 years old	13.5%	17.3%
>25 years old	22.9%	22.7%
Activity: File a complaint with authorities.		
<25 years old	14.1%	12.3%
>25 years old	19.3%	18.8%
Activity: Participate in public demonstrations.		
<25 years old	5.1%	9.4%
>25 years old	7.4%	8.3%
Activity: Organize signed petitions with neighbors.		
<25 years old	15.4%	9.9%
>25 years old	19.1%	14.9%
Activity: Request support from congressmen.		
<25 years old	3.3%	2.5%
>25 years old	4.8%	4.4%

Source: Author's calculations based on ENJUVE.

over this period (corresponding to the general elections of 2000 and 2006), although the percentage of declared voters in the group of 18 to 24 years old was slightly lower in 2008. Political engagement in other forms of activity, beyond voting, as well as interest in and knowledge about politics remains low and stable between 2001 and 2008, as seen in Table 6.2.

There is a dramatic decrease of those who would be willing to sacrifice political freedom in exchange for economic improvement (Difference = –15.1% for the group < 25 years old, and Difference = –15.9 for the rest of the population). A growing percentage of the population believed that the government is becoming more authoritarian, imposing decisions rather than negotiating them (Difference = 12.8% for the group < 25 years old, and Difference = 9.8 for the rest of the population).

Trust in Institutions and Political Figures Table 6.3 gives the percentages of those who distrusted each individual or group. It shows that the level of trust remained fairly stable between 2001 and 2008. There is marginally lower trust in the president and the governor, and substantially lower trust in mayors at the later time period. In addition, although trust in teachers was generally high, more students expressed lack of trust in 2008 than in 2001. In contrast, trust in the Supreme Court was higher in 2008, especially on the part of the younger group. Finally, trust in the police was substantially lower for both groups at the later time period.

Table 6.3

Adults' and Young Adults' Political Mistrust at Two Time Periods: Do You Trust...

Age	2001	2008
The president? (% responding "not at all")		
<25 years old	12.2%	15.6%
>25 years old	12.9%	14.5%
Your governor? (% responding "not at all")		
<25 years old	13.3%	14.6%
>25 years old	11.8%	13.8%
Your mayor? (% responding "not at all")		
<25 years old	17.2%	26.1%
>25 years old	14.8%	25.2%
The church? (% responding "not at all")		
<25 years old	6.0%	6.7%
>25 years old	4.9%	8.8%
Teachers? (% responding "not at all")		
<25 years old	2.4%	6.6%
>25 years old	3.4%	9.2%
The Supreme Court? (% responding "not at all")		
<25 years old	18.7%	10.6%
>25 years old	18.1%	14.8%
The Congress? (% responding "not at all")		
<25 years old	27.3%	20.3%
>25 years old	22.9%	25.2%
The police? (% responding "not at all")		
<25 years old	34.0%	45.1%
>25 years old	34.9%	45.1%

Source: Author's calculations from ENCUP.

CONCLUSIONS

Political participation of youth in Mexico is high with regard to voting behavior but very low with regard to other forms of political engagement. There are few distinctions in the political engagement of the older and younger groups surveyed or across the period from 2001 to 2008, in spite of more competitive electoral politics and significant changes in media openness and the number of political organizations. Satisfaction with democratic institutions and political actors is relatively low for both groups and in some areas declining over time. This may explain the lack of political involvement and could be attributed to the perceived failure of the governments after the 2000 election to improve living conditions for the population.

The stagnation of political attitudes and behavior during a period of political transition is indicative of how ingrained these beliefs and traits are, and perhaps suggestive of the fact that political knowledge, attitudes, and behavior are shaped at a young age, reinforced by older relatives´ attitudes, and more difficult to change after adolescence. Once political understandings and practices become shared in the form of a dominant political culture, a number of social institutions, including political and social organizations, families, and schools, may engage in practices that reflect and reproduce those values and practices. Therefore, changes in political institutions alone do not bring about changes in how people experience and make democracy a way of life, thus putting at risk any progress toward the institutionalization of democratic institutions if reforms are not accompanied by educational programs.

Schools are arguably the social institutions with the greatest autonomy to engage in practices that can challenge the dominant political values, teaching youth civic culture and practices more aligned with democracy as a way of life than with democracy as solely electoral participation. The Mexican education system has undertaken curricular reforms oriented toward those goals at the primary and secondary level. Youth descriptions of their schools suggest that these are environments more supportive of some of the basic forms of democratic engagement, such as tolerance and participation, than families. However, as the small differences in political practice of the younger among youth relative to their older peers examined in this chapter suggest, the process that translates those educational changes into changed political culture in Mexico has yet to bear fruit. Beyond the reforms in the curriculum of civic education that Mexico and other Latin American countries have implemented, the reforms need to extend to the pedagogical practices and school culture to seriously influence students.

This chapter showed that in Mexico low levels of political engagement correlate with low levels of knowledge and low levels of political participation, besides electoral participation. These also relate to low levels of trust and tolerance. However, lack of knowledge alone does not explain low levels of political engagement. Very small percentages of the population engage in forms of political action, which they believe are effective in achieving desired changes.

In contrast to literature in North America documenting limited political engagement of youth in political institutions but more engagement in grassroots organizations, evidence from Mexico shows lack of engagement in any form of political or social organization, even though Mexican youth are altruistic and engage in individual forms of assistance to others, a finding requiring further research.

IMPLICATIONS OF THESE FINDINGS FOR RESEARCH AND POLICY

A large percentage of the population in Latin America is young. In a number of countries, this cohort of youth is the largest it will be in the predictable future. For this reason, their political views and engagement are of great consequence to the future politics in the region. Latin American youth express limited support for democracy as well as limited levels of tolerance for difference. A large percentage of them would be willing to trade democracy for economic security. The incorporation of youth into more democratic forms of engagement does not obviously follow from more competitive politics. Unless democratic elections are accompanied by effective strategies of political socialization and incorporation of the young into democratic processes and practices, the observed stagnation in political engagement should be expected to continue with the ensuing stagnation in governance. Democracy cannot function on the charisma of elected leaders alone.

The very low levels of knowledge of political institutions and of the political process suggest that it is imperative to teach more effectively to youth. This would require explicit efforts on the part of political parties, civil society organizations, and schools, to reach out to youth and look for ways to incorporate and mobilize them. Among those actions, opening pathways to leadership within political organizations for youth figures would be an opportunity to increase the legitimacy of political institutions. Similarly, serious work to increase the effectiveness and accountability of political institutions and actors might contribute to dispel the deep-seated mistrust that youth and non-youth alike profess for them. Educating youth on the political process, as a way to support their participation and engagement, is another potential avenue for reform.

If a new form of political incorporation is to meet youth where they are, it should explore engaging them through electronic media and sports, areas where youth already participate significantly more than any other population group. Similarly, these forms of incorporation should build on the solidarity youth display toward others in private philanthropic acts, and find ways to build toward collective action (see Fox et al., this volume; and Beaumont, this volume). In any case, interventions aimed to incorporate youth in Mexico should explore new communication media and bridge out to other forms of involvement in immediate community issues including traditional forms of communication and organization to bridge across generations.

The research implications of this study are that the sources of low levels of trust of Mexican youth in political institutions should be investigated as well as the fact that a sizable percentage of them declare that they would demonstrate if their candidate did not win an election. An area that needs more attention is the study of the political engagement and views of youth who are in a social limbo, neither studying nor working, not only because of the sheer size of this population group, but because of the potential challenges for governance their alienation may represent. This is, unfortunately, a problem common in the developing countries (see Kassimir & Flanagan, this volume), but it appears to be an urgent issue in Mexico and one for which there is no simple solution.

REFERENCES

Calderon Gongora, G. (2008). La confianza de los jóvenes en las instituciones y el rompecabezas democrático. *Jóvenes, Revista de Estudios sobre Juventud, No. 29,* 30–42. Instituto Mexicano de la Juventud, México, D.F., México.

Fernandez Poncela, A. M. (2009). Desafección política juvenil: Desconfianza, desinteres y abstencionismo. *Casa del Tiempo. Revista de la Universidad Autonóma Metropolitana, 2(18),* 83–89, Universidad Autónoma Metropolitana.

Flores Vega, L. (2007). La transición mexicana: Cultura e identidad política en los jóvenes. Identidades juveniles y cultura. *Jóvenes, Revista de Estudios sobre Juventud, No. 27,* 111–127. Instituto Mexicano de la Juventud, México, D.F., México.

Fundación en Este Pais (2005). Lo que piensan nuestros maestros encuesta nacional sobre creencias, actitudes y valores de maestros y padres de familia de la educación básica en México. *Este Pais, 169,* 4–16.

Guevara, G., & Tirado, F. (2006). Conocimientos cívicos en Mexico: Un estudio comparativo internacional. *Revista Mexicana de Investigación Educativa, 11(30),* 995–1018, Consejo Mexicano de Investigación Educativa.

Instituto Mexicano de la Juventud (2005). Encuesta Nacional de Juventud (ENJUVE), [Data File and code book], retrieved from http://www.bdsocial.org/inmujeres/ENJUVE 2005/ENJ2005.sav.zipINEGI (2006). II Conteo de Población y Vivienda 2005. Resultados Definitivos. Tabulados Básicos (electronic resource). Retrieved from http://www.inegi.org.mx

Kaufmann, D., Kraay, A., & Mastruzzi, M. (2009). *Governance Matters VIII: Governance Indicators for 1996–2008.* World Bank Policy Research, June 2009, The World Bank Group.

Latinobarómetro. Annual report 2008. Retrieved from http://www.latinobarometro.org, Corporación Latinobarómetro.

Meixueiro, , G. (Ed.) (2007). *Conocimiento y accesibilidad: Condiciones para el ejercicio de los derechos de los jóvenes.* México: Centro de Estudios Sociales y de Opinion Pública de la Cámara de Diputados del H. Congreso de la Unión.

O'Donell, G. (1993). Estado, democratización y ciudadanía. *Nueva Sociedad, No. 128,* 62–87. Fundación Friedrich Ebert Stiftung.

Oueda, L., & Martinez, P. (2007). Jóvenes Mexicanos. Encuesta Nacional de Juventud 2005, Centro de Investigación y Estudios sobre Juventud, Instituto Mexicano de la Juventud, México.

Palma, R., & Paola, V. (2007). Democracía y juventud en México: Un reto de confianza institucional. *Jovenes. Revista de Estudios sobre Juventud*, enero-junio 64–83.

Reimers, F. (2007). The study of civic education when democracy is in flux: Analyzing the impact of empirical research in policy and practice in Latin America. *International Journal of Citizenship Teaching and Learning, 3(2)*, 5–21.

Secretaría de Educación Pública. (2005). *Educación Secundaria, Formación Cívica y Ética, Programas de Estudio.* México.

Secretaría de Educación Pública (2006). *Formación Cívica y Ética. Secretaría de Educación Pública*. México.

Secretaría de Gobernación. (2003). *Encuesta Nacional sobre Cultura Política y Prácticas Ciudadanas (ENCUP),* [Data File and code book], retrieved from www.encup .gob.mx

Torney-Purta, J. (2009). International psychological research that matters for policy and practice. *American Psychologist, 84(8)*, 825–837.

Torney-Purta, J. (2005). *Beyond rhetoric to empirical evidence: Fourteen-year-olds' understanding of treats to democracy, economic principles, and political institutions in the Americas* (2005 March). Paper presented at the Annual Meeting of the Comparative and International Education Society, Stanford, CA.

Torney-Purta, J., & Amadeo J. (2004). *Fortalecimiento de la democracía en las Américas a traves de la educacion civica: Un análisis empírico que destaca las opiniones de los estudiantes y los maestros.* Washington, DC: Organization of American States. [English title: *Strengthening democracy in the Americas through civic education: An empirical analysis of the views of students and teachers.*]

Torney-Purta, J., Lehmann, R., Oswald, H., and Schulz, W. (2001). Citizenship and education in twenty-eight countries. Civic knowledge and engagement at age fourteen. Amsterdam: The International Association for the Evaluation of Educational Achievement.

UNDP (2004). *Democracy in Latin America. Towards a Citizens Democracy*. Retrieved from http://democracyreport.undp.org/Downloads/Report_Democracy_in_Latin_America_New.zip

CHAPTER 7

Citizenship Education: A Critical Look at a Contested Field

HELEN HASTE
Harvard University and University of Bath, United Kingdom

INTRODUCTION

THE CONCEPT OF citizenship, and therefore any discussion of civic education, has become contested in recent decades, for a number of reasons. So it is necessary to look critically at agendas for both curricula and research in civic education and to unpack their implicit assumptions. To fail to do so may lead us inadvertently to perpetuate pedagogic procedures that are inadequate to current conditions, or to act less than critically as agents of political agendas that we should have scrutinized. If we cast a critical eye on assumptions and models, we may not only provide better education but also push forward theory and method in education and associated disciplines. In this chapter, I shall critically explore issues that have become salient as a consequence of geopolitical events, as well as of developments in the social sciences and in technology.

It is not unreasonable to argue that work in social science on civic behavior and education largely rested until a couple of decades ago on a U.S.-based model of what comprised democracy and therefore on U.S. models and how to inculcate young people into democratic competence. Furthermore, much early work also was based on a model of human development derived from the then-dominant social-learning theory. Political socialization implied a top-down process in which essentially passive young people were molded by *socializing agents* into *citizens*.

Major geopolitical events have challenged assumptions about the universality of any single form of democracy. Extensive international research has demonstrated the diversity of civic education goals and practices (Torney-Purta, Schwille, & Amadeo, 1999). The pattern of political activity in many nations from the mid-sixties began widening the definition of civic action and, therefore, the parameters of citizenship from a narrow focus on voting and campaigning for parties to a recognition of informal civic action and of community involvement. Recent developments in personal communication devices and networks have greatly expanded the scope of political activism.

Substantive shifts in psychological and education theory are focusing attention on the growing individual as an active agent, in dialogic relation to the social and cultural context. This moves the analytic emphasis toward a socially constructed and mediated development of identity and agency, in which the experience of action is at least as important as the acquisition of knowledge.

In summary, the chapter will address the following questions:

What are the challenges to models of human development and what are their implications for the development of civic identity and for pedagogy?

What is contested about citizenship?

What challenges to implicit models of democracy arise from international data and geopolitical change?

What is the impact of new technologies?

What caveats should be raised about political demands and expectations that underpin curricula in civic education?

MODELS OF DEVELOPMENT AND EDUCATION—THE CHALLENGES

As a starting point, I will consider how contemporary models of human development as a cultural process provide a framework for understanding how cultural narratives, identity, and the social construction of values and status are central to civic engagement. Much writing about civic education and engagement has been dominated by an implicit socialization model of human development. Indeed, the term *political socialization* is widely used in the field as a catchall phrase covering everything from parental influence to civics classes. First, this implies a passive human being, shaped by external social forces. It is out of step with contemporary developmental theory, in which the growing individual interacts *as an active agent* with her environment. A second influence on these approaches is traditional social psychology, in which the model is of knowledge (cognition) *leading to* action, mediated via motivational (affective) factors. This research tended to focus on values as enduring and trait-like attitude and ideology structures, which are presumed to have a casual relation to action.

Challenges to both these models come from contemporary theories, specifically from Vygotskian developmental theory and from social constructionist and discursive approaches within social psychology. Both focus on the dynamic and dialogic processes by which people actively negotiate meaning within a sociocultural context (Vygotsky, 1978; Wetherell, Taylor, & Yates, 2001). We are not merely the passive recipients of a top-down conduit of knowledge and values. We are tool-users who interact with our world as agents, and our tool-using experience frames the way that we interpret our world (Wertsch, 1998; Haste, 2008). This resonates with the distinction within pedagogy between fore-fronting *knowledge* (and its transmission) in education, and fore-fronting *praxis*. Experience first brings the young person to awareness of an issue through actual contact with it. Second, through action around or upon the issue, the individual gains the skills, motivation, and confidence for competent engagement.

For a critical understanding of citizenship education we need to consider such debates and approaches. They direct attention to the cultural, social, historical, and political context in which civic action and civic-related responses take place, and within which the individual co-constructs meaning. This means looking at how values are *used* (Billig, 1995; Haste, 2004). Values and beliefs are not just fixed entities such that by mapping them we understand a person's (or a group's) perception of the world. Values are the lens through which individuals filter and process information and experience. A value is not just a point on a Likert scale of agree-disagree; it carries with it explanations for events, narratives, norms, and prescriptions. John chooses point 4 on a pro-vegetarianism scale because he considers it unethical to squander the planet's resources on pasturing cattle when the land could feed many more if wheat were grown; Jane chooses the same point because she believes in the sanctity of all life. John's response is contextualized within Green values; Jane's comes from Buddhism. John might be happy to eat *wild* meat because it has been reared without cost to grain production; Jane would not.

By looking at values as *actions upon* our experience and our world, we recognize that they are part of a dynamic, and dialectical, social process. This also allows us to understand a phenomenon that mystifies traditional social psychologists—that people are inconsistent. Potter and Wetherell's groundbreaking work (1987) showed that people (in their case, New Zealanders) can move swiftly from invoking one cultural narrative that supports liberal views on immigration, to another narrative that is decidedly xenophobic. Billig showed people holding the apparently inconsistent views that the British Royal Family are an outmoded waste of money, and at the same time are the best form of symbolic state leadership, especially when compared to presidents (Billig, 1992). This is because different aspects of the situation have become salient *at that point in the dialogue.* Would Potter and Wetherell's New Zealanders vote for a more restrictive or more liberal immigration policy? Would Billig's respondents vote to abolish the monarchy or would they attend the parade when the Queen visits their town? It depends on which value is made salient by the current rhetoric and context.

To understand how political reasoning is mediated through language, dialogue, and cultural discourse, we must also look beyond a person's thought and values, and consider the social and cultural processes within which the individual negotiates meaning. These processes operate in two ways. First, dialogue between the self and significant persons, parents, teachers, and peers scaffolds development, and is also the crucible for debate and negotiation. Second, cultural discourses, narratives, explanations, and justifications frame what is taken for granted as normative, as well as what is seen as problematic and to be questioned or justified. Even more important, it determines what is *comprehensible* within any cultural context. Individual reasoning and values must be understood within the context of the individual's culture. Further, to understand how citizenship and its cultural purposes, boundaries, categories, and values are defined within a culture, we must decode how these are storied, explained, and justified and how they sustain current power relations. Educators need to pay attention to these processes in considering how to foster both engagement and critical awareness.

CONTESTED CITIZENSHIP STATUS AND IDENTITY

Definitions of citizenship status set the backdrop for the development of the individual citizen and also the goals and constraints for any education agenda. They also set the parameters of civic identity and therefore for the motives that support civic participation. Contestations of citizenship status nudge us to reflect critically upon the assumptions we bring to this topic. A number of questions frame how citizenship status is defined in theory and practice:

- What does it mean to be a citizen? Is this a definition of inclusion (and therefore of exclusion)? If so, what are the cultural justifications behind the criteria that include or exclude? By what routes is inclusion automatic? Who has power over what is defined as a *good* citizen?
- How should outsiders, the marginal, or the undocumented be treated, and how is such treatment related to the cultural narratives of civic identity?
- If being a citizen implies specific expectations of behavior and values, what objectives and whose purposes do they serve?
- What are educators doing when they foster such objectives—in what are they complicit? How can education in citizenship act as a challenge or counter to dominant political forces—and how far should it go?

Citizenship status is liminal; it sets the boundary rules for immigrants or for excluded groups within a society. Benhabib describes it thus:

> Citizenship and practices of political membership are the rituals through which the nation is reproduced spatially… The history of citizenship reveals that these nationalistic aspirations are ideologies; they attempt to mold a complex, unruly and unwieldy reality according to some simple governing principle of reduction, such as national membership. Every nation has its others, within and without (2004, p. 18).

Governments create legitimizing hurdles that grant entitlement and facilitate the acceptable immigrant. In periods when immigration is encouraged, entitlement may be relatively straightforward, but even then, nations may exclude particular categories for the purpose of maintaining a certain citizen profile. An example is the exclusion of "non-white" immigrants from Australia between 1901 and 1973. Those targeted were Asians, whose energy, endurance, and flexibility, combined with a willingness to accept a low standard of living, were seen as a threat to the emerging Australian way of life. In practice, this made Australia an exclusively white European immigrant culture that also marginalized the indigenous people. Several countries have a citizenship test designed to ensure a basic knowledge of the legislative and government structures and to equip the immigrant to develop a positive identity with the mores of their new nation. These tests are frequently and unintentionally amusing in what they reveal about supposed national characteristics and pastimes. They often include particular accounts of history that purportedly are common knowledge and that are components of indigenous national pride. A consequence is that new immigrants often acquire arcane knowledge that few native-born inhabitants possess.

Exclusion and inclusion criteria are indications of a nation's self-definition. This self-definition is constructed on the identity of those current inhabitants who have the power to define and regulate identity. As Anderson describes, this identity, this "imagined community," is supported by symbols, narratives, and discourses that tell the stories explaining and supporting the nation's worldview (Anderson, 2006). I will explore two examples: the role of the hero and of threats.

The cultural hero has a crucial narrative role. Heroes are presented to young people systematically as part of civic and moral education. Their carefully edited and embellished stories embody the virtues and behavior desired in a good person—and citizen. Their struggles (and the hero narrative always includes overcoming obstacles whether these are childhood hardship or an oppressing enemy) are supposed to inspire young people with the determination to emulate them. National heroes—those who are constructed as being the architects or the saviors of the nation—are clothed not only in national identity but in the attributes deemed symbolic of the true member of the nation. Schwartz describes how Lincoln's iconography changed from being a folk hero, rough-mannered, direct, and honest—the antithesis of the Eastern elite—to being the august and dignified leader purveying wisdom and authority, symbolically seated in a temple surrounded by his iconic messages for the people (Schwartz, 1990).

The hero may fight the nation's external enemy or may struggle against internal opposition. The literature for children in the United States is heavily populated with both historical and fictional characters who either resisted the British, or, later in history, were instrumental in creating a fairer society for various minority or underprivileged groups. Here the story is of justice in accordance with late twentieth-century moral and civic values. British children's literature in the colonial period was heavily imbued with imperial values and virtues, including an ethnic hierarchy based both on inherent, innate qualities and on the performance of appropriate deeds. Even foreign heroes who serve these narratives become appropriated. Neither William Wallace nor Robert the Bruce were Scottish, yet both are designated as essential heroes of the Scottish struggle against the English (Reicher & Hopkins, 2001).

Discourses of threat justify exclusion and inclusion criteria. In times of military threat, whether formal or related to terrorism, the overt exclusion of those who may take aggressive action is enhanced by a legitimizing counterpoint of general paranoia about invasion. A wide swathe of people becomes suspicious simply on the basis of physical characteristics.

Such anxieties are not only about the threat from militants. They include cultural threat in the form of fears that alien forces will undermine the dominant culture through their different social practices. At its most basic, cultural threat is that the perceived *other*, whose religion, mode of dress, and eating habits are seen as alien, threatens one's national identity. Stereotypes of the other often have sexual connotations, being either over-sexed or effeminate, as Southern Europeans have historically been cast by both the British and Anglo-Americans.

Caricatures of the other reliably erupt during internecine strife. More sophisticated are the arguments around the invasion of alien values and of cultural pollution. Current Western anxieties around Islam center largely on the presumed evangelism and intolerance in Islam toward the dominant Christian (or secular) culture, and the resulting fear that the immigrants will impose, by legal means, an alien system of law on the nation (Haste, 2006; Spencer, 2008). The fact that in most Western countries the Muslim population is statistically quite small, and therefore their potential power is very slight, does not diminish the anxiety. (In France and Germany, Muslims comprise about 7% of the population, in England 3%, and in the United States less than 1%). The anxiety seems to encompass the fear that all Muslims, including moderate and sophisticated individuals, will become militant fundamentalists, and that this group may achieve sufficient power to influence mainstream practices.

A somewhat different "threat" comes from the numbers of potential immigrants and a perceived imbalance of cultural representation. The world is seeing the largest migrations ever; between 1910 and 2000, the world's population increased threefold, and its migrant population sixfold. Suarez-Orozco argues that both host and immigrant groups are reconstituted and reframed by the process of integration (Suarez-Orozco, 2004).

How does a nation ensure that newcomers will contribute to the nation's good and not become a cultural, political, or economic threat? How do a nation's policies of admission and assimilation sustain its avowed ideology—whether this is a liberal, tolerant, multifaceted ethic (such as Canada, the UK, or The Netherlands), a policy of full assimilation into the dominant culture (such as France and the United States), or a more conservative policy of exclusion or enculturation to maintain a particular cultural or ethnic mainstream (such as Israel, or at one time, Australia)? The identities of young people of any nation, whether they are majority or minority group members, are substantially bound up with their nation's narratives of inclusion and exclusion.

The rhetoric of cultural threat is in continual tension with a liberal ethic of tolerance and multiculturalism, but both are driven by the goal of sustaining national values. It is a major tenet of most Western societies that the nation should be open to diversity and that the good citizen embraces the value that many perspectives should be validated. That is why the most insidious cultural threat comes from those immigrants whose value system does not embrace this ethic (Kymlicka, 1995). Benhabib defines the problem as *political membership*. First there are the tensions between the demands of liberal democracy and the demands of the nation state: "Transnational migrations bring to the fore the constitutive dilemma at the heart of liberal democracies: between sovereign self-determination claims on the one hand and adherence to universal rights on the other" (Benhabib, 2004, p. 2).

We should explore not only the formal legal dimensions of citizenship status but also the hidden constraints and facilitations within a society. To be an effective citizen—to exercise the normal rights of citizenship—requires agency and the infrastructures to enable that agency. However, many who are fully accredited citizens, according to the law, are denied agency by overt and covert discrimination, absence of the skills needed to enact citizenship (including education), lack of financial or other material resources, or unequal power relations. In many countries, the history of civil rights movements is as much about the implementation of legally existing rights and entitlements to disadvantaged or excluded groups as it is about the change in laws in order to provide those rights. In critically scrutinizing citizenship, we must pay attention to the gap between a presumed norm of entitlement and the actual reality. Empowered groups are often disenfranchised and hidden by social barriers. It is often only through analysis of these covert barriers that the nature and remedy for disenfranchisement becomes evident.

CITIZENSHIP IN THE GLOBAL WORLD; THE PARADOXES OF GLOBALIZATION

What is the scope of citizenship that a young person will enter? Citizenship status is frequently discussed in the context of the nation state, an entity with legal and geographical boundaries that is presumed to subsume local or group identities. Most writing on citizenship education is from within the culture of the writer's nationality. However boundaries are becoming less clear. First, with greater economic mobility (not just immigration), increasing numbers of people are living and working across national boundaries. Their children attend international schools and may have rarely lived in the home nations of either parent: Where is their national identity located? There is considerable push for a *European* identity, in part to forge commitment to the larger Europe, and in part to diminish parochial nationalism and potential conflicts, but also in part to approach an ideal of supranational identity that echoes global citizenship. However, current data suggest that national identity still outweighs allegiance to Europe.

The concept of *global citizenship* carries mixed value. For some, it entails transcending national boundaries and particularly nationalistic sentiments, and also implies a responsibility to the larger world community and to the planet's ecological needs. It is unlikely ever to have legal status, though arguably entitlement to internationally agreed and sanctioned human rights would approach this. It has moral appeal to many young people and therefore has educational implications for motivating engagement in global causes.

The concept of globalization is also contested. On the one hand it is associated with multinational capitalism, exploitation, and inequality. On the other hand, where it focuses on the expansion of communication without boundaries, it has much the same moral import as the global citizen: transcendent and libertarian. This is a concept that McLuhan envisaged in the "global village" that he saw resulting from new technology—in that case, television (McLuhan, 1964; Wolfe, 2003). This implication of globalization has been fueled by the rapid development of technologies that enable anyone with the equipment to communicate worldwide, and the equipment is available to almost everyone in industrial societies at low cost. As Friedman argues, now "the world is flat"—meaning that many traditional boundaries such as geography, communication constraints, and outmoded ideas are dissolving, and the skills for interacting across such boundaries have become both normative and essential (Friedman, 2007). Already we see young people who are communicating freely across international boundaries through a variety of messaging and social networks. This blurs the psychological boundaries of identity framed within the nation state, as well as civic obligations defined by such boundaries.

The ambiguities of globalization are also evident when we unpack the meaning of individuals' relationship to the nation state. Nussbaum, for example, argues that the nation state is a concept accessible to all citizens, which transcends individual greed and self-interest (Nussbaum, 2008). One of the problems of seeking a universal sentiment of concern for humans as a whole is that people are highly particularistic in their attachments and commitments. We care about those close to us, and our identity is strongly associated with a nation that is united by a common view of symbols, history, and location. This is Anderson's imagined community. Although globalization and being a citizen of the planet are appealing, they miss this key psychological point.

THE McDONALD AND DISNEY "WORLD CITIZEN"?

An aspect of globalization that stirs concern among many is cultural imperialism. Waves of books in recent decades have reflected on the extent to which American media dominate the world, and many have called them the agents of cultural imperialism, as they purvey American values, images, and symbols (Barber, 1995). What sometimes seems the universal presence of Disney's world in children's lives is one aspect, but so is the pervasiveness of brand names as status symbols for the young everywhere. Said (and others) argue that the Western worldview has been fed by the *othering* of the East. A mixture of fascination with the exotic and a resistance to understanding the richness of the others' perspective generates a mythology that legitimates its rejection (Said, 1993).

In reaction, as Barber argues, non-Western cultures can argue both that Western imperialists intend the destruction of other cultures and that they are ridden with immorality. These provide a moral justification for rejecting Western ideas (for example, the recent issue of AIDS treatment in South Africa), or for mounting an aggressive defense against perceived incursion, as in versions of Islamic jihadism. These are just some of the paradoxes of globalization.

More interactive models counter the image of a one-way traffic of ideas that dominates scenarios like these. Jenkins, for example, argues that rather than a one-way conduit, we are seeing *convergence* (Jenkins, 2006). This rests on new technology. Even in a world that is dominated by top-down media and its moguls, there is space for the audience's modification and adaptation, selective appropriation and reconstruction. How cultures and individuals receive these messages is infinitely various. It is easier to see the *transport* of an image from its source and its appearance at the endpoint than to interpret the *incorporation* of that image into the local culture. With interactive technology, and the diffusion of monolithic media into a huge variety of channels, the appropriation process is not passive. The message is actively mediated through local mores and symbols. As it is selectively assimilated, its meaning is changed.

How the child in Bangkok reads the Disney character is not the same as how the child in Los Angeles does—each will distill the message through his or her cultural lenses. It is in the use of new interactive technology that Jenkins sees the creation of something new that is not a minor modification of the U.S. narrative and image to fit local frames of meaning. Instead, both Western and non-Western young people *incorporate and reconstitute* a range of cultural images. This is a two-way process of cultural diffusion that does not rely on mega-media corporations but can be generated by young people on their own technology, or by small independent media groups. At the same time, we must not ignore the potential corporate appropriation and exploitation of this cosmopolitanism.

CONTESTED CITIZENSHIP PRACTICES: THE NATURE OF "DEMOCRACY"

The pervasive model of democracy found in much civics education curricula in the United States reflects a specific model of democratic processes and the skills required for it. Democratic processes are intertwined with culture, history, and national identity. This has been vividly demonstrated, for example, in the ways that post-Soviet states (and other emergent democracies) constructed their own versions of the democratic state, which bore only modest resemblance to the models in the United States or the United Kingdom but were derived from their own history (Haste, 2004; Andrews, 2007). Such nations sought models of democracy from periods when they threw off a colonial or conqueror's yoke, or ended feudalism. Their heroes were the liberators of that time. This is also illustrated in the chapter-length national case studies covering background principles underlying civic education that were provided by Lithuania, the Czech Republic, Hungary, and Bulgaria, as they prepared to participate in the IEA Civic Education Study (Torney-Purta, Schwille, & Amadeo, 1999) and in the questions submitted for national civics subtests dealing, for example, with Michael the Brave, a Romanian hero from the early 1600s.

The underlying principles of the democratic state also vary. Freedom of religion, and freedom from centralized government, are not the major rhetorical principles of most European states, east or west. These are the heritage of the United States, which was founded on the search for religious toleration and the creation of an autonomous community. Socialism, for example, is regarded even by conservative Europeans as a valid system for maximizing equality. Labeling leaders in the United States pejoratively as *socialist* for espousing mildly liberal policies is ideologically incomprehensible to Europeans. In their histories, all European states experienced forms of socialist idealism during the nineteenth and twentieth centuries, and most have or have had mainstream socialist parties.

Second, data from international studies such as the IEA 28-nation survey of civic education also show the diverse assumptions about the goals of civic education and about desirable and normative forms of engagement (Torney-Purta et al., 2001). One example is volunteering, which is central to conceptions of the good citizen in the United States. In countries with a highly developed welfare state (such as Sweden) or in formerly Communist nations such as the Czech Republic or Hungary, where it meant imposed community activity, it may even be resented (Flanagan et al., 1999; Torney-Purta, Schwille, & Amadeo, 1999). International projects such as these make explicit the extent to which U.S. definitions of democracy are rooted in its own history and traditions.

The construction of, and experience with, democracy is different in stable and transitional societies. The United States and many western European states have had stable systems of government for a long period. Their main form of democracy is representational, with regular elections. The ordinary citizen's primary access to power is via lobbying their representative, or using the media and pressure groups to influence public opinion and government policy. In transitional societies these structures may not be in place. If the individual citizen has potential power, it is through membership of unstable groups struggling to establish their position. Such periods can be both deeply frustrating and exhilarating (Andrews, 2007). Countries where violations of civil and political liberties are prominent in recent history create a climate where young people are especially interested in learning about how they can participate in the international protection of human rights (Torney-Purta, Wilkenfeld, & Barber, 2008). Accounts of the immediate post-Soviet era show young people who were very active in movements for change veering between high optimism and deep disillusion (Van Hoorn et al., 2000; Markova, 2004). Similar data come from South Africa (Abrahams, 1995; Haste & Abrahams, 2008).

CONTESTED PRACTICES: CIVIC ACTION

The model of what constitutes *civic action* is rooted in conceptions of the purposes and processes of the democratic state. Historically (and still for many political scientists), the core of civic action and the democratic state has been voting and conventional party support, so the political panic is around "why don't more young people vote?" Since the 1960s, the informal civic action of liberationist and emancipatory social movements, especially around civil rights and the environment, has brought making one's voice heard into the civic action and skills arena, and raised questions about its place in the goals of civic education (Sigel & Hoskins, 1981; Kaase, 1999; Zukin et al., 2006).

The place of community action, helpfulness, and service in defining youth civic engagement has been problematic for some models of citizenship insofar as it does not relate to party or voting activity, though other models have included it as part of public domain engagement. The development of communitarian theory links community action causally to the process of becoming more conventionally political, as well as identifying such action as a core element of the creation of social capital and therefore of effective democracy (Putnam, 2000). Despite considerable criticism of aspects of this argument, empirical studies of the relationship between helping or community activity and later civic participation do suggest that it can be a route to civic efficacy. A number of studies show that participation in community action can be a route to a more critical understanding of political and social forces provided that there are opportunities for reflection on the part of the participants (Yates, 1999; Morgan & Streb, 2001; Westheimer & Kahne, 2004).

These perspectives challenge the assumption that politics is mainly about party agendas. Two writers who explore this are Giddens (1991, 1994) and Beck (1992). The ideological boundaries of emancipatory social movements cut across the Left-Right spectrum and do not follow conventional party lines. They are heavily imbued with moral rhetoric and they also reflect a change in how democracy functions (Harré, Brockmeier, & Muhlhausler, 1999). When such social movements exert effective pressure on mainstream politics, this shifts the balance of power from the representative legislative body to something closer to grassroots democracy. A successful social movement goes beyond lobbying; it changes the culture. Protest movements, once seen as manifestations of unconventional political activity—and even a threat to social order—have become cornerstones of democracy. Beck argues that the disenchantment with politics as conventional procedures has paradoxically broadened the base of democracy by creating powerful voices that cannot be ignored. Both Beck and Giddens show that social movement activity is a response to issues that are perceived as personally relevant and entailing personal responsibility. Equipping young people to be effective in such activities is at least as important as equipping them to vote.

It is clear that a compelling issue can engage—and mobilize—a citizen. Though this may lead to a wider party-oriented perspective, the motivation for civic action comes from personal connection and a desire to have an effect in the public domain—whether with respect to social injustice or perceived risks to one's own life domain. The phrase *the personal is political* is a salient and powerful part of the rhetoric of emancipatory and liberationist movements (Haste, 1994; Yuval-Davis & Werbner, 1999). The strong moral component in many of these issues breaks the traditional boundary between the moral and the political, the personal and the political, and public and private domains, opening up a rather different path to explaining how people become engaged (Haste & Hogan, 2006; Klandermans, 1997). Empirical studies on engagement show that people, especially young people, become involved in civic action primarily by one of two routes: They accompany friends to an event and their initially social motivation leads to a commitment to the group and the cause, or they are moved or upset by something and become motivated to take action, often with moral support from others (Haste, 1990; Andrews, 1991; Colby & Damon, 1992; Goodwin & Jasper, 2003). Young people who have had experiences of effective agency tend to be active in adult life (Youniss, McLellan, & Yates, 1997).

The study by Yates (1999) considers some of these processes. She observed young middle-class Black students participating in a soup kitchen as part of a school exercise over several weeks. Initially the young people saw the homeless as piteous, and as alcohol or drug abusers. They also expected them to be Black. Their experience changed their perceptions, seeing instead misfortune, pride, and greater diversity. Many began to understand their own expectations. Some also came to question the role of the city's policies in contributing to homelessness.

These sensitivities depended on opportunities for reflection. Studies of similar exposure show little effect without such reflection. Seider found that white middle-class suburban students, who started out with liberal views, became more *conservative* when exposed to information about and contact with the homeless (Seider, 2008, 2010). Many of these young people's families were products of the American dream—anyone can make it if they try. Seeing homeless people who were demographically very like themselves challenged their worldviews and made them anxious.

Identifying what engages young people in civic participation also entails understanding how young people define the civic domain. Numerous studies show that when asked about their interest in politics, young people respond overwhelmingly negatively. However, when asked about their interest in specific political issues, such as the environment, social injustice, or wars, a much higher level of interest is evident (Hahn, 1998).

CATEGORIES OF CIVIC PARTICIPATION

Several writers have classified young people's civic action by differentiating conventional from more proactive engagement. Bennett, Freelon, and Wells (this volume), for example, distinguish the *dutiful* from the *actualizing* citizen. Westheimer and Kahne (2004) present a tripartite model that explicitly incorporates a hierarchy of social justice-oriented action. Torney-Purta (2009), in a cluster analysis of young people from five Eastern and five Western European countries, distinguishes social justice-oriented citizenship and conventionally oriented citizenship as well as finding relatively large groups of disengaged or alienated adolescents.

A slightly different picture emerges from a recent British study of more than 1,000 British young people aged between 11 and 21, which explored different profiles of values and action (Haste, 2005; Haste & Hogan, 2006). Value items, some of which were drawn from the IEA Civic Education questionnaire, asked first about the criteria of the good citizen. Second, social concerns and values were tapped by asking on what issues the respondents would like to influence the government. Third, a question about their expected future actions was used as a proxy for normative assumptions about appropriate adult civic behavior (rather than as a measure of actual prediction of their own activities).

Additionally, a measure of actual current engagement was their recent civic-related activities. Three-quarters had participated in the last two years in civic action ranging from helping in community activities, to running for office in school or college, to boycotting products.

- The most important criterion of *being a good citizen* was obeying the law. This was closely followed by voting in elections, protecting the environment, and helping the community. Over half thought that promoting human rights, following political issues in the news and talking with family and friends about them was important, and nearly half thought it was important to protest against an unjust law.
- The *level of social concern* was high, particularly among girls. This parallels the IEA data, which showed that gender differences in civic knowledge and activities have lessened in recent decades (Torney-Purta et al., 2001).
- Provision of good health care and opportunities for young people ranked high as issues on which they would like to influence the government, closely followed by social problems such as racism, drugs, and controlling crime.
- Nearly three-quarters expected, as adults, to vote in elections, nearly half expected to work with an organization to help people in need, more than half expected to sign a petition, and 30% expected to take part in a peaceful protest. Only 14% expected to join a political party. This parallels the IEA Civic Education Study across countries where it was also the case that adolescents neither trusted political parties nor saw themselves as potential members (Torney-Purta et al., 2001).

Using principal components factor analysis, we identified profiles of values, concerns, and civic norms among these British young people. Four distinct profiles of civic engagement and related recent action emerged. *Active monitoring* comprised paying attention to current events and discussing them, as well as being concerned about social issues, but it was not associated with recent civic action, whereas the other three profiles were. *Conventional participation* included values and activities relating to voting and elections. *Making one's voice heard* was associated with valuing and expecting future protest or pressure group activity and was associated with recent action. *Helping in the community* brought together the values and recent and future actions around community activity and support, and was also associated with support for Green issues and the environment.

In addition to the patterns of values and activities that emerged, there was further support for the links between moral and political motivation. One of the best predictors both of action and of social concern was the item *I am often upset by events in the news.*

These profiles largely support the distinctions I explored earlier between different kinds of civic engagement. They suggest that a simple dichotomy between conventional and activist engagement may not appropriately or fully differentiate the range of motives that move young people to civic action.

CITIZENSHIP PRACTICES: THE ROLE OF NEW TECHNOLOGY

Technology has exploded in the last decade. While what are often called *new technologies* have been around for some time—and have been used in support of civic action—their full implications for a rethink of the nature of civic action are only recently becoming appreciated (Haste, 2009). Bennett, Freelon, and Wells's chapter (this volume) comprehensively reviews data on the impact of new technology on civic action. In this chapter, I will address some critical perspectives.

New technologies enable the individual to be an active agent in accessing, modifying, and disseminating information on a potentially global scale, almost instantaneously. This is a major shift in power. When advanced media and information retrieval technology was primarily in the hands of government, corporations, or teachers in schools, it was possible to control what information was both available and valid. While libraries have been repositories of knowledge where the citizen could find out a great deal with diligent research, this required skill, motivation, and the organization both of the search and its results. Classically, governments have controlled the public's knowledge either by censorship or media pressure, or by carefully constructed consultations that conform to the government's agenda.

Classically, the teachers' role has been to structure and scaffold children's path through both skills and material. It is argued that new technology democratizes, because these restrictive structures no longer have the same impact.

In real-world politics, there are numerous manifestations of new technology in action. The first such event is generally seen to be the massive demonstration against the World Trade Organization (WTO) meeting in Seattle in 1999 by 50,000 people, who were summoned by messaging and e-mail. Since then we have seen many anti-war demonstrations, worldwide, instigated by electronic communication. In 2009, anti-government activists organized a demonstration of 10,000 people in Chisinau, the capital of former Soviet satellite Moldova, within 18 hours of an unpopular election result being declared.

New technology opens up many opportunities for individual and small-group civic action and empowerment. In that sense it is undoubtedly *democratizing*. It also poses problems for governments. Without massive censorship, it is very difficult to constrain these bottom-up activities and communication. Even countries with centralized controls are having difficulty in limiting access to the Internet. Juris sees the process as part of a wider change in worldview; he describes the "cultural logic of networking," by which he means changing the underlying metaphors of social action: "The self-produced, self-developed and self-managed network becomes a widespread cultural ideal, providing not just an effective model of political organising but also a model for re-organising society as a whole" (2004, p. 353). This reflects a pattern of horizontal connection, open information, and decentralized collaboration that many writers connect to new technology's civic—and community—potential (Poortinga & Pidgeon, 2003; Hampton, 2004; Nash, 2008).

In principle, everyone with the technology and basic skills can access every piece of information in the history of the world. As sophisticated handheld devices with Internet capability become more accessible, user-friendly, and cheap, this will expand even further (Dede, 2007, 2009). There will still be inequality but it will be greatly reduced—in the same way that, 40 years ago, television ownership became essential at all economic levels. However, access to such rich information does not of course guarantee its productive use. One of the goals of future education must be to structure critical selection and effective deployment of materials and these rich resources (Buckingham, 2007; Cliff, O'Malley, & Taylor, 2008).

This way of accessing information requires educators to rethink some basic assumptions. First, the young person becomes an active seeker with, nominally, no restraints. She is in control of what she decides is of interest or relevant, needing only to know how to navigate Google and Wikipedia.

Second, she is able, in many cases, to modify the sites that she accesses: She is a collaborator in the creation and the processing of knowledge (Reich, 2008). Many sites are deliberately designed to be cumulative in this way, requiring editing skills that young people are fast acquiring. Thirdly, it is highly likely that she will work collaboratively, with friends with whom she has face-to-face contact, or with people she has never met and who may not even be from the same region of the world.

She is also likely to be participating in complex gaming. Contrary to early stereotypes of lonely male nerds escaping into a virtual fantasy world that made no demands on social skills, we now see that video games can develop considerable organizational and leadership skills, managing team members in highly complex moves in an elaborate game scenario (Shaffer, 2006; Salen, 2008; Gee, 2007a, 2007b). She will also be learning to manage multiple selves, via her avatars in games and also multiple versions of her real self in the public networking of sites such as Facebook and in blogging. She will be able to move between the demands of different face-to-face groups in her social world, each of which represents itself via a specific set of symbols, codes, and styles (Maffesoli, 1996; Riley, 2008; Riley, Griffin, & Morey, 2010). Gaming requires attention, motivation, and perseverance for long stretches of time, often coupled with long-delayed rewards (Vass, 2008). Gaming also requires multitasking, cognitively complex and rapid problem solving, and information processing, all of which take place within a collaborative and interactive context.

Finally, all this can be communicated rapidly to a wide range of people. No longer does the individual citizen have to go through the gatekeepers of media to make his or her voice heard. The huge proliferation of blogs—in 2008, over 112 million were tracked worldwide, with probably over 70 million more in China—represents the desire and willingness of people to air their views and engage with others, whether sharing common values or attempting to persuade public opinion.

Educators need to shift their perspectives away from the top-down conduit model in which the teacher facilitates and scaffolds how and what children learn. Instead they need to use a more bottom-up model in which the teacher is the choreographer of children working collaboratively and critically, as agents in their own learning. It is important to realize that this is not something added on, in the way that the computer in the classroom corner is often merely an extension of library access that fits into traditional pedagogic style. It requires transformation in managing the learning process.

Many teachers are attempting this, though currently more in affluent schools, which have good equipment and whose students possess their own equipment. Until the gap in access to technology is narrowed by the wider availability of more sophisticated handheld devices, this will remain.

However, the required shift is in the *mindset*. Currently many people see the extensive activity of young people in interaction with their technology as a kind of play that has no place in the classroom. As long as young people are primarily text-messaging their friends under the desk during class, this opinion is reasonable. In many cases, teachers are far behind their pupils in their use of and understanding of technology, and so do not have an appreciation of its potential.

The missing mindset is the translation of the skillful participation that currently characterizes many young people's leisure activities and communication, into educational philosophy. What is currently seen as *play* becomes instead the infrastructure of school and college *work*. Merely grafting some of these practices and schools on to the curriculum misses the point. It is a different way of engaging with knowledge and information resources, as Dede, Buckingham, and others argue. The concept of the individual scholar, working alone and in competition with other scholars for the best individual grades or recognition, is being challenged. Assessment that focuses on such individual production rather than assessing collaborative activity is shortsighted.

There are numerous ongoing efforts to generate games for educational purposes—everything from science to moral and civic education. Some successful examples simulate activities quite commonly found in the traditional curriculum but use the scope of new media to extend their potential. For example, *River City*, developed by Dede and his team at Harvard Graduate School of Education, creates a virtual geographical and social space in which students can generate hypotheses, test them, and do exploratory investigations into the distribution of various infestations that might be the cause of disease in the city. It simulates the processes of epidemiological and ecological research far beyond a usual field trip (see http://www.gse.harvard.edu/~dedech/).

In addition to using such approaches across the curriculum, data suggest that participating in leisure video games is beneficial for civic education (Kahne, Middaugh, & Evans, 2008; Flanagan & Nissenbaum, 2007; Lenhart et al., 2008). Bennett, Freelon, and Wells review many of these studies. Such games provide the opportunity for taking part in discussion on civic issues, and participating in the life of a community, including as a civic leader, in collaboration with large numbers of other players As one example, Kahne, Middaugh, and Evans (2008) explored participation in (leisure) games in which players helped others, organized groups or guilds, explored social or ethical issues, learned about a problem in society, or had to make decisions about how a community, city, or nation should be run. They found that while the *quantity* of game playing does not correlate with civic participation, game characteristics and the context of play do. These data support the findings, from real-life community experience and classroom interaction, that participation enhances civic awareness when young people are forced to confront and question their own assumptions.

NEW TECHNOLOGY: A CRITICAL PERSPECTIVE

There are also caveats and concerns about young people's use of technology and the extent to which it is liberating and expanding. One of the consequences of becoming effective in managing multiple online selves might be that, as Riley argues, communication technologies create a situation where people understand aspects of themselves as only truly meaningful when they are offered up for the consumption of others (2008). Even though she is, in general, positive about new technology, Turkle (2004) warns that while a simulation such as a video game may give students insight, they may not be learning the same concepts or modes of thinking about a problem that they would in a hands-on situation. For example, in making something from a design in the "real" world, one is constantly encountering and dealing with slight mismatches between the design and the materials being used; in the virtual world the design neatly turns into the desired product, without glitches. Learning to manage the glitches is often a crucial part of the learning experience, especially in science. To give an example, in the simulated *River City*, no one falls into the polluted lake or contaminates her specimen jar with mud.

One pessimistic interpretation is that despite their increased sense of efficacy, youth are becoming disengaged from conventional political activity but more involved in consumer politics. Even for those who become more civically involved, there are problems. What happens, for instance, if no one responds to an individual's blogs? How can we control offensive blogs and the communities whom they serve? The bottom line must be: How can educators develop civic curricula that enable young people to achieve the full *critical* and political as well as personally empowering potential of Information and Communication Technology (ICT)?

Coleman (2008) sees a tension between those who want to manage e-democracy and those who have sampled its empowering potential. In the management model of education, young people are regarded as apprentice citizens in the process of transition. Their apprenticeship entails learning how to exercise responsible judgment in a risky and complex world, including seeing the Internet as an anarchic realm that is unsafe for young people "not only because their social innocence might be exploited by predators but also because they are politically vulnerable to misinformation and misdirection" (p. 191). In contrast, those youth who aspire to autonomous e-citizenship refuse to see themselves as apprentice citizens; they argue for themselves on agendas of their own making. The very anarchy of the Internet appeals, as a "relatively free space in which untrammelled creativity and acephalous [headless] networks can flourish" (p. 192).

Coleman also sees challenges. Managed e-citizenship overprotects young people and distorts the political world with its emphasis on friendliness, deliberation, and consensus, producing "a virtual community of well-trained democrats who would be lost in any real political party, trade union or local council" (p. 192). On the other hand, autonomous e-citizenship can be dislocated from the structures and processes of effective power, paying little attention to opposing views or entering into deliberative debate and focusing mainly on single issues.

Managed citizenship is attractive to those who fail to appreciate (or wish to avoid) the real potential of new technology and act as though it was merely an add-on to current procedures. For example, critics of the emerging Organisation for Economic Co-operation and Development (OECD)'s agenda for a *civic education e-democracy programme* see it as designed to mold citizenship into a narrow, quiescent, and consumerist model of civic action (Ververi, 2008; Hoskins & Mascherini, 2008). They argue that OECD objectives suggest that e-democracy might be exclusively operated by government as a means of disseminating information and controlling decision making, dialogue, networking, and the political agenda. New technologies will make these more facile and controllable.

CONSTRAINTS AND LIMITATIONS ON CIVIC ENGAGEMENT

The foregoing has largely focused on the question of how education can facilitate critical use of new technologies and thus expand empowerment and competence. There are, however, other constraints. Discussions of the achievement gap in civic activity vary from concerns about knowledge to concerns about efficacy and alienation (see Levinson, this volume). Civic knowledge is important, but increasing civic knowledge is not necessarily going to increase thoughtful action of the sort detailed above. Alienation, however, can spring from several sources and can include both lack of empowerment and apathy in relation to the political world. Alienation arising from the marginalization of one's social group and its disenfranchisement either through legal or economic factors is well documented, with higher-income families being considerably more likely to participate in campaign and community work, to contact elected officials, and to protest (Verba, Schlozman, & Brady, 1995).

These constraints are also reflected in opportunities in schools in the United States. Kahne and Middaugh (2008) found that African American and Hispanic students reported less open classroom discussion and fewer opportunities for participation in community service than White students. Asian students reported more opportunities for after-school activities but less experience of open classroom discussion. Students in Advanced Placement (AP) classes reported more civic opportunity experiences. Higher social economic status students were more likely to report learning how laws are made, participating in service activities, and having debates or discussions in class. Wilkenfeld (2009) has explored the contexts of low social economic status neighborhoods as well as schools with primarily low social economic status students and arrived at similar conclusions.

Whether the democratizing power of new technology—especially once it becomes inexpensive enough to extend to the overwhelming majority of young people—will actually translate into greater empowerment and engagement is moot. There is a need to recognize the potential power of new technology in civic education and action, and the importance of providing a strong critical scaffolding. This includes opportunities for participation as well as information organization using new technologies.

THE POLITICAL AGENDA

My final critical point addresses the political agenda and its demands. As we have seen, when nations are in the process of creating an exclusion/inclusion boundary for those who will be accepted as new citizens, they frame their definition of citizenship and the hurdles to reach it to achieve the goal of producing a particular kind of culture. Civic education curricula can implicitly act as the agency of political structures and their reproduction, not only in *what* is taught but *how* it is taught. Even if we as social scientists are happy to be complicit in these agendas, it behooves us to be critically aware of them and how they operate.

Regimes other than our own, especially when viewed at a historical or geographical distance, seem quite transparent in how they shape their civic education around their goals of both social control and desired social order. This is especially obvious with totalitarian regimes where the symbols and slogans are often blatant and where youth movements are explicit in their goals and structures. It is less obvious in democratic societies. Yet with hindsight we can, for example, see how the British education system, between 1850 and 1960, prepared the young for their role in a military, empire-building, and empire-governing culture and how changing American values have been mirrored in curricula as well (Orrill, 1997).

In any political agenda of democracy we need to be sensitive to the government's objectives. Is democracy primarily about managing social order and social control, or is it also about tackling social issues? And if so, what count as social issues? As an example, Nussbaum (1999) writes of 10 human needs, "functional capabilities" or entitlements, without which life is incomplete. Her *political* position is that it is the function of a good political system to meet the needs of its citizens. But for her this is also a *moral* imperative. These needs include bodily, social, and emotional domains, and practical reason. They form an indivisible set in that "a life that lacks any one of these capabilities, no matter what else it has, will fall short of being a good human life" (p. 42). Because these human capabilities exert a moral claim on the political system, they translate into rights, and she argues that it is incumbent on any democratic government to provide the conditions under which such capabilities can flourish.

These capabilities can be manifested in a variety of ways and they adapt to a wide range of cultural conditions. A critical lens on political agendas requires us *both* to consider how any civic education program is moving toward Nussbaum's capabilities *and* to take a critical look at how they are being implemented and defined. To what extent do they map on to, or profoundly clash with, the agendas of the parties that have current potential power—in any Western nation? And to what extent might young people's concerns, those that motivate their engagement, relate to Nussbaum's criteria?

A CRITICAL LOOK AT THE (LIKELY) FUTURE

Given international concerns, civic education is likely to gain an even higher profile in the future. The enlargement of the curriculum to include innovative methods such as forms of gaming is likely. The official civic agenda, however, may conflict with what young people are already doing. The use of blogs and wikis for making one's voice heard, and creating transnational pressure groups, is very likely to increase, especially for morally charged issues such as the environment or violations of human rights. At the same time, there will be more consumer-related online activism and also more partisan/interest group activism of less liberal tone, which could proliferate further under perceived threats (such as immigration or terrorism).

There are, however, major uncertainties. One is about dominant values. Economic pressures in conjunction with immigration and other perceived cultural threats may precipitate a more conservative, exclusionary, and public mood. Currently, the cultural values that inform civic education are primarily liberal: concern about under-privilege, diversity, rights, freedom of choice, and the environment. A more hostile economic environment, or even a moral reaction against a consumer-hedonic culture, could precipitate a considerable value shift.

Will young people feel more empowered to express their views? Might governments succeed in limiting online power, or delegitimizing its use?

To what extent will empowerment from technology be used for civic participation, and to what extent will it be diverted into consumerist action or self-promotion? Motivation for civic participation rests on a combination of personal efficacy as well as moral and social concern. In their absence, apathy and alienation may be a response.

Despite the opportunities that interactive media provide for new ways of knowing and working, technology is often still used as an adjunct to traditional education methods, or as merely another source of information, not as a way of transforming how information is used. To a large extent, the basic metaphor of school-based learning has been that the teacher facilitates and channels information to students, in ways designed to maximize the students' ability to process and retain it. Opportunities for students to learn through praxis or through discussion and collaboration are usually choreographed to direct such opportunities toward a known successful outcome. The teacher has a central role as orchestrator, even if off the scene. The primary target is the learner's performance, as an individual, often in competition with others.

Actions by students to change information (for example, editing and modifying wikis) sidestep the role of the teacher as manager and authority and blur the boundaries between expert and novice. Interactive technologies are inherently bottom-up, in the sense that they are driven by the agent who is acting upon the information. They are, potentially if not exclusively, collaborative. Many claim that this is a *metaphor* of democracy and interacting with it is an *act* of democracy. But it can also be a metaphor of anarchy. The apparent lack of boundaries, including boundaries between individual and collaborative thought and action, contrasts with conventional education and particularly with a model in which achievement depends on the individual working alone. This is a profound tension. It may be misguided to assume that current institutions can graft on new technologies to existing practices. In order to take advantage of new technologies, and to bring into formal civic education the increasingly routine practices and skills of the rest of the student's world, schools will need to rethink the top-down model of education. They will need to find ways to facilitate, and orchestrate, these bottom-up and collaborative practices productively and critically, in order to foster the next generation of effective civic agents.

REFERENCES

Abrahams, S. (1995). *Moral reasoning in context: The construction of the adolescent moral world under apartheid.* Unpublished doctoral dissertation, Harvard Graduate School of Education.

Anderson, B. (2006). *Imagined communities.* London: Verso.

Andrews, M. (1991). *Lifetimes of commitment*. Cambridge: Cambridge University Press.

Andrews, M. (2007). *Shaping history*. Cambridge: Cambridge University Press.

Barber, B. (1995). *Jihad vs. McWorld: Terrorism's challenge to democracy*. New York: Ballantine Books.

Beck, U. (1992). *Risk society*. Thousand Oaks, CA: Sage Publications.

Benhabib, S. (2004). *The rights of others: Aliens, residents and citizens*. New York: Cambridge University Press.

Billig, M. (1992). *Talking of the royal family*. London: Routledge.

Billig, M. (1995). *Arguing and thinking*. Cambridge: Cambridge University Press.

Buckingham, D. (2007). *Beyond technology: Children's learning in the age of digital culture*. Cambridge: Polity Press.

Cliff, D., O'Malley, C., & Taylor, J. (2008). *Future issues in socio-technical change for UK education*. Bristol: Futurelab.

Colby, A., & Damon, W. (1992). *Some do care*. New York: Free Press.

Coleman, S. (2008). Doing IT for themselves: Management v. autonomy in youth e-citizenship. In L. Bennett (Ed.), *Civic life online: Learning how digital media can engage youth*. Cambridge, MA: MIT Press.

Dede, C. (2007). Reinventing the role of information and communications technologies in education. In L. Smolin, K. Lawless, & N. Burbules (Eds.), *Information and communication technologies: Considerations of current practice for teachers and teacher educators* (pp. 11–38). (NSSE Yearbook 2007 [106:2]). Malden, MA: Blackwell Publishing.

Dede, C. (2009). Immersive interfaces for engagement and learning. *Science, 323(5210)*, 66–69.

Flanagan, C., Johnson, B., Botcheva, L., Csapo, B., Bowes. J., Macek, P., Averina, L., & Sheblanova, E. (1999). Adolescents and the "social contract": Developmental roots of citizenship in seven countries. In M. Yates & J. Youniss (Eds.), *Roots of civic identity* (pp. 135–155). Cambridge: Cambridge University Press.

Flanagan, M., & Nissenbaum, H. (2007). A game design methodology to incorporate social activist games. *CHI*, April–May.

Friedman, T. (2007). *The world is flat*. New York: Picador.

Gee, J. P. (2007a). *Good video games and good learning*. New York: Peter Lang.

Gee, J. P. (2007b). *What video games have to teach us about learning and literacy*. New York: Palgrave Macmillan.

Giddens, A. (1991). *Modernity and self-identity: Self and society in the late modern age*. Cambridge: Polity Press.

Giddens, A. (1994). *Beyond left and right: The future of radical politics*. Cambridge: Polity Press.

Goodwin, J., & Jasper, J. M. (2003). *The social movements reader*. Oxford: Blackwell Publishing.

Hahn, C. (1998). *Becoming political*. Albany: SUNY Press.

Hampton, K. (2004). Networked sociability online, offline. In M. Castells (Ed.), *The network society: A cross-cultural perspective* (pp. 217–232). Cheltenham: Edward Elgar.

Harré, R., Brockmeier, J., & Muhlhausler, P. (1999). *Greenspeak: A study of environmental discourse.* Thousand Oaks, CA: Sage Publications.

Haste, H. (1990). Moral responsibility and moral commitment: The integration of affect and cognition. In T. Wren (Ed.), *The moral domain* (pp. 315–359). Cambridge, Mass: MIT Press.

Haste, H. (1994). *The sexual metaphor.* Cambridge, MA: Harvard University Press.

Haste, H. (2004). Constructing the citizen. *Political Psychology, 25(3)*, 413–440.

Haste, H. (2005). *My voice, my vote, my community*. Nestlé Social Research Programme Report # 4. Croydon: The Nestlé Trust.

Haste, H. (2006). Assets, aliens or asylum seekers? Immigration and the UK. *UNESCO Prospects, 26(3)*, 327–341.

Haste, H. (2008). Constructing competence: Discourse, identity and culture. In I. Plath (Ed.), *Kultur-handlung-Demokratie: Diskurse ihrer Kontextbedingungen* (pp. 109–134). Wiesbaden: Verlag für Sozialwisshenschaften.

Haste, H. (2009). What is "competence" and how should education incorporate new technology's tools to generate "competent" civic agents? *The Curriculum Journal, 20(3)*, 207–223.

Haste, H., & Abrahams, S. (2008). Morality, culture and the dialogic self: Taking cultural pluralism seriously. *Journal of Moral Education, 37(3)*, 377–394.

Haste, H., & Hogan, A. (2006). Beyond conventional civic participation, beyond the moral-political divide: Young people and contemporary debates about citizenship. *Journal of Moral Education, 35(4)*, 473–493.

Hoskins, B., & Mascherini, M. (2008). Measuring active citizenship through the development of a composite indicator. *Social Indicators Research, 90(3)*, 459–488.

Jenkins, H. (2006). *Convergence culture: Where old and new worlds collide.* New York: New York University Press.

Juris, J. (2004). Networks of social movements: Global movements for global justice. In M. Castells (Ed.), *The network society: A cross-cultural perspective* (pp. 341–362). Cheltenham: Edward Elgar.

Kaase, M. (1999). Interpersonal trust, political trust and noninstitutionalised political participation in Western Europe. *West European Politics, 22(3)*, 1–21.

Kahne, J., & Middaugh, E. (2008). *Democracy for some: The civic opportunity gap in high school* (CIRCLE Working Paper 59). Medford, MA: CIRCLE.

Kahne, J., Middaugh, E., & Evans, C. (2008). *The civic potential of video games.* MacArthur Foundation. Retrieved from http://www.digitallearning.macfound.org

Klandermans, B. (1997). *The social psychology of protest.* Oxford: Blackwell Publishing.

Kymlicka, W. (1995). *Multicultural citizenship: A liberal theory of minority rights.* New York: Cambridge University Press.

Lenhart, A., Kahne, J., Middaugh, E., Macgill, A. R., Evans, C., & Vitak, J. (2008). *Teens, video games and civics*. Retrieved from http://www.pewinternet.org

Maffesoli, M. (1996). *The time of the tribes: The decline of individualism in mass society.* London: Sage Publications.

Markova, I. (2004). *Trust and democratic transition in post-communist Europe. Proceedings of the British Academy, 123.* Oxford: Oxford University Press.

McLuhan, M. (1964). *Understanding media: The extensions of man.* Cambridge, MA: MIT Press.

Morgan, W., & Streb, M. (2001). Building citizenship: How student voice in service-learning develops civic values. *Social Science Quarterly, 82(1)*, 154–169.

Nash, N. (2008). Future issues in socio-technical change for UK citizenship: The importance of "place." *Beyond Current Horizons review paper*, Challenge #2, Bristol: Futurelab.

Nussbaum, M. (1999). *Sex and social justice.* New York: Oxford University Press.

Nussbaum, N. (2008). Towards a globally sensitive patriotism. *Daedalus*, Summer, 78–93.

Orrill, R. (Ed.). (1997). *Education and democracy: Re-imagining liberal learning in America.* New York: College Entrance Examination Board.

Poortinga, W., & Pidgeon, N. F. (2003). *Public perceptions of risk, science and governance.* Norwich: University of East Anglia Press.

Potter, J., & Wetherell, M. (1987). *Discourse and social psychology.* Thousand Oaks, CA: Sage Publications.

Putnam, R. (2000). *Bowling alone: The collapse and revival of American community.* New York: Simon & Schuster.

Reich, J. (2008). Reworking the web, reworking the world: How Web 2.0 is changing our society. *Beyond Current Horizons review paper*, Challenge #2, Bristol: Futurelab.

Reicher, S., & Hopkins, N. (2001). *Self and nation: Categorisation, contestation and mobilisation.* Thousand Oaks, CA: Sage Publications.

Riley, S. (2008). Identity, community and selfhood: Understanding the self in relation to contemporary youth cultures. *Beyond Current Horizons review paper*, Challenge #2, Bristol: Futurelab.

Riley, S., Griffin, C., & Morey, Y. (2010). The case for "everyday politics": Evaluating neo-tribal theory as a way to understand alternative forms of political participation, using electronic dance music as an example. *Sociology. 44(2)*, 1–19.

Said, E. (1993). *Culture and imperialism.* New York: Alfred A. Knopf.

Salen, K. (2008). *The ecology of games.* Cambridge, MA: MIT Press.

Schwartz, B. (1990). The reconstruction of Abraham Lincoln. In D. Middleton & D. Edwards (Eds.), *Collective remembering.* Thousand Oaks, CA: Sage Publications.

Seider, S. (2008). *Literature, justice and resistance: Engaging adolescents from privileged groups in social action,* (Unpublished doctoral dissertation). Harvard Graduate School of Education, Cambridge, MA.

Seider, S. (2010). Teaching social justice in the suburbs. In A. Howard & R. Gaztambide-Fernandez (Eds.), *Ahead of the rest: Class privilege and educational advantage in the United States.* New York: Rowan and Littlefield.

Shaffer, D. W. (2006). *How computer games help children learn.* New York: Palgrave Macmillan.

Sigel, R., & Hoskins, M. (1981). *The political involvement of adolescents.* New Brunswick, NJ: Rutgers University Press.

Spencer, R. (2008). *Stealth Jihad: How radical Islam is subverting America without guns or bombs.* Washington, DC: Regnery Publishing.

Suarez-Orozco, C. (2004). Formulating identity in a globalised world. In M. M. Suarez-Orozco & D. B. Qin-Hilliard (Eds.), *Globalization: Culture and education in the new millennium* (pp. 173–202). Berkeley, CA: University of California Press.

Torney-Purta, J. (2009). International psychological research that matters for policy and practice. *American Psychologist, 64*, 822–837.

Torney-Purta, J., Schwille, J., & Amadeo, J. (1999). *Civic education across countries: Twenty-four national case studies from the IEA Civic Education project*. Amsterdam: International Association for the Evaluation of Educational Achievement (IEA).

Torney-Purta, J., Lehmann, R., Oswald, H., & Schultz, W. (2001). *Citizenship and education in twenty-eight countries: Civic knowledge and engagement at age fourteen*. Amsterdam: International Association for the Evaluation of Educational Achievement (IEA).

Torney-Purta, J., Wilkenfeld, B., & Barber, C. (2008). How adolescents in 27 countries understand, support and practice human rights. *Journal of Social Issues, 64(4)*, 857–880.

Turkle, S. (2004). The fellowship of the microchip: Global technologies as evocative objects. In M. Suarez-Orozco & D. B. Qin-Hilliard (Eds.), *Globalization: Culture and education in the new millennium* (pp. 97–113). Berkeley, CA: University of California Press.

Van Hoorn, J., Komlosi, A., Suchar, E., & Samuelson, D. (2000). *Adolescent development and rapid social change.* Albany, NY: SUNY Press.

Vass, E. (2008). New technology and habits of mind. *Beyond Current Horizons review paper*, Challenge #2, Bristol: Futurelab.

Verba, S., Schlozman, K. L., & Brady, H. E. (1995). *Voice and equality: Civic voluntarism in American politics.* Cambridge, MA: Harvard University Press.

Ververi, O. (2008). The civil society project. *Beyond Current Horizons review paper*, Challenge #2, Bristol: Futurelab.

Vygotsky, L. (1978). *Mind in society*. Cambridge, MA: Harvard University Press.

Wertsch, J. (1998). *Mind as action*. New York: Oxford University Press.

Westheimer, J., & Kahne, J. (2004). Educating the "good" citizen: Political choices and pedagogical goals. Retrieved from http://www.democraticdialogue.com/Ddpdfs/WestheimerKahnePS.pdf

Wetherell, M., Taylor, S., and Yates, S. J. (2001). *Discourse theory and practice.* Thousand Oaks, CA: Sage Publications.

Wilkenfeld, B. (2009). Does context matter? How the family, peer, school and neighborhood contexts relate to adolescents' civic engagement. (Working Paper #64) Medford, MA: CIRCLE at Tufts University.

Wolfe, T. (2003). Foreword. In S. McLuhan & D. Staines (Eds.), *Marshall McLuhan: Understanding me.* Cambridge, MA: MIT Press.

Yates, M. (1999). Community service and political-moral discussions among adolescents: A study of a mandatory school-based program in the United States. In M. Yates & J. Youniss (Eds.), *Roots of civic identity* (pp. 16–31). Cambridge: Cambridge University Press.

Youniss, J., McLellan, J. A., & Yates, M. (1997). What we know about engendering civic identity. *American Behavioral Scientist, 40*, 620–631.

Yuval-Davis, N., & Werbner, P. (1999). *Women, citizenship and difference.* London: Zed Books.

Zukin, C., Keeter, S., Andolina, M. W., Jenkins, K., & Della Carpini, M. X. (2006). *A new civic engagement? Political participation, civic life and the changing American citizen.* New York: Oxford University Press.

SECTION II

GROWING INTO CITIZENSHIP: DEVELOPMENT, SOCIALIZATION, AND DIVERSITY

RESEARCH ON THE development of civic engagement has blossomed in recent years as researchers in developmental psychology have joined political science and other disciplines in studying this topic. However, existing developmental theories have not been fully tapped and research has disproportionately focused on older youth. At some time periods, researchers may have focused too much attention on formal educational processes as the major influence on socialization. Furthermore, attention to development and socialization requires sensitivity to the increasing diversity of youth in the United States and many other countries. These chapters adopt a broadened perspective on development, socialization, and education addressing theory, the role of young people's developmental level, and other influences such as the media, school, politics, and families. All are considered in the context of cultural diversity. The authors attempt to address past deficiencies of research and policy and to develop a research agenda for studying the development of civic engagement into the twenty-first century.

The chapter by Wilkenfeld, Lauckhardt, and Torney-Purta discusses ways in which civic development is like other aspects of human development, especially cognitive and social development, and therefore may be examined under the lens of general theories in developmental science. These include Bandura, Kohlberg, Turiel, Selman, Erikson, and Bronfenbrenner; the chapter also discusses theories specific to youth development developed by Larson and Watts. More extensive attention to theory is necessary for the generation of stronger research questions and approaches to measurement.

The chapter by Metzger and Smetana reviews research on adolescents' reasoning about pro-social behavior and how its findings could inform civic involvement. Psychological research utilizing a social-cognitive perspective to examine adolescents' beliefs, reasoning about and interpretation of political issues, the social contract, democratic principles, and human rights is considered. Reasoning about civic responsibility and conceptualizations of the type of civic obligation inherent in various types of civic behavior are also relevant to engagement.

The chapter by Astuto and Ruck argues that early childhood is an underexamined age period providing a foundation for civic engagement. Young children develop executive functions and pro-social skills during quality play experiences that are critical to the development of later civic engagement. The early childhood classroom context is the first representation of the greater society for young children. It should be possible to construct classroom practices, curricula, and school policies to support the precursors of civic identity and engagement in young children.

The chapter by Finlay, Wray-Lake, and Flanagan addresses the implications of the current prolonged transition to adulthood for civic identity formation. Lifelong civic commitments are shaped by the institutional opportunities available as a generation comes of age. There is an institutional lacuna, especially for youth who do not attend four-year colleges. Evidence about the civic benefits from institutions such as four-year colleges, community colleges, community or youth organizations, and service or training programs points to new institutional models that are developmentally grounded.

The chapter by Flanagan, Stoppa, Syvertsen, and Stout explores the theme of trust and schools, drawing from research on trust between teachers, principals, and parents. It also considers the dynamics in schools that develop trusting dispositions among students. Particular features of school climates (student solidarity, teachers' insistence on a civil climate of mutual respect) are foundations for the younger generation's beliefs about people being fair and trustworthy. Stereotypes that parents hold about schools as unsafe spaces may have a negative impact on perceptions of democratic teaching practices.

The chapter by Levinson finds the civic empowerment gap in the United States as large and disturbing as the reading and math achievement gaps that have received significant attention. The chapter describes five approaches that could potentially lessen this civic gap for historically disenfranchised youth: reducing the dropout rate, improving civic education across K–12 education, engaging students in co-constructing empowering civic historical narratives, infusing experiential civic education throughout the curriculum, and providing powerful civic learning and engagement opportunities for urban teachers.

The chapter by McLeod, Shah, Hess, and Lee also focuses on the gap in participatory engagement between those with high and low levels of educational attainment. Non-college bound youth have lower levels of news use and political discussion, as well as civic participation. These gaps tend to widen from early to later adulthood, and Internet news audiences remain stratified in terms of education. Scholars and policy-makers increasingly recognize the substantial positive influences of both education and communication on youth socialization into public life.

The chapter by Bennett, Freelon, and Wells argues that young people have largely abandoned traditional news while they have become more enthusiastic in their consumption, production, and critique of online political information. There is a corresponding change from orientation toward established civic authorities (*dutiful citizenship*) to one that favors self-motivated and personally networked action (*actualizing citizenship*). However, the youth civic Web remains largely oriented toward dutiful citizenship and is out of step with the civic preferences of many young people.

The chapter by Jensen addresses the civic and political lives of immigrant youth in the United States including research from psychology, political science, sociology, and anthropology. Immigrant youth are similar to their native peers of comparable demographic characteristics in civic engagement. Having a strong cultural identity can serve as a conduit to immigrant youths' civic and political engagement. Furthermore, discrimination can be a catalyst for immigrant youth to enter the civic and political arena in order to counter injustices. Implications are drawn for policy and civil society.

The chapter by Seif examines Latina/o immigrant youth's civic engagement and activism. When socioeconomic variables are controlled for, immigrant youth exhibit rates of civic engagement that are comparable to non-immigrants. The schools that serve working class immigrant youth must be improved so the civic training reaches the standards of more affluent educational institutions. Undocumented youth face the contradiction of being included in public schools and excluded from the nation-state. This chapter makes a strong plea both for continuing research and for needed policy attention.

The chapter by Russell, Toomey, Crockett, and Laub continues the focus on disenfranchised youth by addressing lesbian, gay, bisexual, and transgender (LGBT) youth. School-based Gay-Straight Alliances (GSAs) are an example of how LGBT youth have organized and taken leadership roles in educational advocacy movements to create safe environments for themselves and their peers in schools. Youth voice in contemporary movements paves the way for future civic engagement among LGBT and allied straight youth. Implications for policy are drawn.

Development, socialization, and diversity form the core of research on youth, including youth civic engagement. These 11 chapters illustrate the diversity of topics and approaches to these three areas. Research on civic engagement from childhood through early adulthood shows the same robustness and breadth as research in any other topic related to this age group.

CHAPTER 8

The Relation between Developmental Theory and Measures of Civic Engagement in Research on Adolescents

BRITT WILKENFELD
University of Maryland

JAMES LAUCKHARDT
Fordham University

JUDITH TORNEY-PURTA
University of Maryland

ALTHOUGH RESEARCH ON civic engagement has increased in recent years, theory generation on the development of civic engagement has been less prolific. Theoretical foundations of other topics in developmental science, such as prosocial development or moral action and identities, have received greater attention (e.g., Colby & Damon, 1995; Hart, 2005). As a result, much of the research and measurement in the area of youth civic engagement has not been theoretically based. Insufficient theory from which to generate hypotheses can be problematic for a field of research. Furthermore, studies generally have been descriptive or correlational rather than longitudinal or experimental; there has been little empirical testing of hypotheses.

The purpose of the chapter is to discuss the ways in which civic development is like other aspects of human development and therefore may be examined under the lens of general theories in developmental science. The aim is to provide examples of developmental theory that relate to civic development and engagement in the first section of the chapter, and then to discuss the limited amount of theory that has been generated directly related to civic development. We will address the current disconnect between theory and measurement in this field and will describe a recent attempt to use theory in the early phases of an international civic engagement project and later in that project to apply developmental concepts to youth participation.

BACKGROUND

The surge in research on adolescent civic engagement can be attributed in part to the belief by some scholars that the participation of youth in society has decreased compared to previous generations (Putnam, 1996, 2000). However, other lines of research indicate a steady increase in youth volunteering since the 1970s and a recent increase in political activities such as voting and making political donations (National Conference on Citizenship, 2006). Although research on youth civic engagement has been on the rise, the absence of theoretically based research questions and measurement has hindered productive debate and the application of findings to practice.

Civic engagement is a part of young people's development that corresponds in important ways with other aspects of development, particularly its social and cognitive aspects. In this chapter we make the case for a reciprocal relation between theory generation in developmental science and civic engagement research. We start by reviewing several theories in developmental science and address their potential relevance to research on civic engagement. The theories were chosen based on their focus on cognitive and social domains of development, their specific discussion of adolescence, and their relevance to the civic domain. We discuss four cognitive and social theories (social cognitive theory, Kohlberg's theory of moral development, domain theory, and role taking theory), and also examine theories from the psychoanalytic and contextual perspectives (psychosocial theory and ecological systems theory, respectively). There are several developmental principles that all of these theories incorporate, even if they diverge in their specific theoretical assumptions or the details of the processes they describe:

1. Adolescents are active participants in their own development.
2. Development is bidirectional such that adolescents influence their environment just as the environment is having an influence on them; socialization is reciprocal.
3. Development is both continuous and discontinuous, is influenced by both learning and maturation, and occurs in a variety of settings.
4. Opportunities for development differ across the life span and for individuals growing up in different contexts.

In addition to the six developmental science theories mentioned above, we also analyze theories developed specifically for their potential contribution to developmental research on civic engagement. Finally, we consider the importance of theory for the generation of research questions and approaches to measurement.

Developmental theory is relevant to research in the field of civic engagement because of the value of understanding the processes behind changes in civic values, motivations, and identities during childhood and adolescence. Most research has emphasized adolescence, thus the field has really not grappled with civic development from childhood through late adolescence (or adulthood). While the adolescent period includes young people's transition into active political participation, there are likely to be precursors to participation. Understanding the mechanisms that underlie the connection between early development and later engagement is critical to designing programs and policies to promote civic development.

DEVELOPMENTAL THEORIES AND CIVIC ENGAGEMENT

Social Cognitive Theory

An early recognition that people learn and display certain behaviors through the observation of others is found in theories such as those of Miller and Dollard (1941). Conceptual frameworks guiding research in this era, including social learning theory, concentrated on the environmental influence on behavior, often discounting the role of thinking or cognition. Albert Bandura, a prominent social learning theorist, expanded on this approach by adding the missing cognitive component in his book *Social Learning Theory* in 1977. Social cognitive learning theory, as it was called beginning with his subsequent book in 1986, concentrates on the environment's influence on behavior but also pays particular attention to personal characteristics, cognitive factors, and affective factors in human development. Neither version of this theory is developmental in the strict sense of attending to age progression and change; Bandura assumes that the same social or social-cognitive learning principles apply at every age (Astuto et al., this volume; Finlay et al., this volume). However, social cognitive theory has been used in youth civic engagement research because concepts such as self-efficacy and observational learning in this theory are clearly relevant to youth civic engagement. These and other concepts will be discussed further in the next section.

The factor that Bandura (1989) believed to have the most significant influence on a person's behavior is his or her sense of self-efficacy. Self-efficacy is the confidence in one's ability to control and execute the actions required to deal with current and future situations (Bandura, 1995, 1997). Incorporated into self-efficacy is the perceived ability to take actions that result in desired outcomes and prevent undesired ones (Bandura, Caprara, Barbaranelli, Pastorelli, & Regalia, 2001). There are four principal sources serving as the basis for self-efficacy judgments: performance mastery experiences, judgments of capabilities in comparison with social models, social influences and persuasion, and physiological and emotional states (Bandura, 1995). These sources are likely to contribute to the development of civic or political efficacy in addition to a more globalized efficacy.

The manner in which the four principal sources mentioned above can contribute to the development of civic or political efficacy is illustrated here with the example of an adolescent leading a protest against a school board's decision to close a school. If the protest, and the associated pressure on the school board, contributes to the abandonment of the board's plan to close the school, this successful outcome will contribute to the adolescent's belief that her civic participation can make a difference (an example of performance mastery experience). Perhaps other community members or students attempted to organize efforts to sway the school board but could not mobilize people or initiate change. The young person was successful and therefore would evaluate herself as highly capable in comparison to others, which would be likely to contribute to higher efficacy (an example of self-judgment in comparison to social norms). Receiving positive feedback from other young people and adults would reinforce feelings of self-efficacy. Feedback could also come in the form of others choosing the individual to lead future protests (reflecting social influences and persuasion). Finally, the emotional "high" from successful civic participation would increase positive feelings and confidence, since physiological and emotional states also contribute to efficacy judgments. All of these sources of self-efficacy judgments are consistent with the proposition that an individual feels more efficacious about being able to complete a future task upon successful completion of a current one (Bandura, 2001). See Beaumont (this volume) for an extended application of Bandura's theory to the growth of political efficacy in college students. Specific kinds of civic engagement such as service learning have been shown empirically to relate positively to later civic engagement (Astin, Vogelgesang, Ikeda, & Yee, 2000; Hart, Donnelly, Youniss, & Atkins, 2007; Youniss & Yates, 1997, 1999). It is likely that efficacy is one of the major links between early and later civic participation.

Groups of people can also feel efficacious about their change efforts. Bandura describes collective efficacy as "a group's shared belief in its conjoint capabilities to organize and execute the courses of action required to produce given levels of attainment" (Bandura, 1997, p. 477). Building on the concept of individual self-efficacy, collective efficacy represents the collective beliefs and power of group members to produce desired outcomes. A strong sense of self-efficacy plays a significant role in perceived collective efficacy (Fernández-Ballesteros, Díez-Nicolás, Caprara, Barbaranelli, & Bandura, 2002). Collective efficacy is especially relevant to civic engagement in that being active as a citizen usually involves working with others to achieve a common goal.

One way in which youth are given the opportunity to work with others to achieve a common goal is through community service. Through schools, religious institutions, and community organizations, young people can work together to effect change in issues such as public health or environmental preservation. The experience of working with others and developing a sense of collective efficacy in addition to individual self-efficacy has been found to be important to civic development (Pasek, Feldman, Romer, & Jamieson, 2008). More research is needed to differentiate the importance of self-efficacy and collective efficacy, however.

Bandura (1997) also developed theory about political efficacy, defined as the belief and confidence that one can use political action to produce desired outcomes. Political efficacy is comprised of internal political efficacy, which refers to one's perceived ability to influence political decisions, and external political efficacy, referring to perceptions of the response of the government to individuals' efforts (see Beaumont, this volume). It is important to note the connection that Bandura (1997) makes between the development of political efficacy in a young person and a young person's sense of efficacy to influence the behaviors of adults in institutions of which they are a part (e.g., schools, community centers, and religious institutions). Bandura claims that if children feel that they are able to influence the actions of adults in societal institutions, they may generalize that feeling of efficacy to politics and feel that they can have an influence on government as well (Bandura, 1997). One reason that voter turnout among young people historically is lower than other age groups may be that they do not feel efficacious about their vote; youth believe that nothing will change as a result of their choosing one candidate over another (Delli Carpini, 2000). However, voter turnout among 18- to 29-year-olds increased in the 2008 U.S. presidential election (CIRCLE, 2008), indicating that various attempts to mobilize young people were effective. By specifically reaching out to young voters, the campaigns were sending a message that politicians listened to young people, which may have increased their sense of external political efficacy.

Bandura (1986) has asserted that learning occurs through direct interactions with, or indirect observations of, others' behavior and the associated consequences. Observational learning, also termed modeling, is a way to convey social norms, values, and other thoughts, feelings, and behaviors. Modeling plays an important role in socializing because it affects attitudes and emotional dispositions toward others, toward issues, and regarding the worth of certain behaviors (Bandura, 1989). Behavior can be intentionally observed and then manifested in an individual's behavior. Even when explicit observation is not occurring, however, expectations of behavior are often cognitively processed and internalized (Bandura, 1986). Intentional and unintentional observational learning is especially important to recognize in the socialization of civic behavior. Some of the early political socialization studies employed questions about the child's perspective on whose attitudes he or she was copying (Hess & Torney, 1967, reissued 2006); the internalization of parents' attitudes was part of what the authors called the identification model of political socialization. Other researchers interviewed both parents and children to identify attitude similarities (Jennings & Niemi, 1974). These and more recent studies have found evidence for political modeling, including findings that children's and adolescents' civic behavior and attitudes tend to be consistent with their parents' behavior and attitudes (Andolina, Jenkins, Zukin, & Keeter, 2003; Hart, Atkins, Markey, & Youniss, 2004; Zaff, Malanchuk, Michelsen, & Eccles, 2003).

Mapping the construct of modeling onto youth civic engagement, Torney-Purta (1995) described the process by which political socialization occurs through interactions with parents and peers. Adolescents start with cognitive structures (based on prior experience, biological development, and other factors), but cognition is changed through exposure to new ideas or perspectives, reading about political topics, and discussion of political and social issues. Through social relationships, adolescents participate in the collaborative construction of knowledge, meaning that cognitive structures are created and changed when young people interact with others. For example, an adolescent may have an established stance on an environmental issue such as global warming. Her stance, that global warming is not a serious problem, could be based on her own experience (e.g., the lack of any drastic change in weather in her town) and exposure to her parents' attitudes (e.g., overhearing criticism of scientists as alarmists). Discussion and debate in the classroom, exposure to other students' perspectives, and reflection over different sides of the issue could lead to the adolescent developing a new perspective. Through interactions with others and exposure to new ideas she has created new cognitive structures. Of course, some beliefs will remain stable and continue to serve as the lens through which new information is interpreted. Therefore, political socialization is not merely imposed onto young people, but rather youth are active participants in the construction of their knowledge, political ideals, and values.

Reflection plays an important role in both directly reinforced learning and observational learning, and therefore is relevant to civic engagement. As students reflect on the impact that they personally have or have observed in a certain situation, they may feel more efficacious in similar situations. Alternatively, critical reflection may contribute to a lack of efficacy through cynicism or frustration. Not only has reflection in a civic engagement activity been shown to support Bandura's views about social cognition (Wilkenfeld & Torney-Purta, 2005), but the reflection that takes place in activities such as community service has also been linked to the impact of service participation on moral development (Youniss & Yates, 1999). Furthermore, adults who participate in the reflection process also serve as coaches and models. Hence, the reflection component of social cognitive theory also has implications for research on civic education and policies to promote it. It suggests the importance of asking research respondents explicitly about links between experiences such as volunteering and classroom discussion of community problems, for example.

Theories of Moral Development

Kohlberg's perspectives. Theories of moral development can also inform the study of civic and political engagement. In his developmental theory, Lawrence Kohlberg (1976) proposed that moral functioning involves the understanding of justice and fairness, and that this understanding is the basis for distinguishing right from wrong. Moral development occurs throughout the life span with progress through six stages of moral reasoning. Stage theories offer a particular view of development. Movement from one stage to the next can be considered growth or progress but may also be conceptualized as a rejection and reconstruction of earlier views. Through an awareness of its contradictions and inadequacies, the logic of an existing stage is rejected and a new stage is created.

At first glance, Kohlberg's (1969, 1976) theory of moral development may not seem directly relevant to the study of civic and political engagement because civic engagement is not believed to develop in stages. However, reasoning about moral issues bears some similarity to reasoning about political issues. When reasoning about complex issues, there are seldom clear choices, at least for individuals who make informed and reasoned political choices rather than following the lead of parents or peers or the dictates of a particular party. Therefore moral reasoning (as well as reasoning in general) seems relevant to certain political choices. Interesting lines of future inquiry include whether moral and political development occur in parallel, and whether moral reasoning drives political behavior (or vice versa).

Kohlberg's measurement of moral development also provides guidance regarding the measurement of civic or political development. In particular, the dilemmas used in research on moral reasoning suggest ways to study political reasoning. The researcher could prepare a political or civic dilemma, for example, about citizens' rights or about loyalty to a nation. Early political socialization research indicated that younger children are more likely than older children to agree that it is acceptable for a political leader to lie to another country if the lie protects the country's citizens (Hess & Torney, 1967, reissued 2006). Using scenarios modeled on those in research on moral development, children and adolescents of different ages could be given a scenario in which a political leader has lied about a public matter and claims that it is because of a desire to protect the people in that nation. Young people could be asked to give their reasoning about whether this was or was not the right thing to do and why. In other words, Kohlberg's theory of moral development could inform civic development research by providing an approach to measurement as well as to studying differences in political reasoning between age groups.

Rest, Narvaez, Thoma, and Bebeau (2000) take a neo-Kohlbergian perspective in their assertion that moral development can be understood in terms of schemas rather than stages. Similar to Kohlberg's (1969) stages, moral schemas allow for change when new knowledge is acquired and new experiences affect a person's view on specific issues. However, transitions between schemas are more gradual than the discrete movement from one stage to the next as postulated by Kohlberg. The three schemas proposed by Rest et al. (2000) are personal interest ("what is best for me"), maintaining norms (guided by societal norms, rules, and obeying authority), and post-conventional (enhanced and flexible understanding of societal and moral constructs). Using the previous example, an individual's stance on whether a leader should have lied might be the same throughout adolescence, but the reasoning could change depending on the particular schema reflected. An adolescent who reflects the personal interest schema would reason that the leader was justified as long as the adolescent and his or her family remained safe and secure. The adolescent's reasoning under the norm maintenance schema might involve a belief that leaders have so much authority that their lies are not to be judged in the same way as those of private citizens. Using the post-conventional schema, a more complex balancing of the value of truthfulness against the protection of the common good might be made.

Nearly 40 years ago the work of Adelson and his colleagues took a similar approach (Adelson & Beall, 1970). They assessed adolescents' conceptions of law and government using hypothetical scenarios set on a desert island where residents were presented with social problems to solve in a setting that lacked established laws and government. The researchers noted that young adolescents were especially likely to express an obedience orientation toward law, while a pragmatic or popular-will orientation was more common among older adolescents.

Research on character education or service learning has attended to moral development processes more fully than has research in civic or political education. Assessment of the reasoning that characterizes responses to hypothetical dilemmas could make a greater contribution to understanding the development of civic values, attitudes, and behaviors than it has in the past.

Domain theory. In a further departure from Kohlberg's (1969) theory of moral development, Eliot Turiel has proposed that moral development does not occur in stages; rather it is through distinct conceptual domains that moral and social reasoning develop. Instead of a global understanding of the social world that is distinctly different in each stage, domain-specific knowledge develops simultaneously in distinct domains (Turiel, 1983). According to domain theory (Turiel, 1983, 1998), people's judgments of right and wrong, or of appropriate and inappropriate behavior, are affected by whether the judgment falls in one of three domains: moral, social convention, or personal jurisdiction. The moral domain involves fairness, rights, and the welfare of others. Judgments of social conventions pertain to societal-based regularities and expectations that promote group functioning. Personal jurisdiction involves issues of personal choice and agency.

Researchers have begun to inquire about whether adolescents' conceptions of civic engagement fall in the moral, social convention, or personal jurisdiction domain (Metzger & Smetana, this volume). The appropriate domain will likely vary based on the type of civic engagement and level of individual commitment. A major contribution of domain theory to research on civic engagement is that measures used in studies based on domain theory (e.g., semi-structured interviews and story-reaction methods) might be useful in surfacing information about the processes behind civic-related decisions (Killen, 2007).

Theory of Role Taking

Robert Selman's (1976) theory of role taking is also relevant to civic engagement research because, as with the previous theories, it takes a social cognitive perspective (Selman et al., this volume). Additionally, this theory has been the basis for exploring measures of psychosocial maturity to be used to evaluate character education programs (Schulz, Selman, & LaRusso, 2003). Perspective taking is a key concept in this theory and in civic engagement. A coordinated understanding of the different perspectives (of individuals, groups, or even society as a whole) is important for young people when they participate in processes such as interpersonal negotiation. This was clear from Selman's early work (1976, 1980) and is even more explicit in his recent book (2003). Being civically or politically active inevitably involves interacting with others who take different positions on issues and resolving conflicts that may result.

The third and fourth levels of the development of perspective discussed by Selman (1976, 1980, 2003) are especially relevant to civic engagement.

As development advances to these levels, adolescents have the ability to view their own thoughts, feelings, and behavior from the other's perspective. They also recognize that others can do the same. Finally, adolescents can also "distinguish between one's own point of view and a more generalized perspective that might be taken by an 'average' member of the group" (Muuss, 1982, p. 516). Since civic activism often involves groups of people with both common and divergent goals or perspectives, this ability is critical to the development of civic engagement.

At advanced levels of development, the individual also has the ability to take a societal perspective. An individual with this ability can step back and understand the various points of view being presented and how they affect others in the group. Being able to understand that members of a group share mutual as well as individualized goals is among the qualities of an effective citizen. This understanding also contributes to individuals feeling that they are responsible for doing their part as active citizens.

Selman's theory of role taking and social awareness (1980, 2003) delineates the development of several abilities that are important for civic engagement. Researchers could address ways to specify, refine, and expand these developing competencies to make them more specific to the political domain. The fact that a survey instrument has been developed relating to psychosocial maturity as formulated in this theory is a helpful first step.

Psychosocial Theory

Another developmental theory that could inform examination of adolescents' civic engagement is Erik Erikson's (1968) psychosocial theory of development. Psychosocial theory encompasses life-span development and each stage represents a specific crisis or tension that requires resolution (either positive or negative) before the individual advances to the next stage. Development is seen as cumulative; therefore, the positive or negative resolution of a crisis affects later stages and functioning.

All eight life stages proposed by Erikson have implications for the development of civic engagement. Three specific stages are discussed here, starting with the crisis experienced in infancy—trust versus mistrust. Most infants are able to establish a trusting relationship with their parents, which will lay the foundation for future trusting relationships. Flanagan and colleagues (this volume) have described social trust as an important factor contributing to youth civic engagement. To some extent, the trust developed early in life may underlie social trust in adolescence, either directly or indirectly as an extension of social trust in childhood. Understanding more about this connection may explain the strong association between parental behavior and attitudes and the level of youth civic engagement.

According to Erikson, school-aged children are at the developmental stage in which they must face the task of industry versus inferiority. The child tries to develop a sense of self-worth by refining skills and developing feelings of efficacy. Understanding what happens at this stage could aid in understanding factors that contribute to a child's sense of competence and agency in the civic domain. Providing children with age-appropriate activities that involve altruistic behavior in the community could assist in developing a sense that one's actions can have positive results, which is the core of a sense of industry.

The last stage discussed here is adolescence, the developmental stage in which identity versus diffusion is the issue. Adolescents explore multiple roles and identities in an effort to define themselves. Political and civic identity has, however, rarely been studied from a psychosocial perspective. Erikson (1958) mentions political identity as the individual's sense of connectedness with others and an investment in a collective future. As Youniss and Yates eloquently stated, "As youth focus inwardly to find self-sameness (continuity with the past), they must also look outward to form relationships with society's traditions" (1997, p. 22). Therefore, a pivotal component of identity formation is an understanding of one's role in society. The development of a general identity in terms of worldview and values may translate to feelings about society, but development of a specific political identity is a more critical component of civic engagement. Although a clear, empirically supported distinction has not been made between generalized identity and civic or political identity, there are studies that attempt to understand youth identity issues as they relate to civics and politics (Flanagan, Syvertsen, Mitra, Oliver, & Sethuraman, 2005; Goossens, 2001; Torney-Purta, Lehmann, Oswald, & Schulz, 2001).

Erikson's (1968) theory of development takes a life-span perspective and suggests directions for examining the precursors of adolescent civic engagement. Additionally, the developmental crises faced at each stage suggest age-appropriate measures. Psychosocial theory also offers some guidance in designing measures of three concepts important in civic engagement: trust, sense of industry, and identity. Empirical research is needed to determine the extent to which psychosocial conflicts faced by the individual are reflected in the civic domain, however.

Ecological Systems Theory

In a contextual theory of development, Urie Bronfenbrenner (1979) describes the multiple interacting influences on development throughout the life span, ranging from micro- to macro-level factors. Ecological systems theory posits that individuals learn and develop as a result of multiple interacting systems of influence over time (Bronfenbrenner, 1979, 2005). In addition to the ongoing interaction between the individual and the systems of influence, the systems also are interdependent with each other. Indeed, development is affected by the direct influence of each system, as well as the indirect influences of distal systems operating through more proximal systems. The nested systems of the ecological model include the individual's microsystem, mesosystem, exosystem, and macrosystem.

The system that is most proximal to the adolescent is the microsystem, which includes individuals and societal institutions that directly interact with youth through interpersonal relationships and recurring patterns of activity (Bronfenbrenner, 1989). Because of their proximity to the individual, components of the microsystem directly affect development. Different aspects of the microsystem environment are more salient depending on the age of the individual. For young children, the family and home have the largest influence, but as children grow older and explore their surroundings they experience additional influences, including school and peers. The influence of each context may change over time, especially given interactions with other contexts. An initial microsystem that influences civic development is the family. Some research on civic engagement has emphasized the role of family socialization early in life (Flanagan & Sherrod, 1998). If parents are active in civic pursuits and are involved in the democratic process, their children are more likely to be involved as well (McIntosh, Hart, & Youniss, 2007). It may also be the case that at a young age, children are given the opportunity to participate in certain family processes much like adolescents and adults have the opportunity to participate in the decision-making processes in society. Other components of the microsystem are associated with youth civic engagement, including peer groups (Zaff et al., 2003), schools (Torney-Purta, Barber, & Wilkenfeld, 2007), and youth organizations (Hart & Kirshner, 2009).

The interactions between individuals and settings of the microsystem make up the adolescent's mesosystem (Bronfenbrenner, 1989). In the mesosystem, relationships between multiple settings have the potential for an additional influence on development. For example, the connection between parents and the school can enhance positive outcomes. Parental involvement in the school may provide additional opportunities for learning outside the classroom, such as field trips to the state capitol building or city hall. Some qualitative research has also identified conflict between microsystems, for example, the views of civic processes found in school textbooks and everyday life experiences in the family and neighborhood (Rubin, 2007).

The exosystem also involves the interaction between individuals and settings; however, only one component of the relationship is from the adolescent's microsystem. Since a necessary requirement for being contained in the exosystem is that one of the aspects is not in a person's microsystem, the influence of relationships and processes in the exosystem on development is indirect (Bronfenbrenner, 1989). A frequently mentioned exosystem is the connection between an adolescent's parents and the parents' workplace; however, the connection between an adolescent's school and the neighborhood in which the school is located also relates to adolescents' outcomes, including civic attitudes and behavior (Wilkenfeld, 2009). Also included in the exosystem are local school boards, community groups, and public policies that affect youth through their school and families (e.g., state policies regarding the maximum income level for students to receive free lunch at school or state curriculum frameworks in social studies).

The most remote system of influence on adolescent development is the macrosystem. The macrosystem includes the overarching attitudes and ideologies that characterize the broader social context and frame other systems of influence. Although the effect is indirect, these larger societal processes permeate all stages and domains of development because they are by definition a "societal blueprint" (Bronfenbrenner, 1989, p. 228). The macrosystem is especially relevant to the study of civic development. A collectivist society may place specific emphasis on helping others and being involved in one's community as opposed to an individualistic society, which may promote concern for individual wishes or needs. Indeed, research has found country differences in outcomes such as adolescents' civic commitment (Flanagan, Bowes, Jonsson, Csapo, & Sheblanova, 1998). Even more obvious, however, is how the structure of government within a society can impact an individual's knowledge base and ability to become civically active. In a study examining 27 countries (utilizing data from the International Association for the Evaluation of Educational Achievement [IEA] Civic Education Study), adolescents in countries whose governments were active in international human rights dialogue had greater knowledge and understanding of the United Nations and the Convention on the Rights of the Child than those in countries where the government was less active in this international discourse (Torney-Purta, Wilkenfeld, & Barber, 2008).

Each of the systems described by Bronfenbrenner (1979) plays a significant role in civic development, but the interaction between the systems offers the most promising opportunities for new research on civic engagement. For example, a particular community may not provide an individual with opportunities to become civically involved, but other aspects of the individual's microsystem may provide such opportunities, for example, by joining with parents in volunteer activities. The interactions between these systems of influence and their relation to civic engagement have rarely been systematically studied. Use of Bronfenbrenner's (1979) theory also promotes multidisciplinary research in that different disciplines have traditionally studied the different levels of influence. Research on civic engagement would benefit from a multidisciplinary approach that incorporates concepts and theories from psychology, sociology, political science, anthropology, and economics, as well as social work and education.

The theories discussed in this section provide foundations on which theories of civic development might be formulated. Although research on civic engagement could benefit from concepts and measurement inspired by the theories discussed here, these perspectives are infrequently found in research on civic and political development. The theories discussed in the next section pertain specifically to the development of civic engagement.

THEORIES SPECIFIC TO CIVIC ENGAGEMENT

Theories about development in social and cognitive domains are well established, but few have been applied to the investigation of civic development. In contrast, there are two theories that directly address the civic domain, but they are in the early stages of elaboration and use by researchers. In this section, we discuss these two theories: Larson's work with colleagues on a theory of motivational change and engagement (Pearce & Larson, 2006; Wood, Larson, & Brown, 2009) and Watts's psychological theory of sociopolitical development (Watts, Griffith, & Abdul-Adil, 1999; Watts, Williams, & Jagers, 2003). These theories are not central in developmental science because the scope of their application is different.

Theory of Motivational Change

Pearce and Larson (2006) utilized interviews and a grounded theory approach to address the need for theory in understanding the motivation behind youth participation in and commitment to civic action. Their work focuses on linking profiles of organizations with experiences of youth that promote youth participation (such as peer interaction and leader support). The theory, developed primarily from qualitative data, stresses that participation in youth programs fosters feelings of self-reliance and responsibility and gives adolescents the opportunity to exercise individual choice and fulfill clearly stated expectations (Larson, Pearce, Sullivan, & Jarrett, 2007; Wood et al., 2009).

In some of their studies, the researchers found evidence for a three-stage engagement process. First, the youth have to be present in the setting, whether it is required or of their own volition. Second, they need to feel a personal connection to the organization's mission, and third, the activities in which they participate need to generate intrinsic motivation. This approach to theory development suggests ways to operationalize different aspects of civic action involved in youth participation in organizations and programs, as well as providing information to guide the development of a set of constructs to be included in assessments. Theoretically based empirical research can then be used to revise and more fully develop the theory.

Theory of Sociopolitical Development

In the second theory of civic engagement, developed by Watts and colleagues (Watts et al., 1999, 2003), the researchers define sociopolitical development as "the evolving understanding of the political, economic, cultural, and other systemic forces that shape society and one's status in it, and the associated process of growth in the relevant knowledge, analytical skills, and emotional faculties necessary to engage in political activity" (Watts, Armstrong, Cartman, & Guessous, 2008). This theory was developed from a liberation psychology perspective (also drawing from the cognitive psychology and spirituality literatures).

Each of the five stages delineated in the theory incorporates the concept of critical consciousness, because of its perceived contribution to sociopolitical development (Watts et al., 1999, 2003). Critical consciousness is defined conceptually in a way that distinguishes between the mechanisms and outcomes of oppression (Freire, 1990). It is a process that involves critically analyzing socially constructed norms and beliefs, and associated institutions. Additionally, the theory suggests that spirituality in the form of belief in a higher power can play a supportive role for an individual and can provide the motivation to become an advocate for change (Watts et al., 1999).

The theory of sociopolitical development is more developmental than some other empowerment theories in community psychology because of its premise that the impact of events on individuals is cumulative over time. The chronology of this process is represented within the five stages laid out by the theory. The first stage of sociopolitical development is the acritical stage. Persons in this stage believe that there are minimal differences in resources based on group membership and that individuals have complete control over their place in society. The second stage of sociopolitical development is the adaptive stage. Individuals in this stage are able to recognize that there may be institutional asymmetry but choose to adopt a defeatist attitude. The precritical stage is the third stage, at which point individuals become more concerned about the asymmetries and inequalities that exist and correspondingly less complacent. In the fourth stage of sociopolitical development, the critical stage, individuals have a desire to learn more about the inequalities in society and come to realize that activism and advocacy are necessary to combat these injustices. In the fifth and final stage of sociopolitical development, the liberation stage, involvement in social action and community actions stimulates the awareness of oppression (Watts et al., 1999, 2003).

Watts and colleagues (1999) suggest a series of key questions designed to enhance consciousness and promote the movement of the individual through the stages. For example, young people in early stages can be asked to consider why affluent children are allowed to take their books home from school while impoverished children cannot. In higher stages young people are asked what they can do to confront systemic problems of injustice.

In order to elaborate the theory of sociopolitical development, Watts et al. (1999) conducted interviews with African American males, a population that has historically experienced oppression. The researchers found that critical consciousness increased among the young men who participated in a particular program. Key action questions were asked of the participants in order to facilitate progression through the five stages (discussed above). Unfortunately, the researchers were not able to determine which factors actually contribute to critical consciousness, or whether or not critical consciousness does in fact lead to civic action. However, the empirical results allowed the investigators to more clearly define the social analysis and worldview portions of their theory.

Watts and colleagues (2008) describe four elements of a conceptual model: a worldview and social analysis, a sense of agency, awareness of the opportunity structure, and behavior representing societal involvement. An individual's analysis of society ranges from the notion that people get what they deserve due to their own actions and pursuit of opportunities (stage 1), to an acknowledgement of social institutions that influence individuals' lives (stage 3). Watts et al. (2003) posit that increased awareness of social injustices increases the likelihood of social activism. However, the relationship between knowledge and awareness of social injustice and actually taking action is moderated by a sense of agency and the opportunity structure for action (Watts et al., 2003). As an individual's sense of agency and the available resources to take action increase, the relation between social analysis and social involvement is postulated to become stronger.

The work of Watts and colleagues in attempting to understand the role of critical consciousness in civic development takes a different direction from the other theories presented here. The empirical work associated with it is at a relatively early stage, however.

This section provided examples of the use of specific theories to guide research on civic engagement. The associated research illustrates the complicated interplay between theory and empirical research that is essential to growth of a new research area. With the exception of these two theories, there has been little theory generation specifically dealing with civic and political development. The perceived inadequacy of relevant theories results in studies not being consistently guided by theories or even by well-explicated conceptual frameworks.

MEASUREMENT OF CIVIC AND POLITICAL DEVELOPMENT

Theories incorporate concepts or constructs that are linked to each other, and measures are the operationalization of those constructs. To date, researchers have assessed a wide array of civic behaviors and attitudes. However, because there has been little common measurement across studies (in part because measures have not been theoretically based), the empirical landscape is not coherent. Flanagan and Faison (2001), Sherrod and Lauckhardt (2009), and Torney-Purta (2002) have each proposed that there are multiple components of civic engagement. However, there is insufficient evidence about which basic factors underlie civic behaviors and attitudes. Identifying these underlying factors is essential for understanding the process of development in this area.

In the first half of this chapter, we described several developmental theories and made recommendations about how the concepts and assumptions of each could inform measurement of civic engagement. In this section we describe research that is methodologically strong but less firmly grounded in theory.

Flanagan, Syvertsen, and Stout (2007) developed a measure that assessed a range of behaviors, attitudes, and opinions related to civic engagement and civic knowledge. The measure combined original items with items from other instruments, such as the California Civic Index (Kahne, Middaugh, & Schutjer-Mance, 2005), the Civic Engagement Questionnaire (Keeter, Zukin, Andolina, & Jenkins, 2002), and the Civic Education Study survey (Torney-Purta et al., 2001). Flanagan et al. (2007) used the combined measure in a cross-sectional study of youth aged 12 to 18 years.

Principal components analysis (PCA) was used to determine what dimensions were assessed, and structural equation modeling (SEM) was then used to test for latent constructs. The PCA and SEM analyses revealed 45 underlying constructs related to civic engagement. These constructs were then grouped into the following 14 categories: civic behaviors, attitudes toward elected officials and government, conventional civic engagement, alternative civic engagement, political efficacy, attitudes regarding equality and injustice, conception of types of citizens, parents' civic engagement, political discourse, values, media consumption, school climate, personal beliefs and trust, and knowledge of government and electoral politics (Flanagan et al., 2007).

This study made important contributions to the measurement of civic engagement. The researchers incorporated items from previous research, provided evidence of good psychometric properties, and demonstrated underlying constructs of civic engagement. The drawback is that theory did not explicitly guide the choice of items on the measure, or predictions about the constructs. However, it is clear that some of the civic constructs identified statistically relate to constructs discussed by developmental theorists: political efficacy (Bandura), equality and injustice (Kohlberg, Turiel, and Watts), and school climate (Bronfenbrenner), to name a few. Furthermore, as is true for most research in this field, the sample studied consisted entirely of adolescents, so the study offers little guidance for measurement at younger ages.

Andolina and colleagues (Andolina, Jenkins, & Keeter, 2002; Andolina et al., 2003) have not explicitly articulated a theory of civic engagement, but their empirical work also has the potential to lead to theory development. In a multiphase multi-method study of civic engagement among 15- to 25-year-olds, the researchers created a measure of youth civic engagement based on qualitative and quantitative data. They conducted focus groups to hear young people's thoughts about civic engagement, including opinions and definitions of commonly used terms in the field, such as citizenship, volunteering, and community (see Torney-Purta, Amadeo, & Andolina, this volume). This information was then used to develop a measure to assess these constructs. After piloting with telephone and Internet surveys, the final instrument was a survey of civic and political engagement. Constructs that emerged include (but are not limited to): competence for civic action, political voice, expectations for engagement in electoral politics, expectations for unconventional political engagement, and alternative ways of expressing political voice. However, as with Flanagan et al. (2007), Andolina et al. (2002, 2003) did not rely on theory to guide their measurement development.

This approach to measurement development, while time consuming, offers a promising approach for future development of measures. However, the starting place should be theory followed by qualitative and quantitative data collection. The approach could also be applied to research with young children since there is relatively little information on the civic outcomes of children (with no large-scale studies since Hess & Torney, 1967, reissued 2006; and Moore, Lare, & Wagner, 1985). Understanding how elementary school children conceive of what it means to be a citizen is an important first step for research on school-aged children. Examining what teachers and parents believe important to teach children about citizenship is another potentially useful strategy. Focus groups of parents, teachers, and researchers may be a productive approach to understanding civic engagement at earlier ages than adolescence. These types of efforts may be important to the development of age-appropriate assessments of civic engagement, and would contribute to our understanding of the early precursors of civic engagement (Astuto & Ruck, this volume).

While the measurement efforts described in this section represent scientifically sound approaches that have generated psychometrically valid assessments, they often refer only tangentially to a theoretical foundation.

The combination of theory and methodological rigor has the potential to drive and advance research in the field of youth civic engagement.

AN INTERNATIONAL STUDY OF ADOLESCENTS' CIVIC ENGAGEMENT: THEORY, METHODOLOGY, AND ANALYSIS

Using Theory to Inform Design and Measurement in Civic Engagement Research

In one of the few studies to examine national differences in civic engagement among adolescents, Torney-Purta et al. (2001) assessed 14-year-olds in 28 countries (and 17-year-olds in 16 countries in a related study; Amadeo, Torney-Purta, Lehmann, Husfeldt, & Nikolova, 2002). Cross-cultural research demands careful attention to measurement, and the rigorous consensus-building process in this study ensured the appropriate meaning of the instruments in all participating countries.

Torney-Purta and a group of international colleagues (Torney-Purta et al., 2001) implemented this two-phased cross-sectional study of 14-year-olds, the IEA Civic Education Study (CIVED). The first phase involved an in-depth investigation into the nature of civic education in 24 countries, including national case studies and interviews with national experts and leaders in education. Based on qualitative data collected during this phase, it was determined that there were a number of content topics that were deemed to be essential for 14-year-olds to understand across the participating nations. With consultation from individuals from six countries, these topics were classified into three larger content domains: the meaning of democracy and democratic institutions (including citizenship), national identity and international relations, and issues of social cohesion and diversity. Two instruments (a test and a survey) were designed to cover content within each of these domains. These instruments and related items from other sources can be found on a web site developed by the Education Commission of the States (n.d.).

During the second phase of the study, researchers developed the assessment and survey through pre-piloting and piloting. The final assessment measures students' knowledge of fundamental democratic principles and skills in applying civic knowledge to interpreting political materials. The second instrument is a survey of students' attitudes toward civic issues, conceptions of democracy and citizenship, attitudes toward immigrants and minority groups, patriotic feelings, sense of political efficacy, and expected civic participation. Items reflecting all three content domains (discussed above) were included, and 20 scales were developed utilizing confirmatory factor analysis and item response theory. Additionally, this study included a teacher survey and an administrator survey, obtaining different perspectives about civic engagement and civic education.

The researchers for the international study collaboratively developed a theoretical framework that guided the study's design and measurement. This was called the Octagon Model (Torney-Purta et al., 2001, p. 21). It incorporated concepts from ecological systems theory, especially elements of the macrosystem such as political institutions and the country's international position (Bronfenbrenner, 1989), and ideas about legitimate peripheral participation from situated learning theory (Lave & Wenger, 1991). From the study's inception these theories informed its design, research questions, and measures. As the study progressed, the qualitative data from the national case studies became a somewhat stronger influence on the content of the multiple-choice achievement test questions. This was in part to ensure that each participating nation could recognize its own expectations and aims for civic education in the achievement test that students took. However, many of the topics of attitudinal questions in the survey reflected dimensions of the Octagon Framework (e.g., attitudes toward immigrants, attitudes toward one's nation, and trust in political institutions). A post-hoc attempt to apply concepts from several developmental theories to these data in order to understand youth civic engagement was conducted several years later; this is discussed further in the next section.

Using Theoretical Concepts in Secondary Analysis of Civic Engagement Data

Psychological theories have generally been absent from the study of service learning as a type of civic engagement just as they have been ignored more generally. In this section, we give a brief example of the application of concepts from multiple theoretical perspectives to the measurement of civic engagement, though it is a post-hoc examination. This particular analysis examined data from four countries from the IEA Civic Education Study (Chile, Denmark, England, and the United States) to look at the effects of volunteering and of learning in school about community problems on several civic engagement outcomes.

In formulating the analysis, Torney-Purta, Amadeo, and Richardson (2007) began by constructing a chart of concepts derived from three of the theorists discussed above (Erikson, Bandura, and Watts) and from Lave and Wenger. The researchers identified common concepts across theories that could guide analyses of civic engagement.

The first concept was trust or social cohesion, which relates to one of the crises in Erikson's theory. Trust was exemplified in the IEA CIVED data in measures of trust in the government and trust in the media. Generalized social trust develops early in life and may be related to more specific trust of governmental institutions. A second concept that emerged was political identity and meaningful practice, which also relates to a developmental crisis discussed by Erikson (discussed in a previous section) and also to Lave and Wenger (see Torney-Purta, Amadeo, & Andolina, this volume).

A third concept was efficacy, which is discussed as industry, agency, and empowerment by Erikson, Bandura, and Watts. The CIVED data included a measure of internal political self-efficacy. More theory-driven research could be conducted, using either developmental theories or the more specific theory of sociopolitical development as the foundation, to better understand the concept of efficacy. One line of inquiry is whether industry and agency are equivalent to self-efficacy, or whether they are precursors. Another question is whether self-efficacy in the political realm is an extension of a deep-seated personality characteristic or is more situation specific.

The fourth and fifth civic concepts that were identified by Torney-Purta et al. (2007) and that were exemplified in the CIVED data were prosocial attitudes and sense of community. These concepts may exemplify the higher stages of sociopolitical development discussed by Watts, to the extent that they reflect an understanding of systemic forces and a critical analysis of social issues.

The use of concepts found across four theories linked to reliable measures in the CIVED provided coherence to an analysis that related service learning experiences (defined as a combination of volunteering and learning in school about community problems) to several measures of civic engagement. This attempt to link theories to measures took place after the fact (rather than being an explicit part of the research design), but it shows the potential of concepts derived from theories in this area. Generally speaking, in designing assessments it is often valuable to find concepts that have an important role in more than one theory. In the field of civic engagement, trust, identity, efficacy, and some aspects of prosocial attitudes are among those concepts (Metzger & Smetana, this volume).

One of the intriguing findings of the analysis undertaken by Torney-Purta et al. (2007) was that in England participating in volunteer activities by itself appeared to be sufficient to promote an enhanced sense of efficacy. In contrast, in the United States, efficacy was found to be highest among students who studied community problems in school in addition to volunteering outside of school. These findings indicate that not only can international research benefit from a theoretical base, but also that international research may contribute to further theory development. International comparisons allow us to investigate what civic engagement means (and how it might be measured) within different cultural and political contexts. Other analyses have shown both consistencies and inconsistencies across countries. For instance, in all 28 countries involved in the Civic Education Study, students' individual civic knowledge predicted their expectations of future voting behavior (Torney-Purta et al., 2001). However, features of the political context in these countries (specifically the governments' international participation in human rights dialogue) predicted specific aspects of civic knowledge (Torney-Purta et al., 2008). In other international research, more frequent discussion of politics or public issues with friends predicted higher political participation among youth in Belgium and Canada, but being part of a network characterized by racial and religious diversity was only beneficial in Belgium (Harell, Stolle, & Quintelier, 2008). International research is important because it can inform our conception of civic engagement as multidimensional and can lead to a better understanding of the contexts in which it is developed. However, theoretical assumptions often differ between regions (such as Asia, Europe, North America) as well as between social science disciplines. This makes theory development and theory-based measurement challenging in studies involving several countries and a range of investigators. A theory such as that of Bronfenbrenner may be used to frame research questions, but specific choices concerning the design and the content of measurement need to be legitimated in each participating country. Finally, any theoretical approach adopted in an international study needs to be able to take adequate account of the context at several levels (Torney-Purta, 2009).

CONCLUSION

Research on the development of adolescent civic engagement should have a solid theoretical foundation in order to produce conceptually justified research questions and measures. Theory-driven research that informs methods and measures has the potential to enhance the rigor of studies, facilitate continuity of measures between studies, enhance interpretation of findings and comparisons across studies, and contribute to our understanding of civic development and the processes and contexts in which it occurs. There are particular challenges in interdisciplinary work, because the assumptions on which theories are based and the criteria by which they are judged differ widely in different disciplines. Foundations and professional associations, which often tend to focus on research within a single discipline, could contribute to this area by making explicit efforts to diversify the theoretical perspectives that they encourage in their requests for proposals for funding, meeting plans, and publications.

REFERENCES

Adelson, J., & Beall, L. (1970). Adolescent perspectives on law and government. *Law & Society Review, 4(4)*, 495–504.

Amadeo, J., Torney-Purta, J., Lehmann, R., Husfeldt, V., & Nikolova, R. (2002). *Civic knowledge and engagement: An IEA study of upper secondary students in sixteen countries*. Amsterdam: International Association for the Evaluation of Educational Achievement.

Andolina, M., Jenkins, K., & Keeter, S. (2002). Searching for the meaning of youth civic engagement: Notes from the field. *Applied Developmental Science*, *6*, 189–195.

Andolina, M., Jenkins, K., Zukin, C., & Keeter, S. (2003). Habits from home, lessons from school: Influences on youth civic engagement. *PS: Political Science and Politics*, *36*, 275–280.

Astin, A., Vogelgesang, L., Ikeda, E., & Yee, J. (2000). *How service learning affects students*. Los Angeles: Higher Education Research Institute, University of California, Los Angeles.

Bandura, A. (1977). *Social learning theory*. New York: General Learning Press.

Bandura, A. (1986). *Social foundations of thoughts and action: A social cognitive theory*. Englewood Cliffs, NJ: Prentice-Hall.

Bandura, A. (1989). Social cognitive theory. *Annals of Child Development*, *6*, 1–60.

Bandura, A. (1995). Exercise of personal and collective efficacy in changing societies. In A. Bandura (Ed.), *Self-efficacy in changing societies* (pp. 1–45). New York: Cambridge University Press.

Bandura, A. (1997). *Self-efficacy: The exercise of control*. New York: Freeman.

Bandura, A. (2001). Social cognitive theory: An agentic perspective. *Annual Review of Psychology*, *52*, 1–26.

Bandura, A., Caprara, G. V., Barbaranelli, C., Pastorelli, C., & Regalia, C. (2001). Sociocognitive self-regulatory mechanisms governing transgressive behavior. *Journal of Personality and Social Psychology*, *80*, 125–135.

Bronfenbrenner, U. (1979). *The ecology of human development*. Cambridge, MA: Harvard University Press.

Bronfenbrenner, U. (1989). Ecological systems theory. In. R. Vasta (Ed.), *Annals of child development: Vol. 6. Six theories of child development: Revised formulations and current issues* (pp.187–249). Greenwich, CT: JAI Press.

Bronfenbrenner, U. (2005). *Making human beings human: Bioecological perspectives on human development*. Thousand Oaks, CA: Sage Publications.

CIRCLE. (2008, December). *Young voters in the 2008 presidential election* (Fact Sheet). Medford, MA: Author.

Colby, A., & Damon, W. (1995). The development of extraordinary moral commitment. In M. Killen, & D. Hart, (Eds.), *Morality in everyday life* (pp. 342–370). Cambridge: Cambridge University Press.

Delli Carpini, M. X. (2000). Gen.Com: Youth, civic engagement, and the new information environment. *Political Communication*, *17*, 341–349.

Education Commission of the States (n.d.). *Resources to assess student civic competencies and school climate*. Retrieved on April 23, 2009: www.ecs.org/qna

Erikson, E. (1958). *Identity: Youth and the life cycle*. New York: International Universities Press.

Erikson, E. (1968). *Identity: Youth and crisis*. New York: W. W. Norton.

Fernández-Ballesteros, R., Díez-Nicolás, J., Caprara, G. V., Barbaranelli, C., & Bandura, A. (2002). Determinants and structural relation of personal efficacy to collective efficacy. *Applied Psychology: An International Review*, *51*, 107–125.

Flanagan, C. A., Bowes, J. M., Jonsson, B., Csapo, B., & Sheblanova, E. (1998). Ties that bind: Correlates of adolescents' civic commitment in seven countries. *Journal of Social Issues, 54(3)*, 457–475.

Flanagan , C., & Faison, N. (2001). Youth civic development: Implications of research for social policy and programs. *Social Policy Report, 15(1)*, 3–14.

Flanagan, C.A., & Sherrod, L. (1998). Youth political development: An introduction. *Journal of Social Issues, 54(3)*, 447–456.

Flanagan, C. A., Syvertsen, A. K., Mitra, D., Oliver, M. B., & Sethuraman, S. S. (2005). *Randomized field design of implementation of Student Voices in Pennsylvania schools: A final report.* Philadelphia: Annenberg Public Policy Center.

Flanagan, C. A., Syvertsen, A. K., & Stout, M. D. (2007, May). *Civic measurement models: Tapping adolescents' civic engagement* (CIRCLE Working Paper No. 54). College Park, MD: CIRCLE (The Center for Information and Research on Civic Learning and Engagement).

Freire, P. (1990). *Education for a critical consciousness.* New York: Continuum.

Goossens, L. (2001). Global versus domain specific status in identity research: A comparison of two self-report measures. *Journal of Adolescence, 24*, 681–689.

Harell, A., Stolle, D., & Quintelier, E. (2008). *Network diversity and political participation: A complication or asset?* (2008, July 3–4). Paper presented at the Conference on Comparative Perspectives on Political Socialization, Bruges, Belgium..

Hart, D. (2005). Adding identity to the moral domain. *Human Development, 45*, 257–261.

Hart, D., Atkins, R., Markey, P., & Youniss, J. (2004). Youth bulges in communities: The effects of age structure on adolescent civic knowledge and civic participation. *Psychological Science, 15(9)*, 591–597.

Hart, D., Donnelly, T. M., Youniss, J., & Atkins, R. (2007). High school community service as a predictor of adult voting and volunteering. *American Educational Research Journal, 44(1)*, 197–219.

Hart, D., & Kirshner, B. (2009). Civic participation and development among urban adolescents. In J. Youniss & P. Levine (Eds.), *Engaging young people in civic life.* Nashville: Vanderbilt University Press.

Hess, R., & Torney, J. (1967). *The development of political attitudes in children.* Chicago: Aldine. (Reissued 2006 by Transaction Press.)

Jennings, M. K., & Niemi, R. (1974). *The political character of adolescence: The influence of families and schools.* Princeton: Princeton University Press.

Kahne, J., Middaugh, E., & Schutjer-Mance, K. (2005). *California Civic Index* [Monograph]. New York: Carnegie Corporation and Annenberg Foundation.

Keeter, S., Zukin, C., Andolina, M., & Jenkins, K. (2002). *The civic and political health of the nation: A generational portrait.* College Park, MD: The Center for Information and Research on Civic Learning and Engagement.

Killen, M. (2007). Children's social and moral reasoning about exclusion. *Current Directions in Psychological Science, 16*, 32–36.

Kohlberg, L. (1969). Stage and sequence: The cognitive-developmental approach to socialization. In D. Goslin (Ed.), *Handbook of socialization theory and research* (pp. 347–480). Chicago: Rand McNally.

Kohlberg, L. (1976). Moral stage and moralization: The cognitive-developmental approach. In T. Lickona (Ed.), *Moral development and behavior: Theory, research and social issues* (pp. 84–107). New York: Holt, Rinehart, & Winston.

Larson, R. W., Pearce, N., Sullivan, P. J., & Jarrett, R. L. (2007). Participation in youth programs as a catalyst for negotiation of family autonomy with connection. *Journal of Youth and Adolescence, 36(1)*, 31–35.

Lave, J., & Wenger, E. (1991). *Situated learning: Legitimate peripheral participation.* Cambridge: Cambridge University Press.

McIntosh, H., Hart, D., & Youniss, J. (2007). The influence of family political discussion on youth political development: Which parent qualities matter? *Political Science and Politics, 40*, 495–499.

Miller, N. E., & Dollard, J. (1941). *Social learning and imitation*. New Haven, CT: Yale University Press.

Moore, S., Lare, J., & Wagner, K. (1985). *The child's political world: A longitudinal perspective*. New York: Praeger.

Muuss, R. (1982). Social cognition: Robert Selman's theory of role taking. *Adolescence, 17*, 499–525.

National Conference on Citizenship (2006, September). *America's Civic Health Index: Broken engagement*. Washington, DC: National Conference on Citizenship.

Pasek, J., Feldman, L., Romer, D., & Jamieson, K. H. (2008). Schools as incubators of democratic participation: Building long-term political efficacy with civic education. *Applied Developmental Science, 12(1)*, 26–37.

Pearce, N., & Larson, R. (2006). How teens become engaged in youth development programs: The process of motivational change in a civic activism organization. *Applied Developmental Science, 10(3)*, 121–131.

Putnam, R. (1996). The strange disappearance of civic America. *American Prospect, 7*, 34–48.

Putnam, R. (2000). *Bowling alone: The collapse and revival of American community.* New York: Simon & Schuster.

Rest, J., Narvaez, D., Thoma, S., & Bebeau, M. J. (2000). A neo-Kohlbergian approach to morality research. *Journal of Moral Education, 29(4)*, 381–395.

Rubin, B. (2007). "There's still not justice": Youth civic identity development amid distinct school and community contexts. *Teachers College Record, 109(2)*, 449–481.

Schultz, L., Selman, R., & LaRusso, M. (2003). The assessment of psychosocial maturity in children and adolescents. *Journal of Research in Character Education, 1(2)*, 67–87.

Selman, R. L. (1976). Social-cognitive understanding. In T. Lickona (Ed.), *Moral development and behavior: Theory, research, and social issues* (pp. 108–123). New York: Holt, Rinehart & Winston.

Selman, R. L. (1980). *The growth of interpersonal understanding: Developmental and clinical analysis.* New York: Academic Press.

Selman, R. L. (2003). *The promotion of social awareness: Powerful lessons from the partnership of developmental theory and classroom practice.* New York: Russell Sage.

Sherrod, L. R., & Lauckhardt, J. (2009). The development of citizenship. In R. Lerner & L. Steinberg (Eds.), *Handbook of adolescent psychology* (pp. 372–408). Hoboken, NJ: John Wiley & Sons.

Torney-Purta, J. (1995). Psychological theory as a basis for political socialization research. *Perspectives on Political Science, 24(1)*, 23–41.

Torney-Purta, J. (2002). The school's role in developing civic engagement: A study of adolescents in twenty-eight countries. *Applied Developmental Science, 6(4)*, 203–212.

Torney-Purta, J. (2009). International research that matters for policy and practice. *American Psychologist, 64(8), 822–837.*

Torney-Purta, J., Amadeo, J., & Richardson, W. (2007). Civic service among youth in Chile, Denmark, England and the United States: A psychological perspective. In M. Sherraden & A. McBride (Eds.), *Civic service worldwide: Impacts and inquiries* (pp. 95–132). Armonk, NY: M. E. Sharpe.

Torney-Purta, J., Barber, C., & Wilkenfeld, B. (2007). Latino adolescents' civic development in the United States: Research results from the IEA Civic Education Study. *Journal of Youth and Adolescence, 36*, 111–125.

Torney-Purta, J., Lehmann, R., Oswald, H., & Schulz, W. (2001). *Citizenship and education in twenty-eight countries*. Amsterdam: International Association for the Evaluation of Educational Achievement.

Torney-Purta, J., Wilkenfeld, B., & Barber, C. (2008). How adolescents in twenty-seven countries understand, support, and practice human rights. *Journal of Social Issues, 64(4)*, 857–880.

Turiel, E. (1983). *The development of social knowledge: Morality and convention.* Cambridge, UK: Cambridge University Press.

Turiel, E. (1998). The development of morality. In W. Damon (Series Ed.) & N. Eisenberg (Vol. Ed.), *Handbook of child psychology: Vol. 3. Social, emotional, and personality development* (5th ed., pp. 863–932). New York: John Wiley & Sons.

Watts, R., Armstrong, M., Cartman, O., & Guessous, O. (2008). *Findings on a theory of youth sociopolitical development* (2008, March 24–28). Paper presented at the American Educational Research Association 2008 Annual Conference, New York, NY.

Watts, R., Griffith, D., & Abdul-Adil, J. (1999). Sociopolitical development as an antidote for oppression-theory and action. *American Journal of Community Psychology, 27*, 255–271.

Watts, R., Williams, N., & Jagers, R. (2003). Sociopolitical development. *American Journal of Community Psychology, 31*, 185–194.

Wilkenfeld, B. (2009, June). *Does context matter? How the family, peer, school, and neighborhood contexts relate to adolescents' civic engagement* (CIRCLE Working Paper No. 64). Medford, MA: CIRCLE (The Center for Information and Research on Civic Learning and Engagement).

Wilkenfeld, B., & Torney-Purta, J. (2005). *Outcomes associated with undergraduate students' service-learning experiences.* Unpublished manuscript, University of Maryland, College Park, MD.

Wood, D., Larson, R. W., & Brown, J. (2009). How adolescents come to see themselves as more responsible through participation in youth programs. *Child Development, 80(1)*, 295–309.

Youniss, J., & Yates, M. (1997). What we know about engendering civic identity. *American Behavioral Scientist, 40,* 620–631.

Youniss, J., & Yates, M. (1999). Youth service and moral-civic identity: A case for everyday morality. *Educational Psychology Review, 11,* 361–376.

Zaff, J. F., Malanchuk, O., Michelsen, E., & Eccles, J. (2003, March). *Promoting positive citizenship: Priming youth for action* (CIRCLE Working Paper No. 05). College Park, MD: CIRCLE (The Center for Information and Research on Civic Learning and Engagement).

CHAPTER 9

Social Cognitive Development and Adolescent Civic Engagement

AARON METZGER
West Virginia University

JUDITH G. SMETANA
University of Rochester

CITIZENS OFTEN REFER to political activities like voting as doing one's *civic duty*. This notion of civic duty also surfaces in reference to other civic activities such as participation in community service or even the avoidance of public littering. However, it is often unclear exactly what people mean by either the terms *civic* or *duty*. From a developmental science perspective, the two components of this colloquial term are interesting because there has been extensive empirical research concerning children's and adolescents' conceptual understanding of both. Specifically, a great deal of political science and psychological research has investigated individuals' understanding of civic or political knowledge, attitudes, and beliefs (Flanagan, 2005; Furnham & Stacey, 1991; Haste & Torney-Purta, 1992; Thomlinson, 1975). Researchers studying moral and prosocial development have had a long-standing interest in the development of conceptions of obligation and duty (Eisenberg, Fabes, & Spinrad, 2007; Kohlberg, 1971; Smetana, 2006). However, research has not examined how individuals apply beliefs about duty to their notions of the civic. That is, little research has examined how individuals reason about political, community, and civic engagement.

Social-cognitive processes are inherently a part of civic and community participation. For instance, individuals must reason and then decide about their candidate of choice when voting in elections and deciding which political party they are going to join. Protesters join political and social protests and causes based on their conceptualization of the issues at stake. People avoid or even actively boycott certain products based on their beliefs about companies' practices. In the same way, individuals' beliefs about disadvantaged individuals and their own responsibility to ameliorate the plight of the disadvantaged influence the types of community service in which they choose to engage. Thus, cognitions and beliefs are central to how individuals view themselves in relation to civic and community institutions. They affect whether individuals will become civically involved, as well as the form that such involvement will take.

Nevertheless, research on adolescent civic development has focused primarily on adolescents' civic behaviors. Research has examined demographic and family variables that predict adolescents' volunteering and political activities (Duncan & Stewart, 1996; Hart, Atkins, & Ford, 1998; Nolin, Chaney, & Chapman, 1997; Pancer & Pratt, 1999; Smetana & Metzger, 2005; Youniss, McLellan, & Yates, 1999), and adolescents' civic activity as a means of facilitating adult civic involvement (Sherrod, Flanagan, & Youniss, 2002). In this research on adolescents' civic behavior and volunteering, adolescents primarily have been asked about the types of activities in which they *are* involved or *plan to be* involved. Less empirical attention has been paid to ways in which individuals conceptualize civic activities and whether and how individuals apply notions of duty to community and political participation. Even adolescents who are not currently involved may hold beliefs about involvement, and these adolescents might still judge community service or political activity as actions in which citizens *should* engage. Furthermore, from a developmental perspective, research has shown that there are age-related changes in children's and adolescents' social reasoning (Smetana & Villalobos, 2009). It is important to understand these age trends as they apply to reasoning about civic involvement.

In this chapter, we review research from a social-cognitive perspective that has examined topics relevant to civic involvement, including research, which has examined adolescents' civic concepts and notions of duty. Conceptualizations of civic involvement entail prosocial reasoning, or beliefs about one's responsibility to help or aid others through community service or other forms of civic engagement. We begin this chapter by briefly reviewing research that has examined adolescents' reasoning about prosocial behavior in interpersonal contexts and discuss how findings from this research, particularly when it has considered developmental processes and individual differences, could inform civic involvement. We then review research that has examined adolescents' reasoning about political issues and political concepts, such as democracy and human rights, as well as studies considering adolescents' conceptualizations of civic institutions and their relationship to individuals. This section ends with a review of recent research that specifically examines adolescents' reasoning about civic obligation and various types of civic behavior. Finally, we conclude with some directions for future research. Throughout this review, we highlight the diverse methodologies utilized in social-cognitive research and discuss ways in which these methodologies could be employed in future empirical investigations of adolescent civic development (see Wilkenfeld, Lauckhardt, & Torney-Purta, this volume).

PROSOCIAL REASONING

Historically, political scientists interested in civic development have investigated the ways in which individuals obtain the information necessary for political engagement such as knowledge about government structure and political process (Furnham & Stacey, 1991; Stradling, 1977; Delli Carpini & Keeter, 1996). Civic, political, and community involvement entail more than just knowledge of the structure of governmental and social institutions, however. Civic engagement is intended to benefit individuals or contribute to social and community organizations. It is also expected that individuals engage in these actions because they feel motivated or even obligated to contribute to political institutions and their community. Thus, civic involvement can be seen as a specific type of prosocial activity. There is a long tradition in developmental psychology of investigating children's and adolescents' prosocial behavior, typically defined as voluntary behavior that is intended to benefit another individual (see Eisenberg, Fabes, & Spinrad, 2007, for a review). Most of this research has focused on predicting children's prosocial behaviors or examining emotional states, such as sympathy, that accompany prosocial behavior. Other research has looked at how children and adolescents conceptualize different prosocial actions. These studies have examined the normative development of prosocial reasoning and have viewed prosocial reasoning as developing through a series of hierarchical stages. In addition, this research has examined individual differences in prosocial reasoning, as well as domain differences in individuals' reasoning about various types of prosocial acts.

Development of prosocial reasoning. Social-cognitive developmental research has examined age-related changes in children's and adolescents' reasoning about prosocial acts. In this research, more mature development typically is described in terms of acts that are intrinsically motivated by internalized values, goals, and self-rewards rather than by external forces (Mussen & Eisenberg, 2001). Eisenberg found a five-level sequence of age-related changes in prosocial reasoning (Eisenberg, 1990; Eisenberg, Miller, Shell, McNalley, & Shea, 1991). As they develop, young children move from hedonistic reasoning to reasoning that reflects concerns with pleasing others, greater sympathy, and more perspective-taking in preadolescence. In adolescence, individuals begin to utilize internalized, abstract principles in their reasoning about prosocial behavior (Eisenberg, 1990; Eisenberg, Fabes, & Spinrad, 2007). In addition, adolescents become more concerned with living up to their own personal ideals and see engaging in prosocial behavior as consistent with this self-image. Some research has found that prosocial behaviors increase somewhat with age (Eisenberg et al., 2005). However, this research has also found that less mature levels of prosocial reasoning, such as hedonistic reasoning, reappear in late adolescence. In addition, a recent growth curve analysis of rural adolescents found that prosocial behavior declined across early and middle adolescence but increased slightly in late adolescence (Carlo, Crockett, Randall, & Roesch, 2007). However, research also has found that prosocial moral reasoning may increase again in early adulthood (Eisenberg, Cumberland, Guthrie, Murphy, & Shepard, 2005). This pattern of findings in early adulthood is especially significant, given the importance of civic involvement during this age period and survey data, which point to lower levels of several types of civic and political activity in early adulthood (see Finlay et al., this volume).

In addition, research has found that lasting individual differences in prosocial orientation (including behaviors and reasoning) have their origins in early childhood but are firmly established for most by adolescence (Eisenberg, Guthrie, Murphy, Shepard, Cumberland, & Carlo, 1999), and remain stable into early adulthood (Eisenberg, Guthrie, Cumberland, Murphy, Shepard, Zhou, & Carlo, 2002). Young children who engaged in more spontaneous prosocial behaviors compared to their peers had higher levels of both self-reported sympathy and perspective-taking in early adulthood. There are also consistent gender differences in prosocial reasoning. In childhood and adolescence, girls tend to be more prosocial in their behavior, reasoning, and affective response (sympathy) than boys (Eisenberg et al., 2007). In a meta-analysis of over 100 studies of moral reasoning, Jaffee and Hyde (2000) found that girls tended to use slightly more care-oriented prosocial reasoning than boys, although this difference was moderate.

Reasoning about different types of prosocial behavior. Based on social domain theory, researchers also have examined adolescents' reasoning about different types of prosocial behavior. Social domain theory postulates that individuals develop different types of social knowledge, in particular moral, conventional, and personal knowledge (Smetana, 2006; Turiel, 2006). Moral concepts are obligatory, universally applicable, and not contingent on social agreement or regulatory authority. Social conventions are arbitrary, agreed-upon regulations that coordinate behaviors and interactions within specific social contexts. In contrast to morality, social conventions are alterable and contingent on authority or rules. Both the moral and social conventional domains are different from the personal domain, which includes actions that pertain only to the self. Personal actions are neither regulated by conventional authority nor subject to moral concern, but instead include concepts of the self and decisions involving personal preference.

In one study, children, adolescents, and college students ranked different types of potentially positive acts (e.g., sharing lunch, giving to charity, holding a door open for someone) according to which was the most "right" and gave domain-related justifications for each act. Participants were more likely to apply moral justifications to events that were ranked as most right and more social-conventional justifications for events that were ranked as less right (Smetana, Bridgman, & Turiel, 1982). In semi-structured interviews, Kahn (1992) asked children whether a protagonist in different stories should share with their classmates (or engage in other prosocial acts) and whether it would be permissible for the protagonist not to do so. Whereas children generally conceived of prosocial activities as acts that individuals should perform, more than half of the participants did not view such acts as obligatory. In the same way, adolescents may evaluate different types of civic behavior as involving different domains of social knowledge. For example, taking a proactive stand toward racial discrimination may be seen as a moral act, while picking up litter is seen as more social conventional.

Prosocial reasoning and behavior. Researchers have posited that prosocial behavior is linked to prosocial reasoning, including greater social sensibility and feelings of responsibility. The expected associations have been observed (Eisenberg et al., 2007), but several situational and individual variables, such as emotions, have been found to moderate the relationship between reasoning and behavior. For instance, children are more likely to help children in need when they report high levels of sympathy for the children (Miller, Eisenberg, Fabes, & Shell, 1996).

In addition, the association between prosocial reasoning and behavior is enhanced when the cost to the individual performing the prosocial act is high (Eisenberg & Shell, 1986). A time-consuming prosocial behavior that conflicts with other desired activities or one that involves a great deal of effort may be unattractive to an adolescent because of its high personal cost. Hart and Fegley (1995) studied the moral reasoning and self-concepts of 15 African American and Latin American adolescent exemplars, who were nominated by community members for their extensive participation and community service or exceptional care for others. There were no differences between care exemplars and a matched control group in level of moral reasoning, but compared to controls, care exemplars were more likely to describe themselves in terms of positive, moral, caring personality traits. This is similar to other research, which has found that older adolescents often point to moral values and social responsibility as reasons for their prosocial behaviors (Carlo, Eisenberg, & Knight, 1992).

In summary, researchers have studied both normative developmental patterns as well as individual differences in prosocial reasoning using structural-developmental and social domain theoretical models. Research also has investigated associations among prosocial reasoning and prosocial behavior together with cognitive and affective processes such as perspective-taking and sympathy. There are multiple ways in which prosocial reasoning research could contribute to a comprehensive understanding of civic development. Active civic behavior requires that individuals feel motivated or obligated to become involved. Such obligation may grow out of individuals' prosocial attitudes toward those in need, which may lead to involvement in community service. However, these attitudes might also affect how adolescents view their relationship to broader civic and political institutions. This expanded vantage point could lead to other forms of civic participation such as contributing to a political campaign or joining a political or social protest. Thus, adolescents' civic development may be linked with their developing prosocial reasoning, but there is more than one pathway to any particular civic behavior.

Adolescents' reasoning about civic engagement also may be linked to their thinking about civic and political institutions. In the next section, we review research that has investigated adolescents' civic and political beliefs.

RESEARCH ON POLITICAL BELIEFS

Historically, two lines of research have examined children's and adolescents' political beliefs and understanding. Political scientists have focused on how individuals acquire beliefs and attitudes from social contexts including schools or intergenerationally from parents (Jennings & Niemi, 1968; Verba, Schlozman, & Brady, 1995). The theoretical assumption underlying much of this research is that individuals' belief systems are actively socialized by parents or schools and that political reasoning is acquired through the absorption and assimilation of political messages from the environment. In fact, research has shown that adolescents often hold political attitudes that are similar to those of their parents, especially when parents are more politically active (Jennings, 2002). In contrast, according to constructivist theories of development (Hunt, 1969; Smetana & Villalobos, 2009), individuals actively create their own meaning systems through dynamic interactions with the environment. Thus, the focus of social-cognitive research on political reasoning has been on individuals' active construction of social understanding. A great deal of social-cognitive research on political reasoning (too much to review here) was conducted in the 1970s. We discuss shifts in the focus of this research with a greater emphasis on more current studies.

Several aspects of political reasoning have been examined, including the normative development of political concepts. Research also has explored how children and adolescents reason about institutional authority, types of government, and democracy, as well as how adolescents reason about individuals' relationships to these institutions in their conceptualizations of human rights and civic responsibility. In addition, variables that may account for differences in political beliefs, such as individual differences in religious beliefs, socioeconomic status, and ethnic background, have been investigated. Finally, research has explored associations between adolescents' political reasoning and their civic and community activities.

Development of political thought and moral reasoning. One avenue of research has been to describe how individuals develop political belief systems or political ideologies. A great deal of this research has viewed political reasoning as developing through a series of hierarchical stages that parallel the stages described for cognitive development (Piaget, 1970). For instance, some researchers have described political thinking as developing from an orientation toward personal and authoritarian views of political issues in early childhood toward a comprehensive view of social structures involving more general principles in late adolescence (Weinreich-Haste, 1986).

This developmental model of increasing sophistication and abstraction in adolescents' political thought is similar to findings of several early researchers who examined age-related changes in political reasoning. For instance, Adelson and colleagues (1971; Adelson & O'Neil, 1966) utilized hypothetical situations in which adolescents (ages 11 to 18) were asked to imagine that 1,000 people venture to an island to start a new society. Adolescents were asked about the types of government and laws that this hypothetical society might form. In these studies, adolescents' reasoning was found to develop from a personalized, concrete assessment of laws and social institutions in early adolescence to a more sociocentric view in middle to late adolescence. At later ages, adolescents were able to discuss political topics in more abstract ways.

Similarly, Connell (1971) conducted semi-structured interviews with 112 Australian youth who ranged in age from 5 to 16 years. Connell had anticipated that children's reasoning would reflect political ideas children heard from parents and the media. Instead, children's and adolescents' interview responses did not point to a simple reproduction of adult ideas, but instead, demonstrated a stage-like progression in thinking. At the earlier stages, young children displayed intuitive reasoning that was lacking in concrete details about politics. By early adolescence, participants were able to discuss the relationship between multiple political actors, including a more sophisticated understanding of governmental power and the role of political parties. Middle adolescents displayed more ideological thinking. Their reasoning was more abstract, and they were able to discuss societies and polities as wholes rather than focus on fragmented communities or individuals.

More recently, Torney-Purta (1991, 1992, 1994) utilized a social-cognitive model to explore adolescents' developing understanding of political concepts. She examined the developmental trajectory of adolescents' political understanding and proposed that adolescents actively make sense of their social world and construct meaning systems through the development of cognitive structures called schemata. As they develop cognitively, individuals become able to reason at more mature levels about political issues. When adolescents encounter new political information that cannot be assimilated into their current cognitive structures, or schemata, the cognitive structure must be adapted in order to accommodate the new information.

To assess developmental patterns in adolescents' political reasoning, Torney-Purta (1992) used methods that captured adolescents' active construction of political concepts. For instance, she measured adolescents' political understanding by mapping adolescents' responses to a series of political dilemmas such as the finance minister of a developing country who cannot pay interest on the country's debt and must decide what to do. This methodology, which utilized think-aloud problem solving, allowed for a detailed description of adolescents' cognitive structures used in solving political problems, as well as the limits of their current political schemata. Adolescents ranged dramatically in the complexity of their reasoning regarding political, social, and economic systems. She divided adolescents' political responses into groups ranging from "pre-novice" to "expert" based on their ability to comprehend multiple aspects of the political issue, including constraints (obstacles) to successful political actions and the interconnection between different actions. Adolescents at higher stages of political cognitive development had a more nuanced understanding of the complexities involved in political issues and also had the cognitive resources to comprehensively apply this knowledge to different political issues.

Concepts of government, democracy, and human rights. In addition to studying the normative development of political reasoning, research also has investigated how adolescents conceptualize societal institutions and how they place limits on individual freedoms and rights. For instance, social-cognitive research has explored children's and adolescents' conceptualizations of institutional authority and participatory government. This research has examined how adolescents reason about different types of government, as well as how adolescents conceptualize democracy. Adelson and O'Neil (1966) found that adolescents' views of government shifted from allowing the government to have limitless authority in early adolescence to questioning the power of leaders, especially when it came to control over individual freedoms and rights, in late adolescence. More recently, Emler (1992) argued that children develop sophisticated conceptualizations of institutional authority in early childhood and that these conceptualizations are rooted in the relationship to authority that children learn at school. While young children often have been found to view institutional authority as absolute, Emler also found that children viewed the enactment of authority as contingent on consensus and negotiation.

Governments take many forms, and beliefs about the limits of institutional and governmental authority may differ for adolescents who live under different political systems. Research has shown that young children differentiate between forms of government, state their preference for a specific form of government, and make judgments about the legitimacy of different forms of government to enact laws protecting human rights. Helwig (1998) had Canadian children ages 6 to 11 make judgments about their preference for different types of government, such as representative democracy, direct democracy, democracy by strict consensus, pure meritocracy, and pure oligarchy. Children in this study preferred democratic forms of government, and children's justifications for this preference focused on notions of political fairness. In addition, older children were less likely to consider laws that limited individual rights and freedoms as unacceptable if they were passed by democratic rather than non-democratic forms of government. Recent research has shown that with age, adolescents' views on democracy become more nuanced (Helwig, Arnold, Tan, & Boyd, 2007). In responding to hypothetical scenarios involving the fairness of different types of government, adolescents 12 to 19 years old from Canada and both urban and rural areas of China preferred democratic over non-democratic forms of government. However, while younger adolescents favored direct democracy, older adolescents (15- to 18-year-olds) were more aware of the pragmatic limitations of direct democracy (the need to have all citizens vote on every issue). They instead preferred representative democracy, in which democratic voice was fulfilled through the election of individuals who had the time to more fully participate in government action (and a mandate from the voters).

Other research has specifically examined adolescents' conceptualizations of democracy. Early work on adolescents' reasoning about democracy is primarily focused on whether adolescents could adequately describe central aspects of democratic forms of government. Adolescents' conceptions of democracy were studied more recently in a cross-national study of adolescent political engagement and political knowledge (referred to as the IEA Civic Education Study, conducted in 28 countries) (Torney-Purta, 2002; Torney-Purta, Lehmann, Owald, & Schulz, 2001). In addition to measuring civic behavior in these different countries, the researchers investigated adolescents' civic knowledge and knowledge of democratic principles. There was consensus across countries that free elections, allowing citizens to publicly criticize the government, and having a diversity of news media were good for democracy. However, there were also some differences in reasoning about what was good or bad for democracy among adolescents from different countries. In Chile, for example, young people did not recognize that some acts, such as having courts and judges influenced by politicians or having political leaders give jobs to members of their families, constitute threats to democracy (Torney-Purta, Amadeo, & Richardson, 2007).

Flanagan, Gallay, Gill, Gallay, and Nti (2005) studied views of democracy in 700 12- to 19-year-old racially diverse adolescents. They asked participants to provide open-ended responses to the question "What does democracy mean to you?" Given the strong production demands of this task, it is not surprising that only 53% of the adolescents were able to supply at least one correct, codable definition of democracy. In this study, adolescents' correct definitions of democracy were divided into three themes: individual rights, representative rule, and civic equality. These definitions were offered in relatively equal frequency, indicating a great deal of heterogeneity in adolescents' reasoning about democracy. Parents' education was not associated with adolescents' different definitions. However, the IEA study previously described found parents' education to have a strong association with students' conceptual knowledge of democracy across nations (Torney-Purta, Lehmann, Oswald & Schulz, 2001) (see also Levinson, this volume).

However, civic involvement involves more than concepts of government and civic institutions. It also entails beliefs about the relationship between individuals and these civic institutions. Social-cognitive research on political reasoning has examined this relationship primarily by exploring individuals' concepts of human rights, which have long been considered a central aspect of adolescents' political understanding. Early survey studies seemed to indicate that American children and preadolescents had very limited knowledge about concepts such as rights (Gallatin & Adelson, 1970).

More recently (in 1999), the IEA Civic Education Study, which included nationally representative samples of students studied cross-nationally, included three knowledge items about international human rights (Torney-Purta, Wilkenfeld, & Barber, 2008). They also obtained information about the extent to which the governments of 27 of these countries mentioned human rights in their reports to United Nations (UN)-affiliated groups. Adolescents were more likely to know the purpose of the Convention on the Rights of the Child if they lived in countries that mentioned international human rights in their reports to UN agencies. Students who had positive experiences of participatory democracy as part of their school climate also were more knowledgeable about human rights.

As critics have noted (Helwig & Turiel, 2002; Neff & Helwig, 2002), these large survey studies do not obtain adolescents' rationales or justifications for their judgments. It is sometimes useful to ask children to make judgments about the legitimacy of human rights in scenarios where they conflict with other social and moral concerns. In a series of studies, Helwig (1995, 1997; Helwig & Jasiobedzka, 2001) examined children's and adolescents' conceptions of human rights using social domain theory. Helwig (1995) explored children's, adolescents', and college students' judgments and justifications regarding civil liberties (freedom of speech and freedom of religion). Participants evaluated stories in which characters exercised civil liberties in either unconflicted situations or conflict situations. In the *conflict* stories, exercising civil liberties conflicted with competing moral concerns regarding human welfare, harm to others, justice, and rights or conventional concerns (referring to arbitrary, agreed-upon regulations that coordinate behaviors and interactions within specific social contexts). For example, participants made judgments about a situation where it was required that new members of a religion be severely beaten with wooden sticks. Thus, a moral concern (physical harm) was in conflict with a right (freedom of religion). The *unconflicted* situations had no such competing concerns. All participants viewed freedom of speech and freedom of religion as universal rights in unconflicted scenarios. However, participants' judgments of the conflict situations were not as clear-cut, as civil liberties were sometimes subordinated to competing social and moral concerns.

Other research has shown that adolescents are capable of making judgments about human rights in situations where the context of the scenario is manipulated (Helwig, 1997). Even young children espoused concepts of freedom of speech and religion as rights regardless of the context, but older participants, and especially college students, viewed parental limitations on children's religious freedom in the home as appropriate. More recent research has shown that adolescents in other countries and cultures, including adolescents in both rural and urban settings in China, hold a diverse array of concepts about individual rights (Lahat, Helwig, Yang, Tan, & Liu, 2009). In this study, Chinese adolescents completed a questionnaire composed of nine scenarios in which children's desires to exercise a right, such as freedom of speech, were in conflict with the wishes of authority figures or with potential obligations to others. While some age and location differences emerged, adolescents from both Canada and China endorsed a wide array of personal rights.

Reasoning about civic responsibility. Developing an understanding of government and of civic and political rights is essential to civic development. This lays the foundation for an appreciation of the relationship between the individual and civic institutions. However, civic involvement often requires service on behalf of one's community or contributions to a political cause. This type of service switches the relationship between the individual and civic institutions; through civic involvement, individuals are acting *prosocially* toward these institutions. Similar to the research on prosocial development discussed earlier, researchers have explored how individuals reason about civic responsibility.

Early on, researchers studying political reasoning were interested in how individuals reasoned about the public good. Their research focused on how adolescents balanced individual rights with beliefs about what is best for the citizenry as a whole. Gallatin and Adelson (1970) had children and adolescents choose whether individuals in hypothetical scenarios should engage in a behavior that contributed to the good of their community even when doing so necessitated giving up an individual freedom. Participants were asked whether individuals who did not have children should still be forced to pay an education tax or whether men over a certain age should be required to get yearly medical exams. Interestingly, compared to younger children, adolescents emphasized the public good rather than personal rights for some issues, but focused more on individual rights for others. Thus, adolescents balanced notions of the responsibility to the public good with beliefs about individual freedoms and choice. This is similar to Helwig's (1995, 1997) findings on adolescents' reasoning about situations where social and moral concerns conflict with human rights.

More recently, developmental researchers have postulated that adolescents gradually develop knowledge of the social contract, or the "deal that inheres between persons and their society" (Flanagan, 2000, p. 191). With age, children develop theories about the social order through interacting with and interpreting the prevailing ethos and values of their society. Adolescents develop beliefs about the types of rights and benefits they can expect from societal institutions, as well as the types of behavior institutions and the state can expect from citizens. For instance, within democratic societies, the hope is that adolescents will develop beliefs about the importance of social responsibility, involved citizenship, and contributing to the well-being of their communities.

Research has found that adolescents view social responsibility as entailing different types of civic activity. In a study by Haste and Hogan (2006), British youth ranging in age from 11 to 21 completed a survey regarding normative civic action. Principal components analysis yielded five components: voting, conventional political participation, community helping, "making one's voice heard" activities (e.g., protesting), and joining organizations. However, adolescents may judge some forms of civic involvement to be more obligatory and important than others. In fact, research has shown that adolescents from different countries do differentially value different types of civic involvement (Torney-Purta, 2002); adolescents tend to focus on concrete behaviors such as obeying laws, conventional forms of political participation such as voting, and community activities. Other forms of political participation, such as participation in political parties, political protest, or taking part in public discourse about important issues were seen as less important.

In a cross-sectional study of 312 late adolescents from a middle-class suburban high school, Metzger and Smetana (2009) examined adolescents' judgments and justifications for different forms of civic involvement. Participants' civic concepts were assessed by adolescents' ratings of obligation to engage in the behavior, rankings of the importance of engaging in the behavior, and justifications for the behavior. Three types of civic involvement were assessed: community service, standard political involvement such as voting, and involvement in social movements (e.g., protesting for a cause). Adolescents' judgments and justifications indicated that they treated involvement in community service as a moral issue. These activities were seen as obligatory, worthy of great respect, and important. They also were justified primarily with moral justifications. Interestingly, standard political activities such as voting were rated as being even more obligatory than community service, but they were treated as conventional in the other ratings and justifications. The findings also showed that adolescents treated involvement in social movements as far less obligatory and worthy of respect than standard political involvement or community service. It is important to realize, however, that community service and political participation may have a different meaning in different countries. For instance, youth in the United States have been found to volunteer at higher rates than youth in other countries, especially in Nordic and post-Communist countries (Torney-Purta et al., 2001, p. 142).

In contrast to the characterization of adolescents as being individualistic and apathetic regarding political participation (Weller, 2006), the majority of adolescents in the Metzger and Smetana (2009) study viewed citizens as obligated to be involved in various forms of civic activities. Only a small percentage of students reported that it was "not at all wrong" for citizens in the United States to avoid participation in political or community service activities. However, the results also suggested that adolescents have complex views about their social and civic world and that they evaluate the distinctive features of different kinds of civic involvement.

In summary, some research assessing adolescents' reasoning about civic and political institutions has found that most individuals generally move from more individual and concrete views of political issues and civic institutions in childhood to more sociocentric, abstract, and complex reasoning in late adolescence. Other empirical work has investigated political reasoning, especially beliefs about human rights, from a social domain perspective. This research has focused on heterogeneity in adolescents' reasoning and the different forms of social knowledge they bring to bear on these issues. An understanding of political institutions and a comprehension of civil liberties are important facets of civic reasoning. However, civic involvement also involves prosocial action in service of these institutions. Research has examined how an understanding of civic responsibility, including beliefs about the common good and the social contract, develops. More recent research has assessed moral judgments about different types of civic involvement. This research has shown that most adolescents find both mainstream political involvement and community service to be obligatory aspects of citizenship.

CONTEXTUAL INFLUENCES ON ADOLESCENTS' CIVIC AND POLITICAL BELIEFS

In addition to examining normative consistencies and developmental changes in children and adolescents' understanding and beliefs about government, human rights, and civic responsibility, research has examined contextual influences on reasoning. This research has examined the intersection among religious, political, and civic beliefs, as well as how parents influence these beliefs. Other research has examined the effects of demographic characteristics such as sex, socioeconomic status, and ethnicity on civic beliefs.

Flanagan et al.'s (2005) research on adolescents' reasoning about democracy, discussed previously, also found that adolescents' age, parental education, and report of their families' political discussions were associated with adolescents' ability to articulate at least one correct definition of democracy. In addition, adolescents' endorsement of specific definitions of democracy varied according to their individual beliefs. Adolescents' personal values and the values and political beliefs endorsed by their families were associated with the likelihood of stating a specific definition. For instance, adolescents who saw social vigilance and materialism as essential values were more likely to endorse individual rights in their definitions of democracy, whereas adolescents whose families valued responsibility for the environment and for other people were more likely to stress civic equality in their definitions. Other research has found that cultural and religious beliefs may influence adolescents' reasoning about limitations on freedom of speech. For instance, Muslim youth were less likely to endorse freedom of speech, which was offensive to Muslim religious teachings, than were Dutch majority youth in the Netherlands (Verkuyten & Slooter, 2008).

Religious and cultural beliefs are not the only variables that influence adolescents' political reasoning. Research also has examined the effects of socioeconomic status. For instance, Flanagan and Tucker (1999) investigated variations in adolescents' explanations for three different political issues: unemployment, poverty, and homelessness, as a function of socioeconomic status. Distinctions were made between individual and dispositional reasons and situational, societal, and structural reasons. Interestingly, compared to adolescents from higher socioeconomic status families, adolescents from lower socioeconomic status families held individuals more responsible for social problems and believed that America provided more equal opportunities for all. They were also more likely to endorse materialism as a personal value and reported that their family valued self-reliance more than compassion and social responsibility. The authors argued that adolescents from poorer families may hold individuals responsible for social advancement because they may see access to increased financial opportunities as dependent on their own individual effort. Other researchers also have found associations between socioeconomic status and political reasoning. Raajimakers, Verbogt, and Vollebergh (1998) found that compared to well-educated adolescents, poorly educated adolescents showed more variability in their political attitudes.

The relationship between social class and views of the social contract may differ for adolescents from different countries. For instance, Flanagan and Campbell (2003) compared attitudes toward governmental responsibility between adolescents from former socialist countries (e.g., the Czech Republic) and adolescents from America and Australia. They assessed adolescents' beliefs about whether their society was a meritocracy, where "anyone who was willing to work could get ahead," and whether "the government should provide social entitlements." Adolescents from former socialist countries were less likely to view their country as a meritocracy and more likely to state that the government should provide social entitlements than did adolescents from free-market countries. However, these relationships were qualified by interactions between social class and country of origin. Middle-class adolescents in free-market countries questioned the merit-based nature of their societies more, whereas middle-class adolescents from former socialist countries were less likely to state that the government should give entitlements.

Ethnicity also may impact adolescents' political beliefs and attitudes. Ethnic minority youth feel less politically efficacious (Lopez, Levine, Both, Kiesa, Kirby, & Marcelo, 2006). They evaluated statements such as "I am able to have an impact on my community" less positively than did ethnic majority youth. However, survey data also show that ethnic minority youth volunteer and contribute to churches and charities at a relatively high rate (Lopez et al., 2006).

Sanchez-Jankowski (2002) provided a theoretical framework for conceptualizing civic engagement across different ethnic groups. Sanchez-Jankowski asserted that due to the historic rejection from mainstream political and community involvement, ethnic minority groups view civic responsibility and action in terms of activities that directly help their communities. When youth realize that the historical endeavors of their group to become involved in the broader social order have been repudiated, they may become more interested in problems and policies in their immediate environment. For instance, research has shown that adolescents from a variety of ethnic backgrounds had higher levels of civic commitment when they felt a sense of connectedness with their communities (Flanagan, Cumsille, Gill, & Gallay, 2007). Adolescents' ratings of the importance of items such as "serving my country" or "helping the less fortunate" were associated with how adolescents viewed the levels of trust, collective efficacy, and inclusiveness within their communities.

Sanchez-Jankowski's theoretical framework can be seen to involve some social cognitive appraisal. Youth evaluate types of involvement. They assess their cultural group's relationship to different types of social institutions and the special needs of their own culture. Therefore, youth are actively selecting their civic activities. In fact, research has shown that ethnic minority youth do prioritize civic and political issues that more directly impact their own ethnic group. For instance, a study drawn from the IEA Civic Education Study's data compared the civic knowledge and attitudes of adolescents from different ethnic groups in the United States. When making judgments about the relative importance of different political issues, Hispanic adolescents were more likely to prioritize immigration issues than were youth from other ethnic groups. This shows that Hispanic youths' political beliefs were influenced by an awareness of the special political needs and obstacles of their cultural group (Torney-Purta, Barber, & Wilkenfeld, 2007).

Finally, although it has received less empirical attention, gender is another important dimension of individual differences in civic reasoning and development. Metzger and Smetana (2009) found that adolescent boys' and girls' judgments about different types of civic responsibility differed slightly. Boys judged political involvement (e.g., voting) to be more important and obligatory than girls, who, in turn, prioritized community service more than did boys. This finding is similar to the gender differences in prosocial reasoning discussed previously and also is consistent with the results of surveys that find that girls tend to volunteer at slightly higher levels than boys (Eisenberg et al., 2007). It could be that girls' more advanced prosocial reasoning leads them to focus on community service, as this type of civic involvement directly affects the welfare of others.

A great deal of individual variability has been found in adolescents' reasoning about a wide range of political issues, such as democratic forms of government and civil liberties. Thus, research on political reasoning has moved from a focus on normative developmental patterns to research that has assessed individual differences and contextual influences. Adolescents' reasoning about their obligation to become involved with civic and community institutions is influenced by a variety of demographic factors, including socioeconomic status, country of origin, ethnicity, and gender. It also is influenced by psychological factors such as religious beliefs and beliefs about individual responsibility. Future research should continue to explore how these factors affect adolescents' civic development, including how individual differences may impact the relationship between adolescents' civic beliefs and behavior (see Finlay, this volume; Torney-Purta et al., this volume).

CIVIC BEHAVIOR AND CIVIC REASONING

As noted earlier, research on civic engagement has been primarily concerned with adolescents' activities and behaviors. Indeed, the goal of developmental research in this area is to understand the factors that can help to produce an active and engaged polity (Flanagan & Faison, 2002). Thus, if social-cognitive research is to make a meaningful contribution to our understanding of adolescent civic engagement, adolescents' beliefs, attitudes, and reasoning regarding political issues should be associated with civic behavior.

Rational choice theories of motivation postulate that individuals choose to participate in civic activities for personal gain. In contrast to these utilitarian justifications, however, Verba and his colleagues (Verba, Schlozman, & Brady, 1995) found that among Americans, civic involvement stemmed primarily from individuals' beliefs that they had a responsibility to participate and "do their share" in contributing to the common good. They justified their civic engagement by pointing to moral values or notions of social responsibility. Similar explanations for civic behavior were found in a study of adolescent civic commitments in seven countries including the United States (Flanagan, Jonsson, Botcheva, Csapo, Bowes, & Macek, 1998). In all seven countries, youth who were committed to civic goals such as improving their communities or helping the poor were more engaged in volunteer activities in their communities. Similar associations between holding relevant norms or beliefs about what good citizens do and individuals' intention to vote, join a political party, and volunteer were found in Chile, Estonia, Finland, Greece, Switzerland, and the United States (Richardson & Torney-Purta, 2008).

Participation in civic activities also has been found to be associated with other civic beliefs, such as social trust. Social trust, which reflects a general positive belief about people (Flanagan, 2003), is a critical facet of democratic societies (see also Flanagan, this volume). Individuals who are high in social trust are thought to have a strong desire to participate in their communities. Research has shown that involvement in community groups and volunteering leads to increased social trust and that engagement in multiple, diverse activities is associated with even higher levels of social trust (Flanagan, Gill, & Gallay, 2005). Engagement in organized and civic activities also has been linked with more sophisticated political reasoning. For instance, Flanagan et al. (2005) found that older adolescents' participation in community- or school-based extracurricular activities was associated with a greater likelihood of correctly defining democracy, whereas participation in faith-based groups or student government was not. However, the causal relationship between political reasoning and engagement in civic activities is unclear. Yates and Youniss (1996) conducted a short-term longitudinal study to investigate the process by which adolescent civic involvement might lead to the creation of a political-moral identity. They examined essays written by a small sample of urban, primarily minority adolescents before and after they had volunteered at a soup kitchen. Students' essays were examined for their level of *transcendence*. This reflected the extent to which adolescents placed their daily activities within a historical framework, such as utilizing their experiences at the shelter to reflect on justice, responsibility, society, or political processes that influence homelessness. Working at the soup kitchen led to a significant increase in the quantity of transcendent statements.

The association between civic reasoning, transcendence, and civic involvement is not limited to community service. Duncan and Stewart (2007) examined associations between personal political salience and individuals' engagement in women's rights and civil rights activism. The authors defined personal political salience as the degree to which individuals felt that politically charged historical events (for instance, the Vietnam War, the civil rights movement) were personally meaningful to them. Individuals who felt more connected to historical political events, as measured by personal political salience, engaged in more social movement political activities.

More recent events, such as the events of September 11, 2001, also may impact individuals' political views and behavior. Sherrod, Quinones, & Davita (2004) had college students fill out surveys that measured their experiences of the events of September 11. The study measured different types of reactions, such as terrorism fears, prejudice, desires for retaliation, and the desire to show support for the United States. The students also rated the importance of items that measured their attitudes toward inequality, self-preservation and terrorism, social causes, and conservative morality. Intercorrelations indicated that students who responded to the events of September 11 with fears about terrorism viewed concerns about equality, self-preservation and terrorism, and conservative morality as especially important. In contrast, students who reacted with prejudice and desires for retaliation viewed concerns about quality of life and social causes as of relatively little importance. Thus, adolescents' interpretations of an important historical event were associated with their political views.

In the study by Metzger & Smetana (2009) discussed previously, associations between adolescents' judgments and their involvement in different activities also were examined. Adolescents who were more involved in civic and organized activities viewed community service, standard political involvement, and social movement involvement as more obligatory and more worthy of respect. However, analyses of adolescents' involvement in different types of activities showed that adolescents' civic beliefs and behavior were linked in domain-specific ways. Specifically, adolescents who were more involved in volunteer and service activities judged involvement in community service to be more obligatory and more worthy of respect. In addition, adolescents who were more involved in political activities judged both standard political and social movement activities to be more obligatory and more worthy of respect. While the cross-sectional nature of the study did not allow for causal inferences, this research shows that adolescents' civic behavior is associated with their reasoning about civic involvement.

Other researchers have noted, however, that adolescents are often involved in more than one activity, and different patterns of involvement may be associated with adolescents' civic conceptualizations. For instance, adolescents' involvement in heterogeneous activities was found to be linked to higher levels of social trust (Flanagan, Gill, & Gallay, 2005). Metzger (2007) examined whether different profiles of adolescent organized and civic activity were associated with adolescents' civic beliefs and reasoning. Six categories of adolescent activity involvement (school, community, religious, political, volunteer/service, work for pay) were examined using cluster analysis. Six activities profiles were derived: an *uninvolved* (low on all activities), a *just work* group (low on everything except work), *no work* (moderate activity involvement, low levels of work), *no church* (moderate activity involvement and work, but low church involvement), *church and work* (high levels of church involvement and work, but low levels of every other activity), and *multiply involved* (high levels of all forms of involvement). Ratings of obligation and respect for three types of adult civic involvement (community service, political involvement such as voting, and involvement in social movements) were examined for these profiles.

Generally, students classified in the activity profiles that entailed greater involvement across activities (multiply involved, no church, no work) gave higher ratings of obligation and respect for all types of activities than did teens clustered in profiles reflecting less involvement. However, profiles that highlighted primarily work or church (just work, and church and work profiles) prioritized civic involvement less. A great deal of research has found that for adolescents, working longer hours is associated with a host of negative developmental outcomes, including cynical attitudes toward work and increased materialistic attitudes (Greenberger & Steinberg, 1986). Materialism is often considered to be at odds with civic mindedness or prosocial reasoning, which could explain why adolescents who worked more judged involvement in civic activities to be less obligatory and less worthy of respect. Given that several theorists have argued that religious involvement may increase adolescent civic engagement (Crystal & DeBell, 2002; Furrow, King, & White, 2004; Hunsberger, Pratt, & Pancer, 2001; Youniss, McLellan, & Yates, 1999), it is also interesting that profiles entailing greater church involvement were associated with judgments of less respect and obligation for different types of civic involvement.

Some of the individual differences in adolescents' political reasoning can be accounted for by adolescents' involvement in different types of civic activities. Research has begun to address connections between adolescents' civic behavior and political reasoning and beliefs. Such associations are consistent with a constructivist view of development, as adolescents' engagement with their community and with civic institutions is connected to their beliefs about individuals' responsibility to contribute to community and political institutions. Thus, social-cognitive research may provide valuable insights into how adolescents coordinate their civic reasoning and their civic involvement.

CONCLUSIONS

Adolescents' reasoning about prosocial behavior has been a persistent topic of interest in developmental psychology. The research reviewed in this chapter demonstrates that prosocial reasoning is relevant to understanding adolescents' civic involvement. It entails prosocial behavior directed toward civic and community institutions or classes of people, such as the less fortunate or the homeless. However, little research has explicitly examined these connections. A profitable direction for future research is to examine associations between adolescents' developing prosocial reasoning and civic involvement.

Political scientists have had a long-standing interest in individuals' understanding of their civic and political world, and there has been a renewed interest in these issues among developmental scientists. This has led to a new understanding of adolescents' beliefs concerning others and their complex and multifaceted views of their relationships to civic and political institutions. Social-cognitive perspectives can illuminate adolescents' reasoning about civic obligations and their links to civic and community activity. Research demonstrates that adolescents reason in sophisticated ways about civic duty and that civic duty is a multifaceted notion that can entail both moral and conventional concepts.

Traditionally, civic development research has focused on civic behavior, which is seen as transmitted from parents to children through socialization. Considering social-cognitive processes shifts the focus to how adolescents come to understand civic institutions and how they actively construct an understanding of their relationships and obligations to civic institutions.

In this view, parents, teachers, and other socializing agents are important in civic development, but children's and adolescents' beliefs and interpretations must be considered. Furthermore, earlier cognitive-developmental research was based primarily on Kolhberg's (1971) theory and focused on examining age-related changes (stages) in understanding. In contrast, more recent social-cognitive research incorporates a concern for individual, demographic, and contextual variables that may situate individuals' judgments and reasoning. Through active civic engagement, adolescents not only construct beliefs about their relationship to these institutions, but also learn how their engagement might significantly influence or even change those institutions. Thus, a social-cognitive approach to civic development has the potential to elucidate how individuals become fully functioning and aware civic participants. This research can help to explain the different beliefs, motivations, and knowledge systems associated with different forms of civic behavior.

FUTURE DIRECTIONS

As this chapter demonstrates, children and adolescents are capable of reasoning about their civic and political world. Therefore, the next step will be to further explore how these concepts are coordinated with civic activity. Our research (Metzger & Smetana, 2009) provides one model for how this research could be conducted. Future research on adolescent civic reasoning would be enhanced by adopting the types of methods used in social-cognitive research. For instance, future research could benefit from the more open-ended interview methods and hypothetical dilemmas utilized by researchers studying political and prosocial reasoning. These methods would provide additional insight into adolescents' thinking about civic involvement, including situations where reasoning about civic involvement conflicts with other civic, social, or moral concerns. Previous research has primarily examined adolescents' more abstract beliefs. Exploring adolescents' reasoning about conflicting situations (e.g., joining a protest or boycotting a product may negatively affect a merchant's commercial activity, or family or social obligations may interfere with opportunities for community service) would provide greater insight into adolescents' developing civic beliefs.

Research on adolescents' civic reasoning also could use the available research on normative social-cognitive developmental processes in adolescence. Adolescents' decision making (Lewis, 1981) and knowledge about political institutions becomes more sophisticated and abstract in late adolescence, and this may affect adolescents' ability to effectively choose and reason about forms of civic action (see Wilkenfeld et al., this volume). As discussed in this chapter, recent research has begun to examine how individual differences in religious or social beliefs and demographic characteristics affect civic development. These may moderate the relationship between adolescents' civic beliefs and behavior. Future civic development research should examine how gender, socioeconomic status, and ethnicity impact adolescents' views of civic responsibility and their coordination of civic behavior and beliefs. In addition, affective processes such as sympathy or patriotism or ideological or political attitudes may be associated with adolescents' beliefs about civic engagement and should be studied.

As detailed here, political scientists have had a long-standing concern with the development of political reasoning. More collaboration between political and developmental scientists could be very fruitful in examining associations between various belief systems and different types of civic behavior. More generally, future social-cognitive research on civic development will benefit from interdisciplinary efforts, which could lead to more sophisticated theories and methods and produce findings that can be used to shape social policy.

However, the ultimate goal of civic development research is to increase both adolescents' and adults' active engagement. Despite slightly higher voter turnout among young adults in the 2008 U.S. presidential election, few youth consistently engage in civic or political behavior. Therefore, there is a need among researchers to attend to promoting civic activity. Findings from research on the ways in which individuals coordinate civic beliefs, political attitudes, and engagement could contribute to knowledge of normative development in this area, but it also has the potential to inform education programs aimed at increasing adolescent civic involvement. Social-cognitive researchers should collaborate with educators to create comprehensive civic education programs that include cognitive and affective components. Such programs could teach adolescents the skills necessary for civic behavior. They could also help them to develop the ability to coordinate community service with feelings of empathy toward the less fortunate, as well as balance political forms of participation with feelings of obligation toward civic and community institutions. We have reviewed research that demonstrates adolescents' diverse and sophisticated reasoning about civic and political issues. Capitalizing on adolescents' developing cognitive skills in education programs could challenge students to think constructively and form their own beliefs about the importance of civic responsibility.

Adolescents' social life has been described as involving an increase in privileges with a parallel expansion of responsibilities (Levesque, 2002). Further investigation of adolescents' conceptualization of civic behavior would help elucidate the ways in which young people view their expanded responsibilities, as well as their beliefs about community service and political engagement. In addition, Helwig's (2007) research on adolescent political reasoning has referred to democratic rights and decision making as the two core components of democratic reasoning. As discussed in this chapter, beliefs about civic responsibility and civic participation may constitute a potential third component of democratic reasoning. Future research from a social-cognitive perspective could contribute to our understanding of adolescents' developing civic reasoning and how they actively construct their beliefs about civic duty.

REFERENCES

Adelson, J. (1971). The political imagination of the young adolescent. *Daedalus, 100,* 1013–1050.

Adelson, J., & O'Neil, R. P. (1966). Growth of political ideas in adolescence: The sense of community. *Journal of Personality and Social Psychology, 4,* 295–306.

Carlo, G., Crockett, L. J., Randall, B. A., & Roesch, S. C. (2007). A latent growth curve analysis of prosocial behavior among rural adolescents. *Journal of Research on Adolescence, 17,* 301–324.

Carlo, G., Eisenberg, N., & Knight, G. (1992). An objective measure of adolescents' prosocial moral reasoning. *Journal of Research on Adolescence, 2,* 331–349.

Connell, R. W. (1971). *The child's construction of politics.* Melbourne University Press: Carlton, Victoria.

Crystal, D., & DeBell, M. (2002). Sources of civic orientation among American youth: Trust, religious valuation, and attributions of responsibility. *Political Psychology, 23,* 113–132.

Delli Carpini, M. X., & Keeter, S. (1996). *What Americans know about politics and why it matters.* New Haven: Yale University Press.

Duncan, L. E., & Stewart, A. J. (1996). Still bringing the Vietnam War home: Sources of contemporary student activism. *Personality & Social Psychology Bulletin, 21,* 914–924.

Duncan, L. E., & Stewart, A. J. (2007). Personal political salience: The role of personality in collective identity and action. *Political Psychology, 28,* 143–164.

Eisenberg, N. (1990). Prosocial development in early and mid-adolescence. In R. Montemayor & G. Adams (Eds.), *From childhood to adolescence: A transitional period? Advances in adolescent development: An annual book series, Vol. 2* (pp. 240–268). Thousand Oaks, CA: Sage Publications.

Eisenberg, N., Cumberland, A., Guthrie, I. K., Murthy, B. C., & Shepard, S. A. (2005). Age changes in prosocial responding and moral reasoning in adolescence and early adulthood. *Journal of Research on Adolescence. Special issue: Moral development, 15,* 235–260.

Eisenberg, N., Fabes, R., & Spinrad, T. (2007). Prosocial development. In N. Eisenberg, W. Damon, & R. M. Lerner (Vol. Eds.), *Handbook of Child Psychology: Vol. 3 Social, Emotional, and Personality Development* (6th ed., pp. 646–718). Hoboken, NJ: John Wiley & Sons.

Eisenberg, N., Guthrie, I., Cumberland, A., Murphy, B., Shepard, S., Zhou, Q., & Carlo, G. (2002). Prosocial development in early adulthood: A longitudinal study. *Journal of Personality & Social Psychology, 82,* 993–1006.

Eisenberg, N., Guthrie, I., Murphy, B., Shepard, S., Cumberland, A., & Carlo, G. (1999). Consistency and development of prosocial dispositions: A longitudinal study. *Child Development, 70,* 1360–1372.

Eisenberg, N., Miller, P. A., Shell, R., McNalley, S., & Shea, C. (1991). Prosocial development in adolescence: A longitudinal study. *Developmental Psychology, 27,* 849–857.

Eisenberg, N., & Shell, R. (1986). The relation of prosocial moral judgment and behavior in children: The mediating role of cost. *Personality and Social Psychology Bulletin, 12,* 426–433.

Emler, N. (1992). Childhood origins of beliefs about institutional authority. *The Development of Political Understanding: A New Perspective: New Directions for Child Development, 56,* 65–77.

Flanagan, C. A. (2000). Social change and the "social contract" in adolescent development. In L. Crockett & R. Silbereisen (Eds.), *Negotiating adolescence in times of social change* (pp. 191–198). New York: Cambridge University Press.

Flanagan, C. A. (2003). Trust, identity, and civic hope. *Applied Developmental Science, 7,* 165–171.

Flanagan, C. A. (2005). Volunteerism, leadership, political socialization, and civic engagement. In M. Gazzaniga (Ed.), *The new cognitive neurosciences* (2nd ed., pp. 721–745). Cambridge, MA: MIT Press.

Flanagan, C. A., & Campbell, B. (2003). Social class and adolescents' beliefs about justice in different social orders. *Journal of Social Issues, 59,* 711–732.

Flanagan, C. A., Cumsille, P., Gill, S., & Gallay, L. S. (2007). School and community climates and civic commitments: Patterns for ethnic minority and majority students. *Journal of Educational Psychology, 99,* 421–431.

Flanagan, C. A., & Faison, N. (2002). Youth civic development: Implications of research for social policy and programs. *Social Policy Report,* Society for Research in Child Development.

Flanagan, C. A., Gill, S., & Gallay, L. (2005). Social participation and social trust in adolescence: The importance of heterogenous encounters. In A. Omato (Ed.), *Processes of community change and action* (pp. 149–166). Mahwah, NJ: Erlbaum.

Flanagan, C. A., Jonsson, B., Botcheva, L., Csapo, B., Bowes, J., & Macek, P. (1998). Adolescents and the "social contract": Developmental roots of citizenship in seven countries. In M. Yates & J. Youniss (Eds.), *International perspectives on community service and civic engagement in youth* (pp. 135–155). New York: Cambridge University Press.

Flanagan, C. A., Gallay, L. S., Gill, S., Gallay, E., & Nti, N. (2005). What does democracy mean? Correlates of adolescent views. *Journal of Adolescent Research, 20,* 193–218.

Flanagan, C. A., & Tucker, C. (1999). Adolescents' explanations for political issues: Concordance with their views of self and society. *Developmental Psychology, 35,* 1198–1209.

Furnham, A., & Stacey, B. (1991). *Young people's understanding of society.* New York: Routledge.

Furrow, J., King, P., & White, K. (2004). Religion and positive youth development: Identity, meaning, and prosocial concerns. *Applied Developmental Science, 8,* 17–26.

Gallatin, J., & Adelson, J. (1970). Individual rights and the public good: A cross-national study of adolescents. *Comparative Political Studies, 3,* 226–244.

Greenberger, E., & Steinberg, L. (1986). *When teenagers work: The psychological and social costs of adolescent employment.* New York: Basic Books.

Hart, D., Atkins, R., & Ford, D. (1998). Urban America as a context for the development of moral identity in adolescence. *Journal of Social Issues, 65,* 513–530.

Hart, D., & Fegley, S. (1995). Prosocial behavior and caring in adolescence: Relations to self-understanding and social judgment. *Child Development, 66,* 1346–1359.

Haste, H., & Hogan, A. (2006). Beyond conventional civic participation, beyond the moral-political divide: Young people and contemporary debates about citizenship. *Journal of Moral Education, 35,* 473–493.

Haste, H., & Torney-Purta, J. (1992). Introduction. The development of political understanding: A new perspective. *New Directions for Child Development, 56,* 1–10.

Helwig, C. (1995). Adolescents' and young adults' conceptions of civil liberties: Freedom of speech and religion. *Child Development, 66,* 152–166.

Helwig, C. (1997). The role of agent and social context in judgments of freedom of speech and religion. *Child Development, 68,* 484–495.

Helwig, C. (1998). Children's conceptions of fair government and freedom of speech. *Child Development, 69,* 518–531.

Helwig, C. (2007, April). *The development of judgments and reasoning about democratic decision making in mainland China and Canada.* Discussion presented at the biennial meeting of the Society for Research in Child Development, Boston, MA.

Helwig, C., Arnold, M. L., Tan, D., & Boyd, D. (2007). Mainland Chinese and Canadian adolescents' judgments and reasoning about the fairness of democratic and other forms of government. *Cognitive Development, 22,* 96–109.

Helwig, C., & Jasiobedzka, U. (2001). The relation between law and morality: Children's reasoning about socially beneficial and unjust laws. *Child Development, 72,* 1382–1393.

Helwig, C. C., & Turiel, E. (2002). Children's social and moral reasoning. In P. Smith & C. Hart (Eds.), *Blackwell handbook of childhood social development* (pp. 476–490). Malden, MA: Blackwell Publishing.

Hunsberger, B., Pratt, M., & Pancer, M. (2001). Adolescent identity formation: Religious exploration and commitment. *Identity: An International Journal of Theory and Research, 1,* 365–386.

Hunt, J. M. (1969). The impact and limitations of the giant of developmental psychology. In D. Elkind & J. Flavell (Eds.), *Studies in cognitive development: Essays in honor of Jean Piaget.* New York: Oxford University Press.

Jaffee, S., & Hyde, J. S. (2000). Gender differences in moral orientation: A meta-analysis. *Psychological Bulletin, 126,* 703–726.

Jennings, M. K. (2002). Generation units and the student protest movement in the United States: An intra- and intergenerational analysis. *Political Psychology, 23,* 303–324.

Jennings, M., & Niemi, R. (1968). The transmission of political values from parent to child. *American Political Science Review, 62,* 169–184.

Kahn, P. H., Jr. (1992). Children's obligatory and discretionary moral judgments. *Child Development*, *63*, 416–430.

Kohlberg, L. (1971). From is to ought: How to commit the naturalistic fallacy and get away with it in the study of moral development. In T. Mischel (Ed.), *Psychology and genetic epistemology* (pp. 151–235). New York: Academic Press.

Lahat, A., Helwig, C., Yang, S., Tan, D., & Liu, C. (2009). Mainland Chinese adolescents' judgments and reasoning about self-determination and nurturance rights. *Social Development*, *18*, 690–710.

Levesque, R. J. (2002). *Adolescents and the law: Preparing adolescents for responsible citizenship.* Washington, DC: American Psychological Association.

Lewis, C. C. (1981). How adolescents approach decision: Changes over grades seven to twelve and policy implications. *Child Development*, *52*, 538–544.

Lopez, M. H., Levine, P., Both, D., Kiesa, A., Kirby, E., & Marcelo, K. (2006). *The 2006 civic and political health of the nation: A detailed look at how youth participate in politics and communities*. Medford, MA: CIRCLE (The Center for Information and Research on Civic Learning and Engagement). Retrieved November 13, 2007, from http://www.civicyouth.org/PopUps/2006_CPHS_Report_update.pdf

Metzger, A. (2007). *Domain-specific judgments of civic and political engagement in late adolescence: Associations with adolescent activity involvement* (Doctoral dissertation). University of Rochester (2008). Retrieved from Dissertation Abstracts International: Section B: The Sciences and Engineering, Vol. 68(8-B), p. 5613.

Metzger, A., & Smetana, J. G. (2009). Adolescent civic and political engagement: Associations between domain-specific judgments and behavior. *Child Development*, *80*, 433–441.

Miller, P. A., Eisenberg, N., Fabes, R. A., & Shell, R. (1996). Relations of moral reasoning and vicarious emotion to young children's prosocial behavior toward peers and adults. *Developmental Psychology*, *32*, 210–219.

Mussen, P., & Eisenberg, N. (2001). Prosocial development in context. In A. Bohart & D. Stipek (Eds.), *Constructive and destructive behavior: Implications for family, school, and society* (pp. 103–126). Washington, DC: American Psychological Association.

Neff, K. D., & Helwig, C. (2002). A constructivist approach to understanding the development of reasoning about rights and authority within cultural contexts. *Cognitive Development*, *17*, 1429–1450.

Nolin, M., Chaney, B., & Chapman, C. (1997). *Student participation in community service activity.* Washington, DC: U.S. Department of Education, National Center for Educational Statistics.

Pancer, S., & Pratt, M. (1999). Social and family determinants of community service involvement in Canadian youth. In M. Yates & J. Youniss (Eds.), *Roots of civic identity* (pp. 32–55). New York: Cambridge University Press.

Piaget, J. (1970). *Structuralism*. New York: Harper & Row.

Raajimakers, Q., Verbogt, T. F., & Vollebergh, W. A. (1998). Moral reasoning and political beliefs of Dutch adolescents and young adults. *Journal of Social Issues, 54*, 531–546.

Richardson, W. K., & Torney-Purta, J. (2008). Connections between concepts of democracy, citizen engagement, and schooling for 14-year-olds across countries.

In B. C. Rubin & J. M. Giarelli (Eds.) *Civic education for diverse citizens in global times* (pp. 79–103). New York: Lawrence Erlbaum Associates.

Sanchez-Jankowski, M. (2002). Minority youth and civic engagement: The impact of group relations. *Applied Developmental Science, 6*, 237–245.

Sherrod, L., Flanagan, C., & Youniss, J. (2002). Dimensions of citizenship and opportunities for youth development: The what, why, when, where, and who of citizenship development. *Applied Developmental Science, 6*, 264–272.

Sherrod, L., Quinones, O., & Davita, C. (2004). Youth's political views and their experience of September 11, 2001. *Applied Developmental Psychology, 25*, 149–170.

Smetana, J. G. (2006). Social-cognitive domain theory: Consistencies and variations in children's moral and social judgments. In M. Killen & J. Smetana (Eds.), *Handbook of moral development* (pp. 119–153). Mahwah, NJ: Erlbaum.

Smetana, J. G., Bridgeman, D. L., & Turiel, E. (1982). Differentiation of domains and prosocial behavior. In D. L. Bridgman (Ed.), *The nature of prosocial development* (pp. 163–183). New York: Academic Press.

Smetana, J. G., & Metzger, A. (2005). Family and religious antecedents of civic involvement in middle class African American late adolescents. *Journal of Research on Adolescence, 15*, 325–352.

Smetana, J. G., & Villalobos, M. (2009). Social-cognitive development during adolescence. In R. L. Lerner & L. Steinberg (Eds.), *Handbook of adolescent psychology, Vol. 1* (3rd ed., pp. 187–208). New York: Wiley-Blackwell Publishing.

Stradling, R. (1977). *The political awareness of the school leaver.* London: Hansard Society.

Thomlinson, P. (1975). Political education: Cognitive developmental perspectives from moral education. *Oxford Review of Education, 3*, 241–267.

Torney-Purta, J. (1991). Schema theory and cognitive psychology: Implications for social studies. *Theory and Research in Social Education, 19*, 1991.

Torney-Purta, J. (1992). Cognitive representations of the political system in adolescents: The continuum from pre-novice to expert. *The Development of Political Understanding: A New Perspective, 56*, 11–25.

Torney-Purta, J. (1994). Dimensions of adolescents' reasoning about political and historical issues: Ontological switches, developmental processes, and situated learning. In J. Voss & M. Carretera (Eds.), *Cognitive and instructional processes in history and social sciences* (pp. 103–121). Hillsdale, NJ: Erlbaum.

Torney-Purta, J. (2002). The school's role in developing civic engagement: A study of adolescents in twenty-eight countries. *Applied Developmental Sciences, 6*, 203–212.

Torney-Purta, J., Amadeo, J., & Richardson, W. (2007). Civic service among youth in Chile, Denmark, England and the United States. In A. McBride & M. Sherraden (Eds.), *Civic service worldwide: Impacts and inquiry* (pp. 95–132). Armonk, NY: M. E. Sharpe.

Torney-Purta, J., Barber, C., & Wilkenfeld, B. (2007). Latino adolescents'civic development in the United States: Research results from the IEA Civic Education Study. *Journal of Youth and Adolescence, 36*, 111–125.

Torney-Purta, J., Lehmann, R., Owald, H., & Schulz, W. (2001). *Citizenship and education in twenty-eight countries: Civic knowledge and engagement at age 14.* Amsterdam:

International Association for the Evaluation of Educational Achievement. Retrieved from http://www.terpconnect.umd.edu/~iea

Torney-Purta, J., Wilkenfeld, B., & Barber, C. (2008). How adolescents in twenty-seven countries understand, support and practice human rights. *Journal of Social Issues, 64(4)*, 857–880.

Turiel, E. (2006). The development of morality. In. N. Eisenberg, W. Damon, & R. Lerner (Eds.), *Handbook of child psychology, Vol. 3: Social, emotional, and personality development* (6th ed., pp. 789–857). Hoboken, NJ: John Wiley & Sons, Inc.

Verba, S., Schlozman, K. L., & Brady, H. E. (1995). *Voice and equality: Civic volunteerism in American politics.* Cambridge, MA: Harvard University Press.

Verkuyten, M., & Slooter, L. (2008). Muslim and non-Muslim adolescents' reasoning about freedom of speech and minority rights. *Child Development*, *79*, 514–528.

Weinreich-Haste, H. (1986). Kohlberg's contribution to political psychology: A positive view. In S. Modgil & C. Modgil (Eds.), *Lawrence Kohlberg: Consensus and controversy* (pp. 337–361). Philadelphia: The Falmer Press.

Weller, S. (2006). Skateboarding Alone? Making social capital discourse relevant to teenagers' lives. *Journal of Youth Studies*, *9*, 557–574.

Yates, M., & Youniss, J. (1996). Community service and political-moral identity in adolescents. *Journal of Research on Adolescence*, *54*, 248–261.

Youniss, J., McLellan, J. A., & Yates, M. (1999). Religion, community service, and identity in American youth. *Journal of Adolescence, 22*, 243–253.

CHAPTER 10

Early Childhood as a Foundation for Civic Engagement

JENNIFER ASTUTO
New York University

MARTIN D. RUCK
City University of New York

HISTORICALLY, RESEARCH ON civic engagement has focused on how youth, and more recently emerging adults, develop a civic or political orientation (Flanagan & Sherrod, 1998). Individual beliefs, attitudes, and knowledge of politics are common areas of research interest. These research foci are well justified. Most youth and young adults are hypothetical thinkers, consider multiple perspectives, and reason logically (Keating, 1990). Because of these skills, measurement of attitudes, beliefs, and behaviors is, for the most part, straightforward. Adolescence is also a time when sociopolitical factors can enhance developmental processes and outcomes. Youth respond to their changing environment and so, present practitioners and policy-makers with an opportunity to move them toward positive citizenship.

Hence, a developmental focus on adolescence and youth for research on civic engagement is understandable. Less empirical attention has been placed on the developmental roots of civic identity, that is, when civic identity begins to appear in children. Although a considerable amount of theorizing about the processes surrounding young children's political socialization exists (Dawson & Prewitt, 1969; Easton & Dennis, 1969; Hess & Torney, 1967; Powell, 2003), there is little current empirical research shedding light on early childhood antecedents to youth civic engagement. Are there early childhood developmental competencies that predict later civic behavior? Can early childhood settings provide unique opportunities for engagement in activities, which serve to facilitate and encourage prerequisites for later civic involvement? That is, what is the developmental foundation for youth civic engagement?

This chapter examines available evidence that suggests early childhood may be an overlooked or underexamined foundation for civic engagement, or both. We begin by providing a brief history of youth civic engagement research and note the absence of empirical work on the topic with young children. We then examine the germane work and developmental theory on early childhood competencies that may speak to later civic engagement in children and adolescents. We also consider a children's rights perspective in a brief overview of the UN Convention on the Rights of the Child as a guide for developmental scientists interested in civic engagement. Then, we consider how young children's participation or engagement in cognitively rich and language-rich socialization practices, such as play, may serve as a significant developmental context for later civic engagement. In concluding comments, we consider directions for future research, policy, and practice.

THE HISTORY OF CIVIC ENGAGEMENT RESEARCH WITH YOUNG CHILDREN

During the 1950s to the 1970s, there were a number of scholars from sociology, psychology, and political science who focused on young children's development of political understanding and awareness of political and civic symbolism. They were interested in capturing how early socialization contributed to the development of party affiliation, civic awareness, and political development (reviewed by Dudley & Gitelson, 2002; Sapiro, 2004). Most of these early investigations assumed that early childhood and adolescence provided the contexts for the development of cognitive and affective structures that were germane to later political choices, behaviors, and attitudes (Berti, 2005). In the earlier part of this period, empirical studies were captured under the umbrella of *political socialization* research (Stacey, 1978). Stimulated by theoretical frameworks such as an early version of social learning theory, systems theory, and psychoanalytic theory, there was an effort to identify antecedents of adult political engagement in childhood (Wilkenfeld et al., this volume). Some note that the focus on early socialization during the 1950s reflected the state of developmental science at the time (Flanagan & Sherrod, 1998). Large surveys and questionnaires were utilized to examine the relationship between children's political beliefs and their parents' views or the congruence of children's attitudes toward political issues with their teachers (Hess & Torney, 1967; Greenstein, 1965). However, these methods systematically excluded children younger than 7 years of age because of developmental limitations on survey measurement (Berti, 2005; Moore, Lare, & Wagner, 1985).

Later in this period, a perfect storm of theoretical inspiration and methodological creativity led to a focused examination on how political views *developed*, which supported the inclusion of younger children in research investigations. This shift has been attributed to the power of Piagetian theory as a dominant force in cognitive-developmental theory and thought (Berti, 2005); this work also supported the use of individual interviews as an effective data collection method with children as young as five years old. Connell (1975), an Australian psychologist, examined ways in which young children constructed their ideas about politics in line with their thinking about the social world more broadly. Hess and Torney (1967) proposed four frameworks, including the cognitive developmental model, as ways of understanding how children aged 7 to 13 developed their orientations to political authority and law, as well as citizens' participation. Easton and Hess's (1962) statement suggesting that the "truly formative years" of an individual within a political system are between ages 3 and 13 was echoed in Greenstein's (1965) work *Children and Politics*. This seminal piece summarized the importance of identifying the developmental roots of political socialization: "In general, the more important a political orientation is in the behavior of adults, the earlier it will be found in the learning of the child" (Greenstein, 1965, p. 12).

Studies with young children focused on an array of topics (Berti, 2005). The work of Moore et al. (1985) examined 5-year-olds' understanding of their political system and followed them for several years. There were methodological limitations to this study, in particular the use of the type of analysis that would have been suitable for cross-sectional rather than longitudinal data. However, this work represents one of the few longitudinal data collections on political understanding in early childhood. Topics including the judicial system (Demetriou & Charitides, 1986), law (Tapp & Kolhberg, 1971), concepts of country and nationality (Jahoda, 1964), understanding and definitions of altruistic behaviors (Austin et al., 1991), as well as views of adults' economic and political worlds (Furth, 1980) were explored with younger children (many of these studies are reviewed, as ways of understanding precursors to adolescents' views about society, in Torney-Purta, 1990). Together, these investigations provided the foundation for understanding how American children understand their political world, examining issues such as holding benign images of the president (Easton & Dennis, 1969; Greenstein, 1965; Hess & Torney, 1967). This work generated a detailed view of political understanding in early childhood; however, because reviews are available elsewhere, this research is not reviewed in this chapter (Barrett & Buchanan-Barrow, 2002; Berti, 2005).

Civic engagement continued to flourish as an important area of inquiry for researchers after the 1970s, with most samples representing youth ranging from 11 to 18 years old. One reason why researchers focused on this population was related to the engagement of youth and young adults in social movements at the time (e.g., civil rights and anti-Vietnam war protests) (Flanagan & Sherrod, 1998). Only recently, however, has an effort been made to focus on racially, ethnically, and socioeconomically diverse populations (Fridkin, Kenny, & Crittenden, 2006; Rubin, 2007; Russell, 2002; Sanchez-Jankowski, 2002). The work of Torney-Purta and colleagues (IEA; International Association for the Evaluation of Educational Achievement, Torney, Oppenheim, & Farnen, 1975; Torney-Purta, 2002; Torney-Purta, Lehman, Oswald, & Schulz, 2001; Torney-Purta, Schwille, & Amadeo, 1999) notably expanded our knowledge of and interest in youth civic education and knowledge outside of the United States. The IEA study of the 1970s found that the attitudes of 10-year-olds were somewhat less differentiated than those of 14-year-olds (Torney, Oppenheim, & Farnen, 1975). With few exceptions, however (e.g., Austin et al., 1991; Berti & Andriolo, 2001; Brophy & Alleman, 2002; Stevens, 1982), the focus on younger children inherent in the earlier work did not survive in mainstream American and European research on the topic.

Most recently, scholars are again calling for a downward extension of the age ranges involved in the study of civic engagement (Flanagan, 2003; Sherrod, 2002). Recognizing the growth of civic identity as a developmental process influenced by varying social contexts and experiences that are formative during early childhood requires both methodological creativity and robust theoretical thinking. Stewart & McDermott (2004) suggest that trends in civic engagement are influenced by macro-level factors, which are important at all life stages, and that early events are critical in shaping later civic engagement orientations:

> We may expect then, both historical change in patterns of civic engagement and generation to play some role in structuring the pattern within a single period, or for different generations at the same time but at developmentally different life stages (p. 190).

Similarly, Rosenblum (1998) made clear that civic engagement had a developmental course and that developmental scientists had something unique to contribute to its study. The idea that social events experienced during the formative years are critical to later development is, of course, not new (Mannheim, 1928, 1972).

There is no solid evidence regarding the longitudinal impact of early socialization on later civic engagement outcomes. As a result, we can only speculate about how an examination of young children's skills and experiences during preschool and kindergarten contexts may inform an understanding of developmental trajectories of civic identity.

EARLY CHILDHOOD COMPETENCES AND LATER CIVIC ENGAGEMENT

Early childhood settings, such as classrooms, are the first representation of greater society for young children. Not only does this context function to introduce young children to democratic processes and values, but it also may be the most fundamental context in developing the necessary competencies and skills for future civic engagement in the polity. During the remainder of this chapter, we introduce a conceptual framework for exploring how early childhood settings may lead to later civic engagement behaviors, attitudes, and beliefs (see Figure 10.1). We start by identifying and defining executive functions and prosocial skills as competencies, which are nurtured through quality play experiences in early childhood contexts, and lead to later civic engagement behaviors, attitudes, and beliefs in youth. By *quality play* we mean play that is complex, where children are encouraged to explore their interests in ways that promote language, creativity, and problem solving. We argue that quality play experiences in early childhood settings promote and nurture the necessary skills for later engagement.

Extensive research has contributed to the belief that behaviors such as attachment style, delinquency, high achievement, social competence, and aggression can be traced to early childhood, as early as infancy (Renken,

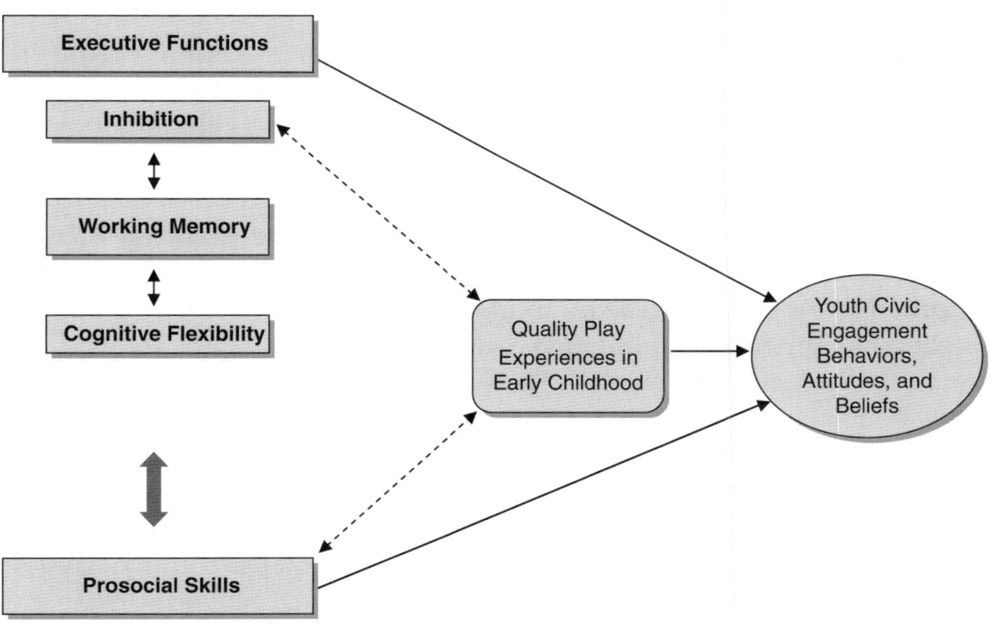

Figure 10.1 Hypothesized Model of Early Competence, Opportunities for Quality Play, and Later Youth Civic Engagement.

Egeland, Marvinney, Mangelsdorf, & Sroufe, 1989; Reynolds, Ou, & Topitzes, 2004; Bohlin, Hagekull, & Rydell, 2000). In contrast, most of what we know about the development of civic engagement is based on adolescence and early adulthood as its formative stages. However, a close examination of the development of cognitive and socio-emotional competencies during early childhood raises opportunities for researchers interested in civic engagement. As children broaden their social circles and have increased cognitive demands and expectations from formal school settings, they are introduced to notions of citizenship, belongingness, and democratic values (Dewey, 1938, 1944; Erwin & Kipness, 1997; Flekkoy & Kaufman, 1997). For example, not only are young children expanding their language and developing more complex concepts through engagement in activities such as play, they are also learning to develop and follow social rules and operate with others who may have different affective responses and cognitive perspectives. These early childhood educational experiences may provide the fertile ground for later attitudes, behavior, and beliefs about citizenship and engagement in the political and civic domain. Early childhood experiences play a powerful role in developing notions of the democratic process, and as Berti (2005) noted:

> ... although young children appear to lack a conceptual political domain, even in a very rudimentary form, they construct a set of interconnected concepts in the context of personal relations within the family, kindergarten, and peer groups, which provide some of the threads necessary for weaving true political concepts (p. 77).

If we consider the behaviors, attitudes, or beliefs of youth who are civically engaged, we can theorize which early developmental competencies are required to lead to such later civic engagement processes and outcomes. Although these relationships have yet to be tested empirically, two areas, which may account for many of the skills that serve as precursors to later civic outcomes, include executive functions (EFs) and prosocial behavior. Although interrelated, these developmental competencies may build the foundation for later adolescent and early adulthood civic orientations and capacity in important, and unique, ways.

EXECUTIVE FUNCTIONS AND PROSOCIAL SKILLS: PRECURSORS TO LATER CIVIC ENGAGEMENT?

Executive functions (EFs), also known as cognitive controls, represent the intersection of cognitive and social-emotional competencies that have not been conceptualized as fundamental developmental skills for later civic engagement. Although variation in definitions of EFs exist, most experts agree that three core EFs are inhibition, working memory, and cognitive flexibility (Diamond, Barnett, Thomas, & Munro, 2007). Inhibition refers to a child's ability to inhibit one desirable action to attend to the requirements of another. Working memory is the ability for children to hold relevant information in their minds, while manipulating or utilizing additional information in an effort to gain greater understanding, and relates to the ability to use information to develop complex concepts. Finally, cognitive flexibility is the ability to adjust to differing demands or priorities—to shift perspectives. All of these skills conceptually relate to abilities required to proactively and productively engage in society. For example, acquiring strong working memory skills enables youth to grasp the complexity of democratic values and develop dynamic solutions to social problems within their local context.

Most research, however, has examined the relationship of these abilities to schooling. EFs have been linked to a variety of skills required for academic readiness in young children and success in later grades. For example, in a meta-analysis of six longitudinal studies, which included two nationally representative samples, kindergartners' attentional control skills predicted later grade math and reading scores (Duncan et al., 2007). Working memory is important for preschool language skills (Adams & Gathercole, 1995; Blair & Razza, 2007), math skills (Blair & Razza, 2007; Espy et al., 2004), as well as later school success in both language and math domains (Barrouillet & Lepine, 2005; De Beni, Palladino, Pazzaglia, & Cornoldi, 1998; Gathercole, Pickering, Knight, & Stegmann, 2004; Savage, Cornish, Manly, & Hollis, 2006; Swanson & Kim, 2007). Inhibitory control independently predicts both preschool math and language abilities (Blair & Razza, 2007; McClelland et al., 2007). Later school-year success in math (Bull & Scerif, 2001; Passolunghi & Siegel, 2001) and language (Fiebach, Ricker, Friederici, & Jacobs, 2007; Savage et al., 2006) domains are also predicted by inhibitory control during preschool years.

Executive functions also relate to prosocial behaviors in important ways. Some have argued that the role of prosocial behavior in maintaining social relations is critical, and that research on prosocial behavior assists in understanding cognitive development (Hartup, 1995). For example, prosocial behavior is based on socio-cognitive abilities such as recalling past events and interpreting others' needs (Trivers, 1971; Selman & Kwok, this volume). In an effort to identify the types (and dosages) of experiences young children require to develop healthy adolescent civic identities, we must consider the independent as well as interactive contributions of EFs and prosocial competencies to this process.

Prosocial behaviors of young children are defined by action (e.g., sharing, cooperation, helping) and affective and motivational dimensions (e.g., honesty, respect for others' rights and feelings) (Radke-Yarrow, Zahn-Waxler, & Chapman, 1983; Metzger & Smetana, this volume). According to cognitive-developmental theories, prosocial behavior is mediated by the young child's understanding of themselves and others (Baldwin, 1897; Kohlberg, 1969; Mead, 1934/1974; Piaget, 1932/1965). Although prosocial behaviors such as making helpful suggestions and comforting others are evident in children as early as their second year of life (Young, Fox, & Zahn-Waxler, 1999), other prosocial behaviors continue to emerge as children typically enter formalized school settings. Relational inclusion—when young children include others in activities and play and interactions—is a common form of prosocial behavior found in preschool and kindergarten age children (Greener & Crick, 1999). This skill contributes to a child's repertoire of social behaviors, which allows them to fluidly invite others to join social groups that may represent different goals (e.g., imaginative play, problem solving). Here, we see how the opportunity to exercise relational inclusion in early childhood contexts mirrors the group social norms needed for youth to engage and invite discussion with others who hold competing goals or beliefs (e.g., views on national health-care policy or pro-choice rights). Thus, children who have adequate EFs engage in complex prosocial behaviors in early childhood, which theoretically support later behaviors and skills needed by youth to become productive members of society (e.g., complex language and reasoning skills, affective regulation skills, and perspective-taking abilities).

The acquisitions of EFs and prosocial skills shape young children's experiences in different ways. Over the past 20 years, research on teachers' views of young children's school readiness has shifted from academically oriented skills to social skills (Heaviside & Farris, 1993; Lin, Lawrence, & Gorrell, 2003; Piotrkowski, Botsko, & Matthews, 2001). The five skills reported to be most essential for a nationally representative sample of 3,000 kindergarten teachers included: (1) tells needs and thoughts, (2) is not disruptive, (3) follows directions, (4) takes turns and shares, and (5) is sensitive to others. Respectively, 84%, 79%, 78%, 74%, and 62% of teachers rated these particular skills as either very important or essential (Lin et al., 2003). Because teachers are more likely to engage in positive ways with children who display prosocial behaviors (Kuklinski & Weinstein, 2000), children with a variety of these behaviors are likely to be exposed to quality learning environments and to adult-child interactions leading to overall positive outcomes. For example, evidence suggests that young children who have access to prosocial models will more likely interact with peers in similar ways, both concurrently and prospectively (Bandura, 1977; Fisch, Truglio, & Cole, 1999). This finding raises the question of whether children who are identified by teachers as having poor EFs and prosocial skills are less likely to have experiences and be introduced to activities that promote language development, reasoning skills, and social-emotional competencies—the fundamental skills for later engagement of youth in society more broadly.

EARLY CHILDHOOD SETTINGS AS A CONTEXT OF DEVELOPMENT OF CIVIC ENGAGEMENT

Where do young children have an opportunity to develop EFs and prosocial behaviors? In studies of early development, settings such as neighborhoods (Brooks-Gunn, Duncan, Klebanov, & Sealand, 1993), schools (Duncan & Raudenbush, 1999), family (Bradley & Corwyn, 2006), and peers (Rubin, Bukowski, & Parker, 1998) have been found to make critical contributions to varied developmental processes and outcomes. In civic engagement research with youth and young adults, research that examines contexts provides important theoretical frameworks for understanding the development of civic beliefs, attitudes, and behavior (Flanagan, Cumsille, Gill, & Gallay, 2007; Wilkenfeld, 2009). As a result, it seems important to examine the role of early childhood contexts in the emergence of civic engagement through EF and prosocial competencies. For the purposes of this chapter, we will focus on one context, early childhood classrooms, and ask how they may be a useful setting to explore questions regarding pathways to civic identity.

Early childhood classrooms are powerful socializing agents. According to Bronfenbrenner and Morris (1998), classroom settings are part of a child's proximal influences, having a significant impact on their budding skills and capacities. Preschool or kindergarten settings are the first "outside of the home" contexts for many American children (Miller & Olson, 2000). In this way, early childhood classrooms represent the first template of society for young children. It is here that four- or five-year-olds are introduced to the way rules that apply to all are developed, learned, and followed; to how authority (outside of familial figures) is recognized; and to individual rights and responsibilities as they make up an ongoing process. Consistent with models of development such as Piaget, Kohlberg, and others, these learning experiences are complementary to the developmental needs of the young child. For example, at approximately 4 years of age, children acquire the capacity to identify what attitudes, skills, and behaviors are acceptable among a group of peers in the classroom, and thus learn how a democracy functions (Flekkoy & Kaufman, 1997).

Can we identify particular activities in early childhood education that create such learning experiences? Classroom-based play provides the context for the development of executive functions (Diamond et al., 2007) and for overall increases in prosocial behavior in preschoolers (Howes & Phillipsen, 1998). Specifically, engagement in complex imaginative play is linked to the development of executive-function skill, which includes different elements such as controlling emotions, resisting impulses, and exerting self-control and discipline (Barnett et al., 2008; Diamond et al., 2007). These skills include children's ability to follow rules, pay attention, and control emotions, and are vital for school readiness (Eisenberg & Fabes, 1992). And we argue that these skills are also critical for the development of youth citizenship and engagement in a democratic society. For example, if play provides opportunities for young children to function in democratic ways, solve problems, communicate effectively, and express opinions, then a quality play context also provides a unique template for engagement in society. It is here where children learn to become an active member of a group, follow rules, and contribute to the development of ideas. These foreshadow the skills (and behaviors) of a civically engaged adolescent.

To find examples of early childhood settings to support the idea that children as young as 4 years old learn how to become *young citizens*, we look outside of the U.S. context. Although there is no nation where democratic practice in schools has been completely adopted, citizenship education is being experimentally implemented in school curriculums around the world. For example, in the United Kingdom a large proportion of schools share the philosophy that children are active participants in their curriculums (Hart, 1992; Kerr & Cleaver, 2009). Encouraging participation in the classroom challenges and supports children to become active agents in their schools and communities (National Healthy School Standard [NHSS], 2004). *The journey of participation* is a new concept introduced by NHSS (2004) that encompasses schools' efforts to promote shared power and responsibility in decision making, exercising individual rights, and supporting the socio-emotional development of students.

Priestland Campus in Hampshire, England, has implemented peer support as a platform for promoting democracy and civic engagement in their infant classroom among their Year 2 pupils. Students are trained to staff a *friendship stop*, where lonely children are able to seek support (NHSS, 2004). In Australia, the South Australian Curriculum Standards and Accountability (SACSA) framework outlines required elements to be included in a new curriculum for all government schools and children's services, which is based on social constructivist theories and promotes the development of civic responsibility (Department of Education Training and Employment, 2001). In the early years, specifically ages three to five years, children are encouraged to refine and develop social, cultural, and linguistic skills for establishing and maintaining relationships and friendships, in order to navigate and influence their communities. Self and social development is enhanced through a curriculum in which children are supported in developing and contributing their opinions as well as demonstrating positive ways to challenge injustice, which contributes to empowerment and a strong sense of self (SACSA).

The International Step by Step Association (ISSA) was established in the Netherlands in 1999 and is currently operating within countries in Europe, Asia, and North and South America. A core principle in the program's philosophy is fostering democratic principles and ideas in children, which is accomplished through early childhood programs that encourage children to make choices, to accept responsibility, to learn independently and cooperatively, and to be tolerant and respectful of differences (ISSA, 2009). Classrooms in the ISSA program are organized around developmentally appropriate learning and activity centers, where the organization of the environment encourages peer learning and gives children the opportunity to make decisions on a daily basis; activity centers are tailored to the interests and learning level of each age group. The role of the teacher is outlined as creating a climate for learning, exemplifying the qualities that should be developed in children, interacting with children during work and play, observing and listening to children, and planning developmentally appropriate learning activities (ISSA).

Early childhood is a viable context for a new direction in civic engagement research in the United States. Furthermore, U.S. preschool programs, such as Head Start, can learn from programs across the world, such as those described above, about how to promote the early foundations of civic engagement. In the next section, we examine how even young children are citizens deserving of opportunities for participation and engagement; this view of children's rights provides support for the view of the importance of early childhood contexts for later civic engagement.

CHILDREN AS CITIZENS

As Carlson and Earls (2001) noted, "In the closing decade of the Twentieth century a new era in the history of childhood was ushered in by adoption of the United Nations Convention on the Rights of the Child" (p. 12). The Convention on the Rights of the Child (CRC; U.N. General Assembly, 1989), which has been ratified by the majority of nations of the world, with the exception of the United States and Somalia, outlines children's political, social, economic, civic, and cultural rights. Many argue that this document has already had a considerable impact in terms of how children and youth are viewed and treated around the world (Hart, 1997) and has the potential for greater influence if governments take the Convention's provisions seriously (Andrews & Kaufman, 1999; Torney-Purta, Wilkenfeld, & Barber, 2008).

The CRC (1989) consists of a Preamble and 54 Articles addressing the rights of the child and the responsibilities of states' parties in implementing those rights. The Convention also reflects the view that children have a right to take an active role in many of the decisions regarding their own lives. In fact, almost a quarter of the articles making up the CRC are related to children's participation or self-determination. The CRC attempts to strike a balance between children's protection and participation rights. The balance between protecting children's rights while at the same time allowing opportunities for participation or self-expression is clearly reflected in the fundamental tenets that underpin the CRC, "the best interests of the child" (Article 3), "the evolving capacity of the child" (Article 5), and "the dignity of the child" (Preamble).

By viewing children as individuals worthy of rights and freedoms, the CRC challenges the limitations of views of children only as individuals to be taken care of or protected (Ruck & Horn, 2008). In addition, by being viewed as citizens, children correspondingly have the right to participate fully in family, culture, and social life (CRC, 1989). As Minow (1990) stated, "Including children as participants alters their stance in a community from things or outsiders to members... Rights discourse implicates its users in a form of life, a pattern of social and political commitment" (p. 297–298).

A growing body of research examines children's and adolescents' knowledge and understanding concerning human rights and civil liberties. A complete consideration of the literature on young people's conceptions of rights is beyond the scope of this chapter, but the interested reader is referred to Helwig (2006) as well as Peterson-Badali and Ruck (2008) for complete reviews (also Metzger & Smetana, this volume; Wilkenfeld, this volume). However, it will serve our purposes to provide a brief elaboration of the findings most relevant to this chapter.

Some of the first work on children's understanding of their rights was carried out by Melton (1980), who employed a cognitive-developmental stage model, where one global orientation is said to characterize the child's thinking across various contexts or situations. He found that children's conceptions of rights progressed through three distinct levels from egocentric to more abstract modes of thought. Children at Level 1 (around 6 years of age), viewed rights as privileges that could be granted or taken away by those in authority. By Level 2 (found mainly in 8- to 13-year-olds), children view rights as being based on fairness and obedience to rules. Finally, in Level 3 (found in a minority of 13-year-olds), rights are seen in terms of abstract principles.

More recently, work on this topic has favored a contextual or domain-specific approach, which sees the growth of children's understanding of rights and civil liberties as related to the gradual accumulation of domain-specific knowledge (Turiel, 1998). According to this perspective, children will use different forms of reasoning to assess a wide range of social situations regarding rights. Using this approach, researchers have found that by around 10 years of age, most children view participation and decision making as important children's rights (Ruck, Keating, Abramovitch, & Koegl, 1998). In addition, Helwig (1995, 1997) reported that, in contrast to the earlier work of Melton (1980), abstract concepts of freedom of speech and religion were found in some children as young as six years of age.

Finally, some of this work has focused on whether there are differences in terms of how children think about protection (nurturance) and participation (self-determination) rights. Ruck and colleagues (Peterson-Badali, Morine, Ruck, & Slonim, 2004; Ruck, Abramovitch, & Keating, 1998; Ruck, Peterson-Badali, & Day, 2002) found that children and early adolescents (8-, 10-, and 12-year-olds) viewed protection rights as more salient than participation rights, while older children (14- and 16-year-olds) viewed both types of rights as meaningful in children's lives. Similar findings have recently been reported in cross-cultural work (Cherney & Perry, 1996; Lahat, Helwig, Yang, Tan, & Liu, 2009). Ruck et al. (1998) suggest that younger children's preference for nurturance over self-determination may be due to their greater familiarity with being cared for and protected and having fewer opportunities for participation and self-expression. Taken together, these findings suggest that how children think about rights reflects how they understand and experience rights in their own lives (Ruck et al., 1998, 2002).

As indicated explicitly in the CRC, children are entitled to be heard and there is no lower age limit imposed on the right to participate (Lansdown, 2001). Article 12 of the CRC provides the clearest expression of children's right to democratic participation:

> State Parties should assure to the child who is capable of forming his or her own views the right to express those views freely in all matters affecting the child, the views of the child being given due weight in accordance with the age and maturity of the child.

While the CRC offers little explicit reference to foundational theories of child development, developmental theory is nevertheless implicit in the CRC (Daiute, 2008; Hart, 1997; Lansdown, 2001, 2005). For example, state parties will provide children with rights "in a manner consistent with the evolving capacities of the child" (CRC, 1989, Article 5). Such language speaks to the fact that while younger children may not have the ability to engage in the types of democratic participation evidenced in older children and adolescents, young children benefit from opportunities (or the right) to participate actively, be taken seriously, and engage in decision making according to their developmental capacities, individual needs, and with appropriate adult or parental support and guidance (Flekkoy & Kaufman, 1997; Ochaita & Espinosa, 1997, 2001).

There is ample evidence of what democratic participation looks like in older children and youth across a range of contexts in this volume. However, there is less information available with respect to the participation of younger children. A number of scholars (Carlson & Earls, 2001; Hart, 1997; Lansdown, 2001) have provided examples of children's democratic decision making in various participatory programs and projects in countries around the world. However, in most cases, the children involved in these participatory programs and projects range in age from middle childhood through adolescence. Despite the value of these programs for providing opportunities for children to exercise their citizenship through active participation in decisions affecting their daily lives, there remains a dearth of information pertaining to frameworks regarding the democratic participation of younger children.

However, there are compelling examples of consultation projects in the United Kingdom where young children, often under the age of eight, were able to express their opinions (to policy-makers and legislators) on issues such as physical punishment, health services, citizenship, children's rights, and asylum-seeking (Hyder, 2002). Like their adult counterparts, children in the UK have the legal right to be consulted with and to express their viewpoints and wishes with regard to decisions made about services concerning them (Walker, 2001). In such cases, young children are able (with the assistance and partnership of adults) to play an active role in decisions that affect their lives, challenge the status quo, expose inequitable treatment, and achieve social justice.

Finally, there are clear positive benefits in terms of personal growth and development, such as self-esteem, initiative, autonomy, and responsibility (Covell & Howe, 2001; Deslandes, Potvin, & Leclerc, 2000; as cited in Day, Peterson-Badali, & Ruck, 2006) that result from children's democratic participation in matters and decisions that affect them.

Allowing the child to participate freely and fully in the cultural, recreational, and artistic life of the community enables the full development of the child (Flekkoy & Kaufman, 1997). As a result, proponents of children's rights would argue that children have or should have the right to play. In the next section, we focus specifically on the child's right to play and its value in terms of thinking about the possibilities for civic engagement in early child development.

CHILDREN'S RIGHT TO PLAY IN EARLY CHILDHOOD

The CRC (1989) also recognizes the development of the child as it relates to "...the right of the child to engage in play and recreational activities appropriate to the age of the child..." (Article 31). Because *play* is one of the earliest opportunities where citizenship is exercised, it becomes a unique context to study overall civic engagement.

The relationship of quality play to cognitive and social-emotional development has been well documented. In a recent randomized study, those children who participated in an early childhood education setting that implemented a curriculum with a strong emphasis on play had improved executive functions, and overall classroom quality increased (Barnett et al., 2008). Early studies have linked play to a variety of developmental processes including cognitive functioning and impulse control (Saltz, Dixon, & Johnson, 1977), representational competence (Pederson, Rook-Green, & Elder, 1981), mathematic readiness (Yawkey, 1981), linguistic/literacy abilities (Pellegrini, 1980), and the development of social problem-solving skills (Fisher, 1992). More recent studies examining the use of literacy materials during play experiences in early childhood programs demonstrate an increase in children's use of these materials and engagement in literacy acts (Bergen & Mauer, 2000; Einarsdottir, 2000; Stone & Christie, 1996). Language-rich play activities facilitate children's reading and writing skills (Saracho, 2001), as well as improved narrative structure and narrative recall abilities (Kim, 1999). Smith and Dutton (1979) found that children provided with play opportunities were more effective at problem solving than those who received direct training for a task. Saracho (2001) has shown that kindergarten classrooms can be literacy-enriched, helping children learn to read and write effectively through play activities. Kim (1999) demonstrated that children who engage in pretend play have better developed narrative structure and narrative recall abilities. In a longitudinal study, Wolfgang, Stannard, and Jones (2001) found block play in preschool settings to be related to later math achievement in seventh grade and high school.

Cumulatively, this body of research suggests that play is an essential component of early childhood experience and that it enhances child development in a variety of areas; we propose that one of those areas is civic engagement (although we do not know of empirical research to support this claim). Hart (1992) argues that play in the classroom as well as in the community helps children to find meaningful roles in their communities and to discover their own rights and responsibilities for participating with others in community development. He suggests that from an early age, children need to collaborate with one another and have the support of adults to achieve the developmental gains that are essential for participation. We need research on civic engagement to consider how a child's right to play reflects a fundamental social experience, which creates the foundation for later active adult citizenship. We believe that early childhood settings that do not encourage quality learning experiences such as play are depriving individuals of an opportunity to flourish that will benefit society.

CHALLENGES TO OPPORTUNITIES FOR PLAY

A challenge to maintaining valuable play experiences within early childhood classrooms emerged in light of well-intentioned education reform policy. The inception of the U.S. No Child Left Behind Act (2002) set forth several tenets for public education that shifted early childhood classroom practices in schools. A major philosophical change in the expectations we have for young children, and the type of experiences offered in early childhood settings, is likely to remain for years to come. For example, some states proposed legislation that will require standardized testing for children as young as four years old. These pressures have shaped the practices in early childhood settings and place a large emphasis on didactic skill building. As a result, opportunities for engagement in quality play have been disappearing. School districts have decreased activities in elementary school education, such as recess, creative arts, and physical education to allow more class time for reading and mathematics (Ginsburg, 2007). Astuto & Allen (under review) present evidence from an urban school region that playtime in kindergarten is competing with rote academic activities.

Recent research highlights the amount of time lost in preschool settings serving low-income children (Justice, Mashburn, Hamre, & Pianta, 2008). Although the efforts of NCLB were to increase quality instruction and decrease the amount of time young children engaged in off-task, unstructured *play-time* (Good Start, Grow Smart, 2008), children from low-income backgrounds in the United States appear to be getting neither high-quality play nor academic skill development. This finding suggests an urgent need to improve the opportunities for all children, especially low-income, young children to engage in cognitively stimulating, language-rich, quality play during the early school years. The point of this chapter is that we need to consider how these experiences have the potential to lead to sustainable, democratic, and engaged generations of youth.

While the disappearance of child-centered activities and the increase in test preparation in early childhood, as a result of NCLB in the United States, is largely absent from the empirical literature, it is being documented in the popular media. The priority given to play has been declining as it is increasingly viewed as a practice interfering with classroom practices, rather than an important educational tool. Frost (2007) notes that the increased emphasis on standardized tests shifts the focus of education toward skill development and away from other social-emotional competencies. He comments that kindergartens and preschools:

> ... are no longer a place for play ... no longer a place for lessons on cooperation and sharing ... Now, 3- to 5-year-olds, some still wetting their pants, not knowing how to stand in line, sit in a circle, or follow simple instructions, spend much of their time drilling skills and prepping for tests. (p. 226)

Olfman (2005) further suggests that the accountability established by No Child Left Behind has created a disconnect between the developmental tasks of childhood and the skill-based curricula and test prep being required in kindergarten classrooms. She also questions the ultimate purpose and goals of education and comments:

> If the mandate of the public school system is to support children's capacity to become thoughtful, caring, creative citizens capable of exercising independent judgment and freewill, then treating age appropriate play-based curricula as expendable diversions in preschool and kindergarten is not the answer. (p. 206)

It is suggested that children in early childhood classrooms that emphasize *academics* over play, including rote learning activities and test prep, are likely to be more anxious, perfectionist, more dependent on adults, less proud of their work, and more likely to conceptualize problems as having only one right answer (Golinkoff, Hirsh-Pasek, & Singer, 2006).

We need to think critically about what types of early education experiences foster the development of civic engagement in older children. Examining which early childhood classroom experiences provoke independent, complex thought, creativity, and socialization among peers is an important step in the direction of identifying pathways to civically engaged youth and young adults in the United States.

RESEARCH, PRACTICE, AND POLICY IMPLICATIONS

In this chapter we argue that quality play provides a unique developmental context for later civic engagement. As challenges to sustaining opportunities for quality play in early childhood settings continue, it will be necessary to identify ways to diminish the impact. In the following paragraphs, we offer suggestions for producing a sustainable focus on the importance of quality play for young children in America.

Supporting children's right to play may lead to increased awareness of the importance of play in early childhood. Despite the failure of the United States to yet ratify the CRC, it still provides a useful framework for supporting the inherent dignity and equality of the child. Stakeholders and policy-makers who are interested in expanding the discourse around protecting children's play in early childhood and school settings should consider using the CRC to raise awareness of the child's right to play. Organizations like the International Step by Step Association (ISSA, 2009), discussed earlier in this chapter, provide an infrastructure that may influence the fostering of democratic principles and ideas in American early childhood classrooms. ISSA is currently operating within countries in Europe, Asia, and North and South America.

Productive dialogue, however, isn't enough. Early childhood settings should implement curricula that encourage and support the use of quality play. One such curriculum is called Tools of the Mind (Bodrova & Leong, 2007). Implemented in 12 states in the United States, serving 18,000 children,

Tools has been shown to promote executive functions in children from diverse economic backgrounds (Diamond et al., 2007). Based on Vygotskian principles, Tools emphasizes the use of rich, imaginary play to increase children's ability to *master* their ideas.

Lastly, millions of dollars have been spent on developing, implementing, and evaluating early childhood classroom quality assessment tools. Yet, none of the nationally implemented or recognized assessments considers seriously the *quality* of play as core to overall classroom quality. Although new assessments of *play* are being developed (Astuto, Allen, & Cooke, under review), the field lacks a systematic and reliable way to examine the variations in classroom-based play that young children in the United States experience. This area of research is crucial as we consider the predictive nature of early experience and later civic engagement. That is, early childhood classroom quality, defined in part by the presence of quality play opportunities, may not only lead to greater cognitive and social-emotional outcomes for young children, but later civic participation and engagement in American youth.

CONCLUSION

The literature reviewed in this chapter suggests that early childhood is an overlooked developmental context for promoting civic engagement, particularly in the United States. Through developmentally appropriate activities such as quality play, young children develop competencies that may serve to strengthen their later civic engagement orientation. Children as citizens are entitled to human rights and freedoms, including the right to play (CRC, 1989, Article 31). Education reform policies in the United States, such as the current NCLB Act, reflect our views and beliefs about how children should spend their time in early education classrooms. It is time that the value of play be recognized in education reform policies. One possible unintended consequence of current policies such as NCLB is the disappearance in periods devoted to quality play for young children. We propose that diminishing opportunities for play and socialization in early childhood education may risk the potential of a robust development trajectory affecting areas such as later civic engagement. And this result, in turn, could compromise the healthy development of both children and our society.

We join others (Flanagan, 2003; Sherrod, 2002) in a call for an increased theoretical and empirical effort to explore the roots of civic engagement in early childhood. This effort will require innovative designs, methods, and measures to address the unique challenges of conducting research with young children. For example, the lack of construct stability from early childhood through adolescence in civic engagement must be addressed as a critical issue for longitudinal study attempts.

An expansion of civic engagement research into early childhood, particularly with a focus on the impact of classroom settings, will have important implications for policy and practice. As we learn more about the pathways to civic engagement, we can construct school-level supports, classroom practices, curricula, and school policies in general to programmatically support the precursors of civic identity in young children.

REFERENCES

Adams, A.-M., & Gathercole, S. E. (1995). Phonological working memory and speech production in pre-school children. *Journal of Speech and Hearing Research, 38*, 403–414.

Andrews, A. B., & Kaufman, N. H. (1999). *Implementing the U.N. Convention on the Rights of the Child: A standard of living adequate for development.* Westport, CT: Praeger.

Astuto, J., & Allen, L. (under review). Building blocks or taking tests: How are kindergarten children spending their day?

Astuto, J., Allen, L., & Cooke, J. (under review). The development of the Early Childhood Time-Use Scale (ECTUS).

Austin, A. M.-B., Schvaneveldt, J. D., Lindauer, S. L.-K., Summers, M., Braeger, T., Robinson, C., & Armga, C. (1991). A comparison of helping, sharing, comforting, honesty, and civic awareness for home care, day care, and preschool children. *Child and Youth Care Forum, 20(3)*, 2–34.

Baldwin, J. M. (1897). *Social and ethical interpretations in mental development: A study in social psychology*. New York: Macmillan.

Bandura, A. (1977). *Social learning theory*. New York: General Learning Press.

Barnett, W. S., Jung, K., Yarosz, D., Thomas, J., Hornbeck, A., Stechuk, R., & Burns, S. (2008). Educational effects of the *Tools of the Mind curriculum:* A randomized trial. *Early Childhood Research Quarterly, 23(*3), 299–313.

Barrett, M., & Buchanan-Barrow, E. (2002). Children's understanding of society. In P. K. Smith & C. H. Hart (Eds.), *Blackwell handbook of childhood social development* (pp. 491–512). Oxford, UK: Blackwell Press.

Barrouillet, P., & Lepine, R. (2005). Working memory and children's use of retrieval to solve addition problems. *Journal of Experimental Child Psychology, 91(3)*, 183–204.

Bergen, D., & Mauer, D. (2000). Symbolic play, phonological awareness, and literacy skills at three age levels. In K. A. Roskos & J. F. Christie (Eds.), *Play and literacy in early childhood: Research from multiple perspectives* (pp. 45–62). New York: Erlbaum.

Berti, A. E., & Andriolo, A. (2001). Third graders' understanding of core political concepts (law, nation-state, government) before and after teaching. *Genetic, Social and General Psychology Monographs, 127(4)*, 346–377.

Berti, A. E. (2005). Children's understanding of politics. In M. Barrett & E. Buchanan-Barrow (Eds.), *Children's understanding of society* (pp. 69–103). New York: Psychology Press.

Blair, C., & Razza, R. P. (2007). Relating effortful control, executive function, and false belief understanding to emerging math and literacy ability in kindergarten. *Child Development, 78(2)*, 647–63.

Bodrova, E., & Leong, D. (2007). *Tools of the mind: A Vygotskian approach to early childhood education.* Upper Saddle River, NJ: Pearson/Merrill Prentice Hall.

Bohlin, G., Hagekull, B., & Rydell, A. M. (2000). Attachment and social functioning: A longitudinal study from infancy to middle childhood. *Social Development, 9(1),* 24–39.

Bradley, R. H., & Corwyn, R. F. (2006). The family environment. In L. Balter & C. S. Tamis-LeMonda (Eds.), *Child psychology: A handbook of contemporary issues* (pp. 493–520). New York: Psychology Press.

Bronfenbrenner, U., & Morris, P. A. (1998). The ecology of developmental processes. In W. Denton (Series Ed.) & R. M. Lerner (Vol. Ed.), *Handbook of child psychology: Theory* (5th ed., Vol. 1). New York: John Wiley & Sons.

Brooks-Gunn, J., Duncan, G. J., Klebanov, P. K., & Sealand, N. (1993). Do neighborhoods influence child and adolescent development? *American Journal of Sociology, 99,* 353–395.

Brophy, J., & Alleman, J. (2002). Learning and teaching about cultural universals in primary-grade social studies. *The Elementary School Journal, 103(2),* 99–114.

Bull, R., & Scerif, G. (2001). Executive functioning as a predictor of children's mathematics ability: Inhibition, switching and working memory. *Developmental Neuropsychology, 19(3),* 272–293.

Carlson, M., & Earls, F. (2001). The child as citizen: Implications for the science and practice of child development. *International Society for the Study of Behavioral Development Newsletter, 2(38),* 12–16.

Cherney, I., & Perry, N. (1996). Children's attitudes toward their rights: An international perspective. In E. Verhellen (Ed.), Monitoring children's rights (pp. 241–250). Netherlands: Martinus Nijhoff Publishers.

Children Act 1989, (c.41). [online] HMSO1989. Retrieved from http://www.hmso.gov.uk

Connell, R. W. (1975). *Child's construction of politics.* Melbourne: Melbourne University Press.

Covell, K., & Howe, R. B. (2001). Moral education through the 3R's: Rights, respect and responsibility. *Journal of Moral Education, 30,* 31–42.

Daiute, C. (2008). The rights of children, the rights of nations: Developmental theory and the politics of children's rights. *Journal of Social Issues, 64(4),* 725–748.

Dawson, R. E., & Prewitt, K. (1969). *Political socialization.* Boston: Little, Brown and Co.

Day, D. M., Peterson-Badali, M., & Ruck, M. D. (2006). The relationship between maternal attitudes and young people's attitudes toward children's rights. *Journal of Adolescence, 29,* 193–207.

De Beni, R., Palladino, P., Pazzaglia, F., & Cornoldi, C. (1998). Increases in intrusion errors and working memory deficits of poor comprehenders. *The Quarterly Journal of Experimental Psychology, 51(A),* 305–320.

Demetriou, A., & Charitides, L. (1986). The adolescent's construction of procedural justice as a function of age, formal thought, and sex. *International Journal of Psychology, 21,* 333–353.

Department of Education Training and Employment (2001). South Australian Curriculum, Standards and Accountability Framework (SACSA). Adelaide, Australia: Author. Retrieved from www.sacsa.sa.edu.au/index_fsrc.asp?t=LA

Deslandes, R., Potvin, P., & Leclerc, D. (2000). Links between adolescent autonomy, parental involvement, and school success. *Canadian Journal of Behavioural Sciences, 32*, 208–217.

Dewey, J. (1938). *Experience and education*. New York: The Free Press.

Dewey, J. (1944). *Democracy and education*. New York: The Free Press. (Original work published in 1916)

Diamond, A., Barnett, W. S., Thomas, J., & Munro, S. (2007). Preschool program improves cognitive control. *Science, 318*, 1387–1388.

Dudley, R. L., & Gitelson, A. R. (2002). Political literacy, civic education, and civic engagement: A return to political socialization? *Applied Developmental Science, 6(4)*, 175–182.

Duncan, G. J., & Raudenbush, S. W. (1999). Assessing the effects of context in studies of child and youth development. *Educational Psychologist, 34*, 29–41.

Duncan, G. J., Dowsett, C. J., Claessens, A., Magnuson, K., Huston, A. C., Klebanov, P., Pagani, L. S., Feinstein, L., Engel, M., Brooks-Gunn, J., Sexton, H., Duckworth, K., & Japel, C. (2007). School readiness and later achievement. *Developmental Psychology, 43(6)*, 1428–1446.

Early, D., Maxwell, K. L., Burchinal, M., Bender, R. H., Ebanks, C., Henry, G. T., & Zill, N. (2007). Teachers' education, classroom quality, and young children's academic skills: Results from seven studies of preschool programs. *Child Development, 78(2)*, 558–580.

Easton, D., & Hess, R. D. (1962). The child's political world. *Midwest Journal of Political Science, 6(3)*, 229–246.

Easton, D., & Dennis, J. (1969). *Children in the political system*. New York: McGraw-Hill.

Einarsdottir, J. (2000). Incorporating literacy resources into the play curriculum of two Icelandic preschools. In K. A. Roskos & J. F. Christie (Eds.), *Play and literacy in early childhood: Research from multiple perspectives* (pp. 77–90). New York: Erlbaum.

Eisenberg, N., & Fabes, R. A. (1992). Emotion, regulation, and the development of social competence. In M. S. Clark (Ed.), *Review of personality and social psychology: Vol. 14. Emotion and social behavior*. Newbury Park, CA: Sage.

Erwin, J. E., & Kipness, N. A. (1997). Fostering democratic values in inclusive early childhood settings. *Early Childhood Education Journal, 25(1)*, 57–60.

Espy, K. A., McDiarmid, M. M., Cwik, M. F., Stalets, M. M., Hamby, A., & Senn, T. E. (2004). The contribution of executive functions to emergent mathematic skills in preschool children. *Developmental Neuropsychology, 26*, 465–486.

Fiebach, C. J., Ricker, B., Friederici, A. D., & Jacobs, A. M. (2007). Inhibition and facilitation in visual word recognition: Prefrontal contribution to the orthographic neighborhood size effect. *Neuroimage, 36*, 901–911.

Fisch, S. M., Truglio, R. T., & Cole, C. F. (1999). The impact of Sesame Street on preschool children: A review and synthesis of 30 years' research. *Media Psychology, 1*, 165–190.

Fisher, E. P. (1992). The impact of play on development: A meta-analysis. *Play and Culture, 5(2)*, 159–181.

Flanagan, C. (2003). Trust, identity, and civic hope. *Applied Developmental Science, 7(3)*, 165–171.

Flanagan, C., Cumsille, P., Gill, S., & Gallay, L. S. (2007). School and community climates and civic commitments: Patterns for ethnic minority and majority students. *Journal of Educational Psychology, 99(2)*, 421–431.

Flanagan, C., & Sherrod, L. (Eds.). (1998). Political development: Youth growing up in a global community. *Journal of Social Issues, 54(3)*, 447–456.

Flekkoy, M. R., & Kaufman, N. H. (1997). *The participation rights of the child: Rights and responsibilities in family and society*. Bristol, PA: Jessica Kingsley.

Fridkin, K. L., Kenney, P. J., & Crittenden, J. (2006). On the margins of democratic life: The impact of race and ethnicity on the political engagement of young people. *American Politics Research, 34(5)*, 605–626.

Frost, J. L. (2007). The changing culture of childhood: A perfect storm. *Childhood Education, 83(4)*, 225–230.

Furth, H. G. (1980). *The world of grown ups: Children's conceptions of society*. New York: Elsevier.

Gathercole, S. E., Pickering, S. J., Knight, C., & Stegmann, Z. (2004). Working memory skills and educational attainment: Evidence from National Curriculum assessments at 7 and 14 years. *Applied Psychology, 18*, 1–16.

Ginsburg, K. R. (with the Committee on Communications and the Committee on Psychosocial Aspects of Child and Family Health). (2007). The importance of play in promoting healthy child development and maintaining strong parent–child bonds. *Pediatrics, 119*, 182–191.

Golinkoff, R. M., Hirsh-Pasek, K. A., & Singer, D. G. (2006). Why play = learning: A challenge for parents and educators. In D. G. Singer, R. M. Golinkoff, & K. Hirsh-Pasek (Eds.), *Play = learning: How play motivates and enhances children's cognitive and social–emotional growth* (pp. 3–14). New York: Oxford University Press.

Good Start, Grow Smart (GSGS). (2008). A White House initiative. Retrieved from www.ed.gov.

Greener, S., & Crick, N. R. (1999). Children's normative beliefs about prosocial behavior: What does it mean to be nice? *Social Development, 8*, 349–363.

Greenstein, F. I. (1965). *Children and politics.* New Haven: Yale University Press.

Hart, R.A. (1992). Children's participation: From tokenism to citizenship. UNICEF International Child Development Centre, Florence, Italy.

Hart, R. A. (1997). *Children's participation: The theory and practice of including young citizens in community development and environmental care*. New York: UNICEF.

Hartup, W. W. (1995). The three faces of friendship. *Journal of Social and Personal Relationships, 12(4)*, 569–574.

Heaviside, S., & Farris, E. (1993). *Public school kindergarten teachers' views on children's readiness for school (NCES No. 93–410)*, U.S. Department of Education, Office of Educational Research and Improvement, Washington, DC.

Helwig, C. (1995). Adolescents' and young adults' conceptions of civil liberties: Freedom of speech and religion. *Child Development, 66*, 152–166.

Helwig, C. (1997). The role of agent and social context in judgments of speech and religion. *Child Development, 68*, 484–495.

Helwig, C. (2006). Rights, civil liberties, and democracy across cultures. In M. Killen & J. Smetana (Eds.), *Handbook of moral development* (pp. 185–210). New Jersey: Lawrence Erlbaum.

Hess, R. D., & Torney, J. V. (1967). *The development of political attitudes in children.* Chicago: Aldine. (Reissued by Transaction Press, 2006)

Howes, C., & Phillipsen, L. (1998). Continuity in children's relations with peers. *Social Development, 7(3),* 340–349.

Hyder, T. (2002). Young children's rights in action: The work of Save the Children's Centre for Young Children's Rights. In B. Franklin (Ed.), *The new handbook of children's rights* (pp. 311–326). New York: Routledge.

International Step by Step Association (ISSA). (2009). http://www.issa.nl/activities.html

Jahoda, G. (1964). Children's concepts of nationality: A critical study of Piaget's stages. *Child Development, 35(4),* 1081–1092.

Justice, L. M., Mashburn, A., Hamre, B., & Pianta, R. (2008). Quality of language and literacy instruction in preschool classrooms serving at-risk pupils. *Early Childhood Research Quarterly, 23,* 51–68.

Keating, D. P. (1990). Adolescent thinking. In S. Feldman & G. Elliott (Eds.), *At the threshold: The developing adolescent* (pp. 54–89). Cambridge, MA: Harvard University Press.

Kerr, D., & Cleaver, E. (2009). Strengthening education of citizenship and democracy in England: A progress report. In J. Youniss & P. Levine (Eds.), *Engaging young people in civic life* (pp. 235–72). Nashville, TN: Vanderbilt University Press.

Kim, S. Y. (1999). The effects of storytelling and pretend play on cognitive processes, short-term and long-term narrative recall. *Child Study Journal, 29(3),* 175–191.

Kohlberg, L. (1969). Stage and sequence: The cognitive-developmental approach to socialization. In D. A. Golsin (Ed.), *Handbook of socialization theory and research* (pp. 347–480). Chicago: Rand McNally.

Kuklinski, M. R., & Weinstein, R. S. (2000). Classroom and grade level differences in the stability of teacher expectations and perceived differential teacher treatment. *Learning Environments Research, 3(1),* 1–34.

Lahat, A., Helwig, C., Yang, S., Tan, D., & Liu, C. (2009). Mainland Chinese adolescents' judgments and reasoning about self-determination and nurturance rights. *Social Development, 18(3),* 690–710.

Lansdown, G. (2001). *Promoting children's participation in democratic decision-making.* Florence: Innocenti Research Centre.

Lansdown, G. (2005). *The evolving capacities of the child.* Florence: Innocenti Research Centre.

Lin, H. L., Lawrence F. R., & Gorrell, J. (2003). Kindergarten teachers' views of children's readiness for school. *Early Childhood Research Quarterly, 18 (2),* 225–37.

Mannheim, K. (1928). The problem of generations. In P. G. Altbach & R. S. Laufer (Eds.), *The New Pilgrims: Youth Protest in Transition* (pp. 101–138 in 1972 P.). New York: David McKay and Company.

Mannheim, K. (1972). The problem of generations. In P. G. Altbach & R. S. Laufer (Eds.), *The new pilgrims* (pp. 101–135). New York: McKay. (Original work published 1928)

McClelland, M. M., Cameron, C. E., Connor, C. M., Farris, C. L., Jewkes, A. M., & Morrison, F. J. (2007). Links between behavioral regulation and preschoolers' literacy, vocabulary, and math skills. *Developmental Psychology, 43*, 947–959.

Mead, G. H. (1934/1974). *Mind, self and society*. C. W. Morris (Ed.). Chicago: University of Chicago Press.

Melton, G. B. (1980). Children's concepts of their rights. *Journal of Clinical Child Psychology, 9*, 186–190.

Miller, A. L., & Olson, S. L. (2000). Emotional expressiveness during peer conflicts: A predictor of social maladjustment among high-risk preschoolers. *Journal of Abnormal Child Psychology, 28(4)*, 339–352.

Minow, M. (1990). *Making all the difference: Inclusion, exclusion, and American law*. Ithaca, NY: Cornell University Press.

Moore, S. W., Lare, J., & Wagner, K. A. (1985). *The child's political world: A longitudinal perspective*. New York: Praeger.

The National Healthy School Standard (NHSS). (2004). Promoting children and young people's participation. Crown Copyright.

No Child Left Behind Act of 2001, Pub. I, No. 107–110, 115 Stat. 1425 (2002).

Noble, K. G., McCandliss, B. D., & Farah, M. J. (2007). Socioeconomic gradients predict individual differences in neurocognitive abilities. *Developmental Science, 10(4)*, 464–480.

Ochaita, E., & Espinosa, M. A. (1997). Children's participation in family and school life: A psychological and developmental approach. *International Journal of Children's Rights, 5*, 279–297.

Ochaita, E., & Espinosa, M. A. (2001). Needs of children and adolescents as a basis of justification of their rights. *International Journal of Children's Rights, 9*, 313–337.

Olfman, S. (2005). *Childhood lost: How American culture is failing our kids*. New York: Praeger Publishers.

Passolunghi, M. C., & Siegel, L. S. (2001). Short-term memory, working memory, and inhibitory control in children with difficulties in arithmetic problem solving. *Journal of Experimental Child Psychology, 80(1)*, 44–57.

Pederson, D. R., Rook-Green, A., & Elder, J. L. (1981). The role of action in the development of pretend play in young children. *Developmental Psychology, 17(6)*, 756–759.

Pellegrini, A. D. (1980). The relationship between kindergartners' play and achievement in prereading, language, and writing. *Psychology in the Schools, 17(4)*, 530–535.

Peterson-Badali, M., Morine, S., Ruck, M. D., & Slonim, N. (2004). Predictors of maternal and child attitudes towards children's nurturance and self-determination rights. *Journal of Early Adolescence, 24*, 159–179.

Peterson-Badali, M., & Ruck, M. D. (2008). Studying children's perspectives on self-determination and nurturance rights: Issues and challenges. *Journal of Social Issues, 64(4)*, 749–770.

Piaget, J. (1932/1965). *The moral judgment of the child*. London: Free Press.

Piotrkowski, C. S., Botsko, M., & Matthews, E. (2001). Parents' and teachers' beliefs about children's school readiness in a high-need community. *Early Childhood Research Quarterly, 15*, 537–558.

Powell, K. A. (2003). *Creating Kidspace: The Structure of Civic Participation in a Landscape Architecture Service-Learning Course*. Paper presented at the International Conference on Civic Education, New Orleans, LA, November 16–18, 2003.

Radke-Yarrow, M., Zahn-Waxler, C., & Chapman, M. (1983). Children's prosocial dispositions and behavior. *Handbook of child psychology: Socialization, personality and social development, 4*, 469–545.

Renken, B., Egeland, B., Marvinney, D., Mangelsdorf, S., & Sroufe, L. A. (1989). Early childhood antecedents of aggression and passive-withdrawl in early elementary school. *Journal of Personality, 57(2)*, 257–281.

Reynolds, A. J., Ou, S. R., & Topitzes, J. W. (2004). Paths of effects of early childhood intervention on educational attainment and delinquency: A confirmatory analysis of the Chicago child-parent centers. *Child Development, 75(5)*, 1299–1328.

Rosenblum, N. L. 1998. *Membership and morals: The personal uses of pluralism in America*. Princeton, NJ: Princeton University Press.

Rubin, B. (2007). "There's still no justice": Youth civic identity development amid distinct school and community contexts. *Teachers College Record, 109(2)*, 449–481.

Rubin, K. H., Bukowski, W., Parker, J. G. (1998). Peer interactions, relationships, and groups. In N. Eisenberg (Ed.), *Handbook of child psychology* (pp. 619–700). New York: John Wiley & Sons, Inc.

Ruck, M. D., Abramovitch, R., & Keating, D. (1998). Children's and adolescents' understanding of rights: Balancing nurturance and self-determination. *Child Development, 64*, 404–417.

Ruck, M. D., Keating, D. P., Abramovitch R., & Koegl, C. J. (1998). Adolescents' and children's knowledge about rights: Some evidence for how young people view rights in their own lives. *Journal of Adolescence, 21*, 275–289.

Ruck, M. D., Peterson-Badali, M., & Day, D. (2002). Adolescents' and mothers' understanding of children's rights in the home. *Journal of Research on Adolescence, 12(3)*, 373–398.

Ruck, M. D., & Horn, S. S. (2008). Charting the landscape of children's rights. *Journal of Social Issues, 64(4)*, 685–700.

Russell, S. T. (2002). Queer in America: Citizenship for sexual minority youth. *Applied Developmental Science, 6(4)*, 258–263.

Saltz, E., Dixon, D., & Johnson, J. (1977). Training disadvantaged preschoolers on various fantasy activities: Effects on cognitive functioning and impulse control. *Child Development, 48(2)*, 367–380.

Sanchez-Jankowski, M. (2002). Minority youth and civic engagement: The impact of group relations. *Applied Developmental Science, 6(4)*, 237–245.

Sapiro, V. (2004). Not your parents' political socialization: An introduction to a new generation. *Annual Review of Political Science, 7*, 1–23.

Saracho, O. N. (2001). Enhancing young children's home literacy experiences. *International Journal of Early Childhood Education, 5*, 135–141.

Savage, R., Cornish, K., Manly, T., & Hollis, C. (2006). Cognitive processes in children's reading and attention: The role of working memory, divided attention, and response inhibition. *British Journal of Psychology, 97(3)*, 365–385.

Sherrod, L. (2002). *What's wrong with bowling alone: Youth and politics.* Presented at Fordham University Colloquium, New York, NY.

Smith, P. K., & Dutton, S. (1979). Play and training in direct and innovative problem solving. *Child Development, 50(3)*, 830–836.

Stacey, B. (1978). *Political socialization in Western society: An analysis from life-span perspective.* London: Arnold.

Stevens, O. (1982). *Children talking politics.* Oxford: Martin Roberston.

Stewart, A. J., & McDermott, C. (2004). Civic engagement, political identity, and generation in developmental context. *Research in Human Development, 1(3)*, 189–203.

Stone, S. J., & Christie, J. F. (1996). Collaborative literacy learning during sociodramatic play in a multiage (K–2) primary classroom. *Journal of Research in Childhood Education, 10(2)*, 123–133.

Swanson, L., & Kim, K. (2007). Working memory, short-term memory, and naming speed as predictors of children's mathematical performance. *Intelligence, 35*, 151–168.

Tapp, J. L., & Kohlberg, L. (1971). Developing senses of law and legal justice. *Journal of Social Issues, 27(2)*, 65-90.

Torney-Purta, J. (1990). Youth in relation to social institutions. In S. Feldman & G. Elliott (Eds.), *At the threshold: The developing adolescent* (pp. 457–478). Cambridge, MA: Harvard University Press.

Torney-Purta, J. (2002). The school's role in developing civic engagement: A study of adoelscents in twenty-eight countries. *Applied Developmental Science, 6(4)*, 203–212.

Torney-Purta, J., Lehman, R., Oswald, H., & Schulz, W. (2001). *Citizenship and education in twenty-eight countries: Civic knowledge and engagement at age fourteen.* Amsterdam: IEA. Retrieved February 22, 2010 from http://www.terpconnect.umd.edu/~jtpurta

Torney, J. V., Oppenheim, A. N., & Farnen, R. F. (1975). *Civic education in ten countries: An empirical study.* New York: Halsted Press of John Wiley and Stockholm: Almqvist and Wiksell.

Torney-Purta, J., Schwille, J., & Amadeo, J. (1999). *Civic education across countries: Twenty-four national case studies from the IEA Civic Education Project.* Amsterdam: IEA.

Torney-Purta, J., Wilkenfeld, B., & Barber, C. (2008). How adolescents in twenty-seven countries understand, support and practice international human rights. *Journal of Social Issues, 4(4)*, 857–880.

Trivers, R. L. (1971). The evolution of reciprocal altruism. *The Quarterly Review of Biology, 46(1)*, 35–57.

Turiel, E. (1998). The development of morality. In W. Damon (Series Ed.) & N. Eisenberg (Vol. Ed.), *Handbook of child psychology: Vol. 3, Social, emotional, and personality development* (5th ed., pp. 863–932). New York: John Wiley & Sons.

United Nations General Assembly. (1989, November 17). *Adoption of a convention on the rights of the child.* New York, NY.

Walker, S. (2001). Consulting with children and young people. *The International Journal of Children's Rights, 9*, 45–56.

Wilkenfeld, B. (2009). *Does context matter? How the family, peer, school and neighborhood contexts relate to adolescents' civic engagement* (CIRCLE Working Paper 64). Medford, MA: Tufts University, CIRCLE.

Wolfgang, C. H., Stannard, L. L., & Jones, I. (2001). Block play performance among preschoolers as a predictor of later school achievement in mathematics. *Journal of Research in Childhood Education, 15(2)*, 173–180.

Yawkey, T. D. (1981). Sociodramatic play effects on mathematical learning and adult ratings of playfulness in five year olds. *Journal of Research and Development in Education, 14*, 30–39.

Young, S. K., Fox, N. A., & Zahn-Waxler, C. (1999). The relations between temperament and empathy in two year olds. *Developmental Psychology, 35*, 1189–1197.

CHAPTER 11

Civic Engagement during the Transition to Adulthood: Developmental Opportunities and Social Policies at a Critical Juncture

ANDREA FINLAY
The Pennsylvania State University

LAURA WRAY-LAKE
The Pennsylvania State University and
Claremont Graduate University

CONSTANCE FLANAGAN
The Pennsylvania State University and
University of Wisconsin—Madison

Adolescence and the transition to adulthood are developmental periods when civic values and commitments take shape. During this time, identity formation is a critical developmental task as young people explore moral and ideological commitments (Damon, 2001; Erikson, 1968; Hart, 2005) and options for education, employment, marriage, and parenthood (Arnett, 2000). Civic exploration and engagement during the transition to adulthood, when such opportunities are available, can solidify civic identities and political positions thereafter, as political ideologies tend to crystallize by the end of the third decade of life (Jennings, 1989).

In this chapter, we first summarize what is known about civic engagement during the young adult years and place those findings in the context of the prolonged transition to adulthood that is now common in the developed world. The transition to adulthood has become increasingly protracted as more young people continue to pursue higher education, postpone the choice of a career path, depend on their parents for support, and delay marriage and parenthood (Settersten, Fursternberg, & Rumbaut, 2005). We address the civic implications of this protracted transition for individuals and for democracy. Second, we review evidence suggesting that recent cohorts of young adults are turning away from traditional forms of civic participation such as political party and organizational membership. Third, we discuss four-year colleges, the institution that serves large numbers of young adults and offers many opportunities to develop civic skills. Fourth, we summarize existing knowledge about the potential of institutions such as community colleges, community-based youth organizations, and service and training programs to bolster civic engagement among young adults who do not attend four-year colleges. In addition, we review the common elements across institutions and programs that provide structure and guidance for young adults' civic development during this transitional period. Finally, we turn to policy and summarize a set of recommendations for enhancing and expanding opportunities for civic engagement during the transition to adulthood.

CIVIC DEVELOPMENT DURING ADOLESCENCE AND THE TRANSITION TO ADULTHOOD

Adolescence

Many studies suggest that civic involvement in adolescence is associated with a range of positive outcomes in adulthood. Participation in high school extracurricular activities of many kinds including community service consistently predicts both community involvement and conventional political participation in adulthood (Jennings & Stoker, 2004; McFarland & Thomas, 2006; Oesterle, Johnson, & Mortimer, 2004; Smith, 1999). Short-term longitudinal studies across adolescence also conclude that community service participation predicts greater intentions to participate civically in adulthood (Johnson, Beebe, Mortimer, & Snyder, 1998; Metz & Youniss, 2005). Adolescence and young adulthood are ideal times to develop civic skills and competencies, and participation in organizations may help establish social networks where members are then recruited into political activities (Flanagan, 2004). Youth also begin to construct a relationship with society that continues into adulthood and is manifested via civic action (Youniss, McLellan, & Yates, 1997). Thus, substantial evidence points to life-span continuity in civic engagement, beginning in adolescence, and to the central role of civic identity in that process.

Civic engagement in the adolescent years is distinctly different from young adulthood engagement for three primary reasons. First, adolescents spend the majority of each day in school. They are a captive audience while attending school, and school is the main public institution through which young people are recruited into civic life. Thus, adolescence represents a last formal opportunity to utilize social resources before high school graduation, after which paths diverge and there is no clear public institution that engages young adults. Second, although youth are in the midst of exploring their viewpoints, they are still focused on their families and friends and have not had the experiences of living on their own that they will have as young adults. In higher education or work settings, young people may encounter more heterogeneous social groups, and as a result of these experiences, they may start to think more systematically about larger political and social structures that affect their lives. Third, adolescents have not yet attained legal rights that come with adulthood. At age 18, for example, individuals become eligible to vote, serve on a jury, join the military, and sign legal and financial contracts without parental consent. Thus, young adults have full access to the rights and responsibilities of citizenship, and this access widens the possibilities for civic engagement.

Even with the advantages toward involvement that young adulthood provides, adolescence is generally more conducive to civic development given that adolescents are a captive audience in public schools. Despite evidence of unequal access to civic opportunities in schools (Kahne & Middaugh, 2008), society devotes vast public resources to adolescents compared to young adults. Civic opportunities for adolescents include school-based service projects, extracurricular activities, and community organizations geared toward this age group; adolescents can get recruited into civic activities by the mere fact of being in these institutions. In contrast, civic opportunities, especially provided by public dollars, become scarce as youth transition into adulthood.

The Transition to Adulthood

Young adulthood, the developmental period following adolescence, has become increasingly protracted in Western countries with delayed marriage and childbearing and more time spent in school (Arnett, 2000). Arnett has suggested that young or *emerging* adulthood is a distinct developmental phase with five key indicators. First, compared to adolescence, young adulthood is characterized by heterogeneity and unpredictability in developmental pathways. Second, young adults tend to feel subjectively that they are in a distinct life phase. They no longer feel they are adolescents but have yet to take on the full responsibilities of adulthood, such as marriage, career, and parenthood. Third, individuals spend time exploring their identities in the areas of work, love, and worldviews, which gives them an expanded task of identity exploration compared to adolescents. Finally, Arnett claims that young adults are uniquely optimistic about their futures and self-focused on their own pursuits compared to individuals at other periods of life. Certainly, however, these characteristics are most true of white, middle-class adults in industrialized countries.

Scholars have noted that rates of civic involvement are low in young adulthood when compared to later adulthood. Jennings and Stoker's (2004) longitudinal examination of a 1965 cohort across ages 18 to 50 revealed that involvement in civic organizations was highest in adolescence and midlife and lowest during the transition to adulthood. Furthermore, analyses of different cohorts indicated that, at least for voting, civic engagement may be increasingly delayed for younger generations, yet these cohorts catch up to the rates of previous generations in midlife after they have settled into adult roles (Flanagan & Levine, 2010). Indeed, according to life-cycle theories, stable patterns of political engagement take shape once people have settled into adult roles such as marriage, parenting, and home ownership (Kinder, 2006). These adult roles help individuals to establish roots in communities and give them a vested interest in community affairs. During their 30s and 40s individuals are more likely to be in jobs, relationships, and families that make them political stakeholders and recruit them into civic life. For example, adults with school-age children are more likely to attend school board meetings and care about school policies. Similarly, individuals who purchase homes may be asked to join their local neighborhood associations. The delay in civic engagement among young adults may also be explained by a lack of institutional supports: Jennings and Stoker interpreted their results of lower volunteering and social trust in young adulthood by arguing that there are fewer supportive structures and institutional imperatives in the young adult years, making it necessary for individuals to identify civic opportunities for themselves.

Thus, there is some empirical support for the life-cycle perspective that argues for lower civic engagement during young adulthood. However, there is also reason to believe that young adulthood is an ideal time to build a civic ethic and foster long-term civic commitments. Young adulthood is characterized by tolerance and is a time to explore political ideas and alternative points of view, and to wrangle with others in the solution of political issues. Moreover, with residential shifts and changing environments, young people are exposed to diverse social networks that may challenge their existing worldviews (Alwin, Cohen, & Newcomb, 1991). The capacity for reflective thinking and examining the bases of ideas and opinions is more likely to develop when ideas are challenged by opposing information or points of view (Fischer, Yan, & Stewart, 2003). An awareness of social justice may be key to fostering civic engagement and can also boost persistence. For example, adolescents at risk of dropping out of high school participated in a social justice program that altered their attitudes toward school, improved their reading and writing skills, and ensured graduation (Cammarota, 2007). Critical consciousness is another technique used with high school students to raise awareness of social contexts and oppression through the discussion of rap songs and videos; over the course of one critical consciousness program, critical thinking skills improved among participants (Watts, Abdul-Adil, & Pratt, 2002). Techniques that facilitate social justice and critical consciousness can also be used with young adults, yet their potential has not yet been fully realized.

Encounters with heterogeneous groups can facilitate reflective judgment in young adults. Programs offered on college campuses aimed at increasing integration and promoting democratic citizenship among students have been effective through the use of lectures, readings, and group discussions conducted under the rules of civic discourse (Gurin, Nagda, & Lopez, 2004). For example, students who participated in a quasi-experimental study in their first year of college were more likely in their fourth year to endorse democratic sentiments such as motivation to take the perspective of others, acknowledgment of commonalities among diverse individuals, appreciation of group differences, and increased civic activities as compared to control participants.

These experiences need not take place in the classroom: Opportunities to participate in collective efforts to resolve civic issues would also harness young adults' predominant characteristics of exploration and tolerance for others. For those continuing into higher education, post-secondary institutions usually provide opportunities for critical reflection and heterogeneous encounters that stimulate civic engagement. For non-college-bound youth, finding such opportunities and developing civic skills and competencies fall onto their shoulders and may not be a priority as individuals struggle to establish themselves in adult roles of work and family (Zaff, Youniss, & Gibson, 2009). In fact, non-college-bound youth face additional life challenges that impede their civic participation. These include lower job prospects, less financial security and thus reduced opportunities for homeownership, weaker civic infrastructures in their neighborhoods, and fewer available programs that facilitate involvement in civic life. Thus, the class divide in civic participation becomes even more amplified during the transition to adulthood. Creating similar experiences where young adults who are not attending 4-year colleges can examine diverse ideas and engage in collective efforts is essential to counteracting the civic divide.

The Class Divide in Civic Engagement

There is a notable class divide in civic engagement in the United States. Individuals of lower education and income are less likely to participate in voting, volunteering, and other civic behaviors (see Levinson, this volume). The positive association between civic involvement and education has been called "the best-documented finding in American political behavior research" (Nie, Junn, & Stehlik-Barry, 1996, p. 31). The class divide in engagement challenges the tenets of democracy that the interests of all individuals be represented in government and is not unique to the United States: Studies show political interest and voter turnout to be highest among the most advantaged in Britain and lowest among those with few educational or employment qualifications (Bynner, 2005; The Electoral Commission, 2005). The IEA Civic Education Study showed a significant association between measures of parental educational background and likelihood of voting among 17- to 19-year-olds in Chile, the Czech Republic, Denmark, and Estonia (Amadeo, Torney-Purta, Lehmann, Husfeldt, & Nikolova, 2002).

Within the United States, young people in poor neighborhoods and low-income school districts have been shown to have lower levels of civic knowledge, fewer opportunities for engagement, fewer adults available to model civic participation, and lower rates of participation in voting (Atkins & Hart, 2003; Brown, Moore, & Bzostek, 2003; Hart & Atkins, 2002; Skocpol, 2004; Wilkenfeld, 2009). Non-college-bound youth exhibit lower rates of civic participation including voting, volunteering, and boycotting than their college counterparts (Zaff et al., 2009). Parental and family circumstances also contribute to the civic disadvantage that accrues during childhood and adolescence. Young people growing up in homes with well-educated parents who give time and money to political groups are more likely to be politically active and involved than youth without these resources (Verba, Burns, & Lehman, 2003). These and other studies have found that broad measures of family disadvantage are associated with lower rates of voter turnout; for example, growing up in a single-parent household or in a household with an income of less than $10,000 reduces voter turnout by about 5% (Pacheco & Plutzer, 2008). Given the developmental importance of civic experiences in adolescence and young adulthood for lifelong engagement, these early disparities in civic opportunities reflect a serious social issue.

The class divide in civic engagement is part of a broader class divide in incorporation into society. The number of 18- to 24-year-olds who are disconnected or alienated from social institutions is growing with 14% of young people in this age group unemployed, having no degree beyond high school, and not enrolled in school or the military (Jekielek & Brown, 2005). Disconnected youth are difficult to reach during the transition to adulthood, given that they are no longer required to attend school and limited institutional supports are available for youth who do not pursue higher education. For youth who rely on public support systems such as foster care, the transition to adulthood can be particularly perilous. Some of the most vulnerable youth are aged out of public support when they reach age 18 and have limited familial or institutional scaffolding that other young people enjoy (Collins, 2001; Osgood, Foster, Flanagan, & Ruth, 2006). Community colleges, community-based youth organizations, and national service programs (e.g., AmeriCorps) have the potential to provide experiences that promote civic competencies and incorporate a broader range of young people into society as they are transitioning to adulthood. A review of generational differences in the civic engagement of young people can offer insights into the relationships between institutional supports and engagement.

GENERATIONAL DIVIDES IN CIVIC ENGAGEMENT

The attitudes, habits, and political identities of each generation are formed in the context of the key issues and the institutional opportunities characterizing the historical moment during which members of each generation become young adults (Jennings, 1989; Mannheim, 1952/1997). Indeed, generational theorists have long argued that the politics of a society will change as younger generations replace their elders in the political process. We first review civic engagement from a historical, generational perspective, and then summarize by putting these trends in economic and policy contexts.

Civic Trends by Generation

Across generations, youth are less likely than their elders to vote, but recent studies have made more nuanced comparisons between the civic orientations of the *Dot Nets* (born between 1976 and 1984), *Generation Xers* (born between 1964 and 1976), *Baby Boomers* (born between 1946 and 1964), and the *World War II Generation* (WWII; born between 1930 and 1946). Compared to the oldest two generations, youth in Generation X held higher values of individualism and materialism, had lower levels of social trust, and were less likely to belong to community organizations than were the other generations (Bengtson, Biblarz, & Roberts, 2002; Jennings & Stoker, 2004; Putnam, 2000). Some argue that Baby Boomers are more loosely connected to community and political organizations than their parents from the WWII generation. However, Rotolo and Wilson (2004) found that Baby Boomers were involved but took part in different types of activities than their parents. Dot Nets and Generation Xers have been shown to be less likely to vote and participate in political parties and campaigns compared to previous generations; in addition, Dot Nets have reported paying less attention to political affairs and current events and talking less about politics than the three older generations (Keeter, Zukin, Andolina, & Jenkins, 2002). Other evidence suggests that Dot Nets, due to the protracted transition to adulthood, may have delayed the habit of regular voting (Flanagan & Levine, 2010). It appears that this group will reach levels of voting similar to older generations at a later point in their life cycle. Some of this delay may reflect this generation's delay in settling into adult roles in relation to work, family, and home ownership, as life-cycle theorists argue that regular patterns of voting are established within the context of these adult roles.

A few recent studies have investigated the civic engagement of *Millennials* (born after 1985), the most recent cohort of youth coming of age. A report by CIRCLE (Kiesa et al., 2007) revealed that Millennials attending four-year institutions were ambivalent about formal politics and disliked polarizing political debates, yet were more engaged in volunteer work, local communities, and social issues than Generation Xers had been when they were in college. Recent cohorts of youth 18 to 25 have voted in presidential elections at record-setting rates; youth voting rates were up 11% in 2004 and increased another 2% in 2008 (Kirby & Kawashima-Ginsberg, 2009). As evidence of the class divide described above, however, voting rates were much lower for youth not attending college and those not holding a high-school degree (CIRCLE, 2008; Zaff et al., 2009).

Other research suggests that younger generations are choosing to participate in society through activities other than conventional politics. Younger generations are just as active as older generations in volunteering, fundraising, and solving problems in their communities, according to recent surveys (Keeter et al., 2002). Some scholars have suggested that current generations of young people are taking the lead on new forms of participation such as political consumerism and lifestyle politics (Bennett, 2008; Micheletti & Stolle, 2006). Furthermore, youth often explore new forms of political activism (Flanagan, Syvertsen, & Wray-Lake, 2007). For example, young people are increasingly turning to online communities as a means of self-expression (Bennett et al., this volume; Xenos & Foot, 2008). The evidence to date about whether younger generations are turning to new forms of civic engagement is suggestive rather than conclusive. Furthermore, the societal implications of changes in younger generations' modes of involvement need further investigation through studies that illuminate the meaning that individuals give to various types of participation (see Torney-Purta, Amadeo, & Andolina, this volume). In summary, as generations come of age, they grapple with particular issues and find forms of civic engagement that help define them as a distinct generation.

The Role of Institutions and Policies

Individuals currently transitioning to adulthood are finding new ways of engaging such as blogging and citizen journalism, but conventional forms are still very much a part of their civic repertoire. Attention to the historical contexts and institutional support offered to different generations can help to clarify the extent and meaning of civic engagement. The historical context when a generation comes of age shapes their political interest and issues. A comparison of the economic and policy contexts of the WWII generation and today's youth, for example, reveals key differences in institutional supports.

The WWII generation came of age when a plethora of civic opportunities were available. In this regard, lessons from the World War II generation are illustrative. This group of individuals has been called the *Long Civic Generation* (Putnam, 2000) and the *Greatest Generation* (Brokaw, 1998) for their extraordinary levels of involvement in community organizations and civic life. However, as young adults, this generation greatly benefited from programs and institutional supports that were part of Roosevelt's New Deal or were established after World War II. These supports included the GI Bill for education and programs such as the Civilian Conservation Corps, designed to provide ways for young men who were out of work during the Depression to earn money while contributing to society. Furthermore, experiencing World War II undoubtedly contributed to this generation's patriotism and community contributions.

In contrast, especially since the 1970s, there has been an erosion of many government support programs. The increasing cost of higher education combined with decreasing financial support available for students has resulted largely from policy changes. First, educational support is more often offered as loans rather than scholarships, burdening students long after they have finished their educations. Second, Pell Grants have not kept up with the cost of higher education and students must often work to supplement their grants. The workplace has also been restructured. Private workplace benefits such as health care, unemployment compensation, and retirement pensions were once part of the safety net for many American workers, but there has been a *privatization of risk*, such that individuals increasingly must fend for themselves (Hacker, 2006). These decreased institutional supports have occurred during the same period as a radical restructuring of the economy in the United States. Many jobs in the new economy are part-time, of shorter tenure, and carry fewer benefits. Job instability is especially acute for African American men (Bluestone & Rose, 1997). Compared to the years between 1946 and 1972, when changes in a person's employment typically reflected promotions and raises, changes in employment in recent years are more likely to be associated with demotion, unemployment, or displacement to other careers (Carnavale, 1995). Moreover, for younger generations today, globalization has changed the conditions of work life, job stability, and young people's ability to set down roots in a community—and thus the timing of their political engagement.

In conclusion, a historical perspective on civic engagement reveals a story of young people's struggles as each generation defines and refines the meaning of civic engagement in the context of their circumstances. A comparison of the economic opportunities available in different historical periods when young people come of age underscores the need to take a serious look at the institutional opportunities available for current and future generations of young people as they transition to adulthood.

Primary Institutions Supporting Civic Engagement During the Transition to Adulthood

Institutional contexts provide opportunities to incorporate young people into society in traditional ways, such as through employment, higher education, and professional organizations, and have the potential to simultaneously promote connection to civic life. First we consider four-year and community colleges, as higher education offers the most widely available forms of institutional support for young adults. We then discuss community organizations and other service and training programs that offer civic opportunities for young adults.

Civic Opportunities Provided by Four-Year Colleges

Historically, four-year colleges have been the primary institution providing opportunities to civically engage those in late adolescence and early adulthood. Indeed, colleges and universities often offer more than job skills, academic and career counseling, and broader competencies that prepare individuals to join the workforce; they also offer opportunities to acquire political knowledge and civic skills both inside and outside the classroom. A recent review has identified a range of activities at four-year institutions that have positive effects on students' community orientation and commitments such as: student engagement in diversity workshops, interaction with diverse groups of peers, discussions of social and political issues with fellow students, membership and participation in student organizations, and participation in learning communities and collaborative learning (Pascarella & Terenzini, 2005). Young people's experiences at college are especially influential for their social and political views. Exposure during college to others' viewpoints has been shown to influence individuals as much as 50 years later (see Alwin et al., 1991 for U.S. students; Frazer & Emler, 1997 for students in the United Kingdom).

There are several examples of programs on college campuses that are designed to increase civic engagement. The Political Engagement Project (PEP) studied students in 21 special programs in higher education institutions around the country (Colby, Beaumont, Ehrlich, & Corngold, 2007). These programs included activities such as collegial living units where students engaged in civic discussions and community service, summer or semester-long programs, and traditional courses enhanced with visits from local leaders. A wide-ranging survey administered prior to and just after these experiences showed increases in sense of political identity, skills, and other forms of engagement. These increases were especially substantial for students who entered the programs with low levels of political interest (Beaumont, Colby, Ehrlich, & Torney-Purta, 2006).

Decades ago, civic and moral learning was a core part of higher education, but more recently civic learning in many institutions has been relegated to extracurricular activities (Colby, Ehrlich, Beaumont, & Stephens, 2003). Some argue that higher education currently promotes knowledge too far removed from public life (Boyte, 2008; Flanagan, 2006). Students need opportunities both in and out of classrooms to discuss controversy in a civil fashion, struggle with ethical and moral dilemmas, and take responsibility for the public problems facing society. However, in making decisions about how much public engagement to expect or how many resources to expend on civic opportunities, college and university administrators often face a dilemma. Some students and parents see higher education as an investment in private gains (for the student) with public gains for the community or the society in a distant second place (Carnegie Foundation & CIRCLE, 2006). Yet experiences with the community and society may provide the richest learning moments for students. For example, service-learning projects developed in collaboration with members and agencies in the community benefit communities and take into account the historical relationship of the university and the community in which students engage while also encouraging a deeper learning of course content. Civic and moral maturity can be developed during the young adult years, but opportunities must be created on college campuses that connect students with the community and promote social responsibility. Four-year colleges often provide an atmosphere that supports civic development and engagement among young people, and there is a national higher education organization, Campus Compact (www.compact.org), dedicated to campus-based civic engagement. Despite their laudable efforts, insufficient adherence to the civic mission of universities and lack of financial support for college attendance stand in the way of fully realizing the potential civic benefits of higher education.

Challenges faced by four-year colleges. More than two-thirds of U.S. high-school graduates enter colleges within a year of graduation (U.S. National Center for Education Statistics, 2005). However, only 60% of those who begin higher education at four-year colleges complete their degrees within five years, a percentage that has remained relatively stable since the 1970s. There are also gender and ethnic differences in educational attainment (Lopez & Marcelo, 2006). Women are more likely to obtain a bachelor's degree by age 25 than are men. Among various ethnic and racial groups, Hispanics are the least likely to obtain a bachelor's degree.

Finances represent a significant barrier to enrollment and retention at colleges. Recent statistics show that more than half of 16- to 24-year-olds enrolled in college are employed (U.S. Department of Education, 2008). Individuals can earn an educational award through volunteer participation in AmeriCorps (Corporation for National and Community Service, 2004), but tuition payments awarded through the program are not enough to enable a person to attend college full-time without supplemental incomes. In sum, although four-year colleges and universities represent the most prominent institutional avenue for young adults to gain civic opportunities, these challenges mean that a considerable proportion of young adults are left out.

Civic Opportunities Provided by Community Colleges

Community colleges provide affordable higher education, vocational training, and civic experiences. Once known as junior colleges and designed to ease the transition into four-year institutions (Travis, 1995), community colleges have expanded to include high-school-level remedial classes, continuing education, and vocational programs to move adults of all ages into the workforce (Sanchez & Laanan, 1998; Smith & Vellanti, 1999). Community colleges were created to provide these diverse educational opportunities at low tuition costs, and open enrollment is key (Dowd, 2003). These policies make two-year institutions ideal for students who do not have the academic background or the financial resources to attend four-year colleges yet seek post-secondary educational opportunities.

As with four-year colleges, the mission of many community colleges includes a civic theme (Sanchez & Laanan, 1998; Smith & Vellanti, 1999; Travis, 1995). Fujimoto (1999) argues that community colleges have a responsibility to civically educate and prepare underrepresented individuals for life in the community. Pacheco and Plutzer (2008) provide evidence that disadvantaged youth who attend two-year community colleges accrue civic benefits similar to those who attend four-year colleges. In their analysis, disadvantage was defined by both exogenous factors (e.g., disadvantaged neighborhoods or school, parents with minimal educational background) and personal experiences (e.g., dropping out of high school, early parenthood). Attending a four-year institution was associated with a 10% to 14% higher voting rate for Hispanic, Black, and White students. However, the results for two-year institutions were even more dramatic. Community college attendance was associated with a 25% higher voting rate for White students and a 100% higher voting rate for Black students.

The mechanisms underlying the community college effects on voting are unclear. Perhaps students were contacted on campus to register and to vote or they interacted through their classes with more politically active individuals who modeled civic interest. Regardless of the mechanism, Pacheco and Plutzer's (2008) analyses clearly suggest that community colleges provide opportunities to reduce civic disparities among disadvantaged young people, particularly those from ethnic minority backgrounds. Community colleges are another place for community members to have experiences with diverse individuals, thus exposing young people to different worldviews considered important for developing civic commitments. Community colleges also link students to job opportunities and other community organizations and thus are a conduit for incorporation into the broader community. As Verba, Schlozman, and Brady (1995) demonstrate, political participation is higher among individuals who are in jobs, institutions, or organizations where they can get recruited into civic life.

Challenges of community college populations. Enrollment and retention in community colleges are among the challenges to many young adults' civic development. Graduation rates at community colleges average less than 35% (National Center for Education Statistics, 2005). Enrollees often have to balance school with work and family obligations (Sanchez & Laanan, 1998). In one study, for example, students of parents with low or no postsecondary education were found to complete fewer credit hours, have lower grades, and work more hours per week than students with moderately or highly educated parents (Pascarella, Wolniak, Pierson, & Terenzini, 2003). Thus, these students likely have little time to engage in civic activities. A study using focus groups of potential, current, and former community college students suggested that support services such as child care, funding for books, as well as academic and personal counseling available at flexible hours would be valuable in helping non-traditional students complete their educations (Matus-Grossman, Gooden, Wavelet, Diaz, & Seupersad, 2002). Policy experiments increasing financial aid and structuring learning communities for students have shown some success in student retention and course completion (Brook & Richburg-Hayes, 2006; Scrivener et al., 2008). Programs such as these encourage young adults to enroll and remain in school, and school contexts provide structured opportunities for civic learning and engagement that are difficult for individuals to seek out alone.

Civic Opportunities Provided by Community Organizations

A wide range of community organizations exist that engage young adults in civic life. Below, we discuss existing evidence and civic possibilities for engaging young adults in community-based youth organizations, youth activism, and political parties. Though most of the literature on these opportunities focuses on adolescents, our review suggests that these structures offer promising yet untapped potential for young adults.

Community-based youth organizations. Extracurricular activities and community-based youth organizations are contexts where adolescents develop civic skills and motivations. Longitudinal analyses of national data suggest that certain extracurricular activities, such as debate and public performance, are better than others (e.g., sports) in promoting later adult civic engagement (McFarland & Thomas, 2006). Youth organizations are often promoted as opportunities for adolescents to become engaged and competent adults (Roth, Brooks-Gunn, Murray, & Foster, 1998), and community-based organizations can offer avenues for youth to civically engage and practice adult roles (Flanagan, 2004). Young people engage in a wide range of community and school-based organizations and even initiate their own (Sherrod, Flanagan, Kassimir, & Syvertsen, 2006). Likewise, these organizations can encourage a wide range of civic skills and motivations. Before the widespread availability of service learning in schools, civic skills were gained largely through community-based organizations (e.g., Scouts, Boys and Girls Clubs) where youth worked collectively on projects for the broader community. However, unlike schools, community-based organizations are not available everywhere and child-saturated communities are less likely to have community groups or the adults available to volunteer in them (Hart & Atkins, 2002). Furthermore, engagement in community projects is higher in high school when young people are a captive audience and falls precipitously in early adulthood when individuals are on their own to identify opportunities and join organizations.

Youth activism. Youth activism distinguishes itself from service learning and mainstream youth development programs in being youth-led rather than adult-led and being motivated by the desire to redress perceived injustice rather than to provide service to a community more generally. The model borrows from community organizing and often involves a critical analysis of social, political, and economic power. It emphasizes issues identified by young people and actions led by young people to improve their everyday lives. Adults are involved as partners to train youth in community organizing, analyses of power structures, and strategies for institutional change. Importantly, young people act as agents of change and report a strong sense of power, collective problem solving, and leadership (Kirshner, 2007; O'Donoghue, 2006; Watts & Flanagan, 2007). Typically youth organizing and activism involve young people in marginalized communities who are collectively addressing issues directly relevant to them (Ishihara, 2007; Kwon, 2006; Lewis-Charp, Yu, & Soukamneuth, 2006).

Prominent themes in youth activist projects include reform of public education in response to the poor quality of urban schools, community development projects that include marginalized youth challenging gentrification, as well as issues related to the criminal justice system including racial profiling. Many youth activism projects incorporate elements of youth culture, such as music or technology, and also educate young people about the history of activism. For example, in an African American neighborhood in California, a local community organization focused on fostering a shared sense of racial and cultural identity across participants through workshops designed to help youth reflect on their shared experiences (Ginwright, 2007). As a result, youth participated in local political affairs and began to adopt feelings of personal responsibility for civic change. Youth activists can also develop social networks by interacting with other adults of various ages as they plan collective action (see Fox et al., this volume). Community-based youth organizations as well as youth activism have the potential to expose adolescents and young adults to people of different ages, backgrounds, and education levels because of their focus on issues of concern to diverse groups. However, community organizations may not put a priority on engaging young adults and fewer youth may be recruited into these organizations, thus limiting the potential benefits offered by such programs.

Political parties. Local political parties are one type of community-level organization that historically has been successful at garnering support for candidates and mobilizing voters, but young people are less often approached to participate than older age groups (Shea & Green, 2004). Typically, political parties get out the vote by appealing to people who have regularly voted with the party; resources are concentrated on the *base* because they are the most reliable group. First-time voters are not typically seen as part of the base. Furthermore, in their study of local political parties, Shea and Green found that local leaders generally had few ideas for ways to recruit youth members.

Since Shea and Green's study, however, there have been dramatic changes in political party strategies. Howard Dean's campaign successfully utilized the Internet in recruiting young voters, and social networking sites such as Facebook, MySpace, and YouTube became outlets for many candidates during the 2008 presidential election and beyond. The fact that Obama took 68% of the vote of those under 30 (CIRCLE, 2008) may have been, in part, a case of youth resonating with the message of hope in his campaign. Likewise, analysis of the Monitoring the Future study of high-school seniors has revealed historical trends over 30 years showing that periods when young people feel that government and elected officials can be trusted are also periods when they tend to express optimism about the world (Syvertsen, Wray-Lake, Flanagan, Briddell, & Osgood, under review).

Civic Opportunities Provided by Service and Training Programs

Service and training programs refer to national service programs where young adults serve their country and/or communities in various capacities, and simultaneously receive job and life skills training as part of the program. The service experiences offered are quite diverse, yet these kinds of programs share the benefit of offering multidimensional opportunities for young adults to build civic skills and prepare for future careers. Below, we discuss the historical example of the Civilian Conservation Corps, and then turn to AmeriCorps, the Armed Forces, and YouthBuild.

Civilian Conservation Corps. A famous historical example of a successful service and training program is the Civilian Conservation Corps (CCC) of the 1930s, which provided young men with a means to generate income for their families, contribute to environmental conservation in the United States, and promote the development of society during the Great Depression (Bass, 2003). The CCC enrolled more than three million members from 1933 to 1942 and was the first and largest national service program in the United States. Young men from families in need and veterans worked on environmental projects such as flood control and prevention of soil erosion as well as building public facilities in national and state parks in exchange for room and board and a small stipend. The benefits of this program included functional literacy programs and technical training for skills pertinent to their field of employment (Gorham, 1992). Socially, CCC participants interacted with other young men while in camp and were mentored by older individuals guiding the service experiences. Participation in CCC projects instilled feelings of camaraderie with peers of diverse socioeconomic backgrounds and encouraged an ethic of working together to solve community and societal problems. The CCC is an interesting historical example of the merits of national service programs and serves as a model for current national service programs for today's young adults such as the AmeriCorps National Civilian Conservation Corps (Corporation for National and Community Service, 2009).

AmeriCorps. AmeriCorps is a national service program that encompasses local and state voluntary organizations (Corporation for National and Community Service, 2004). The vast majority of participants are under the age of 30, but participants across age groups devote a year to service work in exchange for a modest living stipend (enough to cover living expenses for most participants) and an educational award. The Corporation for National and Community Service (2008) compared AmeriCorps participants to individuals who sought information about but did not enroll in AmeriCorps. AmeriCorps participants had stronger perceptions of connection to their communities, greater ability to understand problems within their communities, higher confidence in their ability to work with the local government in leading a community-based movement, and more participation in community affairs. AmeriCorps participants were also more likely to be working in the public sector after completing their service and reported higher life satisfaction than comparison group members. Even eight years after joining the program, the civic benefits of the AmeriCorps program persisted (Corporation for National and Community Service, 2008). AmeriCorps provides opportunities for young people of all backgrounds to engage in communities and also to see the impact of their work.

Developmentally, programs like AmeriCorps provide a natural next step for recent high-school or college graduates because they offer opportunities for exploration of personal goals in relation to social issues. Indeed, peaks of enrollment are seen at ages 18 and 22 (Corporation for National and Community Service, 2008). In addition, 36% of participants reported having received public assistance or lived in public housing prior to their service work, indicating that national programs can provide opportunities for disadvantaged youth. In subgroup analyses, individuals of color who participated in AmeriCorps were more likely than a comparison group of individuals of color to choose a career in public service. AmeriCorps members from disadvantaged circumstances were also more likely than comparison group members to be employed in the public sector. Another national program, Youth Corps, which is designed specifically for disadvantaged youth, saw increases in civic engagement among African American males including increased reports of social and personal responsibilities and reports of greater likelihood of voting (Jastrzab, Blomquist, Masker, & Orr, 1997).

At the critical developmental juncture when young adults are consolidating their civic identities and values, immersion in well-organized volunteering appears to have lasting benefits both to individuals and for society. The majority of AmeriCorps State and National participants remain in their communities for the duration of their service and contribute directly to the communities they are from. The Edward M. Kennedy Serve America Act (PL 111-13) added more slots in AmeriCorps programs and increased the educational stipend (Flanagan & Levine, 2010). In addition, new Corps are being added in areas such as public service, emergency preparedness, heath care, and the environment. With this Act, more young adults will be able to remain in their communities while exploring career options and working on civic issues. More analyses are needed, but AmeriCorps is one potential route through which youth from disadvantaged circumstances can be empowered to improve their lives through education and training while also bettering their communities.

Armed Forces. The Armed Forces includes explicit civic experiences and is a next step for many young people finishing high school or college. Time in the military appears to socialize an ethic of civic participation. Studies indicate that veterans are more likely than non-veterans to vote (with the exception of veterans from the war in Vietnam) (Teigen, 2006). Analyses of the Current Population Survey in 2005 showed that volunteering was higher among African American and Hispanic veterans, but not among veterans overall (Nesbit & Reingold, 2008). Though the reasons for the association between military service and civic participation need further investigation, it may be that U.S. military activities create a sense of solidarity or instill a long-term ethic of service to the country.

Although we could not find any current research on the mechanisms by which military experiences facilitate civic engagement, there is some evidence that the military may be a promising venue for increasing civic engagement for non-college-bound youth (Zaff et al., 2009). A program for at-risk youth modeled after the National Guard offers some important insights. ChalleNGe combines community service work, job skills training, and mentoring to foster responsible citizenship (National Guard Youth ChalleNGe Program, 2005, 2008). Designed to prevent high-school dropout and problems with the juvenile justice system, youth are enrolled in a residential program where they are matched with mentors. For one year after completing the residential phase, these mentors provide guidance as the participants return to higher education, join the military, or rejoin their communities. Early results from an experimental evaluation indicate that youth in ChalleNGe were far more likely than controls to earn a GED or diploma (Bloom, 2010). Further evaluation is needed to determine the extent to which the community service and responsible citizenship components of the ChalleNGe program were responsible for improving civic engagement among participants and whether civic commitments were sustained after the post-program year. This program holds promise for facilitating the development of civic engagement among at-risk youth.

YouthBuild. Another program designed for low-income youth, YouthBuild, combines community service with general education and job skills training (YouthBuild, 2009). Young people between the ages of 16 and 24 participate in the program, which entails alternating between an educational program to obtain a GED or high-school diploma and working on construction sites building housing for homeless and low-income individuals. The program develops youth leadership and civic skills through structures for governing their own community service project and participating in tasks related to their projects (e.g., helping get permits for building sites). YouthBuild has a strong theoretical model, and a follow-up survey of graduates of the program found positive civic outcomes (Hahn, Leavitt, Horvat, & Davis, 2004); however, a rigorous evaluation of the program has yet to be completed.

In summary, despite some evaluations of these programs, the effectiveness of national policy initiatives and training programs for improving civic engagement among young adults has not been rigorously tested. However, these programs hold promise especially for youth who do not attend four-year or community colleges. Combining service work with training and education serves three purposes. First, skills training in combination with actively employing those skills through service is a hands-on method of helping young people develop a repertoire of abilities. The combination also gives young adults examples of settings in which these skills can be employed. Second, service work can show young people what they have to contribute. When combined with education and training, young people who see their contributions valued are likely to increase their sense of efficacy or agency (Beaumont, this volume; Schwartz, Cote, & Arnett, 2005; Wilkenfeld, this volume). Third, these programs can offer an explicit civic ethic that challenges participants to understand their roles and responsibilities in society. Scientifically rigorous evaluations are certainly needed, but these programs may offer a route through which youth, especially those from disadvantaged circumstances or who are struggling to transition into adulthood, can be empowered to more fully engage in society.

ELEMENTS OF SUCCESSFUL PROGRAMS THAT SUPPORT CIVIC ENGAGEMENT DURING THE TRANSITION TO ADULTHOOD

Identifying the elements that make particular programs successful with young adults is a vital step. There are five elements that appear to be crucial for successful programs: (1) an explicit civic orientation and opportunities for building civic skills, (2) mentoring by supportive adults, (3) structured guidelines that encourage program completion, (4) exposure to diverse social networks, and (5) a clear focus on young adults. Although these elements have neither been present in the majority of programs nor been rigorously evaluated, available evidence suggests that programs including these components can provide young adults with the support and experience they need to consolidate their civic identities.

First, explicit civic goals along with opportunities to acquire basic civic skills are necessary parts of the mission of an organization. Westheimer and Kahne (2004) detail various civic goals of organizations that are associated with three different types of citizens. Personally responsible citizens are generally developed through programs that emphasize integrity and self-discipline. Participatory citizens need to acquire skills to engage in civic life, to learn how community-based organizations are run, and to develop trust that can lead to civic commitments. Justice-oriented citizens need to be able to analyze social and political injustices and to devise strategies for change to which they are committed. A recent analysis of 14-year-olds in the United States and four Western European nations indicated that a substantial group of adolescents in each country is committed to social justice ideals, yet holding these ideals is not associated with any particular commitment to action (Torney-Purta, 2009). These young people believe in rights for immigrants and minority groups, for example, but do not hold themselves responsible for doing anything about the injustices they see. Thus, it is important that the civic goals of an organization be grounded in action rather than ideals alone. No single program will teach every skill, yet by outlining explicit civic goals a collection of organizations can help develop a range of civic competencies among young people.

Second, supportive adult role models appear crucial to the success of these programs. Mentoring programs can empower youth to participate politically (Youniss & Hart, 2005). Furthermore, mentoring can provide positive social relationships for young people, build their cognitive skills through informal conversation as well as direct instruction, and promote identity development (Rhodes, Spencer, Keller, Liang, & Noam, 2006). Some programs already incorporate adult mentors into their designs; for example, as noted above, the National Guard Youth ChalleNGe program matches high-school dropouts with adult mentors for a minimum of one year after completion of the program.

A third element of strong programs is having structured guidelines that encourage program completion. Programs structured with rules generated by members provide predictability and opportunities to practice personal responsibility as well as responsibility to the group (Billig, 2007; National Youth Leadership Council, 2009). A few programs currently available to young adults, including AmeriCorps and YouthBuild, integrate service with training and have specific goals such as completing the construction of a house. The training youth receive is related to their service projects, the skills learned are put to immediate use, and the emphasis is on collective action. By tying civic experiences to concrete goals, youth are taught valuable lessons about fulfilling their commitments and working for long-term results. Furthermore, individuals can see the results of their work and thus, they may acquire a sense of agency and efficacy. Structure can also take the form of scheduled routine activities that build camaraderie (e.g., morning calisthenics practiced by City Year volunteers). The sense of camaraderie built by a shared routine, an area of great strength in the military, can foster commitment to completing the specific guidelines of service. As youth are transitioning to adulthood, many structured aspects of their lives fall away; programs with manageable goals seem to promote self-efficacy and have the potential to foster a long-term commitment to civic engagement.

Exposure to diverse social networks represents a fourth element of successful programs. Heterogeneous interactions can occur through exchanges with adult mentors, other program participants, or individuals who benefit from their service. Diverse social networks are a crucial part of young people's service experiences (Finlay, Flanagan, & Black, 2007). Interacting with people from different backgrounds not only challenges existing worldviews but also may lead to envisioning alternate futures for themselves. For example, coming to know civic leaders can be inspirational for forming civic identities.

Fifth, a focus on young adults as part of an organization's mission is crucial to assisting in the transition into adulthood. Research has indicated that actively recruiting youth into organizations, providing young adults with a voice in the organization, and encouraging supportive, respectful relationships with adult organizers are all essential to developing a feeling of place and importance in an organization (Zeldin, 2004). In our view, civic opportunities are much less accessible for young adults than for adolescents; whereas organizations that focus on both groups of young people are certainly important, a more explicit emphasis on young adults in programs is sorely needed.

CONCLUSIONS: POLICY AND PROGRAM RECOMMENDATIONS

Thus far, we have identified a number of challenges to being fully civically engaged during the transition to adulthood, enumerated particular strengths that characterize many individuals in this developmental period, and reviewed the most prominent institutions and programs that support civic engagement for young adults. Given that the protracted transition to adulthood means that many youth have fewer formal opportunities for civic development, it is necessary to consider this issue at both the local and national policy levels. Policies that could support civic engagement among young adults include promoting retention in higher education, strengthening the civic mission among institutions of higher education, prioritizing a commitment to the development of young adults in existing organizations, and rigorously evaluating a range of programs for non-college-bound youth to determine what best supports their civic development during the transition to adulthood.

Increasing enrollment and retention in higher education. First, policies aimed at increasing financial, educational, personal, and family support are crucial to improving enrollment and retention in post-secondary education. Financial aid, child care, enhanced counseling, learning communities, and skills-based training available on college campuses are specific forms of support that can keep young adults of diverse backgrounds enrolled in college. Enrollment and retention in institutions of higher education are essential for allowing students to take advantage of civic opportunities on campuses.

Revitalizing civic missions in higher education. Policies are needed that further revitalize and energize the civic mission of four-year and community colleges. Laudable steps have been taken in this direction in the past 10 years (such as those by Campus Compact), but more work is needed. Some colleges have community service as a graduation requirement, but these service requirements are sometimes disconnected from in-depth consideration of social issues, collective action, and discipline-based curriculum in the classroom. Done without these deeper considerations, college students' service to disadvantaged individuals can sometimes cultivate an *us*-versus-*them* attitude. Any college course that is designed to address social issues could utilize participation in the community as an extension of classroom discussions.

Second, educational institutions should increase their support for the growth of public scholarship—the collection and sharing of knowledge as a public good—on their campuses (Flanagan, 2006). Higher education institutions, especially land grant institutions in the United States, should be further encouraged to integrate research, teaching, and outreach. The original concept of the land grant institution of higher education was that research not be relegated to the realm of experts but informed by applied practice. Recent research on higher education has shown that the promotion of public scholarship in faculty's teaching and research is more likely in institutions where the leadership sees this as a key role of the institution (Colby et al., 2003). In order for public scholarship to become a mainstream approach to teaching and research, these efforts should be adequately valued in the tenure and promotion process.

Strengthen service and training programs. We have already outlined five key elements of successful programs for young adults, and likewise, we recommend several policies to strengthen community programs for young adults. Community organizations could prioritize young adult participation both as members and as leaders within the organization by assigning responsibility for leadership tasks. If funding were tied to young adult membership and leadership, community organizations would have incentives to develop civic participation among this age group. For service programs like AmeriCorps, increasing stipends and educational awards should be a top policy priority, and the Kennedy Serve America Act is one positive step in this direction. If AmeriCorps participants were paid a living wage, individuals would not have to find additional work to supplement their stipends, allowing them to work full-time to improve their communities and develop civic skills. Volunteering rates are lowest among 19- to 24-year-olds as compared to younger and older groups (Kawashima-Ginsberg, Marcelo, & Kirby, 2009), indicating that social policies related to volunteering should target the transition to adulthood years. One guideline might be that service-work participants receive equivalent benefits to military participants for an equivalent year of work. Health-care and educational benefits should also be enhanced to increase the feasibility of participating full-time in such national service programs.

Evaluate promising programs. Finally, rigorous evaluations of current programs are crucial to creating defensible programs that have a positive impact on the civic engagement of individuals during the transition to adulthood.

Though some evidence has been gathered about the civic benefits of programs such as AmeriCorps, we need to more fully determine which aspects of these programs are linked with civic outcomes. More attention needs to be paid to the kinds of civic skills that can be effectively fostered by the various aspects of these programs. Attention should also be given to understanding which populations are best served by various programs. For example, ChalleNGe serves one type of population, whereas the population targeted by AmeriCorps is more diverse.

Understanding the kinds of programs that meet the needs of all youth during this transition and acting on this knowledge by instituting policies at various levels that disseminate information about these programs to youth are important and immediate goals for shaping the civic identities of the next generation of adults. By utilizing existing knowledge about supporting civic engagement in diverse contexts such as higher education, community-based organizations, and service and training programs, as well as conducting careful evaluations of these programs, we can build opportunities that work to equip young adults with the skills and experiences necessary to become actively participating members of society. As individuals transition to adulthood and take on adult social roles, the extent and quality of their civic participation is setting the stage for engagement across the life span.

REFERENCES

Alwin, D. F., Cohen, R. L., & Newcomb, T. M. (1991). *Political attitudes over the lifespan: The Bennington women after fifty years*. Madison, WI: The University of Wisconsin Press.

Amadeo, J., Torney-Purta, J., Lehmann, R., Husfeldt., V., & Nikolova, R. (2002). *Civic knowledge and engagement: An IEA study of upper secondary students in sixteen countries*. Amsterdam: IEA. Retrieved from http:www.terpconnect.umd.edu/~iea

Arnett, J. (2000). Emerging adulthood: A theory of development from the late teens through the twenties. *American Psychologist, 55*, 469–480.

Atkins, R., & Hart, D. (2003). Neighborhoods, adults, and the development of civic identity in urban youth. *Applied Developmental Science, 7*, 156–164.

Bass, M. (2003). *National service in America: Policy (dis)connections over time* (Working Paper 11). College Park, MD: CIRCLE.

Beaumont, E., Colby, A., Ehrlich, T., & Torney-Purta, J. (2006). Promoting political competence and engagement in college students: An empirical study. *Journal of Political Science Education, 2*, 249–270.

Bengtson, V. L., Biblarz, T. J., & Roberts, R. E. L. (2002). *How families still matter*. Cambridge, MA: Cambridge University Press.

Bennett, W. L. (2008). Changing citizenship in the digital age. In W. L. Bennett (Ed.), *Civic life online: Learning how digital media can engage youth* (pp. 1–24). Cambridge, MA: The MIT Press.

Billig, S. H. (2007). *Unpacking what works in service-learning: Promising research-based practices to improve student outcomes.* St. Paul, MN: National Youth Leadership Council.

Bloom, D. (2010). Programs and policies to assist high-school dropouts in the transistion to adulthood. In M. Waters, G. Berlin, & F. Furstenberg (Eds.), *Transistion to adulthood: The Future of Children, 20(1)*, 89–108.

Bluestone, B., & Rose, S. (1997). Overworked and underemployed. *The American Prospect, 31*, 58–69.

Boyte, H. C. (2008). Public work: Civic populism versus technocracy in higher education. In D. W. Brown & D. Witte (Eds.), *Agent of democracy* (pp. 79–102). New York: Random House.

Brokaw, T. (1998). *The greatest generation*. New York: Random House.

Brook, T., & Richburg-Hayes, L. (2006). *Paying for persistence: Early results of a Louisiana scholarship program for low-income parents attending community college*. New York: MDRC.

Brown, B., Moore, K., & Bzostek, S. (2003). *A portrait of well-being in early adulthood: A report to the William and Flora Hewlett Foundation*. Washington, DC: Child Trends.

Bynner, J. (2005). Rethinking the youth phase of the life course: The case for emerging adulthood? *Journal of Youth Studies, 8*, 367–384.

Cammarota, J. (2007). A social justice approach to achievement: Guiding Latina/o students towards educational attainment with a challenging, socially relevant curriculum. *Equity & Excellence in Education, 40*, 87–96.

Carnavale, A. P. (1995). Introduction. In S. J. Rose, *Declining job security and the professionalization of opportunity.* Research report 95-04 (May). Washington, DC: National Commission for Employment Policy.

Carnegie Foundation, & CIRCLE. (2006). *Higher education: Civic mission and civic effects*. New York: Carnegie & CIRCLE.

CIRCLE. (2008). *Young voters in the 2008 presidential election*. Medford, MA: CIRCLE.

Colby, A., Beaumont, E., Ehrlich, T., & Corngold, J. (2007). *Educating for democracy: Preparing undergraduates for responsible political engagement*. San Francisco: Jossey-Bass.

Colby, A., Ehrlich, T., Beaumont, E., & Stephens, J. (2003). *Educating citizens: Preparing America's undergraduates for lives of moral and civic responsibility*. San Francisco: Jossey-Bass.

Collins, M. E. (2001). Transition to adulthood for vulnerable youths: A review of research and implications for policy. *The Social Service Review, 75*, 271–291.

Corporation for National and Community Service. (2004). *Serving country and community: A longitudinal study of service in AmeriCorps*. Washington, DC: Corporation for National and Community Service, Office of Research and Policy Development.

Corporation for National and Community Service. (2008). *Still serving: Measuring the eight-year impact of AmeriCorps on alumni*. Washington, DC: Office of Research and Policy Development.

Corporation for National and Community Service. (2009). AmeriCorps NCCC. Retrieved August 12, 2009, from http://www.nationalservice.gov/about/programs/americorps_nccc.asp

Damon, W. (2001). To not fade away: Restoring civil identity among the young. In D. Ravitch & J. Viteritti (Eds.), *Making good citizens: Education and civil society*. New Haven, CT: Yale University Press.

Dowd, A. (2003). From access to outcome equity: Revitalizing the democratic mission of the community college. *Annals of the American Academy of Political and Social Science*, *586*, 92–119.

The Electoral Commission. (2005). *Election 2005: Turnout. How many, who and why?* Retrieved October 20, 2005, from http://aceproject.org/ero-en/regions/europe/UK/Election2005turnoutFINAL.pdf/view

Erikson, E. H. (1968). *Identity: Youth and crisis*. New York: W. W. Norton.

Finlay, A. K., Flanagan, C., & Black, S. (2007). *Service as a developmental opportunity: Building connections for vulnerable youths* (Growing to Greatness 2007). Saint Paul, MN: National Youth Leadership Council.

Fischer, K. W., Yan, Z., & Stewart, J. (2003). Adult cognitive development: Dynamics in the developmental web. In J. Valsiner & K. Connolly (Eds.), *Handbook of developmental psychology* (pp. 491–516). Thousand Oaks, CA: Sage Publications.

Flanagan, C. (2004). Volunteerism, leadership, political socialization, and civic engagement. In R. M. Lerner & L. Steinberg (Eds.), *Handbook of adolescent psychology* (2nd ed., pp. 721–745). Hoboken, NJ: John Wiley & Sons, Inc.

Flanagan, C. (2006). Public scholarship and youth at the transition to adulthood. *New Directions for Teaching and Learning*, *105*, 41–50.

Flanagan, C., & Levine, P. (2010). Civic engagement and the transition to adulthood. In M. Waters, G. Berlin, & F. Furstenberg (Eds.), *Transition to adulthood: The Future of Children*, *20(1)*, 159–179. Princeton: Brookings. www.futureofchildren.org.

Flanagan, C., Syvertsen, A., & Wray-Lake, L. (2007). Youth political activities: Sources of public hope in the context of globalization. In R. Silbereisen & R. M. Lerner (Eds.), *Approaches to positive youth development* (pp. 243–256). Los Angeles: Sage Publications.

Frazer, E., & Emler, N. (1997). Participation and citizenship: A new agenda for youth politics research? In J. Bynner, L. Chisholm, & A. Furlong (Eds.), *Youth, citizenship and social change in a European context* (pp. 171–195). Aldershot, England: Ashgate.

Fujimoto, J. (1999). The Los Angeles community colleges: Pathways to urban change. *New Directions for Community Colleges*, *107*, 55–66.

Ginwright, S. A. (2007). Black youth activism and the role of critical social capital in Black community organizations. *American Behavioral Scientist*, *51*, 403–418.

Gorham, E. B. (1992). *National service, citizenship, and political education*. New York: State University of New York Press.

Gurin, P., Nagda, B. A., & Lopez, G. E. (2004). The benefits of diversity in education for democratic citizenship. *Journal of Social Issues*, *60*, 17–34.

Hacker, J. (2006). The privatization of risk and the growing economic insecurity of Americans [Electronic Version]. Retrieved June 27, 2009, from http://privatizationofrisk.ssrc.org/Hacker/

Hahn, A., Leavitt, T. D., Horvat, E. M., & Davis, J. E. (2004). *Life after YouthBuild: 900 YouthBuild graduates reflect on their lives, dreams, and experiences*. Somerville, MA: YouthBuild U.S.A.

Hart, D. (2005). The development of moral identity. In G. Carlo & C. P. Edwards (Eds.), *Nebraska Symposium on Motivation: Vol. 51. Moral motivation through the lifespan* (pp. 165–196). Lincoln, NE: University of Nebraska Press.

Hart, D., & Atkins, R. (2002). Civic competence in urban youth. *Applied Developmental Science, 6*, 227–236.

Ishihara, K. (2007). *Urban transformations: Youth organizing in Boston, New York City, Philadelphia, and Washington D.C.* (Occasional Paper No. 09). New York: Funders' Collaborative on Youth Organizing.

Jastrzab, J., Blomquist, J., Masker, J., & Orr, L. (1997). *Youth Corps: Promising strategies for young people and their communities* (No. 1-97). Cambridge, MA: Abt Associates, Inc.

Jekielek, S., & Brown, B. (2005). *The transition to adulthood: Characteristics of young adults ages 18 to 24 in America*. Washington, DC: Child Trends.

Jennings, K. M. (1989). The crystallization of orientations. In M. K. Jennings & J. van Deth (Eds.), *Continuities in political action* (pp. 313–348). Berlin, Germany: DeGruyter.

Jennings, K. M., & Stoker, L. (2004). Social trust and civic engagement across time and generations. *Acta Politica, 39*, 342–379.

Johnson, M. K., Beebe, T., Mortimer, J. T., & Snyder, M. (1998). Volunteerism in adolescence: A process perspective. *Journal of Research on Adolescence, 8*, 309–332.

Kahne, J., & Middaugh, E. (2008). *Democracy for some: The civic opportunity gap in high school* (Working Paper 59). Medford, MA: CIRCLE.

Kawashima-Ginsberg, K., Marcelo, K. B., & Kirby, E. H. (2009). *Youth volunteering in the States: 2002 to 2007*. Medford, MA: CIRCLE.

Keeter, S., Zukin, C., Andolina, M., & Jenkins, K. (2002). *The civic and political health of the nation: A generational portrait*. New Brunswick, NJ: CIRCLE.

Kiesa, A., Orlowski, A. P., Levine, P., Both, D., Kirby, E., & Lopez, M. H., et al. (2007). *Millennials talk politics: A study of college student political engagement*. College Park, MD: CIRCLE.

Kinder, D. (2006). Politics and the life cycle. *Science, 312*, 1905–1908.

Kirby, E., & Kawashima-Ginsberg, K. (2009). *The youth vote in 2008*. Medford, MA: CIRCLE.

Kirshner, B. (Ed.) (2007). Special issue: Youth activism as a context for learning and development. *American Behavioral Scientist, 51*, 367–379.

Kwon, S. A. (2006). Youth of color organizing for juvenile justice. In S. Ginwright, P. Noguera, & J. Cammarota (Eds.), *Beyond resistance! Youth resistance and community change: New democratic possibilities for practice and policy for America's youth* (pp. 215–228). New York: Routledge.

Lewis-Charp, H., Yu, H. C., & Soukamneuth, S. (2006). Civic activist approaches for engaging youth in social justice. In S. Ginwright, P. Noguera, & J. Cammarota (Eds.), *Beyond resistance! Youth resistance and community change: New democratic possibilities for practice and policy for America's youth* (pp. 21–36). New York: Routledge.

Lopez, M. H., & Marcelo, K. (2006). *Fact sheet: Youth demographics*. College Park, MD: CIRCLE.

Mannheim, K. (1952/1997). The problem of generations. In M. Hardy (Ed.), *Studying aging and social change: Conceptual and methodological issues* (pp. 22–65). Thousand Oaks, CA: Sage Publications (original work published in 1952).

Matus-Grossman, L., Gooden, S., Wavelet, M., Diaz, M., & Seupersad, R. (2002). *Opening Doors: Students' perspective on juggling work, family, and college*. New York: MDRC.

McFarland, D. A., & Thomas, R. J. (2006). Bowling young: How youth voluntary associations influence adult political participation. *American Sociological Review, 71*, 401–425.

Metz, E., & Youniss, J. (2005). Longitudinal gains in civic development through school-based required service. *Political Psychology, 26*, 413–437.

Micheletti, M., & Stolle, D. (2006). Political consumerism. In L. Sherrod, C. A. Flanagan, R. Kassimir, & A. B. Syvertsen (Eds.), *Youth activism: An international encyclopedia*. Westport, CT: Greenwood Publishing.

National Center for Education Statistics. (2005). *College persistence on the rise? Changes in 5-year degree completion and postsecondary persistence rates between 1994 and 2000*. Washington, DC: U.S. Department of Education.

National Guard Youth ChalleNGe Program. (2005). *2005 Performance and accountability*. Chantilly, VA: AOC Solutions, Inc.

National Guard Youth ChalleNGe Program. (2008). National Guard Youth ChalleNGe Program [Electronic Version]. Retrieved November 16, 2008, from http://www.ngycp.org/aboutus.php

National Youth Leadership Council. (2009). *Growing to greatness 2009: The state of service learning*. St. Paul, MN: National Youth Leadership Council.

Nesbit, R., & Reingold, D. A. (2008). *Soldiers to citizens: The link between military service and volunteering* (Working Paper #10). Austin, TX: RGK Center for Philanthropy and Community Service.

Nie, N. H., Junn, J., & Stehlik-Barry, K. (1996). *Education and democratic citizenship in America*. Chicago: University of Chicago Press.

O'Donoghue, J. L. (2006). "Taking their own power": Urban youth, community-based youth organizations, and public efficacy. In S. Ginwright, P. Noguera, & J. Cammarota (Eds.), *Beyond resistance! Youth resistance and community change: New democratic possibilities for practice and policy for America's youth* (pp. 229–246). New York: Routledge.

Oesterle, S., Johnson, M. K., & Mortimer, J. T. (2004). Volunteerism during the transition to adulthood: A life course perspective. *Social Forces, 82*, 1123–1149.

Osgood, D. W., Foster, E. M., Flanagan, C., & Ruth, G. R. (2006). Introduction: Why focus on the transition to adulthood for vulnerable populations? In D. W. Osgood, E. M. Foster, C. Flanagan, & G. R. Ruth (Eds.), *On your own without a net: The transition to adulthood for vulnerable populations* (pp. 1–26). Chicago: University of Chicago Press.

Pacheco, J. S., & Plutzer, E. (2008). Political participation and cumulative disadvantage: The impact of economic and social hardship on young citizens. *Journal of Social Issues*, *64*, 571–593.

Pascarella, E. T., & Terenzini, P. T. (2005). *How college affects students. Volume 2: A third decade of research*. San Francisco: Jossey-Bass.

Pascarella, E. T., Wolniak, G. C., Pierson, C. T., & Terenzini, P. T. (2003). Experiences and outcomes of first-generation students in community colleges. *Journal of College Student Development*, *44*, 420–429.

Putnam, R. D. (2000). *Bowling alone*. New York: Simon & Schuster, Inc.

Rhodes, J. E., Spencer, R., Keller, T. E., Liang, B., & Noam, G. (2006). A model for the influence of mentoring relationships on youth development. *Journal of Community Psychology*, *34*, 691–707.

Roth, J., Brooks-Gunn, J., Murray, L., & Foster, W. (1998). Promoting healthy adolescents: Synthesis of youth development program evaluations. *Journal of Research on Adolescence*, *8*, 423–459.

Rotolo, T., & Wilson, J. (2004). What happened to the "Long Civic Generation"? Explaining cohort differences in volunteerism. *Social Forces*, *82*, 1091–1121.

Sanchez, J. R., & Laanan, F. S. (1998). Economic benefits of a community college education: Issues of accountability and performance measures. *New Directions for Community Colleges*, *104*, 5–15.

Schwartz, S., Cote, J., & Arnett, J. (2005). Identity and agency in emerging adulthood: Two developmental routes in the individualization process. *Youth and Society*, *37*, 201–229.

Scrivener, S., Bloom, D., LeBlanc, A., Paxson, C., Rouse, C. E., & Sommo, C. (2008). *Opening Doors: A good start: Two-year effects of a freshman learning community program at Kingsborough Community College*. New York: MDRC.

Settersten, R. A., Jr., Fursternberg, F. F., Jr., & Rumbaut, R. G. (Eds.). (2005). *On the frontier of adulthood: Theory, research and public policy*. Chicago: University of Chicago Press.

Shea, D. M., & Green, J. C. (2004). *The fountain of youth: Political parties & the mobilization of young Americans*. College Park, MD: CIRCLE.

Sherrod, L., Flanagan, C. F., Kassimir, R., & Syvertsen, A. K. (Eds.). (2006). *Youth activism: An international encyclopedia*. Westport, CT: Greenwood Press.

Skocpol, T. (2004). Civic transformation and inequality in the contemporary United States. In K. Neckerman (Ed.), *Social inequality* (pp. 729–767). New York: Russell Sage Foundation.

Smith, E. S. (1999). Effects of investment in the social capital of youth on political and civic behavior in young adulthood: A longitudinal analysis. *Political Psychology*, *20*, 553–580.

Smith, J. L., & Vellanti, F. A. (1999). Urban America and the community college imperative: The importance of open access and opportunity. *New Directions for Community Colleges*, *107*, 5–13.

Syvertsen, A. K., Wray-Lake, L., Flanagan, C. A., Briddell, L., & Osgood, D. W. (under review). Divergent paths: Time trends in youth's civic and political engagement for college and non-college bound youth.

Teigen, J. M. (2006). Enduring effects of the uniform: Previous military experience and voting turnout. *Political Research Quarterly, 59*, 601–607.

Torney-Purta, J. (2009). International research that matters for policy and practice. *American Psychologist, 64*, 825-837.

Travis, J. E. (1995). Rebuilding the community: The future for the community college. *Community College Review, 23*, 45–61.

U.S. Department of Education. (2008). *Section 5: Contexts of postsecondary education*. Washington, DC: National Center for Education Statistics.

U.S. National Center for Education Statistics. (2005). *College enrollment of recent high school completers: 1970–2005*.

Verba, S., Burns, N., & Lehman, K. (2003). Unequal at the starting line: Creating participatory inequalities across generations and among groups. *The American Sociologist, 34*, 45–69.

Verba, S., Schlozman, K. L., & Brady, H. E. (1995). *Voice and equality: Civic voluntarism and American politics*. Cambridge: Harvard University Press.

Watts, R., Abdul-Adil, J., & Pratt, T. (2002). Enhancing critical consciousness in young African American men: A psycho-educational approach. *Psychology of Men and Masculinity, 3*, 41–50.

Watts, R., & Flanagan, C. (2007). Pushing the envelope on youth civic engagement: A developmental and liberation psychology perspective. *Journal of Community Psychology, 35*, 779–792.

Westheimer, J., & Kahne, J. (2004). What kind of citizen? The politics of educating for democracy. *American Educational Research Journal, 41*, 1–30.

Wilkenfeld, B. (2009). *Does context matter? How the family, peer, school and neighborhood contexts relate to adolescents' civic engagement* (Working Paper No. 64). Medford, MA: CIRCLE report and College for Citizenship and Public Service, Tufts University.

Xenos, M., & Foot, K. (2008). Not your father's Internet: The generation gap in online politics. In W. L. Bennett (Ed.), *Civic life online: Learning how digital media can engage youth* (pp. 51–70). Cambridge, MA: The MIT Press.

Youniss, J., & Hart, D. (2005). Intersection of social institutions with civic development. *New Directions for Child and Adolescent Development, 109*, 73–81.

Youniss, J., McLellan, J. A., & Yates, M. (1997). What we know about engendering civic identity. *American Behavioral Scientist, 40*, 620–631.

YouthBuild. (2009). YouthBuild U.S.A. Retrieved from http://www.youthbuild.org/site/c.htIRI3PIKoG/b.1223921/k.BD3C/Home.htm

Zaff, J. F., Youniss, J., & Gibson, C. M. (2009). An inequitable invitation to citizenship: Non-college bound youth and civic engagement. Washington, DC: PACE (Philanthropy for Active Civic Engagement).

Zeldin, S. (2004). Youth as agents of adult and community development: Mapping the processes and outcomes of youth engaged in organizational governance. *Applied Developmental Science, 8*, 75–90.

CHAPTER 12

Schools and Social Trust

CONSTANCE FLANAGAN
The Pennsylvania State University and
University of Wisconsin-Madison

TARA STOPPA
Eastern University

AMY K. SYVERTSEN
The Pennsylvania State University and
Search Institute

MICHAEL STOUT
Missouri State University

Schools are the institution with the most universal mandate for incorporating younger generations of Americans into the polity. Many state constitutions justify public school financing based on the role of schools in ensuring a healthy democratic culture (Carnegie Corporation & CIRCLE, 2003). Often this refers to the content of instruction, including the basic reading, writing, arithmetic, and social studies skills that enable individuals to interact and function in society. While instruction is important for advancing the civic mission of schools, knowledge and skills alone cannot promote civic interest, action, and commitment. Students also need opportunities to work together, to voice their views, and to hear those of fellow students. Through such wrangling and working together, students get to know one another, appreciate the perspectives of fellow members of the school community, and learn to trust others.

In this chapter, we frame schools as public spaces where members of the public, especially younger members, gather. We contend that the relationships and processes in schools, sometimes referred to as the informal curriculum or climate in which learning takes place, are critical to ensuring a healthy democratic culture. In our work we have explored the mechanisms through which schools promote democratic dispositions and feelings of membership in a collective body, what we have dubbed a *sense of the public* in students. The democratic disposition at the center of our project is young people's faith in humanity or social trust, their beliefs that people—in general—are trustworthy and fair rather than out for their own gain.

Drawing from the political science literature, we know that social trust is critical to the functioning of a democratic society: Adults who have faith in humanity, who believe that people generally are fair and trustworthy are more likely to participate in public life by joining community groups, voting, and giving of their time and money for the common good of their communities. In short, those who trust others are more likely to pitch in and make democracy work (see Putnam, 2000; Uslaner, 2002).

However, the literature on social trust has primarily focused on adults. Despite the likelihood that our beliefs about other people and whether we can trust them have strong foundations in our experiences in childhood and adolescence, most of the research on social trust focuses on those 18 years old and older. Our interest has been on the developmental foundations of a person's faith in humanity or social trust, a disposition that we believe is enhanced when young people recognize that their fates are linked with others. This realization of linked fates, this sense that *we're all in this together* occurs through repeated practices that reinforce feelings of group membership, belonging, and solidarity. Such feelings are likely to motivate individuals to act in trustworthy ways that benefit the group and not only the self. Thus, school practices that reinforce a sense of solidarity, or identification with the group, should boost young people's trust in others. Here, we approach the theme of schools and trust in several ways: First, we show that, by virtue of being a member of a community of learners at school, by having a voice, and by identifying with fellow members of the institution, young people develop the disposition to trust a more generalized *other*. This disposition to trust others occurs over time through repeated experiences of social inclusion and group identity formation. Our major point here is that when others at school make a young person feel that she belongs and is an important part of the school, a group or collective identity becomes a core aspect of the youth's identity. This, in turn, increases the likelihood that the young person will see the similarities between herself and others and will develop a sense that we're all in this together. Social trust increases when the similarities between oneself and others are salient (Uslaner, 2002).

Second, we argue that young people are more motivated to act on behalf of a common good when they feel a sense of connectedness and bonding with fellow students and a sense of trust in their teachers. Here, we consider how adolescents respond to a hypothetical dilemma where a peer is planning to "do something dangerous" that poses harm to others at school. Among the most studied dimensions of school climate is students' sense of community with fellow classmates. Within the context of educational research, community is defined as a space where individuals share a group identity, care about each other, and work toward common goals (e.g., Battistich, Solomon, Watson, & Schaps, 1997). Building on the literature on students' sense of connectedness, belonging, and cohesion at school, we develop a civic argument, specifically, that the connectedness and solidarity students feel with teachers and classmates will motivate them to take action if the safety and security of fellow members of the school community are at risk. In other words, we contend that inclusive school climates promote trust and a sense of social responsibility for the common good.

Third, we develop the theme of schools and trust from a different vantage point—that of parents' perceptions of schools as trustworthy and safe institutions. Framing public schools as institutions of democracy, we examine whether the public's negative stereotypes about schools compromise the civic mission of schools. Parents represent a major part of the public, especially as stakeholders in the public schools. We contend that when they hold stereotypes about schools as untrustworthy, unsafe, or insecure, it undermines the trust between families and schools as they work together to raise civically minded young people. In summary, we take an ecological perspective (Bronfenbrenner & Evans, 2000), arguing that schools and the practices in them are embedded in other relational contexts. The capacities of schools to effect a sense of the public and to boost social trust are either reinforced or constrained by what goes on in other contexts of children's lives (e.g., families, faith- and community-based organizations) and their parents' lives and by the quality of the relationships across those settings. We employ data from three studies to buttress and illustrate these three points.

RELATIONAL TRUST AND EFFECTIVE SCHOOLS

Before describing these studies, we summarize the research on trust as a critical factor in schools as effective organizations. In this regard, two programs of research focusing on relationships among teachers and between teachers, principals, and parents are highly relevant. Hoy and Tschannen-Moran (1999) describe five components of trust among the faculty of an effective school. These reflect both beliefs in one another and standards individuals hold for their own behavior: benevolence or confidence that others care about one's well-being, and that one can count on their good intentions; honesty or being true to one's word and accepting responsibility for one's actions; reliability or predictability in the sense of being counted on for the good of the group;

competence or the capacity to do one's job; and openness or transparency in sharing relevant information for the good of the school community. They show that these facets covary and form a coherent construct of trust. Theoretically, Tschannen-Moran and Hoy (2000) argue that trust is needed in schools because schools are contexts of interdependence where the interests of each party can only be realized by reliance on others in the setting. This very fact of interdependence brings with it some level of vulnerability, that is, one's trust in others may be disappointed. But good teaching involves taking risks and accepting personal vulnerability as a potential cost. Innovations in education are more likely to be effective in schools where relational trust among teachers and between teachers and the administration is high. This is the conclusion reached by Bryk and Schneider (2002) in their studies of school reform in Chicago. Teachers are more willing to experiment, to try new things, and are less fearful about their personal vulnerability in taking such risks when levels of trust, respect, and caring are integral to the functioning of the school. In fact, the work of Bryk and Schneider and that of Hoy and Tschannen-Moran (2009) support the conclusion that trust relations within a school and between schools and families are essential for student achievement, innovation, and school reform. Thus, trust is an organizational element that is important not only for the role of schools in supporting democracy but also for their role in promoting students' academic achievement.

The authors' insights concerning the importance of relational trust to the effectiveness of urban schools is derived from earlier work on Catholic schools (Bryk, Lee, & Holland, 1993). In those, largely urban, schools, parents put their faith in the teachers' professional judgments about how best to teach their children and supported the teachers' efforts. But the teachers shared a moral commitment to the education and well-being of each child entrusted to them. They believed that each child deserved a good education and was capable of learning and that it was the teachers' moral obligation to ensure the right to a first-rate education to each of their students.

Trust relations, then, are a moral resource in private as well as public schools. But the right to education is a right of the public, and public schools have a historical mission to provide an education to all children, regardless of their family's ability to pay. In our national quest for school reform policies that can deliver on that right, we would do well to heed Bryk and Schneider's (2002) conclusions about relational trust and urban school reform. They found that, collectively, teachers were more willing to innovate in schools characterized by high levels of trust, respect, and caring and conclude that adults in such contexts share a moral commitment to educate all of the students and to act in the interests of the common good of the school community. Teachers in such schools believe that all children are capable of learning. The teachers and administration identify with the school and believe in its mission of educating the children entrusted to them by parents. Relational trust, then, reflects a shared sense of mission, of common purpose realized through collective efforts. To paraphrase our earlier point, not only does trust reflect a realization that we're all in this together, but that the *this* that *we are in together* is the mission of educating the next generation. As a group, teachers are more likely to assume the risks of innovation implied in urban school reform to the extent that they feel the administration respects them as persons and as professionals. Both the actions and the perceived intentions of the administration are integral to the faculty's trust. Relational trust operates, as Bryk and Schneider summarize, on perceptions of doing the right thing for the right reasons.

The work discussed thus far has focused primarily on trusting relationships among adults in schools. Next, we turn to a deeper look at the qualities of relationships—between teachers and students, and students with fellow students—that shape the dispositions of younger generations toward greater faith in humanity.

SOCIAL RESPONSIBILITY AND PREVENTION PROJECT

The claims about schools and trust in this next section are drawn from three studies based upon the Social Responsibility and Prevention Project, a three-year longitudinal study of more than 1,000 5th through 12th graders, their parents, and teachers from 29 elementary, middle, and high schools in seven rural, suburban, and small-urban school districts in the northeastern United States. Eighty percent of the students were from European American, 10% African American, 7% Latino American, and the rest were from other backgrounds. Families reflected a broad spectrum of social classes with 20% of parents reporting household incomes below $30,000 and 10% with incomes above $100,000.

A common set of school climate variables is used in each of the studies discussed. These studies are based on students' and parents' reports of two features of the school climate: first, a democratic authority structure in which teachers trust and respect students, encourage them to voice their views and respect one another's views, and insist on principles of tolerance as the basis for discussion and dissent; and second, school solidarity in which students feel a sense of collective identity with fellow students and with the school as an institution (i.e., that students at the school care about one another, feel like they are an important part of the school, keep the school looking good, and have a sense of spirit and pride in being part of the school). Both of these features have been identified as key elements that define a school as a caring community that promotes students' sense of belonging and civic responsibility (Battistich et al., 1997; Torney-Purta, 2002). These dimensions are quite similar to those that teachers identified in the aforementioned work on effective urban schools, that is, (1) a sense of identification with the school and solidarity with fellow teachers and (2) support from the authority, in their case the principal, to express their opinions. As noted, Bryk and Schneider (2002) refer to these elements as *relational trust* and contend that this typifies a school context in which individuals share a moral commitment to act in the interests of the collective.

SCHOOLS AS MINI POLITIES

Drawing from Dewey's (1916) assertion that local community is where democracy happens, we conceive of schools as *mini polities*, or public spaces where, through repeated actions in everyday practices, younger generations learn about and help to define what it means to live in a democratic society. Dewey emphasizes the importance of communication in creating a sense of the public and in transforming local community experiences into the *Great Community*. He writes, "Without such communication the public will remain shadowy and formless … Till the Great Society is converted into a Great Community, the Public will remain in eclipse. Communication can alone create a great community" (Dewey, 1927, p. 142). The fact that Dewey refers both to communication and community and the common root of both terms, that is, *building together*, is relevant for the theses we lay out in this chapter. In particular, for younger generations to appreciate that they are part of a public (*We, the people*), they need opportunities to build a community of shared interests and goals, have a voice, listen to one another's perspectives, and find common ground. Trust is both essential for and an outcome of that process.

Participation in the life of the school (the mini polity, as we have dubbed it) creates a foundation from which youth develop affective connections to the broader society and learn to exercise their rights and responsibilities as citizens (Flanagan, 2003; Flanagan, Cumsille, Gill, & Gallay, 2007). The ways in which adult authorities and students in the school treat one another, deal with differences, and work toward collective goals are the bases on which young people's ideas about democracy and civil society are formed. In the next section, we discuss the theoretical bases for the roles of adult authorities in creating democratic climates for learning and of school solidarity in the development of students' social trust.

ADULT AUTHORITIES

Teachers are adult authority figures who wield power over young people's lives. Thus, they play a critical role in educating children about democratic principles and about trust in the democratic process of decision making.

Young people's concepts of political authority are constructed from their experiences with adult authorities who exert power over their lives, in this case, at school. Bandura (1997) alluded to this idea in his observation that "... children's beliefs about their capabilities to influence governmental functioning may also be partially generalized from their experiences in trying to influence adults in educational and in other institutional settings with which they must deal" (p. 491). Similarly, according to political socialization theory, the younger generation's support for the political system evolves from their beliefs in the responsiveness of political authorities to people like them, that is, to parents and other adults in their social networks (Easton & Dennis, 1967). We agree but contend that, rather than distal relationships to elected leaders in government, it is the proximate experiences young people have with teachers and other local adult authorities (e.g., youth program leaders, coaches, police, and community leaders) that are the bases for their beliefs about the responsiveness of the political system to people "like them" (Flanagan et al., 2007).

Empirical studies have shown positive associations between students' reports of open classroom climates in which teachers encourage students to express their views and students' tolerance and open-mindedness (Berman, 1997; Torney-Purta, 2002), sense of social responsibility rather than alienation (Flanagan et al., 1998; Torney-Purta, 2009), and commitment to the democratic ideals of patriotism, tolerance, and helping people in need (Flanagan et al., 2007; Torney-Purta, Richardson, & Barber, 2004). These associations are very similar in European countries and in the United States. We have dubbed such open classroom climates *civil climates for learning* and argue that, by participating in such settings, students learn about the phenomenon of trust. First, they learn that trust is based on freedom—one's own and that of others, and consequently, trusting implies some vulnerability. Second, they develop an appreciation of the reciprocal relationship between trust and trustworthiness.

To create and maintain an open classroom climate requires commitment on the part of both teachers and students. For teachers, this commitment is both philosophical and pedagogical. Moving away from the transmission model of education, teachers who effectively nurture an open classroom environment believe deeply in their responsibility to educate the whole student. That is not to say these teachers compromise or abandon their job of teaching students disciplinary content, but rather that teachers who buy into this philosophy take the time when exploring new ideas and principles to let students express their opinions, even when those opinions challenge the teacher's own views (Torney-Purta & Wilkenfeld, 2009).

When teachers create a civil climate for learning and an open exchange of opinions in their classrooms, they are teaching several aspects of the phenomenon and practice of trust. First, by giving students' opinions serious consideration, even when they conflict with the teacher's own views, teachers are giving students practice in disagreeing in a civil fashion and in negotiating authority. They are also conveying a sense of trust in their students. The teacher, who could maintain his/her authority by making and enforcing the rules and procedures, instead invites students to share in the governance of the classroom. In this sense, he/she treats students as his/her equal and encourages them to share the rights and responsibilities entailed in governance. Democracy means rule by and sovereignty of the people, and teachers who engage in shared governance practices are developing the skills of democratic governance in their students.

In the process, students learn what it means for an adult authority to consider them worthy of trust. In turn, when teachers treat students as trustworthy, students develop a confidence in their capacities to participate in democratic decision making, which, ultimately, extends to their civic agency in society. In choosing to teach in this way, the teacher accepts some level of vulnerability. The students might not rise to the occasion and the teacher's faith in them might be thwarted. Trust, however, is premised on freedom, and it is because people are free to decide for themselves that trust is a foundation for democratic governance. So, in creating open climates for learning, teachers are giving their students practice in exercising freedom, respecting the rights of fellow members of the school community, and learning about the vulnerabilities and responsibilities that the exercise of freedom entails.

Second, in creating an open climate for exchange of views, teachers express their expectation that students treat one another with respect. In so doing, they set standards for how members of a civil society should treat one another. By insisting on respect for the diverse views of fellow students, teachers are imparting norms of tolerance, a foundational principle that binds us as Americans (Walzer, 1990, 1997). In such learning contexts, students should come to appreciate the reciprocal relationship between trust and trustworthiness (Deutsch, 1958; Erikson, 1950), that is, *the teacher has placed her faith in us and we should live up to those expectations by respecting our fellow students*. Research has also shown that having a trusting relationship with a teacher is associated with a student trusting the validity of knowledge imparted by that teacher (Raider-Roth, 2005). Social trust is positively related to a sense of shared norms and a feeling of being part of the same moral community (Uslaner, 2002). Thus, we contend that, by creating an open classroom climate for learning and a respectful exchange of views, teachers enable students to appreciate that they are part of the same moral community, a realization that should augment their social trust.

School Solidarity

According to Aristotle (1947), a particular form of friendship, civic friendship, is what holds states together. Without the comity and trust implied in relationships between fellow citizens who appreciate that they share a common fate, neither institutions nor laws nor any formal characteristics of a political system will in themselves support governance. Bonds of affection, and of mutual concern in friendships are formed through being in the same contexts, working on common projects, and finding common purpose. Again, and as Phan (2008) asserts, social trust is enhanced by a sense that "we're all in this together" (p. 23), that is, that we share a common fate.

Within the context of students' lives, this sense of shared fate can be captured in their experiences of being united as a student body. Notably, a student body can form in contention with the administration or teachers at a school or as a body that is respected by those adults as an integral part of the school. We emphasize the latter and choose the term *school solidarity* to capture students' feeling of attachment to the school, their sense that students are integral to and respected members of the school community and thus are proud to identify with the institution. School solidarity, therefore, broadly captures students' feelings of pride in and identification with their educational institution and with fellow members therein.

National longitudinal studies have shown that students' sense of institutional connectedness in high school is a significant predictor of various forms of political and community engagement in young adulthood (Duke, Skay, Pettingell, & Borowsky, 2008; Smith, 1999). Further, motivational, developmental, and social psychologists have all pointed to the importance of *identification* with an organization or group as a dynamic underlying cooperation, commitment, and a sense of responsibility for the whole (Pearce & Larson, 2006; Rutkowski, Gruder, & Romer, 1983; Ryan & Deci, 2000), even when the demonstration of responsibility for the group entails personal sacrifice (Baumeister & Leary, 1995; Brewer & Gardner, 1996; Dawes, van de Kragt, & Orbell, 1990). Reports of solidarity and feelings of connectedness at school are positively correlated with students' commitments to civic behavior in both Eastern and Western Europe (Flanagan et al., 1998, Torney-Purta, 2009) and with trust in schools as well as trust in political institutions in countries as different as Colombia and the United States (Torney-Purta, Barber, & Richardson, 2004). Thus, students' sense of solidarity at school should boost social trust because it increases youths' realization of their interdependence with fellow human beings.

Likewise, in literature on social trust, the development of a collective identity via engagement in associations is thought to socialize cooperation and tolerance and ultimately to boost trust (Boix & Posner, 1988; Hooghe,

2003). Feelings of solidarity capture the sense of belonging to something larger than oneself, which, when satisfied, has a positive impact on our perceptions of others (Baumeister & Leary, 1995). In summary, a considerable body of work points to the likelihood that social trust should be positively impacted by feelings of solidarity with fellow students and of pride of membership in the institution of the school.

Students' sense of solidarity is not the same as their sense of school spirit, although there is probably some overlap. The overlap would be in the sense of belonging to the institution that the two constructs capture. These feelings of connectedness to community institutions such as the school are the predictors of civic engagement in young adulthood, as is noted above. School spirit can also connote support for the school's athletic teams. That feeling of solidarity would be what scholars of social trust refer to as bonding social capital, a resource that could be related to trust in a generalized other. The question is how wide the network of *others* such bonding reflects and whether the internal bonds of trust and loyalty are maintained by excluding others on the outside (Portes, 1998). The social dynamics in some schools reflect a hierarchy in which athletes, especially *stars*, live by a different set of rules than those governing the rest of the student body.

Results of Our Empirical Work

School Solidarity Boosts Students' Social Trust Our first study focused on developmental patterns of social trust and was based on the reports of early, middle, and late adolescents whom we followed over several years. We measured their levels of social trust in years two and three of our longitudinal study in addition to asking them to assess two dimensions of school climate, that is, the perception of their classroom authority structure as democratic and their sense of school solidarity.

Student solidarity at school, as we conceive it, is horizontal, not hierarchical, and reflects students' perceptions that, in general, the students at their school care about one another, even fellow students that they do not know well, and that they feel a sense of pride in being an important part of the school community. We found that students' feelings of school solidarity did boost social trust over a two-year period. Controlling for multiple factors, including levels of social trust and school solidarity (as reported by individual students in the prior year), the democratic climate of their classroom, and their interpersonal trust, adolescents' reports that they felt a sense of solidarity and pride of membership in their school predicted significant increases over two years in their social trust (Flanagan & Stout, in press). And, although levels of social trust declined with age, these effects of school solidarity held for all age groups. We concluded that adolescents' social trust is shaped by feelings of belonging and of having a sense of collective identity at school.

Reports of a democratic climate at school affected social trust indirectly through reports of student solidarity. In other words, when youth felt that teachers at their school respected students' autonomous opinions and encouraged a respectful exchange of views, it increased their sense of school solidarity which, in turn, boosted social trust over time. The positive effect of respect from adult authorities on adolescents' social trust is consistent with longitudinal work showing that levels of social trust are higher among adults who, as youth, reported that their parents and teachers respected their autonomy (Damico et al., 2000; Uslaner, 2002). Notably, in the research on effective urban schools, respect from the authority in power (in that case, the administration) was a critical element in teachers' relational trust and commitment to the mission of the school.

However, the indirect effect of teaching practices that we uncovered, operating through students' feelings of solidarity, led us to another conclusion concerning how classroom dynamics may boost social trust. Teaching practices that encourage a respectful exchange of views may build feelings of collective identity which, in turn, enhance youth's trust in people. This interpretation is consistent with experimental work using the prisoner's dilemma, which has shown that a period of discussion preceding the game tends to build group identities and cooperation (Orbell, van de Kragt, & Dawes, 1988). Thus, we conclude from the first study presented above that civil climates for learning create the public space for developing a shared sense of identity. Through that collective identity, these teaching practices boosted social trust.

This first study also revealed age differences in the patterns and correlates of social trust. Not only did the cross-age comparisons point to an inverse relationship between age and social trust, but the longitudinal data also showed declines over two years for each age group. Further, adolescents' beliefs hardened with age. Although there was a strong correlation between adolescents' social trust at Time 1 and Time 2, the strength of that correlation increased between early, middle, and late adolescence. Thus, whereas young people's faith in humanity was more malleable in early adolescence, it was more hardened by late adolescence.

The results from this first study have several implications for policy. First, classroom and school climates and the quality of student-teacher relationships matter: Teaching content but ignoring process undermines the role of schools in developing students' democratic dispositions, and policies that base accountability on testing alone undermine trust in the professionalism and judgment of teachers. According to analyses of national data on civic education, our schools need to do a better job in this regard. These analyses show that democratic procedures such as teachers' promoting civil discussion of public issues are not common practices even in civics classes (Hess, 2009; Campbell, 2007; Niemi & Junn, 1998). Second, for teaching practices to boost social trust, they have to impact students' sense of shared or collective identity. Thus, it is important to pay attention not just to caring relationships in teacher-student interactions but also to practices that promote students' attention to and consideration of fellow students' views. In this regard, work on deliberative dialogues and classroom discussions of controversial issues that increase students' perspective taking is relevant for policy and practice (Hess, 2009). Third, school climates that promote a sense of solidarity with others and provide a civil climate for learning matter at all ages, because but intervening in early adolescence may be more fruitful because social trust is more malleable at this age. National educational policies and teacher education programs should attend to these relational and process aspects of classroom climate because they are as important as curricular content for learning.

Acting on Behalf of the "Public Good" Besides building faith in humanity, how might school climates motivate students to act on behalf of the common good? In the next study, we addressed this question by looking at the factors that motivate students to act to prevent harm to fellow members of their school community. This work draws on John Dewey's (1927) observation that a "public" forms when citizens come together around issues of common concern and when those citizens recognize they have "a common interest in controlling these consequences" (p. 126). Conceiving of schools as public spaces for learning, we hypothesized that students would be more inclined to protect those spaces and the people therein to the extent, borrowing from Dewey, that they understood themselves as members of the public with common interests. Thus, we added a civic dimension to the literature on school violence by studying whether students' sense of belonging to the school community and their trust in teachers would motivate them to protect fellow members of the school community.

We presented the students in our study with the following hypothetical situation: "Suppose some kid was talking about doing something dangerous at school." The students were then asked to rate the likelihood that they would use four different response strategies: intervene directly (e.g., tell the kid not to do it), talk to an adult, tell a friend but not an adult, and ignore it. Unlike the latter two response options, the former strategies represent action on behalf of others. We contend that taking action to help others is a manifestation of social responsibility (see Selman & Kwok, this volume).

What factors were related to the likelihood that youth would do something to prevent harm to others at school? To answer this question, we examined whether students' willingness to endorse each of the response strategies varied based on three dimensions of perceived school climate: (1) the democratic authority structure created by teachers in which students are encouraged to voice their views, (2) the sense of school solidarity experienced by the student body, and (3) students' personal sense of integration or acceptance at school.

We found that adolescents' perceptions that their teachers create a democratic environment that is fair and open, as well as their sense of solidarity with classmates and feeling like they personally fit in, each made a unique, positive contribution to the prediction of adolescents' motivation to act on behalf of the common good—that is, their willingness to intervene directly with the peer or to approach a teacher or principal, or both, with their concerns about a hypothetical peer's plan to do something dangerous. However, it was only students' perceptions of the authority structure as democratic and their personal sense of acceptance at school that predicted their refusal to ignore a peer's plan to act dangerously. In other words, when students felt their teachers were responsive and trusting of students and when those students felt a personal sense of belonging at school, they would refuse to stand by and do nothing in the face of potential harm to others at school. Taken together, these findings demonstrate the association between perceiving the school climate as democratic and inclusive and students' motivation to speak up and take action when the safety of themselves, their classmates, and their teachers is compromised.

Drawing from previous work on barriers to peer intervention (e.g., National Research Council and Institute of Medicine, 2003), we also tested whether the relationship between students' perceptions of their school climate and willingness to intervene on behalf of others was mediated by their belief that disclosing their concerns to an adult might result in trouble for themselves or their classmate. As expected, youth were more likely to say they would ignore their peer's dangerous plan or talk about it among friends (but not with an adult) to the extent that they believed that going to an adult would result in more trouble. Not surprisingly, students who espoused this fear were also less likely to say they would approach adults at school with their concerns about a peer's dangerous intentions.

These results have implications for policy, especially concerning zero tolerance policies. For most adolescents, divulging a peer's confidence is a difficult decision that may be intensified by a zero tolerance climate. As was reflected in our findings, the more students believed that going to a teacher or principal would result in trouble, the more likely they were to ignore a peer's dangerous plan or simply talk about it with a friend but not an adult in a position to intervene. Such bystander or ignoring behaviors are problematic. Not only does bullying, for example, harm individual students, it also compromises the safety of schools as public spaces for learning, where students and teachers from diverse backgrounds can share different perspectives and ideas in a context free from derision. School policies and the practices of teachers and administrators can go a long way in ensuring that classrooms and schools are safe spaces where all students can learn. However, the onus for taking action often falls on students who are more likely than teachers to be privy to instances of bullying or aware of rumors of potential violence.

There is mounting evidence of adolescents' willingness to take action against bullying, victimization, substance use, or violence (see summary in Syvertsen, Flanagan, & Stout, 2009). That is, when the safety of others is compromised, most young people appear willing to respond by taking socially responsible action. Results from our second study show that the inclination to act on behalf of others, and for the common good, is enhanced when students have trusting relationships with teachers, a sense of personal inclusion, and a perception of solidarity in the student body.

Parents' Perceptions of Schools as Trustworthy Institutions Acknowledging the negative stereotypes about the safety and trustworthiness of schools, our third study highlights the challenges for schools to function as mini polities and to effectively develop students' democratic dispositions. Students and parents provide two sources of information about dimensions of their students' school's climate and relationships therein. Parents' views about schools as institutions and how trustworthy, safe, and secure they are compared to when the parents were children provide an additional source of information relevant to the public's trust in schools and how that relates to the development of social trust.

The public's trust in schools is essential to the civic vision of public education. As Tschannen-Moran and Hoy (2000) highlight, trust implies that individuals believe in the reliability, competence, and security of an institution to carry out its tasks and to serve their collective interests. By trusting in an institution, individuals form attachments and become connected to its purpose. In this way, trust invites participation and encourages individuals to work toward sustaining the institution and its mission. Importantly, by promoting connections to society, institutional trust also helps to foster social trust and to build social capital (Devos, Spini, & Schwartz, 2002; Duke et al., 2008; Uslaner, 2002).

Although many Americans agree that public schools are important civic socializers (Rose & Gallup, 2000), there is accumulating evidence that suggests their faith in public education as an institution has declined. Annual public opinion surveys regarding the state of public education tracked by Phi Delta Kappa and the Gallup Organization consistently show that, although many Americans espouse favorable views of their local schools, most report feeling cynical about the nation's schools in general. For instance, in a recent poll, while almost three-quarters of American parents surveyed rated the school attended by their eldest child as above average, less than one-fourth thought public schools in general merited similar scores (Bushaw & Gallup, 2008). Correspondingly, data from another national poll of adults indicate that U.S. confidence in institutions, including its public schools, has approached its lowest point in over three decades (Gallup Organization, 2008). Such trends are clearly troublesome and point to a growing disconnection between the public and public schools.

Many factors likely contribute to the negative perceptions of public schools. For instance, although evidence suggests that incidents of school-related violence are relatively rare, many Americans believe that their children still are unsafe at school (Cornell, 2006). In the aftermath of several highly publicized school shootings in the 1990s and 2000s, many parents and students continue to report fearfulness of schools as increasingly violent places. A survey conducted by Arnette and Walsleben (1998) revealed that 40% of parents with children in high school reported that they were "somewhat" or "very" worried about their child's safety at school. Similarly, findings from a Pew Research Center (2000) poll indicated that nearly three-fourths of parents feel that the widely publicized school shooting in Columbine, Colorado, had significantly altered their perception of their children's safety at school.

Although all acts of violence are lamentable, we contend that these fears, largely fueled by media sensationalism and public misperception, are simply inconsistent with the facts surrounding school violence and have served to create a false stereotype of America's schools (Cornell, 2006). Indeed, results from several large-scale studies demonstrate that violent events in public schools have actually decreased in the past decade and that most homicides involving school-aged children have not taken place in schools (e.g., Centers for Disease Control and Prevention, 2004; U.S. Department of Education, 2001). In spite of this evidence, we believe that the culture of fear and negative stereotypes, such as those surrounding school violence, impair the capacities of schools to fulfill their democratic functions.

In order to better understand the implications of such perceptions of schools on the democratic mission of education, we asked parents to compare their views of the trustworthiness of schools now with their lived experiences as children (Stoppa & Flanagan, in press). Parents were asked to rate their perceptions of schools using a *Less Trustworthy, Safe, or Secure* (1) to *More Trustworthy, Safe, or Secure* (5) rating scale. Responses were then recoded as "Untrusting" (1, 2) or "Trusting" (3, 4, 5). We then compared these groups with the parents' and the students' ratings of relationships in their own schools—that is, the extent to which teachers in their school encouraged a democratic climate of exchange and mutual respect (democratic authority structure) and the degree to which students felt a sense of solidarity and connection to the institution of their school (school solidarity).

Our findings indicated that the majority of parents (63%) reported orientations of distrust toward schools, whereas considerably fewer (37%) reported orientations of trust. Mean comparisons of trusting versus untrusting parents' perceptions of the schools that their own child attended revealed that trusting parents saw their son's or daughter's school in a more positive light, that is, they reported a more democratic authority structure in their children's schools relative to untrusting parents and also perceived greater school solidarity in their children's schools compared to untrusting parents.

Additionally, we conducted a series of analyses to compare mean differences among students in regard to perceptions of their school's democratic authority structure and school solidarity based upon parents' trusting versus untrusting orientations toward the institution of schools. The pattern of results among students was similar to the pattern observed among their parents. Specifically, students whose parents reported trusting orientations toward the institution of schools perceived their schools to have a more democratic authority structure compared to students whose parents held untrusting orientations. Likewise, students whose parents reported trusting orientations perceived a greater sense of solidarity in their school relative to students whose parents held untrusting orientations. Notably, additional analyses indicated that these differences in students' and parents' perceptions were not based on the students' experiences, for example, of bullying or social exclusion.

Thus, we concluded that negative stereotypes about public schools as institutions are a lens through which parents and students view climates and relationships in their own local schools. Such global perceptions, therefore, hold important implications for how parents and children approach relationships with schools in their communities at the local level. As these data demonstrate, when parents hold negative stereotypes about schools in general, these views may be corrosive to both their own and their children's perceptions of their immediate school environment. Parents who hold more favorable perspectives on schools as institutions in general, however, tend to have and to inspire more positive affective ties to local schools.

As a democratic institution, public education depends, in large part, upon its relationship with the citizenry. To carry out its civic mission, public schooling requires a commitment from the people and a shared investment from the polity in its purpose. Trust in and commitment to our public schools are essential in sustaining this vision (Matthews, 1997). The results from our third study suggest that holding negative stereotypes about schools (which other studies find have little basis in fact) undermines relationships between parents and schools, and colors students' perceptions of the social dynamics and relationships in their own schools.

REFLECTIONS ON THE DEMOCRATIC ROLE OF SCHOOLS

Perhaps more than any other institution, the public school introduces younger generations to and develops their capacities for participating in a democratic society. It is the setting in which most Americans spend a significant portion of their childhood and adolescence. In addition, because public education is a right granted to all U. S. citizens, in theory the public school should offer direct opportunities for participation and institutional involvement irrespective of traditional social boundaries. In light of this unique level of accessibility and inclusive scope, the public school constitutes an essential space for the promotion and practice of democratic skills and ideals (Covaleski, 2007).

In *The Public and its Problems* (1927), Dewey recognizes the powerful forces that work against the realization of a public: corporate capital, unbridled self-interest, and the media and communication that numb the sensibilities of the public. In this chapter, we have argued that public schools offer unique possibilities for the realization of a public because they are spaces where the principles and practices of living in a democratic society get interpreted and negotiated by each new generation. Drawing from our program of work, we have shown that certain practices in schools play a particular role in nurturing democratic dispositions such as social trust and a motivation to act to protect fellow members of the public. Our thesis is that it is in trusting relationships with teachers and in solidarity with fellow students that younger generations develop democratic dispositions, a public identity, and the motivation to act on behalf of the common good. We have emphasized the need for trusting relationships between teachers, administrators, students, and parents in fulfilling those goals, and we have shown that negative stereotypes about schools as unsafe and untrustworthy institutions compromise relationships within the institution and consequently the democratic functions of public schools.

In research on effective schools, teachers identify similar dimensions of the organizational climate at school that Bryk and Schneider (2002) have labeled relational trust. Teachers in more effective schools report a sense of identification with the school and solidarity with fellow teachers and also encouragement from the principal or authority figure to express their opinions (Tschannen-Moran & Hoy, 2000). Further, teachers' trust in their colleagues predicts collaboration in educational improvement activities (Tschannen-Moran, 2009). Bryk and Schneider contend that relational trust enables innovation because it reflects an environment in which individuals share a moral commitment to act in the interests of the collective.

Public schools in the United States have always served two competing goals: preparing younger generations for jobs in the capitalist market and preparing them for civic participation in a democratic society. Each of these goals has been more or less prominent at different periods in our history (Carnoy & Levin, 1985). In recent decades, the discourse on accountability in schools has focused on student achievement, primarily in math, science, and literacy (see Astuto & Ruck, this volume, for a discussion of the accountability discourse concerning elementary education). These are critical dimensions on which to assess our public schools, because citizens should not leave decisions that affect the public good (e.g., environment, economic inequality) to experts alone. Literacy, numeracy, and scientific understanding are important capacities required for citizens to make informed judgments about policies in their society.

However, a focus on achievement to the neglect of students' civic dispositions and skills is a policy that undermines the democratic mission of education. We need a larger definition of accountability than the current one, which relies on testing discrete (and, as many claim, narrow) domains of knowledge. Besides the inflated reliance on standardized tests, the civic mission of schools also has been compromised by trends toward privatization in schooling (Molnar, 2005). In an incisive essay, Covaleski (2007) points out that a discussion of the meaning of *the public* and its relevance for democratic life has been missing from the debates on school reform. Furthermore, he points to a subtext in the critiques of public schools, part of a larger politics over the past several decades in which blind faith in the market drove policies in many sectors, which resulted in the privatization of our common wealth, our things owned in common, and our republic (*res publica*), including our public schools.

Educational policies also need to be scrutinized to assess whether they are enforcing the promise of equal opportunity. Unequal educational outcomes (by race and class) have long plagued public schooling in the United States. However, typically, attention is paid only to unequal outcomes such as high-school graduation rates or performance on standardized math and reading tests. Far less attention is paid to the unequal opportunities students have for civic practice. As one large study of California's public schools found, opportunities for developing civic skills and knowledge vary widely across school districts and even within schools for students from differing socioeconomic backgrounds. These investigators found clear correlations between the number and quality of civics classes and the socioeconomic status of the students served by a school (Kahne & Middaugh, 2009). Similar disparities have been identified in New York City with schools that serve college-bound students more likely to have an array of opportunities (Devine, 1996). Opportunities for involvement in extracurricular activities (such as political simulations, debate, student government, and even service learning), which build civic skills and are known to predict civic involvement in adulthood, are less likely to be found in schools in poorer communities (Kahne & Middaugh, 2009; Carnegie and CIRCLE/Civic Mission of Schools, 2003; Levinson, this volume).

Finally, there are significant differences in disciplinary practices between schools that serve privileged and poor populations, with the latter having little practice in participating in the formation of school or classroom codes of conduct, since disciplinary and learning functions are separated. In many schools serving disadvantaged populations, classroom instruction is managed by teachers and administrators, but the school is under the control of a non-teaching security (police) force that makes and enforces disciplinary codes (Devine, 1996; Fine, 1994; Fox et al., this volume). Such inequities have been the focus of a number of civic activism projects successfully led by students (sometimes with their teachers) in disadvantaged school districts (Larson & Hansen, 2005).

By focusing on public schools, we do not assert that it is only in public schools that the democratic dispositions of future generations are formed. In fact, the practices that have been our focus—mutual respect between teachers and students; exchange of contrasting views; deliberation and finding common ground; and feelings of belonging, solidarity, and pride with others and the institution—are processes that happen in private and public schools alike. Indeed, there is some evidence that Catholic schools do a better job than public schools in redressing social inequalities, reducing disparities between more and less advantaged students, and leveling the playing field for students' achievement (Bryk, Lee, & Holland, 1993). Of course, the parents who send their children to Catholic schools and the teachers who teach in them share a core set of values that unites them as a community and facilitates the learning process. Bryk et al. (1993) contend that the vision of the Catholic schools in their study was one that Dewey promoted as the purpose of schools—to provide democratic education and advance the common good of students and of society (see also the discussion of Kohlberg's just community schools in Levine & Higgins-D'Alessandro, this volume).

In deciding to focus on public schools, we are also cognizant that the bureaucracy of large public school systems can pose barriers to democratic education. Meier (2002) has shown that the freedom to experiment in charter schools is a plus in enabling teachers to trust their students and their creative instincts, and to take chances that invite into the learning community those students who are typically marginalized by mainstream practices. But universal public education has been America's democratic experiment. Not only is education heralded as the great equalizer of opportunity, the leveler of the playing field, but it is also the means by which ordinary citizens develop the skills and dispositions for self-governance (Mann, 1848). Democracy in the United States challenged rule by an aristocracy as well as the elite models of education that maintained such rule. Long ago, Thomas Jefferson (1820/1989) linked education to rule of and by the people when he said, "I know of no safe repository of the ultimate powers of the society—but the people themselves. And if we think them not enlightened enough to exercise control with a wholesome discretion, the remedy is not to take it from them, but to inform their discretion by education."

ACKNOWLEDGEMENTS

Support for the empirical studies summarized in this chapter was provided by Grant RO1 DA005629 from the National Institute on Drug Abuse awarded to Constance Flanagan.

REFERENCES

Aristotle (1947). Nicomachean ethics (W. D. Ross, Trans.). In R. McKeon (Ed.), *Introduction to Aristotle*. New York: Random House.

Arnette, J. L., & Walsleben, M. C. (1998). *Combating fear and restoring safety in schools.* Rockville, MD: Juvenile Justice Clearinghouse.

Bandura, A. (1997). *Self-efficacy: The exercise of control*. New York: Freeman.

Battistich, V., Solomon, D., Watson, M., & Schaps, E. (1997). Caring school communities. *Educational Psychologist*, *32*, 137–151.

Baumeister, R. F., & Leary, M. R. (1995). The need to belong: Desire for interpersonal attachments as a fundamental human motivation. *Psychological Bulletin*, *117*, 497–529.

Berman, S. (1997). *Children's social consciousness and the development of social responsibility*. New York: State University of New York Press.

Boix, C., & Posner, D. (1988). Social capital: Explaining its origins and effects on government performance. *British Journal of Political Science*, *28*, 686–695.

Brewer, M. B., & Gardner, W. (1996). Who is this "We"? Levels of collective identity and self representations. *Journal of Personality and Social Psychology*, *71*, 83–93.

Bronfenbrenner, U., & Evans, G. W. (2000). Developmental science in the 21st century: Emerging theoretical models, research designs, and empirical findings. *Social Development*, *9*, 115–125.

Bryk, A. S., Lee, V. E., & Holland, P. B. (1993). *Catholic schools and the common good.* Cambridge, MA: Harvard University Press.

Bryk, A. S., & Schneider, B. (2002). *Trust in schools: A core resource for improvement*. New York: Russell Sage.

Bushaw, W. J., & Gallup, A. M. (2008). The 40th annual Phi Delta Kappa/Gallup poll of the public's attitudes toward the public schools. *Phi Delta Kappan*, *90*, 9–20.

Campbell, D. E. (2007). Sticking together: Classroom diversity and civic education. *American Politics Research, 35(1)*, 57–78.

Carnegie Corporation & CIRCLE. (2003). *The civic mission of schools.* Retrieved from http://www.civicmissionofschools.org/campaign/documents/CivicMissionofSchools.pdf

Carnoy, M., & Levin, H. M. (1985). *Schooling and work in the democratic state*. Stanford: Stanford University Press.

Centers for Disease Control and Prevention. (2004). Violence-related behaviors among high school students—United States, 1991–2003. *Morbidity and Mortality Weekly Report*, *53*, 651–655.

Cornell, D. G. (2006). *School violence: Fears versus facts.* Mahwah, NJ: Lawrence Erlbaum.

Covaleski, J. (2007). What public? Whose schools? *Educational Studies*, *42*, 28–42.

Damico, A. J., Conway, M. M., & Damico, S. B. (2000). Patterns of political trust and mistrust: Three moments in the lives of democratic citizens. *Polity*, *32*, 377–400.

Dawes, R. M., van de Kragt, A., & Orbell, J. (1990). Cooperation for the benefit of us—not me, or my conscience. In J. J. Mansbridge (Ed.), *Beyond self-interest*. Chicago: University of Chicago Press.

Devos, T., Spini, D., & Schwartz, S. H. (2002). Conflict among human values and trust in institutions. *British Journal of Social Psychology*, *41*, 481–494.

Dewey, J. (1927). *The public and its problems*. New York: Holt.

Dewey, J. (1916). *Democracy and education*. New York: The Free Press.

Duke, N. N., Skay, C. L., Pettingell, S. L., & Borowsky, I. W. (2008). From adolescent connections to social capital: Predictors of civic engagement in young adulthood. *Journal of Adolescent Health*, *44*, 161–168.

Easton, D., & Dennis, J. (1967). The child's acquisition of regime norms. *American Political Science Review*, *61*, 25–38.

Flanagan, C. A. (2003). Developmental roots of political engagement. *PS: Political Science and Politics*, *36*, 257–261.

Flanagan, C. A., Bowes, J., Jonsson, B., Csapo, B., & Sheblanova, E. (1998). Ties that bind: Correlates of adolescents' civic commitments in seven countries. *Journal of Social Issues*, *54*, 457–475.

Flanagan, C., Cumsille, P., Gill, S., & Gallay, L. (2007). School and community climates and civic commitments: Processes for ethnic minority and majority students. *Journal of Educational Psychology*, *99*, 421–431.

Flanagan, C. A., & Stout, M. (in press). Developmental patterns of social trust between early and late adolescence: Age and school climate effects. *Journal of Research on Adolescence.*

Gallup Organization (June 20, 2008). *Confidence in Congress: Lowest ever for any institution.* Retrieved from http://www.gallup.com/poll/108142/Confidence-Congress-Lowest-Ever-Any-US-Institution.aspx

Hess, D. (2009). *How schools can foster a new intellectual freedom: Preventing tyranny by nurturing controversy.* e-Library: Taylor and Francis; also, New York: Routledge.

Hooghe, M. (2003). Participation in voluntary associations and value indicators. *Nonprofit and Voluntary Sector Quarterly*, *32*, 47–69.

Hoy, W. K., & Tschannen-Moran, M. (1999). Five faces of trust: An empirical confirmation in urban elementary schools. *Journal of School Leadership, 9,* 184–208.

Jefferson, T. (1820/1989). Letter to William Charles Jarvis, September 28, 1820. As quoted in National Research Council (U.S.), *Improving Risk Communication*. National Academy of Sciences, Washinton, DC: National Academy Press.

Kahne, J. E., & Middaugh, E. (2009). Democracy for some: The civic opportunity gap in high school. In J. Youniss & P. Levine (Eds.), *Policies for Youth Civic Engagement*. Nashville, TN: Vanderbilt University Press.

Mann, H. (1848). *Education and prosperity*. From his Twelfth Annual Report as Secretary of Massachusetts State Board of Education.

Matthews, D. (1997). The lack of a public for public schools. *Phi Delta Kappan, 78,* 740–744.

Meier, D. (2002). *In schools we trust: Creating communities of learning in an era of testing and standardization*. Boston: Beacon Press.

Molnar, A. (2005). *School commercialism: From democratic ideal to market commodity.* New York: Routledge.

National Research Council and Institute of Medicine. (2003). *Deadly lessons: Understanding lethal school violence.* Washington, DC: National Academy Press.

Niemi, R. G., & Junn, J. (1998). *Civic education: What makes students learn.* New Haven: Yale University Press.

Orbell, J. M., van de Kragt, A., & Dawes, R. M. (1988). Explaining discussion-induced cooperation. *Journal of Personality and Social Psychology, 54,* 811–819.

Pearce, N. J., & Larson, R. W. (2006). How teens become engaged in youth development programs: The process of motivation change in civic activism organization. *Applied Developmental Science, 10,* 121–131.

Pew Research (2000, April 19). *A year after Columbine: Public looks to parents more than schools to prevent violence.* Washington, DC: Pew Research Center for the People and the Press.

Phan, M. B. (2008). We're all in this together: Context, contacts, and social trust in Canada. *Analyses of Social Issues and Public Policy, 8,* 23–51.

Portes, A. (1998). Social capital: Its origins and applications in modern sociology. *Annual Review of Sociology, 24,* 1–24.

Putnam, R. D. (2000). *Bowling alone: The collapse and revival of American community.* New York: Simon & Schuster.

Raider-Roth, M. B. (2005). Trusting what you know: Negotiating the relational context of classroom life. *Teachers College Record, 107,* 587–628.

Rose, L. C., & Gallup. A. M. (2000). The 32nd annual Phi Delta Kappa/Gallup poll of the public's attitudes toward the public schools. *Phi Delta Kappan, 82,* 41–57.

Rutkowski, G. K., Gruder, C. L., & Romer, D. (1983). Group cohesiveness, social norms, and bystander intervention. *Journal of Personality and Social Psychology, 44,* 545–552.

Ryan, R. M., & Deci, E. L. (2000). Self-determination theory and the facilitation of intrinsic motivation, social development, and well being. *American Psychologist, 55,* 68–78.

Smith, E. S. (1999). Effects of investment in the social capital of youth on political and civic behavior in young adulthood: A longitudinal analysis. *Political Psychology, 20*, 553–580.

Stoppa, T. M., & Flanagan, C. A. (in press). Parents' perceptions of public schools and implications for youth civic development.

Syvertsen, A. K., Flanagan, C. A., & Stout, M. D. (2009). Code of silence: Students' perceptions of school climate and willingness to intervene in a peer's dangerous plan. *Journal of Educational Psychology, 101*, 219–232.

Torney-Purta, J. (2002). The school's role in developing civic engagement: A study of adolescents in twenty-eight countries. *Applied Developmental Science, 6*, 203–212.

Torney-Purta, J. (2009). International research that matters for policy and practice. *American Psychologist, 64*, 822–837.

Torney-Purta, J., Barber, C., & Richardson, W. (2004). Trust in government-related institutions and political engagement among adolescents in six countries. *Acta Politica, 39*, 380–406.

Torney-Purta, J., & Wilkenfeld, B. (2009). *Paths to 21st century competencies through civic education classrooms: An analysis of survey results from ninth-graders.* Chicago, IL: American Bar Association Division for Public Education.

Tschannen-Moran, M. (2009). Fostering teacher professionalism in schools: The role of leadership orientation and trust. *Educational Administration Quarterly, 45*, 217–247.

Tschannen-Moran, M., & Hoy, W. K. (2000). A multidisciplinary analysis of the nature, meaning, and measurement of trust. *Review of Educational Research, 70*, 547–593.

U.S. Department of Education. (2001, February/March). *Community update* (No. 85). Washington, DC: U.S. Department of Education.

Uslaner, E. M. (2002). *The moral foundations of trust.* Cambridge, UK: Cambridge University Press.

Walzer, M. (1990). What does it mean to be an "American"? *Social Research, 57*, 591–614.

Walzer, M. (1997). *On toleration.* New Haven, CT: Yale University Press.

CHAPTER 13

The Civic Empowerment Gap: Defining the Problem and Locating Solutions

MEIRA LEVINSON
Harvard University

THE PURPOSE OF this chapter is to demonstrate that there is a profound *civic empowerment gap* in the United States—as large and as disturbing as the nationally recognized reading and math achievement gaps—and to argue that schools can and should help address this gap. There is widespread recognition that political power is distributed in vastly unequal ways among U.S. citizens. As the American Political Science Association's Task Force on Inequality and American Democracy memorably put it, "Citizens with low or moderate incomes speak with a whisper that is lost on the ears of inattentive government, while the advantaged roar with the clarity and consistency that policymakers readily heed" (APSA Task Force on Inequality and American Democracy, 2004, p. 651). Less poetically, but as powerfully, Bartels (2008) recently demonstrated that "political influence seems to be limited entirely to affluent and middle-class people. The opinions of millions of ordinary citizens in the bottom third of the income distribution have *no* discernible impact on the behavior of their elected representatives" (p. 5). Both scholars and educators can do much more to clarify the role of schools in contributing to and ameliorating this problem. The purpose of this chapter is to clarify the ways in which schools, understood both as contextually located civic institutions and as primary deliverers of civic education, can and must help address this unjust civic empowerment gap, especially among historically disenfranchised populations.

The first section begins by defining good citizenship, and by extension, the aims of good civic education. I then demonstrate the existence of a broad and deep civic empowerment gap across all dimensions of good citizenship—civic and political knowledge, skills, attitudes, and behaviors—

and argue that this gap challenges the stability, legitimacy, and quality of our democratic republic. In the second section, I suggest that we focus on *de facto* segregated urban schools as crucial sites for addressing the civic empowerment gap. The third section then recommends five specific approaches that could improve access to high-quality civic education and experiences, especially among historically disenfranchised youth. These include reducing the dropout rate, improving the quantity and distribution of civic education across K–12 education, engaging students in co-constructing empowering civic historical narratives, infusing experiential civic education throughout the curriculum, and providing powerful civic learning and engagement opportunities for urban teachers.

CITIZENSHIP AND THE CIVIC EMPOWERMENT GAP

What are the components of citizenship, and what does it mean to be a good citizen? These questions must be answered prior to any discussion about the aims or content of civic education. Can you be a good citizen if you don't vote? What if you vote, but are uninformed about most of the issues and candidates, or vote solely on the basis of a single issue? How important is it to be law-abiding? Is being economically self-sufficient a hallmark (or even a precondition) of good citizenship? How should we judge the act of protesting injustice via civil disobedience against the act of sacrificing oneself on the battlefield? Depending on how one answers these questions, one's judgment about what makes for good civic education will be radically different.

In this chapter, I adopt the definition set forth in *The Civic Mission of Schools*, as it integrates many disparate strands of belief and ideology about citizenship:

> Civic education should help young people acquire and learn to use the skills, knowledge, and attitudes that will prepare them to be competent and responsible citizens throughout their lives. Competent and responsible citizens:
>
> 1. Are informed and thoughtful; have a grasp and an appreciation of history and the fundamental processes of American democracy; have an understanding and awareness of public and community issues; and have the ability to obtain information, think critically, and enter into dialogue among others with different perspectives.
> 2. Participate in their communities through membership in or contributions to organizations working to address an array of cultural, social, political, and religious interests and beliefs.
> 3. Act politically by having the skills, knowledge, and commitment needed to accomplish public purposes, such as group problem solving, public speaking, petitioning and protesting, and voting.

4. Have moral and civic virtues such as concern for the rights and welfare of others, social responsibility, tolerance and respect, and belief in the capacity to make a difference.

—(Carnegie Corporation of New York & CIRCLE, 2003, p. 4).

One virtue of this characterization of good citizenship, and hence of good civic education, is that it is capacious without being simplistic. Within this definition, good citizens may be those who vote, protest, boycott, run for office, join political parties, join civic organizations, commit acts of civil disobedience, circulate e-mail petitions, write influential political blogs, "tweet" or text message about political events being kept under a news blackout, and attend neighborhood council meetings. Good citizens may not, however, merely keep to themselves; simply not being a burden to others is not sufficient for good citizenship. In this respect, this definition rejects the ideal of the "personally responsible citizen," as Westheimer and Kahne describe in their influential article, "What Kind of Citizen" (Westheimer & Kahne, 2004, p. 239), but encompasses their ideals of both "participatory" and "justice-oriented" citizens. Participatory citizens believe that "to solve social problems and improve society, citizens must actively participate and take leadership positions within established systems and community structures," while justice-oriented citizens believe that one must "question, debate, and change established systems and structures that reproduce patterns of injustice over time" (Westheimer & Kahne, 2004, p. 240, Table 1). Participatory and justice-oriented citizens frequently disagree about the most fruitful acts to take as citizens—and hence also would disagree about the best approaches to citizenship education—but they both embrace the importance of knowledgeable, skillful, active involvement in civic and political institutions in order to improve society. The definition of good citizenship given above clearly would recognize both kinds of citizens as good citizens.

On the downside, this definition arguably privileges traditional modes of civic action that are both increasingly outdated and unrepresentative of a range of actions and behaviors that have historically been important civic tools of members of disadvantaged, oppressed, or marginalized groups, or any combination of the three. For example, various Web 2.0 activities such as uploading a video to YouTube and interacting through social networking sites such as Facebook or Ning do not obviously fit into the categories and actions described above, despite their increasingly evident civic importance (see Bennett, Freelon, & Wells, this volume). This definition also seems to exclude artistic production and expression such as hip-hop music and videos, poetry slams, and graffiti—all of which have arguably been used especially by young, often poor, people of color in the United States and elsewhere to critique contemporary power structures and civic institutions. Furthermore, it fails to credit the civic intentionality and implications of "everyday . . . forms of resistance" by "relatively powerless groups: foot dragging, dissimulation, desertion, false compliance, pilfering, feigned ignorance, slander, arson, sabotage, and so on" (Scott, 1985, p. xvi). Finally, emphasis on public and collective forms of engagement likely overlooks the ways in which especially members of historically disadvantaged groups may be "pillars of their communities" without participating collectively in public activities. A well-known community elder, for example, may exert considerable civic influence by modeling rectitude, advising youngsters about how to behave, and serving as an informal but final arbiter of community disputes, even though he takes part in no obvious "public" activities. These are all arguably significant civic roles, actions, and dimensions of influence that are not obviously included in the definition above.

It is nonetheless worth proceeding with this definition—and with the measures of civic engagement that follow from the definition—for a couple of reasons. First, we don't have good quantitative measures of most of the forms of civic engagement listed in the above paragraph. Scholars who study civic engagement in the United States have relatively good quantitative measures of rates of voting, government contact, political discussion in the home, boycotts, and even protest participation (among many others). But they don't have good measures of use of social networking tools for civic engagement, or of how civic engagement is expressed and enacted through art or music, hip-hop culture, informal neighborhood leadership, or calculated subversion. A more expansive definition would incorrectly suggest that my analysis of demographic measures of civic empowerment was capable similarly of being more expansive, which it is not.[1] Second, traditional forms of engagement still matter with respect to empowerment. People who vote regularly, contact politicians and other government officials, speak up in public meetings, join civic organizations, and donate money to both candidates and civic causes almost invariably have more civic and political power in the United States in the early twenty-first century than those who do not. Since this chapter is about civic empowerment, we need to take these traditional measures of civic engagement into account, even at the cost of privileging them over other modes that are more accessible to and more frequently employed by members of historically disadvantaged groups. This risks creating a circular and apparently deficit-oriented argument in which I place certain groups at the bottom of a civic empowerment gap, precisely because I discount forms of civic engagement in which they are particularly

1 Qualitative data and research are obviously also crucial to documenting and understanding the multiple dimensions and patterns of civic engagement and empowerment.

involved. But gaps need not imply deficits, and it does no one any good to ignore the specific harms suffered by those who cannot or do not deploy traditional levers of civic and political power. Thus, I will rely upon this definition of good citizenship—and correlatively, of the desirable outcomes of good civic education—despite its acknowledged limitations.

Central to this definition are civic *knowledge*, *skills*, *attitudes*, and *behaviors*. Good citizens need to be *knowledgeable* about politics, history, government, and current events; they need to be *skilled* communicators, thinkers, deliberators, and actors; they need to be *concerned* about the common good in addition to their own self-interest, and to *believe* it is possible and worth trying to make a difference through public action; and they need to *become involved* in public or community affairs, through some combination of voting, protesting, contacting public officials, mobilizing others, contributing time or money to causes or campaigns, participating in community groups, and other appropriate actions. No matter where one lands on the participatory versus justice-oriented continuum, or on the civic versus political continuum (Zukin, Keeter, Andolina, Jenkins, & Delli Carpini, 2006; Lopez, Levine, Both, Kiesa, Kirby, & Marcelo, 2006), these four attributes are necessary to be a good citizen. On all of these measures, there is evidence of a profound gap between many non-White, immigrant, and especially low-income youth and adults, on the one hand, and White, native-born, and especially middle-class or wealthy youth and adults, on the other (see Jensen, this volume; Seif, this volume).

Knowledge and Skills

As early as in the fourth grade and continuing into the eighth and twelfth grades, African American, Hispanic, and poor students perform significantly worse on the National Assessment of Educational Progress' (NAEP) test of civic knowledge than White, Asian, and middle-class students (U.S. Department of Education, Institute of Education Sciences, National Center for Education Statistics, & National Assessment of Educational Progress (NAEP), 2007; Lutkus, Weiss, Campbell, Mazzeo, & Lazer, 1999). On the 2006 NAEP Civics Assessment, for example, White 4th and 8th graders who were poor (i.e., eligible for free or reduced-price lunch) performed as well as middle-class and wealthy (ineligible for free or reduced-price lunch) African American and Hispanic students—and significantly better than poor African American and Hispanic students. Asian students' results were mixed. Within each racial/ethnic group, poor students earned significantly lower scores than middle-class and wealthier students (computed using data from IES: National Center for Education Statistics, 2007). Similar disparities appear in American ninth graders' scores on the 1999 IEA test of civic knowledge and skills (Baldi, Perie, Skidmore, Greenberg, & Hahn, 2001, Tables 4.1 and 4.5; Torney-Purta, Barber, & Wilkenfeld, 2007). Immigration status also seems to influence students' mastery of civic knowledge and skills. Students who haven't lived in the United States their whole lives performed significantly worse on the 1998 NAEP Civics Assessment than students who have always done so, with scores directly related to the number of years living in the United States (IES: National Center for Education Statistics, 2007); similar results hold for ninth graders' performance on the IEA CIVED test (Torney-Purta, Barber, & Wilkenfeld, 2007). This shouldn't be surprising, since it is predictable that the longer students live in the United States, the more they will learn about U.S. government and democracy. But it does set the stage for civic and political participation gaps between native-born and naturalized citizens, as I discuss below.

These results for youth are, unsurprisingly, echoed in studies of adults. In a comprehensive study of adults' civic and political knowledge, Delli Carpini and Keeter (1996) conclusively demonstrate that "men are more informed than women; whites are more informed than blacks; those with higher incomes are more informed than those with lower incomes; and older citizens are more informed than younger ones." These disparities are not small: out of the 68 questions asked in the 1989 Survey of Political Knowledge, for example, "In no case was the percentage correct for blacks as high as for whites or for low-income citizens as high as that for upper-income ones." Similarly, three-quarters of Black Americans scored below all but the bottom quarter of White Americans; more than three-quarters of poor respondents scored below the top three-quarters of their middle-class counterparts (Delli Carpini & Keeter, 1996, p. 157, also Tables 4.8 and 4.9, Figure 4.1; see also Verba, Schlozman, & Brady, 1995, Table 12.4; and The Pew Research Center for the People and the Press, 2007, for independent corroborating data). These patterns can manifest themselves in startling ways. In 2004, for example, when I was teaching eighth grade in a Boston public school that served predominantly low-income, first- and second-generation immigrant students of color, none of my 27 homeroom students knew that July 4th celebrates the signing and publication of the Declaration of Independence (see Hart & Atkins, 2002, for a similar story).

It is undoubtedly true that these surveys and tests of political and civic knowledge and skills are both limited and biased in a number of ways. Relevant political and civic knowledge are defined overwhelmingly by middle-class, native-born, White scholars, educators, and policy-makers, who care about federal and especially electoral politics. They privilege both modes and content of civic knowledge that are familiar to and valued by such groups. Thus, the 1989 and 2007 Pew Surveys of Political Knowledge, cited above, ask respondents to identify the Speaker of the House and other public officials, answer specific questions about impending federal legislation and policies, name foreign leaders, and answer questions about domestic and foreign affairs (The Pew Research Center for the People and the Press, 2007). Other political knowledge and skills are arguably of far greater relevance to many low-income youth of color living in urban neighborhoods. My eighth-grade students, for example, eloquently made the case that I—a White, middle-class woman living in a middle-class Boston neighborhood—would have a hard time understanding and negotiating the politics of "the hood" in which they lived. I certainly would have flunked a test that asked me to identify members of the locally relevant power structure: who controlled what block; which housing projects I could safely enter as a resident of another project; or which social workers, police officers, and housing authority representatives could be trusted and which were to be avoided (see, e.g., Ayers & Ford, 1996).

Even independent of a race-, class-, or context-based analysis of what kinds of political knowledge matter, there is little agreement between those who design tests of students and those who design adult surveys about what kinds of civic knowledge count. As Niemi and Sanders (2004) point out, "NAEP quizzes students almost exclusively about political structures and institutions, whereas adult 'tests' focus mostly on contemporary politics (personalities and policies) . . . raising questions about the meaningfulness of the items on which students are tested" (p. 327). They go on to conclude, "The kind of information routinely sought from students is simply not essential for them to have as adults" (p. 337).

Even if these measures of civic knowledge for adults or children are incomplete, skewed, or poorly justified, both the sheer lack of knowledge as well as the consistency of the differences matter and should be troubling. Traditionally measured civic knowledge is clearly and directly correlated with higher levels of political participation and expression of democratic values including toleration, stable political attitudes, and adoption of "enlightened self-interest" (Galston, 2001; Delli Carpini & Keeter, 1996). One's capacity for civic empowerment is greater if one knows about both political structures and institutions as well as about contemporary politics than if one does not know of these things. It is easy to imagine how people who don't know who their elected representatives are, what the White House's position is on various high-profile policy disputes, or how a bill becomes a law, may find it harder to influence civic life than those who do (Hart & Atkins, 2002). These domains of knowledge aren't all that matter. But it would be hard to claim that they are irrelevant to the distribution of power in society. Thus, demographically predictable patterns in the distribution of knowledge in these domains presage a disturbing civic empowerment gap.

People who are poor and non-White are also demonstrably less likely to develop traditional civic skills via education, the workplace, or participation in voluntary associations—three of the primary venues in which individuals have the opportunity to develop and practice communication, analysis, organization, and leadership skills relevant to civic and political participation. This is because they are likely to leave school sooner, to have attended worse schools, to have lower-status jobs, and to participate less in voluntary associations. Churches may ameliorate, but certainly do not solve, this civic skills opportunity gap (Verba, Schlozman, & Brady, 1995, Chap. 11). Again, I contended almost daily with this gap as an urban middle-school teacher. My eighth-grade students frequently struggled to negotiate conflicts without getting into fights; they interacted ineffectually with authority figures and ended up in trouble despite their best intentions not to; and they relied on me to teach them even such basic skills as how to use a phone book and talk on the phone in a professional manner because they had never seen these skills modeled by others. Similarly, I frequently watched in frustration (and assisted when I could) as deeply committed and caring parents often failed to advocate effectively for their children because they didn't have the necessary communication skills (see Lareau, 2000, 2003 for a compelling account of this problem). This gap in civic knowledge and skills thus impacts not just individuals' interactions with government officials or politicians but also their everyday experiences at school and in their communities.

Behavior and Participation

There has been a fair amount of media coverage of the voting gap based on race, ethnicity, income, and education level. In the presidential election of 2004, for example, Hispanic and Asian voting-age citizens voted at a rate only two-thirds that of eligible Whites (approximately 45% versus 67%, respectively) (U.S. Census Bureau, 2005, Table 4a), while people living in families with incomes under $15,000 voted at about half the rate of those living in families with incomes over $75,000 (45% versus 80%, respectively) (U.S. Census Bureau, 2005, Table 9). Likewise, 11% fewer naturalized versus native-born citizens voted, which is a cause for concern since 20% of the U.S. population is first- or second-generation immigrant (U.S. Census Bureau, 2005, Table 13; see also DeSipio, 2001).

Despite widespread excitement about Barack Obama's candidacy and media coverage suggesting huge increases in youth and minority turnout, 2008 presidential election voting rates almost exactly replicated the disparities seen in 2004. While 65% to 66% of White and Black voting-age citizens voted in the 2008 presidential election, for example, barely half of Hispanic, Asian, Native American, or other voting-age citizens did so (McDonald, 2009). The voting gap between native-born and naturalized citizens in 2008 also exactly replicated the results in 2004 (65% versus 54%). Similarly, in both 2004 and 2008, voting rates of citizens with less than a high-school diploma persisted at less than 40%, compared with a little over half of citizens with a high-school diploma choosing to cast their ballot, participation by almost three-quarters of citizens who had attended college, and voting rates of over 80% of those with post-graduate education (McDonald, 2009). And finally, half of those with an income under $15,000 voted, versus 79% of those with an income over $100,000 (U.S. Census Bureau, 2008). It is worth remembering that these voting rate disparities persisted despite the extreme competitiveness of the Democratic primary election and the historic nature of the 2008 presidential campaign.

Significant behavior disparities also persist beyond voting. Reliable analyses of political participation, as measured by membership in political parties, campaign donations, campaign volunteering, participation in protests, contacting an elected official, and so forth, show vast disparities linked with class, education, and race. People who earn over $75,000 annually are politically active at up to *six times* the rate of people who earn under $15,000, whether measured by working for a campaign, serving on the board of an organization, or participating in protests (Verba, Schlozman, & Brady, 1995, p. 190, Figure 7.2). Broader measures of civic participation—belonging to any group or organization, working on a community problem, volunteering, attending a community meeting, or even just wearing a campaign button or putting a political bumper sticker on one's car—also seem to be highly unequally distributed by educational attainment. The 2008 Civic Health Index, for example, found that 81% of young adults with no college experience were "not very engaged" civically according to these and similar measures, as compared to 41% of young adults with some college experience (National Conference on Citizenship, 2008). Latinos, too, are far less involved in all of these activities than Whites or Blacks, and Blacks are more likely to participate in "outsider" activities such as protests rather than "insider" activities such as campaign donations or direct contact with officials (Verba, Schlozman, & Brady, 1995, Chap. 8; Nie, Junn, & Stehlik-Barry, 1996; see also Wolfinger & Rosenstone, 1980). Hispanic young adults (ages 18 to 24) in particular have much lower rates of voter registration and community involvement than their White and Black peers (Verba, Schlozman, & Brady, 1995; Lopez, 2003; Lopez, Levine, Both, Kiesa, Kirby, & Marcelo, 2006, p. 20).

It is important to note that the forecast is not entirely grim. Recent immigration reform efforts, including rallies, marches, and protests surrounding support for the DREAM Act and opposition to the 2006 proposed congressional immigration bill, mobilized significant numbers of Hispanic and first- and second-generation immigrant youth and adults. Most likely as a result of these protests, more immigrant youth reported participating in protests in 2006 than native-born youth (Lopez et al., 2006; Seif, this volume). In addition, African American youth and to a lesser extent Asian American youth ages 18 to 29 are in many ways more politically or civically engaged than their White counterparts as measured by the 2006 and 2008 Civic Health surveys (Lopez et al., 2006; National Conference on Citizenship, 2008; see also Marcelo, Lopez, & Kirby, 2007). This may indicate that the civic participation gap is actually lessening among youth, or at least emphasize that race and ethnicity contribute less than income and education to the civic empowerment gap. However, the data are too recent and context-specific to foster confidence about long-term reductions in the civic behavior gap.

Furthermore, even if the promising trends continue, the civic participation gap remains enormous in the United States as compared to other developed (and even many less-developed) democracies (Torney-Purta & Amadeo, 2004, pp. 56, 69, 88). There is a tendency in the United States to normalize the demographic difference in participation rates by explaining it away in the same way many did with the reading or math achievement gap a decade ago: "But of course poor people [or Hispanics, etc.] participate less. They don't have the time or financial resources (or education, knowledge) to participate as wealthier people do." This argument doesn't make sense when one considers, for example, the protests in Argentina a few years ago, when hundreds of thousands of poor and middle-class people took to the streets banging pots and pans and ended up forcing the resignations of their political leaders; they were actually following the example set by *piqueteros* (picketers)—unemployed workers who started a nationwide movement for social change in the 1990s and have sustained it for over a decade. If unemployed and uneducated citizens in Argentina (as well as other South American democracies) can demonstrate such high levels of civic and political engagement, poor people in the United States could do the same. This is not to argue that socioeconomic differences in political participation are negligible in other countries. Studies of European, Canadian, and Central American voter turnout rates in the 1980s and 1990s demonstrate that those democracies have an average 10 to 12 percentage point difference in voter turnout between the most- and least-educated citizens—but this is far eclipsed by the United States' 35% gap (Powell, 1986; Lijphart, 1997, p. 3). Furthermore, the participation gap has not always been a major feature even of American civic and political life (see Montgomery, 1993). In the late nineteenth and early twentieth centuries, immigrant incorporation groups, trade unions, fraternal organizations, and political parties regularly mobilized poor, working-class, non-White, and newly immigrant Americans (Skocpol, 1999; Montgomery, 2001, p. 1268ff; Sachar, 1993, pp. 175–176; Freeman, 2002), and participation in civic organizations was extremely widespread (Skocpol, Ganz, & Munson, 2000).

Attitudes

People's decisions to participate in civic life are at least partly determined by their attitudes: whether they believe that individuals can influence government (political efficacy), that they themselves can influence government (individual efficacy), that one has a duty to participate (civic duty), and that one is part of a civic community (civic identity). All of these pro-civic attitudes are disproportionately correlated with both race/ethnicity and class.

Verba, Schlozman, and Brady show, for example, that individuals' political efficacy increases in direct relationship to their income, with the poorest individuals expressing attitudes almost a full standard deviation lower than the wealthiest; it is also significantly correlated with race/ethnicity, with Latinos at the bottom, African Americans in the middle, and White respondents at the top (Verba, Schlozman, & Brady, 1995, Table 12.4). Similarly, a study specifically of young Latinos, African Americans, and Whites (ages 15 to 25) shows equivalent significant individual efficacy differences in their confidence that "I can make a difference in solving the problems of my community" (Lake Snell Perry & Associates & The Tarrance Group, 2002; Carnegie Corporation of New York & CIRCLE, 2003; although, see Hunter & Bowman, 1996; *Washington Post*, Kaiser Family Foundation, & Harvard University, 2000; Baldi, Perie, Skidmore, Greenberg, & Hahn, 2001, for some conflicting research). These efficacy disparities are further reflected in individuals' competing interpretations of controversial political events. A *Newsweek* poll following Hurricane Katrina, for example, showed that twice as many African Americans versus White Americans (65% versus 31%) thought the government responded slowly to the disaster because most of the affected people were African American (Huddy & Feldman, 2006).

President Obama's election and administration may narrow the efficacy gap, but is not likely to eliminate it, if for no other reason than that the gap is utterly rational. White, middle-class or wealthy, college-educated, and native English-speaking citizens living in relatively high social capital neighborhoods undeniably *do* have greater opportunities to influence government or public policy than do non-White, educationally underserved, economically disadvantaged youth and adults living in neighborhoods with limited social and political capital (Jacobs & Skocpol, 2005; Bartels, 2008). Although unjust and profoundly antidemocratic, this fact remains equally true no matter who is president. The problem, however, is that the efficacy gap may be viciously self-reinforcing, if those who correctly view themselves as more able to make a difference become ever more involved while those who question their efficacy withdraw from public civic engagement.

Two other attitudinal components contribute significantly to the civic empowerment gap: namely, individuals' senses of civic identity and civic duty. Dawson has demonstrated in considerable quantitative and qualitative detail the ways in which African Americans' senses of civic membership and responsibility are distinct from non-African Americans' in being focused on the "linked fate" of African Americans as a group (Dawson, 1994, 2001). Immigrant citizens' sense of civic identity is similarly ambiguous. Although their sense of patriotism tends to be as high as or higher than native-born citizens, their sense of themselves as Americans is more tenuous. In interviews I conducted in April 2004 with first- and second-generation Arab-American students, parents, teachers, and community leaders in Dearborn, MI, for example, my interlocutors (most of whom were citizens) consistently referred to "Americans" as "they":

> Interviewer: Three of you are American citizens, born in the United States. But you have consistently throughout the interview ... used the term "Americans" not to refer to yourselves but to refer to others.... [Y]ou talked about Americans as other people. So I'm curious why.
>
> Student: I see what you're trying to get us to say—like we were born here, like, why shouldn't we consider ourselves as regular American people. But I think that we're different because we have to fall back on our parents' background because our parents—that's what they teach us. That's what our culture is. Like our background from our old country and stuff like that.

This echoes other scholars' findings from New York City.

> [Second generation immigrants] used the term American in two different ways. One was to describe themselves as American compared to the culture, values, and behaviors of their parents.... But they also used "American" to refer to the native white Americans that they encountered at school, the office, or in public places, but whom they knew far better from television and the movies. They saw those "Americans" as part of a different world that would never include them because of their race/ethnicity. Many respondents sidestepped this ambivalent understanding of the meaning of being American by describing themselves as "New Yorkers." (Kasinitz, Mollenkopf, & Waters, 2002; see also Stepick & Stepick, 2002)

Similarly ambivalent attitudes and experiences of civic disjuncture have been found among poor, non-White, and immigrant youth (Rubin, 2007; Abu El-Haj, 2008).

Even if these do demonstrate a significant civic empowerment gap along the four dimensions of civic knowledge, skills, attitudes, and behaviors between non-White, immigrant, and especially low-income citizens, on the one hand, and White, native-born, and especially middle- and high-income citizens, on the other, why should we care? I suggest that anyone who believes in the value of democratic governance should recognize how crucial it is to narrow the gap. Individuals' civic knowledge, skills, and attitudes profoundly influence their civic and political behavior, which is concomitantly central to the strength, stability, and legitimacy of democracy. We saw above that civic knowledge is clearly and directly correlated with higher levels of political participation, expression of democratic values, stable political attitudes, and adoption of "enlightened self-interest" (Galston, 2001; Delli Carpini & Keeter, 1996). Individuals' mastery of civic skills is also tied to both their likelihood of civic participation and their effectiveness. "Those who possess civic skills, the set of specific competencies germane to citizen political activity, are more likely to feel confident about exercising those skills in politics and to be effective—or, to use the economist's term, productive—when they do" (Verba, Schlozman, & Brady, 1995, p. 305).

Participation, of course, matters because democratic governance relies on participatory citizens. The legitimacy, stability, and quality of democratic regimes are all directly dependent on the robust participation of a representative and large cross-section of citizens. Governments that appear to serve the interests of only a narrow segment of the population cease to be viewed as democratic, and cease to inspire the loyalty and commitment of those who feel excluded. This poses a direct threat to both their legitimacy and stability. Political violence by citizens is also tightly linked to feelings of disaffection and alienation (Kinder, 1998, pp. 831–832). Furthermore, democratic deliberations and decisions are likely to be of lower quality if people representing only a fairly narrow range of experiences, interests, and backgrounds are involved. Part of the beauty of democracy, when it functions effectively and inclusively, is its ability to create aggregate wisdom and good judgment from individual citizens' necessarily limited knowledge, skills, and viewpoints. To exclude citizens from this process is to diminish the wisdom that the collectivity may create.

Attitudes matter because they constitute the motivational preconditions for civic engagement. Whether one knows nothing about current events or has an advanced degree in political science, whether one is a shy follower or a brilliant orator and leader, if one doesn't believe that civic and political participation can make a difference, then one is not going to participate. Political efficacy is crucial for motivating civic and political engagement. Attitudes of civic duty or obligation are also important motivators: "Citizens with a strong sense of civic duty are about 6 percentage points more likely to turn out to vote in recent presidential elections than are their otherwise comparable counterparts who do not recognize voting as an obligation of citizenship" (Kinder, 1998, p. 832). Verba, Schlozman, and Brady also found that civic obligation was the most important attitudinal predictor for civic activism (Verba, Schlozman, & Brady, 1995, Chap. 4). And finally, identity seems to figure importantly in influencing the character and quality of civic engagement, as political psychologists, philosophers, and others have shown (Damon, 2001, pp. 127, 135; Feinberg, 1998, p. 47).

Above all else, the gaps in knowledge, skills, attitudes, and participation matter because they profoundly diminish the democratic character and quality of the United States.

> Generations of Americans have worked to equalize citizen voice across lines of income, race, and gender. Today, however, the voices of American citizens are raised and heard unequally. The privileged participate more than others and are increasingly well organized to press their demands on government. Public officials, in turn, are much more responsive to the privileged than to average citizens and the less affluent. The voices of citizens with lower or moderate incomes are lost on the ears of inattentive government officials, while the advantaged roar with the clarity and consistency that policymakers readily hear and routinely follow (Jacobs & Skocpol, 2005, p. 1).

Not all of these unequal levels of influence can be attributed to differences in individual levels of knowledge, skills, attitudes, or participation, of course. There are powerful institutional, political, and other factors at work that would likely contribute to the persistence of inegalitarian and undemocratic outcomes even if the gaps explored above were eliminated. The exploding cost of political campaigns and politicians' corresponding dependence upon and attention to wealthy donors provide only one obvious example of the multiple barriers to equal civic empowerment. But it is clear that the civic empowerment gap among individuals is a significant threat to democratic ideals and practice. I suggest that it is important for both the civic and political empowerment of poor, minority, and immigrant individuals, and for the health of the polity as a whole, that we develop means for closing the gap.

DE FACTO SEGREGATED MINORITY SCHOOLS

One important battleground for attacking the civic empowerment gap is the network of mostly urban schools that serve a *de facto* segregated, poor, and minority student population. Fully one-third of Black and Latino students in the United States, and over half of the Black students in the Northeast, attend schools that have a 90% to 100% minority student population (Orfield & Lee, 2006; see also Orfield, Eaton, & The Harvard Project on Desegregation, 1996; Orfield, 2001, Tables 14 and 18). The overwhelming majority of these schools are in urban areas, often central cities. Over half of all schools in the 100 largest school districts were 81% to 100% non-White in 2005 to 2006, and one-fifth of these districts had a non-White student population above 90% (Garofano & Sable, 2008, Table A-8). In practice, therefore, most schools in these districts had a virtually 100% minority population, often from a single race or ethnicity. Detroit, Baltimore, Atlanta, Memphis, and Washington, DC, have over 80% black student enrollment; Brownsville (TX), Santa Ana (CA), San Antonio, and El Paso are more than 80 percent Latino; Los Angeles is almost three-quarters Latino while San Francisco is more than half Asian (Garofano & Sable, 2008, Table A-9). The students in these schools and districts are also generally poor. Half of all students in the 100 largest school districts are eligible for free or reduced-price lunch, and in 21 of these districts, which together serve close to four million students, more than seven out of every ten students are eligible for free or reduced price lunch (Garofano & Sable, 2008, Table A-9 and A-1). Many of these students thus face "double segregation" by both race/ethnicity and class (Orfield & Lee, 2007, p. 5).

The number of these schools serving poor, urban, *de facto* segregated ethnically or racially minority students is likely to increase in upcoming decades. Orfield and his colleagues have exhaustively documented that schools and school districts in the United States are resegregating, not desegregating (Orfield, Eaton, & The Harvard Project on Desegregation, 1996; Orfield, 2001; Orfield & Lee, 2007). This trend will likely accelerate thanks to the Supreme Court's decision in *Parents Involved versus Seattle* ("Parents Involved," 2007), which invalidated race-conscious school assignment policies designed to promote integrated schools in Seattle, Washington, and Louisville, Kentucky. Furthermore, public pressure for integrated schools has diminished considerably. In a 1998 survey, for example, African American survey respondents joined White respondents in ranking racial diversity second from the bottom of their preferred characteristics for a good school (Public Agenda Foundation, 1998); this stands in stark contrast to Blacks' attitudes in the 1970s and 1980s, when integration was a high priority not only in principle but also in practice. Integration is viewed by many as "yesterday's struggle" (Loury, 1997), with greater importance being placed on students' obtaining an "equal opportunity to learn" (Ladson-Billings, 2004), whether in integrated or segregated settings (Horsford & McKenzie, 2008; Walker & Archung, 2003; Shujaa, 1996). African American and Latino political leaders have similarly shifted their focus from integration to equality of opportunity. Leaders of the NAACP, for instance, have held "a formal debate over the virtues of nonsegregated versus black-run schools for black students" (Patterson, 2001, p. 192) and released statements minimizing desegregation concerns (although they did file an amicus brief in support of Seattle's and Louisville's school integration policies). Black mayors in Seattle, Denver, St. Louis, and Cleveland have also led efforts to dismantle desegregation practices (Hochschild & Scovronick, 2003, pp. 48–49; see also Massey &

Denton, 1993), while a leader of La Raza recently asserted, "Having 100% of one ethnicity is not a bad thing" (Bracey, 2009, p. 691). As Justice Clarence Thomas wrote in his concurring opinion in the Seattle and Louisville cases, rejecting the constitutionality of school integration policies, "It is far from apparent that coerced racial mixing has any educational benefits, much less that integration is necessary to black achievement" ("Parents involved," 2007, p. 15). Some prominent scholars have also questioned the desirability of school integration (see, e.g., Bell, 2004, 1980); in Gloria Ladson-Billings' words, "It would be better to have a 'real *Plessy*' than to continue with a 'fake *Brown*'" (Ladson-Billings, 2009). With scholarly, public, and Supreme Court opinions like this, segregated schools will clearly remain a fact of twenty-first century American life.

These schools matter for two other reasons beyond their mere prevalence and staying power. First, Kahne and Middaugh's analysis of several large datasets documents a clear civic opportunity gap between these schools and those that serve wealthier or whiter students, or both:

> [A] student's race and academic track, and a school's average socioeconomic status (SES) determines the availability of the school-based civic learning opportunities that promote voting and broader forms of civic engagement. High school students attending higher SES schools, those who are college-bound, and white students get more of these opportunities than low-income students, those not heading to college, and students of color. (Kahne & Middaugh, 2008, p. 3)

In practice, this means that students in average versus high SES classes are half as likely to report studying how laws are made, barely half as likely to report participating in service activities, and 30% less likely to report having experiences with debates or panel discussions in their social studies classes (Kahne & Middaugh, 2008, p. 16). Since these figures derive from a study only of "average" versus high SES classes, they most likely understate the degree of the disparity between truly impoverished schools and students and those that serve a more privileged student body. But Kahne and Middaugh provide more than enough evidence to demonstrate that poor and non-White students are receiving demonstrably less and worse civic education than middle class and wealthy white students, and that school-level differences are partly to blame.

Second, the civic learning opportunity gap suffered by poor and non-White students especially attending *de facto* segregated urban schools compounds the civic opportunity gaps they face outside of school. Considerable evidence demonstrates that people living in areas of concentrated poverty are significantly less likely to be engaged civically, and to have opportunities for such civic engagement, than those living in more mixed or affluent communities (Alex-Assensoh, 1997; Cohen & Dawson, 1993; Hart, Atkins,

Markey, & Youniss, 2004). Youth in particular face significant impediments in developing civic identities (Atkins & Hart, 2003) or acquiring civic knowledge and skills (Hart & Atkins, 2003) when they grow up in high-poverty urban communities. Since youth who are being educated in *de facto* segregated, non-White, poor urban schools are also almost surely living in *de facto* segregated, poor urban neighborhoods, this means that students attending these schools are facing a civic opportunity gap in their neighborhoods as well as in their schools (Wilkenfeld, 2009).

One can conclude that a large number of poor, ethnically and racially segregated public schools exist; they educate a substantial percentage of ethnic and racial minority students in the United States; their numbers are likely to increase rather than decrease over the coming years, especially as the minority population in the United States also grows (U.S. Census Bureau News, 2008); and they provide significantly fewer and lower-quality civic learning opportunities than schools that serve a whiter and wealthier student population. If we care about political stability, democratic legitimacy, and civic equality, then we must care about what gets taught and learned in these schools—not just for the students' sakes but for our own. This is consistent with condemning the phenomenon of *de facto* segregated schooling as harmful to the students who attend these schools, to the students who don't attend these schools (and who hence are often educated in relatively segregated settings themselves), and to the nation as a whole. There is substantial evidence that the best education for students in a liberal democratic society requires schools that are integrated—integrated ethnically and racially, but also by class, religion, immigration status, and other aspects of family background (Orfield & Lee, 2007; "Parents Involved," 2007, [Stevens, J., dissenting]; American Educational Research Association, 2006; Levinson & Levinson, 2003; Blum, 2002; Reich, 2002; Levinson, 1999; Gutmann, 1995, 1987; Macedo, 1990). But these arguments are irrelevant as regards the current existence and likely future expansion of *de facto* segregated minority schools. These schools pose challenges to U.S. democratic politics *today*, and the students who attend them hence merit attention now, including an appropriate civic education.

WHAT WE CAN DO

Thus far, I have established two things. First, there is a profound civic empowerment gap in the United States that disproportionately muffles the voices of non-White, foreign-born, and especially low-income citizens and amplifies the voices of White, native-born, and especially wealthy citizens. Second, many of these poor, minority citizens attend *de facto* segregated schools when young. Given the high percentage of young people at the lower end of the gap who attend these schools, these schools' documented contributions to the civic learning opportunity gap, and the obstacles to civic empowerment often posed by segregated, economically impoverished settings, we should pay special attention to how civic educational practices in these schools might be reformed in order to combat the civic empowerment gap. This is not to say that school reform will be sufficient. Numerous changes need to be made across multiple sectors of society, including: consistent, same-day voter registration laws; early and expanded voting opportunities; nonpartisan redistricting boards to increase the number of contested elections; political and economic policies that reduce as opposed to increase economic inequality; increased investment in low-income communities; massive reform of the school-to-prison pipeline in poor and minority communities; improved and expanded social service provision; greater challenges to institutional racism; and immigration reform. (See Macedo et al., 2005, for a careful examination of the ways in which electoral, municipal, and voluntary sector policies and practices often impede the quantity, quality, and equality of civic engagement in the United States.) But schools should not be left out of the picture, as they also have an important role to play. My purpose in the rest of this chapter is to provide some constructive suggestions for how *de facto* segregated schools, in particular, can help reduce the civic empowerment gap, and hence help promote true civic and political equality for all Americans.

I recommend five essential reforms specifically for *de facto* segregated, poor and minority, urban public schools.

1. ***Commit to improving urban schools and reducing the dropout rate,*** which reaches nearly 50% in some urban districts. Calls for urban school reform may seem simultaneously banal and absurdly idealistic: Who doesn't support the massive overhaul and improvement of urban schools in the United States in the early twenty-first century, and who has robust confidence in such an overhaul bearing significant fruit? Yet it is a need that nonetheless bears repeating. Both the civic empowerment gap and the quality gap between many impoverished urban versus wealthier suburban schools remind us that our society is inegalitarian and anti-democratic in some fundamental ways. If urban schools were better, and if more students stayed in higher quality schools and graduated, the civic empowerment gap would narrow. Furthermore, higher quality urban education resulting in higher educational attainment among students who attended those schools would likely have a direct effect on these students' civic empowerment, since education is the single most highly correlated variable with civic knowledge, civic skills, democratic civic attitudes, and active civic engagement (Nie, Junn, & Stehlik-Barry, 1996; Galston, 2003).

2. ***Restore civic education to the curriculum.*** The decline in the number, range, and frequency of civics courses offered in U.S. elementary and high schools must be reversed. There is ample evidence that civic education improves civic outcomes (Damon, 2001; Delli Carpini & Keeter, 1996; Galston, 2001; Carnegie Corporation of New York & CIRCLE, 2003; Niemi & Junn, 1998; Torney-Purta, 2002; Torney-Purta, Hahn, & Amadeo, 2001; Kahne & Middaugh, 2008), but resources devoted to it have dropped markedly over the past 30 or 40 years—especially in schools serving minority students. In the 1960s, students regularly took as many as three relevant courses in high school, including civics, democracy, and government; now students tend to take only one—government—and that only in the 12th grade (Carnegie Corporation of New York & CIRCLE, 2003, p. 14; Niemi & Junn, 1998), by which point many poor and minority students have already dropped out. Close to 10% of America's poorest students drop out of high school each year; students from the bottom economic quintile are four-and-a-half times more likely than their peers from families in the top 20% of the income distribution to decide to drop out of high school (Laird, Kienzl, DeBell, & Chapman, 2007, p. 4 and Figure 1). Likewise, barely 70% of Hispanic student youth overall, and only 58% of immigrant Hispanic youth, have graduated from high school by age 24, in comparison with 85% of Blacks, 93% of Whites, and 96% of Asians (Laird, Kienzl, DeBell, & Chapman, 2007, Table 9). If civic education is offered to students only in 12th grade, therefore, then in effect it is disproportionately provided to wealthier, whiter, and native-born citizens.

   Furthermore, it is absurd to think that by offering civic education only a few times over the course of a child's education, we will reliably enable and encourage students to become active, engaged citizens. There is a reason that we require students to take English and math every semester of every year of elementary and secondary school: Mastery takes time and practice. Hence we expect students to engage in ongoing, consistently reinforced learning and coaching with regard to these essential disciplines and practices. If we want students to become masterful citizens, then the same expectations should apply. If we want to narrow the civic empowerment gap, especially by increasing poor, minority, and immigrant students' civic knowledge and skills, then civic education must begin in elementary schools and be a regular part of education kindergarten through 12th grade (and beyond).
3. ***Reform history education in order to help students construct empowering civic narratives that simultaneously cohere with their lived experiences and impel them to civic and political action.*** When we think about how to eliminate the civic empowerment gap, we need to take

seriously what students bring with them into the classroom from their lived experience; from the stories and messages they hear from family members, friends, and neighbors; and from various media sources. Students aren't empty vessels waiting to be filled with appropriate civic attitudes and knowledge; rather, they come into the classroom having already at least partially constructed their own understandings of their civic identity, of their membership in or exclusion from the polity, and even of history's significance and meaning for their own lives. (See Epstein, 1997, 2001, 2009; Wineburg, 2001; VanSledright, 2002; Barton & Levstik, 2004, for further evidence of this attitude and approach.)

When teachers and schools attempt to address the civic empowerment gap, therefore, they need to engage with students' constructions of history, civic membership, political legitimacy, and power relations. They need to recognize that students construct meaning independent of—and hence often in conflict with—the meanings specified by curricula, textbooks, teachers, or other educational authorities (Torney-Purta, 2002; Haste, 2004; Torney-Purta, Barber, & Wilkenfeld, 2007). Educators must therefore overtly and intentionally engage with students' beliefs, attitudes, and narrative schema, which means adjusting instruction from school to school, class to class, and student to student. At the same time, educators must maintain a vision of desirable civic outcomes (including desirable civic and political knowledge, skills, attitudes, and behaviors) that goes beyond what students enter with. Engagement with students' constructed narratives, in other words, does not mean straightforwardly validating them, since the civic empowerment gap cannot be solved simply by reinforcing students' beliefs, attitudes, and differences. Rather, educators need to help students to construct more empowering civic narratives: ones that are truthful but not self-defeating, and that incorporate individuals' and communities' lived experiences while simultaneously justifying and reinforcing a sense of personal and political efficacy, civic membership, and civic duty.

This approach requires a massive change in how and why history is taught in this country, and especially in most urban schools. History education would have to be co-constructed with students, as opposed to delivered as a set of truths to be memorized. Textbooks would need to be used "only [as] reference works," as Diane Ravitch correctly recommends (Ravitch, 2003, p. 156), rather than as primary—let alone sole—sources of knowledge and historical understanding. American history courses, currently taught as a "moderately triumphalist" story of inevitable historical progress toward grand American ideals (Gibbon, 2002; see also Damon, 2001; Ravitch, 2003; Schlesinger, 1993; Stotsky, 2004; Avery & Simmons, 2000), would need to be radically rethought. There would also need to be a shift away from teaching history as a story of individual, larger-than-life heroes to teaching history as a story of collective action by ordinary people (Levinson, 2009). Even the most profound civic changes, led by the greatest and most extraordinary of human beings, are usually brought about by the collective work of ordinary people working together: of "men and women obscure in their labor," as President Obama put it in his Inaugural Address (Obama, 2009). I suggest that one possible model might be found in a civic counter-narrative fostered by many historically segregated African American institutions, including *de jure* and *de facto* segregated schools, Freedom Schools, historically Black colleges and universities, and Black churches. These institutions have often taught a civically empowering historical counter-narrative centered on themes of *struggle*, *obligation*, and *opportunity*. With some imagination and flexibility, teachers and students in other settings could expand upon and incorporate these historical narratives in ways that promote their own civic and political engagement.

Although part of the work of helping students construct empowering civic narratives has to be done in a historical context, recognizing how students interpret the past in relationship to their possible roles in the present, other work needs to be done in a contemporary context. This means changing students' civic and political present by involving them in guided experiential civic learning and other civically empowering pedagogies. Thus, I suggest the following.

4. ***Provide students frequent opportunities to engage in empowering civic practices***: discussion of meaningful, contemporary, and controversial issues; simulations, role plays, and mock trials; classroom and school elections; group collaboration on problems that address community concerns and attitudes in a way that enables students to demonstrate their local knowledge and expertise; and participation in guided experiential civic learning in which they actually *do* civics, not just read about it, including via public policy involvement, youth organizing, participatory action research, or other mechanisms. Civic education needs to become a living part of the school, and it must enable students regularly to exercise their democratic rights and responsibilities. In other words, civic education at its heart must be about active participation, not passive observation. In order to increase students' political and personal efficacy, in particular, and to change students' minds about the value of civic and political engagement more generally, we need to find ways of giving them positive, real-world, civic and political experiences.

What would this look like in practice? Guided experiential civic learning can take a variety of forms, including activities within classrooms and schools as well as those beyond school walls. Students could serve on the school site council, governing board, or diversity committee. They could invite local community leaders to come visit the school and then interview them in small cooperative groups about their accomplishments, the challenges they face, and what motivates them to keep on working for what they believe in. After conducting a "constituent survey" of their peers, students could work together as a class to develop and implement a strategy to improve an aspect of their school. Students could debate current events and then write a letter expressing their opinions to an elected representative or government official. They could participate in a mock trial, conduct a voter registration drive in the school parking lot or before PTA meetings, or create a WebQuest about a policy issue that matters to them. An ambitious teacher could encourage students to research a public policy issue and then make a presentation to local officials, or attend a city council meeting as advocates for their position. Even more ambitiously, a teacher may serve as a facilitator for participatory youth action research projects, in which youth research and act upon problems that they themselves identify and define. Closer to home, students could elect class officers who will collaborate with the teacher on planning field trips and other special activities; or, they could as a class deliberate about and vote on issues including due dates for major projects, the order in which to read class novels, or the consequences for minor disciplinary infractions. Numerous examples, analyses, and evaluations of such approaches are available in the research literature (e.g., Weis & Fine, 2000; Darling-Hammond, French, & Garcia-Lopez, 2002; Westheimer & Kahne, 2002; Kahne & Westheimer, 2003; Noguera, Ginwright, & Cammarota, 2006; Apple & Beane, 2007; Schultz, 2008; Cammarota & Fine, 2008; Delgado & Staples, 2008; Hess, 2009) and from practitioners and civic education organizations. (See www.campaignforthecivicmissionofschools.org for information about and links to over 100 well-vetted curricula, programs, and organizations.)

It's important to note that although these examples range from very simple and straightforward to quite ambitious, they all intentionally build on collective and policy-oriented action. None represent such piecemeal approaches as donating cans to a homeless shelter or spending a morning visiting elderly people in a nursing home. Although both of these activities are noble and may be worthwhile, they don't foster the kind of attention to systemic issues that is important. Nor do they help students recognize the power of their community and of joining together to effect change. Emphasis on communal action is especially important when teaching poor, historically disenfranchised youth who tend to live in poor, historically disenfranchised communities, since collective action is one of the most effective ways to reduce (even if not entirely eliminate) their power differential (Alinsky, 1971).

Research uniformly supports the efficacy of these kinds of active civic learning approaches (Hahn, 1998; Amadeo, Torney-Purta, Lehmann, Husfeldt, & Nikolova, 2002; Westheimer & Kahne, 2002; Kahne & Westheimer, 2003; Carnegie Corporation of New York & CIRCLE, 2003; Kirshner, 2007; Rogers, Morrell, & Enyedy, 2007; Torney-Purta, Barber, & Wilkenfeld, 2007; Hess, 2009). Done well, guided experiential civic education helps students learn and apply a broad range of civic knowledge, develop a number of civic skills, embrace positive civic attitudes, and practice important civic behaviors. It promotes an active, explicitly political conception of citizenship. It can help students make contacts with adults and role models in the community, as well as help the participating organizations and institutions themselves. Guided experiential civic education can motivate students to become civically engaged in the future by contributing to their sense of empowerment and agency, connecting them to adults and peers who model civically engaged behavior, and enabling them to use their knowledge and skills to achieve concrete results. Guided experiential civic learning may also reinforce (or generate) adults' sense of connection to and responsibility and respect for the younger generation, including toward children and young adults who live and are being educated in communities different from those adults' own. These are all extremely important civic outcomes.

5. ***Finally, we need to provide powerful civic learning and engagement opportunities for urban teachers,*** so they can develop these domains of knowledge, skills, attitudes, and habits of participation themselves. Teachers in *de facto* segregated, poor urban schools are often as civically disempowered as their students. Urban teachers work in institutions that are often incredibly bureaucratic, that discourage and even sometimes punish autonomous decision making, and that foster a culture of compliance rather than collaboration. They are chronically underfunded and are buffeted by political and partisan swings in ways that tend to make long-term institutional improvement unlikely. These are not the conditions for building civic skills or civic efficacy among adults, let alone youth. Civic education reform to combat the civic empowerment gap is necessary not just for students, therefore, but for teachers as well.

As schools put these reforms into place, they will provide students and teachers with a set of powerful civic experiences that are likely to increase their sense of personal and political efficacy and trust, and hence to inspire their acquisition of civic knowledge and skills as well as continued productive participation. In doing so, schools will also help strengthen local communities, both via the direct work that students accomplish and by building a new generation of mobilized, empowered adults. Reducing the civic empowerment gap also strengthens democracy. It broadens government's representativeness, increases its responsiveness to diverse individuals and communities, and thereby also reinforces its political legitimacy in the eyes of historically disenfranchised community members. It strengthens schools, as students turn their attention to solving problems collaboratively as opposed to fighting against the system or just checking out. And finally, it promotes civic and political equality and fairness—ideals that are central to our American democracy. These are goals all schools can and should embrace.

REFERENCES

Abu El-Haj, T. R. (2008). 'I was born here, but my home, it's not here': Educating for democratic citizenship in an era of transnational migration and global conflict. *Harvard Educational Review, 77(3)*, 285–316.

Alex-Assensoh, Y. (1997). Race, concentrated poverty, social isolation, and political behavior. *Urban Affairs Review, 33(2)*, 209–227.

Alinsky, S. D. (1971). *Rules for radicals: A pragmatic primer for realistic radicals*. New York: Vintage Books.

Amadeo, J.-A., Torney-Purta, J., Lehmann, R., Husfeldt, V., & Nikolova, R. (2002). *Civic knowledge and engagement: An IEA study of upper secondary students in sixteen countries, executive summary*. Amsterdam: IEA.

American Educational Research Association (2006). *Amicus curiae 10*. Retrieved from http://www.aera.net/uploadedFiles/News_Media/AERA_Amicus_Brief.pdf

Apple, M. W., & Beane, J. A. (Eds.). (2007). *Democratic schools: Lessons in powerful education*. Portsmouth, NH: Heinemann.

APSA Task Force on Inequality and American Democracy (2004). American democracy in an age of rising inequality. *Perspectives on Politics, 2(4)*, 651–689.

Atkins, R., & Hart, D. (2003). Neighborhoods, adults, and the development of civic identity in urban youth. *Applied Developmental Science, 7(3)*, 156–164.

Avery, P. G., & Simmons, A. M. (2000). Civic life as conveyed in United States civics and history textbooks. *International Journal of Social Education, 15(2)*, 105–130.

Ayers, W., & Ford, P. (1996). *City kids, city teachers*. New York: The New Press.

Baldi, S., Perie, M., Skidmore, D., Greenberg, E., & Hahn, C. (2001). *What democracy means to ninth-graders: U.S. Results from the international IEA civic education study* (No. NCES 2001-096). Washington, DC: U.S. Department of Education and National Center for Education Statistics.

Bartels, L. M. (2008). *Unequal democracy: The political economy of the new gilded age*. New York: Russell Sage Foundation.

Barton, K. C., & Levstik, L. S. (2004). *Teaching history for the common good*. Mahwah, NJ: Lawrence Erlbaum.

Bell, D. A. (2004). *Silent covenants: Brown v. Board of Education and the unfulfilled hopes for racial reform*. Oxford: Oxford University Press.

Bell, D. A. (Ed.). (1980). *Shades of Brown: New perspectives on school desegregation*. New York: Teachers College Press.

Blum, L. (2002). The promise of racial integration in multicultural age. In S. Macedo & Y. Tamir (Eds.), *Moral and political education*. New York: New York University Press.

Bracey, G. W. (2009). Our resegregated schools. *Phi Delta Kappan, 90(9)*, 691–692.

Cammarota, J., & Fine, M. (2008). *Revolutionizing education: Youth participatory action research in motion*. New York: Routledge.

Carnegie Corporation of New York, & CIRCLE (2003). *The civic mission of schools*. New York: Carnegie Corporation of New York and CIRCLE.

Cohen, C. J., & Dawson, M. C. (1993). Neighborhood poverty and African American politics. *American Political Science Review, 87(2)*, 286–302.

Damon, W. (2001). To not fade away: Restoring civil identity among the young. In D. Ravitch & J. P. Viteritti (Eds.), *Making good citizens* (pp. 123–141). New Haven and London: Yale University Press.

Darling-Hammond, L., French, J., & Garcia-Lopez, S. P. (Eds.). (2002). *Learning to teach for social justice*. New York: Teachers College Press.

Dawson, M. C. (1994). *Behind the mule: Race and class in African-American politics*. Princeton: Princeton University Press.

Dawson, M. C. (2001). *Black visions: The roots of contemporary African-American political ideologies*. Chicago: Chicago University Press.

Delgado, M., & Staples, L. (2008). *Youth-led community organizing: Theory and action*. Oxford: Oxford University Press.

Delli Carpini, M., & Keeter, S. (1996). *What Americans know about politics and why it matters*. New Haven: Yale University Press.

DeSipio, L. (2001). Building America, one person at a time: Naturalization and political behavior of the naturalized in contemporary American politics. In G. Gerstle & J. Mollenkopf (Eds.), *E pluribus unum? Contemporary and historical perspectives on immigrant political incorporation* (pp. 67–106). New York: Russell Sage Foundation.

Epstein, T. (1997). Sociocultural approaches to young people's historical understanding. *Social Education, 61*, 28–31.

Epstein, T. (2001). Racial identity and young people's perspectives on social education. *Theory into Practice, 40(1)*, 42–47.

Epstein, T. (2009). *Interpreting national history: Race, identity, and pedagogy in classrooms and communities*. New York: Routledge.

Feinberg, W. (1998). *Common schools/uncommon identities*. New Haven: Yale University Press.

Freeman, J. B. (2002). Red New York. *Monthly Review, 54(3)*, 36–42.

Galston, W. A. (2001). Political knowledge, political engagement, and civic education. *Annual Reviews Political Science, 4*, 217–234.

Galston, W. A. (2003). Civic education and political participation. *Phi Delta Kappan, 85(1)*, 29–33.

Garofano, A., & Sable, J. (2008). *Characteristics of the 100 largest public elementary and secondary school districts in the United States: 2005–06* (No. NCES 2008-339).

Washington, DC: National Center for Education Statistics, Institute of Education Sciences, U.S. Department of Education. Retrieved from http://nces.ed.gov/pubs2008/100_largest_0506

Gibbon, P. (2002, 2005). Panel discussion: Why is U.S. History still a mystery to our children? October 1, 2002. Retrieved from http://www.aei.org/events/filter.,eventID.131/transcript.asp

Grossman, L. (2009). Iran protests: Twitter, the medium of the movement. *Time Magazine*. Retrieved from http://www.time.com/time/world/article/0,8599,1905125,00.html

Gutmann, A. (1987). *Democratic education*. Princeton: Princeton University Press.

Gutmann, A. (1995). Civic education and social diversity. *Ethics, 105(3)*, 557–579.

Hahn, C. L. (1998). *Becoming political*. Albany: State University of New York Press.

Hart, D., & Atkins, R. (2002). Civic competence in urban youth. *Applied Developmental Science, 6(4)*, 227–236.

Hart, D., Atkins, R., Markey, P., & Youniss, J. (2004). Youth bulges in communities: The effects of age structure on adolescent civic knowledge and civic participation. *Psychological Science, 15(9)*, 591–597.

Haste, H. (2004). Constructing the citizen. *Political Psychology, 25(3)*, 413–439.

Hess, D. E. (2009). *Controversy in the classroom: The democratic power of discussion*. New York: Routledge.

Hochschild, J., & Scovronick, N. (2003). *The American dream and the public schools*. New York and Oxford: Oxford University Press.

Horsford, S. D., & McKenzie, K. B. (2008). 'Sometimes I feel like the problems started with desegregation': Exploring black superintendent perspectives on desegregation policy. *International Journal of Qualitative Studies in Education, 21(5)*, 443–455.

Huddy, L., & Feldman, S. (2006). Worlds apart: Blacks and whites react to hurricane Katrina. *Du Bois Review, 3(1)*, 1–17.

Hunter, J. D., & Bowman, C. (1996). *The state of disunion: 1996 survey of American political culture, executive summary*. Charlottesville, VA: The Post-Modernity Project, University of Virginia. Retrieved from http://religionanddemocracy.lib.virginia.edu/programs/survey/pubinfo.html

IES: National Center for Education Statistics (2007). NAEP data explorer. Retrieved from http://nces.ed.gov/nationsreportcard/nde/

Jacobs, L. R., & Skocpol, T. (Eds.). (2005). *Inequality and American democracy: What we know and what we need to learn*. New York: Russell Sage Foundation.

Kahne, J., & Middaugh, E. (2008). *Democracy for some: The civic opportunity gap in high school*. College Park, MD: CIRCLE. Retrieved from http://www.civicyouth.org/PopUps/WorkingPapers/WP59Kahne.pdf

Kahne, J., & Westheimer, J. (2003). Teaching democracy: What schools need to do. *Phi Delta Kappan, 85(1)*, 34–40, 57–66.

Kasinitz, P., Mollenkopf, J., & Waters, M. C. (2002). Becoming Americans/becoming New Yorkers: The experience of assimilation in a majority minority city. *International Migration Review, 36(4)*, 1020–1036.

Kinder, D. R. (1998). Opinion and action in the realm of politics. In D. T. Gilbert, S. T. Fiske, & G. Lindzey (Eds.), *The handbook of social psychology* (4th ed., pp. 778–867). Boston: McGraw-Hill.

Kirshner, B. (2007). Introduction: Youth activism as a context for learning and development. *American Behavioral Scientist, 51(3)*, 367–379.

Ladson-Billings, G. (2004). Landing on the wrong note: The price we paid for Brown. *Educational Researcher, 33(7)*, 3–13.

Ladson-Billings, G. (2009). Inching toward equity. *The Forum for Education and Democracy* (2009, June 9). Retrieved from http://www.forumforeducation.org/node/477

Laird, J., Kienzl, G., DeBell, M., & Chapman, C. (2007). *Dropout rates in the United States:* 2005 (NCES 2007-059). Washington, DC: U.S. Department of Education and the National Center for Education Statistics. Retrieved from http://nces.ed.gov/pubs2007/2007059.pdf

Lake Snell Perry & Associates, & The Tarrance Group (2002). *Short-term impacts, long-term opportunities: The political and civic engagement of young people in America.* CIRCLE and The Center for Democracy & Citizenship and the Partnership for Trust in Government at the Council of Excellence in Government.

Lareau, A. (2000). *Home advantage: Social class and parental intervention in elementary education.* Lanham, MD: Rowman & Littlefield.

Lareau, A. (2003). *Unequal childhoods: Class, race, and family life.* Berkeley: University of California Press.

Levinson, M. (1999). *The demands of liberal education.* Oxford: Oxford University Press.

Levinson, M. (2009). 'Let us now praise . . . ?' Rethinking heroes and role models in an egalitarian age. In Y. Raley & G. Preyer (Eds.), *Living in a global world: New essays in the philosophy of education* (pp. 129–161). Oxford: Routledge.

Levinson, M., & Levinson, S. (2003). 'Getting religion': Religion, diversity, and community in public and private schools. In A. Wolfe (Ed.), *School choice: The moral debate* (pp. 104–125). Princeton: Princeton University Press.

Lijphart, A. (1997). Unequal participation: Democracy's unresolved dilemma. *American Political Science Review, 91(1)*, 1–14.

Lopez, M. H. (2003). *Electoral engagement among Latino youth.* College Park, MD: CIRCLE. Retrieved from http://www.civicyouth.org/PopUps/Electoral%20%20Engagement%20Among%20Latino%20Youth.pdf

Lopez, M. H., Levine, P., Both, D., Kiesa, A., Kirby, E., & Marcelo, K. (2006). *The 2006 civic and political health of the nation: A detailed look at how youth participate in politics and communities.* College Park, MD: CIRCLE.

Loury, G. C. (1997, April 23). Integration has had its day. *The New York Times,* p. A23. Retrieved from http://www.nytimes.com/1997/04/23/opinion/integration-has-had-its-day.html?scp=1&sq=&st=nyt

Lutkus, A. D., Weiss, A. R., Campbell, J. R., Mazzeo, J., & Lazer, S. (1999). *NAEP 1998 civics report card for the nation* (No. NCES 2000-457). Washington, DC: U.S. Department of Education, Office of Educational Research and Improvement, and National Center for Education Statistics.

Macedo, S. (1990). *Liberal virtues.* Oxford: Oxford University Press.

Macedo, S., Alex-Assensoh, Y., Berry, J. M., Brintnall, M., Campbell, D. E., & Fraga, L. R. (2005). *Democracy at risk: How political choices undermine citizen participation and what we can do about it.* Washington, DC: Brookings Institution Press.

Marcelo, K. B., Lopez, M. H., & Kirby, E. H. (2007). *Civic engagement among minority youth* (Fact Sheet). College Park, MD: CIRCLE.

Massey, D. S., & Denton, N. A. (1993). *American apartheid: Segregation and the making of the underclass*. Cambridge, MA: Harvard University Press.

McDonald, M. (2009). *2008 current population survey*. (2009, April 6). Retrieved from http://elections.gmu.edu/CPS_2008.html

Montgomery, D. (1993). *Citizen worker: The experience of workers in the United States with democracy and the free market during the nineteenth century*. Cambridge: Cambridge University Press.

Montgomery, D. (2001). Presidential address: Racism, immigrants, and political reform. *The Journal of American History, 87(4)*, 1253–1274.

National Conference on Citizenship (2008). *2008 Civic health index: Beyond the vote*. Retrieved from http://www.ncoc.net/download.php?file=2kccfl36&ext=pdf&name=2008%20Civic%20Health%20Index

Nie, N. H., Junn, J., & Stehlik-Barry, K. (1996). *Education and democratic citizenship in America*. Chicago: Chicago University Press.

Niemi, R. G., & Junn, J. (1998). *Civic education: What makes students learn*. New Haven: Yale University Press.

Niemi, R. G., & Sanders, M. S. (2004). Assessing student performance in civics: The NAEP 1998 civics assessment. *Theory and Research in Social Education, 32(3)*, 326–348.

Noguera, P., Ginwright, S. A., & Cammarota, J. (2006). *Beyond resistance! Youth activism and community change: New democratic possibilities for practice and policy for America's youth*. New York: Routledge.

Obama, B. (2009, January 20 Inaugural address. Retrieved from (via podcast) http://www.telegraph.co.uk/news/worldnews/northamerica/usa/barackobama/4298722/President-Barack-Obamas-inaugural-address-speech-in-full.html

Orfield, G. (2001). *Schools more separate: Consequences of a decade of resegregation*. Cambridge, MA: The Civil Rights Project, Harvard University.

Orfield, G., Eaton, S., & The Harvard Project on Desegregation (1996). *Dismantling desegregation: The quiet reversal of Brown v. Board of Education*. New York: The New Press.

Orfield, G., & Lee, C. (2006). *Racial transformation and the changing nature of segregation*. Cambridge, MA: The Civil Rights Project at Harvard University.

Orfield, G., & Lee, C. (2007). *Historic reversals, accelerating resegregation, and the need for new integration strategies*. Los Angeles: Civil Rights Project/Proyecto Derechos Civiles, UCLA. Retrieved from http://www.civilrightsproject.ucla.edu/research/deseg/reversals_reseg_need.pdf

Parents Involved in Community Schools vs. Seattle School District No. 1, et al. (05-908) and Meredith, Crystal (next friend for McDonald, Joshua) v. Jefferson county Bd. of Education, et al. (05-915), 551 1 (Supreme Court 2007).

Patterson, J. T. (2001). *Brown v. Board of Education: A civil rights milestone and its troubled legacy*. New York: Oxford University Press.

The Pew Research Center for the People and the Press (2007, April 15). What Americans know: 1989–2007. Public knowledge of current affairs little changed by news and information revolutions. Retrieved from http://people-press.org/reports/pdf/319.pdf

Powell, G. B., Jr. (1986). American voter turnout in comparative perspective. *American Political Science Review, 80(1)*, 17–43.

Public Agenda Foundation. (1998). *Time to move on*. New York: Public Agenda Foundation.

Ravitch, D. (2003). *The language police: How pressure groups restrict what students learn*. New York: Alfred A. Knopf.

Reich, R. (2002). *Bridging liberalism and multiculturalism in American education*. Chicago: University of Chicago Press.

Rogers, J., Morrell, E., & Enyedy, N. (2007). Studying the struggle: Contexts for learning and identity development for urban youth. *American Behavioral Scientist, 51(3)*, 419–443.

Rosenzweig, R., & Thelen, D. (1998). *The presence of the past: Popular uses of history in American life*. New York: Columbia University Press.

Rubin, B. C. (2007). 'There's still not justice': Youth civic identity development amid distinct school and community contexts. *Teachers College Record, 109(2)*, 449–481.

Sachar, H. (1993). *A history of the Jews in America*. New York: Vintage.

Schlesinger, A., Jr. (1993). *The disuniting of America*. New York: Norton.

Schultz, B. D. (2008). *Spectacular things happen along the way: Lessons from an urban classroom*. New York: Teachers College Press.

Scott, J. C. (1985). *Weapons of the weak: Everyday forms of peasant resistance*. New Haven: Yale University Press.

Shujaa, M. J. (1996). *Beyond desegregation: The politics of quality in African American schooling*. Thousand Oaks, CA: Corwin.

Skocpol, T. (1999). How Americans became civic. In T. Skocpol & M. P. Fiorina (Eds.), *Civic engagement in American democracy* (pp. 27–80). Washington, DC: Brookings.

Skocpol, T., Ganz, M., & Munson, Z. (2000). A nation of organizers: The institutional origins of civic voluntarism in the United States. *American Political Science Review, 94(3)*, 527–546.

Stepick, A., & Stepick, C. D. (2002). Becoming American, constructing ethnicity: Immigrant youth and civic engagement. *Applied Developmental Science, 6(4)*, 246–257.

Stotsky, S. (2004). *The stealth curriculum: Manipulating America's history teachers*. Washington, DC: Thomas B. Fordham Foundation. Retrieved from http://www.edexcellence.net/doc/StealthCurriculum%5BFINAL%5D04-01-04.pdf

Torney-Purta, J. (2002). The school's role in developing civic engagement: A study of adolescents in twenty-eight countries. *Applied Developmental Science, 6(4)*, 202–211.

Torney-Purta, J., Barber, C. H., & Wilkenfeld, B. (2007). Latino adolescents' civic development in the United States: Research results from the IEA civic education study. *Journal of Youth and Adolescence, 36*, 111–125.

Torney-Purta, J., Hahn, C. L., & Amadeo, J.-A. M. (2001). Principles of subject-specific instruction in education for citizenship. In J. Brophy (Ed.), *Subject-specific instructional methods and activities* (Vol. 8, pp. 373–410). New York and London: JAI Press.

U.S. Census Bureau (2005, May 25). Voting and registration in the election of November 2004. Retrieved from http://www.census.gov/population/socdemo/voting/cps2004.html

U.S. Census Bureau (2008). 2008 Current population survey voting and registration supplement. Retrieved from U.S. Census Bureau: http://www.census.gov/cps/

U.S. Census Bureau News (2008). *An older and more diverse nation by midcentury* (No. CB08-123). Washington, DC: U.S. Census Bureau. Retrieved from http://www.census.gov/Press-Release/www/releases/archives/population/012496.html

U.S. Department of Education, Institute of Education Sciences, National Center for Education Statistics, & National Assessment of Educational Progress (NAEP) (2007). Average scale scores with percentages for civics, grade 8, race/ethnicity used in NAEP reports after 2001 [sdrace] x natl school lunch prog eligibility (3 categories) [slunch3]: By jurisdiction, 2006 (NAEP data explorer). *NAEP 2006 Civics Assessment.* Retrieved from http://nces.ed.gov/nationsreportcard/nde/viewresults.asp?pid=4-2-8-CIV-National---10-SDRACE,SLUNCH3-20063--CR-MN,RP-2-1-1–1-0–2-3–0–1

VanSledright, B. (2002). Confronting history's interpretive paradox while teaching fifth graders to investigate the past. *American Educational Research Journal, 39(4),* 1089–1115.

Verba, S., Schlozman, K. L., & Brady, H. E. (1995). *Voice and equality: Civic voluntarism in American politics.* Cambridge, MA: Harvard University Press.

Walker, V. S., & Archung, K. N. (2003). The segregated schooling of blacks in the southern United States and South Africa. *Comparative Education Review, 47,* 21–40.

Washington Post, Kaiser Family Foundation, & Harvard University. (2000). *Washington Post/Kaiser Family Foundation/Harvard University national survey on Latinos in America* (No. 3023). Washington, DC.

Weis, L., & Fine, M. (2000). *Construction sites: Excavating race, class, and gender among urban youth.* New York: Teachers College Press.

Westheimer, J., & Kahne, J. (2002). Educating for democracy. In R. Hayduck & K. Mattson (Eds.), *Democracy's moment: Reforming the American political system for the 21st century* (pp. 91–107). Boulder: Rowman & Littlefield.

Westheimer, J., & Kahne, J. (2004). What kind of citizen? The politics of educating for democracy. *American Educational Research Journal, 41(2),* 237–269.

Wilkenfeld, B. (2009). Does context matter? How the family, peer, school and neighborhood contexts relate to adolescents' civic engagement (CIRCLE Working Paper 64). Medford, MA: Tufts University, CIRCLE.

will.i.am (Producer). (2008, July 30) *Yes we can.* Retrieved from (via podcast) http://www.youtube.com/watch?v=jjXyqcx-mYY

Williams, M. (2003). Citizenship as identity, citizenship as shared fate, and the functions of multicultural education. In K. McDonough & W. Feinberg (Eds.), *Citizenship and education in liberal-democratic societies: Teaching for cosmopolitan values and collective identities* (pp. 208–247). Oxford: Oxford University Press.

Wineburg, S. S. (2001). *Historical thinking and other unnatural acts: Charting the future of teaching the past.* Philadelphia: Temple University Press.

Wolfinger, R. E., & Rosenstone, S. J. (1980). *Who votes?* New Haven: Yale University Press.

Zukin, C., Keeter, S., Andolina, M. W., Jenkins, K., & Delli Carpini, M. X. (2006). *A new engagement? Political participation, civic life, and the changing American citizen.* Oxford: Oxford University Press.

CHAPTER 14

Communication and Education: Creating Competence for Socialization into Public Life

JACK McLEOD, DHAVAN SHAH, DIANA HESS, AND NAM-JIN LEE
University of Wisconsin—Madison

SCHOLARS AND POLICY-MAKERS in the past decade have come to recognize the positive influences of education and communication on youth socialization into public life, that is, the learning of civic and political practices that have implications for societal and democratic functioning. Reexamination of evidence from older studies and the results of new research have demonstrated the benefits of attaining higher levels of education, taking civics courses, participating in public-spirited school activities, as well as consuming news media and discussing public affairs—both inside and outside the classroom—for civic engagement across the life course. It is thus ironic that, having recently received such acclaim, the contributions of education and communication to citizenship seem to have become weakened and more unequal in their benefits. Young people who are afforded the opportunity to participate in civics courses that include the content and activities that promote active citizens come disproportionately from middle-class and upper-class homes. Budget cutting has limited school activities in less affluent school systems, and the high-school completion rate is almost stagnant, with fewer than 50% of students graduating in many urban schools.

Newspapers and network television news, which did much to inform and motivate young citizens in the latter half of the twentieth century, have fallen into a sharp decline in audience size and news quality. More than a dozen U.S. metropolitan dailies ceased publication during a 12-month period in 2008 to 2009. Youth, especially those not tracking into college, are consuming the richest news sources at lower rates. It is debatable whether the growth of Internet news will be able to make up for the losses in traditional news.

Internet usage is economically stratified, with civically relevant uses among the most educated, and mounting evidence of a persistent digital divide in high-speed access in the home and to access to computers in schools. The digital divide and the resultant democracy divide complicate citizenship, youth socialization, and governance.

Nonetheless, opportunities to address the decline in youth engagement rest in interactions in schools or with mass media. Although opportunities for exposure to content and activities that promote civic socialization in the classroom and via traditional mass media have diminished, innovations in civic socialization focused on building citizenship through discussion of controversial issues in the classroom, and Web-based communication and mobilization strategies show promise. It is these opportunities that are the focus of this chapter.

THE DEMOCRACY DIVIDE

Our special focus is on the *democracy divide* in the United States with respect to the civic and political participation of young people. This democracy divide concerns the gap in participatory engagement between those with high and low levels of educational attainment (see Levinson, this volume). There are numbers of existing and emergent datasets that permit unique insight into the challenges posed by the democracy divide, many of which are publically or commercially available. These datasets, some older and some newer, allow those concerned with adolescent and young adult socialization to understand more fully the intersection of classroom practices, communication patterns, and civic and political engagement. In this chapter, we analyze five of these datasets to answer a series of research questions regarding how young people become competent citizens.

Two of these are older, with less precise measurement, but nonetheless they provide important foundational insights regarding youth socialization: the 2000 Social Capital Benchmark Study (Putnam, 2000) and the 1993 to 2004 DDB Life Style Studies (McLeod, Shah, & Yoon, 2002). Three of these are newer, collected specifically to examine the issue of civic socialization, and thus contain more precise measurement of core classroom and mass media constructs: the 2002 Civic and Political Health of the Nation (CPHN) Study (Keeter, Zukin, Andolina, & Jenkins, 2002; Zukin, Keeter, Andolina, Jenkins, & Delli Carpini, 2006), the 2006 Civic and Political Health of the Nation Study (Lopez et al., 2006), and the 2008 Future Voters study of adolescents 12 to 17 and their parents (Shah, McLeod, & Lee, 2009). Although we rely more on the most recent datasets for our primary analyses concerning the connections between education, communication, and engagement, the insights available from the older studies provide important baseline information about the

Table 14.1
Analyzed Survey Datasets

	Civic and Political Health of the Nation, 2002	**Civic and Political Health of the Nation, 2006**	**Future Voter Study, 2009**	**Social Capital Benchmark Study, 2000**	**DDB Life Style Studies, 1993–2004**
Acronym	CPHN 2002	CPHN 2006	Future Voter Study	Benchmark Study	DDB 1993–2004
Year(s) of data collection	2002	2006	2008 (Short-term Panel)	2000	1993, 1996, 2000, 2004
Population	Youth and adults ages 15 and older	Youth and adults ages 15 and older	Adolescents ages 12–17 and their parents	Adults ages 18 and older	Adults ages 18 and older
Sample size	3,246	2,232	1,325	13,606	3,690 (1993); 3,757 (1996); 3,122 (2000); 3,345 (2004)

shifting nature of these interrelationships. Table 14.1 summarizes basic information about these five datasets (for methodological details, see the online appendix at http://www.journalism.wisc.edu/~dshah/resources.htm).

This chapter's primary purpose is to demonstrate that while there are differences in civic and political participation between young people and older age cohorts, the more serious divide is between people with college education and those without. Those with education beyond high school more frequently engage in virtually all forms of civic and political participation (e.g., community service, voting, participation in public meetings, and boycotting) than those without higher education. The import of this divide lies in its apparent persistence across the life course.

Although education is a predictor of news consumption and civic participation for all age groups, its consequences are especially apparent for adolescents and young adults, who experience vastly different life trajectories if they plan to attend and actually graduate from college. For instance, there were major differences in home media environment, online news use, and civic participation between high-school students tracking toward college and those with lower educational aspirations (2008 Future Voter Study). There was a 31% gap between the two adolescent subgroups in terms of high-speed home Internet access, 26% in terms of any home Internet connection, and 23% in terms of newspaper delivery to the home. There was also a 20% gap in conventional news access via the Internet and a 17% gap in civic participation between those on a college track and those not college bound. This divide portends a serious problem.

There is no reason to believe that this divide will naturally diminish as the groups age. In fact, gaps appear to widen from late adolescence to early adulthood and continue into middle adulthood (McLeod et al., 2002). Consequently, the very groups that are underserved by the political system now will likely receive even less in the future. The negative consequences of the democracy divide extend to society as a whole. A persistent democracy divide existing through the life course calls definitions of participatory democracy into question.

We have known for some time that there is a strong connection between educational attainment and political and civic engagement (Milbrath & Goel, 1977; Verba, Nie, & Kim, 1978; Verba, Schlozman, & Brady, 1995). Yet there is also mounting evidence that what occurs *within* schools with respect to civic education can either spur participation, have no impact, or potentially even produce young people who are less likely to engage in civic and political roles. In 2003, the Carnegie Corporation and CIRCLE convened a large and heterogeneous group that included teachers, educational researchers, professionals from educational groups, political leaders, and both conservative and liberal interest groups to analyze the evidence and formulate a consensus document. The Civic Mission of the Schools (CMS) Report they produced identified six research-based components describing best practices in civic education (Gibson & Levine, 2003). These are instruction in important content, discussions of current events and controversial issues, service learning, participating in extracurricular activities that teach civic skills such as student journalism or school governance, and democratic simulations such as mock trials and Model UN. Many of these recommendations require further testing as to the persistence of gains associated with them and whether they can be scaled up in various social contexts and for various groups.

Despite optimism, there are also caveats about how these components work in practice. Researchers have found that social class matters in powerful ways, with educational attainment the most critical marker. Students with higher SES parents and those who are more academically successful are much more likely to be given the opportunity to engage in civic education that incorporates the CMS components than are other students. Moreover, given the way that class and race intersect in the United States, students who are African American or Latino are much less likely to encounter high-quality civic education than their White or Asian American peers (see Levinson, this volume; Kahne & Middaugh, 2008).

This has important implications throughout the life course, for it is likely related to the development of a constellation of communication skills that are essential for democratic engagement such as news consumption and political conversation. A report by Flanagan, Levine, and Settersten (2009) highlights the potential dangers of disengagement among those lacking a college education. Although the levels of civic and political engagement among young adults have declined overall since the 1970s, the decline has been most dramatic among those without the experience of college education. At this point, half of America's youth do not go to college, with minorities representing a disproportionate percentage. As Figure 14.1 illustrates, newspaper reading, news consumption via the Internet, and political conversation all differ between those with a college education and those without these experiences.

Gaps in frequency of use between the college and non-college respondents in each of four generational categories are indicated by the distances between the points connected by the solid and broken lines. In general, those who were likely to attend, were attending, or had achieved a college education, read newspapers, got Internet news, and engaged in political talk more than those not on track for college. However, the size of the gaps differed greatly among the three communication behaviors. Gaps between education groups were relatively small for newspaper reading, with no difference between education groups among the GenXers. Gaps by education in political talk began at age 18 and were of similar size until age 44. The gap in Internet news use by education was more than double that for newspaper reading and political talk from ages 18 to 22 and on. Unless this gap can be reduced, it will limit the effectiveness of the Internet as a source for

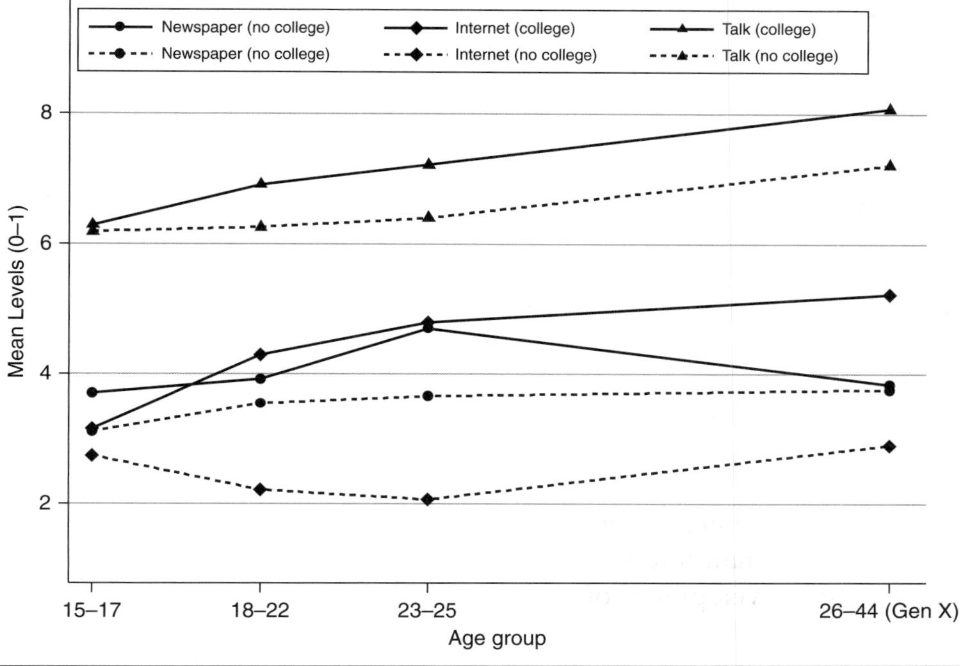

Figure 14.1 Frequency of News Use and Political Talk by Generational Groups

promoting equality in civic participation (see Bennett et al., this volume; Haste, this volume).

The cross-generational trends in gaps are distinctive for exposure to each of the three communication sources. The large gaps in newspaper use among those ages 23 to 25 disappeared as a result of the decline in newspaper reading among the college-educated. Internet news use showed a large gap peaking among the older GenYers (age 23 to 25) but was also strong in the GenXers (ages 26 to 44). Political talk gaps were at a maximum among GenXers. It is unfortunate for the goal of achieving civic equality that the largest educational gaps in communication behaviors promoting civic engagement seems to occur just prior to the years (the 30s) during which the amount of this participation is starting to grow.

One potential approach to addressing these gaps would be concerted efforts toward developing skills and motivations to engage in effective searching for information, listening to other viewpoints, thinking and connecting ideas and perspectives, expressing opinions and ideas, and actively engaging with others in collective action. We call this set of skills and motives *communication competence*, which we discuss below.

COMMUNICATION COMPETENCE AS A CENTRAL CONCEPT

We closely examine the development and role of *Communication Competence* as an important *dimension* of Civic Competence. It includes *media use*, particularly public affairs news, and *interpersonal communication*, in terms of discussion of public affairs and politics, both inside and outside the classroom. Media civic competence (a.k.a. media *literacy*) includes surveillance of the environment; awareness of current events; information search skills; understanding the difference between evidence and inference; distinctions among news, editorial, and public relations or advertising content; reflective thinking about public affairs content; other information-processing strategies; and making cognitive connections between issues that yield more complex issue understanding. Interpersonal civic competence includes interpersonal communication skills such as forming arguments, expressing opinions, listening to other perspectives, turn-taking, active listening, and willingness to collaborate.

Media competence and interpersonal competence are functionally related and highly complementary, and each contributes substantially to civic participation. Many of these skills can be learned through classroom experiences with deliberative discussion about public affairs or social controversies, but are also found in other contexts. Classroom opportunities encouraging deliberative exchanges are a critical precursor to the development of communication competence. These communicative activities help create a stable foundation of competence in youth long after the end of adolescence and in areas extending beyond civic life. That is, communication competence provides a critical set of life skills that can be applied flexibly across contexts, including social interactions, making informed consumer choices (Zukin et al., 2006), and in employment settings (Torney-Purta & Wilkenfeld, 2009). Of course, the consequences for civic life are especially pronounced.

Why is communication competence important for civic engagement? First, it is important because definitions of *civic competence* make the role of practices (participation) central while recognizing other critical aspects of competence such as capacity, knowledge, and judgments of institutions going beyond self-interest. Second, both attentive public affairs media use and civic discussion have been shown in analyses of ANES 2004 data to be effective *mediators* of the influence of education and other social structural variables on civic engagement; 59% of the effects of social structural variables on political knowledge mediated by news attention; 86% of the effects of social structural variables on campaign participation mediated by news attention (McLeod, 2007). Thus, communication competence is not only a contributor to civic engagement but also a conduit for effects of more foundational factors. News use is an important part of the process by which social structural factors, such as education, affect civic and political participation (McLeod et al., 2001; Sotirovic & McLeod, 2004). Interpersonal issue discussion, both face-to-face and online, is an additional mediator of social structural and media influences on engagement (Shah, Cho, Eveland, & Kwak, 2005; Cho et al., 2008).

The discussion and debate of controversial issues in the classroom have been linked to the development of these communication skills, increased political knowledge, and the formation of attitudes that often lead to engagement (Hahn & Tocci, 1990; Hess, 2009) and more directly to various forms of civic activity (Shah et al., 2009). An analysis of data from the IEA Civic Education Study showed that students who reported that interactive discussion was a prominent feature of their classrooms had higher scores on a media literacy measure that required interpreting material from newspapers and distinguishing statements of fact from statements of opinion (Torney-Purta & Wilkenfeld, 2009). While teaching young people how to talk about controversial political issues in schools is not a new concept, evidence suggests that deliberative activities in the classroom have become more accepted within the broader field. For almost a century, many advocates of civic education, especially within the social studies, have called for the infusion of controversial issues in the curriculum. For example, in the early twentieth century, teachers were encouraged to focus on the *problems of democracy* in classrooms. One of the core recommendations of the CMS Report, as noted above, is to "incorporate discussion of current local, national, and international issues and events into the classroom, particularly those that young people view as important to their lives" (Gibson & Levine, 2003, p. 26–27). Communication competence is implicated in each of these recommendations from discussions of current events to learning civic skills through service learning, student media, school governance, and democratic simulations. In short, public affairs media use and issue discussion each have substantial direct and indirect effects on civic and political participation. The multiple roles of communication competence make their relevance to civic engagement self-evident. What is less obvious is the fact that these findings provide important evidence for those forming educational and social policy, since communication *processing* skills are potentially more malleable than other influences on participation, such as social structural characteristics.

THE ROLE OF SCHOOLS IN CREATING COMMUNICATION COMPETENCE

Schools are clearly one of the core institutions that can instill communication competence in young people. The most frequently articulated reason to include controversial issues in the curriculum is the connection between learning how to deliberate over controversies, especially those that focus on public problems, and participating effectively in a democratic society. This connection hinges on a definition of democracy that requires people to engage in high-quality public talk. For example, Mansbridge (1991) posits, "Democracy involves public discussion of common problems, not just silent counting of individual hands" (p. 122). Within this deliberative paradigm, public talk becomes the "valued currency of public life" (Kettering Foundation, 1993, p. 2). Those who hold this conception of democracy advocate the discussion of controversial issues on which individuals hold different views as a form of authentic instruction to prepare young people to participate fully and competently in a form of political engagement that is important in integration with the social world (Newmann & Wehlage, 1995).

It is interesting that another commonly advanced rationale for issues discussion begins with a different presumption. A number of scholars have documented low levels of adult political talk in recent years and urged the schools to work to change this trend (Hibbing & Theiss-Morse, 2002; Conover, Searing, & Crewe, 2002; Mutz, 2006). Regardless of whether one seeks to induct young people into a society where such discussions occur, or rather hopes that the next generation will make political discussions more frequent or even commonplace, advocates of deliberative democracy claim the need for more talk about issues in schools.

Other rationales for issues discussions promote them as *vehicles* for a host of outcomes, some of which are explicitly connected to democratic education.

Examples in this category include the expectation that, via issues discussions, students will: develop an understanding and commitment to democratic values, such as tolerance, equality, diversity, and human rights (Lockwood & Harris, 1985; Oliver & Shaver, 1966; Torney-Purta, Wilkenfeld, & Barber, 2008); enhance their sense of political efficacy (Gimpel, Lay, & Schuknecht, 2003); increase their interest in engaging in public life (Zukin et al., 2006); and learn how to break down historic divides and forge bonds between groups in a society who are markedly different from one another (McCully, 2006). The CMS report summarizes the civic power of controversial issues discussions in a clear and straightforward manner:

> Studies that ask young people whether they had opportunities to discuss current issues in a classroom setting have consistently found that those who did participate in such discussions have a greater interest in politics, improved critical thinking and communications skills, more civic knowledge, and more interest in discussing public affairs out of school. Compared to other students, they also are more likely to say that they will vote and volunteer as adults. (Gibson & Levine, 2003, p. 8)

Thus, the advocacy for issues discussions contains another powerful rationale—the likely connection between this form of democratic education and the development of attitudes, knowledge, and skills linked to informed and engaged citizenship. Issues discussions are advocated also for reasons traditionally associated with schooling outcomes writ large, such as learning important content (Harris, 1996), improving critical thinking, or building more sophisticated interpersonal communication skills (Johnson & Johnson, 1995). It is clear from this list that an ambitious set of aims is attached to controversial political issues discussions in civic education.

In addition to advocating the infusion of controversial issues in the curriculum because of its civic impact, it is also important to note that schools are the most diverse environment that most young people inhabit, notwithstanding the recent trend toward re-segregation. Consequently, they are good sites for such discussions. Most schools contain gender diversity, religious diversity, ethnic diversity, and some degree of racial diversity. Open classroom climates for discussion have been shown to relate to higher support among boys for women's political rights across 28 countries (Barber & Torney-Purta, 2009). The postulated process is that when respectful discussion of issues takes place, boys hear girls expressing opinions that are sometimes similar to and sometimes different from their own and conclude that females have political opinions and rights that should be respected.

Moreover, even classes that appear to be homogeneous along a number of these dimensions likely encompass broader ideological diversity than students encounter in their families or immediate neighbors. The relative diversity of schools makes them particularly good places for controversial issues discussions because it enhances the likelihood that students will be exposed to views that differ from their own and that they will have to explain their own views. This kind of *crosscutting talk* (Mutz, 2006) is markedly different from talk that occurs in an *echo chamber* of similar views.

As a case in point, an ongoing study that examines the nature and range of ideological diversity that exists in high-school social studies courses shows that schools reflect the diversity that exists within the communities to some extent. However, even classes that appear to be extremely homogeneous have a fair amount of ideological diversity. Interviews with students consistently show that they are more likely to recognize and appreciate the ideological diversity in their midst if their teachers include discussions of controversial issues in the curriculum. Many students report that the range of opinions they hear in classes is far wider than in their homes, partially because there are more participants in class discussions, which yields more diversity of viewpoints, but also because the procedures that skillful teachers use bring out the differences of opinion that exist within the group (Hess & Ganzler, 2007; Hess, 2008). We contend that these classroom opportunities are complemented by media use and network discussion outside of school contexts, working together to spur political socialization and civic engagement.

MEDIA USE, NETWORK DISCUSSION, AND THEIR INFLUENCES

It is important to understand how models of communication and youth socialization have changed over the last four decades. The origins of communication approaches to socialization were partially a reaction against the dominant political science functionalist model of the 1960s. The dominant model asserted that it was necessary for citizens to learn a basic set of facts, beliefs, and behaviors reflecting a unified political system. The stability bias of the earlier model, reflected in portraying societies as unified wholes, has given way to focusing on communities as arenas where many forces with differing interests are contending. Forty years of communication research radically altered the conception of youth from a passive recipient of influence to a more active participant in seeking and using information to make sense of the external world. This is not to say that individuals are always systematic and rational in processing information. The new approach asserts that under many circumstances they are active and capable of making connections and going beyond narrow self-interest to work for the common good. It is also important to note that civic potential is by no means fixed in childhood and that changes can and do take place well into adulthood. This parallels changes in the field of developmental psychology from more passive to more active models (Flanagan & Sherrod, 1998, Wilkenfeld et al., this volume).

The idea of an active audience has important implications for learning how youth use media. The early focus on political *outcomes* came at the expense of ignoring *processes* that are vital to democracy. Communication research has gone beyond looking at *how much* media is used to examine the questions of *why* and *how* specific types of content are used. One insight that has arisen from this shift in focus is that time-spent media measures are insensitive to *attention* to specific types of content. Television viewers often combine watching with other activities. Today's youth typically spend more than seven hours a day using media, most of which involves using two or more media simultaneously (Roberts, 2000). It is important to obtain information about the person's typical level of *attention* as well as their *exposure* to particular forms of media content. For television news especially, taking this into account shows much stronger effects on learning than does exposure alone.

Seeking information increases attention to news and facilitates learning while seeking escape or diversion lessens attention and learning. Strategies that individuals use to process information from the news media are crucial to understanding civic engagement. *Reflective thinking* about issues encountered in the news or in conversations with others greatly facilitates forming the connections needed for civic learning and participation while the tendency to *skim or scan* the news for familiar topics is a deterrent to engagement (McLeod et al., 2001; Patterson, 2007). The positive effects of attentive news use are substantially enhanced by discussion of public affairs with others in the person's social network. The processes of deliberation—the thoughtful processing of information from mediated and interpersonal sources, listening to diverse points of view, turn-taking in discussion, and working out compromises—are no less important than adopting attitudes supportive of the political system.

Attentive use of traditional news media made an enduring contribution to civic engagement in the last third of the twentieth century (McLeod & Reeves, 1980; McLeod, Kosicki, & McLeod, 2009; Norris, 2000). Reading of public affairs content in newspapers had the most potent effects, though somewhat selectively in that the college-educated tended to choose higher quality papers and more civically relevant content. Television network news reached massive audiences in their dominance of political campaigns and major news events. Citizens did learn from network news but its effects were less potent than those of newspapers; however, they affected citizens who had not been to college as well as those who had. Somewhat surprisingly, the communication research evidence for these positive effects was not picked up by the general public or by other scholars who instead keep their focus on the negative effects of entertainment television until the benefit of news was popularized at the end of the century (Norris, 2000; Shah, McLeod, & Yoon, 2001).

A cause and consequence of such attentive new media use, public-spirited talk—i.e., discussion about public affairs with friends and family—serves as a critical *mediator* of many of these effects on civic, political, and consumptive forms of participation on the adolescent (Future Voters Study reported in Shah et al., 2009).[1] Although there was some inconsistency in measurement strategies with the two CPHN studies of adults, interpersonal discussion items consistently explained a range of participatory behaviors in both 2002 and 2006. These models indicate that political discussion involving young people plays a major role in youth engagement, mediating prior influences while also contributing uniquely (see Table 1 and Table 2 in the online appendix at http://www.journalism.wisc.edu/~dshah/resources.htm).

Although most of the evidence for positive civic effects of the traditional news media has been based on adult samples, some evidence from early studies indicated that adolescents share in this contribution (Chaffee, McLeod, & Wackman, 1973; McLeod, 2000; McLeod & Brown, 1976). Nonetheless, there were statistically significant if modest gains in news consumption from early to late adolescence that paralleled gains in various indicators of civic engagement: political interest, knowledge, efficacy, and participation (McLeod & Brown, 1976; McLeod, Eveland, & Horowitz, 1995). The gains in news media use and civic engagement extended across the life cycle to age 65. Discussion of issues with friends also became more common across adolescence but the gain was less than that for either news use or civic

[1] Mediation analysis is a research strategy that combines theoretical insights and statistical procedures to provide more complete and sensitive explanations of human behavior. Social science research very often provides empirical evidence of connections between antecedent "causal" variables and conceptually distant outcome "effect" variables without specifying the processes or conditions that can explain the dynamics of why this effect is produced. Better explanations require reducing this distance by specifying the set of variables, often representing processes, that intervenes to mediate the connection between antecedents and their distant outcomes. Various terms describe conceptually the roles of mediating variables in developing theory development. Alternatively, they can transmit, interpret, direct, and contextualize the causal forces of the antecedent conditions into cognitive, affective, or behavioral outcomes. Viewed as the assessment by a set of statistical procedures, mediation is the degree to which controlling the predicted mediating variable can reduce the original association between the antecedent (independent) variable and the outcome (dependent) variable. If the original antecedent to outcome relationship is reduced to zero, total mediation has been achieved; if the original coefficient is reduced significantly but not totally, we can claim partial mediation. To produce mediation of either degree, the mediating variable must be significantly and consistently related to both the antecedent and outcome variables with sufficient strength to the latter that it will remain significant after the control for the antecedent variable is applied in regression or other analyses of the model. Another useful way to describe mediation is that it creates an indirect path from the antecedent variable to the outcome variable through the mediating variable, either eliminating the original direct path (total mediation) or reducing it significantly (partial mediation).

engagement. Family communication patterns also seemed to change during the adolescent years. Parents became more likely to encourage encountering controversial social issues and speaking out and to lessen their demands for avoiding conflict and conformity (Chaffee et al., 1973; McLeod & Brown, 1976). These changes contributed to adolescent civic learning and activity.

More recent research, in particular the IEA Civic Education Study testing in 1999, has not only examined parallel trends but has used HLM analysis to examine media and discussion predictors of several civic outcomes. Reading international news was a significant predictor of both knowledge about human rights and attitudes of political efficacy in an analysis of 14-year-olds across 27 countries (Torney-Purta et al., 2008). Reading national news, as well as discussing politics with parents and having an open climate for discussing issues in the classroom were all associated with narrowing the gap between U.S. Latinos' and non-Latinos' civic knowledge and likelihood of voting (Torney-Purta, Barber, & Wilkenfeld, 2007). Amadeo (2007) examined a subset of the IEA data in Chile, Denmark, and England. These were the only countries that had included a question in the surveys about use of the Internet for news. In all three countries, use of Internet news was significantly correlated with the likelihood of voting. However, in Chile, getting news from newspapers was more highly correlated with electoral participation than was Internet news ($r = .284$ for newspaper and $r = .112$ for Internet).

CHANGES AND CHALLENGES IN THE MEDIA ENVIRONMENT

The growth in news consumption as part of adolescent civic development was encouraging in the past, but the long-term prospects for traditional news media are less positive. Newspaper circulation has been in decline for three decades, and network news viewing has fallen sharply in recent years (Peiser, 2000). For the first time, a majority of younger parents are no longer daily consumers of news and this may reduce the likelihood that their children will become active citizens. Network news is no longer part of the family dinner hour, to the extent that family dinners occur at all. Some even claim that young people now learn as much of their public affairs through late night talk show hosts such as Jay Leno or John Stewart. The falling economic fortunes of the traditional news media have had an additional negative outcome in that they have resulted in shrinking staff and news space, elimination of non-crisis foreign coverage, and increased focus on crime and catastrophes, and on short sound bites from candidates and officials. The 20-year decline in presidential campaign coverage—accompanied by shrinking citizen attention and news effects—was halted only by the intense 2004 and 2008 campaigns (Sotirovic & McLeod, 2008; Shah et al., 2009;

Bennett et al., this volume). The pattern of gradual growth in news media use across age categories in the 1960 to 2000 era is not being reproduced in the twenty-first century. Regular use of traditional news media—newspapers, television news, and radio news—fell by 7% over a recent four-year period (CPHN, 2002, 2006).

Use of Internet by younger cohorts may partly offset the loss in consumption of traditional news media. Adolescents' access to computers and the Internet in schools has grown rapidly in the past decade, but we don't yet know how *access* translates into a pattern of information seeking that might persist into adulthood (Haste, this volume). How computer use is taught in the classroom is doubtless one key to the future contribution of the Internet, and there are some problems here as well. Affluent students are more likely to be guided into learning cognitively complex skills of information search that facilitate processes important to civic activism.

Regular use of Internet news grew by 8% during a recent four-year period (CPHN, 2006; see online appendix Tables 3 and 4). In 2006, regular use of Internet news was only 23% for those under 26, and it exceeded one-third among only one age category, Generation X-ers ages 26 to 37 (34%). It is doubtful in the foreseeable future that Internet news use will reach levels achieved by newspapers and network television news 20 years ago. One hopeful sign is that the majority in each age category continues to use at least one traditional news source regularly (CPHN 2006). Even among the under 26 Millennials, regular use of Internet news (32%) was less common in 2006 than regular use of television network news (37%). However, in our analyses of the Future Voter adolescents' study, there were only modest increases in the regular use of newspapers, television, and Internet news (5%, 5%, and 2%, respectively) among adolescents age 12 to 17 during the primary season of 2008, but more dramatic jumps in political talk and online messaging (11% and 7%, respectively) during this same period.

Particularly noteworthy is the cascading nature of these gaps in use that extend beyond simple access issues. Figure 14.2, which highlights findings from the 2006 CPHN data, begins by showing the gap in access between those with and without the prospect or experience of college aged 15 to 25, with those with access shaded in gray and those without shaded white. When comparing college and non-college bound youth in Internet access, the gap is a sizable 28.4% (64.4% vs. 92.8%). The next level of the graph looks only at those who have Internet access. Among that group, the gap between college and non-college groups in online *news* use is 10% (64.9% vs. 74.9%). Cascading down further, when focusing only on Internet news users, the gap in *regular* online news use between college and non-college bound youth indicates another division approaching 10% (30.7% vs. 40.4%). As this indicates, while the access gap remains large, simply providing

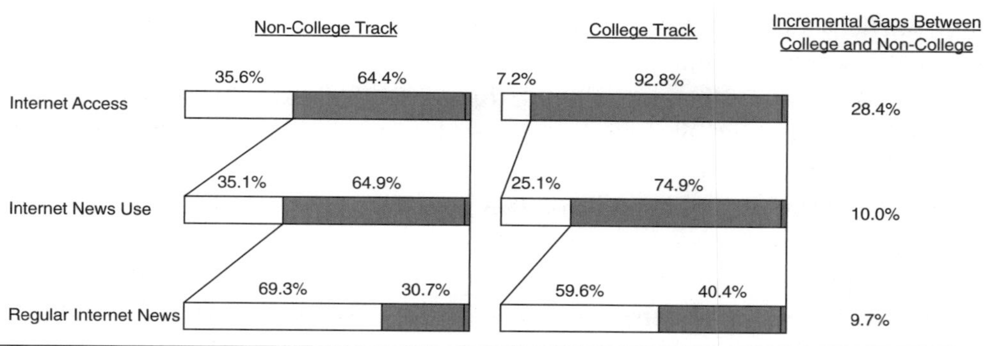

Figure 14.2 Cascading Gaps in Internet Access and News Use

access without encouraging active news consumption is unlikely to eliminate educational gaps.

As these comparisons indicate, we should avoid assuming continuity and an upward trajectory of either communication or civic patterns from adolescence to early adulthood, or any assumptions about the Internet as a civic panacea. Early adulthood is a period of rapid change and differentiation (see Finlay, this volume). The young adult is likely to have moved away from his or her family and its influence into a very different milieu of a new community or neighborhood and life style. Much of the earlier social support for civic engagement from parents, peers, school, and church is removed and new civic allegiances and identities must be formed. Young adults are likely to lack characteristics and ties that strengthen civic engagement. Compared to older adults, they tend to be new to the neighborhood in which they live and anticipate moving away in the next five years. Involved neighborhoods may act as contextual influences on activism beyond the young adult's individual characteristics. Not surprisingly, social interactions with friends and work associates are frequent among young adults, and they play a critical role in all aspect of their lives including the development of their civic identity (Feigenberg, King, Barr, & Selman, 2008; Flanagan et al., 2009; McPherson, Smith-Lovin, & Cook, 2001).

UNDERSTANDING USAGE AND EFFECTS ACROSS THE LIFE COURSE

Communication effects rarely have been evaluated for specific age groups. Newspaper reading, which has the strongest impact on learning and participation for adults generally, is among the strongest positive influences on civic engagement among young adults (see McLeod et al., 2002, reanalysis of the 2000 Social Capital Benchmark Study). Newspaper reading is associated with political interest, civic knowledge, citizen efficacy, volunteering, and civic participation. Further, the strength of effects among young adults was at least as strong as among those over 35. This is supported in analyses of media effects on political knowledge during the 2000 and 2004 election campaigns based on NES data (Sotirovic & McLeod, 2004, 2008). The effects of reading newspaper stories about the campaign were equally strong among the young as among older adults; the youngest (age 18 to 23) showed the most potent effects of any age group.

The problem involved in using newspaper reading as a way of spurring young adult activism seems to be one of low use rather than an inability of youth to learn from print media. Somewhat similarly, television campaign news effects are strongest among the 18 to 23 group eligible to vote for the first time and weakest in the 24 to 30 category. As this indicates, to assess the impact of media use and interpersonal communication on the development of adolescent civic identity, we must consider two factors: the *level* of use and the strength of the *effect*. This is analogous to the distinction between dosage and effectiveness in the evaluation of drugs. For example, it may be that newsmagazines have very few young readers, but they can be highly effective sources of information among those who do read them.

Understanding dosage (level) and potency (effect) is a crucial question for Internet use because of its relatively heavy use among younger adults. For instance, Shah et al. (2001) revealed that Internet use for search and exchange of information was related to both trust in people and in civic participation among the youngest adult cohorts. Again, these Internet effects were stronger than for older adults. The campaign context provides further evidence of stronger Internet effects among young adults than among older citizens. The effect in the 18- to 23-year-old age group was twice as strong as in any other age category. The potential of the Internet to enhance youth activism is thus documented in both its high level of use at least among the college-educated and its generally strong potency of impact among today's youth cohort.

We might expect that the gaps between educational groups in strength of effects (potency) of news use and political discussion stimulating civic participation would parallel the patterns in gaps in levels of use (dosage) shown earlier in Figure 14.1. However, in the 2006 CPHN study, the correlations between each of the three communication behaviors and civic participation revealed at least as many instances of stronger effects among the non-college respondents as of greater potency for the college group (the gap we anticipated).

There was a pattern of weakening effects of exposure to all three of the tested communication sources during the early adult years among those who attended college even while their levels of use of those sources was on the rise. In contrast, the potency of civic participation effects for the non-college groups reached strong levels in the two young adult groups for all three communication sources. This was in spite of their relatively low levels of use. This indicates that the small proportions of non-college youth who used news regularly were very likely to be civically active. The strong communication effects among some non-college young adults provide evidence that disparities in civic participation cannot be attributed to an *inability* to benefit from exposure to civically relevant information in newspapers, online, or from discussion with other people. The main challenge thus is how to increase their levels of exposure to such information.

Status gaps in civic engagement have seldom been examined for adult groups ranging from early through middle adulthood. The civic disadvantages of not having attended college were revealed in a reanalysis of the Benchmark 2000 study (McLeod et al., 2002), where gaps between education groups in the proportion of those volunteering or otherwise civically engaged were maintained in groups as old as 65. Long-term trends in civic participation were also examined in four national DDB Life Style studies over an 11-year period, 1993 to 2004. The pattern of educational gaps across the life course replicated the Benchmark 2000 data.

Evidence from the 2008 presidential campaign of Barack Obama illustrates the effectiveness of Internet-based mobilization strategies but also the persistence of education gaps as obstacles to equal citizen participation. Youth voting reached an all-time high in number of votes cast, the large majority of which went for Obama. The 2008 results can be attributed as much to a failure of the McCain campaign to reach younger voters as to the success of the Obama campaign. Further, while the Obama campaign had remarkable success in mobilizing college-attending and college-educated young adults, there is little evidence that it was able to stimulate turnout among the non-college youth despite the campaign's egalitarian themes. Campaigns tend to the most reachable potential voters, college students and college-educated young adults (Freedman & Goldstein, 1999; Cho et al., 2008).

EFFECTS OF SCHOOL ACTIVITIES, MEDIA USE, AND POLITICAL DISCUSSION ON CIVIC ENGAGEMENT

The two CPHN studies are currently the most comprehensive attempts to examine the effects of curriculum, student activities, classroom deliberation, and conventional and digital news consumption on civic health in the United States. These studies examine a range of relevant civic behaviors and activities, including expressive participation (i.e., letter writing and contacting public officials), civic participation (i.e., volunteerism and community project work), campaign participation (i.e., material or symbolic support of a candidate), and political consumerism (i.e., boycotting or buycotting goods), allowing for forms of participation often overlooked by previous efforts. With their large over-sampling of adolescents and young adults within an otherwise representative sample of adults, these data provide unique insights into the questions of communication competence and civic competence raised above.

Reanalysis of these studies restricted to current students under the age of 25 finds that even when accounting for age, gender, household income, race, and a host of dispositional and structural factors (conservatism, strength of partisanship, educational aspiration, mother's education, residential stability, and church attendance), communication competence mattered for civic engagement, writ large. Specifically, participation in student government and membership in social or political groups in high school was a consistent and robust predictor of all four forms of engagement: expressive civic participation, civic participation in the community, campaign participation, and political consumerism. Likewise, classroom deliberation was positively linked with both civic participation and political consumerism in both the 2002 and 2006 data. Like church attendance, this set of educational activities appears to provide civic skills that become the basis for various forms of engagement, with communication competence clearly among the abilities being developed. That these effects are observed among current students, where variance on these indicators is likely truncated, only adds to their import (Shah et al., 2009).

This is further evidenced by the fact that the benefits of experiences with student government, political groups in school, and classroom deliberation extend well beyond high school into the college years and also by the fact that the effects of these educational activities are largely mediated through communication factors such as conventional and Internet news consumption and political conversation, both inside and outside the classroom. Indeed, in all cases, Internet news consumption was a sizable predictor of expressive participation, which may be partly due to the fact that the Internet is not only a source for news information but also a public sphere populated with political exchanges among citizens in the form of posted comments, political blogs, and other types of online political messaging (Shah et al., 2005; Bennett et al., this volume). In terms of campaign and civic participation and political consumerism, the effect of Internet use appears to be more indirect, working through public affairs discussion inside and outside the classroom. These mediated effects were stronger in 2006 than 2002, when more direct effects were observed in these data. Regardless, the importance of the Internet as a source of political information among young people is apparent in its patterns of direct and indirect effects across this wide range of indicators of civic engagement, from the expressive to the consumptive.

The pattern of effects for conventional news use largely parallels the findings for the Internet, though they were stronger in 2006 than in 2002, when most of the observed effects were only indirect on civic outcomes. In contrast, the more recent CPHN data revealed that conventional news consumption (newspaper and television news use) had direct effects on expressive, civic, and campaign participation, though these effects were also mediated through political discussion. Indeed, consistent with the communication mediation model and its extensions (McLeod et al., 2001; Shah et al., 2005; Shah et al., 2007), both discussions of volunteerism in the classroom and discussion about public affairs with friends and family appear to mediate many of these effects on expressive, civic, political and consumptive forms of participation. When expressive participation is then added to models explaining civic, political, and consumptive forms of engagement, the overall pattern of effects grows stronger, with expressive participation and interpersonal discussion consistently explaining these behaviors across the studies (see Table 5 and Table 6 in the online appendix at http://www.journalism.wisc.edu/~dshah/resources.htm).

Some of these same communications effects processes appear to be at work among young people with few educational advantages. When examining the small subset of respondents in the CPHN data who were over 20 years of age and had not completed high school (N = 173 in 2002 and N = 120 in 2006), Internet news use and public affairs discussion consistently emerge as key predictors of expressive participation. The findings for civic participation are somewhat less clear, with church attendance being the only consistent positive predictor of engagement across the two studies among those who dropped out of high school. Newspaper use and public affairs discussion also explain difference in civic participation among this group in 2002 and 2006, respectively. Internet news use and public affairs discussion also explain campaign participation among high school dropouts, though the former is only significant in 2002. In all of these tests, communication variables are the most powerful predictors in the models, suggesting that news use, especially via the Internet, and interpersonal discussion about public affairs can even play an important role in mobilizing those without high-school diplomas.

CAN COMMUNICATION COMPETENCE DIMINISH THE DEMOCRACY DIVIDE?

If various forms of mediated and interpersonal communication contribute to the civic engagement of adolescents and young adults, even those without the benefits of a high-school diploma, the question becomes: How could these communication processes be better used to further stimulate youth activism?

One approach would be to devise strategies to increase use of news and other content beneficial to civic engagement. Another approach is to focus on teaching youth how to better seek and process information from the content they prefer to use that would facilitate their civic activism. This form of media literacy involves learning cues for focusing attention on certain content, using critical and reflective thinking, and making connections with past information and between isolated facts and issues. In addition, opportunities for discussion and deliberation, potentially about public affairs or documentary content, also may be effective. We argue that this approach is fundamentally concerned with building communication competence.

The traditional news media, such as newspapers and television news, present somewhat different challenges in promoting activism. The problem for using newspapers for activation is largely a matter of how to increase youthful exposure in the face of a decline in readership that is especially noticeable in the youngest cohorts. To the extent that young audiences do read newspapers, the beneficial effects of this activity on civic engagement are equal to those for older adults. Television news viewing is more common than newspaper reading among younger audience, including the less educated, but here the problem is the weakness of its effect on civic engagement. The problem of television news resides in the deficiencies of its content, thus efforts to teach youth how to use it more effectively are not likely to stimulate engagement to the same extent as news media with greater depth of informational and mobilizing content.

This speaks to the broader issue that strengthening the impact of communication on civic engagement is not solely a matter of changing how youth consume news content. Historical changes in news content toward crime and sensational "infotainment" content in both newspapers and television news may be partly responsible for the decline in civic engagement over the last 40 years. While it is difficult to see how those interested in promoting youth activism could effect changes in media content, there are some hopeful signs that news content may be moving in directions more favorable to activism. Concern with declining circulation has lead many publishers to pursue "creating a sense of community" as a goal for their newspaper, supporting both civic journalism and citizen journalism movements. Many local television stations have joined with newspapers in projects of civic/public journalism that include youth. Media professionals claim they are shifting this focus to stories that deal with broader issues and the search for solutions while cutting back on routine coverage of meetings. If these efforts and claims constitute an enduring change in news content, they have the potential to aid youth activism.

The Internet offers great potential for promoting youth activism. It is widely used among both adolescents and young adults, and even has potency among the non-college population. Along with other new media technologies, Internet use has become a part of youth culture providing an area of autonomy and competence beyond that of their parents in many cases. When used for information search and exchange purposes, the Internet has positive effects on civic engagement far stronger than those for older adults. The problem with using the Internet for expansion of youth activism is how to stimulate its use for informational acquisition and public expression purposes in the face of other purposes that are at best irrelevant for activation. While most school assignments involve information search, the lack of adequate training for teachers remains a problem. And, of course, gaps of access and proficiency by socioeconomic status remain sizable, so even with its considerable potency, the dosage remains unevenly distributed.

Given the important relation between education, news media use, political expression, and civic and political engagement, it is clear to many that changes are needed in schooling to reduce the democracy divide. Serious and sustained attention should be directed toward reducing the high-school dropout/push-out rate, given the powerful connection that exists between educational attainment and participation. Putting it simply, effective dropout prevention programs *are* civic education. While much attention in the civic education field concentrates on improving the quality and quantity of civic education in K–12 schools—and ensuring that all students have equal access to this education—it is crucial to emphasize that the impact of these improvements in school-based civic education cannot be felt by young people who aren't attending school.

But working to ensure that young people stay in school will do more to reduce the democracy divide if the opportunities students have to engage in high-quality forms of civic education are present and equally available irrespective of social class. In terms of the relative prominence of civic education in schools, there is evidence that in many elementary and middle schools it has dropped off as a consequence of attention given in the curriculum to literacy and math (the two subjects that No Child Left Behind—NCLB—requires for testing), although that is not the case in most high schools. To ensure that all schools maintain or enhance their focus on civic education, some advocates in the field urge the inclusion of civic education content on assessments mandated by NCLB. While this is promoted as a lever to increase the amount of attention paid to civic education, we are not convinced the quality would be sufficiently high to obtain the payoffs in civic and political engagement. The components of civic education that have shown the most promising effects, such as media literacy programs, classroom discussion of issues, civic simulations, and high-quality student governance opportunities, are almost impossible to assess on standardized tests. Consequently, one potential unintended impact of more testing could be to discourage teachers from engaging their students in the very forms of civic learning that lead to the most robust and varied forms of engagement.

Alternatively, state-, district-, and school-level educational policies that require an emphasis in the curriculum on civic education are probably more likely to result in higher quality learning opportunities, especially if there are adequate resources made available to schools for materials, professional development for teachers, technology, and newspapers. For example, a number of school districts have required by policy that all students in a particular grade participate in curricular-based programs, such as Project Citizen or Kids Voting, that have shown promising results (McDevitt & Chaffee, 2000; McLeod et al., 1995). Additionally, given the impact that news media consumption has on political engagement and the persistent digital divide that exists in the world outside of school, it is especially important for schools to ensure that all students have ready access to digital technology, are given access to the Internet, and are taught how to use it toward civic ends. But as new research so powerfully illustrates, high-quality civic education programs are often not meted out equitably to all students. It may be that state policies that assess equal "opportunities to learn" are necessary to send a clear message to schools that inequality of access to powerful civic education is problematic. It is also the case that government and foundation money that flows to civic education programs should have equality of access standards to encourage schools to shape programs that all students participate in—regardless of academic track or other markers that in practice so powerfully shape who gets what in many schools now.

To conclude, the way in which schooling currently operates in the United States is partially responsible for producing the democracy divide—which is ironic given that its historic purpose in the United States was to promote civic and political engagement. To interrupt this trend and turn it around—to reduce the democracy divide—policies and practices should focus on three goals: Keep more young people in schools, ensure that civic education gets its due in the curriculum, and require that all students within schools have an equal opportunity to the high-quality forms of civic education, building the kind of communication competence that has been shown to influence participation.

IMPLICATIONS AND LIMITATIONS

We have presented a dynamic model of citizenship development in which interdependent communication processes located in the family, schools, media, and peer networks combine to produce communication competence in youth. This model reflects an interdisciplinary approach to theory generation about youth socialization. The intellectual moorings of key concepts we explore are derived from sociology (e.g., social structure and family dynamics), education (e.g., classroom practices and civic curricula), communication (e.g., mass media use and interpersonal discussion), psychology (e.g., learning and attitudes), and political science (civic and electoral participation). This interdisciplinarity also means this model has great potential utility across many different fields and provides robust criteria for policy-based evaluations.

This is especially true for the concept of communication competence. Moving beyond media use or interpersonal talk to a higher level of abstraction makes it easier to transfer this concept to different field spaces. This permits the notion of competence to be applied in a range of settings—at home, at school, at work, with peers, online, and so forth. The evidence indicates that communication competence promotes political learning and sustained patterns of civic activity throughout the life course, which further elevates its value to psychologists, sociologists, and educators. We have considerable empirical evidence consistent with such a theoretical formulation, but there are important limitations of the research designs that generated this evidence, which we address below.

The communication behaviors reported here were limited to the consumption of news and public affairs content of media and discussion of what could be called *serious* topics. Given that this restricted content represents a small portion of the communication activity of youth, we must acknowledge that the myriad of forms of entertainment media content and overwhelming proportion of the social content of the conversations of youth also are like to have important positive and negative civic consequences. The growth of increasingly miniaturized devices for social conversation may either facilitate sharing of information or make it impossible to convey it in a meaningful manner. Accurate measurement of the levels of use and effects of these almost constant and simultaneous activities pose daunting tasks for research.

Our analyses have been restricted to studying communication and civic behavior at the individual level. Of course, we would have preferred to sample actual social networks to validate self-report data, for example. There is a more important theoretical point to be made, however. Youth, even more than older adults, are unlikely to participate alone. For example, many make decisions to participate in the community contingent on the willingness of others to volunteer with them. Further, the opportunities to participate via organizations and associations are unequally distributed geographically in ways that particularly deter activity among the non-college youth living in less affluent neighborhoods. Increasing equality in participation requires increases in targeted social opportunities as well as in individual incentives to become active.

What is needed is larger scale, multi-method studies dedicated to examining the influence of these sorts of factors on youth socialization. This requires two types of approaches: large-scale data integration efforts that merge contextual/geographic information or media/communication content with survey data collections, or different modes of research that include strategies such as classroom observation, experimental testing, field experiments, and textual analysis of course materials and mediated information (see Torney-Purta, Amadeo, & Andolina, this volume). The first of these approaches shows particular promise, as it would allow information about community characteristics, social network properties, and local media ecology to be brought into studies of youth engagement (see Wilkenfeld, 2009, for an example using U.S. census data merged with the IEA Civic Education Study dataset).

Multilevel modeling permits more formal testing of various sorts of civic education policy initiatives. Efforts to subject policy mandates to empirical testing have found that statewide policies may not transfer into changes at the classroom level, with the actual effects on civic outcomes shaped largely by the decisions of individual teachers (Lopez, Levine, Dautrich, & Yalof, 2009). Our concept of communication competence also provides criteria for policy initiatives that can be built around whether developing such competencies in youth has the favorable civic outcomes we contend should result from such interventions. Of course, assessments of improvement and change require longitudinal data, especially panel designs.

Among the datasets we analyzed, only the adolescent Future Voters study had panel data that helps to strengthen assertions about causal direction, but the five-month time period between the first two waves is too short to capture more fundamental changes in the lives of the youth samples. Our analyses of marked differences in levels and effects of communication and participation across the life course used two large Civic and Political Health of the Nation (CPHN) datasets that provide vital information but nonetheless prevent assertions about individual *change* because such cross-section designs confound cohort effects and life-cycle maturational effects. Longitudinal panel designs have become more prevalent in international research on civic engagement, with some work concerned with issues of youth socialization (Schoenbach et al., 1999; Peiser, 2000; de Vrees, 2007). Yet most of the research outside the U.S. context tends to focus on adults and their communication practices, with most centered on European societies. The few exceptions to this trend focus on Latin American civil society and tend to be focused on adult engagement (Rojas, 2009). Clearly, more research on youth socialization in non-Western countries is needed.

To overcome these limitations, it is of primary importance to develop research designs that will trace the trajectories of media use, issue discussions with various partners, and civic learning and behavior from adolescence into early and later adulthood. The term *socialization* implies political learning processes whose effects may carry over into the entire life course. Kurt Lewin, the eminent pioneering social psychologist, advised social scientists of his era to concentrate their research attention on people as they cross crucial junctures in their lives (Lewin, 1947). The transition from late adolescence to early adulthood, from the end of schooling to the start of individuals' occupational lives, is perhaps the most important period for political socialization research. For most young people, this change means a loss of social capital that supports civic engagement. Support from family, peers, and community diminishes, while the demands of the new occupational world delay reintegration.

Longer-term panel studies are expensive enterprises and require painstaking efforts of committed researchers. But Internet-based techniques have been developed that allow a large proportion of panel respondents to be retained over long periods of time. Given the growing body of findings that document the importance of media and interpersonal communication to youth socialization, financial support for such efforts may become more available. The evidence for the interdependent influence of parents, schools, informational media, and peer networks suggests that scholars from a variety of disciplines should be included in longer-term panel research. It also indicates the importance of including macro data from social systems and multilevel analyses in panel designs.

These types of collaborative research strategies are essential for answering the next wave of questions concerning youth socialization and more fully understanding the role of communication competence in building this capability. It is only through these types of efforts that we will gain the insights necessary to address the democracy divide in more systematic ways.

REFERENCES

Amadeo, J. (2007). Patterns of Internet use and political engagement among youth. In P. Dahlgren (Ed.), *Young citizens and new media: Learning for democratic participation* (pp. 125–146). New York: Routledge.

Barber, C., & Torney-Purta, J. (2009). Gender differences in political efficacy and attitudes toward women's rights influenced by national and school contexts: Analysis of the IEA Civic Education Study. In D. Baker & A. Wiseman (Eds.), *Gender equity and education from international and comparative perspectives* (pp. 357–394). Bingley, UK: JAI/Emerald Group Publishing.

Chaffee, S. H., McLeod, J. M., & Wackman, D. B. (1973). Family communication patterns and adolescent political socialization. In J. Dennis (Ed.), *Socialization to politics* (pp. 349–363). New York: John Wiley & Sons, Inc.

Cho, J., Shah, D. V., McLeod, J. M., McLeod, D. M., Scholl, R. M., & Gotlieb, M. R. (2008). Campaigns, reflection, and deliberation: Advancing an O-S-R-O-R model of communication effects. *Communication Theory, 19*, 66–88.

Conover, P. J., Searing, D. D., & Crewe, I. M. (2002). The deliberative potential of political discussion. *British Journal of Political Science, 32*, 21–62.

de Vrees, C. H. (2007). Digital renaissance: Young consumer and citizen? *Annals of the American Academy of Political and Social Science, 611*, 207–216.

Feigenberg, L. F., King, M. S., Barr, D. J., & Selman, R. L. (2008). Belonging to and exclusion from the peer group in schools: Influences on adolescents' moral choices. *Journal of Moral Education, 37*, 165–184.

Flanagan, C., Levine, P., & Settersten, R. (2009, January). *Civic engagement and the changing transition to adulthood*. Boston: CIRCLE report and College for Citizenship and Public Service, Tufts University.

Flanagan, C., & Sherrod, L. (1998). Political development: Youth growing up in a global community. *Journal of Social Issues, 54*, 447–556.

Freedman, P., & Goldstein, K. (1999). Measuring media exposure and the effects of negative campaign ads. *American Journal of Political Science, 43*, 1189–1208.

Gibson, C., & Levine, P. (2003). *The Civic Mission of Schools*. New York and Washington, DC: The Carnegie Corporation of New York and Center for Information and Research on Civic Learning and Engagement (CIRCLE).

Gimpel, J. G., Lay, J. C., & Schuknecht, J. E. (2003). *Cultivating democracy: Civic environments and political socialization in America*. Washington, DC: Brookings Institution Press.

Hahn, C., & Tocci, C. (1990). Classroom climate and controversial issues discussions: A five nation study. *Theory and Research in Social Education, 18(4)*, 344–362.

Harris, D. (1996). Assessing discussion of public issues: A scoring guide. In R. W. Evans & D. W. Saxe (Eds.), *Handbook on teaching social issues* (pp. 289–97). Washington, DC: National Council for the Social Studies.

Hess, D. E. (2008). Controversial issues and democratic discourse. In L. Levstik & C. Tyson (Eds.), *Handbook of research in social studies education* (pp. 124–136). New York & London: Routledge.

Hess, D. E. (2009). *Controversy in the classroom: The democratic power of discussion*. New York & London: Routledge.

Hess, D. E., & Ganzler, L. (2007). Patriotism and ideological diversity in the classroom. In J. Westheimer (Ed.), *Pledging allegiance: The politics of patriotism in American schools* (pp. 131–138). New York: Columbia University Teachers College Press.

Hibbing, J. R., & Theiss-Morse, E. (2002). *Stealth democracy: Americans' beliefs about how government should work*. Cambridge: Cambridge University Press.

Johnson, D. W., & Johnson, R. (1995). *Creative controversy: Intellectual conflict in the classroom* (3rd ed.). Edina, MN: Interaction.

Kahne J., & Middaugh, E. (2008). *Democracy for some: The civic opportunity gap in high school* (Working Paper No. 59). Medford, MA: CIRCLE (The Center for Information and Research on Civic Learning and Engagement).

Keeter, S., Zukin, C., Andolina, M., & Jenkins, K. (2002). *Civic and public health of the nation: A generational portrait*. Medford, MA: CIRCLE (The Center for Information and Research on Civic Learning and Engagement).

Kettering Foundation. (1993). Meaningful chaos: How people form relationships with public concerns. Kettering Foundation.

Lewin, K. (1947). Frontiers in group dynamics: Concept, method, and reality in social science. *Human Relations, 1*, 5–41.

Lockwood, A. L., & Harris, D. E. (1985). *Reasoning with democratic values: Ethical problems in United States history*. New York: Columbia University Teachers College Press.

Lopez, M. H., Levine, P., Both, D., Kiesa, A., Kirby, E., & Marcelo, K. (2006). *Civic and public health of the nation: A generational portrait*. Medford, MA: CIRCLE (The Center for Information and Research on Civic Learning and Engagement).

Lopez, M. H., Levine, P., Dautrich, K., & Yalof, D. (2009). Schools, education policy, and the future of the First Amendment. *Political Communication, 26*, 84–101.

Mansbridge, J. (1991). Democracy, deliberation, and the experience of women. In B. Murchland (Ed.), *Higher education and the practice of democratic politics* (pp. 122–135). Dayton, OH: Kettering Foundation.

McCully, A. (2006). Practitioner perceptions of their role in facilitating the handling of controversial issues in contested societies: A northern Irish experience. *Educational Review, 58*, 51–65.

McDevitt, M., & Chaffee, S. H. (2000). Closing gaps in political communication and knowledge: Effects of a school intervention. *Communication Research, 27*, 259–292.

McLeod, D. M., Kosicki, G. M., & McLeod, J. M. (2009). Political communication effects. In J. Bryant & M. Oliver (Eds.), *Media effects: Advances in theory and research* (pp. 228–251). New York: Routledge.

McLeod, J. M. (2000). Media and civic socialization of youth. *Journal of Adolescent Health, 27*, 45–51.

McLeod, J. M. (2007, August). *Using mediation analyses to develop explanations of communication processes and effects*. Paper presented at the Sungkyunkwan University Conference, Seoul, Korea.

McLeod, J. M., & Brown, J. D. (1976). The family environment and adolescent television use. In R. Brown (Ed.), *Children and television* (pp.199–233). London: Cassell and Collier Macmillan Publishers Ltd., and Beverly Hills, CA: Sage Publications.

McLeod, J. M., Eveland, W. P., & Horowitz, E. M. (1995, August). *Learning to live in a democracy: The interdependence of family, schools and media*. Paper presented at the annual meeting of the Association for Education in Mass Communication, Washington, DC.

McLeod, J. M., & Reeves, B. (1980). On the nature of mass media effects. In S. Withey & R. Abeles (Eds.), *Television and social behavior: Beyond violence and children* (pp. 17–54). Hillsdale, NJ: Lawrence Erlbaum.

McLeod, J. M., Shah, D. V., & Yoon, S. (2002, April). *Informing, entertaining, and connecting: The roles of mass communication for youth civic socialization*. Paper presented at the biennial meeting of the Society for Research on Adolescence, New Orleans, LA.

McLeod, J. M., Zubric, J., Keum, H., Deshpande, S., Cho, J., Stein, S. E., & Heather, M. (2001, August). *Reflecting and connecting: Testing a communication mediation model of civic participation.* Paper presented at the annual meeting of the Association for Education in Journalism and Mass Communication, Washington, DC.

McPherson, M., Smith-Lovin, L., & Cook, J. M. (2001). Birds of a feather: Homophily in social networks. *Annual Review of Sociology, 2*, 415–444.

Milbrath, L.W., & Goel, M. L. (1977). *Political participation: How and why do people get involved in politics?* (2nd ed). Chicago: Rand McNally.

Mutz, D. (2006). *Hearing the other side: Deliberative versus participatory democracy.* New York: Cambridge University Press.

Newmann, F. M., & Wehlage, G. G. (1995). *Successful school restructuring: A report to the public and educators* (Eric Document Reproduction Services No. ED 387925). Madison, WI: Center on Organization and Restructuring of Schools.

Norris, P. (2000). *A virtuous circle: Political socialization in postindustrial societies.* Cambridge: Cambridge University Press.

Oliver, D. W., & Shaver, J. P. (1966). *Teaching public issues in the high school.* New York: John Wiley & Sons, Inc.

Patterson, T. (2007). *Young people and news.* Report from the Joan Shorenstein Center on Press, Politics, and Public Policy, Harvard University.

Peiser, W. (2000). Cohort replacement and the downward trend in newspaper readership. *Newspaper Research Journal, 2*, 11–23.

Putnam, R. (2000). *Social Capital Benchmark Survey.* Saguaro Seminar at the John F. Kennedy School of Government, Harvard University.

Roberts, D. F. (2000). Media and youth: Access, exposure and privatization. *Journal of Adolescent Health, 27S*, 8–14.

Rojas, H. (2009). Strategy versus understanding: How orientations toward political conversation influence political engagement. *Communication Research, 35*, 452–481.

Schoenbach, K., McLeod, J. M., Lauf, E., & Scheufele, D. (1999). Distinction and integration: Sociodemographic determinants of newspaper reading in the USA and Germany, 1974–96. *European Journal of Communication, 14*, 225–239.

Shah, D. V., Cho, J., Eveland, W. P., & Kwak, N. (2005). Information and expression in a digital age: Modeling Internet effects on civic participation. *Communication Research, 32*, 531–565.

Shah, D. V., Cho, J., Nah, S., Gotlieb, M. R., Hwang, H., Lee, N., Scholl, R. M., & McLeod, D. M. (2007). Campaign ads, online messaging, and participation: Extending the communication mediation model. *Journal of Communication, 57*, 676–703.

Shah, D. V., McLeod, J. M., & Lee, N. (2009). Communication competence as a foundation for civic competence: Processes of socialization into citizenship. *Political Communication, 26:1*, 102–117.

Shah, D. V., McLeod, J. M., & Yoon, S-Y. (2001). Communication, context, and community: An exploration of print, broadcast, and Internet influences. *Communication Research, 28*, 464–506.

Sotirovic, M., & McLeod, J. M. (2004). Knowledge as understanding: The information processing approach to political learning. In L. Kaid (Ed.), *Handbook of political communication research* (pp. 357–394). Mahwah, NJ: Lawrence Erlbaum.

Sotirovic, M., & McLeod, J. M. (2008). U.S. media coverage: Persistence of tradition. In J. Stromback & L. Kaid (Eds.), *The handbook of election news coverage around the world.* (pp. 21–40). New York & London: Routledge.

Torney-Purta, J., Barber, C. E., & Wilkenfeld, B. (2007). Latino adolescents' civic development in the United States: Research results from the IEA Civic Education Study. *Journal of Youth and Adolescence, 36,* 111–125.

Torney-Purta, J., & Wilkenfeld, B. (2009). *Paths to 21st century competencies through civic education classrooms: An analysis of survey results from ninth graders* (A Technical Assistance Bulletin). Chicago: American Bar Association, Division on Public Education.

Torney-Purta, J., Wilkenfeld, B., & Barber, C. E. (2008). How adolescents in 27 countries understand, support and practice human rights. *Journal of Social Issues, 64,* 857–880.

Verba, S., Nie, N., & Kim, J. (1978). *Participation and political equality: A seven-nation comparision.* Cambridge: Cambridge University Press.

Verba, S., Schlozman, K. L., & Brady, H. E. (1995). *Voice and equality: Civic volunteerism in American politics.* Cambridge: Harvard University Press.

Wilkenfeld, B. (2009). *Does context matter? How the family, peer, school and neighborhood contexts relate to adolescents' civic engagement.* (Working Paper No. 64). Medford, MA: CIRCLE report and College for Citizenship and Public Service, Tufts University.

Zukin, C., Keeter, S., Andolina, M., Jenkins, K., & Delli Carpini, M. X. (2006). *A new engagement? Political participation, civic life, and the changing American citizen.* New York: Oxford University Press.

CHAPTER 15

Changing Citizen Identity and the Rise of a Participatory Media Culture

W. LANCE BENNETT, DEEN FREELON, AND CHRIS WELLS
University of Washington, Seattle

THE INTERNET AND the networked communication technologies based upon it represent new frontiers for the study of youth civic engagement in the twenty-first century. Unlike print, radio, and television, which are overwhelmingly managed by elites in a top-down fashion, these technologies allow for multidirectional pathways of user-driven production, consumption, appropriation, and pastiche. Moreover, the barriers to entry have in the past few years descended to the point that blogging, social networking (via sites like Facebook and MySpace), and watching videos on YouTube have become integrated into the daily routines of many young people. Despite some persistent socioeconomic divides in access and skills, the growing uses of social technologies have inspired a cautious optimism in some youth civic engagement scholars, who see hope for reversing the decades-long trend of declining civic engagement among younger demographic groups. In this chapter, we examine some of the evidence for and against this optimism, with the aim of identifying policy implications for developing more learning-rich online civic youth communities. We begin by reviewing theory and research suggesting that today's youth are by and large adopting a qualitatively different style of citizenship from their parents, and that the form and content of their media choices reflect this generational split. Next, we explore three distinct avenues of digital citizenship—video production and sharing, social networking web sites, and civic gaming—that attract young people in disproportionately large numbers. Finally, we present results from an original study that evaluated 90 youth civic engagement web sites in terms of the kinds of learning opportunities they offered their users.

AN OVERVIEW OF CONTEMPORARY MEDIA ENGAGEMENT TRENDS

An obvious place to start thinking about the role of media in youth engagement is with consumption of news and related public information. Demographic trends in news consumption make the youth civic engagement outlook seem bleak. Where roughly half of American adults over 30 claim to read the news pages of papers at least several times a week, barely half that number of teenagers make that claim (Patterson, 2007). The television picture is not much better. Hamilton (2004, pp. 85–90) reports that less than 10% of men and women aged 18 to 34 regularly view a nightly network news program, compared to 23% of men and 32% of women over age 50. The ratings for cops and crime reality TV programs beat National Public Radio in every demographic category except men over age 50. Conventional wisdom often points to the Internet as the place where young people encounter public issues. It is true that many teens (43%) say they regularly encounter news online (compared with 33% of those over 30), but closer inspection reveals that most of them (65%) say they just happen upon it, compared to 55% of Internet news users over 30 who say they seek out the news (Patterson, 2007).

Despite marketing efforts to salt the news with topics of interest to younger demographics (whom advertisers pay more to reach), the lack of interest in so-called hard or policy related news has proved an insurmountable obstacle (Hamilton, 2004, pp. 83–85). Pew (2007; 2008) surveys indicate that these trends are long-term and likely irreversible. In 1998 and 2008 Pew asked a survey sample whether they had encountered any news the day before. Overall, there was a rise of from 14 to 19% who reported going without news, but the sharpest rise was among those aged 18 to 24, where "newslessness" rose from 25 to 34%.

Not surprisingly, young citizens fare poorly on general political knowledge tests (identifying figures and issues in the news). For example, only 15% of American 18- to 29-year-olds fit into the high knowledge group in a Pew (2007) survey, compared to 35% of those aged 30 to 49, and 47% of 50- to 64-year-olds. These media trends have become a familiar litany among scholars who pronounce young citizens chronically disengaged. Wattenberg's (2008) careful look at comparable generations of news consumers going back as far as data permit (nearly a century in the case of newspapers) shows that each generation of young people over the past 40 years has dropped substantially in news consumption. For example, 70% of Americans born in the 1930s read newspapers on a daily basis by the time they turned 20, compared to just 20% of those born in the early 1980s. Equally steep declines mark parallel age groups with respect to television news consumption in later decades. In the 1940s, 50s, and 60s, for example, citizens under 30 were about as well informed as older age groups. After the 1970s, each decade saw younger generations become increasingly less informed and less likely to follow political issues and events (with a few notable exceptions such as 9/11). These trends are also true for many other democracies. Wattenberg (2008, p. 5) concludes, "Today's young adults are the least politically knowledgeable generation ever in the history of survey research."

Many scholars have associated these and other patterns in youth disconnection from civic media with declines in voting and other forms of political participation. Yet closer examination of the youth civic landscape indicates a far more complicated picture. For example, survey data analyzed by Zukin, Keeter, Andolina, Jenkins, & Delli Carpini (2006) show that, with the exception of election-related activities, young Americans participate in other areas of public life such as protests and consumer politics at rates comparable to or higher than older age brackets. Moreover, the steady rise of young voter turnout in the 2004 and 2008 elections suggests that the electoral participation gap may be closing.

Nonetheless, the media habits and information trends noted above still cause pessimism about the civic health of our youth. However, if we think differently about how information travels and how it is connected to civic action via social networks enabled by digital technologies, we may also think differently about how young people receive and apply information in their everyday political encounters. Among the early signs of a changing media and information environment was the rise of political comedy as a source of perspective on the news and political elites. Despite concerns expressed by many adults that young people were substituting shallow comedy for in-depth information, it turns out that political comedy audiences are remarkably well informed. Audiences of *The Daily Show* with Jon Stewart and *The Colbert Report* not only skew young, but they are the most knowledgeable of all media audiences (including regular news viewers). Fully 54% of Stewart and Colbert viewers fall into the highest information group in a Pew (2007) survey, compared to just 38% of network evening news viewers who do not watch the comedy programs. Moreover, 21% of the 18 to 29 demographic say they became more engaged in elections through political comedy (Young & Tisinger, 2006; Young & Esralew, 2007). Reflecting the complexity of the contemporary media system, engagement with these programs is not just a television experience; it also occurs online, via video streaming on computers and handheld devices, and by sharing links, clips, and mashups in e-mails and on social networking sites. The contemporary media landscape clearly engages young citizens differently than the legacy media did, in terms of what constitutes information, how it is linked to action options, and how it may be shared over peer networks.

One clear implication of these changes is that the notion of a citizen who receives abstract information through the news as a thing in itself, and then waits for some opportunity such as voting in order to apply it, may fit an older model of citizenship that emerged in a different social era with a different media system than exists today. There is evidence that sweeping social changes in the lived experiences of youth have combined with new information and communication technologies to change the ways in which young citizens tune in, engage, organize, and take action.

CHANGING CITIZEN IDENTITY AND THE NEW MEDIA ENVIRONMENT

It is clear that citizenship is not static. What defines the *good citizen* changes with the political, social, and communication systems of the times (Schudson, 1998). The current *late modern* era, dating from the globalization of societies in the late 1970s onward, is a period of important change in the expression of civic identities. Beginning in the late 1980s and into the 1990s, many observers began to detect important changes in the social and political orientations of recent generations in the post-industrial democracies. For example, in his survey of 43 nations, Inglehart (1997) noted a shift toward a "post-material" politics marked by a diminished sense of the personal relevance of government and growing dissatisfaction with the working of democratic processes. At the same time, younger citizens displayed increased interest in certain political issues including environmental quality, human rights, and consumer politics (Inglehart, 1997; Zukin et al., 2006; Torney-Purta, 2002).

Bennett (1998) has argued that, as a result of these changes, many younger citizens are less inclined to feel a sense of duty to participate politically, while displaying a greater inclination to embrace issues that connect to lifestyle values that can be shared across social networks with peers. By contrast, older generations described by Putnam (2000) and others experience citizenship more in terms of duty to participate in elections, parties, service organizations, and other government-centered activities. Young citizens entering their teens in the early years of the twenty-first century have experienced both generational and developmental changes, coming of age socially and politically in an era of global change that has affected social organization and identity formation in fundamental ways. In particular, the generation sometimes called Generation Y (following the so-called Generation X that came of age in the mid-to-late 1980s) has encountered development challenges associated with having fewer common group membership and social position cues to rely on for personal identification, resulting in greater personal responsibility (and associated stress) in identity expression and management (Giddens, 1991). Among the resources available for expression and experimentation in the development process are social media that enable broad networking through self-oriented content production and sharing via photos, videos, blogs, and ubiquitous texting.

In addition to self-expression and social relationship building through more loosely tied social media networks, young citizens have also adjusted the ways in which they think about credibility and authority. Despite the concern of many adults, young social media users are increasingly comfortable with replacing old gatekeepers such as journalists, teachers, and officials with crowd-sourced information flows developed through information aggregation technologies (e.g., Google news), wikis (e.g., Wikipedia), trusted friend networks (e.g., Facebook, LinkedIn, Move On), and recommendation engines (e.g., Amazon, iTunes).

These social identity and relationship shifts may help explain why many young people see an older civic regime based on membership organizations, public institutions, and officials as hierarchical and artificial. Young media consumers have developed a keen eye for authenticity, and often experience the staged public relations of government as distant and inauthentic (Coleman, 2008; Coleman & Blumler, 2009). They tend to favor more personally expressive or self-actualizing politics, communicated in peer-to-peer networking environments (Bennett, 2007, 2008; Palfrey & Gasser, 2008).

In short, it seems clear that the dominant model of citizenship for the past century, dating from the progressive era, is changing (Bennett, 1998, 2007, 2008; Bennett, Wells, & Rank, 2009). We have termed this legacy model *Dutiful Citizenship* (DC) in light of its core precept that civic engagement is a matter of duty or obligation. It holds that becoming informed consists of consuming information from authoritative sources such as officials, admitted into public discourse through media gatekeepers such as newspapers and television newscasts. By contrast, increasing numbers of (predominantly younger) citizens are motivated by the potential of personally expressive politics animated by social networks where information and action tend to be integrated and authenticated in trusted peer-to-peer relationships that promote engagement. This *Actualizing Citizenship* (AC) style may not lead to learning abstract or factual information, but it can produce knowledge sharing on specific issues around which social action networks emerge. The general outlines of these two models of citizenship are contained in Table 15.1.

The important caveat here is that neither model is superior to the other. Nor are particular individuals (or demographic groups) likely to subscribe exclusively to one model over the other. We are talking about ideal types that highlight general tendencies and trends. Since the DC model has a considerable cultural legacy, most people understand the ideals of connecting with government and being informed, but many AC citizens may see

Table 15.1
Dutiful and Actualizing Styles of Civic Action and Communication

	Civic Style	Communication Logic
Dutiful	• Oriented around citizen input to government or formal public organizations, institutions, and campaigns • Rooted in responsibility and duty • Channeled through membership in defined social groups	• Primarily one-way consumption of managed civic information (from news, partisan organizations, and political ads) • Individual expression most often aimed at specific institutional targets (contacting elected officials, letters to newspapers)
Actualizing	• Open to many forms of creative civic expression, from government to consumer politics to global activism • Rooted in self-actualization through social expression • Personal interests channeled through loosely tied networks	• Lines between content consumption and production blurred • Peer or crowd sourced information (e.g., wikipedia) is authoritative • Interactive content sharing over peer networks that personalize citizen identity and engagement

government as less central, and assemble information from non-news sources in the process of networking with others in personally expressive ways.

While these ideal types are not mutually exclusive, there seem to be broad differences in their related engagement and media use habits across social generations. This does not mean that all members of demographics born after 1980 are AC citizens or that all born before then display only DC qualities. Many young people who grow up today in families that emphasize politics as traditionally practiced continue to acquire DC identifications. Likewise, many senior citizens who participated in the protest and liberation politics of the 1960s and 1970s embrace the more fluid styles of AC politics, tempered by a sense of obligation to follow issues in the news and vote. However, we think that these different civic styles can help account for the often puzzling generational differences in political orientations or socialization found in recent survey research (e.g., Lopez et al., 2006).

The generational shift in civic styles does not mean that young citizens should be given an automatic pass for not knowing who government leaders are or what is going on with key issues in Washington. However, it does suggest that the picture of disengaged and uninformed youth that has haunted the literature for decades may not be as accurate as previously thought. It has long been clear, for example, that young audiences view news with (perhaps appropriate) skepticism, and sample their information more broadly as media genres blur and information channels proliferate (Bennett, 2008). Indeed, the proliferation of media channels and consumer platforms makes the old idea of distributing news or political advertising to large-scale audiences something of a throwback to the mass media era. If we ask about media experiences, we discover that large numbers of youth have all but abandoned television for games, social media, and online video. In fact, young males have become so scarce in television audiences that the Obama campaign in 2008 put ads in video games.

It is challenging to sort out whether changes in the social experiences of youth have spurred the social media revolution, or whether the development of social media has stimulated different patterns of self-expression and social organization. However, it is worth noting that there is nothing inherent in the design of digital media that requires flattened network organizations or interactivity. Indeed the differences in digital media applications between the Obama and McCain campaigns in the 2008 election suggest that media use more reflects social orientation than causes it.

The Changing Media Experience in the 2008 American Presidential Election

The 2008 American presidential election put the spotlight on media and participation trends that have been developing for more than a decade: Youth, who prefer participatory digital media that emphasize content users, may help to produce, consume, and share with others. This means that young citizens are not just the targets of content but active participants in the creation and targeting of content through their social networks. These shifts hold important keys to understanding the nature of youth engagement and the future roles of media in the engagement process.

Surveys by Pew show that digital media came into their own as means of engagement during the 2008 election. Not only did increasing numbers of voters find information online, they also reported sharing that information with others. In comparison to previous elections, staggering numbers gave money (primarily to the Democrats) through small contributions online. Moreover, 50% of young voters 18 to 29 went online for information about campaigns or politics during the primary season, up from 36% in 2004. By contrast, the online news experience of 50- to 64-year-olds was limited to 31% and 36% in 2004 and 2008, respectively (Smith & Rainie, 2008, p. 4). Youth are also far more prolific content creators than older citizens—those 18 to 29 years old are more likely to post original political commentary online than the next three demographic groups combined, and over 50% more likely to use social networking web sites for political purposes (Smith

& Rainie, 2008, pp. 10–11). (We discuss the socio-technological mechanisms underpinning these patterns of content sharing and creation in greater detail in the following section.)

The volume and forms of digital media use suggest an important change in the relationship of young citizens to communication processes, and the possibility of redefining their engagement experiences. The Obama campaign of 2008 offers many examples of the ways in which more conventional (mass) media and newer digital or participatory media experiences can combine to produce a range of different engagement experiences in an electoral context. Going well beyond the Dean campaign of 2004, the War Room command model of campaign communication was integrated in the Obama organization (Silberman, 2009). On the conventional side, the Obama campaign spent record amounts on television advertising, At the same time, the campaign developed and deployed an astonishing array of social media, including blogging communities, twitter feeds, and regular e-mailings of action alerts with embedded video clips featuring the candidate and other campaign leaders exhorting people to organize their own campaign events, donate money, and recruit friends.

An even more telling aspect of this participatory media trend was the large number of digital media artifacts produced and distributed by campaign followers (Jenkins, 2006). Indeed, in both campaigns, the most viewed videos online were not official candidate-endorsed productions but independent productions by supporters. These viral videos on the Obama side ranged from the highly polished *Yes We Can* music video produced by singers will.i.am and Jakob Dylan (with some 24 million views), to the whimsical *Obama Girl* (with nearly 14 million YouTube views), and many more humble DIY mashups. The most-viewed McCain video was *Dear Mr. Obama* (nearly 14 million YouTube views), made by a returning war veteran challenging Obama's war position. And in the blogosphere, Obama received an average of 11,826 daily blog mentions between the launch of his campaign in 2007 through Election Day, compared to 7,370 average daily blog mentions for McCain over the course of his campaign (TechPresident, 2008).

For many younger voters these experiences with digital media seem to have changed their relationship to the election process itself (not just their sense of identification with the candidate) (Waggener-Edstrom, 2008). Young voters—more than any demographic group with the possible exception of Latinos—were instrumental in helping Barack Obama achieve his Electoral College landslide in 2008. Turnout among eligible voters was up to 53% in the 18 to 29 age bracket, representing a 5% gain over 2004, and 11% over 2000 (CIRCLE, 2009). More importantly, those young voters cast roughly two-thirds of their votes for Obama—a 13-point swing to Obama compared to Kerry in 2004. This meant that states not ordinarily in play for the Democrats were importantly involved in the 2008 election. In fact, majorities of voters under 30 sided with the Democrats in all but nine states, with Obama gaining 72% of the youth vote in North Carolina, and unprecedented levels in a number of other states (Jacobson, 2008). Overall, exit polls revealed the Obama majority among voters under 30 at 70%, the largest youth vote swing in the history of exit polling (Fraser & Dutta, 2008).

These trends suggest a possible reversal of decades of youth disconnection from the most important foundation of the democratic process. However, they also suggest something important about the involvement of younger voters in the election, and other aspects of civic life, through their use of social media. To fully understand changes in the youth civic experience, it is necessary to explore the types of participatory civic media operating in the contemporary mediascape. In the following section we examine the dynamics of three distinct forms of digitally mediated engagement: online video sharing, social public networking, and civic gaming.

THE PARTICIPATORY MEDIA SHIFT IN YOUTH CIVIC ENGAGEMENT

The rise of participatory practices centered around social media seems to make a special contribution to a reversing low civic engagement among young people. Our position on the reciprocal dynamic between digital networks and civic and political affairs thus diverges from scholars who claim that digital media will necessarily lead to ideological polarization (Galston, 2003; Sunstein, 2007) or benefit only the already politically engaged (Agre, 2002; Margolis & Resnick, 2000). In this section we describe what is new about digitally mediated civic activity and contrast several prominent forms with their waning 20th-century counterparts. Key cases and research findings drawn from the domains of both electoral and non-electoral politics evidence a broad increase in the capacity of average citizens to seek out, remix, reframe, and create civic and political content—becoming actualizing citizens. Moreover, globe-spanning social networks supported by interactive technologies (and disproportionately adopted by youth) have radically transformed older forms of civic action including protests, journalism, and political campaign mobilization efforts. Although the civic applications of participatory media are numerous, there are inherent limiting factors—including inequities of skill, attention, and opportunity—that significantly skew participation.

Jenkins defines *participatory cultures* as networks of technologically linked individuals that display the following properties:

- Relatively low barriers to artistic expression and civic engagement
- Strong support for creating and sharing one's creations with others

- Some type of informal mentorship whereby what is known by the most experienced is passed along to novices
- Members believe that their contributions matter
- Members feel some degree of social connection with one another (at the least they care what other people think about what they have created) (2006, p. 7)

Participatory cultures coalesce around digital media forms whose properties contrast sharply with traditional or *old* media, which were designed to distribute prepackaged content to mass audiences via one-way transmission channels (Bennett, 2008; Bowman & Willis, 2003; Miel & Faris, 2008). While many of the participatory cases cited in the literature are decidedly non-civic in nature, such as networks of reality-TV fans and pop-culture pastiche artists (Jenkins, 2008), numerous civic participatory cultures have emerged as well. They reflect a distinctly different media and information culture captured in such scholarly concepts as networked individualism (Wellman et al., 2003), the networked public sphere (Benkler, 2006), and actualizing citizenship (Bennett, 2008). All of these perspectives focus on ways in which digital technologies are empowering motivated individuals to engage with others in public affairs. These scholars emphasize that civic participatory cultures are not completely encapsulated within the technological structures that support them. They are best conceptualized as hybrid strategies that combine on- and offline tactics in the service of the civic goal at hand. Three prominent variants of participatory media engagement in which youth are disproportionately represented—online video, social networking, and civic gaming—are discussed below.

Online Video Streaming on-demand video is a rapidly expanding medium, especially among young people. Unlike traditional information outlets, which function as unidirectional content conveyor belts for passive consumers, each online video view represents an individual's conscious choice to actively access the messages found there. By the end of 2007, 70% of U.S. Internet users aged 18 to 29 had visited a video-sharing web site such as YouTube (Rainie, 2008), and 42% of Americans aged 18 to 34 reported watching video online at least weekly (Leichtman Research Group, 2008). Much of this video content is undoubtedly entertainment-oriented, but available evidence indicates that youth (aged 18–29) are more likely to watch online political video clips (such as commercials, speeches, and interviews) than their elders (Smith & Rainie, 2008). This is particularly striking in light of the aforementioned fact that increasing numbers of youth claim to consume no *news* at all (Pew, 2008).

Several key election events of the recent past provide evidence supporting the viability of online video as a vehicle for youth-oriented political messages.

Perhaps the most memorable video of the American 2006 midterm elections was the clip of George Allen, Republican senatorial candidate for Virginia, publicly using a racial slur against a man of Indian descent who was video-recording him at a campaign stop. This single incident has been cited as decisive in Allen's loss at the polls (Kerbel, 2009; Panagopolous, 2007). The fact that his target was college-aged probably did little to endear him to the first-time voter demographic, and the video became one of YouTube's most viewed. Less dramatic but similar clips occasionally materialized on the American national news agenda throughout 2007, among them John McCain singing "Bomb, bomb, Iran" to the tune of the Beach Boys' song "Barbara Ann" and a portrayal of Hillary Clinton as Big Brother in a parody/homage to a classic Apple Computer television advertisement. Many of these clips originate from politically interested citizens armed with inexpensive digital video editing software and digital video recorders for capturing live TV. It has been argued that the "YouTube effect"—co-produced by political outsiders and fueled by youth viewership—has lessened the ability of campaigns to manage their messages (Gueorguieva, 2008; Steinhauser, 2007).

Digital media also appear to be reconfiguring the dynamics of political contention in countries that lack freedom of expression. For example, many young Iranians protesting the results of their 2009 election organized and communicated using text-messaging, Facebook, Twitter, photos, and video. The power to communicate a raw, emotional, and politically potent message bypassing official attempts at censorship was illustrated by the famous video documenting the death of Neda Agha-Soltan, a young woman shot near one of the protests. According to *The New York Times*, the man who recorded the footage was aware of the danger involved in distributing his video. He sent it by e-mail to a friend in Iran, who in turn passed it to Western news outlets and friends in Europe, one of whom posted the video on Facebook, "weeping as he did so" (Stelter & Stone, 2009). Within hours, the wrenching video was being shown on CNN and other news outlets, discussed via Twitter, and accumulating views on YouTube and Facebook (CNN, 2009). Within days it had become a striking symbol (Stelter & Stone, 2009), conveying the youth, idealism, and innocence of the protesters—both within Iran and to a global audience.

As suggested earlier, the potential for large-scale youth engagement via participatory media was demonstrated by the volume of media sharing surrounding Barack Obama during the 2008 American presidential election. During the month prior to the election, the official "BarackObamadotcom" YouTube channel accrued 20 million views for its hosted videos, making it the most viewed YouTube channel, surpassing those of Britney Spears and Beyoncé Knowles. This does not include the copies of Obama videos hosted by users unaffiliated with the campaign. Further, while campaign speeches and political advertisements accounted for a substantial proportion of Obama video views, many of the most popular Obama videos did not resemble traditional hard-news fare. Perhaps the most well-known of these freewheeling election-themed clips featured the aforementioned Obama Girl, a suggestively clothed actress who lip-synched an ode to the Democratic presidential nominee in a 2007 MTV-style video. Dozens of clips released in 2007 to 2008 followed this basic quasi-political formula, providing enterprising remix artists with plenty of opportunities to express their own opinions. It is difficult to measure the mechanisms for secondary engagement with these videos through e-mail forwarding, blogging, and comments on the video sites. However, it is clear that the transmission and modification of content across social networks is responsible for creating viral audiences in the absence of conventional mass media broadcast and scheduled viewing arrangements.

Social Networking The shift in the scope of online social networking technologies from small niche populations to the American mainstream was driven primarily by teenagers (Boyd & Ellison, 2008). For this reason, the most popular social network sites (SNSs) in the United States, MySpace and Facebook, remain havens of youth culture even as older demographics have begun to gravitate toward them (Boyd, 2008; Lenhart & Madden, 2007). Though they are used primarily as spaces to establish new interpersonal ties and reinforce existing ones, SNSs have recently proven effective for disseminating political messages and calls to action independently of traditional, membership-based civic institutions. Civic applications of social networking are especially pronounced among young adults: Nearly a third of the 18–29 age group reports using SNSs for political purposes (Smith & Rainie, 2008). These civic uses include identifying friends' political interests, receiving candidate information, joining political groups, and organizing offline political events.

In 2008, it is not surprising that political SNS uses associated with the election drew considerable popular and scholarly attention. Obama's comparative mastery of online networking was in full evidence throughout the campaign. By Election Day in November, 2008, over two million Americans had signed up for Facebook groups supporting Obama, while only 600,000 had done so for McCain (Fraser & Dutta, 2008). Obama's home-grown social network platform, MyBarackObama, starkly outperformed its counterpart McCainSpace in terms of both audience size and range of available user affordances (Project for Excellence in Journalism, 2008). Obama raised far more money than McCain through social-network–based outreach to small donors (Weisel, 2008), and used his larger supporter database to mobilize canvassing, phone-banking, and in-person networking efforts.

In addition to their efficacy in helping presidential candidates get elected, SNSs are also widely used by other political actors who operate largely in opposition to formal governmental and corporate structures. Social networking technologies are critical tools in the modern antiwar and antiglobalization movements (Bennett, 2008; Bennett, Breunig, & Givens, 2008), which rely on them to recruit and engage interested individuals. Facebook in particular has been used to organize offline protests against powerful interests around the world, including governments in the United States, Myanmar, Colombia, Egypt, South Africa, and Iran.

In much the same fashion, less overtly political protests have deployed the instrumentalities of social networks to attempt to convince political and economic elites to address their concerns. The user communities of Facebook,World of Warcraft, and Second Life have organized online protests and petitions against the parent companies of these services in response to unpopular changes in functionality (Earl & Schussman, 2008; Ondrejka, 2005; Rogers, 2008). While this network activity may resemble traditional consumer pressure movements more than street-storming political activism, the participatory logics that power it are similar. Consistent with this, Earl and Schussman (2008) argue that network-based attempts by fans to petition media corporations may help young people develop *repertoires of contention* that inform future attitudes toward civic engagement.

Civic Gaming One of the frontiers in online youth engagement research evaluates the potential of virtual environments to help young people learn and practice civic skills. The burgeoning literature in this area addresses the civic potential of both commercial games and more topic-specific *civic games*. The available data on young people's gaming reveals the breadth of the potential audience for these approaches. A recent survey found youth gaming a nearly universal phenomenon, with 97% of respondents aged 12 to 17 reporting playing some form of video game (Lenhart et al., 2008). Most promisingly, this study empirically identifies a set of *civic gaming experiences*—incorporating Jenkins's (2006) participatory skills of play, performance, and simulation—that predict youth civic engagement in the offline world. These experiences include helping other players, interacting with a social issue within the context of the game, making decisions about how a community or society should be run, and organizing groups of players in multiplayer games (Lenhart et al., 2008).

The Sims Online and *Second Life* are two examples of for-profit multiplayer gaming environments that were not constructed with civic intentions in mind, but which present players with meaningful civic opportunities (Gordon & Koo, 2008; Jenkins, 2008; Joseph, 2008; Ondrejka, 2008). Jenkins (2008) shows how residents of Alphaville, a virtual city within *The Sims*

Online, addressed their virtual social problems (including prostitution, organized crime, and fraud) through democratic processes closely modeled after their offline equivalents. Ondrejka (2008) takes this argument a step further, contending that *Second Life* should not be considered a game at all, but a "virtual world" distinguished principally by "the ability of residents to generate creations of value within a shared, simulated, 3D space" (p. 231). Thus far, these collaborations have included virtual summer camps for discussing global issues (Joseph, 2008), peer-to-peer teaching of the scripting skills necessary to create *Second Life* objects (Ondrejka, 2008), and simulacra of real-world spaces in which citizens deliberate about the use of the actual spaces (Gordon & Koo, 2008).

The finding that electronic gameplay can yield substantial civic dividends has inspired some civic practitioners and educators to partner with game designers to produce specialized civic games with explicitly pedagogical purposes. They are intended to apply young people's gaming instincts to learn about and brainstorm solutions to specific social and political issues including poverty (Ayiti; see Joseph, 2008), immigration law (ICED: I Can End Deportation), peak oil (World Without Oil), and the aftermath of Hurricane Katrina (Hurricane Katrina: Tempest in Crescent City). Future research can profitably focus on identifying the skills and/or knowledge gains resulting from playing civic games and who is most likely to benefit.

The Limits of Participatory Civic Media Cultures

The foregoing profiles of three relatively new forms of youth-oriented mediated civic engagement do not exhaust the universe of possible civic participatory cultures. Rather, they illustrate some of the most common patterns of civic action built upon networks of loose, interest-based ties. The rise in online video as a political information source reflects an increasing willingness on the part of youth to actively seek out, attend to, and share civic content they perceive as personally relevant or interesting. The use of social networking web sites as distribution channels for traditional and peer-to-peer political messages, ideology-broadcasting, and action alerts illustrates how profit-driven networks can be repurposed to civic ends. Civic gaming is an even more dramatic instance of this process, given the ostensibly frivolous character of video games; it is precisely their lack of explicit connection to the "real" world that makes them attractive environments for the performance and simulation of civic behavior.

Despite the dramatic rise in use of these new forms of media, the potential of mediated civic participatory culture is neither fully realized nor evenly distributed. Two key limiting factors bear mentioning. First, despite the conventional wisdom that young people are *digital natives* with a seemingly inborn understanding of participatory media (Bauerlein, 2008; Palfrey & Gasser, 2008; Tapscott, 2009), not all of them possess the skills necessary to utilize the vast array of digital tools available to them (Hargittai, 2005; Hargittai & Walejko, 2008). Thus, the need for formal training in participatory media skills has recently emerged on the scholarly agenda (Jenkins, 2006; Rheingold, 2008). Second, participatory skills are too often the exclusive province of empowered and self-selected elite. This problem is exacerbated by one of the fundamental characteristics of user-generated content—namely that it tends to follow power-law distributions; a minority of participants produce the vast majority of contributions and receive correspondingly disproportionate attention (Adamic & Glance, 2005; Benkler, 2006; Fisher, Smith, & Welser, 2006; Shirky, 2003).

An important implication is that young citizens need training and opportunities to experiment with online civic participation. Solving the problem of unequal attention means creating online civic experiences that both make sense to a broad range of first-time users and provide motivating feedback (Levine, 2008). In recognition of the need to broaden the civic experience online, there has been rapid growth in sites aimed at engaging young citizens in formal political activities (Montgomery et al., 2004). However, it appears that relatively few offer clear opportunities to learn general civic participation skills beyond joining a particular online community (Bachen et al., 2008). Indeed, there is little in the way of clear conceptualization of what kinds of civic skills various online media sites can offer to young users, and how those skills are best presented.

To begin addressing these problems, researchers at the Center for Communication and Civic Engagement (CCCE) recently completed a study of 90 of North America's most-trafficked youth civic engagement web sites. The aims of this study were: first, to develop definitions and distinct measures of civic learning opportunities that may be learned in online communities; second, to associate civic skills learning with Actualizing and Dutiful citizenship types; and third, to map the distribution of those civic learning opportunities across different kinds of sites in the existing youth civic web sphere.

CIVIC LEARNING AND CITIZENSHIP STYLES IN THE YOUTH CIVIC WEB

Young people have in fact begun to take advantage of many online civic opportunities, but these opportunities are not equally prevalent, comprehensible, or interesting to various elements of their target audiences. As the foregoing discussion has shown, civic action can manifest in a wide variety of contexts, from online games, such as World of Warcraft, to SNSs like Facebook, to web sites created with the express aim of fostering youth engagement such as Youth Noise and TakingITGlobal. Youth Noise is a lively U.S. site with over 100,000 users who discuss various issues and share videos that range from personal life stories to global problems. TakingIT Global is a large online community with users around the world who receive alerts about issues, create profiles, and post actions that they have taken to address problems. Assessing the range of civic learning opportunities online is simplified by focusing on the more explicitly civic sites, which represent a wide array of opportunities for youth to become involved and express themselves on topics such as voting, environmental protection, community service, climate change, and gay rights. Although SNSs like Facebook and MySpace do engage youth in occasional episodes of civic participation, the critical design choices underlying those sites do not communicate clear conceptions of citizenship, nor are they concerned with developing the civic skills of users. By contrast, sites that embrace explicitly civic missions are more likely to offer clearer conceptions of citizenship and civic skills. The question is: What sorts of civic skills are available to members of online communities, and how do they compare to the more formal skills found in civic education programs in schools?

Developing a Typology of Civic Learning Online

Our approach to developing measures of civic learning that might be identified in different online civic youth environments began with a review of the literature on civic learning in schools. From this we derived four general categories considered essential to civic education: *knowledge,* which citizens need to inform their civic decisions; *expression,* skills needed to make one's voice heard; skills for *joining publics* to amplify one's own voice and pursue collective action around issues of common concern; and skills to *take action* (Gibson & Levine, 2003; Niemi & Junn, 1998; Pasek et al., 2008; Syvertsen et al., 2007). A more detailed discussion of this typology and its origins can be found in Bennett, Wells and Rank (2009) and further explication of some of these issues in the chapters by Haste and by Wilkenfeld, Lauckhardt, and Torney-Purta (this volume).

It is clear that each of these broad categories of civic learning may contain some skills more likely to appeal to Dutiful Citizens, while other aspects of learning in the same category may better engage Actualizing Citizens (Bennett, 2007; 2008). For example, knowledge may be delivered through one-way authoritative channels such as teachers, textbooks, or news reports, consistent with a DC citizen style oriented to external authorities and hierarchical relationships. Alternately, knowledge may be derived through shared peer accounts and original experiences more compatible with a personally expressive and socially networked AC style. Of course, both approaches to acquiring knowledge may be combined with salutary results. For example, research in civic education suggests that learning outcomes are enhanced when students have the opportunity to define and lead class activities, discussion, and decision making (Campbell, 2005; Pasek et al., 2008; Torney-Purta, 2002). When no such participatory activities are available, student interest in civic participation is often reduced (Syvertsen et al., 2007). We suggest that this is because more traditional, top-down education methods focus almost exclusively on DC skills and orientations that are less likely to provide for the peer knowledge sharing and networking preferences of AC citizens.

Drawing on this background framework, we developed measures to assess the forms of civic learning available to users of different web sites in our sample of the youth civic web. Specifically, each general category of learning (knowledge, expression, joining, and acting) could manifest in both Dutiful and Actualizing forms. Thus, sites that tell their users what they should know about an issue are offering a DC learning opportunity to acquire knowledge, whereas sites that enable users to cite their own sources of information or share their own experiences are offering an AC opportunity to acquire information. Just as effective classrooms may combine both AC (participatory) and DC (top-down) learning, so may youth engagement sites combine both types of learning. This analytical framework, with the definitions of all eight forms of learning, is displayed in Table 15.2.

Table 15.2

Dutiful and Actualizing Forms of the Four Learning Goals

Civic Learning Opportunity	General Description	Dutiful (DC) Form	Actualizing (AC) Form
Knowledge	Information that citizens should know	Information provided by authorities (e.g., teachers, news reports)	Information created and shared by peers
Expression	Training in effective public communication skills	Training for traditional forms of public address (e.g., letters to editors, government officials)	Training for self-produced digital media (e.g., blogs, wikis)
Joining Publics	Learning how to connect to others through networks and groups	Membership in site-defined, structured organizations	Membership in self-defined networks and groups
Take Action	Actions that engaged citizens can take	Activities defined and offered by authority figures	Activities generated or reported by peers

The leftmost column of Table 15.2 lists the four general categories of learning, as derived from the literature on civic education. We have not included here a fifth general category found in the literature: political orientations such as trust, legitimacy, confidence in institutions, and efficacy, among others. The reason is that these cannot be identified as direct learning opportunities on web sites, but are more likely to be the result of the quality of learning and resulting civic practice (see Beaumont, this volume). To the right of each of our four learning categories is a general definition. In the third and fourth columns, each category of learning is divided into its two forms: Dutiful and Actualizing. For example, within the Knowledge category, we defined information that was provided by the site or other authorities and represented as something visitors should learn as appealing to the Dutiful citizen, while information that was generated and shared among peers is more appealing to the Actualizing type. Similarly, within Take Action, actions specified and recommended by the site or authorities were defined as Dutiful, while those suggested or reported by site users are classified as Actualizing.

Sampling the Youth Civic Web Sphere We applied this civic learning framework to a broad range of youth sites that could be regarded as having an explicitly civic mission, whether recruiting new members to interest organizations or providing spaces for sharing videos and blog posts on matters of concern to adolescents. The sphere of explicitly youth oriented civic engagement sites includes a wide variety of sites that vary by their owners' affiliations (e.g., party, NGO, government, foundation, independent youth activists) and their related conceptions of citizenship, engagement, and democracy (Coleman, 2008). To build our sample, we reviewed literature containing inventories of youth civic sites (Montgomery et al., 2004; Bennett & Xenos, 2004, 2005) and supplemented it with targeted searches, resulting in the identification of 264 primarily U.S. youth civic web sites that were active in May 2008. In order to assess whether different types of organizations differed in models of citizenship and civic learning opportunities they offered users, we sorted the sites into four categories: Online Only sites, which lack offline civic infrastructures (e.g., TakingITGlobal, Idealist.org, Youthnoise); the web sites of government agencies and the major 2008 presidential candidates (e.g., Peace Corps, EPA's youth page, Barack Obama's election site); Community/Service organizations, which emphasize youth leadership and character development (e.g., YMCA, Key Club, and 4H); and Interest/Activist sites, which espouse political-issue-oriented movements or causes (e.g., the youth outreach pages of the NRA, Sierra Club, and ACLU). A complete list of sites in our sample is available in our full project report (Bennett, Wells, & Freelon, 2009).

Using compete.com, a popular Internet traffic-measuring tool, we ranked the sites in each category by the amount of traffic they received in the spring of 2008. We adjusted the final sample slightly by replacing the web sites of national-level organizations with randomly selected local affiliates (e.g., we used a North Carolina chapter of 4H rather than the national organization). We also weighted the sample to include 35 Online Only, 15 Government/ Candidate, 20 Community/Service, and 20 Interest/Activist sites. The over-sample of online only sites enabled us to include a broader spectrum of this rapidly expanding and diverse sector of the web sphere. The slightly smaller government/candidate subsample reflected the relatively smaller offering of youth sites in this sector. All statistical comparisons were corrected for differences in subsample sizes. These sites were then coded for the types of civic learning described in the last section.

Measuring Civic Learning in the Youth Engagement Web Sphere To apply this framework to the web sphere sample, we developed a two-step coding process to avoid confounding the coding decisions for type of civic learning opportunity (knowledge, expression, joining publics, taking action) with decisions about the citizenship style (AC/DC) expressed by each of those opportunities. In the first step, three coders identified the specific pages on each web site that offered one or more of the four categories of learning. Navigating from the home page, they investigated each page linked from the site's main menu bars and searched for any pages containing a general learning opportunity (knowledge, etc.) on each site. This team of coders did not judge whether the opportunity was AC or DC or both. Their catalog of pages that contained some version of each category of learning was then turned over to a different group of coders. These coders applied content analysis codes to each page selected in step one to determine whether a page represented a Dutiful or Actualizing version of the selected learning goal, or whether both forms of the learning goal were present. Each site could be coded as embodying zero or one Dutiful learning opportunity and zero or one Actualizing opportunity for each of the four learning goals. Intercoder agreement for step one was 84.4% overall, and ranged from 82% for Joining Publics to 90% for Take Action; for step two, overall reliability was 91%, and ranged from 78% for the Actualizing knowledge acquisition opportunities to 100% for Dutiful knowledge learning opportunities.

From all 90 sites, our study identified 213 pages on which one or more of the four categories of learning were present, yielding 255 total learning opportunities. The larger number of learning opportunities than pages was due to multiple coding for presence of an AC opportunity and a DC opportunity. Of the 255 civic learning opportunities in the sample, 194 (76%) were classified as DC, and 61 (24%) were coded as AC, indicating a strong overall trend toward the former.

Figure 15.1 depicts the distribution of DC and AC forms of the four civic learning opportunities across the four site types. The cumulative height of each bar represents the percentage of sites of a given type that was coded as manifesting any form (only AC, only DC, or both) of the learning opportunity in question. The gray segments represent the fraction of this percentage in which the DC opportunity appeared without its AC counterpart. The predominance of DC across all site types and nearly all learning opportunities is evident here, with the sole exception being the Online Only category, which accounts for the vast majority of AC opportunities in the sample—42 out of 61 total AC learning opportunities (and all but one of the 19 web pages in which only Actualizing opportunities occurred). This means that roughly two-thirds of the learning opportunities appealing to actualizing civic styles were concentrated in online only site types that constituted just over one third of our sample. When viewed in terms of averages, Online Only sites averaged many more Actualizing opportunities overall (1.2 per site, compared to 0.5 for Government, 0.2 for Community/Service, and 0.4 for Interest/Activist sites).

Despite containing relatively more Actualizing features than the other site categories, Online Only sites are by no means dominated by the AC orientation. As Figure 15.1 also shows, except for the Expression learning goal, Actualizing learning opportunities are most likely to occur alongside

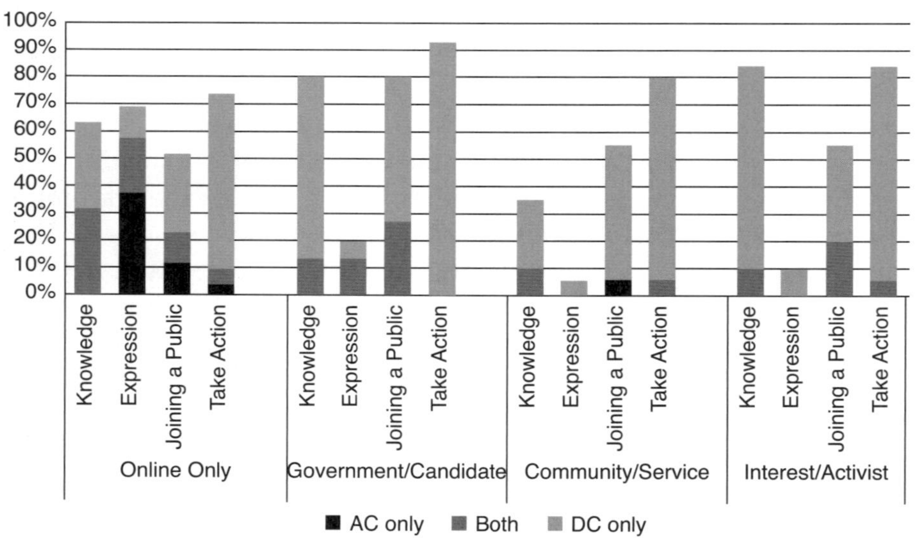

Figure 15.1 Distribution of Civic Learning Opportunities in Four Different Types of Youth Online Communities

Dutiful ones (hence the large *both* bands in most bars) rather than by themselves. And we found relatively few Actualizing opportunities to join publics and take action at all: Only 23% of Online Only sites offered Actualizing Joining Publics opportunities, and only 9% offered Actualizing Take Action experiences.

Figure 15.2 offers a closer look at the kinds of learning opportunities offered by Online Only sites, which are far and away the most balanced in terms of matching the learning opportunities to citizen identity styles. The number of Dutiful learning opportunities per site is displayed along the horizontal axis and the number of Actualizing opportunities appears on the vertical axis. This chart reveals considerable diversity in the number of total learning opportunities offered by these sites (roughly, the spread from lower left to upper right), and the number of Dutiful opportunities (left to right spread). Actualizing opportunities, however, are rather concentrated around one and two per site, and 21 of the 35 sites offer more Dutiful learning opportunities than Actualizing (only six offer more of the latter than of the former).

The Online Only group of sites included several exemplary sites that offered very rich arrays of both Dutiful and Actualizing learning opportunities. The five sites at the top right of the chart, Do Something, Campus

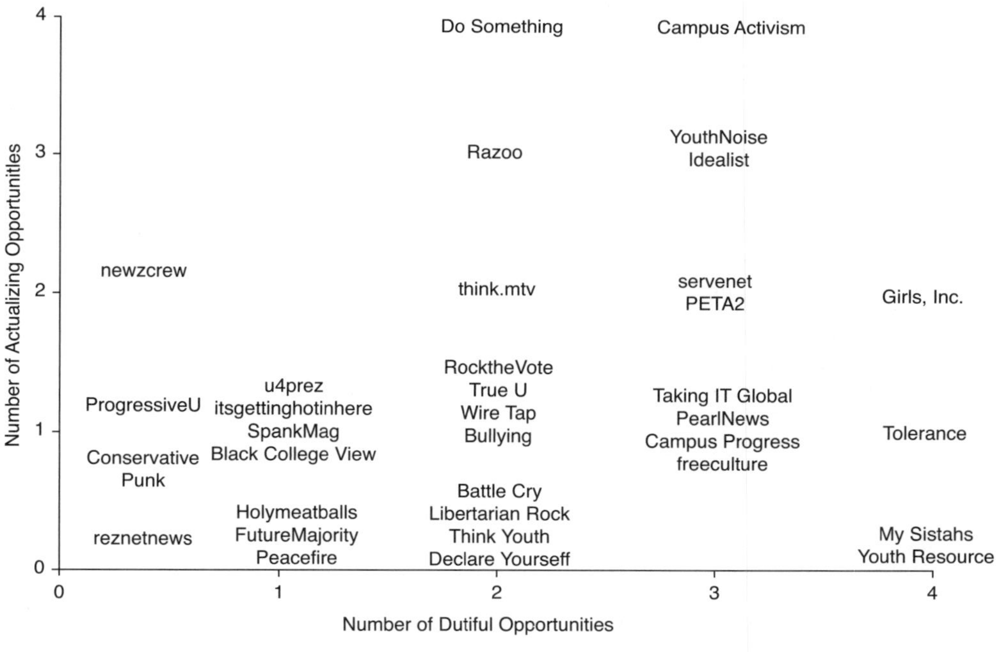

Figure 15.2 Balance of Civic Learning in Online Only Youth Communities Arrayed by Number of Actualizing and Dutiful Opportunities (May 2008)

Activism, Razoo, Youth Noise, and Idealist, were particularly rich, with each one offering three or four Actualizing learning opportunities and two or three Dutiful ones. What set these sites apart? First, it is worth noting the participatory latitude that all five grant to users. Except for Campus Activism, which was a sort of clearinghouse for young activists to post information on campaigns, organizations, and contact information, all of the sites were built on a social networking model. They offered users ways of connecting with social issues on individually defined terms and ample opportunity for individual identity expression, for example, through customizable profiles for themselves and personal friend networks. At the same time, through structure, tone, and content, each of the sites also offered more conventional, Dutiful learning, often in the form of pages with information about specific social issues and suggestions about actions to take to get involved. (For a more thorough exploration of the theory, methods, and implications of this research, see Bennett, Wells, & Freelon, 2009.)

The Current State of the Youth Civic Web Our results indicate that the youth civic web in 2008 hosted an impressive collection of civic learning opportunities. However, the inescapable conclusion is that the online world we observed tended to mirror the school environment in the overall dominance of the Dutiful citizenship model. This likely reflected the generational differences of those who develop school curricula and sponsor online youth sites. Only an exemplary subset of the five Online Only sites noted above appeared to have struck a critical balance between AC and DC, offering young visitors government- and issue-centered civic content alongside interactive opportunities to publicly develop their own understandings of what *civic* means. However, the sites outside the Online Only category tended to resemble K–12 civic curricula content-wise, focusing heavily on DC at the expense of AC. In particular, it seemed likely that many of the major youth civic, service, and interest-based organizations were straightforwardly transferring their offline work and organizational models onto their web sites without taking advantage of the participatory qualities of digitally networked media. We saw this reflected in the ways our four learning categories were presented on their sites: Knowledge was typically presented in terms of information users should absorb rather than create; training to help users Express themselves was rare; where there were opportunities for Joining Publics, they tended to be chances to join the sponsoring organization or predefined chapters, not define and start new groups; and ways of Taking Action were almost always prescribed by the site (and often were simply invitations to contribute financially).

Our findings are similar to those from a survey of the youth civic web sites of seven European countries. The CIVICWEB project analyzed a European sample of youth web sites very comparable to our (mainly) American one, and included sites with diverse organizational backgrounds and approaches. When it came to the use of interactivity as a tool for fostering youth engagement, the researchers found both that overall rates of interactivity were quite low and that "those groups without offline organizational presences are more likely both to promote online participation of some kind and to use bottom-up interactive modes of communication" (Bognar & Aydemir, 2007, p. 136). The authors describe the sites with offline presences as often little more than "leaflet[s] and brochure[s]" for their organizations—a comment reminiscent of our own observations of the American cases. And they similarly conclude that those organizations are to some degree failing to comprehend both their audiences and the possibilities of the new medium, choosing instead to use the Web in a way that "does not differ essentially from the way mass communication functions" (Bognar & Aydemir, 2007, p. 136).

POLICY IMPLICATIONS FOR DEVELOPING ONLINE YOUTH COMMUNITIES

That similarly limited civic learning opportunities appear in youth sites in both North America and Europe—across countries with very different political and civic structures and cultures—speaks to an apparently powerful inertia preventing many sponsoring civic organizations from productively deploying social networking and participatory media affordances for youth. Further investigation into this pattern would be valuable and might help to pinpoint the role of factors such as organizational unwillingness and inability to invest financially in interactive tools; fears of losing physical participants to online activities; fears about the content that unsupervised young people might produce; and, possibly, an age gap reflecting different (AC and DC) citizenship styles between the directors (and funders) of offline organizations and their younger constituents in the online only world.

Whatever the causes of the underutilization of digital media technologies in most online youth communities, organizations around the world would benefit from expanding their visions of what youth can do and learn. As explained above, adolescents' identities are now less defined by membership in conventional parties and community and interest organizations, and more oriented toward expression and information gathering in personal networks. Considerable evidence from the field of civic education suggests that there is resistance from students to learning modes that define civic information and activities exclusively in DC terms. All of this might encourage educational policy-makers, along with the managers of community groups and designers of online environments, to think about ways in which their missions might be better translated for an expressive and heavily networked generation.

However, policy-makers and developers should not conclude from this essay that the ideal approach to online civic learning is simply to turn young people loose in unmoderated environments. Whether the learning environment is the classroom or the online community, civic skills must be actively cultivated to some degree in order to flourish. Some balance between Dutiful and Actualizing modes is desirable, as exemplified on sites such as YouthNoise and Idealist, where Dutiful learning opportunities seem to add structure and context to more Actualizing ones. The question is how to design online civic environments that foster the conditions (and offer the skill-building) necessary for participatory civic learning, while creating spaces to let young people freely and publicly exercise newfound skills. It is clear from examining the development of online communities guided by broader frameworks of civic learning that young people see few boundaries between the personal and the political. Further, resulting forms of expression easily cross boundaries between personal and public issues. The well-meaning aims of many older policy-makers and online developers may miss the importance that young citizens place on self-expression in rich media environments. It is worth noting, for example, that none of the videos produced by either of the presidential campaigns in 2008 came close to the levels of spontaneous viewing and viral sharing gained by a number of independently produced videos.

The availability of autonomous, unmanaged experience is the quality most important for achieving authenticity in the view of young visitors to online environments (Coleman, 2008). The key challenge for those designing such environments is to find ways to build in learning opportunities (from information search functions to digital storytelling guides) without overly managing the ways in which site visitors can use them. Coleman (2008) offers a rich set of policy guidelines encouraging governments, foundations, and nonprofits to create partnerships with younger citizens online that do not involve overly managing the content and activities that may characterize the resulting youth communities.

CONCLUSION

Adolescents and young adults' media orientations are clearly changing. Above all, conventional news and passive mass media consumption are on the wane. At the same time, other participatory forms of direct information sharing and production are on the rise. The use of online sources to get and share information directly seems well established in research on media use in the American election of 2008. The implications of this shift in media engagement will require reflection on and adjustment of our frameworks for understanding the nature of engagement. For example, young people seem inclined to share information that is directly related to action opportunities. This is an important departure from more conventional practices dating from the progressive era of the twentieth century—practices that include receiving independent information from authoritative gatekeepers such as the press, perhaps filtering the information through cues received from civic groups and political organizations, and then connecting the results to individual action at some later point. In the crowd-sourced and socially networked information-action scheme that fits the preferences of Actualizing citizens, information may be shaped by consumers as it is passed along networks. In the process, conventional lines between hard news, soft news, and entertainment genres are blurring as the gate-keeping process itself moves along more fluid networks of trusting relationships among peers. These changing media experiences may produce higher levels of engagement across a broader variety of issues and arenas of action. However, they may not boost scores on classic political information tests, which are based in models of Dutiful citizenship anchored in assumptions about the role of news media in the dissemination of public information.

As mediated public communication is changing, it is important to rethink some of the civic skills that young citizens need in order to participate effectively in this new media environment. Our work on expanding the definitions of basic civic learning to match changing civic styles and media systems suggests that every category of conventional civic learning can be expanded. For example, there may be no substitute for some level of expert *knowledge* about issues and political processes, but this information is likely to be assimilated more effectively if circulated in a context where it can be assembled and organized along with accounts of personal experiences and using a range of sources. Similarly, some standard means of *public expression* such as writing letters or petitions or debating issues may gain credibility if supplemented by digital public voice skills such as blogging, multi-media storytelling, and the uses of wikis and other networked and crowd-sourced forms of public expression. When it comes to *joining groups*, many young people prefer more loosely tied affiliation to formal memberships. This is a clear point of friction for many of the organizations that have attempted to join the online world by simply reproducing their conventional organizations in web sites. By contrast, the sites that exist only in online forms offer more opportunities for young people to create their own associational networks with fewer constraints imposed by memberships and hierarchical relationships. Likewise in the areas of acquiring the skills necessary to *take effective action*, online environments can offer young people chances to plan and execute their own political activities. Yet, few online youth communities seem able to break free from the inclination to manage and program the activities of young citizens, suggesting the lingering influence of the dutiful citizen paradigm on the part of those adults who fund and manage most sites.

Perhaps it is not surprising that when the civic world moves online, many of the trappings of dutiful citizenship move with it, often pushing the rich possibilities of participatory media and social networking technologies to the margins. At the same time, it is clear that those communities that exist only in online forms come closest to utilizing the digital media experiences that young people find appealing in personal and entertainment environments. Participatory civic learning experiences occur predominantly in the online only youth communities. These public networking sites offer examples of where the youth civic media sphere might continue to develop with greater appeal to younger people. While it seems that few of these sites are likely to outpace Facebook in popularity, they might profit from introducing more civic activities that combine the appeal of personalization with the power of social networking.

This online civic world also offers places for teachers and civics curricula to explore in expanding the reach of classroom learning. Many schools are firewalled out of fears of Internet predators or students spending time on their social networking sites when not being monitored. Yet, as the lines between the personal and the political become less meaningful for young people, perhaps our conceptions of what is civic may need to change as well.

REFERENCES

Adamic, L., & Glance, N. (2005, May). *The political blogosphere and the 2004 US election: Divided they blog*. Paper presented at the WWW 2005 2nd Annual Workshop on the Weblogging Ecosystem, Chiba, Japan.

Agre, P. (2002). Real-time politics: The Internet and the political process. *Information Society, 18(5)*, 311–331.

Bachen, C., Raphael, C., Lynn, K. M., McKee, K., & Philippi, J. (2008). Civic engagement, pedagogy, and information technology on web sites for youth. *Political Communication, 25(3)*, 290–310.

Bauerlein, M. (2008). *The dumbest generation: How the digital age stupefies young Americans and jeopardizes our future (or, don't trust anyone under 30)*. New York: Jeremy P. Tarcher/Penguin.

Benkler, Y. (2006). *The wealth of networks: How social production transforms markets and freedom*. New Haven: Yale University Press.

Bennett, W. L. (1998). The uncivic culture: Communication, identity, and the rise of lifestyle politics. *PS: Political Science and Politics, 31(4)*, 741–761.

Bennett, W. L. (2007). Civic learning in changing democracies: Challenges for citizenship and civic education. In P. Dahlgren (Ed.), *Young citizens and new media: Learning democratic engagement* (pp. 59–77). New York: Routledge.

Bennett, W. L. (2008). Changing citizenship in the digital age. In W. L. Bennett (Ed.), *Civic life online: Learning how digital media can engage youth* (pp. 1–24). Cambridge, MA: MIT Press.

Bennett, W. L., & Xenos, M. (2004, August). *Young voters and the web of politics: Pathways to participation in the youth engagement and electoral campaign web spheres* (CIRCLE Working Paper 20). Medford, MA: CIRCLE.

Bennett, W. L., & Xenos, M. (2005, October). *Young voters and the web of politics 2004: The youth political web sphere comes of age* (CIRCLE Working Paper 42). Medford, MA: CIRCLE.

Bennett, W. L., Breunig, C., & Givens, T. (2008). Communication and political mobilization: Digital media and the organization of anti-Iraq war demonstrations in the U.S. *Political Communication, 25(3)*, 269–289.

Bennett, W. L., Wells, C., & Freelon, D. G. (2009, February). *Communicating citizenship online: Models of civic learning in the youth web sphere* (Civic Learning Online Working Paper). Retrieved February 3, 2009, from http://www.engagedyouth.org/blog/wp-content/uploads/2009/02/communicatingcitizeshiponlinecloreport.pdf

Bennett, W. L., Wells, C., & Rank, A. (2009). Young citizens and civic learning: Two paradigms of citizenship in the digital age. *Citizenship Studies, 13*, 103–118.

Bognar, E., & Aydemir, A.T. (2007). *Websites and civic participation: A European overview*. Report of the European Union's CIVICWEB project. Retrieved June 24, 2009, from http://www.wun.ac.uk/nyc/documents/CivicWebEUMainReport.pdf

Bowman, S., & Willis. C. (2003, July). *We media: How audiences are shaping the future of news and information.* Retrieved April 17, 2007, from http://www.hypergene.net/wemedia/weblog.php

Boyd, D. M. (2008). Why youth heart social network sites: The role of networked publics in teenage social life. In D. Buckingham (Ed.), *Youth, identity, and digital media* (pp. 119–142). Cambridge, MA: MIT Press.

Boyd, D. M., & Ellison, N. B. (2008). Social network sites: Definition, history, and scholarship. *Journal of Computer-Mediated Communication, 13(1).*

Campbell, D. E. (2005). *Voice in the classroom: How an open classroom environment facilitates adolescents' civic development* (CIRCLE Working Paper Series). Retrieved March 31, 2009, from http://www.civicyouth.org/PopUps/WorkingPapers/WP28campbell.pdf

CIRCLE (2009). A closer look at the record of the 2008 youth vote. *Around the CIRCLE, 6*, 6–7.

CNN (2009). 'Neda' becomes rallying cry for Iranian protests. *CNN.com*. Retrieved June 26, 2009, from http://www.cnn.com/2009/WORLD/meast/06/21/iran.woman.twitter/

Coleman, S. (2008). Doing IT for themselves: Management versus autonomy in youth e-citizenship. In W. L. Bennett (Ed.), *Civic life online: Learning how digital media can engage youth* (pp. 189–206). Cambridge, MA: MIT Press.

Coleman, S. and Blumler, J., 2009. *The Internet and democratic citizenship: Theory, practice and policy.* New York: Cambridge University Press.

Earl, J., & Schussman, A. (2008). Contesting cultural control: Youth culture and online petitioning. In W. L. Bennett (Ed.), *Civic life online: Learning how digital media can engage youth* (pp. 71–95). Cambridge, MA: MIT Press.

Fisher, D., Smith, M., & Welser, H. T. (2006). *You are who you talk to: Detecting roles in Usenet newsgroups.* Paper presented at the 39th Hawaii International Conference on System Sciences.

Fraser, M., & Dutta, S. (2008, November 19). Barack Obama and the Facebook election. *U.S. News & World Report.* Retrieved March 24, 2009, from http://www.usnews.com/articles/opinion/2008/11/19/barack-obama-and-the-facebook-election.html

Galston, W. A. (2003). If political fragmentation is the problem, is the Internet the solution? In D. M. Anderson & M. Cornfield (Eds.), *The civic web: Online politics and democratic values* (pp. 35–44). Lanham, MD: Rowman & Littlefield.

Gibson, C., & Levine, P. (2003). *The civic mission of schools.* A Report from Carnegie Corporation of New York and CIRCLE: The Center for Information and Research on Civic Learning and Engagement. Retrieved February 11, 2008, from http://www.civicmissionofschools.org/site/campaign/cms_report.html

Giddens, A. (1991). *Modernity and self-identity: Self and society in the late modern age.* Stanford, CA: Stanford University Press.

Gordon, E., & Koo, G. (2008). Placeworlds: Using virtual worlds to foster civic engagement. *Space and Culture, 11(3),* 204–221.

Gueorguieva, V. (2008). Voters, MySpace, and YouTube: The impact of alternative communication channels on the 2006 election cycle and beyond. *Social Science Computer Review, 26(3),* 288–300.

Hamilton, J. T. (2004). *All the news that's fit to sell: How the market transforms information into news.* Princeton, NJ: Princeton University Press.

Hargittai, E. (2005). Survey measures of Web-oriented digital literacy. *Social Science Computer Review, 23(3),* 371–379.

Hargittai, E., & Walejko, G. (2008). The participation divide: Content creation and sharing in the digital age. *Information, Communication and Society, 11(2),* 239–256.

Inglehart, R. (1997). *Modernization and postmodernization: Cultural, economic, and political change in 43 societies.* Princeton, NJ: Princeton University Press.

Jacobson, L. (2008, November 21). Youth vote: Democratic movement or fad? *Stateline.org.* Retrieved March 24, 2009, from http://www.stateline.org/live/details/story?contentId=357447

Jenkins, H. (2006). *Convergence culture: Where old and new media collide.* New York: NYU Press.

Jenkins, H. (2008). *Confronting the Challenges of Participatory Culture: Media Education for the 21st Century.* Retrieved January 29, 2009, from http://www.newmedialiteracies.org/files/working/NMLWhitePaper.pdf

Joseph, B. (2008). Why Johnny can't fly: Treating games as a form of youth media within a youth development framework. In K. Salen (Ed.), *The ecology of games* (pp. 253–266). Cambridge, MA: MIT Press.

Kerbel, M. (2009). *Netroots: Online progressives and the transformation of American politics.* London: Paradigm Publishers.

Leichtman Reseach Group. (2008). *Online video growth fueled by young.* Retrieved March 23, 2009, from http://www.marketingcharts.com/television/online-video-growth-fueled-by-the-young-4523/

Lenhart, A., & Madden, M. (2007). Social networking websites and teens. *Pew Internet and American Life Project.* Retrieved March 25, 2009, from http://pewresearch.org/pubs/118/social-networking-websites-and-teens

Lenhart, A., Kahne, J., Middaugh, E., Macgill, A., Evans, C., & Vitak, J. (2008, September 16). Teens, video games, and civics. *Pew Internet and American Life Project.* Retrieved March 27, 2009, from http://www.pewinternet.org/Reports/2008/Teens-Video-Games-and-Civics.aspx

Levine, P. (2008). A public voice for youth: The audience problem in digital media and civic education. In W. L. Bennett (Ed.), *Civic life online: Learning how digital media can engage youth* (pp. 119–138). Cambridge, MA: MIT Press.

Lopez, M.H., Levine, P., Both, D., Kiesa. A., Kirby, E., & Marcelo, K. (2006). The civic and political health of the nation: A detailed look at how youth participate in politics and communities. *Center for Information and Research on Civic Learning and Engagement.* Retrieved July 2, 2008, from http://www.civicyouth.org/PopUps/2006_CPHS_Report_update.pdf

Margolis, M., & Resnick, D. (2000). *Politics as usual: The cyberspace "revolution."* Thousand Oaks: Sage Publications.

Miel, P., & Faris, R. (2008). *News and information as digital media come of age.* Retrieved February 12, 2009, from http://cyber.law.harvard.edu/sites/cyber.law.harvard.edu/files/Overview_MR.pdf

Montgomery, K., Gottleib-Robles, B., & Larson, G.O. (2004). *Youth as e-citizens: Engaging the digital generation.* Retrieved July 3, 2008, from http://www.centerforsocialmedia.org/ecitizens/index2.htm

Niemi, R. G., & Junn, J. (1998). *Civic education: What makes students learn.* New Haven: Yale University Press.

Ondrejka, C. (2005). *Changing realities: User creation, communication, and innovation in digital worlds.* Retrieved March 26, 2009, from http://papers.ssrn.com/sol3/papers.cfm?abstract_id=799468

Ondrejka, C. (2008). Education unleashed: Participatory culture, education, and innovation in Second Life. In K. Salen (Ed.), *The ecology of games* (pp. 229–251). Cambridge, MA: MIT Press.

Palfrey, J., & Gasser, U. (2008). *Born digital: Understanding the first generation of digital natives.* New York: Basic Books.

Panagopoulos, C. (2007). Technology and the transformation of political campaign communications. *Social Science Computer Review, 25(4)*, 423–424.

Pasek, J., Feldman, L., Romer, D., & Jamieson, K. H. (2008). Schools as incubators of democratic participation: Building long-term political efficacy with civic education. *Applied Developmental Science, 12(1)*, 26–37.

Patterson, T. E. (2007). *Young people and news.* A report from the Joan Shorenstein Center on the Press, Politics, and Public Policy. Kennedy School of Government, Harvard University. Prepared for the Carnegie-Knight Task Force on the Future of Journalism Education.

Pew (2007, April 15). What Americans know: 1989–2007. *The Pew Research Center for the People and the Press.* Retrieved March 31, 2009, from http://people-press.org/reports/pdf/319.pdf

Pew (2008, August 17). Key audiences now blend online and traditional sources. *The Pew Research Center for the People and the Press.* Retrieved March 31, 2009, from http://people-press.org/report/444/news-media

Project for Excellence in Journalism. (2008, September 15). *McCain vs. Obama on the web.* Retrieved March 25, 2009, from http://www.journalism.org/node/12773

Putnam, R. (2000). *Bowling alone: The collapse and revival of American community.* New York: Simon & Schuster.

Rainie, L. (2008, January 9). Video sharing web sites. *Pew Internet and American Life Project.* Retrieved March 24, 2009, from http://www.pewinternet.org/~/media//Files/Reports/2008/Pew_Videosharing_memo_Jan08.pdf.pdf

Rheingold, H. (2008). Using participatory media and public voice to encourage civic engagement. In W. L. Bennett (Ed.), *Civic life online: Learning how digital media can engage youth* (pp. 97–118). Cambridge, MA: MIT Press.

Rogers, R. (2008). Consumer technology after surveillance theory. In J. Kooijman, P. Pisters, & W. Strauven (Eds.), *Mind the screen: Media concepts according to Thomas Elsaesser* (pp. 288–296). Amsterdam: Amsterdam University Press.

Schudson, M. (1998). *The good citizen: A history of American civic life.* New York: The Free Press.

Shirky, C. (2003). *Power laws, weblogs, and inequality.* Retrieved March 13, 2009, from http://www.shirky.com/writings/powerlaw_weblog.html

Silberman, M. (2009, March 13). Welcome to the new media campaign tools of 2012. *Mother Jones.* Retrieved March 24, 2009, from http://www.motherjones.com/politics/2009/03/welcome-new-media-campaign-tools-2012-0

Smith, A., & Rainie, L. (2008). The Internet and the 2008 election. *Pew Internet and American Life Project.* Retrieved March 23, 2009, from http://www.pewinternet.org/~/media//Files/Reports/2008/PIP_2008_election.pdf.pdf

Steinhauser, P. (2007). The Youtube-ification of politics: Candidates losing control. *CNN.com.* Retrieved March 23, 2009, from http://www.cnn.com/2007/POLITICS/07/18/youtube.effect/index.html

Stelter, B., & Stone, B. (2009). Web pries lid off Iranian censorship. *The New York Times.* Retrieved June 26, 2009, from http://www.nytimes.com/2009/06/23/world/middleeast/23censor.html?emc=eta1

Sunstein, C. R. (2007). *Republic.com 2.0.* Princeton, NJ: Princeton University Press.

Syvertsen, A. K., Flanagan, C. A., & Stout, M. D. (2007). *Best practices in civic education: Changes in students' civic outcome* (CIRCLE Working Paper Series). Retrieved July 2, 2008, from http://www.civicyouth.org/PopUps/WorkingPapers/WP57Flanagan.pdf

Tapscott, D. (2009). *Grown up digital: How the net generation is changing your world.* New York: McGraw-Hill.

TechPresident. (2008). *Blog mentions via Technorati 2008.* Retrieved March 24, 2008, from http://techpresident.com/scrape_plot/technorati/2008. Comparisons of McCain and Obama social networks retrieved on November 15, 2008.

Torney-Purta, J. (2002). The school's role in developing civic engagement: A study of adolescents in twenty-eight countries. *Applied Developmental Science, 6(4)*, 203–212.

Waggener-Edstrom. (2008). Survey of voters 35 and under. Retrieved March 4, 2009, from http://www.waggeneredstrom.com/who_we_are/news_recognition/agency_news_6_25_08.asp

Wattenberg, M. P. (2008). *Is voting for young people?* New York: Pearson/Longman.

Weisel, R. (2008, July 15). What is the average size of Obama's contributions and what is the average size of McCain's contributions? *Factcheck.org*. Retrieved March 26, 2009, from http://www.factcheck.org/askfactcheck/what_is_the_average_size_of_obamas.html

Wellman, B., Quan-Haase, A., Boase, J., Chen, W., Hampton, K., Díaz, I., et al. (2003). The social affordances of the Internet for networked individualism. *Journal of Computer-Mediated Communication, 8(3)*.

Young, D. G., & Tisinger, R. (2006). Dispelling late-night myths: News consumption among late-night comedy viewers and the predictors of exposure to various late-night shows. *The Harvard International Journal of Press/Politics, 11*, 113–134.

Young, D. G., & Esralew, S. (2007). *Political participation, engagement, and discussion among viewers of late-night comedy programming*. Paper presented at the 2007 annual meeting of the National Communication Association.

Zukin, C., Keeter, S., Andolina, M., Jenkins, K., & Delli Carpini, M. X. (2006). *A new engagement? Political participation, civic life, and the changing American citizen*. Oxford: Oxford University Press.

CHAPTER 16

Immigrant Youth in the United States: Coming of Age among Diverse Civic Cultures

LENE ARNETT JENSEN
Clark University

THE NATURE OF the civic and political lives of immigrant youth in the United States is important for a number of reasons. First, immigrant youth constitute a notable proportion of American society. In 2007, children under the age of 18 who were foreign-born (first-generation immigrants) or lived with at least one foreign-born parent (second generation immigrants) accounted for 22% of children in the United States (Mather, 2009). Second, they constitute the fastest growing segment of America's youth. The projection is that by 2020, one-third of children in the United States will be immigrants (Mather, 2009). Immigrant youth, then, constitute a sizeable and growing membership of American civil society.

Immigrant children also contribute to changing American demographics. They form a crucial part of an ongoing ethnic and racial transformation of American society. In 2007, 8 of 10 immigrant children under the age of 18 were ethnic or racial minorities. Thus, only 18% were non-Hispanic White whereas 55% were Latino/Hispanic, 16% were Asian, 7% were Black, and the rest were affiliated with other ethnic or racial groups (Mather, 2009). While projections vary somewhat, the expectation is that the United States will have a majority of children who are of ethnic and racial backgrounds other than non-Hispanic White by about 2030 (Mather, 2009; Yen, 2009). Immigrant youth, then, are rendering American society more diverse. How they are received and included into American civil society, and how they conceptualize and contribute to American communities and the political process will have a substantial impact on American society in the decades to come (Sanjek, 2001).

By virtue of being immigrants, many first- and second-generation immigrant youth and their families also have citizenship statuses that are different from non-immigrant Americans. While almost 80% of immigrant children were U.S. citizens in 2000, nonetheless 53% of all immigrant children lived in mixed-citizenship families where at least one member was a citizen and at least one was not. Also in 2005, it was estimated that 11% of children in immigrant families were undocumented and 18% were born in the United States to an undocumented parent (Hernandez, Denton, & Macartney, 2008). Again, the distinctive citizenship experiences of immigrant children and youth make it all the more important to pay attention to their role in American civil society.

Organization, Definitions, and Scope

This chapter will first focus on immigrant youth's rates of civic and political participation. This will be followed by a description of their motives for participating, with special attention to the extent to which having a cultural or ethnic identity is a motivator. Then, we will turn to the question of community and societal reactions to the cultural, ethnic, and racial backgrounds of immigrant youth. Specifically, a number of studies have addressed the impact of discrimination on immigrant youth's identities and their civic and political lives. Next, the chapter will consider how being an immigrant youth may intersect in distinctive ways with the developmental contexts of family, religious institutions, and media in either encouraging or diminishing civic and political engagement. Finally, in the conclusion, we will consider the implications for policy and American civil society of the available research.

Before proceeding, a few definitions and observations about scope are necessary. The present chapter addresses attitudes and behaviors in both the *political* and *civic* realms (e.g., Putnam, 2000). The political realm includes views such as trust in the government and patriotism, and activities such as voting, donating money to political causes, and making contact with public representatives. The civic realm includes attitudes such as social trust, and involvement in school and voluntary associations (e.g., cultural, social, and religious; see Seif, this volume).

As Sherrod, Flanagan, and Youniss (2002a, 2002b) have argued, youth-focused and developmental science research on citizenship needs to pertain not only to political and legal considerations but also to more general civic involvement with others in the community. A focus on both the political and civic realms is also useful because research with American youth in general has shown considerable disengagement from political activities (Galston, 2001), but high rates of engagement for community activities and volunteering (Flanagan, 2004; Torney-Purta, Amadeo, & Richardson, 2007). Furthermore, as I will discuss in more detail, conceptualizing the political and civic realms in broader rather than narrower ways is very apt for immigrant youth.

The term *youth* is used in varied ways within different research traditions. For demographic surveys of immigrant youth included in this chapter, children under 18 years of age were included. For the research described here on immigrant youth's political and civic lives, the participants ranged in age from their early teens to their mid-twenties.

With respect to the civic and political lives of immigrant youth, Stepick and Stepick noted in 2002, "Few researchers have focused on immigrant youth and even fewer have examined issues of civic engagement for immigrant youth" (p. 247). While new studies have been published since then (e.g., Jensen & Flanagan, 2008a), it nevertheless remains the case that the civic and political lives of immigrant youth have received scant research attention. Thus, this chapter will incorporate relevant research with immigrant youth from a number of different disciplines, including psychology, political science, sociology, and anthropology. Furthermore, the chapter also will draw on some findings from research with adult immigrants when they are of relevance to the experiences of youth. Also, given the paucity of research, each main section in the chapter will end by pointing to questions that remain for future research.

Finally, unless otherwise indicated, the research described here is with immigrants in the United States. However, I wish to be clear that immigrants in the United States are very diverse. They vary, for example, in terms of the circumstances that bring them to the country (e.g., refugee versus voluntary), immigration status (e.g., legal versus undocumented), immigrant generation (e.g., first versus second), socioeconomic and employment conditions, educational resources, family composition, religions, languages, and so forth. In 2000, the parents of immigrant children came from more than 125 countries (Hernandez, Denton, & Macartney, 2007). When describing research in the present chapter, I will therefore aim to describe the backgrounds of the immigrants when available.

RATES OF PARTICIPATION

Surveys of the political and civic participation of immigrant youth have been few. However, they suggest that differences between immigrant and non-immigrant youth who are alike on factors such as SES and education are minor. Furthermore, the differences that do exist suggest that immigrant and non-immigrant youths put their civic and political efforts into somewhat different activities.

Lopez and Marcelo (2008) conducted national Internet and telephone surveys that compared first-generation immigrants, second-generation immigrants, and native-born residents between 15 and 25 years of age. The surveys included more than 20 different civic and political items. Results from the Internet survey showed almost no significant differences between the three groups. On the telephone survey, first-generation immigrants were less active than native-born residents on a number of political and civic measures when demographic differences (e.g., SES, gender, and region of the country) were left unadjusted. When these differences were adjusted for statistically, few group differences remained.

With respect to the remaining differences, Lopez and Marcelo (2008) found that there were more *electoral specialists* among native-born residents than first-generation immigrants, where a specialist was someone who had engaged in two or more activities within a specific area (such as electoral politics) within the last 12 months. However, there were more *civic specialists* among second-generation immigrants than native-born residents, and second-generation youth also reported a higher total number of activities than native-born youth.

Another survey compared a total of 1,334 immigrant and native-born first-year college students. Results showed high levels of involvement for all students, and few group differences (Stepick, Stepick, & Labissiere, 2008). Averaged across 23 different political, civic, and social activities, about 80% of the college students reported having been engaged often or very often during their high school years. Among the group differences that did emerge, more native-born residents and second-generation immigrants were registered to vote than first- and one-and-a-half (1.5)-generation immigrants (i.e., persons born abroad who came to the United States prior to 12 years of age). However, native-born residents were lower than some or all of the immigrant groups (first-, 1.5-, and second-generation) on helping non-English speakers, helping a recent immigrant, and helping someone illiterate. This study did not control for demographic differences, but the selection of a college sample probably narrowed potential differences between the immigrant and non-immigrant students.

Huddy and Khatib (2007) also conducted two smaller surveys with students from one college (the sample sizes were 300 and 341). The focus was more on attitudes than behaviors. On seven different measures of patriotism, attention to politics, knowledge of politics, and voting, there were essentially no differences between first-generation, second-generation, and native-born youth.

Taken together, these surveys begin to suggest that on overall rates of political and civic activities, immigrant youth are fairly similar to their native-born peers of comparable demographic characteristics. The surveys also hint that native-born residents may be more involved with electoral politics. At least this may be the case for the kinds of conventional political activities included in the surveys by Lopez and Marcelo (2008), such as displaying a campaign button or sign, and being a member of a political group. Furthermore, the surveys hint that immigrant youth may be more involved with issues of relevance to immigrants (e.g., translation), or that they have encountered among immigrants but that also apply to others (e.g., literacy).

Future Directions

The available findings give direction to future surveys of immigrant youth's civic and political participation. Clearly, future surveys would benefit from broad definitions of the topic at hand (see also Jensen & Flanagan, 2008b). If surveys do not include items that capture the kinds of behaviors that immigrant youth find meaningful and engaging, some of the contributions of immigrant youth will go underreported (Barreto & Munoz, 2003; Junn, 1999). Stepick and his colleagues (2008) have observed that immigrant youth's bilingual and bicultural skills constitute an important resource to the broader community that often is overlooked. In order to arrive at more detailed insights into immigrant youth's civic and political participation, future surveys might also fruitfully differentiate groups not only in terms of immigrant generation but along other lines as well. For example, we know from research on voting among adult immigrants that factors such as ethnicity or race and country of origin matter. Focusing on ethnicity and race, Ramakrishnan and Espenshade (2001) found that among Latinos, the first generation of immigrants was most likely to vote. Among Whites, voting peaked in the second generation of immigrants. For Asians and Blacks, voting was highest among native-born residents. The authors speculated that immigrants' political participation in the United States, in part, is influenced by diverse experiences with inclusion, exclusion, and acculturation.

Focusing on the country of origin, Bass and Casper (2001) found that among adult naturalized immigrants of Asian background, those from India, the Philippines, Vietnam, and South Korea were more likely to vote than those from China. Among naturalized Latinos, Cubans, Guatemalans, and Dominicans reported higher voting participation than Mexicans and Salvadorans. The authors noted that immigrants' political experiences from their country of origin may influence their participation in the United States, where some countries such as India and the Philippines have established histories of holding democratic elections (cf. Rice & Feldman, 1997). While these lines of research focus specifically on adults' voting behavior, they nevertheless highlight diversity among immigrants that future surveys of immigrant youth's civic and political participation might usefully consider.

MOTIVES FOR PARTICIPATING

Clearly, immigrant youth are engaged in a number of civic and political activities. What are their motives for participating? Next, I turn to a discussion of immigrants' cultural motives for political and civic participation, as well as other important motives.

CULTURAL IDENTITY MOTIVES

Historically, the question of how immigrants' incorporation into civil society is influenced by the cultural values they bring with them has been revisited again and again. In the late 1770s, Benjamin Franklin worried about German immigrants' identities and culture. Why, he asked, should "Pennsylvania, founded by the English, become a colony of aliens, who will shortly be so numerous as to Germanize us, instead of us Anglifying them?" (quoted in Degler, 1970, p. 50). In the late nineteenth and early twentieth centuries, at the height of immigrant arrivals from Eastern and Southern Europe, scholars and the public vigorously debated assimilation, the melting pot, and cultural pluralism (e.g., Bourne, 1916; Kallen, 1956; Zangwill, 1975). In an *Atlantic Monthly* article in 1916, for example, Randolph Bourne warned against nationalistic sentiments akin to European ones, and he argued that American civil society would benefit from immigrants contributing their cultural values to a pluralistic mix.

Almost 100 years later, at a time when immigrants are now mostly arriving from Asia and Latin America, Huntington (2004) has been at the forefront of the view that immigrants who maintain a cultural and immigrant sense of self represent a threat to the coherence of American civil society. In his book, "Who Are We? The challenges to America's national identity," Huntington (2004) expressed concern about fragmentation of the national identity due to immigration. Partly echoing Franklin, Huntington worried about the loss of what he termed America's "Anglo-Protestant" culture. Furthermore, Huntington argued that immigrants who have multicultural affiliations will see their loyalties and time divided and hence will put less effort and energy into civic associations, public life, and politics in the United States. "Ampersands"—a term he repeated often—raise the specter of the "erosion of citizenship" and threaten "societal security" (Chap. 8). According to Huntington, immigrants who maintain a cultural identity will pull away from engagement in American civic life.

Interestingly, recent research with immigrant youth (and some work with adults) suggests that having a cultural identity is more of a conduit than an encumbrance to civic and political engagement. Furthermore, immigrant youth's cultural identities are complex, and they find civic expressions that seem considerably more multifaceted and intricate than what commonly is captured by the historical debate.

Testing Huntington's (2004) claim that immigrants who maintain a cultural identity will pull away from American civic life, a mixed-methods study examined the extent to which Asian Indian and Salvadoran immigrant adolescents and their parents spoke of *cultural motives* to account for their involvement or lack thereof in political and civic activities (Jensen, 2008a). Cultural motives included references both to the immigrants' cultures of origin (e.g., Indian and Latino) and self-identification as immigrants (e.g., "being people of different countries"). Findings showed that cultural motives were twice as likely to be mentioned as sources of engagement than disengagement. In fact, cultural motives rarely accounted for lack of participation.

Based on a qualitative theme analysis, the research also differentiated seven different cultural motives of engagement. Of note is that only two of these themes centered on immigrants bonding within their own community—which even by Huntington's standards is not the equivalent of pulling away from civil society. One of the two bonding themes, *Cultural Remembrance*, involved immigrants' desire to remember and maintain values and customs of their culture. The other bonding theme, *the Welfare of the Immigrant or Cultural Communities*, was where immigrants worked politically or civically to ensure or enhance the well-being of their fellow immigrants or compatriots.

Apart from the two bonding themes, the other five themes involved various ways of bridging between the immigrants' cultures and American society. For example, immigrant youth and their parents spoke of being active in American civil society because of *Traditions of Service* taught by their religion or culture. Also, they spoke of their *Appreciation for American Democracy*. This theme often sprung from a comparison of conditions in the United States with those of the country of origin or the world more generally. For example, a second-generation Asian Indian adolescent stated:

> What makes America different from a lot of countries is that the freedom of speech grants people the right to say what they want on any issue, which is good. Definitely good—because it alerts people in things that they might not have been able to break down or able to notice. (Jensen, 2008a, p. 81)

Also, in some cases immigrant youth and their parents spoke not only of acting upon American ideals in the United States, but also of exporting those ideals back to their country of origin. For example, in an effort to enhance gender equality in India, one Asian Indian family had started a scholarship fund for girls in Indian high schools.

Still another theme centered on engagement as a means of *Bridging Communities*—of coming to know others in the United States and them coming to know you. An adolescent immigrant, who passionately prescribed participation in school clubs and extracurricular events, exemplified this theme:

> [Immigrants] should be involved in school! If you're new to the culture, new to life in America, you experience how things are in America, ... because not only are there Americans in these organizations, there's Asians, there's German, there're so many different cultures in these organizations. You see things from many perspectives! (Jensen, 2008a, p. 80)

Taken together, the themes of bonding and bridging show that immigrant youth's cultural identities are multifaceted, and accordingly they form the basis for multiple kinds of engagement with American civil society.

Other research, too, has noted that immigrant youth's cultural identities are a conduit to political and civic involvement. Based on ethnographic work with Indian, Bangladeshi, and Pakistani Muslim immigrant high-school students, Maira (2004) used the terms *polycultural citizenship* and *flexible citizenship* to describe the intersection of their cultural identities and civic involvement. She observed that immigrant youth drew on their multiple cultural identities—religious, nation of origin, panethnic, and so forth—to explain their participation in American civil society. Furthermore, they combined these diverse cultural identities in flexible or changing ways depending upon the specific nature of the civic participation at hand.

As observed by Stepick and his colleagues (2008), immigrant youth's civic participation draws on their bilingual and bicultural skills. The present research, furthermore, indicates that immigrant youth's bicultural (or polycultural) consciousness and experience also are conduits for many kinds of civic and political engagement. (See Jensen [2003] and Jensen, Arnett, and McKenzie [2009] for additional work on multicultural identities, and Leal [2002] for research with adult Latino immigrants on ethnic identity and political behaviors.)

Autonomy and Community Motives

While immigrants have cultural motives for political and civic participation, they are likely to have other important motives as well. What are those? Research has begun to indicate that those motives involve consideration both of the self and the broader community. Excerpts that Stepick and his colleagues (2008) presented from their qualitative work with immigrant youth invoke these dual considerations. For example, a first-generation Haitian adolescent explained that she was doing volunteer service because "[it] is helping people in a way and helping yourself in another way" (p. 63). Along similar lines, an interview study found that African immigrant youth discussed the importance of voting both as an individual right and a duty of democratic citizenship (this study was conducted in Canada; Chareka & Sears, 2006).

Also, another study analyzed immigrant youth's motives for political and civic involvement or lack thereof in terms of three kinds of ethics: Autonomy, Community, and Divinity (Jensen, 2009). Briefly, *Ethic of Autonomy* motives included references to an individual's rights, interests, and well-being. *Ethic of Community* motives pertained to a person's obligations to others, promoting the interests of groups, and interpersonal virtues. *Ethic of Divinity* motives included references to spiritual virtues, and divine authority, lessons, and examples (cf. Jensen, 2008b; Shweder, Much, Mahapatra, & Park, 1997). Findings showed that politically involved youth used more Ethic of Community motives and fewer Ethic of Autonomy motives, compared to politically uninvolved youth. Civically involved and uninvolved youth did not differ on Ethic of Autonomy motives. However, civically involved youth used more Ethic of Community and more Ethic of Divinity motives, compared to civically uninvolved youth. It should be noted, though, that Ethic of Divinity motives were infrequent.

Future Directions

For immigrant youth, then, motives that center on communal and social group considerations seem to be very important to their political and civic engagement. Whether such motives are more important to immigrant youth—who often come from cultures oriented to interdependence—than to American youth more generally, remains for future research to examine. Additionally, immigrant youth are motivated by considerations pertaining to the self and autonomy, and this may especially be the case for civic activities. But again, we need future research to investigate the extent to which immigrant and non-immigrant youth resemble each other in this regard. Finally, for immigrant youth (as for non-immigrant youth) we need additional research to examine the motivational processes of moving from being uninvolved, to becoming involved, to then either staying involved or discontinuing involvement in civic and political activities (Fredricks et al., 2002; Patrick et al., 1999; Pearce & Larsen, 2006).

DISCRIMINATION AND SOCIAL EXCLUSION

Scholars who address the factors that account for migration sometimes differentiate between the *pull* of the receiving country (such as labor recruitment and family unification) and the *push* of the country of origin (such as unemployment and war) (Martin & Zurcher, 2008). While a receiving country may exert a pull on immigrants, there may nevertheless also be a push once immigrants arrive where they are met with misgivings and discomfort, or outright discrimination and social exclusion. Social science scholars have been concerned with the consequences of such discrimination and exclusion on immigrants' understanding of civil society and their place within it (e.g., Rumbaut, 2008; Sanchez-Jankowski, 2002).

Moreover, such concerns may be particularly apt in regard to immigrant youth who developmentally are in the process of forming their identities. Thus, adolescence is a key time where persons go through the process of identifying with some social groups but not others, and for immigrant youth the extent to which they feel included or excluded in their receiving country is likely to be important to their political and civic sense of self. Furthermore, immigrant youth also constitute the coming generation of adult societal members, and hence their commitment to and engagement with American society will matter.

Research has begun to indicate that immigrant youth who experience discrimination also hold more ambivalent or negative attitudes toward American society, compared to youth who do not report discrimination. In a study of more than 5,000 second-generation immigrant adolescents, Portes and Rumbaut (2001) found that negative responses to the statement "There is no better country to live in than the United States" were highest among youth who reported experiences with discrimination. Such responses were especially notable among youth from Haiti, Jamaica, and the West Indies, whom Rumbaut (2008) noted may be most likely to experience racial discrimination.

Also, Wray-Lake, Syvertsen, and Flanagan (2008) examined the relation between social exclusion and trust in the U.S. government among Arab American immigrant youth. They found that 61% of the immigrant youth identified Arabs, Muslims, or Middle Easterners as perceived "enemies" of the United States on an open-ended question stating, "Movies and television programs sometimes show certain countries or groups of people as enemies of America … These days what groups do you think are shown as enemies of America?" (p. 87). Furthermore, these youth were less likely to believe that the U.S. government is responsive to everyone, compared to immigrant Arab youth who did not identify their own cultural, religious, or national group in enemy terms. Wray-Lake and her colleagues concluded that "Exclusion can make the ties that bind individuals to their nation tenuous" (p. 91).

For some immigrant youth, the issue may be further complicated by the fact that they also experience separation or exclusion from their country of origin. For example, Maira (2004), who studied South Asian Muslim immigrant youth at the time of 9/11, observed that critiques of the anti-Muslim backlash were common among the immigrant youth and often coupled with critiques of U.S. nationalism and state powers. Not long after, however, a state-condoned massacre of Muslims took place in Gujarat, India, from which a substantial number of Maira's interviewees and their families originated. Maira thus observed that for these immigrant youth and their families, "there are expressions of the vulnerability that Muslim immigrants have felt, both in the U.S. and 'at home'" (p. 227). Here, then, is the painful downside for immigrants who *bridge* communities, and who sometimes find that their ties across those communities become fragile at both ends.

While experiences with discrimination clearly seem to leave some immigrant youth with diminished social and political trust and uncertainty about where they belong, experiences with discrimination may simultaneously spur political and civic behaviors. In other words, as immigrants feel pushed away, they push back. There are several fairly recent national examples of this phenomenon (see also Waters, 2008). For example, Proposition 187 in California in 1994 seems to have mobilized Latinos (Schildkraut, 2005). The proposition aimed to restrict social services to undocumented immigrants and their children. It passed but was subsequently ruled unconstitutional. Reports indicate that many Latinos regarded the proposition as a direct attack against Latinos in general (Seif, this volume). The Tomas Rivera Center reported that Latino turnout in California in 1994 was 34% higher than in 1990, the previous midterm election. Also, the Field Institute, a public policy research organization in California, reported that nearly half of Latino registered voters in California in 2000 registered after 1994 and that the post-1994 registrants were more likely to be foreign-born than the pre-1994 registrants. These patterns suggest that Proposition 187 promoted a sense of group identification among Latino immigrants (and Latinos more generally) that spurred political mobilization. Similarly, a bill aimed at undocumented foreigners in early 2006 led to demonstrations in cities around the country and student rallies at schools, culminating in a May 1, 2006, "day without immigrants" protest (Lopez & Marcelo, 2008; Martin & Midley, 2006). Again what was perceived as an anti-immigrant bill seems to have rallied immigrants to political action.

Some research with youth also supports this counter-push hypothesis that immigrants engage in civic and political activities as a reaction against discrimination and, more broadly, what they see as injustices. In her ethnographic work, Maira (2004) found that some Muslim immigrant youth took action after 9/11 to counter anti-Muslim sentiments and stereotypes. For example, one Asian Indian immigrant youth wrote the words "INDIA + MUSLIM" on her bag. To her this was a way of signaling that she was Muslim, that Muslims are diverse, and that Muslims are a visible and legitimate part of American society. This youth said, "Just because one Muslim did it in New York, you can't involve everybody in there" (Maira, 2004, p. 226).

Based on their longitudinal work in Miami, Stepick and his colleagues (2008) also reported that previously politically disengaged Cuban immigrant youth became politically active at the time of the Elian Gonzales case. The case took place in 2000 to 2001 when a six-year-old Cuban boy, Elian, survived a raft trip from Cuba to Miami while his mother drowned. His American relatives and the Miami Cuban community wanted Elian to stay in the United States, whereas his father who had remained in Cuba and the Cuban government demanded that he be returned. Elian, in fact, was returned after the U.S. government forcibly seized him from his Miami relatives. According to Stepick and his colleagues (2008), some Cuban immigrant youth explained that they became politically engaged because Cubans were being portrayed negatively and unfairly in national media. As explained by a second-generation Cuban youth:

> All it would show in the news was people, you know, setting trash cans on fire, getting in fights with cops. When you see stuff like that . . . you realize that, you know, they wanted to make us look like angry Cubans. Right? To make everybody hate us. (p. 61)

This youth joined other Latino youth, Cuban and non-Cuban, in keeping daily vigils at the house where Elian stayed.

In interview studies with Salvadoran second-generation youth, Jensen (2008a) also found that some youth were politically and civically engaged as a way to counteract negative reactions to their community, culture, or ethnicity. Explaining why he tutored, one youth said: "because I want more Hispanic people to do better in school and do good. You know, so we won't be stereotyped" (p. 79). In this study as in the ones above, immigrant youth were motivated to be involved in activities such as tutoring, organizing rallies, and demonstrating out of concern with the needs and accomplishments of their immigrant and cultural communities, as well as with the representation and respect afforded these communities within the larger polity.

FUTURE DIRECTIONS

At this time, then, research suggests that experiences with stereotypes, discrimination, and social exclusion are linked to diminished social trust and confidence in the state. At the same time, research also indicates that such negative experiences mobilize some immigrant youth to become engaged in civic and political activities. Future research, however, needs to replicate these findings to establish their robustness and generalizability.

Future studies might also usefully differentiate among different experiences with discrimination. For example, research on discrimination has established a consistent phenomenon known as the *personal-group discrepancy,* where more people report that their ethnic or racial group is a target of discrimination than people who report that they personally have experienced discrimination (e.g., Kessler, Mummendey, & Leisse, 2000). This personal-group discrepancy appears to have implications for immigrants' civic and political lives. In a study with adult Latino immigrants, Schildkraut (2005) found that perceptions of both personal and group discrimination were linked to diminished trust that politicians care about Latino issues, but only personal discrimination was linked to lower trust in the government. More research in this area would be helpful, not only with adults but also with immigrant youth.

Furthermore, future research might examine in more detail the relations between experiences with discrimination, cultural or ethnic identity, and immigrant youth's civic and political lives. Thus in her study with adult Latino immigrants, Schildkraut (2005) also found that immigrants who had experiences with personal discrimination and who self-identified as American were less likely to register and to vote, as compared to immigrants who also reported personal discrimination but self-identified as either Latino or in terms of their national original. On the basis of these results, Schildkraut speculated that ethnic group identifications can assist people in coping with individual discrimination and maintaining connection to the political process.

For immigrant youth, too, cultural identities may be sources of both positive self- and group-regard (e.g., Junn & Masuoka, 2008) that help to push back against discrimination and enter into the civic and political arena. But perhaps, too, cultural identities have a potential downside along the lines of what Rumbaut (1994, 2008) has described as "reactive ethnicity" and "oppositional identities," where in the face of discrimination and exclusion some immigrant youth move away from society as a whole. Such moving away can take the form of psychological and social disengagement from the broader society. In more rare circumstances, it also literally can take the form of moving away from the United States. (For example, see Elliott [2009] for an account of Somali immigrant youth who repatriated, apparently in response to religious, social, and race barriers experienced in the United States, along with a desire to join resistance to the 2006 Ethiopian invasion of Somalia).

Finally, we need future research on the intersections of discrimination, identity, and civic and political participation that gives consideration to the diversity among immigrant youth. Research among adults points to this as an important line of future research. For example, a survey study of adult Mexican Americans and Asian Americans residing in California found that perceptions of discrimination against one's group was a predictor of political engagement for Mexican Americans, but not for Asian Americans (Lien, 1994).

DEVELOPMENTAL CONTEXTS

There is very little research available on developmental contexts of immigrant youth's civic and political lives. Here, then, I will touch on three contexts: family, religious institutions, and media. Family and religious institutions have traditionally been key contexts in the lives of American immigrants. Media are an important context in the lives of most contemporary American youth (Bennett et al., this volume). Rather than reiterating the need for future research in the discussion of each context below, let it simply be stated now that the field seems wide open for studies on how being an immigrant youth intersects with developmental contexts in encouraging or diminishing civic and political involvement.

Given the often high commitment to family that immigrant youth evince (e.g., Stepick et al., 2008), there might be reason to think that these commitments could supersede engagement with civic and political life (Stepick & Stepick, 2002). However, the relation between the family and civic realms may be more complex for immigrant youth. In a study of high-school students, Bogard and Sherrod (2008) found that immigrant youth who felt a strong allegiance to their family also strongly agreed with a measure of civic orientation, which included items prescribing community service, staying informed, and helping the needy.

Adding to the complexity, another study with immigrant adolescents and parents found that the parents were about equally divided in invoking duty to their children as a motive for civic involvement and lack of involvement (Jensen, 2009). On the one hand, some parents spoke of their civic involvement as a way to help their children, set a good example, and stay informed about their children's lives. On the other hand, some parents stated that their responsibilities to their children and families left them without time for civic involvement. What immigrant parents are conveying to their children about the balance between commitments to family and civil society merits further research, as does the question of how immigrant youth themselves view and act on their commitments to these two realms.

Religious institutions have been and continue to be an important context in the social and civic lives of immigrants (Foley & Hoge, 2007). One study with immigrant youth and adults found that half of all study participants' civic activities occurred in the context of religious organizations (Jensen, 2008c). Parenthetically, it might be worth noting that this number is similar to what Putnam (2000) noted for the general American population. Furthermore, the study showed that religious organizations pulled participants evenly across age groups as well as national and religious backgrounds, unlike other institutions such as school, social service groups, and cultural and political organizations.

While the religious context was important for immigrants' civic involvement, findings also showed that few immigrants spoke of religious or spiritual motives when explaining their own civic involvement or why such involvement is important more generally. Only 12% of immigrant adults spoke of religious or spiritual motives, and for youth the comparable number was a mere 3% (Jensen, 2008c). These findings suggest that immigrant youth's (and adults') individual motives for civic involvement might not simply echo those of their developmental contexts, at least not for religious ones.

Media also may impact immigrant youth's civic and political lives. For example, as described above, Wray-Lake and her colleagues (2008) noted how Arab immigrant youth who regarded media portrayals of their culture and religion in a negative light also were more distrustful of the government. Maira (2004) noted how some South Asian Muslim immigrant youth paid close attention to media images of Muslims in the aftermath of 9/11, and then sought in their everyday actions to counter stereotypic images. Stepick and his colleagues (2008) found that media attention to the Elian Gonzales case mobilized Cuban immigrant youth to political action.

Additional research addressing how immigrant youth are influenced by media and how they use media for civic and political action would be very welcome. As an article in the *Economist* (February 7, 2009) addressing the impact of globalization and worldwide electronic media on youth asked: "Will they try to change the world, or simply settle for enjoying themselves?" Certainly, adolescents have more of an interest in media than children or adults (Dasen, 2000; Schlegel, 2001), and perhaps media with their worldwide reach might have particular appeal to immigrant youth whose identities also often cross boundaries (Bennett et al., this volume).

CONCLUSION: IMPLICATIONS FOR POLICY AND POLITY

The research described above on immigrant youth's civic and political lives has implications for policy and for the questions of identity that we face as a nation. The research shows that immigrant youth are different from non-immigrant youth in some respects. Immigrant youth have distinctive civic and political behaviors and motives, and developmental contexts such as family, religion, and media may play distinctive roles in their civic and political lives. Consequently, civics education programs and public policies aimed at promoting youth engagement are likely to be more effective if they go beyond a one-size-fits-all approach (cf. Jensen, forthcoming). In regard to immigrant youth, programs are likely to do be more successful if they to some extent accommodate to the youth's distinctive motives, interests, and behaviors. Furthermore, programs might also take into account that immigrant youth often have strong allegiances to their families, and that immigrant parents potentially may come to see involvement in civil society as part of their parental duty. Thus, civics programs that aim to jointly involve immigrant youth and their families are likely to resonate well.

Also, on the positive side, the research shows that immigrant youth are motivated to bridge between their culture of origin and their new country, and to contribute to civil society. On the negative side, the research indicates that immigrant youth who experience stereotypes and discrimination may come to feel alienated, even oppositional. Consequently, immigrant youth's role in American civil society rests not simply with them, but with the nation as a whole. Levine (2008) has stated that civic and political engagement is sensible when considered from the perspective of *we*. The question that invariably arises in regard to the civic and political incorporation of immigrants into society is the one Huntington asked and that Benjamin Franklin and many others have debated, namely: "Who are *we*?" If current immigrant youth are to both feel and be full members of the polity, they will need to meet with an America of a capacious national identity.

REFERENCES

Barreto, M. A., & Munoz, J. A. (2003). Reexamining the "Politics of In-Between": Political participation among Mexican immigrants in the United States. *Hispanic Journal of Behavioral Sciences*, *25*, 427–447.

Bass, L. E., & Casper, L. M. (2001). Impacting the political landscape: Who registers and votes among naturalized Americans? *Political Behavior*, *23*, 103–130.

Bloemraad, I. (2006). Becoming a citizen in the United States and Canada: Structured mobilization and immigrant political incorporation. *Social Forces*, *85*, 667–695.

Bogard, K. L., & Sherrod, L. R. (2008). Citizenship attitudes and allegiances in diverse youth. *Cultural Diversity and Ethnic Minority Psychology*, *14*, 286–296.

Bourne, R. S. (1916). Trans-national America. *Atlantic Monthly*, *118*, 86–97.

Chareka, O., & Sears, A. (2006). Civic duty: Young people's conceptions of voting as a means of political participation. *Canadian Journal of Education*, *29*, 521–540.

Cyber-hedonism: Virtual Pleasures. (2009, February 7). *The Economist* (London).

Dasen, P. (2000). Rapid social change and the turmoil of adolescence: A cross-cultural perspective. *International Journal of Group Tensions*, *29*, 17–49.

Degler, C. (1970). *Out of our past: The forces that shaped modern America.* New York: Harper & Row.

Elliott, A. (2009, June 11). A call to Jihad, answered in America. *The New York Times*. Retrieved from http://www.nytimes.com/2009/07/12/us/12somalis.html

Flanagan, C. A. (2004). Volunteerism, leadership, political socialization, and civic engagement. In R. A. Lerner & L. D. Steinberg (Eds.), *Handbook of adolescent psychology* (pp. 721–745). Hoboken, NJ: John Wiley & Sons.

Foley, M. W., & Hoge, D. R. (2007). *Religion and the new immigrants: How faith communities form our newest immigrants*. New York: Oxford University Press.

Fredricks, J. A., Alfred-Liro, C. J., Hruda, L. Z., Eccles, J. S., Patrick, H., & Ryan, A. (2002). A qualitative exploration of adolescents' commitment to athletics and arts. *Journal of Adolescent Research, 17*, 68–97.

Galston, W. A. (2001). Political knowledge, political engagement, and civic education. *Annual Review of Political Science, 4*, 217–234.

Hernandez, D. J., Denton, N. A., & Macartney, S. E. (2007). Children in immigrant families—The U.S. and 50 states: National origins, language, and early education (Research Brief Series). University of Albany: Child Trends & the Center for Social and Demographic Analysis.

Hernandez, D. J., Denton, N. A., & Macartney, S. E. (2008). *Children in immigrant families: Looking to America's future*. Social Policy Report. Ann Arbor, MI: Society for Research in Child Development.

Huddy, L., & Khatib, N. (2007). American patriotism, national identity, and political involvement. *American Journal of Political Science, 51*, 63–77.

Huntington, S. P. (2004). *Who are we? The challenges to America's national identity*. New York: Simon & Schuster.

Jensen, L. A. (2003). Coming of age in a multicultural world: Globalization and adolescent identity formation. *Applied Developmental Science, 7*, 188–195.

Jensen, L. A. (2008a). Immigrants' cultural identities as sources of civic engagement. *Applied Developmental Science, 12*, 74–83.

Jensen, L. A. (2008b). Through two lenses: A cultural-developmental approach to moral psychology. *Developmental Review, 28*, 289–315.

Jensen, L. A. (2008c). Immigrant civic engagement and religion: The paradoxical roles of religious motives and organizations. In R. Lerner, R. Roeser, & E. Phelps (Eds.), *Positive youth development and spirituality: From theory to research* (pp. 247–261). West Conshohocken, PA: Templeton Foundation Press.

Jensen, L. A. (2009). To do or not to do: Immigrant motives for civic engagement and disengagement. Unpublished manuscript, Clark University.

Jensen, L. A. (forthcoming). *Bridging cultural and developmental psychology: New syntheses in theory, research and policy*. New York: Oxford University Press.

Jensen, L. A., Arnett, J. A., & McKenzie, J. (forthcoming). Globalization and cultural identity developments in adolescence and emerging adulthood. In S. J. Schwartz, K. Luyckx, & V. L. Vignoles (Eds.), *Handbook of identity theory and research*. New York: Springer Publishing Company.

Jensen, L. A., & Flanagan, C. A. (Eds.) (2008a). Immigrant civic engagement: New translation. *Applied Developmental Science, 12*.

Jensen, L. A., & Flanagan, C. A. (2008b). Immigrant civic engagement: New translations. *Applied Developmental Science, 12*, 55–57.

Junn, J. (1999). Participation in liberal democracy. *American Behavioral Scientist, 42*, 1417–1438.

Junn, J., & Masuoka, N. (2008). Identities in context: Politicized racial group consciousness among Asian American and Latino youth. In L. A. Jensen &

C. A. Flanagan (Eds.), *Immigrant civic engagement: New translation.* Special issue of *Applied Developmental Science, 12,* 93–101.

Kallen, H. K. (1956). *Cultural pluralism and the American ideal: An essay in social philosophy.* Philadelphia: University of Pennsylvania Press.

Kessler, T., Mummendey, A., & Leisse, U. (2000). The personal-group discrepancy: Is there a common information basis for personal and group judgment? *Journal of Personality and Social Psychology, 79,* 95–109.

Leal, D. L. (2002). Political participation by Latino non-citizens in the United States. *British Journal of Political Science, 32,* 353–370.

Levine, P. (2008). The civic engagement of young immigrants: Why does it matter? In L. A. Jensen & C. A. Flanagan (Eds.), *Immigrant civic engagement: New translation.* Special issue of *Applied Developmental Science, 12,* 102–104.

Lien, P. (1994). Ethnicity and political participation: A comparison between Asian and Mexican Americans. *Political Behavior, 16,* 237–264.

Lopez, M. H., & Marcelo, K. B. (2008). The civic engagement of immigrant youth: New evidence from the 2006 Civic and Political Health of the Nation Survey. In L. A. Jensen & C. A. Flanagan (Eds.), *Immigrant Civic Engagement: New Translation,* Special issue of *Applied Developmental Science, 12,* 66–73.

Maira, S. (2004). Youth culture, citizenship and globalization: South Asian Muslim youth in the United States after September 11th. *Comparative Studies of South Asia, Africa, and the Middle East, 24,* 219–231.

Martin, P., & Midley, E. (2006). *Immigration: Shaping and reshaping America.* Washington, DC: Population Reference Bureau.

Martin, P., & Zurcher, G. (2008). *Managing migration: The global challenge.* Washington, DC: Population Reference Bureau.

Mather, M. (2009). *Children in immigrant families chart new path.* Washington, DC: Population Reference Bureau.

Patrick, H., Ryan, A. M., Alfred-Liro, C., Fredricks, J. A., Hruda, L. Z., & Eccles, J. S. (1999). Adolescents' commitment to developing talent: The role of peers in continuing motivation for sports and the arts. *Journal of Youth and Adolescence, 28,* 741–764.

Pearce, N. J., & Larsen, R. W. (2006). How teens become engaged in youth development programs: The process of motivational change in a civic activism organization. *Applied Developmental Science, 10,* 121–131.

Portes, A., & Rumbaut, R. G. (2001). *Legacies: The story of the immigrant second generation.* Los Angeles: University of California Press.

Putnam, R. D. (2007). E pluribus unum: Diversity and community in the twenty-first century. The 2006 John Skytte Prize Lecture. *Scandinavian Political Studies, 30,* 137–174.

Putnam, R. D. (2000). *Bowling alone: The collapse and revival of American community.* New York: Simon & Schuster.

Ramakrishnan, S. K, & Espenshade, T. J. (2001). Immigrant incorporation and political participation in the United States. *International Migration Review, 35,* 870–909.

Rice, T. W., & Feldman, J. L. (1997). Civic culture and democracy from Europe to America. *The Journal of Politics, 59,* 1143–1172.

Rumbaut, R. G. (1994). The crucible within: Ethnic identity, self-esteem, and segmented assimilation among children of immigrants. *International Migration Review, 28*, 748–794.

Rumbaut, R. G. (2008). Reaping what you sow: Immigration, youth, and reactive ethnicity. In L. A. Jensen & C. A. Flanagan (Eds.), *Immigrant civic engagement: New translation.* Special issue of *Applied Developmental Science, 12*, 108–111.

Sanchez-Jankowski, M. (2002). Minority youth and civic engagement: The impact of group relations. *Applied Developmental Science, 6*, 237–245.

Sanjek, R. (2001). Color-full before color-blind: The emergence of multiracial neighborhood politics in Queens, New York City. *American Anthropologist, 102*, 762–772.

Schildkraut, D. J. (2005). The rise and fall of political engagement among Latinos: The role of identity and perceptions of discrimination. *Political Behavior, 27*, 285–312.

Schlegel, A. (2001). The global spread of adolescent culture. In L. J. Crockett & R. K. Silbereisen (Eds.), *Negotiating adolescence in times of social change.* New York: Cambridge University Press.

Sherrod, L. R., Flanagan, C., & Youniss, J. (2002a). Editors' introduction. *Applied Developmental Science, 6*, 173–174.

Sherrod, L. R., Flanagan, C., & Youniss, J. (2002b). Dimensions of citizenship and opportunities for youth development: The *what, why, when, where,* and *who* of citizenship development. *Applied Developmental Science, 6*, 264–272.

Shweder, R. A., Much, N. C., Mahapatra, M., & Park, L. (1997). The "big three" of morality (autonomy, community, divinity), and the "big three" explanations of suffering. In A. Brandt & P. Rozin (Eds.), *Morality and Health.* New York: Routledge.

Stepick, A., & Stepick, C. D. (2002). Becoming American, constructing ethnicity: Immigrant youth and civic engagement. *Applied Developmental Science, 6*, 246–257.

Stepick, A., Stepick, C. D., & Labissiere, Y. (2008). South Florida's immigrant youth and civic engagement: Major engagement, minor differences. In L. A. Jensen & C. A. Flanagan (Eds.), *Immigrant civic engagement: New translation.* Special issue of *Applied Developmental Science, 12*, 57–65.

Torney-Purta, J., Amadeo, J-A, & Richardson, W. (2007). Civic service among youth in Chile, Denmark, England, and the United States. In A. Moore & M. Sherraden (Eds.), *Civic service worldwide: Impacts and inquiry.* Armonk, NY: M.E. Sharpe.

Verba, S., Schlozman, K. L., & Brady, H. E. (1995). *Voice and equality: Civic voluntarism in American politics.* Cambridge, MA: Harvard University Press.

Waters, M. C. (2008). The challenges of studying political and civic incorporation. In L. A. Jensen & C. A. Flanagan (Eds.), *Immigrant civic engagement: New translation.* Special issue of *Applied Developmental Science, 12*, 105–107.

Wray-Lake, L., Syvertsen, A. K., & Flanagan, C. A. (2008). Contested citizenship and social exclusion: Adolescent Arab American immigrants' views of the social contract. In L. A. Jensen & C. A. Flanagan (Eds.), *Immigrant civic engagement: New translation.* Special issue of *Applied Developmental Science, 12*, 84–92.

Yen, H. (2009, May 14). Hispanic, Asian growth slowing, Census says. *Boston Globe*, A17.

Zangwill, I. (1975). *The melting pot: A drama in four acts.* New York: Arno Press.

CHAPTER 17

The Civic Life of Latina/o Immigrant Youth: Challenging Boundaries and Creating Safe Spaces

HINDA SEIF
University of Illinois at Springfield

As demographics shift and immigration is a hotly contested area of civic life in the United States, the civic preparation and participation of Latin American immigrant youth is becoming increasingly important. There is a growing literature on this topic, inquiring into the political and demographic changes that have stimulated this area of inquiry, the challenges of studying this population, and what we currently know and still need to know about immigrant youth civic engagement and activism. At a time when the struggle for immigrant rights in the United States is caught in the crossfire of severe recession and continuing racism, immigrant youth activists offer a ray of hope through their modest yet significant successes. Scholarship on their civic engagement sheds light on ways that youth who live on the fault line between nation-states are creatively forging civic identities, claiming political voices, and making an impact.

Despite assertions that Latin American immigration threatens the vitality of U.S. civic life (Huntington, 2004) and research findings that immigrants are less likely to engage civically than U.S. citizens (Ramakrishnan & Baldassare, 2004; Ramakrishnan & Viramontes, 2006), in 2006, Latinos with varied relationships to the U.S. nation-state led some of the largest political mobilizations in U.S. history (Cano, 2009; Lazos, 2007; Pantoja, Menjívar, & Magaña, 2008). In the 2008 presidential election, Latinos may have provided the margin of victory in swing states (Limonic, 2008). Numerous scholars are revisiting the question of Latina/o immigrant civic engagement to make sense of the gap between common assumptions and academic findings that it is low and their recent, remarkable political activism and influence (Bloemraad & Trost, 2008). Due to the geographic proximity of Latin America, the dependence of Latin Americans on remittances, and the increasing barriers to lawful immigration to the United States from this region (De Genova, 2005), the transnational and human rights dimensions of Latina/o politics challenge traditional paradigms of borders and citizenship.

GROWTH AND DISPERSAL OF LATINA/O IMMIGRANT COMMUNITIES

Although immigrant youth education (Ogbu, 1978; Olsen, 1998; Suárez-Orozco, 1989; Suárez-Orozco, Suárez-Orozco, & Todorova, 2008; Valenzuela, 1999) and family relationships (Foner, 2009) have long been studied, the civic engagement of Latina/o immigrant youth has only recently attracted scholarly attention. This new awareness is partly fueled by changing demographics. English Language Learners are the fastest growing student group in the United States, and as of 2008, 5% of children enrolled in grades K through 12 were immigrants (Pew Hispanic Center, 2009a, p. 4). By 2007, at least half of immigrants under age 18 were of Latin American origin, with 37% of foreign-born minors originating in Mexico (1.1 million), 7% from South America (207,000), and 6% from Central America (175,000) (Pew Hispanic Center, 2009b). As Latin American immigrants disperse throughout the country, they increasingly impact suburban and rural schools in states like North Carolina, Georgia, and Kansas with little experience educating this population (Park, 2009). Unauthorized immigration is intensely debated, and children constituted 12.6% of the undocumented in 2008 (Passel & Cohn, 2009, p. 4). Although the number of undocumented children has not grown since 2003 (Passel & Cohn, 2009, p. ii), these youth are becoming more visible because of legislative battles and organizing efforts that aim to help or hinder their life chances in the United States.

Yet changing demographics only partially explains why the civic engagement of Latina/o immigrant youth is of great consequence. Youth are important change agents and have played key roles in Latina/o social movements. How does their civic participation differ from that of immigrant adults and U.S.-born youth? Latina/o immigrant youth also live at the intersection of a number of key struggles against the criminalization of youth of color and immigrants (HoSang, 2005). Political initiatives that target them include struggles over bilingual education, attempts to restrict the educational access of undocumented students, and federal initiatives to legalize their status. Nevertheless, there are especially strong arguments for incorporating all immigrant children into society. The innocence of children has been highlighted in civil rights struggles, such as the integration of schools and other public facilities. Politically, there is more sympathy for immigrant youth who were brought to this country than for adults, who are largely seen as exercising free will in their decision to migrate. Because immigrant youth have spent much of their lives in the United States, they often have limited exposure to the language, education, and culture of their countries of birth, consider this country their home, and are unlikely to leave the United States.

INCLUSIVE DEFINITIONS OF IMMIGRANT YOUTH CIVIC ENGAGEMENT

When scholars study immigrant youth civic engagement, they face special challenges that include the varied ways that these youth and their civic practices are defined and measured. Most researchers agree that we cannot use the experiences of adult citizens to define and forecast youth civic engagement. Many usual predictors, such as education level and earnings, do not easily translate for immigrant youth who may be too young to attend college, fully engage in the world of work, and vote (Gonzalez, 2008). It is also problematic to use parental patterns to predict immigrant youths' civic engagement because the next generation is more acculturated to the United States.

Jensen and Flanagan (2008) argue that to paint a picture of the civic life of immigrant youth, we must look at their general community involvement. For example, Stepick, Dutton Stepick, & Labissiere (2008) identified and measured four types of activities in their study comparing U.S.-born and immigrant youth in South Florida: (1) political (registering to vote, discussing politics, attending demonstrations); (2) civic (helping others through formal service organizations and programs, e.g., student clubs, or individually, e.g., helping a non-English speaker); (3) expressive group membership (participating in athletics and ethnic organizations); and (4) social (attending church, spending time with peers, helping one's family). This definition, especially its inclusion of certain social pursuits such as spending time with peers and assisting family, is so broad that it blurs the picture of their civic engagement (see Waters, 2008). On the other hand, scholars may fail to fully investigate immigrant youth participation in key political activities (such as volunteering for a candidate) because they assume inactivity due to age and immigration status (Stepick et al., 2008).

Yet as young immigrants and their parents are targeted in divisive, partisan political struggles that include anti-immigrant electoral campaigns and legislative initiatives (such as Proposition 187),[1] non-citizen youth, both

---

[1] Proposition 187 was a 1994 California voter initiative that proposed to bar undocumented immigrants from receipt of public services, including K–12 education, and require police officers and other service providers, such as teachers and healthcare professionals, to report suspected "illegal immigrants" to immigration law enforcement authorities.

documented and undocumented, are participating in get-out-the-vote efforts (Rogers et al., 2008; Seif, 2004, 2008b; S.I.N. Collective, 2007). They may join these endeavors through their affiliations with labor unions or community-based organizations that serve immigrants (Seif, 2008b). Foreign-born Latino youth may have a proclivity to collective political action because of their class and ethnic backgrounds, their limited power as individuals, and in reaction to the draconian political challenges that their families have faced, including policy proposals to bar undocumented immigrants from public schools and to convert unlawful presence in the United States from a violation of civil immigration law into a criminal felony. The challenge is to define their civic engagement in a way that captures its scope yet is not too wide-ranging.

DIVERSITY OF LATINA/O IMMIGRANT YOUTH

The civic engagement of young immigrants can also be hard to assess because of their great diversity and the differing ways that researchers have defined and categorized them. Historically, scholars have called the second generation (children of immigrants born in the United States) "immigrant youth" or have not disaggregated them from first-generation minors (born abroad). For example, a special journal issue of *Applied Developmental Science* on the topic of immigrant youth civic engagement (Flanagan & Jensen, 2008) provides important studies on the topic, yet it also includes research on second-generation youth or does not clearly disaggregate youth born abroad (Jensen, 2008; Junn & Masuoka, 2008; Stepick et al., 2008). Although first- and second-generation youth share immigrant parentage, their experiences may be distinct (Seif, 2004; Suárez-Orozco et al., 2008). All second-generation youth are citizens, yet the first generation may be non-citizens or undocumented; these distinct immigration statuses have an important impact on civic and political activity, including whether youth are or will be eligible to vote. Many young immigrants have lived through long separations from their parents, traumatic border crossings, the disorientation of moving to a new land, and learning a new language (Suárez-Orozco et al., 2008). There are indications that these distinct life events lead to significant differences in their civic participation compared to the children of immigrants who are born in the United States (Lopez & Marcelo, 2008).

Age of entry to the United States also impacts immigrant youth, yet it may be unmarked in scholarship. The one-and-a-half (1.5) generation, generally defined as those born abroad and mostly educated in the receiving country, often have divergent experiences and relationships to the United States and their country of origin compared to second-generation and recently arrived youth. For example, Seif's (2004) study of undocumented 1.5-generation activists in Southeast Los Angeles introduces students who are comfortable in English and Spanish, who serve as mediators for their parents vis-à-vis local institutions, and who cannot fathom returning to their countries of origin. Their daily lives are restricted by their legal vulnerability to deportation, and they face a marginal future. This differs from their siblings and friends who were born in the United States, who even receive more medical care. Compared to the 1.5 generation, the new immigrant students studied by Suárez-Orozco et al. (2008) struggle with English and are more likely to be socially isolated. Furthermore, the 1.5 generation is variously defined, which makes it difficult to compare studies. Young immigrants are also studied at different ages ranging from early adolescence to 30 years old. Although most studies that include immigrant youth do not look at immigration and citizenship status, scholars have begun to examine their great impacts, which are especially relevant to questions of civic engagement and political activity (Abrego, 2006; Gonzalez, 2008; Martínez-Calderón, 2009; Seif, 2004).

Other forms of diversity may impact civic engagement patterns. Latina/o immigrant youth arrive from different countries. Within the dominant group of Mexican immigrants, youth may originate in Mexico City or indigenous communities of rural Oaxaca. Immigrant children and their families come to the United States as refugees, for economic reasons, or both, and they have varied class backgrounds and educational levels. Latina/o immigrant youth have cultural, linguistic, racial, and religious differences. They settle in White neighborhoods isolated from other Latinos and ethnic support systems, and in immigrant enclaves apart from mainstream middle-class culture and resources (Suárez-Orozco et al., 2008). Political context matters in both regions of origin and destination, including local or national political events, presence of opportunities to participate in a social movement, and the changing relations between the United States and sending countries (Brodkin, 2007; Jensen & Flanagan, 2008; Stepick et al., 2008). Cuban adolescents who lived in Miami during the Elián González controversy (Stepick et al., 2008), Mexican immigrants who walked out of California schools to protest Proposition 187 (Seif, 2004), and young Salvadorans who fled political violence with their parents (Suárez-Orozco, 1989) have been shaped by these histories and events. Aside from structural issues, young people also have individual preferences and exercise agency (Valenzuela, 1999). Some have older siblings who model political activism (Sanchez Jankowski, 1986), while others belong to churches that have initiated them into political action (Palacios, 2007). Thus, demographic, geographic, social, economic, political, ethnic, and racial contexts influence immigrant youths' civic engagement opportunities and expressions.

Research in fields such as health (Zúñiga et al., 2005) and education (Ogbu, 1978; Suárez-Orozco, 1989; Valenzuela, 1999) demonstrates that being foreign-born is not only associated with problems; it can also lead to resilience.

Studies that disaggregate the civic engagement of first-generation Latina/o youth can also present a clearer picture of the ways they are disadvantaged or empowered as civic actors compared to their peers, who have deeper roots in the United States and its pervasive racial inequality.

METHODS, THEMES, AND VOICES

The nexus of age, race, and immigration status makes it challenging to identify and study immigrant youth, especially when they are undocumented. Because most work on immigrant youth has been conducted on their education, and schools are a key site of their civic education and engagement, some larger educational studies shed light on their civic life (Olsen, 1998; Suárez-Orozco et al., 2008; Valenzuela, 1999). Similarly, although the experience of immigrant youth was not the focus of Brodkin's (2007) rich anthropological study of the development of youth activists in Los Angeles, approximately half of the activists profiled were immigrants.

Recent research either specifically looks at the civic engagement of immigrant youth or disaggregates them within larger studies of civic engagement. The topic has been approached from a variety of perspectives including psychology and adolescent development, education, political science, sociology, and anthropology. Most research has been qualitative and small-scale, using participant observation, focus groups, interviews, or case studies (Gonzalez, 2008; Rogers et al., 2008; Seif, 2004). This provides a nuanced portrayal of the lives of immigrant youth and their process of civic engagement. Our picture has recently been clarified through analysis of national survey data (Lopez & Marcelo, 2008; Torney-Purta, Barber, & Wilkenfeld, 2006) and longitudinal studies (Stepick et al., 2008). Although quantitative data is more generalizable, it is difficult to find a representative sample of immigrant or Latina/o immigrant youth because of their low frequency in the population and the difficulty of locating them through traditional research methods such as phone surveys (Lopez & Marcelo, 2008).

Scholars are interested in the ways that immigrant youths' civic education and activity compare to that of co-ethnics and other U.S.-born peers. Regarding identity issues, researchers examine how their immigrant or ethnic identity is related to civic engagement and whether these pursuits focus on cultural or immigrant issues or reflect transnational perspectives (Brodkin, 2007; Jensen, 2008; Stepick & Dutton Stepick, 2002). The special role that schools play in immigrant youth civic education, engagement, and activism is a major theme in this field of inquiry (Rogers et al., 2008; Torney-Purta et al., 2006; Torney-Purta, Barber, & Wilkenfeld, 2007). Public schools are charged by the state with teaching the basic skills required for civic life, and instructing students in the functions and importance of democratic institutions. Immigrant students also gain civic and leadership skills by participating in school-sponsored clubs and activities such as student government, tutoring programs, and community service. Through their education, immigrant students join networks beyond the family that incorporate citizen teachers, counselors, and peers (Rogers et al., 2008).

Youth involvement in various immigrant rights struggles is examined, including efforts to pass in-state tuition bills for undocumented students and the 2006 immigration reform protests. Immigrant students are also organizing in support of the federal legislative proposal known as the DREAM (Development, Relief and Education for Alien Minors) Act. This congressional measure, which has become a rallying point for immigrant students and their allies nationally, holds the most promise of unleashing the full civic capacity of approximately 65,000 undocumented youth who graduate from high school each year. If passed, it will provide a pathway to citizenship for qualified immigrants who arrived in the United States as minors, have lived in the country for at least five years, and are of good moral character (National Immigration Law Center, 2009).

The civic engagement and political activism of undocumented youth is a special case that shares some attributes with the situation of other immigrant youth and of undocumented adults but that also has its own characteristics. These distinctions are reflected in related scholarship. For example, because of the difficulty of identifying undocumented youth and gaining their trust, no studies of this population utilize random sampling procedures. The social movement for immigrant rights motivates considerable writing in this area, and a central theme is the ways that silencing, fear, and shame impede undocumented youths' civic engagement (S.I.N. Collective, 2007; Villegas, 2006). In fact, undocumented youth are writing and producing scholarship as part of their activism, blurring the boundaries between research and political action (Madera, 2008; S.I.N. Collective, 2007), researchers and research subjects.

Politics and civic engagement are generally associated with legal citizenship. Thus, critical questions arise in an era when globalization displaces millions across borders to face increasingly restrictive immigration laws. What impact does large-scale, unauthorized migration have on democracy? How do those excluded from formal nation-state membership find ways to participate in the civic life of their adopted homes and countries of origin? When undocumented youth organize for their own rights with documented immigrant and U.S.-born peer allies, they demonstrate creative identifications and citizenship practices as persons formally excluded from the nation-state, a point that will be discussed below. Because general studies of immigrant youth civic engagement and those that focus on the issues of the undocumented diverge, they will be examined separately.

NATIONAL AND REGIONAL STUDIES

Recent analysis of national and regional surveys offers important insights into the civic knowledge and activity of immigrant youth. Torney-Purta et al. (2006) measured the differences in preparation for citizenship between immigrant, non-immigrant, Hispanic, and non-Hispanic youth. Their analysis, conducted from a human development perspective, uses survey data from the IEA Civic Education Study, a nationally representative sample of 2,811 14-year-old students that included 194 non-Hispanic and 92 Hispanic immigrants (Torney-Purta et al., 2006, p. 347). They find that although immigrants' and Hispanic students' understanding of the behavioral norms of citizenship are comparable to non-Hispanic, native-born students', the latter had more positive results in regard to "knowledge of civic concepts, understanding democracy, possessing the skills necessary to understand political communication, expressing positive attitudes toward the nation, and expressing protectionist attitudes toward the nation" (Torney-Purta et al., 2006, p. 352). On the other hand, immigrant and Hispanic youth convey strong immigrant identities and are more likely to support "rights and opportunities" for immigrants (Torney-Purta et al., 2006, p. 352). The authors stress the importance of examining the multiple dimensions of immigrants' civic knowledge and engagement. Perhaps because Latino youth (even those born in the United States) are likely to come from immigrant families with limited civic knowledge and are also likely to attend low-performing schools, they are less civically and politically informed than other students. There is evidence that when some of these characteristics are controlled for, the differences between Latino and non-Latino students diminish (Torney-Purta et al., 2007). Despite often having more limited civic knowledge, Latino adolescents' ethnic and immigrant identifications often serve to expand their understanding of citizenship and immigrant rights.

There is also evidence that among this group, commitments to immigrants and co-ethnics are associated with civic practices. Based on data from the 2006 Civic and Political Health of the Nation Survey, Lopez and Marcelo (2008) find that although young immigrants report less civic engagement than their peers, many of these gaps disappear when demographic variables such as socioeconomic status are controlled for. The survey was conducted soon after the 2006 immigration policy marches. Protest activities were the only arena where immigrant youth showed significantly higher civic engagement levels (Lopez & Marcelo, 2008). Political scientists Setzler and McRee (2005) use the National Longitudinal Study of Adolescent Health to examine patterns of acculturation and civic incorporation of foreign-born, second-generation, and native-born youth. Their sample included 507 first-generation students in grades 7 to 12. They find that "young immigrants are as likely as native youth to embrace core American political values, practice volunteerism, and become politically involved to the extent that their citizenship and socioeconomic circumstances permit" (Setzler & McRee, 2005, p. 17).

Stepick et al. (2008) combine surveys and participant observation in their study of high-school students and college freshmen in Miami, Florida, which, unlike most studies, incorporates Cuban immigrants. They are interested in whether immigrant youth adopt the civic engagement patterns of other youth of color or exhibit distinct behaviors. Using a broad definition of civic engagement outlined previously, Stepick et al. (2008) conclude that immigrant youth's commitments are comparable to those of U.S.-born minorities. However, the volunteer activities of those born abroad are more likely to benefit their ethnic group; they are active in tutoring, use their bilingual skills to help other immigrants, and serve as linguistic and cultural bridges between elders and the broader host society. Like native minorities, they are politically active related to discrimination. The immigrants surveyed are more involved than U.S.-born minorities in sports, an activity that offers a sense of community and demands few English language skills. They report high levels of engagement with churches and family activities (Stepick et al., 2008; see also Suárez-Orozco et al., 2008).

QUALITATIVE PERSPECTIVES

Qualitative inquiries, including studies of immigrant education, shed light on some reasons for the gap between immigrant youth civic knowledge and what appears to be their solid civic engagement. In her ethnography of students at a high school that serves a working class Latino and Mexican immigrant community in Houston, educational scholar Valenzuela (1999) identifies the various factors that sparked school walkouts in 1989. The school had a record of low academic achievement and high dropout rates, and was underfunded compared to others in the district. It was poorly maintained, and the students were given obsolete or broken computers and outdated textbooks. A dearth of qualified personnel led to use of noncertified teachers, a shortage of classes, course scheduling problems, and scarce extracurricular activities.

Although the school had transformed to a Latino majority, there was no corresponding change in school personnel and curriculum. Students demanded more Latino faculty, bilingual counselors, and staff who could communicate with immigrant students and family members, culturally sensitive administration, and an overhauling of the curriculum that mostly ignored Mexican and Latino history and culture. The walkout reminds us that immigrant students and U.S.-born co-ethnics can become civically active in their demand for quality, culturally competent education.

Valenzuela (1999) found that immigrant students' educational progress, friendships, and pursuits varied depending on whether they were from rural or urban regions of Mexico, and their gender and class differences, religious practices, and level of Americanization. For example, immigrant students with limited English language abilities preferred to spend time with other recent immigrants and had difficulty participating in extracurricular activities because of language barriers (see also Suárez-Orozco et al., 2008). Immigrant girls were more likely than boys to help others, and spending time at school was a way to escape the constant supervision of strict parents. Mexico-oriented, 1.5-generation youth were culturally assimilated yet were bilingual and retained pride in their Mexican heritage. These immigrant students were the most likely to participate in mainstream extracurricular activities.

Valenzuela (1999) also discusses the cultural values of Mexican immigrant students. For example, the principle of *educación* "refers to the family's role of inculcating in children a sense of moral, social, and personal responsibility and serves as the foundation for all other learning ... The end state of being *bien educado* is accomplished through a process characterized by respectful relations" (Valenzuela, 1999, p. 23). Because Mexican *educación* is the responsibility of families in addition to schools and emphasizes collective goals rather than individual achievement, this cultural standard may contribute to the robust civic engagement of young Mexican immigrants documented in numerous studies (Bernal, Alemán, & Carmona, 2008; Brodkin, 2007; Seif, 2004).

The developmental study of immigrant youth and education conducted by Suárez-Orozco et al. (2008) also elucidates ways that the immigrant experience both detracts from and promotes civic engagement. Over a period of five years, the researchers followed 309 recently arrived immigrant youth at 100 schools. Like Valenzuela (1999), they found that many immigrant students attend schools that are understaffed, with low academic expectations and hostile and violent peer cultures (Suárez-Orozco et al., 2008). Despite these obstacles, the researchers identify social aspects of the immigrant experience that give these students strong motivation to improve their lives. A driving force of immigration is to provide better opportunities for children. Parents make sacrifices, and their children's success is defined collectively by their ability to elevate their families and communities (Brodkin, 2007; Seif, 2004). Although Suárez-Orozco et al. (2008) focus on the ways that this immigration story influences students' educational motivation, it can also lead to civic and political engagement (Brodkin, 2007; Seif, 2004).

For example, in Seif's (2004) study of undocumented immigrant youth in Southeast Los Angeles who are community and legislative activists, David, a Guatemalan student mentored by second-generation Latino community organizers, testified to the state legislature. He explained that he feels compelled to honor his parents' sacrifices for him by attending college and becoming "someone." From his working-class perspective and against the charges of those who demonize "illegal immigrant" adults, he defines his parents' poorly compensated manual labor as a contribution to the United States. He also wishes to contribute to this society; he feels obligated to his family, his struggling immigrant community, and the country:

> Growing up in the United States has been a difficult transition for me. I would like to acknowledge here today the sacrifices that both my parents made by choosing to bring me to the United States in order to have better opportunities. My parents have worked hard in this country. I too have worked hard. Like them, I would like to contribute to this society. I always knew that education was important. In school I am enrolled in advanced placement courses, extracurricular activities, and I hold a 4.0 GPA. I'm a volunteer with a community-based organization in my neighborhood, and I am involved in working toward bettering our communities. (quoted in Seif, 2004, p. 226)

Yet because of challenging socioeconomic and political contexts and the marginalization of the collective orientation of working-class Latin American immigrants within the dominant U.S. culture of individualism, these strong incentives do not necessarily translate into achievement. Suárez-Orozco et al. (2008) find that this is especially true for recently arrived immigrant youth. In their study, this subgroup of immigrant students is socially segregated and spends time with other newcomers and family members (see also Olsen, 1997). The authors emphasize the special responsibility that non-family mentors assume when they help immigrant youth adjust to their new lives (see also Seif, 2004). Girls were most likely to identify such supportive adults and found them through churches, sports teams, and community centers; however, few immigrant students participated in after-school activities that provided these non-family mentors.

SUMMARY: IMMIGRANT YOUTH CIVIC ENGAGEMENT

In summary, immigrant youth are highly diverse, and their civic engagement varies based on features such as sex, age of immigration, English language ability, and the political contexts of receiving and sending regions. They are also defined in various ways; in order to produce comparable studies, researchers must establish common classifications, such as that of the 1.5 generation. It is also important to disaggregate the first, 1.5, and second generations of immigrant youth for analytical purposes. New immigrant youth are less likely to be comfortable in English and more likely to be socially isolated. One-and-a-half-generation youth born in Mexico may be non-citizens yet are more likely to have a collective rather than an individualistic orientation than their U.S.-born counterparts because they have been reared with the cultural value of *educación*. Such demographic, linguistic, social, and cultural differences have strong implications for civic and political participation.

When socioeconomic variables are controlled, immigrant youth exhibit rates of civic engagement that are comparable to those of non-immigrants. The schools that serve working-class and poor immigrant youth must be improved so the civic training they provide may reach the standards of more affluent educational institutions. Because they often engage in different civic practices than U.S. natives, it is important to define their civic engagement broadly. For example, immigrant youth tend to participate in religious activities and pursuits where English language ability is less important, such as sports, and they assist other immigrants as translators and tutors. Although few recent immigrant youth have non-family mentors, when available, these adults are crucial for their educational achievement and civic development (Seif, 2004). For example, mentors can provide insights into U.S. civic and political life that are unfamiliar to immigrant parents and not imparted in the under-resourced schools in many immigrant neighborhoods. They may involve immigrant students in community organizations, train them as leaders, and expand students' networks in ways that build their civic capacity.

Immigrant youth draw upon cultural and social resources and motivations that can increase their capacity for civic engagement. Their parents have sacrificed to provide better opportunities for their offspring who are motivated to fulfill their end of the immigrant "bargain" (Suárez-Orozco et al., 2008, p. 73) by contributing to their families, neighborhoods, and ethnic communities. Cultural values such as *educación* also emphasize communal responsibility (see also Brodkin, 2007). Ethnic and immigrant identities are strong sources of resilience and civic engagement that should be fostered rather than suppressed.

UNDOCUMENTED IMMIGRANT YOUTH: METHODOLOGIES AND THEMES

Undocumented youths' civic engagement has much in common with that of other young immigrants. It may be impacted by their English language ability and social segregation. Because most Latin American immigrant youth see the persecution and oppression of members of their families, communities, and other co-ethnics on a regular basis, the pursuit of social justice for these groups is a key form of their form of civic engagement (Perez, 2008; Seif, 2004). Yet their precarious status in this country makes daily life, let alone civic participation, very challenging (Solis, 2005). Adolescents without lawful resident status face constant struggles that include the need to work illegally and, because they are ineligible for a driver's license in most states, reliance on public transportation. Their lives in the United States are full of fear—of speaking out, of revealing their identities and concerns in public, and especially of arrest and deportation (Coronado, 2008; Diaz-Strong & Meiners, 2007; Madera, 2008; Martínez-Calderón, 2009; Seif, 2004). The field of civic engagement generally assumes that youth have freedom of mobility and action, and can choose to assemble and engage. While these suppositions are faulty for those who are poor and in communities of color in the United States, they are clearly problematic when one ventures to many countries beyond U.S. borders or looks at the lives of immigrant youth.

Due to the special challenges of researching the undocumented youth population, the few existing studies on their civic engagement are almost exclusively qualitative and generally focus on their controversial political struggles for rights and recognition. Most research is conducted in California, and more specifically, the Los Angeles metropolitan area, the epicenter of immigrant activism (Brodkin, 2007; Madera, 2008). Rare investigations conducted in other geographic regions include J. López's (2007) study of undocumented high-school students in North Carolina and Solis's (2005) research on undocumented Mexican youth and families in New York. Because these studies involve snowball sampling and volunteer recruitment, we know less about students who are not civically active.

This limited research suggests that despite overwhelming obstacles, undocumented youth may be as likely to participate in their schools and communities as other young people and exhibit distinctive civic engagement patterns. Rejected by the nation-state, undocumented youth understand that their life chances and those of their loved ones depend on social change. As is demonstrated by members of immigrant student groups that have emerged on college campuses across the country over the past decade, when gifted and motivated undocumented youth are given opportunities to get involved in immigrant rights and other social justice causes, some become creative and dedicated leaders against the odds.

SCHOOL MEMBERSHIP AND GRADUATION AS TRAUMA

In response to a 1975 Texas law that withheld state funds for educating children without lawful immigration status, the Supreme Court declared that school districts could not exclude undocumented students from public K–12 institutions in its Plyler v. Doe decision (U.S. Supreme Court 457 US 202 Docket: 80-1538, 1982). Although undocumented immigrants do not have many of the rights of U.S. citizens, they are covered under the Equal Protection Clause of the Constitution's 14th Amendment. Briefly, if a state does not provide "equal protection of the law" to all persons within its jurisdiction, it is violating the U.S. Constitution, unless its actions are related to or further a legitimate state interest. The Court found that without basic education and literacy, these immigrant children would grow up like a caste that is unable to live within the structure of our civic institutions, a situation that does not serve a state interest (M. López, 2004). Thus, this landmark decision granted undocumented youth standing in our schools, partly based on their future contributions to U.S. society and civic life (Rogers et al., 2008). With this decision, schools have become a key locus for the civic development of undocumented youth and their parents.

Studies of undocumented immigrants' education provide insight into their civic engagement (Coronado, 2008; Diaz-Strong & Meiners, 2007; Martínez-Calderón, 2009; Rogers et al., 2008). Through schools, students are linked to teachers, peers, counselors, and networks of citizens (Rogers et al., 2008; Gonzales, 2008). They join student clubs and organizations, serve their neighborhoods, develop leadership skills (Gonzales, 2008), and form robust attachments to the United States (Perez, Espinoza, Ramos, Coronado, & Cortes, 2009). For example, Perez et al. (2009) found that school clubs played a "critical role" in facilitating the volunteerism of most of the undocumented students that they interviewed. Many were members of school honor societies, which require community service. Like their documented immigrant peers, undocumented students tend to serve other co-ethnics and immigrants and assist with translation (Rogers et al., 2008).

For undocumented students, there is a contradiction between their educational membership and their exclusion from other social arenas (Gonzalez, 2008; Perez et al., 2009; Rogers et al., 2008; Seif, 2004). As minors, they have an identity as students and are less reliant on driver's licenses, working papers, and other trappings of adult normalcy. Until they reach high school, many undocumented students have limited awareness of their legal status or the future difficulties they face. Rather than a joyful rite of passage, the transition out of 12th grade becomes a traumatic change in identity and status from student to socially stigmatized "illegal alien" or illegal worker (Seif, 2004), and its approach can push youth into either despair or action (Gonzales, 2008; Perez et al., 2009).

THE PARADOX OF SOCIAL REJECTION AND CIVIC ENGAGEMENT

As part of a larger Loss of Talent research study mostly carried out at California's higher education institutions, Perez (2008) asks how illegal status impacts civic engagement patterns. The author hypothesizes that undocumented students will have lower levels of civic engagement because they feel more marginalized and face more discrimination than others. To address this question, 100 undocumented Latino students were recruited for an online survey through messages posted to student listservs. In a follow-up study, 54 students were located for in-depth interviews through e-mail notices sent to undocumented student clubs and flyers distributed in high-school and college classrooms (Perez et al., 2009). Students reported feeling socially rejected. They had substantial time commitments, taking academically rigorous courses and working an average of 12 hours per week during high school and 25 hours per week in college (Perez, 2008). Despite these barriers, 90% of students interviewed recounted civic activity, a level that is even higher than in the general student population (Perez, 2008). Female students reported more social service work and tutoring, and were the most likely to win awards for their civic contributions. The more hours a student was employed, the less they participated civically (Perez, 2008). On the other hand, students with higher GPAs, more extracurricular activities, and greater family responsibilities reported more civic engagement than average.

How do we account for this impressive level of civic action? Rather than give in to hopelessness, students explained that they invest time in community service, volunteerism, and political organizing (Perez et al., 2009). School clubs and churches are important in facilitating these activities. Their service stems from a commitment to social and political ideals. However, it also is a way for students to resist marginalization and demonstrate to themselves and others that they are good people and model citizens (Perez, 2008).

Despite high levels of civic engagement reported by some researchers (Coronado, 2008; Perez, 2008; Perez et al., 2009), other studies demonstrate that undocumented students feel marginalized in organizations that do not focus on their issues (Olsen, 1998; S.I.N. Collective, 2007). This includes Latina/o student groups that overlook immigrant concerns (S.I.N. Collective, 2007) and immigrant groups that overlook youth and student matters (Gonzales, 2008). Undocumented students may be afraid to reveal their immigration status, or their special issues may be ignored or swept aside when raised (S.I.N. Collective, 2007).

This neglect has generated student clubs, organizations, and subcommittees of existing groups that focus on the problems facing undocumented students and advocate for policy changes in schools and at local, state, and federal levels. Their activism has had an impact despite the harsh political and economic climate. Through a movement to enact state legislation that qualifies undocumented students to pay the equivalent of in-state tuition, laws have been enacted in 10 states (CA, IL, KS, NE, NM, NY, TX, UT, WA, WI) that make it more affordable for undocumented students to attend college. Although another in-state tuition law was enacted and later rescinded in Oklahoma, students have helped to block numerous policy proposals across the country that would limit their college access (Rincón, 2008; Seif, 2008a). As I will discuss below, in California (Abrego, 2008) and nationally, they have forged positive identities through their political struggles as alternatives to the stigmatized categorization of "illegal aliens."

UNDOCUMENTED STUDENTS AND THE IN-STATE TUITION MOVEMENT

Although the undocumented cannot legally be excluded from public K–12 schools, their access to higher education is more tenuous. They are generally kept out by cost, and efforts to help undocumented students attend college have focused on their ability to pay in-state tuition and receive financial aid. Seif (2004) examined the successful struggle for California's in-state tuition bill, Assembly Bill (AB) 540, as part of a larger ethnography of the transformation of state legislative politics in Latina/o districts with large immigrant populations. The author traces the connections between legislators of Mexican ancestry who were former student activists and today's students from Mexico and Central America. Undocumented, 1.5-generation teens have become leaders in Southeast Los Angeles because of their high educational achievement compared to their immigrant parents, their English-language abilities, their accepted identity as students, and the mentorship that some receive from local second-generation Latina/o activists (Seif, 2004). Beyond being very painful for the adolescents, their illegal status is a dilemma for Latino immigrant neighborhoods because it demoralizes teachers and fellow students and robs communities of their leaders' full potential (Seif, 2004). Rincón (2008) provides an educational policy history of the national immigrant movement for in-state tuition, with a focus on the story of the first bill passed in 2001, Texas House Bill (HB) 1403. She discusses strategies, organizational forms, and the role of undocumented students in these struggles. The author objects to the reliance on economic arguments or ones that depict young, uneducated immigrants as potential criminals. Rather, she urges students to remain at the center of their movement and assert their human right to education.

Across the United States, dozens of campus-based networks have formed that focus on the needs of students without lawful immigration status. These groups educate others about the plight of undocumented students, advocate for relevant policies and laws, and disseminate information about new in-state tuition laws through outreach. Because highly educated immigrant students face a future of low-paid, illegal employment unless laws change, some college campuses have emerged as dynamic sites of undocumented activism. They have few choices but to advocate on their own behalf (Gonzales, 2008).

At the high school and college levels, undocumented students have played a central role in the partial success of the national in-state tuition movement.

High-achieving and even valedictorian immigrant youth have come out of the shadows and gained public sympathy by telling their personal stories (Rincón, 2008; Seif, 2004). Many also stress their civic contributions in verbal and written accounts. Offering testimony also empowers youth who have hidden and felt ashamed of their legal status by converting their private troubles into a political issue (S.I.N. Collective, 2007). They organize and speak at campus rallies, recount their life histories to journalists, and lobby and testify at government hearings. They advocate for their rights on campus, hold educational forums, gather petitions, organize mock graduations, and even participate in hunger strikes to raise awareness of their plight (Gonzales, 2008; Madera, 2008; Rincón, 2008; Seif, 2004; S.I.N. Collective, 2007). Students travel across the country to lobby, network, and conduct outreach. They use information technologies, including social networking web sites such as Facebook, to publicize their groups and network with other students and associations across the nation (Gonzales, 2008; Rincón, 2008; S.I.N. Collective, 2007).

Young activists engage in these political and civic activities despite the hazards associated with their legal status. They must overcome their fears and assess the danger of arrest and deportation. Students participate in groups with members of mixed immigration statuses, use pseudonyms, and gauge how far they can safely travel to minimize risk (Gonzales, 2008; Rincón, 2008; Seif, 2004). Yet they are committed to speaking for themselves (Gonzales, 2008). Although most immigration reform efforts are currently hampered by the national economic context, these college access victories confirm that immigrant-friendly, regional laws can be enacted when they are associated with the faces and stories of high-achieving, civic-minded youth (Rincón, 2008; Seif, 2004). The in-state tuition laws are new, but there is evidence that their passage also makes it more likely that undocumented students will actively participate in civic life. These political struggles and successes have inspired youth to civic involvement, and undocumented youth who pursue higher education gain more skills and opportunities for this engagement compared to their counterparts who do not attend college. Because of the growing contradiction between their academic preparation and ineligibility for legal employment, undocumented college students are ripe for community participation and activism (Gonzales, 2008; S.I.N. Collective, 2007).

ENFORCEMENT OF HIGHER EDUCATION ACCESS AND OTHER POLICY STRUGGLES

New in-state tuition laws have enabled thousands of undocumented students to attend college, empowered them, and generated more activism (Rincón, 2008; S.I.N. Collective, 2007). They are forging new identities, enforcing these laws and working to expand their scope, pushing for federal legalization, and engaging in other political and policy efforts to help marginalized groups. Abrego (2008) reports that since the California bill's passage, some undocumented youth in the state call themselves *AB 540 students*. This identification highlights their social membership as students and participants in a political struggle (Gonzales, 2008; Rincón, 2008). In California, the in-state tuition law has been poorly enforced by schools and the government (Madera, 2008; Rincón, 2008; Seif, 2008b; S.I.N. Collective, 2007). To address this institutional neglect, the first wave of students to benefit from this legislation formed AB 540 groups on their campuses to enforce the law, organize younger students, and conduct outreach to parents, high schools, and community-based organizations (Gonzales, 2008; Madera, 2008; S.I.N. Collective, 2007). These associations formed the AB 540 College Access Network (Rincón, 2008).

A remarkable account of the impact of the law on the identity and political development of undocumented students was written by the Students Informing Now (S.I.N.) Collective (2007) at the University of California, Santa Cruz (UCSC), a Latina/o student group formed to support higher education access for immigrants (see also Dominguez et al., 2009). The collective offers a "safe space" (S.I.N. Collective, 2007, p. 73) where students without legal status can share their identities, and their concerns are central. Because their group includes Latina/o students with varied legal relationships to the nation-state, members can speak publicly about the plight of undocumented students without placing themselves in jeopardy by revealing their own legal situation. It also provides family-like support for students who struggle to stay in college and face an uncertain future after graduation. This includes emotional, financial, and transportation assistance. Such groups are crucial incubators for undocumented students as active participants in civic life. Although student organizations such as the S.I.N. Collective and Improving Dreams, Equality, Access, and Success (IDEAS) at the University of California, Los Angeles (UCLA) (Madera, 2008) have accomplished near-miracles given their limited resources and power, their efforts are no substitute for institutional enforcement of immigrant students' educational rights.

In addition, student groups in California and across the nation have continued state-level efforts by defending existing state laws that allow students to pay in-state tuition regardless of their immigration status, fending off restrictive legislative proposals and lawsuits, and trying to further expand higher education access for immigrants (S.I.N. Collective, 2007). *Underground Undergrads* (Madera, 2008), a book published from a class project at UCLA's Labor Center, was part of an effort to pass the California Dream Act (Senate Bill 1301, Cedillo), a bill to extend state and university financial aid to AB 540 students. Their goal was thwarted when Governor Arnold Schwarzenegger vetoed the bill.

Undocumented youth are also central to federal immigration reform efforts, including the DREAM Act. Many students are involved in DREAM Act organizing because it offers their best hope for someday using their education by working legally (Martínez-Calderón, 2009). Between 2004 and 2006, immigrant students and their supporters in California organized DREAM Act rallies and engaged in a hunger strike in Los Angeles (Gonzales, 2008; Rincón, 2008). Although student issues were often marginalized in the 2006 immigration reform protests, documented and undocumented immigrant youth and their campus support groups played key roles in the activities (Gonzales, 2008), drawing attention to the intersecting issues of immigrant college access and criminalization (Rincón, 2008). Their civic education, participation in school activism, and organizing efforts for in-state tuition and the DREAM Act prepared undocumented college students to assume leadership (Gonzales, 2008; S.I.N. Collective, 2007).

For participating undocumented youth, the 2006 protests and other activities have led to more empowerment, organizing, and coalition building, including national networking of undocumented students and their groups (Gonzales, 2008). Immigrant student associations have helped mobilize voters in electoral campaigns, advocated for driver's license legislation, and organized against individual deportations (Gonzales, 2008; Rincón, 2008). Like the California students who rejected stigmatized identities by renaming themselves *AB 540 students* a decade ago, many students across the nation are embracing activism and claiming the evocative identities of *DREAM Act students*, *Dream ACTivists*, and *DREAMers*.

SUMMARY: CIVIC ENGAGEMENT AMONG UNDOCUMENTED YOUTH

High-school graduation is an unusual developmental crisis for undocumented youth. They face the contradiction of having been included in public schools but excluded from the nation-state and a painful transition from student to illegal adult worker. They may be motivated to become civically involved to change immigration policy or to improve their communities while they are students with a legitimate place in U.S. society. They become active to feel good about themselves despite the stigma of being considered "illegal immigrants." By emulating active, model citizens, they try to prove that they deserve a place in U.S. society and to position themselves for future legalization programs (Martínez-Calderón, 2009). Despite the risks, these students become visible and offer testimony of their life struggles. Research and writing that sheds light on the ways that undocumented youth contribute to society often serves a dual purpose of activist projects toward granting these students legal status and other rights (Diaz-Strong & Meiners, 2007; Madera, 2008; S.I.N. Collective, 2007).

Undocumented youth are engaged in political organizing on campuses and at local, state, and federal levels to defeat anti-immigrant proposals and enact pro-immigrant policies. Because of the immediacy of these struggles, we have seen a cluster of research and writing on undocumented youth activism despite the difficulties of identifying this population. In-state tuition efforts offer rare cases of successful legislative efforts over the last decade to improve the lives of persons without lawful immigration status. The activism of these young people has significance beyond their numbers because they demonstrate innovative vision and practices of citizenship in a global society where human beings, including children, may not fit into legal categories of national membership.

FUTURE DIRECTIONS

Our knowledge of immigrant youth civic engagement is much greater today than it was a decade ago, yet there is much to learn.

Methods. Because of the challenges of identifying and studying immigrant youth, most studies have been qualitative and small-scale. The recent use of national datasets is a positive development in the field. Researchers should continue to pursue a range of methods to shed light on this topic, and studies that unite quantitative and qualitative analysis should be encouraged. Immigrant education is a rich arena of study that should explicitly incorporate civic education and engagement in schools.

Studying subpopulations. In addition to defining the generations in a consistent manner to make studies comparable, researchers can disaggregate Latina/o immigrant youth in various ways to offer a more nuanced picture. For example, more attention should be paid to the ways that gender and country of origin make a difference in the motivations and processes of immigrant youths' civic and political engagement. Researchers should also be attentive to the impact of immigration status, including the specific patterns of youth with quasi-legal or "In-Between" (Cebulko, 2008) status (e.g., Salvadorans with Temporary Protected Status). Given that migrations from Latin America are increasingly indigenous, it is essential to examine the activities of youth from these communities, especially whether they are able to maintain indigenous cultural practices and forms of civic life.

Geography. Most regional studies on this topic look at youth in California. We need to learn more about their civic and political engagement in other traditional and new immigration states. Beyond urban areas, we know little about the opportunities for civic and political engagement of young immigrants in rural and suburban regions where they increasingly reside.

Addressing weaknesses and building upon strengths. Now that we have identified arenas where immigrant youth are more likely to be civically involved, researchers can shed light on those that are underexplored, such as their participation in religious activities and sports, and identify ways to address weaknesses and promote strengths. The civic education that many Latina/o immigrant youth receive in school and their opportunities to participate in clubs and extracurricular activities are often inferior to those of their more affluent peers. Educators and elected officials should find ways to address these school deficiencies. Given that local community centers, community-based organizations, and non-family mentors are crucial for the civic development of young immigrants, ways to promote these resources in Latino communities should be identified. Immigrant youth are most likely to get involved in their ethnic and immigrant communities, so scholars can find ways to promote their "selective acculturation" rather than "subtractive assimilation" (Portes & Rumbaut, 1996, 2001) to foster their contributions to civic life. The prolific research on the transnational experience of immigrants should also examine the civic and political lives of youth.

Organizing. Despite evidence that information technologies are more widely used to organize by the children of immigrants than their parents (Bloemraad & Trost, 2008), we know little about the ways that immigrant youth employ e-mail, web pages, and texting in their activism and networking (see Bennett et al., this volume). This area of research should be further explored. Given that young immigrants and their concerns may be marginalized in mainstream Latina/o youth organizations, the ways that Latina/o youth of varied immigration statuses civically engage together should be examined. To promote interracial harmony in schools and communities and broad support for immigrant rights, we also need to know more about Latina/o immigrant youth who organize with youth from other backgrounds (see Fox et al., this volume; Jensen, this volume). Young immigrants are using hip-hop, art, poetry, and film to tell their stories; the use of the creative arts in their civic and political life is underexplored.

Undocumented Students and Institutional Policy. We are learning more about the enormous barriers to the civic engagement of undocumented youth, and the courageous and creative ways that some participate against the odds. There is substantial evidence that the passage of in-state tuition laws has promoted their civic and political activity as they advocate for these laws and engage in further political efforts. Such laws should be extended to other states and should be better implemented by schools and state government so the burden of enforcement does not fall on students. Immigrant student groups that have emerged on campuses across the country are dynamic examples of youth activism and engagement that should be further examined. Schools and governments should heed their demands, and they should be assisted through technical assistance and funding.

Less is known about mobilizations for in-state tuition laws in states beyond California and Texas or their advocacy for local and federal policies. These areas of inquiry should be pursued. Because these students are creatively challenging the boundaries of citizenship in a global era, the civic and political engagement of undocumented youth has important implications. Ultimately, we must empower youth raised in a nation where they are legally ostracized to develop and contribute to society to their full capacity. Their struggles for education and a pathway toward U.S. citizenship must be supported.

Acknowledgements

This chapter was made possible through the support of the University of California All Campus Consortium On Research for Diversity (UC ACCORD), the MacArthur Foundation, the Woodrow Wilson International Center for Scholars, UC Berkeley's Center for Latino Policy Research, and the University of Illinois at Springfield. Crucial was the energy and input of immigrant youth activists in California and Illinois who inspire those whose lives they touch. Special thanks to Simón Salinas, Gil Cedillo, and their legislative staffs, and those who worked for California's Assembly Member Marco Antonio Firebaugh. Xóchitl Bada and Jonathan Fox provided feedback and comments, and any remaining weaknesses are my own. This is dedicated to the memory of Marco Antonio Firebaugh (1966–2006), who came from Tijuana to California as a child, authored an in-state tuition law to help the state's students achieve their dream of college regardless of their immigration status, and fiercely advocated for immigrant youth.

REFERENCES

Abrego, L. (2006). "I can't go to college because I don't have papers": Incorporation patterns of Latino undocumented youth. *Latino Studies, 4(3)*, 212–231.

Abrego, L. (2008). Legitimacy, social identity, and the mobilization of law: The effects of Assembly Bill 540 on undocumented students in California. *Law & Social Inquiry, 33(3)*, 709–734.

Bedolla, L. G. (2000). They and we: Identity, gender and politics among Latino youth in Los Angeles. *Social Science Quarterly, 81*, 106–122.

Bernal, D. D., Alemán, E., Jr., & Carmona, J. F. (2008). Transnational and transgenerational Latina/o cultural citizenship among kindergarteners, their parents, and university students in Utah. *Social Justice, 32(4)*, 28–49.

Bloemraad, I., & Trost, C. (2008). It's a family affair: Inter-generational mobilization in the Spring 2006 protests. *American Behavioral Scientist, 52(4)*, 507–532.

Brodkin, K. (2007). *Making democracy matter: Identity and activism in Los Angeles.* New Brunswick, NJ: Rutgers University Press.

Cano, G. (2009). *Political mobilization of Latino immigrants in American cities and the U.S. immigration debate.* Retrieved from Columbia University, Institute of Latin American Studies web site: http://app.cul.columbia.edu:8080/ac/handle/10022/AC:P:29753

Cebulko, K. B. (2008, July). *Documented, undocumented and somewhere in-between: Documentation status and its effects on children of Brazilian immigrants.* Paper presented at the Annual Meeting of the American Sociological Association, Boston, MA.

Coronado, H. M. (2008). *Voices of courage and strength: Undocumented immigrant students in the United States.* Retrieved from UC Santa Barbara Center for Chicano Studies web site: http://escholarship.org/uc/item/43w9p02g

Cortés, R. D. (2008). *"Cursed and blessed": Examining the socioemotional and academic experiences of undocumented Latina/o community college students.* (Doctoral dissertation). Available from ProQuest Dissertations & Theses database (UMI No. 3318524).

De Genova, N. (2005). *Working the boundaries: Race, space, and Mexican "illegality" in Mexican Chicago.* Durham: Duke University Press.

Diaz-Strong, D., & Meiners, E. (2007). Residents, alien policies, and resistances: Experiences of undocumented Latina/o students in Chicago's colleges and universities. *InterActions: UCLA Journal of Education and Information Studies, 3(2).*

Dominguez, N., Duarte, Y., Espinosa, P.J., Martinez, L., Nygren, K., Perez, R., Ramirez, I., & Saba, M. (2009). Constructing a counternarrative: Students Informing Now (S.I.N.) reframes immigration and education in the United States. *Journal of Adolescent & Adult Literacy, 52(5)*, 439–442.

Foner, N. (Ed.). (2009). *Across generations: Immigrant families in America.* New York: New York University Press.

Fry, R., & Passel, J. S. (2009). *Latino children: A majority are U.S.-born offspring of immigrants.* Washington, DC: Pew Hispanic Center. Retrieved from http://pewhispanic.org/files/reports/110.pdf

Getrich, C. M. (2008). Negotiating boundaries of social belonging: Second-generation Mexican youth and the immigrant rights protests of 2006. *American Behavioral Scientist, 52(4)*, 533–556.

Gonzales, R. G. (2008). Left out but not shut down: Political activism and the undocumented Latino student movement. *Northwestern Journal of Law and Social Policy, 3(2)*, 219–239.

HoSang, D. (2005). *Traditions and innovations: Youth organizing in the Southwest.* New York: Retrieved from Funders' Collaborative on Youth Organizing web site: http://www.fcyo.org/media/docs/5037_OccasionalPapers_no8.pdf

HoSang, D. (2006). Beyond policy: Race, ideology and the re-imagining of youth. In S. Ginwright, P. Noguera, & J. Cammarota (Eds.), *Beyond resistance! Youth activism and community change* (pp. 3–20). New York: Routledge.

Huntington, S. P. (2004). The Hispanic challenge. *Foreign Policy, 72(3)*, 30–45.

Jensen, L. A. (2008). Immigrants' identities as sources of civic engagement. *Applied Developmental Science, 12(2)*, 74–83.

Jensen, L. A., & Flanagan, C. A. (2008). Immigrant civic engagement: New translations. *Applied Developmental Science, 12(2)*, 55–56.

Junn, J., & Masuoka, N. (2008). Identities in context: Politicized racial group consciousness among Asian American and Latino youth. *Applied Developmental Science, 12(2)*, 93–101.

Lazos, S. R. (2007). The immigrant rights marches (Las marchas): Did the "gigante" (giant) wake up or does it still sleep tonight? *Nevada Law Journal, 7*, 780–825.

Limonic, L. (2008). *Latinos and the 2008 Presidential Elections: A Visual Data Base*. Retrieved from City University of New York, Center for Latin American, Caribbean & Latino Studies web site: http://web.gc.cuny.edu/lastudies/latinodataprojectreports/Latinos%20and%20the%202008%20Presidential%20Elections%20A%20Visual%20Data%20Base.pdf

López, J. K. (2007). *"We asked for workers and they sent us people": A critical race theory and Latino critical theory ethnography exploring college-ready undocumented high school immigrants in North Carolina.* (Doctoral dissertation). Available from ProQuest Dissertations & Theses database (UMI No. 3262648).

Lopez, M. H., & Marcelo, K. B. (2008). The civic engagement of immigrant youth: New evidence from the 2006 Civic and Political Health of the Nation Survey. *Applied Developmental Science, 12(2)*, 66–73.

López, M. P. (2004). More than a license to drive: State restrictions on the use of driver's licenses. *Southern Illinois University Law Journal, 29*, 91–129.

Madera, G. (Ed.). (2008). *Underground undergrads: UCLA undocumented immigrant students speak out*. Los Angeles: UCLA Center for Labor Research and Education.

Martínez-Calderón, C. (2009). *Out of the shadows: Undocumented Latino college students*. Retrieved from UC Berkeley: Institute for the Study of Social Change web site: http://escholarship.org/uc/item/9zj0694b

National Immigration Law Center. (2009). *Dream Act: Summary*. Los Angeles, CA. Retrieved from http://www.nilc.org/immlawpolicy/dream/dream-bills-summary-2009-03-31.pdf.

Ogbu, J. (1978). *Minority education and caste: The American system in cross-cultural perspective*. New York: Academic Press.

Olsen, L. (1998). *Made in America: Immigrant students in our public schools*. New York: New Press.

Palacios, J. M. (2007). *The Catholic social imagination: Activism and the just society in Mexico and the United States.* Chicago: The University of Chicago Press.

Pantoja, A. D., Menjívar, C., & Magaña, L. (2008). The spring marches of 2006: Latinos, immigration, and political mobilization in the 21st century. *American Behavioral Scientist, 52(4)*, 499–506.

Park, H. (2009, March 13). New to English. *The New York Times*. Retrieved from http://www.nytimes.com/interactive/2009/03/13/us/ELL-students.html

Passel, J. S., & Cohn, D. V. (2009). *A portrait of unauthorized immigrants in the United States*. Washington, DC: Pew Hispanic Center. Retrieved from http://pewresearch.org/pubs/1190/portrait-unauthorized-immigrants-states

Perez, W. (2008, March). *Civic engagement patterns of undocumented immigrant youth in the United States.* Paper presented at the 12th Biennial Society for Research on Adolescence Conference, Chicago, IL.

Perez, W., Espinoza, R., Ramos, K., Coronado, H., & Cortes, R. (2009). *Motives for service: Civic engagement patterns of undocumented immigrant Latino/a youth.* Manuscript submitted for publication.

Pew Hispanic Center. *Mexican immigrants in the United States, 2008.* (2009a). Washington, DC: Pew Hispanic Center. Retrieved from http://pewresearch.org/pubs/1191/mexican-immigrants-in-america-largest-group

Pew Hispanic Center. *Statistical portrait of the foreign-born population in the United States, 2007, Table 19. Living arrangements of children by region of birth.* (2009b). Washington, DC: Pew Hispanic Center. Retrieved from http://pewhispanic.org/files/factsheets/foreignborn2007/Table%2019.pdf

Portes, A., & Rumbaut, R. G. (1996). *Immigrant America: A portrait.* Berkeley: University of California Press.

Portes, A., & Rumbaut, R. G. (2001). *Legacies: The story of the immigrant second generation.* Los Angeles, New York: University of California Press, Russell Sage Foundation.

Ramakrishnan, S. K. (2005). *Democracy in immigrant America.* Palo Alto: Stanford University Press.

Ramakrishnan, S. K., & Baldassare, M. (2004). *The ties that bind: Changing demographics and civic engagement in California.* San Francisco: Public Policy Institute of California. Retrieved from http://www.ppic.org/content/pubs/report/R_404KRR.pdf

Ramakrishnan, S. K., & Viramontes, C. (2006). *Civic inequalities: Immigrant volunteerism and community organizations in California.* San Francisco: Public Policy Institute of California. Retrieved from http://www.ppic.org/content/pubs/report/R_706KRR.pdf

Rincón, A. (2008). *Undocumented immigrants and higher education: Si se puede!* El Paso: LFB Scholarly Publishing.

Rogers, J., Saunders, M., Terriquez, V., & Velez, V. (2008). Civic lessons, public schools, and the civic development of undocumented students and parents. *Northwestern Journal of Law and Social Policy, 3,* 201–218.

Sanchez-Jankowski, M. (1986). *City bound.* Albuquerque: University of New Mexico Press.

Seif, H. (2004). "Wise up!" Undocumented Latino youth, Mexican-American legislators, and the struggle for higher education. *Latino Studies, 2,* 210–230.

Seif, H. (2008a). States open up college to undocumented students. *UC Mexus News, 44,* 21–23.

Seif, H. (2008b). Wearing union T-shirts: Undocumented women farm workers and gendered circuits of political power. *Latin American Perspectives, 35(1),* 78–98.

Setzler, M., & McRee, N. (2005, September). *The civic incorporation of young immigrants in the United States.* Paper presented at the Annual Meeting of the American Political Science Association, Washington, DC.

S.I.N. Collective. (2007). Students Informing Now (S.I.N.) challenge the racial state in California without shame . . . 'SIN verguenza!' *Educational Foundations, 21(1–2),* 71–90.

Solis, J. (2005). Transborder violence and undocumented youth: Extending cultural-historical analysis in transnational immigration studies. In Z. C. Daiute, C.

Beykong, D. Higson, Smith, & L. Nucci (Eds.), *International perspectives on youth conflict and development* (pp. 305–320). New York: Oxford University Press.

Stepick, A., & Dutton Stepick, C. (2002). Becoming American, constructing ethnicity: Immigrant youth and civic engagement. *Applied Developmental Science, 6(4),* 246–257.

Stepick, A., Dutton Stepick, C., & Labissiere, C. Y. (2008). South Florida's immigrant youth and civic engagement: Major engagement, minor differences. *Applied Developmental Science, 12(2),* 57–65.

Suárez-Orozco, C., Suárez-Orozco, M. M., & Todorova, I. (2008). *Learning in a new land: Immigrants, students and American society*. Cambridge, MA: Harvard University Press.

Suárez-Orozco, M. M. (1989). *Central American refugees and U.S. high schools: A psychosocial study of motivation and achievement*. Palo Alto: Stanford University Press.

Torney-Purta, J., Barber, C., & Wilkenfeld, B. (2006). Differences in the civic knowledge and attitudes of adolescents in the United States by immigrant status and Hispanic background. *Prospects: Quarterly Review of Comparative Education, 36(3),* 343–354.

Torney-Purta, J., Barber, C., & Wilkenfeld, B. (2007). Latino adolescents' civic development in the United States: Research results from the IEA Civic Education Study. *Journal of Youth and Adolescence, 36,* 111–125.

Valenzuela, A. (1999). *Subtractive schooling: U.S.-Mexican youth and the politics of caring*. Albany: State University of New York Press.

Vélez, V., Perez Huber, L., Benavides Lopez, C., de la Luz, A., & Solorzano, D. G. (2008). Battling for human rights and social justice: A Latina/o critical race media analysis of Latina/o student youth activism in the wake of 2006 anti-immigrant sentiment. *Social Justice, 35(1),* 7–27.

Villegas, F. (2006). *Challenging educational barriers: Undocumented immigrant student advocates* (Master's Thesis). Available from ProQuest Dissertations & Theses database (UMI No. 1438598).

Waters, M. C. (2008). The challenges of studying political and civic incorporation. *Applied Developmental Science, 12(2),* 105–107.

Zúñiga, E., Stepick, A., Dutton Stepick, C., & Labissiere, X. (2005). *Mexico-United States migration: Health issues*. México D. F.: Consejo Nacional de Población. Retrieved from http://www.healthpolicy.ucla.edu/pubs/Publication.aspx?pubID=155#download

CHAPTER 18

LGBT Politics, Youth Activism, and Civic Engagement

STEPHEN T. RUSSELL, RUSSELL B. TOOMEY, AND JASON CROCKETT
University of Arizona

CAROLYN LAUB
Gay-Straight Alliance Network

LESBIAN, GAY, BISEXUAL, transgender (LGBT) or queer politics are at the forefront of contemporary public debates around the world, particularly in the United States.[1] Only a generation ago LGBT people were invisible and LGBT issues were taboo. Following from the civil rights and women's movements of the mid-twentieth century, and spurred by the sudden impact of the HIV/AIDS pandemic beginning in the 1980s, the gay and lesbian rights movement has ushered in dramatic shifts in public attitudes and opinions, along with unprecedented visibility for LGBT people. These shifts have surfaced persistent personal and cultural tensions regarding the rights of LGBT people, tensions that have led to some of the most heated debates about *morals* and citizenship in the last generation in the United States. Should LGBT people be allowed to serve in the military? Be protected based on their LGBT identities in the workplace? Get married? Adopt children (or be parents)? Indeed, not one of these specific tensions is resolved. Yet it is clear that the movements for visibility, acceptance, and rights for LGBT people are ultimately movements toward civic participation and engagement.

[1] We acknowledge the complexities of language in describing lesbian, gay, bisexual, transgender, and/or queer people and issues. Our use of *LGBT* is intended as an inclusive strategy, but we acknowledge that not all youth choose LGBT sexual or gender identity labels. Although there is great diversity in contemporary sexual identities, LGBT identities remain relevant for the majority of non-heterosexual (Russell, Clarke, & Clary, 2009).

In this context, LGBT young people in the United States grow up in a country that, at the federal level and in most states and localities, denies them access to statuses or institutions that are considered by most to be *basic rights*: military service, marriage and parenthood, and employment nondiscrimination protection. Public debates create politicized and sometimes hostile environments for LGBT people (Rostosky, Riggle, Horne, & Miller, 2009). All contemporary young people navigate the developmental period of adolescence within this context; for LGBT young people these dramatic social changes are the backdrop against which they come to terms with same-sex sexualities and negotiate their sexual identities and coming out. That is, the public discourse about LGBT lives is ever-present: Adolescents are aware of the debates and navigate them—even if unconsciously—on a daily basis.

LGBT youth are in a double-bind when it comes to the civic. There are inherent developmental discontinuities of civic life for youth and for LGBTs and queers. As youth, they are often *pre-citizens*, or citizens-in-waiting. The role of the young person is to adopt a national and cultural civic identity in anticipation of the moment when they reach the status for full participation in civic life. Yet LGBT youth are aware that this day may in fact never come. In contemporary U.S. society (and in many others), sexuality has become a fundamental dimension through which access to and understandings of citizenship are filtered. That is, sexualities—same-sex sexualities in particular—are the basis for defining and categorizing citizenship possibilities. As an LGBT person, one literally may not expect full participation, at least not in the public or political realm if it requires public recognition of LGBT sexuality. Specifically, rights are extended on the condition that they remain in the private realm (Richardson, 2000); movements into public service, the workplace, or public recognition in family life remain forbidden. For LGBT youth, the key issue is that "while they are learning about civic life and their role in it as adolescents, they are simultaneously identifying and exploring a culturally stigmatized identity" (Russell, 2002, p. 259).

In spite of the visibility of LGBT issues in contemporary societies, the role of youth (both LGBT, queer, and heterosexual or *straight*) in the public discourse or debates has been largely tenuous or invisible. At times, children and youth have been cast as potential victims of inferior parenting by LGBT adults. On the other hand, LGBT youth are sometimes seen as vulnerable to rejecting heterosexual family members. In spite of their future stakes in these civic matters, youth and their perspectives have been almost completely absent in discussions of military service and workplace non-discrimination.

One exception has been debates about LGBT issues in education. Foremost in the everyday lives of young people are their experiences in school. Schools are basic for understanding adolescents and their lives, and are particularly relevant as the venue for both teaching about and practicing civic engagement. In debates about LGBT issues in public school activities and curriculum, youth have indeed been central in the debates. Even in this arena, though, they are more often the focus of the debate rather than engaged in it; that is, they are positioned as the objects of debates while their role as participants and debaters is ignored. Youth have been framed as innocent and vulnerable if exposed to LGBT issues at school. However, there are exceptions—times when young people have initiative or been active agents in social change. During the past decade, in several states and many communities, LGBT youth and their heterosexual allies have been fully engaged in public awareness, advocacy, and activism for school policy change.

In this chapter we take up education and schooling as a strategic location for understanding citizenship for LGBT young people. We examine the perspectives of young people regarding LGBT social change in education in the form of school reform. Youth activism for LGBT-inclusive school reform is used as an example of the direct political engagement of young people in social and political change. We point to recent examples in which students are not only engaged in school change, but become active in directly challenging structures and barriers that have characterized educational institutions, whether through individual or group legal action, or community-based activism for social change (Russell, Muraco, Subramaniam, & Laub, 2009). We begin by considering central concepts and processes that frame thinking about youth civic development, and youth activism in particular. With this as a background, we focus on the dilemmas as well as possibilities for contemporary LGBT youth in the civic arena. We then consider the relevance of historical and contemporary thinking about schools and education, and about youth civic engagement, for understanding activism by and for LGBT students. Finally, youth's political activism for state-level school policy reform is illustrated through analyses of student participation in Gay-Straight Alliances (GSAs) in California high schools, and a related case study of mobilization efforts that bring together LGBT and allied young people to lobby for state-level policy and legislative reform regarding LGBT issues in school. Our chapter shows that LGBT youth activism offers a strategic vantage point for understanding youth civic and political development.

LGBT CITIZENSHIP, SOCIAL MOVEMENTS, AND ACTIVISM

The concept of *sexual citizenship* is increasingly used to discuss the relevance of LGBT status for citizenship (Richardson, 2000; Russell, 2002). Specifically, sexual citizenship is defined by sexual rights that can be conceptualized in three dimensions: rights to sexual practice, rights to self-identification, and rights within social institutions and validations of those rights (Richardson, 2000). All three dimensions of sexual rights are relevant for LGBT youth.

At the most basic level, LGBT people should have the right to participate in chosen relationships, including same-sex sexual relationships. It goes without saying that the right to sexual expression is complex when applied to minors for whom there are, in fact, limitations and regulations of sexual practice. Nevertheless, as applied to LGBT youth, they should have the right to the same age- and developmentally appropriate sexual expression that all (heterosexual) youth may have. Second, LGBT people should have the right to self-identify publicly without fear of negative retribution. For full citizenship, current realities require assimilation to heteronormative ideals; that is, to be assured full rights and statuses as a citizen (e.g., access to military service), LGBT persons must maintain their sexual identities in private. Queer identities are, in many cases, barred from public life. For gender nonconforming LGBT people, there is also an imperative for assimilation to gendered norms. For example, it is clear that gender regulation is a typical characteristic of the period of adolescence, and is often focused on the regulation of gendered sexualities, especially for adolescent boys, for whom the *fag discourse* is a pervasive tool of social organization and hierarchy (Pascoe, 2007). Thus for LGBT youth, the right to self-identification applies to freedom from negative retribution for their LGBT status from peers or adults, including school classmates, teachers, or administrators. Yet a growing body of literature suggests that this right remains elusive for LGBT youth. Third, LGBT persons may seek rights within social institutions or through legislation by changing local or state policies; for youth, the most central and obvious public institution that shapes their lives is education. Thus, sexual citizenship is present when students form a GSA on their school campuses or advocate for inclusive school policies at local, state, or federal levels.

The problematics of sexual citizenship are consistent with another developmental discontinuity for LGBT students: They learn their sexual identities in social, peer, or media settings rather than at home, and much of that learning happens in the context of their schools. In contrast, through the processes of racial socialization, ethnic and racial minority youth learn what it means to be a minority person in a majority culture. They learn about the implications of their minority status for becoming civically engaged minority from their family elders (Sanchez-Jankowski, 2002; Umaña-Taylor, Bhanot, & Shink, 2006). This intergenerational process does not happen for most LGBT youth (Russell, 2002). Where do LGBT youth learn about what it means as a queer person to be civically engaged? These youth often do not grow up in homes where parents have experienced what it means to be queer in society: Non-queer parents of LGBT youth cannot teach their children how to navigate a world characterized by sexual prejudice, heterosexism, and homophobia. Youth must learn the navigation of this marginal status either on their own or from others, and in so doing they learn what this identity means for their futures as citizens.

This stark characterization of the lack of family socialization for LGBT identity development remains generally true, yet it is also the case that there are exceptions to this pattern as seen in examples of family acceptance—and even celebration—of the coming out of their LGBT children (Savin-Williams, 2005). However, it is likely that children of LGBT parents face discrimination and harassment due to their parents' LGBT status; one recent study indicates that high-school students generally perceive their schools to be less safe for students who have LGBT parents than for the general student body (Russell, McGuire, Lee, Larriva, & Laub, 2009). In addition, other recent work challenges the idea that coming out is necessarily uncomplicated for youth with LGBT (specifically lesbian) parents. In a study of *second-generation* queer youth, or LGBT children of lesbian parents, a recent study shows that for some second-generation queer youth, gender and generational differences between them and their parents inhibit family socialization processes that might be expected to prepare them for social and civic life as LGBT young adults (Kuvalanka & Goldberg, 2009). While most of the second-generation participants in that study reported that coming out was easier because their parents had experienced coming out as well, a notable number described complex challenges, one of which was the assumption that their coming out must have been easy because of their parents. Many described the concern that their coming out would affirm pejorative assumptions that their parents had caused their LGBT status; some described this factor as delaying their coming out (Kuvalanka & Goldberg, 2009). Thus, the second-generation youth in this study had strong awareness of the political implications of their sexual identities. This work is important because it shows that the coming-out process is not necessarily uncomplicated for LGBT children of LGBT parents. At the same time, these young adults were aware of sociopolitical forces in their lives, a factor that suggests the possibility for greater civic engagement.

LGBT or queer social movements reflect a notion of collective identity proposed by new social movement perspectives, in which individual and group identities merge and empowered individuals become an important site of political strategy and action, in contrast with social movements that primarily coalesce in and act through organizations (Broad, 2002; Taylor & Raeburn, 1995). A commonly cited exemplar of this shift is the process of *coming out*, in which public disclosure of sexual orientation may be used to challenge institutionalized heterosexuality for both personal and political reasons. Specifically, when youth come out at school, they challenge longstanding traditions of heteronormative hegemony: They challenge rituals of adolescent dating and romance, and in doing so, often affront expectations for gendered behavior. These challenges are a form of identity politics that have been criticized as shifting emphasis from public politics and institutional change to safe spaces for self and culture. That is, the focus becomes one of self-acceptance and public affirmation of identities, in contrast to a focus on policies concerned with social organizations or institutions. Yet, Taylor and Raeburn (1995) point out that shifts of activism into arenas of personal life and work entail the possibility of very high long-term costs including harassment, retaliation, injury, or even death. Their arguments are consistent with the experiences of LGBT youth, as a growing body of research demonstrates their heightened risks of verbal and physical harassment, discrimination, and bodily injury (Garofalo, Wolf, Kessel, Palfrey, & DuRant, 1998; Herek, Cogan, & Gillis, 1999; Smith & Smith, 1998; Telljohann & Price, 1993; Williams, Connolly, Pepler, & Craig, 2005). For youth who have little access to power and authority for changing social institutions, activism at school is a logical (if not the singular) venue through which they can exert influence and become engaged in meaningful civic action.

Although not all LGBT youth visibility is voluntary or explicitly political, the social movement literature indicates that, at least when it takes the form of activism, it is likely to have long-term biographical consequences relevant to the civic sphere. Participants in activism, especially high-risk activism, are likely to continue to be active in social movements, maintain their political orientation over time even if no longer regularly involved in activism, have a high level of involvement in conventional political activities, attain higher levels of education, and be employed as helping professionals such as artists, academics, clergy, journalists, lawyers, social workers, and writers (DeMartini, 1983; Marwell, Aiken, & Demerath, 1987; McAdam, 1989; Sherkat & Blocker, 1997). We argue that LGBT youth activism constitutes an important area of sexual minority civic development. It grows out of the constraints, and possibilities, of contemporary sexual citizenship and identity politics, and may yield distinctive pathways for civic engagement.

YOUTH, ACTIVISM, AND CIVIC ENGAGEMENT

With sexual citizenship as a background, we turn to the multiple motivations and methods for youth involvement in civic activities. Sherrod, Flanagan, and Youniss (2002) offer three reasons for youth civic engagement: satisfaction from doing good, a sense of collective efficacy, and contribution to the shared values of one's country or community. In addition to the multiple reasons that youth become engaged, a broad range of activities fall under the civic umbrella. Civic activities range on a continuum from political activities (e.g., voting, attending political rallies) to service activities (e.g., volunteering; Youniss et al., 2002). Yet as minors, youth have little access to legitimate participation. Their arenas of legitimacy involve non-partisan activities: creating civic projects, participation in governance of political and social institutions, and issue-based advocacy (Stoneman, 2002). The formation of high-school GSAs are ways that LGBT youth may be involved in project creation, and thus participate in institutional governance, and might employ issue-based advocacy strategies to advocate for LGBT youth rights in their schools. These examples highlight a few ways that LGBT youth can become engaged in social and political issues in their everyday lives. Stoneman (2002) suggests that, when these legitimate arenas are available to youth, they create the conditions within which youth may become involved in civic activities. Although LGBT youth, like all youth, inevitably participate in the full range of activities, individual access to civic activities varies. On one hand, access may be limited due to the constraints of queer or sexual citizenship. Yet participation in political activities may be greater for these youth because of the salient role LGBT issues currently play in the civic realm. We suggest that the right conditions surrounding initial and continued engagement for LGBT youth include these arenas for possible engagement within a context that is inclusive and supportive—that is, in which youth have access to (or can create contexts for) sexual rights that define their citizenship.

One framework to explain the conditions of whether or not youth become involved includes an examination of the congruence of young people's experiences with societal values with their attitudes toward civic responsibility or their perceptions of their ability to effect change. Rubin (2007) developed a two-by-two quadrant to explain four distinct behaviors (aware, empowered, complacent, and discouraged) that arise from the combinations of dimensions of experience (ranging from congruent to incongruent or disjuncture) and attitude (ranging from passive to active). Youth whose experiences are congruent with society, meaning that their experiences align with the privileges and values of the government, are said to be *aware* if their attitude is one of active participation; they are *complacent* if their experiences are congruent but their attitude toward engagement is passive. Aware youth believe that they have the power to make a difference in the societal policies and practices that affect the lives of those who experience discrimination and prejudice. Within queer movements, *allies*—heterosexual youth who advocate for change and equality for LGBT persons and stand up against homophobia—often fall within the category of aware youth. These youth are aware of their own privileged status in society and work to fight the injustices faced by LGBT individuals. Complacent youth, however, believe that the status quo of society is acceptable and do not see any need for change.

Youth in the disjuncture category (Rubin, 2007) do not experience the privileges, rights, or benefits of general society, nor do they perceive the values of government as congruent to their lived experiences. These youth can be categorized as either *empowered* (those who believe that change is necessary and work toward that change) or *discouraged* (those who believe that change is not possible and that life is just unfair). Because of their different lived experiences, LGBT youth may be actively involved in changing the status quo (empowered youth) or may believe that change is not possible (discouraged youth). One recent study documents the ways that high-school GSA membership and participation are understood to be empowering: When youth gain knowledge and know how to use it, when they feel personal agency, and when they participate in the group and are involved in the empowerment of other youth, they report empowerment (Fox et al., this volume; Russell, Muraco et al., 2009). This model of engagement is useful for understanding the everyday lives and experiences of young people. Its active dimension challenges the notion that the civic capacities are nascent or under development, a shift that acknowledges agency for youth and allows for the possibility of youthful civic action. Indeed, in many instances young people are increasingly taking leadership in political youth movements and are challenging the dominant structures that exist in their everyday lives (Herdt, Russell, Sweat, & Marzullo, 2007).

According to Flanagan (2004), once engaged, youth's participation in civic activities leads to possibilities for the development of ethics of participation and of tolerance. An *ethic of participation* grows from involvement in civic associations and the development of affection for polity and "identification with the public good" (Flanagan, p. 736). Developed affection for polity allows youth to develop trust with the political system and greater society and to challenge the status quo. The relationship between civic associations and social trust is often characterized as reciprocal: Social trust may actually increase or decrease affection for polity. As posited by Flanagan, however, civic opportunities for youth must encourage them to take leadership roles and must involve exposure to *difference*. This work suggests that in the case of youthful civic engagement, we should examine ways that LGBT young people challenge heteronormativity while identifying with a larger good beyond their self-interests. We should look for examples of LGBT youth leadership, but leadership that involves actively engaging with others who are different from themselves. This appears to be precisely what is meant by the "alliance" in *gay-straight alliance*: Queer and non-queer youth form school clubs that are designed to challenge heteronormativity at school, at least in the immediate social space of the club, if not through leadership to actively transform the larger school climate (Griffin, Lee, Waugh, & Beyer, 2004; Russell, Muraco, et al., 2009).

The *ethic of tolerance* described by Flanagan (2004) involves both dissent and empathy for marginalized groups. First, the concept of dissent during adolescence corresponds to the development of autonomy (Flanagan, 2004). Adolescence is characterized as a time when youth begin to understand others' viewpoints and begin to form their own positions on issues, regardless of parental ideologies—a common source of political knowledge for youth (Youniss et al., 2002). The ethic of tolerance, and specifically dissent, allows youth to interact in meaningful ways with others who have differing perspectives on a given issue. The second dimension of Flanagan's conceptualization of an ethic of tolerance is empathy for marginalized groups. Empathy for others is at the heart of a diverse democracy, in that a core American value is to "appreciate difference and respect those differences" (Sherrod et al., 2002, p. 266). In the case of LGBT youth, an ethic of tolerance would be evident in the ways that LGBT youth disagree with and challenge the heteronormativity of schools, and their capacity to connect those actions to the experiences of others who are marginalized. Existing studies of high-school GSAs have pointed to ways that their members understand the pursuit of sexual justice as linked to other social justice struggles (Russell, Muraco et al., 2009), as well as examples of ways that a potentially narrow lens of sexual justice may preclude critical examination of the interconnections of homophobia with racism or classism (Herdt et al., 2007; McCready, 2001).

Certainly ethics of participation and tolerance are relevant for understanding the civic engagement of LGBT youth. Whether framed as *equal rights* or simply as opposition to the heteronormative aspects of youth culture, there is no question that both participation and tolerance are compelling for LGBT youth. However, the model proposed by Flanagan (2004) can also be read from the position of heterosexual privilege: With whom do youth or must youth participate? Who is tolerated? From an LGBT youth perspective, what if you are the one who is marginalized? For LGBT youth, the ethic of participation must include not only the public good but the personal good as well; exposure to difference must be coupled with the development of an understanding of one's queerness as a form of difference, and in relation to heteronormative society. The ethic of tolerance must include not only empathy for the marginalized, but also for the self. That is, for whom must LGBT youth build tolerance: Should they be tolerant of those who marginalize them? Flanagan's framework helps explain the ways that LGBT youth learn that they are (or may be) different from others; LGBT youth and their allies learn to accept differences through tolerance and empathy, and may come to actively embrace it. At the same time, it is they who typically embody difference, or whose status demands empathy. For civic engagement, LGBT youth must not only develop these ethics in relation to others; they must navigate a world that does not typically afford them the same ethical position. The challenge for LGBT youth is to develop these ethics in relation to others, while developing tolerance and empathy for their own marginal status.

Stoneman's (2002) model of participation and Flanagan's (2004) ethics of engagement are intended to include all youth in their conceptualizations. Yet the pathways to engaged citizenship for LGBT youth may be distinct. In fact, LGBT young people are *leading* the movement for LGBT youth rights through participation in queer youth organizations that, in recent years, have focused on the rights of LGBT students and their allies in schools (Herdt et al., 2007; Russell, Muraco et al., 2009).

SCHOOLS AS SITES OF EDUCATION AND RESISTANCE

Schools are a particularly important context for understanding youth development: they are obviously central in the lives of typical contemporary youth. Schools are a context within which youth are meant to learn citizenship, and, practically, one space where many first experience participation in voluntary associations and collective decision making and action. What is important is that attendance is mandated, and yet there is clear evidence that they are not safe places for queer and LGBT youth (Garofalo et al., 1998; Smith & Smith, 1998; Ueno, 2005; Williams et al., 2005). What are the implications—relative to participation and tolerance—for contemporary queer students, as well as their non-queer allies?

Historical understandings of the role of schools in providing civic and political education focused on the promotion of individual personal development and competence, including political development. Little attention has been given historically to the possibility of schools to be sites of active resistance to dominant social and cultural structures that reinforce marginalization based on social class, race, and gender. Likewise, controversy exists as to whether an association between basic civic education and subsequent political involvement exists (Youniss et al., 2002). However, classic understandings of education were extended in the mid-twentieth century through writers who described the radical and transformative possibilities of education.

In his classic work, Dewey (1938/1999) described progressive education as learning that is relevant to the daily lives and experiences of youth; good education has purpose and meaning for both the student and the society. Dewey offered a *theory of experience* based on the premise that the subjective quality of a student's past experiences shapes the understanding and meaning of current and future experiences (Dewey, 1938/1999). The implication for formal education is that teachers must take a student's prior learning and life experiences into account in order to best structure their learning environments and experiences. Thus, the theory highlights the need to understand LGBT students' navigation of heteronormative society and school cultures, and the prior (often discriminatory or marginalizing) experiences that frame their experience of education. However, Dewey did not consider the role of youth or students in challenging dominant structures that defined the educational experience.

Later in the twentieth century, Freire (1970/2006) suggested the possibility that social and political forces were at work in creating inequalities, and that these inequalities were reflected in educational practices and institutions. He theorized that in societies characterized by power imbalances (in his case, colonized nations and peoples), freedom may be frightening to those who are marginalized or powerless. Freedom must be constantly and responsibly pursued; that is, freedom cannot be simply given to those without power. Thus, freedom is an ongoing process or condition of the human experience. Freire argues that freedom can be pursued through education when it is authentic to the student; that is, in conditions when students are permitted and encouraged to incorporate and critique their own experiences of oppression and marginalization. Notably, Freire challenges the student-teacher dichotomy, arguing that true education allows for reciprocal influence: The educator's role is to problematize the world to facilitate students' education while learning from their experiences and perspectives (Freire, 1970/2006). This is the ground upon which ideas of resistance to status quo can be conceptualized, and student- or youth-driven education and social change becomes a possibility.

Drawing from Dewey (1938/1999) and Freire (1970/2006), freedom and true education for LGBT youth must be grounded in or allow attention to their social, cultural, and personal experiences in a heteronormative and homophobic society, and will be defined by their efforts to interrogate and ultimately challenge these sources of power and hegemony. We turn to high-school GSAs as settings in which young people are creating the possibilities for such freedom in education.

GAY-STRAIGHT ALLIANCES AS CIVICS EDUCATION

School is one of the central contexts where LGBT identities become possible. GSAs are voluntary associations (i.e., school clubs) that exist to provide information, support, recreation, and socialization to students, as well as to advocate for LGBT-inclusive school environments (Griffin et al., 2004; Perrotti & Westheimer, 2001). As of 2008, over 3,000 GSAs registered with their national support organization, Gay, Lesbian, and Straight Education Network (GLSEN, 2008).

GSAs and other school clubs focused on LGBT issues can use the role of political activities in many ways: for example, to change school policies (e.g., enumeration of harassment policies to include both sexual orientation and gender identity/expression), to lobby legislators through e-mails or letters, to meet with legislators in person or via telephone, to hold LGBT-related rallies or marches, and to network with other LGBT advocacy organizations (Macgillivray, 2007). In relation to Flanagan's (2004) discussion of tolerance and empathy for marginalized groups, GSAs represent climates where all sexualities and genders are accepted. Herdt et al. (2007) discussed this supportive environment as a context "in which gender and sexual orientation do not matter because, in the views of its members, they should not matter" (p. 246).

Given advances in technology and the state of contemporary youth activism, GSAs are located in an interesting historical moment: There is a shift away from exclusive adult privilege for access to information and resources. GSAs are an interesting social phenomenon in that student participants may have more knowledge and resources about their rights and possibilities, via Internet access and peer groups, than their local education administrators and teachers. That is, students may know more about rights available to them as queer youth than do school teachers and principals (Russell, Muraco et al., 2009). The result is a clash between students' knowledge and experiences of a queer youth social movement, which explicitly includes a discourse about students' education access and rights, and school administrators' or teachers' understandings of the role of education and educators in guiding or managing youthful sexualities. We observe that this tension may be the fertile ground for student engagement and activism.

An Empirical Example: Gay-Straight Alliances and Student Activism

We present data collected from student members of high-school GSAs in California. The GSA Network, a statewide student advocacy organization, collected surveys from LGBT youth and their allies with the mission to empower youth activists to fight homophobia and transphobia in schools. First, at the end of each academic school year, the GSA Network conducts a survey of GSA members who are registered with the Network. These year-end surveys were conducted between 2004 and 2007 (2004, $n = 123$; 2005, $n = 245$; 2006, $n = 254$; 2007, $n = 120$). Approximately 30% of the respondents identified as heterosexual; less than half identify as White, and approximately 20% identify as Latino. Our approach to the analysis of this survey is to examine the themes of participation and tolerance, and personal and sociopolitical attitudes and behaviors. Using qualitative and quantitative data (including student-reported expectations for future civic or political participation), we describe the civic attitudes of the students, illustrate their aspirations for future civic participation, and analyze their interpretations of involvement in the GSA relative to key civic themes.

The second source of data is from a survey of students who participated in 2007 Queer Youth Advocacy Day (QYAD, n = 118). This event included GSA members from across the state who mobilized at the California state capitol to meet with legislators and to lobby for school safety and other LGBT-relevant legislation. Specifically, QYAD 2007 participants lobbied for the passage of two pieces of California legislation: SB777, a bill that clarifies protection for students from discrimination based on sexual orientation and gender identity, and AB537 (known as the *Safe Place to Learn Act*), legislation that provides schools with clarification and guidance on how to comply with state anti-harassment laws and protect students. Approximately 62% of evaluation respondents identified as female; nearly 75% identified as gay, lesbian, bisexual, queer, pansexual, or as having a non-heterosexual identity; and 48% identified as White and 25% as Latino. Based on the analysis of both closed- and open-ended survey items, we consider the civic learning that takes places in this setting created for activism, and the anticipated future civic participation reported by these students.

GSA Year-End Survey: 2004–2007 Results

GSAs serve as a rich context for the legitimate participation in civic activities for LGBT youth and their allies. Several of the major themes and frameworks of civic development and youth activism are illustrated in the youths' responses to questions about their participation in GSA. As described by Stoneman (2002), initial and continued civic participation is conditional on a supportive environment. The majority of participants in each survey year strongly agree that their GSA is a safe place for them to go (i.e., "This year the GSA was a safe place for me to go"; all items on a scale of 1 = strongly disagree to 4 = strongly agree). Furthermore, this percentage grew from 69.7% in 2004 to 77.6% in 2007, a promising trend that documents the growing availability of a safe space for LGBT youth and their allies to mobilize, advocate, and support each other. Additionally, GSAs seem to function as organizations that enable students to learn about and feel a connection to the larger LGBT youth community. This function is evident by the increasing number of participants who strongly agree with the following statement: "This year working with my GSA helped me learn more about the LGBTQ youth community." In 2007, 61.9% of youth strongly agreed with that statement, while the percentage of youth who strongly agreed with this statement in 2004 was much lower, at 46%.

The 2007 year-end survey provides a slightly different context to explore the relationship between civic engagement and student activism around LGBT issues by asking explicit questions about civic activities. In order to better understand youth engagement in civic activities and social justice, we examined youths' responses for salient examples of Flanagan's (2004) ethics of participation and tolerance. In reference to Flanagan's framework, we examined the following open-ended item: "List the things you learned how to do, or got better at doing, through your participation in your GSA." In the most basic form, participation in GSAs initiated interest in politics and civic life in general; as described by one participant, "I learned how to reach out to other people . . . [and] became aware of what's going on around me politically and socially." GSA participation provided youth with experience in leadership roles—a quintessential element for developing an ethic of participation. One youth explained, "I learned to be a better leader, facilitate meetings, organize on campus, and work as a team." For some youth, participation in GSA served the function of building trust in the self and in others; one youth explained, "I finally improved at trusting others and learned to step back a bit," while another youth stated that through GSA participation "I learned . . . not letting myself get hurt by sexual orientation, [how to] handle my parent better, [and how to] handle my friends' remarks better." These examples highlight a few of the ways that GSA participation initiates civic participation, maintains youth engagement, and gives youth experience in leadership roles—all of which are critical for developing an ethic of participation.

Examples of Flanagan's (2004) ethic of tolerance were abundant in the youths' responses. Several youth described that they learned how to speak up for their beliefs, how to tolerate others' points of view, and how to develop tolerance in relation to their own marginal status. Central to the concept of empathy for others, one youth responded:

> As president of the GSA at my high school I learned to become a better leader, to stay more organized, and most importantly I felt like a stronger person for being able to fight homophobia, transphobia, and other injustices. Such 'other' injustices that I recognized in the world also inspired me to become an active officer of my high school's Amnesty International Club.

This student was able to extend the capacity to empathize with the LGBT population and link the pursuit for social justice to other civic arenas. GSA participation also seems to teach youth that they have a legitimate voice with which they can express their beliefs and stand up for themselves and others. This ability to express dissent and tolerance can be found in the following youths' voices: "I learned to stand up for others that need to be stood up for," and "I learned to speak up and defend my beliefs." Participants also expressed that their experience in the GSA allowed them to listen and be tolerant of beliefs that oppose their own. For example, one youth stated, "I've mainly gotten better at stepping away from the crowd, being a leader, and not being afraid of the thoughts and comments of others." Finally, GSAs also provided a space for LGBT youth to learn to tolerate and accept their own marginal status, an example of how the pathway to civic engagement may be distinct for LGBT youth. To highlight this concept, one youth stated that because of participation in GSA, "I learned how to feel accepted."

The 2007 survey included questions about civic participation, as well as follow-up questions for Queer Youth Advocacy Day participants, and we focus here on differences among students in order to point to new avenues of research or practical activist strategy. The survey included an index of civic behaviors that measured youth reports of civic activities that they are willing to do with their GSAs to support safer schools legislation and to become more proactive (activities included voting, writing letters to the editor, attending rallies and protests, and calling, writing, or visiting your legislator or governor). Approximately 44% of youth reported that they would write a letter to the editor for their local newspaper, 48% of all youth stated that they would call, write, or visit their legislator or governor, 60% plan to attend rallies or protests, and nearly 62% plan to vote in the next election after they reach legal age. These numbers are encouraging in the context of the general statistics on adolescents and their expectations for political engagement. In nationally representative study of 1,600 U.S. youth ages 15 to 25 (Lopez et al., 2006), 7% had written a letter to the editor (print media), 11% contacted an elected official, 11% attended a protest, 16% signed an e-mail petition, and 18% signed a paper petition. Compared internationally, results from the 1999 Civic Education Study, which included approximately 90,000 14-year-old students from 28 countries, showed that 80% planned to vote when they were legally able; however, about the same proportion reported that they did not plan to engage in other political activities in the future (Torney-Purta et al., 2001). Thus, the results for GSA members who also attended QYAD show that these youth strongly endorse civic participation.[2]

To examine possible differences by ethnicity, sexual orientation, and gender, we tested bivariate group differences and then multiple regressions predicting the index of civic behaviors. Regarding race and ethnicity, there were no differences in the civic index scores or in any of the individual civic items. We did find differences based on gender and sexual orientation. Specifically, we found that sexual minority youth of both genders, along with heterosexual females, are similar in their willingness to engage in these activities; testing the interaction of sexual orientation and gender, we find that heterosexual males are more reluctant to endorse these future civic

[2] We cannot suggest that youth with civic predispositions select into GSAs and QYAD; it is likely that these organizations attract young people who already have some basis for civic and political awareness and engagement. At the same time, we expect that their endorsement of future civic engagement would be nurtured and strengthened by participation in these organizational activities.

activities. However, closer examination of each behavior separately suggests that this may not necessarily reflect a lesser commitment to LGBT issues, but rather may be a reflection of tactical preferences. Specifically, heterosexual males were not significantly different in attitudes toward attending rallies and protests, or toward voting. However, there was a clear lack of interest in letter writing or interactions with elected representatives. Since the question does not distinguish between meeting with a legislator and other forms of contact, this may reflect a preference for action-oriented activities rather than writing or talking.

A slightly different pattern emerges in the responses to specific questions about participation in Queer Youth Advocacy Day (QYAD). Students who attended QYAD were asked if their lobbying and advocacy training was useful, whether they learned skills that would improve their work as an advocate/activist, and whether they felt empowered by speaking to lawmakers about LGBT issues. Gender was not a distinguishing factor in any of the questions, and there was no difference by sexual orientation in feeling empowered by interacting with lawmakers. However, heterosexuals were less likely to agree that their training was useful or that they learned skills that would help them as an advocate/activist. It is unclear why this difference exists, especially in light of the equivalent feelings of empowerment. Perhaps among GSA members, heterosexual allies are less committed to *activist careers* and so perceive such skills as less useful to them both in the short and long terms. Or they may feel less personal risk while engaging in activism around LGBT issues and so do not perceive such skills as being as valuable as their sexual minority peers.

In addition to this sexual orientation difference, here race or ethnicity appears to be a factor. Students identifying themselves as White were less likely to agree training was useful or report feeling empowered. It may come as no surprise that members of racial and ethnic groups historically excluded from having a political voice feel more empowered and find lobbying and advocacy training more useful.

Overall, youth participation in GSA empowered them to feel more confident about their advocacy skills. Across all four years of evaluation, approximately 60% of youth responded that they strongly agree that "This year after doing things with my GSA, I feel more confident about fighting homophobia, transphobia, and other injustices." Importantly, a large percentage of students each survey year also reported that the school environment for LGBT people got better (2004: 45% to 2007: 58%). While we cannot concretely link the association between the improved school environments and the presence of GSAs, the fact that school environments are perceived to improve over time implies that LGBT-inclusive changes are occurring in schools.

Queer Youth Advocacy Day 2007 Results

We move next to a case study examination of an exemplar of youth advocacy: Queer Youth Advocacy Day (QYAD) 2007. Beyond the GSA year-end survey questions about QYAD, this evaluation allows us to gain insight into the immediate reactions and experiences gained from QYAD participants. The goals of QYAD 2007 were to provide knowledge to LGBT youth and their allies about advocacy and the political system, provide a space and time for youth to come together to advocate for safe school legislation, and to present an opportunity for youth from across California to come together at a central location for networking and to work collaboratively toward change.

After participating in QYAD activities, youth reported an increase in civic knowledge regarding the lobbying process and legislative system (see Table 18.1 for results). The majority of participants report that they agree or strongly agree with statements that suggest that they learned useful tools and new information that aid in civic engagement (e.g., knowledge about legislative system or activist skills). Although no large differences existed between the choice of strongly disagree/disagree and agree/strongly agree on items related to acquired civic knowledge and skills, interesting differences appeared when looking at participant responses at the high end of the scale: agree versus strongly agree. Only 30.8% of students strongly agreed that they knew more about the California legislative system. This suggests that students who participate in advocacy day already have advanced knowledge of the legislative system, *or* when students come together for legislative action more emphasis needs to be placed on the dissemination of legislative process knowledge. Importantly, over 70% of students stated that they felt more confident about their ability to advocate, which suggests that these students did learn valuable tools that will be transferred to future advocacy

Table 18.1
Civic Knowledge Gained from Participation in Queer Youth Advocacy Day, 2007

	Strongly Agree	Agree	Disagree/ Strongly Disagree
I know about how to lobby lawmakers.	53.4%	43.2%	3.4%
I know more about the California legislative system.	30.8%	61.5%	7.7%
I feel more confident about my ability to advocate for safe schools and LGBT youth.	71.2%	25.4%	3.4%
I learned skills that I will use as an activist.	61.9%	37.3%	0.80%

Note: $N = 118$.

engagements. Over half of the students reported that they learned more about how to lobby as a result of participation. One queer, female-identified student demonstrated that this new knowledge would be useful for future advocacy work: "I am going to keep in contact with the legislative system now that I know more on lobbying." Not only did this student demonstrate that she learned knew skills related to lobbying, but she planned to put these skills into action in the future.

Participants also responded to questions related to future advocacy and political action involvement. The large majority of students responded that they plan to vote in the next election as soon as they turned 18 (86.4%), a key predictor of future civic involvement. In response to the question "How are you going to use what you learned?" one straight, female ally wrote: "I will definitely pay close attention to where representatives stand on the issues so my vote in 2008 really counts." The large majority of students also reported that they would likely attend rallies or protests in the future (89%). Fewer students reported that they would participate in the following advocacy activities: call or write legislator (50.8%), visit legislator in his/her district office (42.4%), and write a letter to the editor of my local newspaper (40.7%). Similar to the results in the GSA year-end surveys, a technology shift may be one reason why there were low numbers of youth who reported that they plan to write a letter to a legislator or newspaper: Contemporary generations may instead respond to survey questions about actions such as sending an e-mail to a legislator or responding to an online action alert (see Bennett et al., this volume). Further analyses revealed no similar pattern of civic disengagement among students who reported that they do not plan to vote as soon as they turn 18. Twelve of the 16 students, who reported that they do not plan to vote, do plan to attend future rallies and protests. For these youth, the social atmosphere of a rally or protest may be the reason for engagement, rather than the direct civic nature of the event. Only three students reported that they do not plan to engage in any of the civic activities listed. However, these students did agree that they gained useful tools and information about lobbying and the legislative process at QYAD. It is possible that the subsample of youth who do not plan to engage in future civic activities may include non-citizens of the United States; this is a prerequisite for voting and even for effectively corresponding with legislative representatives. However, this is only speculation as QYAD participants were not asked to identify their status as a U.S. citizen.

Our findings do indicate that the majority of students involved in QYAD, an activity with direct, explicit civic goals, plan to continue engaging in LGBT-related advocacy. Our purpose is not to present QYAD as an intervention that causes continued civic engagement. However, it is valuable to know that when students engage in advocacy activities with specific civic goals, most *plan* to continue to utilize the skills and knowledge gained from participation. We also recognize that the youth who participated in QYAD were already more civically engaged than their peers, thus limiting the generalizability of these results.

IMPLICATIONS AND FUTURE RESEARCH DIRECTIONS

Our review and empirical examples of LGBT youth civic engagements have several implications for policy and practice. We present two examples of opportunities for LGBT adolescents and their straight allies that allow for youth voice and action in civic arenas that have traditionally been closed off to young people. A central focus on youth voice and active participation in civic engagement aligns with the importance of youth governance in organizations or activities that include or influence young people (Zeldin, Camino, & Calvert, 2007). GSAs and QYAD may serve as a model for other youth organizations that serve to build civic engagement capacity—as GSAs and participation in QYAD do give LGBT youth the right to formulate a viewpoint, express it to those with power, and have the viewpoint be taken seriously by those with power (Zeldin et al., 2007). Policy should be implemented that provides youth with this ability and protection, such as the United Nations Convention on the Rights of the Child, which has not been ratified by the United States (Metzger & Smetana, this volume; Torney-Purta, Wilkenfeld, & Barber, 2008). In addition, youth-serving programs and organizations should provide a welcoming environment for all youth to initiate civic engagement for young people who do not feel welcomed in environments that are not overtly accepting of their sexual minority status. For instance, drawing from the safe schools literature, youth-serving organizations might implement nondiscrimination policies that include sexual orientation and gender identity along with other protected categories, or might provide trainings to staff and youth that include information on LGBT issues (O'Shaughnessy, Russell, Heck, Calhoun, & Laub, 2004).

In addition to policy and practice implications, the absence of empirical documentation of LGBT adolescent civic engagement warrants future research. At the most basic level, researchers need to attend to and include multiple forms of diversity (e.g., sexual orientation and identity, race and ethnicity, age, gender, socioeconomic status) in studies of youth civic engagement. Such research would benefit from a multidisciplinary framework. Specifically, civic engagement for LGBT youth is defined by ongoing cultural shifts and political changes, as well as by the family- and person-level processes of individual development from childhood into adolescence. By drawing from human developmental understandings of adolescence, sexual identity development, and family relationships, coupled with historical, cultural, and political analyses of social movements and social change relevant to LGBT lives, multidisciplinary approaches offer the possibility to enhance the knowledge produced about civic engagement for LGBT youth. Although we have begun to document the role of these youth in civic engagement with the two examples provided, future research should begin to examine LGBT youth participation in adolescent organizations and civic activities that are not specific to LGBT issues. This research will provide a foundation for the development of a body of best practices for engaging LGBT youth in youth-serving and civic organizations, and will serve as a catalyst to identify cultural and organizational barriers as well as opportunities for improvement. Further, research should continue to examine the role of LGBT-specific organizations and activities for youth that provide opportunities for civic engagement.

CONCLUSION

LGBT rights are among the defining dimensions of contemporary civic discourse. Adolescence is a crucial period for the development of civic identity and engagement, and today's youth are experiencing that development in a time when the rights and privileges of citizenship for LGBT people are being explicitly debated. For LGBT youth, and their heterosexual allies, the navigation of civic development is historically distinctive, and defined by these cultural tensions. Not surprisingly, these very tensions have created the context for strategic participation by young people in advocacy and activism for full inclusion in education, as well as for leadership in the creation of such a movement for sexual justice and social change. We illustrated these possibilities through analyses of the civic attitudes and expectations of student participants in high-school GSAs in California. Our chapter highlights the attitudes and actions of contemporary young people—both LGBT-identified youth and their straight ally peers—in the arena of LGBT social and political change. Because of the unique period of social debate and change, we show that this youth activism offers a strategic vantage point for understanding youth civic and political development.

Before closing, we acknowledge the complexities of LGBT identities and experiences, and the possibility that discourses about LGBT youth civic engagement may have the potential to reinforce assumptions about youth, sexual minorities, and civic participation that may be limiting. As has been suggested in writing on identity politics (Bernstein, 2002), it is important to question whether LGBT youth activism reifies the injustices that it seeks to eradicate. That is, how might activism for school reform, while embracing a narrative of empowerment and challenging political power structures, simultaneously reinforce notions of youth and LGBT vulnerabilities? In fact, our analyses suggest that this possibility is apparent in the experiences of the GSA participants and the participants in Queer Youth Advocacy Day: The discourse of the *suffering gay youth* is used and learned and reinforced as a provocative (and often effective) tool for political persuasion and social change. It is precisely because it supports and reinforces deeply held stereotypes about *gay youth* that the discourse of struggle is so effective as an advocacy and activist tool. Yet, the irony is that the situation is clearly more complex than a simple *struggling victim* script would suggest (or the *emancipated* or empowered alternative) (Russell, Muraco et al., 2009; Cohler & Hammack, 2007). GSA and QYAD participants reveal that their lives are more complex than *gay* versus *straight*, and that they are actively challenging heterosexism and homophobia in their schools (as well as other intersecting inequalities[3]). Thus, we find examples from these data that suggest the possibility for this activism to engage the primacy of LGBT or queer youth identities while simultaneously questioning those categories and their implications for youth (Loutzenhaiser, 2005). We argue that the possibility to construct a civic identity that may be purposefully malleable—or queer—is at once individually compelling, collectively empowering, and, perhaps, the basis for transformative political activism and change.

REFERENCES

Bernstein, M. (2002). Identities and politics: Toward a historical understanding of the lesbian and gay movement. *Social Science History, 26*, 531–581.

Broad, K. L. (2002). Social movement selves. *Sociological Perspectives, 45*, 317–336.

Cohler, B. J., & Hammack, P. L. (2007). The psychological world of the gay teenager: Social change, narrative, and normality. *Journal of Youth and Adolescence, 36*, 47–59.

DeMartini, J. R. (1983). Social movement participation: Political socialization, generational consciousness, and lasting effects. *Youth & Society, 15*, 195–223.

Dewey, J. (1938/1999). *Experience and education*. Indianapolis, IN: Kappa Delta Pi.

Flanagan, C. A. (2004). Volunteerism, leadership, political socialization, and civic engagement. In R. M. Lerner & L. Steinberg (Eds.), *Handbook of adolescent psychology* (2nd ed.). Hoboken, NJ: John Wiley & Sons.

Freire, P. (1970/2006). *Pedagogy of the oppressed*. New York: The Continuum International Publishing Group.

Garofalo, R. R., Wolf, C., Kessel, S., Palfrey, J., & DuRant, R. H. (1998). The association between health risk behaviors and sexual orientation among a school-based sample of adolescents. *Pediatrics, 101*, 859–902.

[3] Although tolerance for others does not always transcend to other marginalized groups outside of GSAs, some GSAs focus on issues such as race and ethnicity (Russell, 2002; Perrotti & Westheimer, 2001). The issue of whether or not LGBT-related social activism involvement transcends to other issues and other marginalized groups needs further exploration.

GLSEN. (2008). FAQs: Top 5 frequently asked questions from the media. Retrieved April 30, 2008, from http://www.glsen.org/cgi-bin/iowa/all/news/record/1970.html

Griffin, P., Lee, C., Waugh, J., & Beyer, C. (2004). Describing roles that gay-straight alliances play in schools: From individual support to school change. *Journal of Gay & Lesbian Issues in Education, 1*, 7–22.

Herdt, G., Russell, S. T., Sweat, J., & Marzullo, M. (2007). Sexual inequality, youth empowerment, and the GSA: A community study in California. In N. Teunis & G. Herdt (Eds.), *Sexual inequalities and social justice* (pp. 233-251). Berkeley: University of California Press.

Herek, G. M., Cogan, J. C., & Gillis, J. R. (1999). Psychological sequelae of hate-crime victimization among lesbian, gay, and bisexual adults. *Journal of Consulting and Clinical Psychology, 67*, 945–951.

Kuvalanka, A. K., & Goldberg, A. E. (2009). "Second generation" voices: Queer youth with lesbian/bisexual mothers. *Journal of Youth and Adolescence, 38*, 904–919.

Lopez, M. H., Levine, P., Both, D., Kiesa, A., Kirby, E., & Marcelo, K. (2006). The 2006 civic and political health of the nation: A detailed look at how youth participate in politics and communities. College Park, MD: CIRCLE.

Loutzenhaiser, L. (2005). Working fluidity, materiality and the educational imaginary: A case for contingent primacy. *Journal of the Canadian Association for Curriculum Studies, 3*, 27–39.

Marwell, G., Aiken, M. T., & Demerath, N. J., III (1987). The persistence of political attitudes among 1960s civil rights activists. *The Public Opinion Quarterly, 51*, 359–375.

McAdam, D. (1989). The biographical consequences of activism. *American Sociological Review, 54*, 744–760.

McCready, L. (2001). When fitting in isn't an option, or, why Black queer males at a California high school stay away from Project 10. In K. K. Kumashiro (Ed.), *Troubling intersections of race and sexuality: Queer students of color and anti-oppressive education* (pp. 37–54). New York: Rowman & Littlefield Publishers.

Macgillivray, I. K. (2007). *Gay-straight alliances: A handbook for students, educators, and parents*. Binghamton, NY: Harrington Park Press.

O'Shaughnessy, M., Russell, S., Heck, K., Calhoun, C., & Laub, C. (2004). *Safe place to learn: Consequences of harassment based on actual or perceived sexual orientation and gender non-conformity and steps for making schools safer*. San Francisco: California Safe Schools Coalition.

Pascoe, C. J. (2007). *Dude, you're a fag: Masculinity and sexuality in high school*. Berkeley: University of California Press.

Perrotti, J., & Westheimer, K. (2001). *When the drama club is not enough: Lessons from the safe schools program for gay and lesbian students*. Boston: Bacon Press.

Richardson, D. (2000). Constructing sexual citizenship: Theorizing sexual rights. *Critical Social Policy, 62*, 105–135.

Rostosky, S. S., Riggle, E. D. B., Horne, S. G., & Miller, A. D. (2009). Marriage amendments and psychological distress in lesbian, gay, and bisexual (LGB) adults. *Journal of Counseling Psychology, 56*, 56–66.

Rubin, B. C. (2007). "There's still not justice": Youth civic identity development amid distinct school and community contexts. *Teachers College Record, 109*, 449–481.

Russell, S. T. (2002). Queer in America: Sexual minority youth and citizenship. *Applied Developmental Science, 6*, 258–263.

Russell, S. T., Clarke, T. J., & Clary, J. (2009). Are teens "post-gay"? Contemporary adolescents' sexual identity labels. *Journal of Youth and Adolescence, 38*, 884–890.

Russell, S. T., McGuire, J. K., Lee, S.-A., Larriva, J. C., & Laub, C. (2008). Adolescent perceptions of school safety for students with lesbian, gay, bisexual, and transgender parents. *Journal of Gay and Lesbian Issues in Education, 5*, 11–27.

Russell, S. T., Muraco, A., Subramaniam, A., & Laub, C. (2009). Youth empowerment and the high school gay-straight alliance. *Journal of Youth and Adolescence, 38*, 891–903.

Sanchez-Jankowski, M. (2002). Minority youth and civic engagement: The impact of group relations. *Applied Developmental Science, 6*, 237–245.

Savin-Williams, R. C. (2005). *The New Gay Teen*. Cambridge, MA: Harvard University Press.

Sherkat, D. E., & Blocker, T. J. (1997). Explaining the political and personal consequences of protest. *Social Forces, 75*, 1049–1070.

Sherrod, L. R., Flanagan, C., & Youniss, J. (2002). Dimensions of citizenship and opportunities for youth development: The what, why, when, where, and who of citizenship development. *Applied Developmental Science, 6*, 264–272.

Smith, G. W., & Smith, D. E. (1998). The ideology of "Fag": The school experience of gay students. *Sociological Quarterly, 39*, 309–335.

Stoneman, D. (2002). The role of youth programming in the development of civic engagement. *Applied Developmental Science, 6*, 221–226.

Taylor, V., & Raeburn, N. C. (1995). Identity politics as high-risk activism: Career consequences for lesbian, gay, and bisexual sociologists. *Social Problems, 42*, 252–273.

Telljohann, S. K., & Price, J. H. (1993). A qualitative examination of adolescent homosexuals' life experiences: Ramifications for secondary school personnel. *Journal of Homosexuality, 26*, 41–56.

Torney-Purta, J., Lehmann, R., Oswald, H., & Schulz, W. (2001). *Citizenship and education in twenty-eight countries: Civic knowledge and engagement at age fourteen*. Amsterdam, NL: IEA.

Torney-Purta, J., Wilkenfeld, B., & Barber, C. (2008). How adolescents in twenty-seven countries understand, support and practice international human rights. *Journal of Social Issues, 4(4)*, 857–880.

Ueno, Ki. (2005). Sexual orientation and psychological distress in adolescence: Examining interpersonal stressors and social support processes. *Social Psychology Quarterly, 68*, 258–277.

Umaña-Taylor, A. J., Bhanot, R., & Shink, N. (2006). Ethnic identity formation during adolescence: The critical role of families. *Journal of Family Issues, 27*, 390–414.

Williams, T., Connolly, J., Pepler, D., & Craig, W. (2005). Peer victimization, social support, and psychosocial adjustment of sexual minority adolescents. *Journal of Youth and Adolescence, 34*, 471–482.

Younіss, J., Blaes, S., Christmas-Best, V., Diversi, M., McLaughlin, M., & Silbereisen, R. (2002). Youth civic engagement in the twenty-first century. *Journal of Research on Adolescence*, *12*, 121–148.

Zeldin, S., Camino, L., & Calvert, M. (2007). Toward an understanding of youth in community governance: Policy priorities and research directions. *Analise Psicologica*, *xxv*, 77–95.

SECTION III

METHODOLOGICAL AND MEASUREMENT ISSUES IN STUDYING YOUTH CIVIC ENGAGEMENT

Methods and measures have been only weakly connected to theories and research-derived conceptual frameworks in many areas of developmental science. Certainly this has been true for studies of civic engagement in youth. The chapters in this third section deal with a variety of measurement and methodological issues in research on youth civic engagement. They describe evaluations of programs, approaches to selecting research questions, and commonly studied constructs that can be understood in new ways that stimulate better measures.

The chapter by Torney-Purta, Amadeo, and Andolina presents a conceptual framework and multimethod approach to research on youth civic engagement. The first part of the chapter discusses survey research in civic engagement and political socialization. A conceptual framework for research includes individual variables, context variables, and process variables. Three constructs are introduced from communities of practice: the meaning of the civic sphere, civic identity, and civic participation. The chapter contrasts the contributions of surveys and focus groups and outlines policy implications.

The chapter by Beaumont focuses on the sense of political agency and efficacy, a central concept that has been inadequately measured. The chapter adapts psychologists' work on self-efficacy to illuminate processes through which political efficacy develops and analyzes interviews with college students and faculty involved in 21 political engagement programs. Four pathways for developing efficacy are political mastery experiences, models of political efficacy, supportive social networks, and positive political outlooks. The chapter shows ways to match methods to research questions.

The chapter by Higgins-D'Alessandro considers the trans-disciplinary nature of evaluations of character and civic development programs. It introduces a range of strategies to evaluate civic engagement programs. With the upsurge in service learning and out-of-school youth programs intended to promote community involvement and civic awareness, evaluations need to examine the influence of multiple levels of settings and contexts. The chapter also argues for triangulating results from different kinds of measures to optimize validity and credibility.

The chapter by Campbell-Patton and Patton continues the focus on evaluation, examining the limitations of randomized control trials for studying civic engagement programs. These programs tend to be individualized, customized, and innovative interventions developed collaboratively with local partners and young people. The evaluation design should match the program's theory of change and take into account the priority questions and intended uses and users, the costs and benefits of alternative designs, the level of evidence necessary to support decisions, ethical considerations, and utility.

The chapter by Fox, Mediratta, Ruglis, Stoudt, Shah, and Fine draws on the intersections of youth organizing and participatory action research to explore critical youth engagement, in which young people link social inquiry to collective action. Using one participatory action research project and three youth organizing projects as case studies, key elements of critical youth engagement are identified. This chapter outlines an innovative, productive, and infrequently used approach to research on youth civic engagement that can have an impact on both adults and young people who participate.

The chapter by Selman and Kwok describes "informed social reflection," a newly defined construct that examines how civic orientation, ethical awareness, and historical understanding come together when adolescents make decisions. The chapter describes the creation and validation of measures of the quality of a school's civic climate and the sophistication of its students' social awareness or informed social reflection. These can be used to evaluate the impact of programs designed to improve students' capacity to make wise choices as emerging citizens in society and in their own social relationships.

The chapters in this third and final section of the Handbook present several perspectives on the methods and measures of research on youth civic engagement. Enhanced ways of understanding efficacy and participation are proposed, as well as new constructs such as informed social reflection and critical youth engagement. Specific details about how to formulate research questions, how to supplement surveys with interview, observational and focus group methods, and how to tailor evaluation plans to programs' characteristics are discussed.

CHAPTER 19

A Conceptual Framework and Multimethod Approach for Research on Political Socialization and Civic Engagement

JUDITH TORNEY-PURTA AND JO-ANN AMADEO
University of Maryland

MOLLY W. ANDOLINA
DePaul University

INTRODUCTION

RESEARCH ON POLITICAL socialization and civic engagement has produced a substantial number of studies, but the body of work is fragmented. There has been little cumulation of findings because the research questions and measures used in many studies have not been related to clear conceptual frameworks. Some research is also hampered by the lack of psychometrically strong measures that are consistently employed across studies to build a body of conclusions. Other research in this area could benefit from the use of multiple methods.

This chapter will introduce a conceptual framework that is comprehensive and inclusive, and will argue for studies that combine quantitative measures (such as surveys) with qualitative measures (such as focus groups or interviews). The purpose of this chapter is to provide suggestions for better ways of aligning studies and their research questions with designs and methodologies.

Research on civic engagement is an interdisciplinary field, and the perspectives of developmental and educational psychology, political science, and sociology are all important. The major conceptual framework we introduce is the social theory of learning associated with communities of practice

(Lave & Wenger, 1991) adding the concept of efficacy from Bandura's social-cognitive learning theory (Bandura, 1989, 1999). This conceptual framework has the potential to provide a more useful structure within which to develop research topics and assessments than the somewhat scattered lists of concepts and attitudes guiding most current research. The goal is a research framework that will encompass multidimensional views of civic participation (not limited to voting), of political understanding (not limited to factual knowledge), of attitudes or dispositions (not limited to generalized tolerance), and of context (not limited to the formal curriculum).

Although many methods have been used in this field of research, surveys have been particularly dominant. We will argue that whenever feasible, surveys should be supplemented by more open-ended questions administered either in focus groups or individual interviews. We will draw primarily from studies of secondary school and college students, attempting to tear down the artificial boundaries that have existed between studies on these age groups. For example, two recent studies of undergraduates, the Political Engagement Project, which obtained in-depth interviews from university students about their civic engagement experiences to supplement information obtained from surveys (Beaumont, Colby, Ehrlich, & Torney-Purta, 2006; Colby, Beaumont, Ehrlich, & Corngold, 2007; Beaumont, this volume) and the National Civic Engagement Study, which used focus groups of young adults (Zukin, Keeter, Andolina, Jenkins, & Delli Carpini, 2006), have made as significant a contribution to understanding youth political engagement as have studies of middle or high-school students.

The *first* and *second* sections of this chapter discuss survey research in this field and present a conceptual framework delineating variables that are commonly studied. We will suggest ways of expanding and refining research questions and addressing them more systematically. The *third* section will offer suggestions on improving research in civic engagement through the use of multiple methods, especially focus groups in addition to surveys. This section will include a brief overview of how focus group methodology has been used in research on political socialization and civic engagement. The *fourth* section will contrast the contributions of surveys and focus groups, and the *final* section of the chapter will outline policy implications of research based on this conceptual framework and using multiple methods.

SURVEY RESEARCH IN POLITICAL SOCIALIZATION AND CIVIC ENGAGEMENT

One reason that the field of civic engagement research is diffuse is that it has roots in different disciplines that place priority on different topics and prefer different methods of analysis. This has been true for 40 years. To illustrate the major trends and the multiple disciplines that have contributed to this field, a brief overview of survey research in political socialization and civic engagement follows.

Political Socialization Research

In the 1960s, several major projects to study the political attitudes of young people were initiated by political scientists (Greenstein, 1965; Jennings & Niemi, 1975) or involved collaborations between political scientists and psychologists (Easton & Dennis, 1969; Hess & Torney, 1967, reissued 2006), or were initiated by psychologists alone (Adelson & Beall, 1969). These efforts established a subfield of political science called *political socialization research*. This area showed remarkable popularity during the 1960s (seen especially in doctoral dissertations, some of which were later published) and during the 1970s by those interested in understanding the rise of student activism (Barnes & Kaase, 1979). The research largely conceptualized the development of political knowledge and attitudes among young people as a *top-down* learning process that did not distinguish between concerns about characteristics of individuals, processes, and context. The field then experienced a rapid fall in interest (Cook, 1985). Many researchers moved to topics that had a higher profile within their own disciplines. Political socialization research reached its peak in the 1970s and then faded from view, with little work produced in the 1980s and even the early 1990s.

Because of its roots in political science, much of the early research used attitudinal measures adapted from adult surveys (especially the National Election Studies). Questions about political parties sometimes dominated the surveys, although there was evidence that until at least the eighth grade, children did not understand much about the party system. Hess and Torney (1967, reissued 2006) reported interviews with elementary school children to supplement surveys and covered a wide range of topics including attachment to the nation, concepts of political leaders or national institutions and the system of law, sense of political efficacy, and intent to participate. Haste and Torney-Purta (1992) collected articles about the development of political understanding using a variety of methods (ranging from unstructured interviews to think-aloud problem solving to scales developed from social psychology). In the field as a whole, however, no particular method was developed, validated, and then widely used as a paradigm across studies and investigators. This may partially account for the scatter in the research topics addressed and conclusions reached.

By the late 1990s, a number of psychological theories (such as social learning theory and cognitive constructivism), which were in a nascent state during early political socialization research, had been further developed.

With a few exceptions, these theories were infrequently employed by those interested in political socialization, however. Among British scholars (and some in the United States) even the term *political socialization* was criticized as implying a top-down process of indoctrination and failing to attend to issues of power and to discrimination in the everyday lives of young people (Bhavnani, 1991; Haste, this volume).

RESEARCH ON CIVIC ENGAGEMENT IN THE COMMUNITY

The trajectory of research on young people's engagement in the community differed from that of political socialization. The concept of civic engagement was frequently instantiated as service learning or civic service. This topic of research began to rise in popularity at about the time political socialization research began to decline. Civic engagement defined in this way has attracted the attention of some political scientists but has been of more interest to educational researchers, sociologists, and psychologists (see Torney-Purta, Hahn, & Amadeo, 2001). Some research in this field has been linked to the evaluations of particular projects, programs, or curricula (including those in character education, Higgins-D'Alessandro, this volume). The methods associated with this research have not been applied consistently across studies.

Recently, however, the study of service learning and of civic engagement efforts in the school seems to have reached a kind of tipping point, creating a re-emergence in studies that lie between pure political socialization studies and civic engagement studies. Indeed, as the twenty-first century approached, political socialization and civic engagement garnered increased research funding, and younger scholars began to show interest in the field. Political socialization articles have appeared with some regularity in journals across the disciplines, with some journals creating special issues on political socialization or civic engagement (Flanagan & Sherrod, 1998; Niemi & Hepburn, 1995).

RESEARCH ON CIVIC KNOWLEDGE AND ENGAGEMENT IN SCHOOLS

In the mid-1990s, a core of international scholars who had interests in both political and civic matters, particularly in the context of new democracies, organized and conducted the IEA Civic Education Study. This study, which had both a qualitative and a quantitative phase, was initiated by the International Association for the Evaluation of Educational Achievement (IEA) as one in a series of investigations of the purposes of schooling across nations. The study included measures of attitudes, participation, and civic knowledge (Torney-Purta, Lehmann, Oswald, & Schulz, 2001). A number of secondary analyses have looked at issues such as support for human rights in 27 countries (Torney-Purta, Wilkenfeld, & Barber, 2008), the effectiveness of service learning in four countries (Torney-Purta, Amadeo, & Richardson, 2007), or tri-country comparisons (Kennedy, Hahn, & Lee, 2007).

Research Relating to the Center for Information and Research on Civic Learning and Engagement (CIRCLE)

A targeted set of investigations of civic engagement (including both political and civic activities) was promoted by the establishment of the Center for Information and Research on Civic Learning and Engagement (CIRCLE), begun in 2002 at the University of Maryland and relocated at Tufts University in 2008 (www.civicyouth.org). An influential policy paper entitled *The Civic Mission of Schools* was issued (along with working papers and fact sheets). CIRCLE commissioned a large national study of late adolescents and young adults. The study was later published as a book comparing the current youth generation's engagement in civic life to that of older cohorts (Zukin et al., 2006). Levine (2006) built on this work to provide a comprehensive, in-depth look at youth political engagement drawing on cross-disciplinary studies to examine the role of schools in the political socialization process.

The Fragmentary Picture of Civic Engagement from Existing Research

Activities and publications in youth civic engagement have recently increased, but the picture is still fragmented. The only recent published reviews have covered differing approaches to civic curriculum (Abovitz & Harnish, 2006) and views of the field from the point of view of political scientists (Jennings, 2007; Sapiro, 2004). Few pieces of research have a clear conceptual framework to guide the choice of concepts to study, variables to assess, and research problems or research questions to address.

Facing a similar problem in another area of social development, peer relations, Wentzel (2006) suggested a three-part classification of research problems and questions: those that relate to *person variables* (e.g., gender or age), to *context variables* (e.g., in-school or out-of-school), and to *process variables* (e.g., observational learning). This categorization can be applied to research on civic engagement. Studies of political socialization and civic engagement have given attention to the major person variables of age, gender, and sometimes race or ethnic group (though not always in representative samples). Very few studies have an explicit focus on context in spite of the fact that it is clear that the political, economic, and social contexts of a given historical period, as well as the context of the power structure of a given school or community, are important for understanding political and civic engagement

(Torney-Purta, 2009). Even fewer studies deal with underlying processes in an explicit way. In early research, investigators seemed fixated on deciding which *socialization agent* was the most important (family, school, peer group, the media). This was usually addressed in a simplistic way that did not consider issues of process or the relationships among socialization agents. Nor did these researchers recognize that teachers serve as very different kinds of models than parents.

The lack of consistency across studies of civic engagement and political socialization [illegible] endent variables used in differen [illegible] es in the disciplinary training o [illegible] l science most studies have empl [illegible] elections (e.g., party membersh [illegible] d officials' positions). Left out w [illegible] n, such as boycotting products, w [illegible] young people.

A meta-a [illegible] ible at present; most studies do [illegible] for example. However, a syst [illegible] very beneficial but does not cu [illegible] ack of a conceptual framework [illegible] dependent variables pertaining t [illegible] appropriate dependent variab [illegible] es, or dispositions (especially t [illegible] efficacy or agency) and intende [illegible] participation. Both independent variables and dependent variables then could be explored through studies designed with a range of methods including interviews, focus groups, and surveys. This would be an important step toward improving research in this area, which has been conducted with an ever-shifting framework insufficient to anchor strong measurement or strong generalizations. The next section will propose a conceptual framework within which research questions regarding civic engagement might be developed and corresponding measures designed.

IMPROVING RESEARCH IN CIVIC ENGAGEMENT BY IMPROVING THE FRAMEWORK FOR GENERATING RESEARCH QUESTIONS

Lave and Wenger's (1991) work on communities of practice (especially their concepts of meaning, identity, and practice) is an appropriate starting point for a framework that could facilitate researchers' ability to identify major areas of interest in the study of youth civic engagement. This framework has the potential to make research progress more systematic and improve methodology and measurement.

Lave and Wenger see all aspects of the process of learning (and even development) embedded or situated in a social context. Learning is not limited to settings where someone intends to teach something to someone else (such as schools). Learning takes places in a variety of informally organized communities of practice, defined as individuals who are mutually engaged in some kind of joint enterprise and who share a dynamic repertoire of tools, concepts, and narratives or stories (Wenger, 1998; Gauvain & Parke, 2010; McIntosh & Youniss, this volume).

Looking only at school settings where there are formally specified aims of learning impoverishes our understanding of the process of acquiring civic concepts, skills, and dispositions. Looking only at out-of-school settings, such as peer groups or at families, would likewise provide only a partial view. Seeing the individual as a member of a community of practice is analogous to looking at him or her as an apprentice worker or a novice student in the subject area being studied. Individuals belong to several communities of practice, sometimes with others who are much more skilled than they and sometimes with others who are their peers.

Lave and Wenger (1991) also discuss legitimate peripheral participation, a concept developed through observations of apprenticeship situations, for example in a Moroccan tailoring shop. Observing others and acquiring a novice's level of skills and then moving to more skilled actions is a way of becoming progressively more involved in a community of practice. This movement from peripheral to central participation, especially when it is guided or scaffolded by adults or more competent peers, is particularly appropriate in conceptualizations of political and civic life, where opportunities such as voting are not available to those younger than 18. In fact, regularly speaking at an adults' community meeting would usually be thought of as inappropriate for a 14-year-old student, just as it would be inappropriate for a 14-year-old apprentice in a tailor shop to advise a customer about the fit of a suit. Observing the discussion practices at the meeting or the tailor's practices at the fitting are types of peripheral participation, and the novice individual can gradually move from this position to more central involvement.

The concepts associated with learning in Lave and Wenger's work can be used to construct a conceptual model of civic engagement, particularly their concepts of meaning, practices, or action, and identity within a community of belonging. This model is reflected in the concepts in Table 19.1 and has implications for research questions and methodology in research in this field.

We will deal with the concepts of meaning, practices, and identity one at a time. In Lave and Wenger's theory, the *meaning* of experience and the meaning of concepts and skills related to that experience, are shaped by

Table 19.1
A Framework for Generating Research Questions and Appropriate Methods of Assessing Civic Engagement

Dependent Variables	Independent Variables		
	Person (e.g., age, gender, ethnicity, immigrant status, family background, educational expectations)	*Context* (e.g., country, region/city, neighborhood, economic situation, curriculum, climate for discussion, participation opportunities, out-of-school groups, family)	*Process* (e.g., observational learning, apprenticeship, scaffolding by adults)
Meaning (e.g., content knowledge of concepts, of international, national, and local issues, cognitive skills in analyzing information)			
Identity (e.g., party, ethnic, as someone with a particular image or part of a particular group distinct from other groups)			
Agency/Efficacy (e.g., general external, general internal, contextualized, other motives)			
Practice/Action (e.g., electoral, volunteer, voice in debate)			

Note: Columns are based on concepts from Lave and Wenger's Social Theory of Learning and Bandura's Social Cognitive Learning Theory; and on Wentzel (2006).

the communities of practice to which an individual belongs. Educational institutions try to make concepts such as citizenship, democracy, and social justice meaningful to students through pedagogical practices (including lectures, textbooks, and class discussion). But the meaning of these concepts is defined in part by the individual's position in relation to communities of practice both in and outside the school. Students may be relating to a group in their town or city that defines citizenship in a way that excludes them; they may be relating to a neighborhood that gives particular meaning to the concept of power or powerlessness; or they may be relating to groups of peers who imbue the concept of social justice with a particular meaning as they incorporate individuals from different ethnic groups. In Table 19.1, several kinds of knowledge and skills are included, but all may be influenced by the communities of practice of which the young person is a member.

The sense of *identity* is a central concept in communities of practice. We are using the term somewhat more broadly than Lave and Wenger, but their point about connections of identity formation to communities of practice is still appropriate. The concept of identity is found in various forms in other theories as well. In Erikson's (1968) view, the establishment of a personal integrated identity is a central task of the adolescent period and involves the integration or the resolution of the dilemmas of previous stages, such as industry versus inferiority (which is close to the concept of agency or efficacy as it is used in this field).

Breakwell (2001) also includes a sense of self-efficacy as part of identity. She talks about identity in terms of other concepts as well: positive affect or esteem, sense of continuity with the past, and relationships to some societal groups (as well as distinctiveness from others). Political identity can also be seen as the perception of long-term commitments to a political community as central to the self (Colby et al., 2007). Walsh (2004) studied social identities in a mixed method study of adults by asking them "which groups they felt close to." All of these approaches are more satisfying than the views found in the older political socialization literature about the centrality of party identity or identity in relation to a demographic entity (such as a racial group). Membership in a community of practice where political party or ethnic group is central will define an individual's identity to some extent, but there are many other communities of practice in which other identities may be central (social justice activist, environmentalist, dutiful but uninvolved citizen, cool guy distancing himself from adults' norms, and so on).

Efficacy and *agency* are major concepts concerned with motivation toward action, both long and short term. These are not singled out by Lave and Wenger, but both Erikson and Breakwell include similar concepts that can be related to everyday life and the groups with which young people interact. Breakwell (2001), for example, places considerable emphasis on efficacy and observational learning. A sense of efficacy (both individual and collective) is central to Bandura's theory (1989, 1999). For a conceptualization of efficacy, which is expanded from that traditionally found in political socialization studies, see Beaumont (this volume).

Finally, *action* or *practice* is central to any conceptualization in the area of civic engagement. The Internet with its social networking possibilities and online petitions is intriguing, but face-to-face activity also remains important. Young people's connections to different communities of practice present them with different opportunities for action in the present and orientations toward action in the future. Those individuals who are associated with an environmental club as an important community of practice, for example, might favor boycotting certain products, while those for whom a religious organization was an important community of practice might engage in volunteer activity.

Table 19.1 incorporates concepts from Wentzel's discussion of ways to formulate research questions about civic engagement and includes two types of independent variables (persons and contexts) in addition to the processes by which political socialization or civic engagement is assumed to take place. Person variables have been included in many studies (for example, studies of gender differences or differences by age or social class). Research questions about context are becoming more frequent, as researchers look at aspects of schooling, families, or mass media that are associated with civic attitudes or knowledge (Biestra, Lawy, & Kelly, 2009; McLeod et al., this volume). Socialization processes are usually dealt with as part of the assumptions on which a study is based or in the interpretation of findings. For example, Sanchez-Jankowski (1986) considered both context and processes. He provided evidence that among Hispanics, older brothers and sisters were especially important as models and coaches for their younger siblings as they formed their identities related to activist groups. He also found that the available identities for these young people differed between the contexts in his study (two cities in the Southwestern United States). Similarly, Gimpel, Lay, and Schuknecht's (2003) work comparing two different civic environments in Maryland illustrated how the broad context of the community shapes civic socialization processes and outcomes among high-school students.

A conceptual framework such as this one based on communities of practice has considerable potential for making it possible to integrate findings across studies and answer important lingering questions in the field. The research questions relating to person variables are the easiest to formulate. What are the differences by age or gender in political identity (conceptualized in various ways relating to communities of practice or other approaches)? Questions about context and process also can be developed in this framework. In what types of neighborhood contexts do different aspects of school context influence the acquisition of meaningful civic knowledge by students? Does political efficacy play a mediating role in young people's decision to participate in various types of political activities? Some very recent work has begun to touch on related issues of context and process (Pasek, Feldman, Romer, & Jamieson,

2008; Wilkenfeld, 2009), but a systematic review is needed. This conceptual framework (or one like it) could provide a starting point for such a review.

A framework such as that presented in this section and Table 19.1 can contribute to enhancing the research questions being addressed and moving toward a review of what is known and what needs to be investigated. Having a more adequate framework alone cannot improve research methodology, however. Nor can any single study fully incorporate all of these dimensions.

IMPROVING RESEARCH IN CIVIC ENGAGEMENT BY USING MULTIPLE METHODS

After decades of research in which quantitative measurement (written questionnaires or surveys) formed the backbone of research in developmental psychology, recently the value of mixing quantitative with qualitative methods has been seen as essential to formulating a scientific view of child and adolescent development. Yoshikawa, Weisner, Kalil, and Way (2008) discuss the issues in this way:

> We define qualitative data as information that has been collected not in numerical form but in texts, narratives, or observations (including pictures and video). We define quantitative data as information that has been collected in numerical form (e.g., counts, levels, or Likert-format responses) ... Our belief is that the combination of words and numbers can bring us closer to the complexity of developmental change by providing divergent as well as convergent data. (pp. 344–345)

To take an example from adolescents' political development, instead of being limited to information on the number of young adults who have learned specific civic skills in high school and the association between these skills and their levels of efficacy (which a survey study could accomplish), researchers might also observe students' skills and practices when discussing controversial issues in a naturally occurring or constructed small group setting. Qualitative research, while not based on numbers, is still empirical and relies on established principles and procedures to ensure the reliability and validity of the findings (Kirk & Miller, 1986).

Another value to research combining qualitative and quantitative measures is that audiences outside of the academic world can sometimes be more readily convinced of a conclusion germane to policy or practice if they can see the research findings as part of a context rather than as an isolated or artificial procedure.

Scholars in political science have also argued that the nature of human thinking and analysis almost demands qualitative methods at some point in the inquiry process. As Hochschild (1981) explains:

> It is easy to describe simple statements, even if not at all easy to analyze or explain them; survey researchers do an excellent job at this task. But given

> the opportunity, people do not make simple statements; they shade, modulate, deny, retract, or just grind to a halt in frustration. These manifestations of uncertainty are just as meaningful and interesting as the clear, definitive statements of a belief system. (p. 238)

Qualitative research allows the evaluation of participants as individuals and how their thoughts and feelings are shaped by membership in different communities of practice in their schools and neighborhoods.

Surveys and focus groups are among the most frequently used quantitative and qualitative methodologies, and the next sections will focus on them. (For discussion of other qualitative methods, such as interviews and observations, see Beaumont, this volume; Fox et al., this volume; and Metzger & Smetana, this volume.)

Surveys as an Exemplar of Quantitative Methods

Surveys have frequently been used in studies of political socialization and civic engagement to gather information from samples of young people about their attitudes, perceptions, or actions. Often, but not always, these are representative samples. Surveys allow researchers to examine patterns and relationships among variables and to generalize the findings to the larger group being studied.

Surveys are especially valuable in large-scale and comparative studies, such as the IEA Civic Education Study, in which 90,000 14-year-old students from 28 countries and 50,000 upper-secondary students from 16 countries were surveyed (Amadeo, Torney-Purta, Lehmann, Husfeldt, & Nikolova, 2002; Torney-Purta et al., 2001). Its instruments included a test of 38 items assessing civic knowledge and a survey of more than 150 items (forming 19 reliable scales) assessing attitudes and engagement. One of the advantages of these survey measures is that they have undergone widespread pilot testing and information is available about scale dimensions and their reliabilities. These surveys include attitudinal dimensions that are as relevant in a small set of schools as in multiple sites within or across countries.

The National Assessment of Education Progress in the United States also developed multiple-choice knowledge items. In order to make items such as these more broadly available, the Education Commission of the States compiled juried items (including items from the IEA Education Study, also called CIVED, and the National Assessment of Educational Progress, also called NAEP) in the areas of civic knowledge, thinking or cognitive skills, participation skills, civic dispositions, and dispositions to participation (Torney-Purta & Vermeer, 2006; also http://www.ecs.org/qna). Another source is Flanagan, Syvertsen, and Stout (2007), which describes item sets developed for civic behaviors, media, and perceptions of parents, among other topics.

Yet another source is the annual surveys of college freshmen conducted by the Higher Education Research Institute, which have allowed scholars to document trends in political orientations and participation rates among incoming students for over 40 years (see, for example, Pryor et al., 2009).

Well-constructed surveys have certainly enhanced our understanding of civic engagement. Their strengths include generalizability when the samples are representative. A wide range of topics can be covered even in 20 or 30 minutes using survey questions, and the same questions are posed to all respondents. However, there are also limitations and potential pitfalls associated with survey research. First, poorly designed samples may lead to faulty generalizations about the population under investigation. Second, ambiguously worded items or the use of jargon or slang can adversely influence the meaning respondents give to statements and affect the results of the study in unintended ways. Well-written surveys use simple sentence structures, avoid the use of negative statements and absolutes (such as *always* or *never*), and ask respondents to report on issues on which they are likely to have knowledge or experience. When the same instrument is administered across a broad age range in a developmental study, younger respondents may require questions in simple language, but the formulations may seem overly simplistic to older respondents. A third limitation may occur if the response options do not fit the questions. Fourth, a given survey should include groups of items about similar topics so that it is possible to form reliable scales (rather than having to use single item measures with limited ranges). Although surveys are very effective in answering research questions that deal with characteristics of persons (e.g., gender, age, immigrant status) and somewhat effective in answering research questions that deal with context variables (e.g., country, city, school), they are less effective in collecting evidence about process variables. Finally, even when carefully constructed, the respondents may not interpret the survey questions (or response options) in the manner intended by the researcher. Some researchers have developed a pre-testing strategy called cognitive interviewing, in which small samples are interviewed about their interpretation of questions (Greene, Torney-Purta, Azevedo, & Robertson, 2010; Karabenick et al., 2007). However, another powerful way to improve civic engagement research is to combine surveys with focus groups.

Focus Groups as an Example of Qualitative Methods

The social sciences borrowed focus group methodology from market researchers (see Delli Carpini & Williams, 1994, for a historical overview). In general, researchers using focus groups assemble 10 to 12 individuals who are strangers to one another but may share some commonalities (age, race, gender, occupation). Meetings generally last between 60 and 90 minutes (depending on the age of the participants and the depth of the inquiry). While there is a general topic to be discussed and key questions are asked, most focus groups do not follow a strict script. Instead, the group leader guides the conversation, asking participants to discuss ideas in their own terms and allowing them to explore topics in depth. In this way, the participants frame the discussion, rather than responding to the framework of the researcher (Krueger & Casey, 2000). This often provides information that is elusive when surveys are used alone. When participants are given greater control over the discussion of politics and civic life, for example, it becomes possible to evaluate the language they use, the rationales they provide, and the examples they give to understand their perspective on the political world. Focus groups can enrich the researchers' grasp of the meaning of politics and groups important in the individual's identity, as well as context and process variables (see Table 19.1). Many advocates of focus group research argue that one of the key rationales for using this method is that focus groups mirror the way that individuals form their opinions—that is, through discussion and interaction with other people (Gauvain & Parke, 2010; Krueger, 1988; Walsh, 2004).

Generally, individuals are selected by a variety of methods (sometimes but not always a random sample) and the discussion is taped, transcribed, and coded or otherwise evaluated. The method is especially useful when members of the group under investigation are not evenly distributed throughout society (such as activists belonging to a particular organization).

Focus groups are often employed as an early step in survey development, helping to ensure that one has a relatively complete picture of participants' thinking that can be formalized in meaningful questions on a survey. Like qualitative research generally, an advantage of focus groups is that respondents are able to frame the topic using their own language. After listening to the terms and phrases used by focus group participants, survey questions can be developed that reflect the language of the population under study and increase the validity of the results.

One can also use focus groups early in the research process to generate hypotheses, or later as a follow-up to data collection from a survey. For example, in designing a study of citizenship, Conover, Crewe, and Searing (1991) began with focus groups, arguing that they needed to listen to respondents "articulate their own schemata [about citizenship] in their own words" before they could conduct a full-scale study of this concept (p. 805). Other scholars have used focus groups *after* a survey to test key conclusions about the data. After Zukin et al. (2006) created a typology of civic engagement, they conducted focus groups with individuals who were characterized by their survey answers as either uninvolved or highly involved. Discussions with these different groups of individuals provided a means of testing the validity of their survey findings. Hahn (1998) also moved between survey findings and discussions similar to focus groups in her international study of citizenship. This allowed her to identify issues such as the strengths and weaknesses of discussion-based pedagogies using one method, and then to examine the issue more closely using the other method.

Focus groups can be especially helpful in understanding motivations such as efficacy and processes of political socialization. For example, if an individual has taken part in a protest, they can discuss how this participation came about—because of interest in the speakers or being angry over an issue. Or, they might talk about joining a group for social reasons and slowly getting more involved in their political activities. For example, Haste and Hogan (2006) found in a survey of British young people that being upset about an issue was associated with political action. A focus group follow-up could have enriched the understanding of what issues provoked this anger and the process by which individuals moved from emotion to action.

Finally, in conducting a focus group, one can collect data about *group processes* and about points of commonality that may not be obvious from survey findings. If one is interested in how individuals discuss controversial topics such as race or redistribution of income, the focus group provides an opportunity to watch the process unfold and look for unexpected points of disagreement as well as agreement. In a focus group conducted early in the IEA Civic Education Study, adult project leaders from a dozen countries including several post-Communist countries were asked to recount their childhood memories of political experiences. One group member mentioned having a picture on her wall of Lenin as a young boy, and at least half the group echoed, "that picture of Lenin, I had it too."

Of course, there are also some potential drawbacks to focus group research. Although the researcher hopes to create a natural setting for a conversation, it can sometimes feel contrived. Similarly, individual participants will not always feel comfortable revealing their thoughts (especially about controversial topics) in front of strangers. Other concerns relate to the group nature of the research. For example, one participant may have a confrontational approach to political issues that threatens to upset the balance of discussion. Children may have difficulty in responding to each other's ideas in a focus group context, treating it like a class recitation and seeking the moderator's validation of answers as correct. Although a skilled focus group moderator should be able to deal with most of these issues, they need to be considered both during data gathering and data analysis.

Analyzing the data from focus groups often presents a challenge. Even when researchers use structured and well-documented methods, there is room for slippage. If each group takes the discussion in a different direction from a common starting point, the researcher cannot infer what participants in one group would have thought about a topic raised only in another group. Or a scholar may design an investigation of high-school students, expecting to discuss their quasi-political activities, only to discover that students believe that all exercise of political action in their school is forbidden. Scholars have used focus group data either as a precursor or supplement to more traditional survey-based research, or as material that stands on its own. While some researchers rely on focus groups to provide illustrative quotations from narratives, others use complex coding schemes, which may involve a software program that creates a more quantitative analysis of focus group transcripts. There is space in the field for all of these approaches, as long as the chosen methodology is designed to answer the particular research question that has been posed.

Focus Groups Research on Civic and Political Engagement of Youth

Qualitative methods informed many of the early landmark studies in political socialization. While these key works all relied on large-scale surveys, these authors also incorporated techniques ranging from interviews to picture drawing to story writing as they developed their survey instruments (e.g., Greenstein, 1965; Easton & Dennis, 1969; Hess & Torney, 1967). The final versions of the surveys included some illustrations and graphic organizers for responses (e.g., big boxes labeled *YES* and smaller ones labeled *yes*). Some questions were adapted from actual statements made by children in the interviews.

As research on political socialization and youth civic engagement has experienced a revival, there has been a similar rekindling of research using qualitative methodologies, including both focus groups and interviews. For example, in a 2008 volume of *Applied Developmental Science* that focused on youth civic engagement, many of the articles combined survey research with qualitative methods (usually in-depth interviews) to evaluate issues such as the cultural identities of immigrant youth (Jenson, 2008), racial group consciousness (Junn & Masouka, 2008), and young adults' views of the social contract (Wray-Lake, Syvertsen, & Flanagan, 2008). Similarly, Beaumont et al. (2006) and Colby et al. (2007) used in-depth interviews to supplement their survey findings about what types of college programs are most effective in building political competence and engagement in college students. Sirin and Fine (2008) employed personal identity maps drawn by respondents, along with focus groups and surveys in their study of Muslim American young people. Other scholars have published studies based entirely on qualitative research, such as gendered discourse among high school youth (Rosenthal, Jones, & Rosenthal, 2003), and the role of kinship communities in the civic socialization of minorities (Kelly, 2004).

Many researchers use focus groups either as their key form of analysis or in combination with quantitative methods.[1] Focus group research on youth civic engagement has lent both breadth and depth to our understanding of this topic. Some work began about a decade ago and focused on a generation of young adults (born between the mid-1960s and the mid-1970s) who are commonly referred to as Generation X or Generation Xers. A 1996 study sponsored by the Center for Policy Alternatives and *Who Cares?* Magazine ("Youth Voices") used focus groups of 18- to 24-year-olds to supplement the findings from a national survey. The other, "College Students Talk Politics," conducted by The Harwood Group in 1993, relied entirely on a set of focus groups composed of students enrolled in four-year colleges and universities across the country. Both studies argued that the image of Xers as apathetic and lazy was superficial and unfair. Young adults were not active politically in a conventional sense, but the authors concluded that their inaction was based more on their lack of efficacy and their failure to see the relevance of politics to their lives. The researchers also saw signs of hope for this generation, as members expressed a wish for more opportunities to be involved. Focus group discussions illuminated some nuances that had been missed by survey studies.

These findings were echoed and sharpened several years later with the release of "Neglection 2000," a major study of candidates and young adults during the campaigns of 2000 (Freyman & McGoldrick, 2000). This report used a national survey, focus groups of youth in six cities, and a content analysis of television shows to illustrate the deep disconnect between traditional electoral groups and their political practices on one side and the youngest voters on the other. (The authors titled their report *They Pretend To Talk To Us, We Pretend To Vote.*)

Over the next six to eight years, focus-group-based research on young adults continued. One of the largest studies during the time period compared the new youth cohort, labeled *Dot Nets*, to older age cohorts (Generation Xers, Baby Boomers, and Dutifuls) across attitudinal and behavioral measures (Zukin et al., 2006). The authors incorporated focus groups at both the beginning and the end of their project. In the beginning, they convened generationally specific focus groups in four cities across the nation to see if young adults were involved in political and civic life in ways that might not be captured by traditional measures of activism. These early focus groups provided insight about youth attitudes toward civic life (Andolina, Jenkins, Keeter, & Zukin, 2002). In addition, they used these focus groups to develop the language for two large-scale nationwide surveys. Thus, findings

[1] Some scholars rely on in-depth interviews as their qualitative methodology of choice, but this particular chapter discusses focus groups, which some call group interviews. Some of the same principles apply.

from the focus group aided in the development of their survey instrument, allowed them to provide examples to illuminate their findings and illustrate key points, and served as a data source unto itself. For example, the researchers included measures of consumer activism (buying or failing to buy a product because of the conditions under which it was produced) that might not have been added without these focus group discussions. In addition, the authors found that the younger generation provided descriptions of politics as something for "white guys in suits," which became an effective metaphor for their worldview. Lastly, the difficulties young people had in discussing their civic duties was a finding in itself.

As mentioned earlier, one of the results of the Zukin et al. study was a typology of civic engagement, developed from respondents' answers to questions on a survey. In order to test the validity of these findings, the authors administered the survey to a random sample and then convened two focus groups: one of citizens characterized as *uninvolved* by their survey responses; one of *engaged* citizens. The focus group discussions revealed that the differences found in the survey were reflective of differences in real life. Not only were engaged citizens more involved in the civic and political life of their communities, they spoke with a deeper understanding of and commitment to engagement, which was reflected in the language they used and even the ways in which they approached issues of public policy. This is an example of the way that an identity, in this case as an engaged citizen, can shape the meaning of events and the way they are discussed.

Indeed, it is through focus group research that we have gained insight into a variety of topics related to youth civic and political engagement. Studies have revealed that young adults who refrain from politics experience a sense of powerlessness in the communities of practice that are important to them (O'Toole, Marsh, & Jones, 2003), the preference among youth for local, positive, non-sensationalized news as well as the diversity of their news consumption habits (Sherr, 2004), and the key sources of election news and information among young voters (Wells & Dudash, 2007). Kahne, Chi, and Middaugh (2006) included focus groups as part of a larger research project about high-school civic education. Including students' perspectives in their analysis helped them to "understand survey responses and identify issues and reasoning that were not captured in surveys (e.g., why they found simulations or exposure to role models so valuable)" (p. 6).

Political scientists studying young people have found focus groups to be especially valuable in providing nuances to their understanding of adolescents and young adults. For example, focus group discussions can reveal modes of expression or role models for behavior or means of networking and communicating that may be familiar in youth culture but unfamiliar to the researchers. Indeed, a focus group methodology is particularly useful when a scholar from one generation is attempting to understand members of another age cohort. Focus group members will often frame the discussion around events or experiences that have special meaning to members of their generation but may be unfamiliar to those who are older. Or they may identify with communities of practice that the researcher may know little about. In the study of college students sponsored by Kettering Foundation and described earlier, focus groups were held on college campuses nationwide. At the time, scholars had empirical evidence for young adults' withdrawal from political life (such as voting rates) but didn't know if such inaction was a result of apathy or disgust. These focus groups shed light on the issue.

More recently, in partnership with the Center for Information and Research on Civic Learning and Engagement (CIRCLE), Kettering funded a follow-up study, with researchers conducting 47 different focus groups with almost 400 college students (Kiesa et al., 2007). The replication allowed a comparison over time, provided insight into a new generation of youth, and once again afforded a more nuanced understanding of young adults' expectations and frustrations with the political world. Although the study revealed a youth cohort that is more politically engaged than their predecessors in the 1990s, it also indicated that college students continued to prefer community service to political action. In addition, the researchers found that the plethora of options for getting news had not resulted in increased knowledge or efficacy but instead had left youth feeling overloaded by news media outlets that they didn't necessarily trust.

Others have found focus groups to be especially beneficial when studying minority groups. Cohen (2006) used findings from focus groups of African American youth in Chicago to illustrate how current conceptualizations of the political have limited applicability to minority youth. Cohen describes these 18- to 21-year-olds as engaging in a "politics of invisibility"—essentially "making themselves invisible to authority figures like the police, teachers, and correction officers that they believe are out to 'get them'" (p. 7). The findings from these groups also shaped a survey instrument designed to capture the political reality of African American youth.

Finally, focus groups have been used to identify young people's misconceptions, especially in relation to topics that might be found in school curriculum. For example, educational researchers in Australia aimed to study the political experiences of 5- to 11-year-old children (Howard & Gill, 2000). They wanted to provide suggestions for a new national curriculum in Australia that would go beyond an information-based approach and would instead "provide children with the space in which to discuss and explore their own and others' emerging conceptions of power and politics" (Howard & Gill, 2000, p. 377). The interactions among children in these groups were characterized by substantial give and take and showed an increasing grasp of power relations among older participants. The discussions were also useful in showing misconceptions held by the young, for example, that political leaders get their positions by passing a difficult basic skills test. More sobering, most of the 11-year-olds had little or no understanding of how electing someone to office led to having leaders in power who were supposed to represent the views of the individuals who elected them. To summarize, a survey could indicate that the child knew what elections were but would not show that children failed to grasp the process of representation. A survey could indicate whether the school had a student council, but only a more qualitative technique like a focus group could indicate on which issues it was thought to be effective.

Lessons Learned from Focus Group Research

A few common themes emerge from these studies. For one, focus group analysis has helped scholars to better understand young adults' lack of involvement in political and civic life and gaps in their knowledge. Instead of simply looking at voting trends and labeling young adults as apathetic or ignorant, qualitative research has revealed the varied ways in which young adults are involved in public life (besides voting) and provided a more nuanced understanding of their reasons for abstaining (e.g., alienation, absence of a sense of efficacy, a lack of key skills). Further the types of misconceptions that are common among young people can be identified. Focus groups have enabled scholars to sharpen their survey instruments by expanding definitions of political acts, as well as shaping the language in each item to be more meaningful to pre-adult audiences. Focus groups have also allowed those who hope to spur youth civic engagement a means of creating policy prescriptions. For example, in a series of studies at Fordham University over several years, scholars used both survey research and focus groups to better understand youth attitudes about political and civic engagement and to explore these concepts in detail with the ultimate goal of determining how best to promote engagement (Sherrod, 2003). Focus group discussions provide the space and framework for exploring various interventions that could be attempted in a specific context or provide instances of a particular process. This would be much more difficult to investigate in a closed-ended survey.

CONTRASTING QUANTITATIVE (SURVEY) AND QUALITATIVE (FOCUS GROUP) METHODS IN STUDYING CIVIC ENGAGEMENT

The large majority of research in political socialization, up until quite recently, relied on survey measures with infrequent use of multiple methods such as focus groups. Scholars have documented how many young people are involved in political and civic life, key factors associated with their activism, how they compare to earlier cohorts of youth, and much more. However, when reviewing the lessons revealed by quantitative work, we should be careful not to ignore the insights from complementary studies that have used qualitative methods.

To return to the distinctions made in the early part of the chapter, qualitative research is often focused on understanding a particular *process*, for example, how individuals interpret the meaning of political messages. Such practices do not always translate easily to a set of response categories in a closed-ended survey. When respondents are given the time and space to tell their own stories, they can illuminate elements of the process that would be lost in a more constrained investigation. Thus, qualitative research often uncovers thinking or suggests theories that the researcher did not consider prior to collecting data (Kirk & Miller, 1986). Finally, qualitative research can often involve a diverse group of scholars, which has the potential to position the findings in a broader, cross-disciplinary discussion.

Table 19.2 summarizes general aspects of surveys and focus groups, respectively, and by their complementary nature suggest the value of multiple methods in studies of socialization and civic engagement. This table also indicates some of the ways in which survey and focus group research can be contrasted with respect to dimensions of communities of practice. In relation to *meaning*, more complex and nuanced meanings of information and behavior can be accessed in a focus group than in a survey. In relation to *identity*, although racial and ethnic identity are clearly important, a more qualitative approach allows individuals to describe their identity in relation to a variety of groups. They can say how each of those groups serves as a community of practice for them and the process by which their identity has developed over time. In studying *efficacy or agency*, qualitative methods such as focus groups can surface narratives of political efficacy (or lack of efficacy), which are much more informative than knowing whether an individual agrees or disagrees that "the government is like the weather; there is nothing people can do about it" (a commonly used efficacy survey item). Finally, surveys can estimate how often the average young person engages in given political *activities* but fails to give information about why participation begins or continues and with whom the individual interacts.

In summary, qualitative research is used in a variety of ways. For some scholars, it is their sole method of inquiry. Others use qualitative techniques to elaborate empirical findings or to add depth through quotations in the words of young people. Still others rely on qualitative research as a methodological tool to sharpen the language used in survey instruments that contain mostly closed-ended questions.

Table 19.2
A Comparison of Survey and Focus Group Methods in the Study of Civic Engagement

	Survey	Focus Group
Using current slang	Avoids because individual respondents interpret differently	Can uncover phrases or terms meaningful to the group being studied
Using provocative statements	Avoids terms such as *none*, *all*, *never*, *always*	May stimulate discussion with controversy
Questioning	Standardized	Non-standardized; directed by participants' responses
Asking for memory of a specific instance	Plays a minor role	Asks for details and narratives associated with a topic
Sampling	Random	Purposeful
Understanding *meaning*	Uses simple statements to minimize alternative interpretations of meaning	Searches for in-depth alternative meanings and/or clarification of meanings
Ascertaining dimensions of *identity*	Examines individuals' identity by party, gender, or ethnicity	Seeks to understand how individuals would describe themselves
Studying *efficacy*	Often limited to internal and external efficacy	Can examine narratives of collective efficacy
Examining *activities*	Asks what respondents do and how often	Probes why, how, and with whom participants engage

CONCLUSIONS AND POLICY IMPLICATIONS

Our discussion of research on political socialization and youth engagement offers several suggestions that would increase its power for making recommendations about policy or the design of interventions. One problem with making policy recommendations from available research is the lack of a clear conceptual framework, which can generate research questions that lead to an accumulation of knowledge about the characteristics of persons and contexts that support engagement. Our framework, which includes both categories of potential independent variables (persons, contexts, and processes) and constructs from which to derive dependent variables (meaning, identity, efficacy, and action) is proposed as a step in the solution of this problem. Many important questions could be asked about how contexts in schools or neighborhoods condition the nature of ethnic group, SES, and gender differences in identity or efficacy, to give just one example.

Another problem constraining the relevance of research to policy is with limitations that exist when surveys are the sole method used in research. The mindsets of those who fund the research as well as of the researchers themselves need to be considered. A number of our recommendations, therefore, are directed to those who fund research and formulate the rubrics by which research is judged before it is brought to the attention of individuals who formulate policy or plan interventions. First, we recommend support by federal agencies and private foundations for cumulative reviews of findings (within a conceptual framework, one example of which has been discussed) and for the secondary analysis of existing datasets as preliminary steps to designing new studies or programs. Second, we recommend the design of explicit mechanisms (for example, electronic communication, conferences, or publications) to foster awareness among researchers in one discipline of methodologies and research findings from other disciplines. In writing this chapter, some of the assumptions, methodologies, and results that were familiar to the two authors who were psychologists differed from those that were familiar to the political scientist. This should go beyond political science and developmental or social psychology to include organizational and community psychology as well as sociology and anthropology. Some of these partnerships might take place in cross-national collaborations.

Third, we recommend the fostering of partnerships between organizations and institutions that are developing civic engagement programs and scholars interested in assessing the impacts of such programs and drawing generalizations from them (see Higgins-D'Alessandro, this volume). Because programs are designed to be implemented in specific contexts and with specific age groups, this could help focus research on aspects of meaning, identity, efficacy, and action that are especially relevant in particular settings or for particular young people.

Fourth, potential advocates for a particular policy or policy approach are important parts of the audience for research findings. The information needed by individuals serving in advocacy roles may not be identical to the information needed by policy-makers and their staffs. However, both groups are more likely to be persuaded by cumulative reviews (not scattered findings) and by information that can be seen in a context.

Finally, we recommend support for multimethod studies that employ both quantitative and qualitative measures, capitalizing on the advantages and minimizing the disadvantages of each. At present these studies are sometimes thought to be too risky or too expensive. In our view, until such research becomes more widely accepted and supported, we will have an insufficient foundation upon which to build enhanced youth civic engagement.

REFERENCES

Abovitz, K. K., & Harnish, J. (2006). Contemporary discourses of citizenship. *Review of Educational Research, 76(4)*, 653–690.

Adelson, J., & Beall, L. (1969). Adolescent perspectives on law and government. *Law and Society Review, 495.*

Amadeo, J., Torney-Purta, J., Lehmann, R., Husfeldt, V., & Nikolova, R. (2002). *Civic knowledge and engagement. An IEA study of upper secondary students in sixteen countries.* Amsterdam, NL: IEA. Retrieved from http://www.terpconnect.umd.edu/~iea

Andolina, M. W., Jenkins, K., Keeter, S., & Zukin, C. 2002. Searching for the meaning of youth civic engagement: Notes from the field. *Applied Developmental Science, 6(4)*, 189–195.

Bandura, A. (1989). Social cognitive theory. In R. Vasta (Ed.), *Six theories of human development. Annals of Child Development* (Vol. 6, pp.1–60). Greenwich, CT: JAI Press.

Bandura, A. (1999). Social cognitive theory: An agentic perspective. *Asian Journal of Social Psychology, 2*, 21–41.

Barnes, S., & Kaase, M. (1979). *Political action. Mass participation in five Western democracies.* Beverly Hills, CA: Sage Publications.

Beaumont, E., Colby, A., Ehrlich, T., & Torney-Purta, J. (2006). Promoting political competence and engagement in college students: An empirical study. *Journal of Political Science Education, 2*, 249–70.

Bhavnani, K-K. (1991). *Talking politics: A psychological framing for youth in Britain.* Cambridge: Cambridge University Press.

Biestra, G., Lawy, R., & Kelly, N. (2009). Understanding young people's citizenship learning in everyday life: The role of contexts, relationships, and dispositions. *Education, Citizenship and Social Justice, 4(1)*, 5–24.

Breakwell, G. (2001). Social representational constraints upon identity processes. In K. Deaux & G. Philogene (Eds.), *Representations of the social: Bridging theoretical traditions* (pp. 251–282). London: Blackwell.

Cohen, C. (2006). African American youth: Broadening our understanding of politics, civic engagement and activism. SSRC web forum on Youth Activism. Retrieved from http://ya.ssrc.org/african/Cohen

Colby, A., Beaumont, E., Ehrlich, T., & Corngold, J. (2007). *Educating for democracy: Preparing undergraduates for responsible political engagement.* San Francisco: Jossey-Bass.

Conover, P. J., Crewe, I. M., & Searing, D. D. (1991). The nature of citizenship in the United States and Great Britain: Empirical comments on theoretical themes. *Journal of Politics, 53(3)*, 800–832.

Cook, T. E. (1985). The bear market in political socialization and the costs of misunderstood psychological theories. *American Political Science Review, 79*, 1079–1093.

Delli Carpini, M. X., & Williams, B. (1994). The method is the message: Focus groups as a method of social, psychological, and political inquiry. *Research in Micropolitics, 4*, 57–85.

Easton, D., & Dennis, J. (1969). *Children in the political system: Origins of political legitimacy*. New York: McGraw Hill.

Erikson, E. (1968). *Identity: Youth and crisis*. New York: Norton.

Flanagan, C., Syvertsen, A., & Stout, M. (2007). Civic measurement models: Tapping adolescents' civic engagement (CIRCLE Working Paper 55). College Park, MD: CIRCLE.

Flanagan, C. A., & Sherrod, L. R. (1998). *Journal of Social Issues, 54(3)*, 447–456.

Freyman, R., & McGoldrick, B. (2000). *Neglection 2000: They pretend to talk to us, we pretend to vote*. Third Millennium Project.

Gauvain, M. & Parke, R. (2010). Socialization. In M. Bornstein (Ed.), *Handbook of cultural developmental science* (pp. 239–258). New York: Psychology Press.

Gimpel, J. G., Lay, J. C., & Schuknecht, J. E. (2003). *Cultivating democracy: Civic environments and political socialization in America*. Washington, DC: Brookings Institution Press.

Greene, J., Torney-Purta, J., Azevedo, R., & Robertson, J. (2010). Using cognitive interviews to explore elementary and secondary school students' epistemic cognition. In L. Bendixen & F. Feucht (Eds.), *Personal epistemology in the classroom.* (pp. 368-405). Cambridge: Cambridge University Press.

Greenstein, F. I. (1965). *Children and politics*. New Haven: Yale University Press.

Hahn, C. (1998). *Becoming citizens: Comparative perspectives on citizenship education.* Albany, NY: SUNY Press.

Haste, H., & Hogan, A. (2006). Beyond conventional civic participation, beyond the moral-political divide: Young people and contemporary debates about citizenship. *Journal of Moral Education, 35(4)*, 473–494.

Haste, H., & Torney-Purta, J. (Eds.). (1992). *The development of political understanding*. San Francisco, CA: Jossey-Bass (New Directions in Child Development).

Hess, R. D., & Torney, J. (1967, reissued 2006). *The development of political attitudes in children*. Chicago: Aldine Publishing Company.

Hochschild, J. (1981). *What's fair? American beliefs about distributive justice*. Cambridge, MA: Harvard University Press.

Howard, S., & Gill, J. (2000). The pebble in the pond: Children's construction of power, politics and democratic citizenship. *Cambridge Journal of Education, 30(3)*, 357–378.

Jennings, M. K. (2007). Political socialization. In R. Dalton & H-D. Klingemann (Eds.), *Oxford handbook of political behavior.* Oxford: Oxford University Press.

Jennings, K., & Niemi, R. (1975). Continuity and change in political orientations: A longitudinal study of two generations. *The American Political Science Review, 69(4)*, 1316–1335.

Jenson, L. A. (2008). Immigrants' cultural identities as sources of civic engagement. *Applied Developmental Science, 12(2)*, 74–83.

Junn, J., & Masouka, N. (2008). Identities in context: Politicized racial group consciousness among Asian American and Latino youth. *Applied Developmental Science, 12(2)*, 93–101.

Kahne, J., Chi, B., & Middaugh, E. (2006). Building social capital for civic and political engagement: The potential of high-school civics courses. *Canadian Journal of Education, 29(2)*, 387–409.

Karabenick, S., Woolley, M. E., Friedel, J. M., Ammon, B. V., Blazevski, J., Rhee Bonney, C., De Groot, E., Gilbert, M. C., Musu, L., Kempler, T. M., Kelly, K. L. (2007). Cognitive processing of self-report items in educational research: Do they think what we mean? *Educational Psychologist, 42(3)*, 139–151.

Kelly, D. C. (2004). Civic view of young adult minorities: Exploring the influences of kinship communities and youth mentoring communities on prosocial civic behaviors (CIRCLE Working Paper 25). College Park, MD: CIRCLE. Retrieved from http://www.civicyouth.org

Kennedy, K., Hahn, C., & Lee, W-O. (2007). Constructing citizenship: Comparing the views of students in Australia, Hong Kong, and the United States. *Comparative Education Review, 52(1)*, 53–91.

Kiesa, A., Orlowski, A. P., Levine, P., Both, D., Kirby, E. H., Lopez, M. H., & Marcelo, K. B. (2007). *Millenials talk politics*. College Park, MD: CIRCLE and the Kettering Foundation. Retrieved from http://www.civicyouth.org

Kirk. J., & Miller, M. L. (1986). *Reliability and validity in qualitative research*. Newbury Park, CA: Sage Publications.

Krueger, R. A. (1988). *Focus groups: A practical guide for applied research*. Newbury Park, CA: Sage Publications.

Lave, L., & Wenger, E. (1991). *Situated learning: Legitimate peripheral participation*. Cambridge: Cambridge University Press.

Levine, P. (2007). *The future of democracy: Developing the next generation of citizens*. Boston: University Press of New England.

Niemi, R., & Hepburn, M. (1995). The rebirth of political socialization. *Perspectives on Political Science, 24(1)*, 7–17.

O'Toole, T., Marsh, D., & Jones, S. (2003). Political literacy cuts both ways: The politics of non-participation among young people. *Political Quarterly, 74*, 349–360.

Pasek, J., Feldman, L., Romer, D., & Jamieson, K. H. (2008). Schools as incubators of democratic participation: Building long term political efficacy with civic education. *Applied Developmental Science, 12(1)*, 26-37.

Pryor, J. H., Hurtado, S., DeAngelo, L., Sharkness, J., Romero, L. C., Korn, W. S., Tran, S. (2009). "The American Freshman: National Norms for Fall 2008." Los Angeles: Higher Education Research Institute (HERI), University of California, Los Angeles (UCLA) Graduate School of Education & Information Studies. Retrieved from http://www.heri.ucla.edu

Rosenthal, C. S., Jones, J., & Rosenthal, J. A. (2003). Gendered discourse in the political behavior of adolescents. *Political Research Quarterly, 56(1)*, 97–104.

Sanchez-Janowski, M. (1986). *City bound: Urban life and political attitudes among Chicano youth*. Albuquerque: University of New Mexico Press.

Sapiro, V. (2004). Not your parents' political socialization: Introduction for a new generation. *Annual Review of Political Science, 7*, 1–23.

Sherr, S. (2004). News for a new generation report 1: Content analysis, interviews, and focus groups (CIRCLE Working Paper 16). College Park, MD: CIRCLE. Retrieved from http://www.civicyouth.org

Sherrod, L. R. (2003). Promoting the development of citizenship in diverse youth. *PS: Political Science and Politics, 36*, 287–292.

Sirin, S., & Fine, M. (2008). *Muslim-American youth: Understanding hyphenated identities through multiple methods.* New York: NYU Press.

Torney-Purta, J. (2009). International research that matters for policy and practice. *American Psychologist, 64(8),* 825–837.

Torney-Purta, J., Amadeo, J., & Richardson, W. (2007). Civic service among youth in Chile, Denmark, England and the United States: A psychological perspective. In M. Sherraden & A. McBride (Eds.), *Civic service worldwide: Impacts and inquiries* (pp. 95–132). Armonk, NY: M. E. Sharpe.

Torney-Purta, J., Hahn, C., & Amadeo, J. (2001). Principles of subject-specific instruction in education for citizenship. In J. Brophy (Ed.), *Subject-specific instructional methods and activities* (Vol. 8, pp. 373–410). Amsterdam: Elsevier Science.

Torney-Purta, J., Lehmann, R., Oswald, H., & Schulz, W. (2001). *Citizenship and education in twenty-eight countries: Civic knowledge and engagement at age fourteen.* Amsterdam: IEA. Retrieved from http://www.terpconnect.umd.edu/~iea

Torney-Purta, J., Wilkenfeld, B., & Barber, C. (2008). How adolescents in twenty-seven countries understand international human rights. *Journal of Social Issues, 64(4),* 857–880.

Torney-Purta, J., & Vermeer, S. (2004, updated version 2006). *Developing citizenship competencies from kindergarten through grade 12: A background paper for policymakers and educators.* Denver, CO: Education Commission of the States, 32 pages. Retrieved from http://www.ecs.org

Walsh, K. C. (2004). *Talking about politics.* Chicago: University of Chicago Press.

Wells, S. D., & Dudash, E. A. (2007). Wha'd'ya know? Examining young voters' political information and efficacy in the 2004 election. *American Behavioral Scientist, 50*(9), 1280.

Wenger, E. (1998). *Communities of practice: Learning, meaning, and identity.* Cambridge: Cambridge University Press.

Wentzel, K. R. (2006). Developing and nurturing interesting and researchable ideas. In C. Conrad & R. Serlin (Eds.), *The Sage handbook for research in education: Engaging ideas and enriching inquiry.* Thousand Oaks, CA: Sage Publications.

Wilkenfeld, B. S. (2009). A multilevel analysis of context effects on adolescent civic engagement: The role of family, peers, school, and neighborhood. Unpublished doctoral dissertation, University of Maryland, College Park.

Wray-Lake, L., Syvertsen, A. K., & Flanagan, C. A. (2008). Contested citizenship and social exclusion: Adolescent Arab American immigrants' views of the social contract. *Applied Developmental Science, 12(2),* 84–92.

Yoshikawa, H., Weisner, T., Kalil, A., & Way, N. (2008). Mixing qualitative and quantitative research developmental science: Uses and methodological choices. *Developmental Psychology, 44(2),* 344–354.

Zukin, C., Keeter, S., Andolina, M. W., Jenkins, K., & Delli Carpini, M. X. (2006). *A new engagement? Political participation, civic life and the changing American citizen.* New York: Oxford.

CHAPTER 20

Political Agency and Empowerment: Pathways for Developing a Sense of Political Efficacy in Young Adults

ELIZABETH BEAUMONT
University of Minnesota

INTRODUCTION

THE NOTION OF a *sense of political efficacy*—the belief that political change is possible and that we have the capacity to contribute to it through deliberate judgments and actions—is a core component of human agency and empowerment to act in the world. Perceptions of political efficacy are widely recognized as vital to democratic dispositions and actions in young people and adults. Research on the civil rights movement, for example, indicates that political efficacy among blacks was crucial for sustaining the movement against great odds and personal costs (McAdam, 1982, 1988). Sense of political efficacy forms a powerful nexus between our personal motivations, choices, and values, and our political interactions and behaviors. Drawing together insights from political science and psychology helps explicate what a sense of political efficacy is, why it is important for self-development and democratic institutions, and some of the processes through which it emerges in young people. This chapter offers a multi-perspective view of the sense of political efficacy, drawing on student and faculty interviews from a major study of undergraduates' political learning experiences to illustrate the interplay of social and psychological processes in political life. This approach adopts an interdisciplinary framework including psychologists' views about self-efficacy. It also includes young people's reflections on their political experiences and capacities and emphasizes the powerful role that well-supported political learning experiences can play in students' sense of political efficacy, agency, and empowerment.

Developing political efficacy involves gaining political confidence and a sense that one's everyday choices and actions matter and can contribute meaningfully to political goals. We can see such a gain in political confidence in one student's description of herself before and after participating in a semester program focused on understanding and addressing urban problems:

> Well, I would say that prior [to the program] I was just like a spectator, maybe, and now I'm more willing to take part in creating change. And before also I think I lacked confidence and didn't think what I did could make a difference and now I think it would.... And I guess I didn't have the political framework with which to look at things because I just wasn't interested in it.... Initially I had a sense of hopelessness that I couldn't do anything, that I'd have to do things in the larger [national] scheme for there to be any difference. I realized that I could just do things at my level and be effective. That makes me more confident of what I do.

This chapter identifies four pathways of political learning that can help undergraduates from different backgrounds develop greater faith in their capacities for political judgment and action: (1) skill-building political mastery experiences: challenging but achievable experiences that foster political skills and include ongoing guidance and reflection; (2) models of political efficacy and involvement: a variety of politically active and confident role models to observe and emulate; (3) social encouragement, supportive relationships and networks, and inclusion in political community: meaningful connections to politically engaged peers, community members, and groups; and (4) empowering and resilient political outlooks: interactions that foster hope, courage, and perseverance.

PERSPECTIVES ON POLITICAL EFFICACY FROM POLITICAL SCIENCE AND PSYCHOLOGY

A sense of political efficacy is our confidence in our abilities to understand the political realm and act effectively in it, and our belief that these judgments and actions are meaningful and worthwhile. Thus, our sense of political efficacy overlaps with our sense of ourselves as political agents, and our feelings of political empowerment. Political scientists call the self-perception of political capacity *internal political efficacy*, and began studying it in the 1950s, describing it as "the feeling that political and social change is possible, and that the individual citizen can play a part in bringing about this change" (Campbell, Gurin, & Miller, 1954, p. 187). For psychologists, a sense of political efficacy is a type of self-efficacy expressed in a particular domain, and they similarly define it as "belief that one can produce effects through political action" (Bandura, 1997).

The sense of political efficacy described in this chapter centers on individuals' perceptions and evaluations of their capacities for political judgment and action. Sense of political efficacy is neither the same as our actual political effectiveness, or *objective political efficacy,* nor is it the same as our perceptions of political institutions' openness to change, or our sense of *external efficacy* or *government responsiveness*. Nor is it identical to *regime support* or *trust* in political institutions (Niemi, Craig, & Mattei, 1991).

For example, educational psychologists' work shows that sense of self-efficacy is not the same as beliefs about expected outcomes, and that such perceptions are often better predictors of behavior (Schunk & Pajares, 2004). Similarly, political science research shows that self-efficacy in the political realm can operate differently than beliefs about government responsiveness or political trust. Among Black youth in the 1960s during the Civil Rights movement, high levels of political efficacy coincided with considerable distrust of institutions and cynicism; and there is evidence that civic education efforts can simultaneously boost sense of political efficacy *and* political cynicism (Rodgers, 1974; Liebschutz & Niemi, 1974; Abramson, 1977). More generally, when a strong sense of personal political efficacy is combined with feeling somewhat distrustful or angry about political institutions or policies, this can motivate political action, although severe cynicism is usually debilitating (Gamson, 1968; Abramson, 1983; Levi & Stoker, 2000).

A variety of theoretical and empirical work demonstrates the power of a sense of political efficacy. People who believe they have the capacity to make a meaningful difference are often motivated to act, regardless of whether they trust the political system or believe those in power are likely to listen, as with movements for political change in the Baltic States during the early 1990s.

As work on social movements suggests, there is overlap between our individual sense of political self-efficacy and our *perceptions of collective political efficacy,* or our beliefs about a group's abilities to act effectively in politics. Psychologists show that collective efficacy is rooted in self-efficacy, but they are not the same (Bandura, 1993, 1997). For example, a parent may be confident in her own political capacities but thinks her PTA is too disorganized to accomplish its goals. Or, a member of an active PTA may feel collectively efficacious, yet lack confidence in his own abilities.

In general, however, an individual's sense of her own political efficacy and her sense of collective political efficacy are mutually supportive. Politics is a realm in which much depends on the interplay of cooperation and conflict between different groups and forces. As a result, developing both individual and collective efficacy is crucial for much democratic involvement, from supporting an electoral campaign to joining a political protest or boycott. Thus, the primary focus of this chapter is on how young people gain an individual sense of political efficacy, recognizing that this usually dovetails with gaining a sense of collective efficacy. Together, these feelings of political agency form vital foundations for self-development and for the social capital and collective action on which communities and democracies depend (Putnam, 2000; Brehm & Rahn, 1997).

THEORETICAL ROOTS: POLITICAL AUTONOMY, POLITICAL COURAGE, AND DEMOCRATIC EXPERIENCE

The term *political efficacy* was not widely used until the 1950s, when political scientists began studying it through surveys. But concepts related to political agency and efficacy possess a long lineage in the history of political thought. Among the many perspectives political theorists offer, three broad sets of ideas form the theoretical underpinnings of political efficacy.

POLITICAL AUTONOMY AND MORAL AGENCY

One intellectual foundation is Immanuel Kant's theory of autonomy or self-directedness, which rests on critical thinking and moral judgment. Kant argues that our judgments determine both what is *possible* and how we should act. He treats human autonomy as involving judgment, intention, and possibility—not as an autonomy dependent on results or narrowly instrumental thinking. We have a responsibility to *ourselves* to align our actions with our judgments. We should always try to work for what we think is right even if we cannot always succeed, and we should see such actions as personally meaningful. This counters the instrumental perspective that we should act only when we know our actions will produce desired results. Thus, Kant's notion of human autonomy and moral agency form a crux of political efficacy: Even when we know we can't fully control outcomes, we can still decide what we think ought to be the case. We should feel a sense of responsibility to ourselves to act on our best judgments and try, to the best of our abilities, to influence the world around us.

POLITICAL LEAPS OF FAITH: FACULTIES FOR POLITICAL FREEDOM AND COURAGE

A second theoretical foundation for sense of political efficacy emerges from the emphasis classical and republican traditions place on the belief in a human faculty for political freedom, a faculty stemming from our capacity to act in the political realm (Pocock, 1975; Skinner, 1990; Pettit, 1997). Hannah Arendt, for example, interpreted the classical conception of political freedom as a human "faculty of beginning." Each person constitutes a new beginning and possesses the power to begin "something new on our own initiative" and set in motion new chains of events through political words and deeds (Arendt, 1958, p. 9, pp. 147–149; 1961, pp. 166–167, 170–171).

The cornerstone of this faculty for political freedom is the belief in our political initiative and capacity, or our sense of political efficacy. Viewed from the perspective of classical political thought, sense of political efficacy is a political disposition for conscious action comprising political judgment, skill, and courage (1961, pp. 153–154). Our faculty for political freedom stands in stark contrast to fatalistic and passive outlooks that treat politics as uncontrollable whims of fate or fortune.

This does not mean a naive belief that one's political actions will achieve a desired result. As Arendt put it, our capacity for political action involves our rational knowledge that "objectively... the chances that tomorrow will be like yesterday are always overwhelming" (1961, pp. 170–171). Yet as Kant's notion of autonomy suggests, we need to recognize our ability for purposeful response to political forces and historical circumstances. We are born into a world that precedes and constrains us but must view ourselves as political agents possessing the potential to enact change despite what may feel like an "infinite improbability" of doing so (Arendt, 1961, pp. 169–170).

Political Transformation through Shared Democratic Experience and Interaction

For many political theorists, democratic experience itself is the cornerstone for developing agency, political capacities, and courage for political action (Dewey, 1927; Arendt, 1958, 1961; Warren, 1992). Drawing ideas from thinkers like Rousseau and Mill, for example, a range of contemporary political theorists urge that when people engage in political discussion and action with others, for example as members of small New England town meetings, these experiences are as important for self-transformation through sense of political efficacy as they are for the political outcomes they produce (Pateman, 1971; Mansbridge, 1980, 1999; Barber, 1984). If people are never provided with opportunities to work with others on political goals, they may never form a sense of themselves as capable political agents. Thus, sense of political efficacy is reciprocal with concrete democratic experience and interaction.

Tracing these philosophical roots shows that feelings of political efficacy are crucial for democracy, and they are not the same as regime support or political complacency. While some early political scientists suggested links between efficacy and relatively unquestioning support for the political system (Easton 1975; Dennis, 1968, p. 89), psychologists looking at the same data identified efficacy as a motivation for citizens' critical activity between election cycles (Hess & Torney, 1967).

Feeling politically efficacious involves a sense of political autonomy, skill, and courage to act in ways that may support *or* critique and challenge existing political policies and leadership. Part of political efficacy is the conviction that the beliefs and actions of politicians and experts are not all that matter for democracy. One's own and others' political judgments and activities matter and can be exercised skillfully. There is value and dignity in taking deliberate political action, even when those actions are unlikely to reach hoped-for consequences. This theoretical lineage helps show that political efficacy forms a vital circuit between political judgments, skills, and actions, and is vital for self-development as agents and for involvement that sustains democratic governance.

SENSE OF POLITICAL EFFICACY IN RELATION TO PARTICIPATION, SOCIOECONOMIC STATUS, CIVIC RESOURCES, AND POLITICAL SOCIALIZATION

Turning to modern empirical work, five decades of national surveys of adults demonstrate that political efficacy is among the most important influences on political participation and has significant, positive associations with political knowledge, political interest, paying attention to the news, and many other political dispositions (Almond & Verba, 1963; Campbell, Gurin & Miller, 1954; Nie, Verba, & Petrocik, 1976; Morrell, 2003). As its theoretical roots suggest, a sense of political efficacy involves a network of bridges to cognitive, motivational, and behavioral facets of political life.

Political science usually studies efficacy as an influence on participation, rather than as an outcome, and relies strongly on cross-sectional surveys that reveal broad patterns of associations between levels of efficacy and contemporaneous influences. These patterns show that sense of political efficacy is not uniform or evenly distributed, but varies greatly across the population. In general, those who are wealthier and more highly educated, as well as White, male, middle-aged, and more politically knowledgeable, are most likely to feel politically efficacious and to participate in politics (Finkel, 1985; Verba, Schlozman, & Brady, 1995). Those who possess few of these political advantages and resources, including young people, generally, are likely to feel little political efficacy.

Political science identifies several sets of influences that help explain differences in levels of political efficacy among people: (1) political participation; (2) socioeconomic status (SES), including education levels, race, and gender; (3) civic resources, including political knowledge, skills, motivations, social networks, and experiences; and (4) political socialization, including the learning and experiences of young people in families and schools.

Partly because of its link with socioeconomic position, some scholars view efficacy as a function of status, reflecting reasonable calculations regarding the costs and benefits of political involvement (Abramson, 1977). Such factors are undeniably important, but sense of political efficacy can be adequately explained neither as a mere reflection of one's position in the social hierarchy nor through a simple model of *homo economicus* making rational choices about achieving narrow self-interest. Black Americans, for example, often have levels of political efficacy and rates of participation much higher than their socioeconomic status would predict because they have gained motivation and a sense of capacity through other pathways (Verba & Nie, 1972; Shingles, 1981).

Indeed, influential studies suggest that the strong associations between socioeconomic status and political self-efficacy stem largely from the role status plays in helping people acquire civic resources important for political engagement (Beck & Jennings, 1982). The civic resources that help us feel politically efficacious include cognitive, informational, motivational, and social and cultural resources, especially politically relevant knowledge, skills, orientations, social networks, and political experiences. These are often gained through high-quality education, high-status jobs, and inclusion in community groups and social networks that invite political involvement (Verba, Schlozman, & Brady, 1995; Rosenstone & Hansen, 1993). From this perspective, high status coincides with political efficacy because it serves as a vehicle for acquiring civic resources that boost political confidence.

A smaller body of work on political socialization, including panel studies surveying the same individuals over time, shows that sense of political efficacy and the constellation of civic resources that build efficacy—political knowledge, skills, motivations, and experiences—are shaped by young people's experiences in families, schools, extracurricular activities, and communities (Beck & Jennings, 1982, p. 98; Langton & Karns, 1969). This research identifies key social learning experiences that contribute to political efficacy and engagement: whether one grew up in a home where parents were politically interested and talked about politics; taking classes involving learning about or discussing politics; open classroom environments and participation in class decision making or school governance; participating in student clubs and extracurricular activities; and political skill-building experiences (Jennings & Niemi, 1974, 1981; Niemi & Junn, 1998; Jennings & Stoker, 2004; Sears & Levy, 2003; Torney-Purta, Wilkenfeld, & Barber, 2008). But most large-scale political socialization studies relying on general measures cannot examine the specific processes and mechanisms at work in such efficacy-enhancing experiences. For this, psychology is especially valuable.

THE PSYCHOLOGY OF SELF-EFFICACY

Psychologists do not typically focus on sense of political efficacy per se, but they study development of self-efficacy perceptions, or a person's beliefs about her abilities in a given domain, as well as collective efficacy perceptions (Bandura, 1977, 1997). Three decades of research, including experimental research, on young peoples' and adults' experiences in schooling, health, athletics, organizations, and other settings suggest that self-efficacy guides our judgments and actions through four general psychological and social processes: cognitive, motivational, affective, and selection processes (Bandura, 1994; Wilkenfeld, Lauckhardt, & Torney-Purta, this volume).

THINKING PROCESSES: POLITICAL JUDGMENT AND ASPIRATION

Operating through cognitive processes, having a sense of efficacy in a given domain affects goal setting by enhancing our ability to grapple with complex information and tasks. When people face difficult circumstances, those with a greater sense of efficacy exhibit stronger analytic thinking and remain focused on their goals, while those with less sense of agency often begin feeling confused or overwhelmed and lowering their aspirations. People who feel efficacious can visualize success scenarios that inspire and guide their actions. People who doubt their efficacy are more likely to focus on things that could go wrong and give up.

In this way, sense of self-efficacy helps us grapple with the uncertainty and contingency that characterizes the world of politics by strengthening analytical abilities and fostering high aspirations. Our sense of political efficacy influences political interest and willingness to undertake political action because it involves basic confidence that we can think and act skillfully in this complex milieu. As political theorists suggest, sense of political efficacy operates through political judgment and political imagination—the kinds of political beginnings we can conceive, the chains of events we visualize, and the political possibilities and futures we envision as achievable goals.

MOTIVATIONAL PROCESSES: POLITICAL COMMITMENT, RESILIENCE, AND PERSEVERANCE

Perceived efficacy in a particular setting also affects motivation, shaping the sense of value and commitment we place on our actions, the short-term goals we set, how much effort we are willing to expend, how long we will persevere, and how resilient we are to setbacks (Bandura, 1997). When people gain confidence in their political abilities, for example, they are more likely to perceive politics as important and relevant to their own lives. Moreover, the stronger the sense of self-efficacy in a given domain, the more willing people are to confront challenges and risk failure. As theorists like Hannah Arendt suggest, possessing political courage is important for civic undertakings, which, like most social projects, are inherently challenging (Arendt, 1961).

One key motivational process through which perceived efficacy works is causal attribution. When people who feel efficacious experience failure, they tend to believe that they didn't put in enough effort; if they persevere, they will eventually succeed. Those without efficacy, in contrast, often attribute their failure to their lack of ability; no matter how hard they worked at something, they would probably not succeed. This resilient mode of interpreting challenges and bouncing back from failures is especially important in politics, where nearly all important goals, whether elections or grassroots community work, require long-term effort and fortitude.

Emotional and Affective Processes: Political Confidence and Hopefulness

As it interacts with cognitions and motivations, perceived self-efficacy also influences emotional states, especially affective reactions to frustration and failure. When people feel hopeless or cynical about their prospects for meaningful political action—or even if, in some senses they are more objectively realistic about the difficulty of achieving political goals—they are more likely to avoid political activities or to give up quickly.

Feelings of efficacy help reduce the extent to which people feel stress, anxiety, or helplessness when they engage in difficult activities. Strong feelings of efficacy also counter perceptions that circumstances are intractable or beyond our control, contributing to a more positive long-term outlook. As a result, when people gain a sense of political efficacy, their confidence in their political capacities makes them more likely to believe that their concerted effort can make a difference, and more likely to view challenges as opportunities to work toward ambitious goals.

As George Bernard Shaw quipped, "The reasonable man adapts himself to the world," while "the unreasonable one persists in trying to adapt the world to himself. Therefore all progress depends on the unreasonable man" (1903/2009). From this perspective, a sense of political efficacy is not "reasonable" in the sense of rationally calculating outcomes, and it can counteract politically disempowering cynicism and apathy that undermine democratic action. It can help us find gratification, inspiration, and value in political life and feel hopeful about the role we can play.

Selection and Social Processes: Formative Interests and Relationships

Finally, and in relation to the other three psychological processes, our self-efficacy can shape the broader trajectories of our lives by influencing the things we find interesting, the activities we select, and the people with whom we interact (Bandura, 1997). A sense of efficacy can move us toward particular interests, values, skills, and relationships and groups. This can have enduring influence because the influences and incentive structures in different environments can promote or thwart certain abilities and values long after we make an initial choice. For example, careers, often selected based on our sense of our abilities, form an ongoing basis for our further growth through the opportunities and relationships they provide.

Similar selection processes color many political activities, often beginning with small undertakings and over time creating formative interests and relationships that lead to more intensive and long-lasting patterns of political involvement. One study of political development in undergraduates, the Bennington College study, showed that political changes women experienced as undergraduates persisted over many decades because the friends, spouses, careers, and civic activities they chose after graduation both reflected and solidified their political trajectories (Newcomb, Koening, Flacks, & Warwick, 1967; Alwin, Cohen, Theodore, & Newcomb, 1991). Individuals who were politically active during the civil rights era, or who served in the Peace Corps, often report that the sense of their abilities and the relationships they formed served similarly formative functions.

In addition to identifying the rubric of psychological processes involved in developing a sense of self-efficacy, scholars have identified four major sources through which perceived self-efficacy and collective efficacy emerge in many domains. Developing efficacy relates to *mastery experiences*, or direct experiences with the activities and tasks involved in a given realm; *vicarious experiences* gained through role models; *social persuasion*; and *affective states* (Bandura, 1997). These offer an initial framework for identifying pathways of political learning that can contribute to a sense of political efficacy.

EXAMINING POLITICAL LEARNING AND POLITICAL EFFICACY IN UNDERGRADUATES

What does an emerging sense of political efficacy look like in young people, and what types of concrete experiences are involved in supporting and promoting political confidence and agency? This next section presents results from a study of college courses and extracurricular programs that included a focus on promoting political engagement among undergraduates. I adapt psychologists' typology of sources of self-efficacy to frame students' reflections on their political learning and sense of themselves as political actors.

The data come from the three-year Political Engagement Project study of nearly 1,000 students participating in 21 college courses and programs across the United States during a three-year study period from 2002 to 2005. The purpose of the study was to understand how young people become more politically informed and involved. All of the programs included at least one active learning experience that prior work suggested contributes to political engagement. These included extensive political discussions; interaction with political leaders or activists as guest speakers or mentors; politically related internships, community placements, or extended service learning; political research or action projects; and political simulations, such as mock assemblies and Model U.N. (Kuh & Associates, 2005; Astin, 1993; Torney-Purta, 2002).

The sites represented different student populations, institutional contexts, and program types: summer institutes; a semester in Washington program; summer and academic-year, politically related internship programs; extracurricular programs; multi-year living-learning programs; as well as several academic courses. The academic courses in the study were drawn from fields including political science, public policy, American studies, urban affairs, history, and environmental science. Many were aimed at the general college population, fulfilling graduation requirements. There were also several interdisciplinary programs related to leadership development, diversity, and community involvement. Thus, the programs diverged in substantive focus and extent of students' self-selection. Including programs and settings that differed in many respects increased the potential for findings that are not limited to any one type of learning experience or participant.

To provide a faceted view, the study used a mixed-method approach and relied on a quasi-experimental repeated measures design in which students serve as their own controls (Cook & Campbell, 1979; Torney-Purta, Amadeo, & Andolina, this volume). We conducted a survey of students before and after their participation (here called the pre-post survey). Four students from each program were interviewed by phone. These 45- to 75-minute interviews included two randomly selected students from each program and two students identified by instructors as having become more politically engaged (not necessarily the most academically successful students). Instructors were not told which students had been interviewed. In addition, program leaders were interviewed and surveyed, and syllabi, program descriptions, and other materials such as students' assignments were collected. More detailed accounts of participating programs, survey instrument results, interviews, and materials are reported in Colby, Beaumont, Ehrlich, and Corngold (2007a, 2007b), and Beaumont, Colby, Ehrlich, and Torney-Purta (2006).

A brief description of two of the courses and programs in the study illustrates some of their approaches to promoting political efficacy.

Democracy Matters

Democracy Matters is a non-partisan extracurricular program that started at Colgate University and has spread to dozens of college campuses across the United States. The Democracy Matters campus groups have student leaders who receive ongoing mentoring and opportunities to participate in learning workshops at Colgate University. The program helps students who are frustrated about current democratic processes get involved in campus, community, state, and national projects related to campaign finance reform, fair elections, voter protection, and other reform efforts. By initiating and participating in political action projects on and beyond their campuses, participants in Democracy Matters are gaining a deeper understanding of political processes. They are learning the history behind current electoral processes and how new legislation gets enacted or stalled. Importantly for efficacy, their work on various democratic reforms helps them acquire and apply a set of practical political skills, such as how to gain visibility for their efforts, run meetings, lobby, and form coalitions with other student and community groups (Colby et al., 2007b).

Introductory American Politics and the Youth Urban Agenda

A second example is a large introductory American Government course at Wayne State University in which students participate in creating and implementing a *Youth Urban Agenda*. The course includes content included in typical introductory courses and fulfills a university requirement at this diverse urban university in Detroit, Michigan. The Youth Urban Agenda, created by the late Otto Feinstein and recently adopted more widely, begins by asking students to work in small groups to identify the local issues they believe are most important for civic groups and public officials to address. The small student groups then come together in a large convention to hammer out a single agenda, which is then used as the basis for political action and communication, such as engaging with high-school students and with community groups, as well as with local political officials and candidates and the press (Perry & Wilkenfeld, 2006).

These experiences help students develop a range of political skills for deliberating and organizing: learning how to make a case for one's political view, discussing conflicting political goals and priorities, and building coalitions. Students also learn methods for influencing politics by using their political agendas to gain broader community support and exert pressure on local politicians to respond to community priorities and problems. Actively creating, publicizing, and carrying out a political agenda takes students beyond the facts and theories that dominate most political science courses. Participating in political activities focused on problems that are relevant to students' own lives and communities helps many feel much more politically efficacious.

Although these two programs draw different students and operate in different ways, both sought to promote participants' sense of themselves as competent political actors. Indeed, interviews with faculty and instructors revealed that increasing political agency and efficacy was an important goal for most of the 21 sites in the study, though they did not necessarily use the term. For example, one professor described wanting to help students "come to see themselves as having what it takes to make changes happen." Moreover, goals related to gaining self- and collective political efficacy often overlapped with other types of political engagement goals, such as motivating students for political involvement by interesting them in political issues beyond electoral politics, making them feel that ordinary people could understand and influence political processes and policies, and giving them a sense of solidarity with peers and others to achieve civic goals over the long term.

The remainder of this section deals with results from the 21 programs considered together. The pre-post surveys had a 70% or higher response rate within each program; undergraduates who participated in the study were generally representative of the college student population, showing the full range of parental educational levels, our proxy for socioeconomic status, and a considerable degree of racial diversity.[1] Slightly more than one-third identified themselves as racial or ethnic minorities. About one-fifth were immigrants, while about one-third had at least one parent from another country. As in higher education more generally, the programs included more women than men (60% vs. 40%). Thus, the programs drew many students from groups that tend to be less involved in political life or at higher risk for opting out of political involvement, including many minorities, first-generation college students, students with lower socioeconomic status,

[1] A total of 863 students completed the pre-survey, representing a response rate of 86%. 732 students completed the post-survey, representing a response rate of 76%. 680 students completed both pre- and post-surveys for a 70% pre-post response rate. The repeated measures analyses of variance (ANOVA) reported here is based on a subsample of 481 students: Respondents were removed from the full sample if their pre- and post-responses did not reflect the actual beginning and/or end of a long-term program and a random sample of 60 students was drawing from a disproportionately large course of more than 200 students in order to prevent skewing the data too much in favor of the effect of one program.

immigrants, and women (Lay, Gimpel, & Schuknecht, 2003). A fair portion of participants were political science or public policy majors, but more than two-thirds had other majors crossing the arts, humanities, social sciences, sciences, and professional fields.

The survey also showed that students participated in these courses and programs for many reasons. Self-selection based on initial political interest played an important role for about half of the students. The other half were drawn to these programs primarily to fulfill college requirements or because of a professor's reputation. It was possible to focus on the experiences of students who were more politically interested at the outset as well as those who were less politically interested (more typical undergraduates and young adults).

Basic analysis of the pre-post survey data shows that, overall, students who participated in these political learning programs increased their sense of political efficacy after completing the programs (Significant pre-post main effect from Analysis of Variance with time as within-subjects factor, $p < 0.001$, partial eta squared = 0.384). The moderate effect size reflected in the partial eta squared shows that a fair proportion of the variance in students' efficacy levels is attributed to the effect of the intervention, indicating that these increases are practically as well as statistically significant.

As a whole, students also made significant gains on other important political outcomes, including sense of politically engaged identity, political understanding, civic skills, and expectations for future political action. However, the size and number of shifts varied between students who entered the programs with more political interest and those with less initial political interest (Beaumont, Colby et al., 2006).[2] Importantly, there were no patterns of movement toward either more politically liberal or conservative stances nor were there shifts in political party affiliations. This mitigated potential fears that political learning programs involve latent political indoctrination.

For detailed quantitative analysis using a multilevel model to trace the role of some features of political learning on the achievement of a sense of political efficacy, see Beaumont, Greene, & Torney-Purta (in press). However, complex political learning processes cannot be adequately understood through survey analysis alone. The psychological framework of self-efficacy

[2] The outcomes examined included a sense of politically engaged identity, interest in reading about politics in the newspaper, current events knowledge, and more foundational types of political knowledge, skills of political influence and action, and intentions to engage in conventional electoral activities and activities expressing *political voice*. (Repeated measures analyses of variance with time as a within-subjects measure showed significant main effects for these dependent variables, all of which were highly significant at the $p <= 0.001$ level for Pillai's Trace measure and had effect sizes in the small to moderate range of Cohen's $d = 0.19 - 0.49$).

is particularly useful for analyzing the perspectives faculty and students offered in interviews.

APPLYING A PSYCHOLOGICAL FRAMEWORK TO POLITICAL LEARNING: FOUR PATHWAYS TO A SENSE OF POLITICAL EFFICACY

Fostering efficacy is challenging because it must confront skepticism about politics as well as helplessness and inertia that stem from the not unrealistic perception that it is hard for people to successfully intervene in complex political processes. To promote political efficacy, programs in the Political Engagement Project used a variety of teaching approaches, from political action projects like those included in Democracy Matters and in the American Government course at Wayne State, to politically focused service learning and internships, to mentoring and structured reflection. Such activities may operate differently. Hearing a talk by a state representative on transportation issues and creating a project to try to change campus transportation policies are not interchangeable learning experiences, for example. Both could contribute to sense of political efficacy, however.

The developmental processes involved in promoting sense of political efficacy appear similar to those psychologists identify for self-efficacy in other settings but may operate distinctly in the realm of political learning. Here, I map students' and faculty's descriptions of political learning onto four main social and psychological channels that feed into a robust sense of political efficacy: (1) skill-building political mastery experiences; (2) models of political efficacy and involvement; (3) social encouragement, supportive relationships and social networks, and inclusion in political community; and (4) empowering and resilient political outlooks. This analysis complements prior examination of political motivation and experience, tracking some similar territory while bringing a different set of analytic lenses to bear (Beaumont et al., 2006; Colby et al., 2007; Battistoni & Hudson, 1997; Kahne & Westheimer, 2006).

Skill-Building Political Mastery Experiences

In the political realm, this pathway for promoting efficacy involves providing young people with opportunities to become skilled and confident actors in the public arena through hands-on, guided experiences. Just as theoretical and empirical political scientists stress the importance of hands-on civic experience, psychologists similarly emphasize experience as the most important source of self-efficacy, particularly when individuals confront and learn to master the tasks and activities in a specific domain (Bandura, 1997). Successful experiences usually create higher self-efficacy, while repeated failures reduce it, with the crucial qualification that self-efficacy is filtered by individuals' perceptions of circumstances. In other words, *evaluations of* and *attributions for* experiences and their outcomes are crucial. For example, students who get a high grade on an assignment but think it was extremely easy are not likely to increase self-efficacy in that subject. Or, if a student fares poorly on an assignment but uses a successful strategy to revise it, she is more likely to sustain self-efficacy (Cleary & Zimmerman, 2004).

The Need to Balance Meaningful Political Challenges with Modest Successes: Significant and *Doable Political Goals* Acquiring mastery in any given domain, including the world of politics, does not mean conquering easy experiences or those in which everything goes smoothly. To develop the kind of aspiration, skill, and persevering commitment involved in robust political agency, we need complex, real-world political experiences that are recognized as meaningful for issues and people we care about, and in which we overcome difficulties by trying different strategies and making continued efforts. But to gain proficiency and confidence through complex experiences we also need ongoing guidance or mentoring from people with greater expertise who can suggest how to break larger undertakings into smaller components or help cope with problems.

For most program leaders, trying to increase students' confidence as political agents involved some type of guided political mastery experiences—through political action projects on campus or in the community, or political internships or working with community groups. As one professor for a course on community organizing said, concrete political learning projects build political skills and commitments and "makes political learning real." Not every political experience offers equal potential for gaining mastery or efficacy, and understanding the relationship between the significant and the doable is important. Young people often get caught in a trap of thinking it is only valuable to work on the most high-profile political goals, like *world peace*. Because they view such goals as impractical, they wind up feeling discouraged. When they plan a doable activity, such as a meeting for people worried about ethnic conflict, they may say, "I can have this meeting, but it won't bring world peace." The goal shared by many program leaders is to build efficacy by helping students identify political goals and projects in which "they can couple something genuinely significant in terms of [their] values and where they can do something that is actually possible."

Thus, the ongoing guidance from program leaders often involves helping students choose undertakings that are personally meaningful or valuable for an issue they care about. Then the students set incremental, achievable political goals within larger undertakings. This involves helping students see broader significance in achievable concrete goals, develop skills, and make plans for carrying out steps to attain those goals. They can recognize the skills they gain and the modest successes they achieve as satisfying in themselves and as crucial progress toward larger goals.

For example, a leader of the Democracy Matters program said that it is often hard to see progress in politics (and to feel political agency), when working toward a big goal, like changing campaign financing. As a result, "If we can get students to see some of the more subtle things as progress then we've made a huge impact on them," and redefining success can help fuel a sense of efficacy and long-term political engagement. Students working on projects involving campaign finance reform efforts through Democracy Matters, for instance, came to view their political experiences as successful when they saw that "We made this an issue on our campus." In other words, if you asked people on their campus about the major issues students care about, the issue of money in politics would be one of them. Or, students might define success as meaning that the Democracy Matters group became a known and influential entity on campus, or that the group sponsored events with other campus or community groups, or that they did a few concrete things that gave them a sense of achievement: "We went into the local high school, we went to the legislature to lobby; had a successful evening event, had a great article in the newspaper."

Other students and faculty talked often about small gains achieved through the political projects in their programs. These included successful experiences with electoral politics, such as getting face-to-face meetings with staffers at state assemblies to talk about issues students were working on, or helping get local candidates elected or local ballot initiatives passed, often by narrow margins. Students got the sense that they were helping to shape the political playing field.

The greater portion of students' political experiences involved less conventional and non-electoral forms of politics, including political education and advocacy, communication, and organizing. Students created a workshop on transportation alternatives for faculty, staff, and students for a political program that focused on environmental issues. When two deans attended the students' transportation workshop and asked many questions, the students felt their ideas had been heard and seeds that were planted would eventually sprout into policy changes: The workshop "really made a difference or at least made a positive step in helping educate people about alternatives to driving their cars." Another student, who was concerned about pollution runoff in a local river, undertook a political action project that brought together a group of political officials and other stakeholders to discuss the pollution and identify possible solutions. Although the student didn't solve the problem of runoff, he felt a sense of personal accomplishment for getting various stakeholders with competing interests to sit down together to discuss the problem.

Connecting to Values, Gaining Skills, and Making Incremental Progress The interviews often revealed ways program leaders tried to help students set some shorter-term goals connected to their political values and the larger issues they cared about, see how to apply their skills, and learn how to take incremental steps toward broader goals like large-scale policy changes. This does not mean that instructors were trying to convey simplistic understandings of politics. In fact, most said that they wanted students to gain a healthy realism about the complexity and difficulty of political action. A professor who leads a course focused on community involvement and leadership in Appalachia suggested that she wanted to help students "unlearn their expectations or stereotypes so that they can learn a more complex, more realistic, and more motivating approach" to political involvement in the community. Political empowerment means helping students see where the openings and opportunities are for political action in one's community: "Understanding what you *can* change, as well as what can't be changed, or the givens, is crucial for developing a robust sense of efficacy." Her method included a version of political mastery experiences: student projects with community organizations. Through these activities, participants get "the experience of making maybe just a small difference by completing a project," so that they see themselves as having applied skills that led to real achievements by the end of the course.

For students, the opportunity to work on concrete political goals and tie their work to political values, political power, and political change is novel and empowering. As one student said, "I like actually trying to *do* something. I had never done anything before so when it came time to do a project I was sort of hesitant at first, but once I got involved I realized it was not as hard or as monumental as I had built it up to be in my mind."

Guided political mastery experiences played a big role in political efficacy. One student described trying to "raise awareness of the political disenfranchisement that's taken place at [his university]. Basically, we are not part of either of the cities in the area—and students can't vote in most local elections or on other local issues." This young man was not able to change the policy or win voting rights for students. Indeed, a major part of his political learning involved recognizing what a difficult problem this was, and to see that his short-term strategy for trying to address it was insufficient:

> With my project I thought I could have the whole thing wrapped up by the end of the semester. I thought I'd march into the City Council, present my ideas very eloquently, and they would sit there and nod and agree with me and by the end of the semester, we'd be a part of [the city] and we'd have our voting rights in [the city]. But by about mid-semester I realized this might not happen because there's so much work to do.... It would have made more sense to work with some sort of political organization but I thought I could do

> it on my own.... One thing I'm going to take away is that political action is more successful with a group than by yourself and that it will take time, more like a couple of years than a couple of months, to get this solved.

Importantly, through ongoing guidance and positive support from instructors and peers, the student did not feel demobilized by his failure to solve the voting rights issue. He had succeeded in raising awareness on his campus because many students had come to see this as a serious injustice, and he believed that, over time, an increasing number of people and groups would commit to working on the problem. Thus, his positive evaluation of the small goals he achieved, rather than the big goal he failed to achieve, allowed him to feel more politically efficacious. One turning point for his feeling of political agency and resiliency came when he wrote a paper analyzing his project. Reflecting made him realize that even though he hadn't come close to realizing his initial goal, "I've been doing things; I'm making progress. That experience got me thinking; I didn't realize how much I had actually done... and I was pretty proud of myself."

Models of Political Efficacy and Involvement

A second channel for developing political efficacy is through role models and vicarious experience gained by observing, interacting with, and emulating people who are politically involved and confident. We do not always need to engage firsthand in activities to gain confidence in our abilities. Rather, our level of self-efficacy can be influenced through observing others, such as peers, parents, or teachers, engaging in activities (Schunk & Pajares, 2004). In addition to the efforts faculty and program leaders made to model political efficacy, many programs provided students with a variety of speakers and mentors who could convey compelling and adaptive styles of political thinking. Interviews indicated that students often found the political figures they interacted with or learned about personally inspiring, kindling their confidence.

Ordinary People and Mold-breakers We might assume that the best role models for developing a sense of political efficacy are those who are most highly accomplished or most politically powerful. But research suggests the most powerful role models are those with whom we can identify. Moreover, *coping models* who show confidence and the ability to adapt when they confront challenges or make mistakes are often the most powerful (Kitsantas, Zimmerman, & Cleary, 2000). To some extent, to feel politically efficacious, we need to see that people like us possess a confident outlook in the face of different kinds of political experiences. Seeing people similar to ourselves working on political goals, making mistakes, adapting strategies, developing skills, exerting effort, and gaining some success through sustained work can make us believe that we, too, have these kinds of capacities. Such *existence proofs* make political efficacy feel like a genuine option and help us imagine undertaking similar activities, achieving similar political goals, and being similar kinds of people in the future.

Young people have few opportunities to interact with politically engaged role models in the absence of special programs. One student, for example, said that meeting local political leaders and activists and coming to realize that many of them were relatively ordinary people like him before deciding to get involved in politics changed his view that political processes are "beyond my control" and that only certain kinds of people are politically active. He went on to say:

> After sitting in class with the mayor of [a local town], I realized she's just a regular person like we are, so that really helped make that connection... she was just a mom that had kids in the educational system who heard about a couple of things and then went door-to-door, got involved... and now she's this big political voice [in the local community].

For some programs in the study, models of political efficacy came from studying political history and learning about how past social movements developed. One young woman, for example, said that after a candidate she liked lost an election, she had been politically inspired by seeing a documentary on the political career of Harvey Milk, the openly gay former mayor of San Francisco who fought against discrimination based on sexual orientation before he was assassinated: Milk had run for political office four times before he was elected. "He didn't fit the mold—or the standard idea of what you have to be to be a political leader, someone like Bill Clinton or George Bush." This example and other readings in this students' program made her believe that "you don't always have to fit into the mold or the norm to effect change." Many important political figures have been outsiders who gained influence through their willingness to keep trying despite obstacles and multiple failures. Because so many young people perceive politics as involving those born with political advantages of wealth, race, and gender, seeing unconventional political figures often convinced them that there is space in politics for different faces and ideas.

Models of Political Choices and Visions of Political Resilience Interacting with people from various backgrounds who have gotten involved in different ways not only introduces students to multiple styles of action, but it allows students to observe and emulate models of real-life political choices, civic commitment, and resilience. A professor at a campus that draws many students who are often the first in their families to attend college told us that students are looking for models of the kinds of political paths people pursue through their choices about careers and community activities. She found that one of the best ways for fostering political efficacy in the young adults she worked with:

> ... is for them to have experience and contact with people who aren't cynical or complacent.... You present models of some political choices that students may not see, especially our students, who are often just looking to get a better job and a decent source of income.

One of her major strategies for providing such models was through community presenters. These were people from community organizations that the students were working with, political leaders, community activists, who had chosen certain careers because of their political commitments. Students can see "that people like themselves make these choices and devote a fair amount of either their professional or their community life working in politics."

A student from this course spoke of being particularly inspired by a community presenter from a local Kentucky group that fought to prevent an old army depot from burning gases and materials that would produce toxic fumes. Hearing his group's experiences impressed her that it's more than a cliché that "people can make a difference if they get together with others." Many stories from political figures and mentors gave students realistic encouragement and a sustainable feeling of political confidence. They revealed that even major accomplishments usually began with and continued to depend on small-scale, everyday kinds of actions carried out by relatively ordinary people acting together, not just statesmen or national figures. As one student from a program on city politics reported, he was amazed by the perseverance of the community group he worked with in Chinatown; each time their efforts for small community improvements, like sanitation, met opposition, instead of giving up in frustration, "they tried harder the next time."

Many faculty members worked to ensure that their programs provided a supportive atmosphere for students to develop efficacy connected to their own political commitments and styles by providing examples of political involvement from people with different commitments and affiliations, stressing that there is no single *best* model of political agency. A young man participating in a program focused on city politics, for example, said that political speakers spoke about different pathways of involvement at different scales of politics. "You don't have to be mayor, or whatever. You can simply be a parent at a school board meeting... Each person has a say in a different way."

Other program leaders talked about introducing students to people who have been involved in politics for many years as a way of giving students models for weathering the kinds of frustrations and failures that are part of any complex political undertaking. As one program leader put it, students learn from these kinds of models that politics is "a marathon, not a sprint" and that persistence and long-term perspective are needed for success in most political goals.

Social Encouragement, Supportive Relationships and Networks, and Inclusion in Political Community

Our sense of efficacy can be either enhanced or lowered by the kinds of groups or communities to which we belong and the feedback and social persuasion we receive from them. This third set of formative experiences through which young people develop political agency builds from social relationships and interactions and encouragement for political involvement they provide. Not surprisingly, people who are persuaded verbally that they have the capacity to succeed at a given activity are likely to undertake greater effort. Being told frequently that we can't do something often becomes a self-fulfilling prophecy.

But cheerleading alone can't build a robust sense of efficacy in the political realm, or any other realm. If we are given unrealistic appraisals of our abilities, we are not likely to retain a sense of efficacy. Nearly every faculty and program leader told us that young people have strong radars for identifying hypocrisy or "happy talk" disconnected from political reality. What is more useful for shaping perceptions of our capacities is not lofty rhetoric about the importance of civic duty for democracy but feedback that allows us to see how specific things we do and learn can move us forward toward goals (Cleary & Zimmerman, 2004).

Many programs emphasized providing political encouragement and a support network for students' political engagement in two ways that often intersected. One is extensive forms of feedback, reflection, and discussion. A second is by helping students develop relationships and a sense of connectedness to groups that value their sense of political agency. Interviews suggested that participating with other students, or having a chance to reflect with peers on political experiences in internships, community placements, and service learning, was especially useful.

The Role of Feedback, Reflection, and Discussion As the discussion of political mastery experiences indicates, encouraging students often took the form of helping them redefine what it means to participate effectively in politics. Faculty and students told us that when the programs began, students often thought of politics as a hugely overwhelming, distant, and largely mysterious set of forces. They saw politics as a "dark territory." And students often had very unrealistic, abstract, or textbook-based views of what it means to be part of politics: "I thought before that being politically engaged meant that you had to be a legislator or a protestor." The student who worked to try to get voting rights for students in local elections said that before his program, he thought of politics as "a rich man's hobby."

Because young adults often have such disempowering views of politics, helping them gain efficacy is not a matter of sending them out into a political internship or a campus project and leaving them to their own devices. Rather, it involves providing support through ongoing guidance, feedback, and reflection: giving students information about how politics works in different settings, talking about different strategies of political action and why they either succeed or fail or produce unintended consequences, providing interpretive frameworks for thinking about what politics involves, and discussing ways that students' political actions are making a difference. A leader of the Democracy Matters group, for example, described reflection processes as "the yeast that makes the bread rise" for political learning. A student from another program described intensive reflection. Trying to connect political theory and political practice in weekly reflection papers was difficult, but "then when you did think hard enough, you did find them. . . . It was a good challenge in a way because it really made you think deeper than you otherwise would."

Sense of Connectedness, Solidarity, and Inclusion in Political Community

Processes of guidance and reflection often contributed not only to students' political judgment, but to students' development of a strong sense of belonging to a community where politics was seen as important and where members' political goals and actions were supported. Because many young people had never felt included in politically engaged groups or communities, they tended to perceive political life as something "for other people." By giving students an opportunity to find mutual political interests and goals, share experiences, process their reactions, learn coping skills, and jointly develop strategies for handling challenges, they are helping to co-create and form a politically empowering community and coming to see peers as a support network for political engagement.

Students gained crucial support by developing a sense of connectedness with each other, solidarity with communities, and relevance to democratic processes. Many students talked about the strong sense of community they felt within their programs. One student contrasted this with his other college courses:

> You are in a small community of people, other students that are doing the same things as you, interested in the same things as you. And, they're really people you can trust and I think that's huge because in other college courses you are not; that kind of community is not really facilitated at all. You're lucky if you walk out knowing anybody's name at the end of the semester.

For many other students, forming relationships with peers who were simultaneously involved in political learning was one of the most important experiences. Many saw these as enduring friendships that would help them sustain their own political goals and open them to different political perspectives. They saw that even close-knit communities involve intense political disagreements and can grow from these conflicts. For example, one student who participated in a living-learning program described feeling a sense of peer community and mutual respect when discussing controversial topics:

> If you really know someone you'll respect them more in a heated debate than if you don't know them. And when you build a bond with someone because you live with them, eat meals together, going to social activities with them, sitting in the classroom with them, then you can respect their opinion and actually listen to what they have to say instead of shutting them out and just wanting to express your own opinion.

Rather than feeling threatened, she found that:

> Some of my opinions changed because I respected the people who made the opposite argument, respected them enough to actually listen to what they had to say to understand their points of view and sometimes wound up agreeing with them on some points in the end.

For this young woman, forging a strong sense of political community empowered her, in part by making her less anxious about disagreement, more willing to participate in the political fray, and more open to learning from new ideas. Her political judgments mattered to others, and she felt that people can disagree strongly in politics while retaining civility and respect. This helped her feel that real-life political conflicts need not be demonizing, as she had often perceived them.

Another student described an additional benefit of a strong sense of peer community: Getting feedback from members of her program was crucial for helping her cope with some of the overwhelming aspects of her political experiences. This student interned for a nonprofit working to help victims of torture, by giving presentations at local schools and developing educational materials. When she looked back at the things that kept her from feeling overwhelmed by the seeming intractability of the problem, she said, "It helped that I had a community where twice-weekly meetings allowed students to discuss their various experiences and get each others' takes on them." It was particularly useful to her, when she was feeling despondent, to have a group where she could "just say it" and feel supported.

In many of the programs, students were working with other groups on campus or in the community, often gaining a sense of collective political efficacy together with self-efficacy. Developing personal connections to these groups helped students recognize the interdependence of individuals and communities, helped them see themselves as agents capable of acting deliberately within larger systems, and helped them see the power of collective action for politics. One young man, for example, said that meeting politically active people was "an affirmation of hope" that made him feel less "stuck" by feelings of political cynicism and more "determined" about his own political goals. Fostering a sense of connectedness to, solidarity with, or inclusion in various politically involved groups and communities was a planned component of several programs. For some faculty, developing these relationships and connections was a crucial method for counteracting feelings of disempowerment. A professor teaching an American politics course in a state university said that because her students were often the first in their families to attend college, they tended to believe that "People like them . . . don't have much to contribute" to the political realm. As one of her students said:

> Before I took this, I hadn't been involved in any kind of political action or community service, and when I started I didn't know [political engagement] was a central part of the course and I thought those things were for other people and not me.

She and other program leaders working with students from lower socioeconomic status backgrounds, racial or ethnic minorities, and recent immigrants saw promoting political efficacy among these groups as a particular challenge. This professor tried to give students a sense of inclusion in and qualifications for participating in the political domain by having them undertake politically focused service learning that connected them to political offices, organizations, and nonprofits working in their own communities.

Students in many of the programs that included political experiences in their local communities told us about the relationships they had formed. One student said that the most important thing she gained from her political internship for an organization working with troubled youths was "building relationships with the kids," as well as "building relationships with people from all over the country" working on similar issues. It was these relationships that made her feel that her ongoing political involvement mattered very much to these groups.

The many strands of interconnection to other people and the political issues facing them made students see politics as something relevant to people's everyday lives and concerns. One student said that her internship working for a community group teaching English made the connection between political policies and everyday life very real: "Being exposed to so many immigrants and refugees especially, I could see how different policies were affecting them."

Empowering and Resilient Political Outlooks

Cultivating political confidence and a positive outlook on one's political capacities and the possibility of meaningful political action is a key element of developing a strong sense of political agency. The final set of political development processes taps into the fact that our beliefs about our abilities depend on both rational evaluations of the effects of our actions and on our emotional states and perceptions. When we feel stressed, depressed, frustrated, or despondent, for example, we are likely to feel less self-efficacy. Thus, promoting political efficacy often entails promoting more positive political outlooks and finding ways to reduce the kind of cynicism, apathy, distaste, and hopelessness young people and adults often feel toward all things political, even the term *politics* itself.

Balanced Optimism: Places for Hope and Places for Criticism To be clear, promoting a positive outlook and reducing political cynicism is not the same as encouraging political naïveté, blind idealism, or uncritical endorsement of the status quo. Just as superficial praise has little lasting effect on self-efficacy in other domains, it is unlikely to promote enduring political efficacy. Nor would such an approach be appropriate in academic settings. But political learning can temper cynicism and build efficacy if it helps students recognize openings to shape the political world within real constraints. In fact, research suggests that people are politically involved when they feel politically efficacious themselves but are skeptical about existing political institutions, which leads them to believe that political influence "is both possible and necessary" (Gamson, 1968, p. 48). Cultivating a political outlook that is hopeful, empowering, and resilient involves promoting balanced optimism and realistic commitment that continued efforts are important, and that they contribute to meaningful political change and progress toward democratic ideals (Gutmann, 1987).

Many of the methods for promoting positive outlooks overlapped with the other three channels for promoting political efficacy, since models of efficacy, political guidance and feedback, and supportive social networks can help students feel the intrinsic and social rewards of political involvement and expose them to positive outlooks for political change.

In providing guidance and feedback on students' political experiences and learning, most faculty and program leaders intentionally recognize both the challenges and the opportunities for small and incremental successes. As a leader of Democracy Matters said, "While we are critical [of the current campaign finance system], we are not doomsayers"; program leaders and students needed to maintain a balance in "hope versus despair." Students in many different programs talked about gaining a balanced political outlook, such as a student who participated in a program focused on urban challenges, and who felt both more hopeful and more critical:

> I guess I'm more hopeful. I wouldn't say I'm optimistic. I'm hopeful, like Cornel West says, there's a difference between hopefulness and optimism. I

> wouldn't say I'm so pessimistic, but more critical. I don't know how much faith I have in politics, but I'm not necessarily pessimistic, I'm just critical of it.

A student from a program focused on community issues in rural Appalachia shared similar reflections, describing the kind of "critical hopefulness" he had developed, even though other people sometimes "think I'm negative because I believe that the problems run so deep." Interactions with various political groups and the guidance that program leaders provided for political experiences helped make students more aware of "places for hope," as one young woman working on welfare reform put it, as well as places where there is not much realistic opportunity for change right now.

Integrity, Solidarity, and the Rewards of "Trying to Make a Difference" Some faculty and program leaders used an approach to changing students' outlooks on political efficacy that helped students take a critical step back from their cynicism. While there are many things young people might not like about the current political system, "that's what we're given to work with." While "cynicism and complacency can be accurate responses to a corrupt political system," the "alternative to trying to make a difference" is to reinforce that system. Students were simultaneously learning, from political role models, from their own political experiences, and from the communities they were forming with peers that political involvement entails many personal and social rewards even when it is not fully successful. There is self-integrity in working toward one's values, and an enriching sense of community and solidarity of doing so together with others.

Many students took the circular problem of political cynicism seriously and began to feel a sense of personal accountability to work on political problems. One student who participated in the Youth Urban Agenda, for example, said he came away feeling:

> If you just sit on the sidelines and complain and don't do anything to make your complaints heard, then whatever agenda is put forth and it's passed, then you have informally or indirectly agreed with it because you haven't done anything. So, if you're passive, then you get just what comes. And if you're active, then you'll fight it.

His experience "set a precedent for me to start to become involved in my community on a local level." This involved both a sense of agency and self-responsibility: "It more or less made me have a sense of accountability. . . . So there's something I can do and this class gave me the tools in which to do that."

As this example illustrates, an important way of supporting engagement involved helping students connect their values to their political actions and recognize the intrinsic rewards of acting in accordance with one's commitments. Students saw, in many political figures they met, role models who felt a sense of responsibility to act on their values, even in the face of political challenges, and who gained dignity and self-respect in doing so.

One young woman who viewed the existing political system as being stacked unfairly against racial minorities described herself as having developed a keen sense of responsibility for acting on her own political values, in part because of the solidarity she felt with other people who currently felt "voiceless" in American democracy.

> Part of the empowerment [gained from the program] was that I can do something about the political situation in the country—even if I'm in the minority, I'm still a voice. And that there should be a place for all voices in this country, and not all voices get listened to right now. And part of my responsibility is making that known.

CONCLUSIONS

From voting for an underdog candidate to protesting a school's decisions to raise tuition, democratic participation is akin to philosopher Soren Kierkegaard's notion of a *leap of faith*, an act of risk-taking under conditions of uncertainty, without any guarantee of success, based on personal belief and commitment (Kierkegaard, 1841/1974). In the political sphere, we must have primary faith in ourselves and others, and courage and confidence for civic action. By drawing together perspectives from political science and psychology, we can more fully understand the connections between a sense of political efficacy and the political confidence, courage, and commitment involved in democratic action. This allows us to appreciate the importance of efficacy, but also indicates why it is particularly difficult to acquire. Examining concrete ways in which undergraduates gain political confidence illustrates how four main pathways and related mechanisms can contribute to the web of experiences, perceptions, and relationships that foster a sense of political efficacy.

Political theory, empirical political science, and psychology remain three largely separate enterprises. Although scholars share overlapping concerns with political efficacy, they draw on different types of knowledge and evidence and do not take advantage of opportunities to borrow and build across disciplinary tables. This would come as a surprise to early political scholars from Aristotle to Machiavelli to Weber, all of whom treated politics as an *interdisciplinary* subject involving integral relationships between political ideas, human motivations, and social institutions. This separation is unfortunate because of the cross-fertilization that comes from bringing the different, but often complementary and enriching, lenses offered by each discipline to bear on sense of political efficacy. This provides a multifaceted view that includes historical and wide-angle perspectives on efficacy's theoretical roots and its broad patterns of relationships with civic resources in different populations, as well as finer-grained perspectives on the underlying social and psychological channels of political development. Taken together, these perspectives help us better understand how people learn to construct democracy and how the interplay between individuals, ideas, institutions, and everyday practices contributes to this construction.

Bringing these fields into conversation also allows us to see some shortcomings and areas for growth within each. The roots of political efficacy identified by political theorists reveal the importance and difficulty of trying to study and meaningfully measure this complex set of perceptions, but theorists often eschew attending to these concrete challenges. Empirical political science includes a remarkable number of studies in which sense of political efficacy plays a role, but its measures are typically very general, individualistic, and decontextualized, and few studies are concerned with understanding the development of political efficacy in different contexts or populations. Psychologists, meanwhile, have done considerable work on the development of self-efficacy in various settings, but very little on *political* self-efficacy. Their insights on developmental processes involved in academics and sports, for example, do not always transfer to political contexts. As a result, despite wide recognition of how important political efficacy is, we continue to know too little about how to foster it; this concern largely falls between the interdisciplinary cracks.

Taking the perspective offered by psychology suggests an important shift in the way political scientists often treat political agency and the civic resources that contribute to political efficacy and engagement generally. Empirical political science usually focuses on individuals and broad populations, generalizable measures, and static indicators rather than the nuances of contexts and dynamic forces, and it usually treats efficacy as "given" rather than malleable. There has been little interest in formulating and examining meaningful hypotheses about how political efficacy develops and operates.

Adapting psychologists' work on self-efficacy to concrete political learning experiences, such as those described by students in this study, encourages us to adopt a broader and deeper view of the sources and operation of efficacy-enhancing civic resources. Sense of political efficacy is not fixed and does not develop in isolation or through highly individualistic reasoning, but develops dynamically through social settings and interactions. A number of contextual features play a role in shaping our political experiences and our interpretations of those experiences. Rather than viewing political resources and motivations like efficacy as fixed individualistic assets that some people either possess or lack, based largely on socioeconomic status, such a perspective understands political resources as emerging from and being constructed through social interactions and perceptions in civic contexts (see Levinson, this volume). Most importantly, such political resources and contexts can be actively *created*—and *co-created by students themselves*—through well-designed political learning programs.

Based on this study of undergraduates at 21 colleges and universities in the United States, and building on insights from political science and psychology, we can suggest that political learning programs will have the best chance to engender a vibrant sense of political efficacy if they consciously attend to creating the four pathways to political efficacy, and then help students establish their own individual and collective trajectories down these paths:

- Cultivate guided, skill-building political mastery experiences that balance complex, meaningful, real-life political challenges with small successes and encourage students to connect political values and skills with incremental progress.
- Provide a variety of politically efficacious and involved role models that allow students to see how "people like them" have engaged in politics and weathered challenges, which might include historical as well as contemporary figures.
- Foster encouraging and supportive relationships and social networks that give students a strong sense of connection to and inclusion in politically engaged networks of peers and community members working on issues they care about.
- Engender positive, empowering, resilient political outlooks by giving student balanced optimism, not naïve cheerleading, about democracy and politics, helping them see places for hope as well as places for criticism, and revealing the valuable sense of dignity, community, and solidarity that can come from an active political life.

Working in concert, these features of political learning experiences are particularly important for helping young people develop confidence in their political judgments and actions.

Unfortunately, despite strong evidence from multiple disciplines indicating how important direct and meaningful political experience is for developing a sense of political efficacy and agency, young people's political experiences are typically left to happenstance and the influence of individual backgrounds. There are few politically focused learning programs on college campuses, in high schools, or in communities that reach out to youth from different backgrounds. This leaves many young adults, particularly those who lack other routes for gaining valuable civic resources, with few pathways and opportunities to move toward political agency and empowerment.

ACKNOWLEDGEMENTS

Many thanks to my partners from the Political Engagement Project, Anne Colby, Thomas Ehrlich, and Joshua Corngold, as well as Judith Torney-Purta and many faculty and program participants. Support for this research was provided by a grant from the University of Minnesota and the McKnight Landgrant Professorship; the initial study was generously supported by the Atlantic Philanthropies, the Carnegie Corporation, the Carnegie Foundation, CIRCLE, the Ford Foundation, the Hewlett Foundation, and the Surdna Foundation.

REFERENCES

Abramson, P. R. (1977). *The political socialization of Black Americans: A critical evaluation of research on efficacy and trust.* New York: Free Press.

Abramson, P. R. (1983). *Political attitudes in America.* San Francisco: W. H. Freeman.

Almond, G. A., & Verba, S. (1963/1989). *The civic culture.* Boston: Little Brown.

Alwin, D. F., Cohen, R., Theodore, L., & Newcomb, T. L. (1991). *Political attitudes over the life span.* Madison, WI: University of Wisconsin Press.

Arendt, H. (1958). *The human condition.* Chicago: University of Chicago Press.

Arendt, H. (1961). *Beyond past and future: Eight exercises in political thought.* New York: Viking Press.

Astin, A. W. (1993). *What matters in college? Four critical years revisited.* San Francisco, CA: Jossey-Bass.

Bandura, A. (1977). Self-efficacy: Toward a unifying theory of behavioral change. *Psychology Review, 84,* 191–215.

Bandura, A. (1993). Perceived self-efficacy in cognitive development and functioning. *Educational Psychologist, 28(2),* 117–148.

Bandura, A. (1994). Self-efficacy. In V. S. Ramachaudran (Ed.), *Encyclopedia of human behavior* (Vol. 4, pp. 71–81). New York: Academic Press.

Bandura, A. (1997). *Self-efficacy: The exercise of control.* New York: Freeman.

Barber, B. (1984). *Strong democracy.* Berkeley, CA: UC Press.

Battistoni, R., & Hudson, W. (Eds.). (1997). *Experiencing citizenship.* Washington, DC: American Association of Higher Education.

Beaumont, E., (in press). Building political agency, addressing political inequality: A multilevel model of political efficacy. *Journal of Politics.*

Beaumont, E., & Battistoni, R. M. (2006). Beyond Civics 101: Rethinking what we mean by civic education. *Journal of Political Science Education, 2(3),* 241–247.

Beaumont, E., Colby, A., Ehrlich, T., & Torney-Purta, J. (2006). Promoting political competence and engagement in college students: An empirical study. *Journal of Political Science Education, 2(3),* 249–270.

Beck, P., & Jennings, M. K. (1982). Pathways to participation. *American Political Science Review, 76,* 94–108.

Brehm, J., & Rahn, W. (1997). Individual-level evidence for the causes and consequences of social capital. *American Journal of Political Science, 41(3),* 999–1023.

Campbell, A., Gurin, G., & Miller, W. E. (1954). *The voter decides*. Evanston, IL: Row, Peterson and Company.

Cleary, T. J., & Zimmerman, B. J. (2004). Self-regulation empowerment program: A school-based program to enhance self-regulated and self-motivated cycles of student learning. *Psychology in the Schools, 41*, 537–550.

Colby, A., Beaumont, E., Ehrlich, T., & Corngold, J. (2007a). *Educating for democracy*. San Francisco, CA: Jossey-Bass.

Colby, A., Beaumont, E., Ehrlich, T., & Corngold , J. (2007b). *Educating for democracy: Additional resources*. Retrieved November 15, 2009, from http://72.5.117.129/dynamic/downloads/Weinberg.pdf

Conover, P., & Searing, D. (2000). A political socialization perspective. In L. M. McDonnell, P. M. Timpane, & R. Benjamin (Eds.), *Rediscovering the democratic purposes of education*. Lawrence, Kansas: University Press of Kansas.

Cook, T., & Campbell, D. (1979). *Quasi-experimental design*. Chicago: Rand McNally.

Craig, S. C., & Maggiotto, M. A. (1982). Measuring political efficacy. *Political Methodology, 8(3)*, 85–109.

Craig, S. C., Niemi, R. G., & Silver, G. E. (1990). Political efficacy and trust: A report on the ANES pilot study items. *Political Behavior, 12(3)*, 289–314.

Dennis, J. (1968). Major problems of political socialization research. *Midwest Journal of Political Science, 12(1)*, 85–114.

Dewey, J. (1927). The public and its problems. In J. A. Boydston (Ed.), *The collected works of John Dewey. The later works, 1925–1953*. Carbondale and Edwardsville: Southern Illinois University Press.

Easton, D. (1975). A re-assessment of the concept of political support. *British Journal of Political Science, 5*, 435–457.

Easton, D., & Dennis, J. (1967). The child's acquisition of regime norms: Political efficacy. *American Political Science Review, 61*, 25–38.

Finkel, S. E. (1985). Reciprocal effects of participation and political efficacy: A panel analysis. *American Journal of Political Science, 29(4)*, 891–913.

Galston, W.A. (2001). Political knowledge, political engagement, and civic education. *Annual Review of Political Science, 4*, 217–234.

Gamson, W. (1968). *Power and discontent*. Homewood, IL: Dorsey Press.

Gutmann, A. (1987). *Democratic education*. Princeton, NJ: Princeton University Press.

Hess, R., & Torney, J. (1967). *The development of political attitudes in children*. Chicago: Aldine. (Reissued 2006 by Transaction Press)

Jennings, M. K., & Niemi, R. G. (1974). *The political character of adolescence: The influence of family and schools*. Princeton, NJ: Princeton University Press.

Jennings, M. K., & Niemi, R. G. (1981). *Generations and politics: A panel study of young Americans and their parents*. Princeton, NJ: Princeton University Press.

Jennings, M. K., & Stoker, L. (2004). Social trust and civic engagement across time and generations. *Acta Politica, 39*, 342–379.

Kahne, J., & Westheimer, J. (2006). The limits of political efficacy: Educating citizens for a democratic society. *PS: Political Science & Politics, 39*, 289–296.

Kant, I. (1785/1991). *The groundwork of the metaphysics of morals*. Trans. Herbert J. Paton. New York: Harper & Row.

Kierkegaard, S. ([1841] 1974). *Fear and trembling*. Trans. Walter Lowrie. Princeton, NJ: Princeton University Press.

Kitsantas, A., Zimmerman, B. J., & Cleary, T. (2000). The role of observation and emulation in the development of athletic self-regulation. *Journal of Educational Psychology, 91*, 241–250.

Kuh, G., Schuh, J. H., Whitt, E. J., & Associates. (2005). *Student success in college: Creating conditions that matter.* San Francisco, CA: Jossey-Bass.

Langton, K. P., & Karns, D. A. (1969). The relative influence of the family, peer group, and school in the development of political efficacy. *Western Political Quarterly, 22(4)*, 813–826.

Lay, C. J., Gimpel, J. G., & Schuknecht, J. E. (2003). *Cultivating democracy: Civic environments and political socialization in America*. Washington, DC: Brookings Institution Press.

Levi, M., & Stoker, L. (2000). Trust and trustworthiness. *Annual Review of Political Science, 3*, 475–507.

Liebschutz, S. F., & Niemi, R. G. (1974). Political attitudes among black children. In R.G. Niemi & Associates (Eds.), *The politics of future citizens*. San Francisco, CA: Jossey-Bass.

Madsen, D. (1987). Political self-efficacy tested. *American Political Science Review, 81(2)*, 571–582.

Mansbridge, J. (1980). *Beyond adversary democracy*. New York: Basic Books.

Mansbridge, J. (1999). On the idea that participation makes better citizens. In S. Elkin & K. E. Soltan (Eds.), *Citizen competence and democratic institutions*. University Park, PA: Penn State University Press.

McAdam, D. (1982). *Political process and the development of Black insurgency, 1930–1970.* Chicago: University of Chicago Press.

McAdam, D. (1988). *Freedom Summer*. New York: Oxford University Press.

Morrell, M. E. (2003). Survey and experimental evidence for a reliable and valid measure of internal political efficacy. *Public Opinion Quarterly, 67*, 589–602.

Newcomb, T. M., Koenig, K. E., Flacks, R., & Warwick, D. P. (1967). *Persistence and change: Bennington College and its students after 25 years*. New York: John Wiley & Sons.

Nie, N., Junn, J., & Stehlik-Barry, K. (1996). *Education and democratic citizenship.* Chicago: University of Chicago Press.

Nie, N., Verba, S., & Petrocik, J. R. (1976). *The changing American voter.* Cambridge, MA: Harvard University Press.

Niemi, R. G., Craig, S. C., & Mattei, F. (1991). Measuring internal political efficacy in the 1988 national election study. *American Political Science Review, 85(4)*, 1407–1413.

Niemi, R. G., & Hepburn, M. A. (1995). The rebirth of political socialization. *Perspectives on Political Scienc*e, *24*, 7–16.

Niemi, R. G. & Junn, J. (1998). *Civic education: What makes students learn*. New Haven: Yale University Press.

Pateman, C. (1970). *Participation and democratic theory.* Cambridge: Cambridge University Press.

Perry, A. D., & Wilkenfeld, B. S. (2006). Using an agenda setting model to help students develop & exercise participatory skills and values. *Journal of Political Science Education, 2(3)*, 303–312.

Pettit, P. (1997). *Republicanism: A theory of freedom and government*. Oxford: Clarendon Press.

Pocock, J. G. A. (1975). *The Machiavellian moment: Florentine political thought and the Atlantic republican tradition*. Princeton, NJ: Princeton University Press.

Putnam, R. (2000). *Bowling alone*. New York: Simon & Schuster.

Rodgers, H. (1974). Toward an explanation of the political efficacy and political cynicism of Black adolescents: An exploratory study. *American Journal of Political Science, 18*, 257–282.

Rosenstone, S. J., & Hansen J. M. (1993). *Mobilization, participation, and democracy in America*. New York: Macmillan.

Sapiro, V. (2004). Not your parents' political socialization: Introduction to a new generation. *Annual Review of Political Science, 7*, 1–23.

Schunk, D. H., & Pajares, F. (2004). Self-efficacy in education revisited: Empirical and applied evidence. In D. M. McInerney & S. Van Etten (Eds.), *Big theories revisited* (pp. 115–138). Greenwich, CT: Information Age.

Sears, D. O., & Levy, S. (2003). Childhood and adult development. In D. O. Sears, L. Huddy, & R. Jervis (Eds.), *Handbook of political psychology*. New York: Oxford University Press.

Shaw, G. B. (1903/2009). *The revolutionist's handbook and pocket companion*. Cambridge, MA: The University Press (1903). Retrieved November 15, 2009, from http://www.bartleby.com/157/5.html

Shingles, R. D. (1981). Black consciousness and political participation: The missing link. *American Political Science Review, 75*, 76–91.

Sigel, R. S., & Hoskin, M. B. (1981). *The political involvement of adolescents*. New Brunswick, NJ: Rutgers University Press.

Skinner, Q. (1990). The Republican idea of liberty. In G. Bock, Q. Skinner, & M. Viroli (Eds.), *Machiavelli and republicanism*. Cambridge: Cambridge University Press.

Torney-Purta, J. (2002). The school's role in developing civic engagement: A study of adolescents in twenty-eight countries. *Applied Developmental Science, 6*, 203–212.

Torney-Purta, J., Wilkenfeld, B., & Barber, C. (2008). How adolescents in twenty-seven countries understand, support and practice human rights. *Journal of Social Issues, 64(4)*, 857–880.

Verba, S., & Nie, N. H. (1972). *Participation in America*. New York: Harper & Row.

Verba, S., Schlozman, K., & Brady, H. (1995). *Voice and equality: Civic voluntarism in American politics*. Cambridge, MA: Harvard University Press.

Warren, M. (1992, March). Democratic theory and self-transformation. *American Political Science Review, 86*, 8–23.

Wolfinger, R. E., & Rosenstone, S. J. (1980). *Who votes?* New Haven, CT: Yale University Press.

CHAPTER 21

The Transdisciplinary Nature of Citizenship and Civic/Political Engagement Evaluation

ANN HIGGINS-D'ALESSANDRO
Fordham University

INTRODUCTION

THIS VOLUME REVIEWS a range of research about young people's capacities and attitudes as they prepare to undertake the responsibilities of democratic citizenship, participating in civic life, voting, and volunteering. While there is only a small body of evaluation research on civic education and civic and political engagement programs, this work shows a positive relationship between the civic knowledge and activities of adolescents and youth and their attitudes toward and their actual later activities, such as participating civically, voting, and volunteering. This chapter introduces the idea that evaluation research can contribute to knowledge in the fields of citizenship and civic or political engagement education by becoming a transdisciplinary science. Evaluation as a transdisciplinary science means that evaluation studies not only assess current theories and knowledge in a substantive field but they also contribute new theoretical ideas and knowledge to that field. This chapter first highlights basic research findings and reviews evaluation research of citizenship education and civic or political engagement programs and then raises a range of issues and challenges inherent in evaluation and introduces ideas from the evaluation literature that can be helpful for advancing these fields. From a transdisciplinary perspective, good evaluation research not only demonstrates what works, the extent to which interventions affect outcomes, and overall program impact, but it also addresses questions about how and why programs work, thus adding new theoretical and practical knowledge. The chapter begins with a brief history of applied research in the United States and concludes with a short section about how educational settings and youth organizations can build evaluation capacity.

THE GROWING RECOGNITION OF THE IMPORTANCE OF EVALUATION RESEARCH: A BRIEF HISTORY OF PUBLIC POLICY AND RESEARCH IN THE UNITED STATES

The tension that exists today in the politics of evaluation is between accountability and system responsivity. The climate in the United States, especially in education and social services, has stressed accountability but is now beginning to lean toward emphasizing responsiveness to needs and ideas for structural change in schooling and service delivery as well. The emphasis by states and cities on the accountability aspects of the No Child Behind (NCLB) legislation is an example. This bipartisan law has required national standardized testing of students and assessments of schools by setting annual yearly progress criteria as a way of holding schools accountable for ensuring that all students learn and perform at grade level. The unintended but predictable consequence of making accountability the highest priority for evaluation research is that evaluators have focused on what can be measured with existing types of measures. This limits insights to already defined and measured constructs and curtails new theoretical work.

In contrast, system responsivity focuses on continuous improvement of interventions and programs using evaluation strategies to build theory as well as identify and strengthen weak linkages in program delivery across multiple levels and diverse groups of stakeholders. These responsive evaluations often lead to new insights but may have limited ability to make inferences regarding scaling up and generalizability.

The pendulum seems to swing between accountability and responsivity—from evaluations grounded in linear models focused on describing causal chains, assessing well-defined goals, and optimizing the generalizability of results, to evaluations with community goals designed by all stakeholders for the purpose of improving the program. As Levine and Higgins-D'Alessandro (this volume) point out, all evaluations embody particular values that are essential in interpreting evaluation results. Additionally, these same values become important in setting evaluation goals and choosing research designs and methods.

Quantitative evaluation methods are usually grounded in linear models, and the program theory that describes a program's effectiveness typically uses causal language. For example, the implementation of a particular program leads to changes in school climate and teacher strategies, which in turn produce increased student civic and political commitment and participation for some groups of students (and perhaps not for others). Such program theories focus on well-defined and measurable goals and often use constructs and instruments validated in previous research.

By contrast, qualitative methods are used to assess broad program and community goals when the purpose of the evaluation is to improve a local program or examine its effectiveness from the perspectives of multiple stakeholders. Here evaluators seek to understand the goals of an intervention from these perspectives and either negotiate about differences or seek consensus about program goals and how to assess them.

Societal perspectives on science and its relationship to public welfare and societal improvement have evolved over the years toward a fuller recognition that scientific work contributes to the public welfare in complex and often indirect ways. Evaluation research has had an important role in this evolution.

A BRIEF HISTORY OF THE SOCIAL CONTRACT BETWEEN SCIENCE AND SOCIETY

The fundamental social contract between science and society has changed since its first persuasive articulation in the 1945 government report, *Science: The Endless Frontier* (Bush, as cited by Molas-Gallart & Davies, 2006), which asserted that scientific research was the key to U.S. welfare and security. This report argued that basic research was essential for developing new knowledge that could inform applied research and technological development that, in turn, would lead to new products and processes. There was a strong focus on the development of measurement techniques, instruments, and assessment tools into the 1960s. According to Jacobs (2003), this marked the birth of evaluation research, which relied heavily on using these new valid and reliable measures to assess program outcomes. However, critics argued that society's needs were not being met by such evaluations because there was too often a mismatch between what the available good measures assessed, the more varied sets of outcomes that interventionists wanted assessed versus what the public wanted to know.

By the 1970s the social contract between society and science had changed, requiring that science demonstrate social relevance and focus on targeted and problem-oriented research. Federal grant programs were set up to encourage universities to be centers where ideas, social programs, and products were generated and to undertake research designed to improve society. Universities began to forge links with industry, school systems, and social and health services; these links remain strong today. This led to preferences for research and program development that focused on specifying and measuring outcomes and net effects. Social scientists imported the ideas of rigor and research designs used in laboratory studies, especially randomized controlled trials (RCTs). RCTs are called the *gold standard* because this method allows researchers to make strong causal inferences and to generalize their findings. When the research designs of the laboratory sciences were used to assess the benefits of alternative types of social programs, problems with scaling up laboratory designs became apparent. Using the tools of basic science maintained a kind of accountability but also narrowed the vision. Moreover, implementing RCT designs to evaluate multisite, multilevel, large-scale projects proved daunting; often the initial random selection of sites was compromised. In addition, implementation across sites as well as across levels within sites was often uneven. In some sites, there might be no implementation (for reasons such as staff departures or failure to recruit sufficient participants to form control and experimental groups of sufficient size). Compromises to RCT designs affect both the ability to make causal inferences and to generalize the results (see Campbell-Patton & Patton, this volume).

EVALUATION RESEARCH COMES INTO ITS OWN

The Golden Age of social programs was the 1960s and 1970s (Rossi & Wright, 1984). The need for Great Society programs to be evaluated created the modern interdisciplinary evaluation field; at one time, 500 to 600 private firms as well as existing university-based research institutes had government contracts to conduct evaluation research (Rossi & Wright, 1984). Although randomized controlled trials (RCTs) of demonstration projects of proposed national programs were implemented (e.g., the negative income tax), almost all evaluations of these proposed Great Society programs showed very minimal effects (Rossi & Wright, 1984). In 1966 Campbell and Stanley published their seminal work on quasi-experimental designs for evaluating educational research (a term they coined, according to Rossi and Wright, 1984) in response to the need for alternative designs that would keep internal validity threats low. Alternative designs were needed because RCTs were expensive; maintaining the fidelity of large multisite and multiyear projects was extremely difficult; and their results often came too late to inform social policy decisions.

Also changing political priorities intervened. Because of the minimal results and the stronger *states rights ideology* of the Reagan administration, federal money was given to states to launch many smaller and more local programs instead of national programs. This led to two major changes in evaluation theory and research. First, because a myriad of small programs had limited budgets, there was an upsurge in small-scale evaluation studies. Because the goals of these startup local programs were less clear than those defined by the government for the previous large-scale demonstration projects, using qualitative approaches that allowed evaluators to work with stakeholders in formulating program goals made sense. Local program designers and implementers often did not come from universities and research institutes. Rather they were practitioners who did not always consider how immediate outcomes in the form of changes in behavior or utilization of services would relate to long-term goals such as being an engaged citizen. Different stakeholders had different expectations about whether a program's goals were short or long term and how they matched up with the program's activities and with student/client needs (Scriven, 1977; Guba & Lincoln, 1981).

Second, in the early 1980s Rossi and Freeman (as retrospectively reported in Rossi & Freeman, 1993) and then others developed the idea of *comprehensive evaluation*, composed of five components that they laid out as related logically and sequenced through time. Today, we treat these components as a list of alternative types of evaluation:

1. Research to justify a program's focus and design
2. Needs assessment
3. Implementation research to explore alternative delivery systems
4. Program implementation monitoring
5. Impact assessment

In the 1980s and 1990s, quasi-experimental designs were used to evaluate large national programs such as Head Start. They too became controversial, often because evaluation measures were not well matched to the program activities and goals. More importantly, questions were raised about the extent to which causal inferences could be made and research results generalized from quasi-experimental designs. Recently, scholars such as West (2009) and Shadish and Cook (2009) have argued that specific kinds of quasi-experimental designs (e.g., regression discontinuity and interrupted time series designs) and selection procedures (e.g., identifying all covariates and using propensity scoring for matching samples) allows causal inferences to be made with a similar degree of confidence as randomized experiments.

Scholars of evaluation (Rossi & Wright, 1984; Rossi, Lipsey, & Freeman, 2004) suggested criteria for matching the purpose of an evaluation to the goals of a program. The Joint Committee on Standards for Educational Evaluation (1994) stressed methodological appropriateness for varying purposes and stakeholders. Developing program or intervention theories and logic models that explicate the decision processes and components of a program and then testing those models using structural equation modeling (SEM) or hierarchical linear modeling (HLM) has become a popular way to define appropriateness from a quantitative perspective. However, when evaluation is new to a field, as with civic education and engagement, it is important first to ground program theories and logic models in developmental, social psychological, organizational, and educational theories and basic research. Otherwise, SEM, HLM, and other data analytic techniques can lead to post hoc explanations of findings without tests of other reasonable alternatives.

Since the 1970s, further innovations in research designs and data analytic techniques have flourished. Nonetheless, the gold standard of RCTs remains, transformed in the late 1980s and early 1990s into outcomes-based accountability (OBA) and hailed as a new approach for large-scale federal projects (Jacobs, 2003). OBA is not always appropriate, but policy-makers and funders often insist on this approach for small or new programs, for which qualitative or formative evaluations may be more useful and appropriate. There are several kinds of evaluation strategies for each type of quantitative evaluation identified by Rossi, Lipsey, and Freeman (2004). In addition, qualitative evaluation has developed into distinct types as well such as participatory, empowerment, critical theory, responsive, and so forth. (Patton, 2002; also see Campbell-Patton & Patton, this volume). Since about 2002, mixed methods evaluations employing both quantitative and qualitative methods have been gaining in popularity (for an early example of multimethod evaluation guidance for civic-related programs, see Torney-Purta, 1998).

In summary, debates are flourishing about different theoretical and methods-led approaches to evaluation, and the field is examining the limits of approaches and techniques. Evaluators are writing about evaluation as a transdisciplinary science in which it is seen as contributing substantively to other fields (Preskill & Donaldson, 2008). This is the situation that evaluators of civics and citizenship education interventions enter today. They have many choices, but a clear rationale for choosing among evaluation theories and designs with regard to the specific content and goals of civics and citizenship education has not been articulated. Taking a transdisciplinary perspective encourages evaluators to make choices that can simultaneously assess a specific program and contribute to the field of civic or political education and engagement. In addition, two sets of parameters can guide evaluation efforts. First, evaluations should be developed within the context of the most robust and current research findings in the field. Second, evaluations should be connected to documents developed by national groups that provide criteria by which to judge citizenship education. The first tells us what we know and the second provides guidelines and goals offered by national leaders in the field. The next two sections summarize these two sets of parameters.

SUMMARY OF ROBUST RESEARCH FINDINGS

This volume deals with a wide variety of ideas about how to prepare young people for citizenship and about ways in which the contexts of students' lives as well as their personal characteristics influence their learning, their personal views, and their commitment to citizenship. This section summarizes several robust research and evaluation findings, which provide useful parameters for making decisions regarding which evaluation theories, goals, and designs are appropriate in specific instances. They constitute the first of Rossi and Freeman's (1993) necessary evaluation components given earlier—the research to justify a program's focus and design.

1. Research shows strong relationships between both explicit civic instruction and interactive discussion of current national and local issues and the depth of students' civic knowledge (Carnegie Corporation & CIRCLE, 2003; Niemi & Junn, 1998; Baldi, Perie, Skidmore, Greenberg, & Hahn, 2001; Lutkus, Weiss, Campbell, Mazzeo, & Lazer, 1999; Torney-Purta, Lehmann, Oswald, & Schulz, 2001; Torney-Purta & Wilkenfeld, 2009).
2. The importance of a positive and participative school culture is sometimes related to citizenship outcomes (Flanagan et al., 1999; Torney-Purta, 2002; Torney-Purta, Wilkenfeld, & Barber, 2008), sometimes shows no relationship (Kahne & Sporte, 2008), and sometimes shows a mixed relationship (Niemi & Junn, 1998; Lutkus et al. 1999).
3. There is some evidence that citizenship education changes students' attitudes and skills as well as their intentions to engage in civic activities as adults (Kahne & Sporte, 2008; Torney-Purta et al., 2008), and other research that found no evidence (Print & Coleman, 2003).
4. Even though some studies cited previously (Baldi et al, 2001; Lutkus et al., 1999; U.S. Department of Education, 2007; Levinson, this volume) show that African American and Hispanic students and students living in poverty perform less well on civics education tests, further analyses of the IEA data (Torney-Purta & Wilkenfeld, 2009) demonstrate that school SES and climate may partially account for these outcomes. They showed that students in low SES schools had higher levels of civic knowledge but lower levels of civic efficacy when teachers used traditional lecture presentations versus interactive methods. These findings were moderated by the open climate of the school, which positively impacted both outcomes across all levels of SES. In addition, Sporte and Middaugh (2008) found that classroom SES also impacted student civic learning; students in low SES classrooms performed more poorly. These results highlight how important it is to seriously consider the contexts of schooling and to identify implementation processes.

5. We have limited knowledge about the influence of venues other than formal education on youth's attitudes toward their own developing citizenship, nor do we understand much about the paths of learning, the specific mechanisms or processes by which organizations, including schools, affect citizenship attitudes, sense of identity, or behaviors (Hart, Atkins, & Matsuba, 2008; Dudley & Gitelson, 2002; Youniss, McLellan, & Yates, 1997; Watts, Armstrong, Cartman & Guessous, 2008; Torney-Purta, Amadeo, & Andolina, this volume; McIntosh & Youniss, this volume).

NATIONAL EFFORTS TO STRENGTHEN CITIZENSHIP EDUCATION

National efforts in a field can sharpen the focus of evaluation research. Polls show that Americans hold schools and teachers primarily responsible for the citizenship education of our youth (Stern, 2009); thus, projects that aim to strengthen these efforts have broad support. Several national organizations, both public and private, in the past decade have focused their efforts on strengthening, redefining, and revitalizing citizenship education. While space does not allow discussion of these national projects to set goals for citizenship education, the following examples suggest that this is a good time for educators, practitioners, and evaluators to consider the goals embodied in these national efforts and to design evaluation research conducted across a range of theoretical perspectives. To give just a few selected examples of national crosscutting efforts, in 1999 the National Association of Secretaries of State launched the New Millennium Project to identify the source of problems with youth political engagement and electoral participation. At about the same time, the National Center for Learning and Citizenship was established at the Education Commission of the States to examine state policies and to focus on the needs of policy-makers for measures of civic outcomes and school climate. In 2001, the National Council for the Social Studies issued a position paper on creating effective citizens. In 2003, a major consensus document, *The Civic Mission of Schools,* was issued by CIRCLE and the Carnegie Corporation of New York and served as a founding document for The Civic Mission of Schools Campaign.

Historically, schools and teachers have made commonsense efforts to educate young people to become responsible members of society. However, scholars and practitioners of citizenship education recognize that the associations between what they teach, what children experience, and how they act as citizens are complex and difficult to study. The focus and content of programs vary widely but include: teaching democratic principles and governance structures, U. S. history and government, and current events in classrooms; having school-based political or civic outreach field experiences; involving students in outside school projects that conduct critical analyses of current political issues through research and advocacy; and trying to make schools themselves more democratic (through interactive discussion in the classroom, classroom or school democratic decision making, and a participatory school climate). With the goal of contributing theoretical and practical knowledge as well as assessing programs, evaluations should address the following questions:

- How does each of these strategies, as part of schooling or out-of-school experiences during adolescence, serve the goal of creating an enlightened, engaged, and responsible citizenry?
- How can evaluations characterize the many different efforts of citizenship education in ways that best align with their philosophies and goals as well as their outcomes?
- How can evaluations best conceptualize and examine the processes and mechanisms that underlie the associations found among civic and citizenship strategies and practices and student, teacher, and other adult mentor, and program outcomes?

The next sections address these questions by highlighting evaluations of a wide range of citizenship education efforts.

CURRENT EXAMPLES OF EVALUATION RESEARCH IN CIVIC EDUCATION AND ENGAGEMENT

The two primary vehicles for explicit teaching of citizenship education in schools are civics courses and experiential civic engagement such as service-learning or community outreach programs. In addition, the rights and responsibilities of citizenship are the implicit goals of youth organizations, some specifically focused on enhancing political and civic knowledge, others focused on leadership and other skills. The following sections discuss the research and evaluation findings of studies of the various types of school-based and out-of-school interventions.

Civic Education

Research evidence shows that civics courses increase knowledge, affect attitudes, and promote participation. They are taken in either the 9th or 12th grades, usually for one semester. Niemi and Junn's (1998) analysis of the 1988 National Assessment of Educational Progress (NAEP) data found substantially higher civic knowledge when civics courses covered a wide range of topics and included discussions of current events; this analysis controlled for gender, ethnicity, home environment, and prior interest. High-school graduates who had the *We the People* curriculum that is used in both the United States and increasingly internationally (Branson, in preparation) performed substantially better on civic knowledge and other political engagement indicators than polls show for the general public. However, fully 30% of young people do not get civics courses either because they have dropped out of school (15%) or do not take them for other reasons (15%) (Branson, in preparation). Kahne and Middaugh (2008) found that schools increase inequalities by not providing equal civic preparation to all students, especially minorities and those with low academic performance.

Some research has proposed and tested models to explain the effects of civic curriculum on student attitudes and behaviors. McDevitt and Kiousis (2004, 2006) found that the *Kids Voting USA* curriculum increased the use of news media and familial discussions of political issues. Both a short-term and a longer-term impact study of the effects of this program found positive results. Students showed immediate increases in political interest, a sense of political efficacy, and knowledge of local and state government (Pasek, Feldman, Romer, & Jamieson, 2008). A model of the effects on these graduates a year or two later found that only those who felt politically efficacious and were attentive to political issues were more likely to vote (Pasek et al., 2008). Most studies show that civic education increases civic knowledge and has a positive effect on political attitudes and intentions to vote as adults when it includes participative activities at the middle- and high-school levels.

SCHOOL-BASED SERVICE LEARNING

A decade ago, Youniss, McLellan, and Yates (1997) theorized that youth commit to present and future civic engagement when they can directly participate in political or civic activities, especially community service and service learning (usually defined as a combination of volunteering and school-based curriculum or reflection on the volunteer experience). Hart, Donnelly, Youniss, and Atkins (2007) confirmed that service learning, whether voluntary or required, as well as extracurricular activities, predict adult volunteering and voting. Service learning and volunteering includes a range of activities from occasional cookie sales or regularly tutoring younger students to occasional or regular service in soup kitchens or homeless shelters. Evidence of the effectiveness of civically or (sometimes) politically oriented service learning on future indicators of citizenship such as voting is stronger than programs that present service as a form of personal helping (Torney-Purta, Amadeo, & Richardson, 2007; Beaumont, this volume).

Many civically oriented service-learning programs are designed to avoid politics (Westheimer & Kahne, 2000, 2004). Political engagement and discussion of political issues is seen by some teachers as controversial, and they are reticent to tackle it due to fears of being accused of indoctrination. Althof and Berkowitz (2006) argue that the same is true for youth organizations that engage adolescents in volunteer work. The orientation toward personal helping evident in many service-learning and community service programs may in part account for the preference of high-school females to engage in service more than males. In contrast, males prefer politically oriented activities (Torney-Purta, 2002).

An examination of service learning in 10 schools showed that those programs that gave students real responsibilities, decision-making power, and ownership resulted in student gains in political engagement and tolerance toward out-groups; students' self-concepts were enhanced, as well (Morgan & Streb, 2001). In an explicitly political outreach program, *Public Achievement,* elementary, middle-, and high-school students in seven communities worked for one school year on public issues of their choosing with the support of teachers, college students, and community mentors who taught political concepts and skills and advised on developing feasible projects. Several small evaluations demonstrated that students developed a range of political skills from chairing meetings and public speaking, to deliberating, negotiating, and writing (Boyte, 2003).

Gifted high-school student members of a three-week residential summer service-learning program were compared to peers in an accelerated academic residential three-week program. Both programs were held on the same university campus. The service-learning program combined academic learning, community service, field trips, meetings with politicians, and guest lectures. The pre-intervention and six-month follow-up survey evaluation showed that the service-learning group became more aware of political and civic issues and felt more responsible for improving their communities; however, analyses comparing the two groups found no differences at either time on broader indices of civic engagement. Both spent fewer than 10 hours a month in community service, and almost all in both groups said they would register to vote when they turned 18 (Lee, Olszewski-Kubilius, Donahue, & Weimholt, 2007).

These studies offer some insight into what makes service-learning programs effective citizenship education; however, they also raise issues. Are the effects of consecutive programs offered from elementary through high school cumulative or is there an age or time period when service learning is the most effective vehicle for citizenship education? Do the capabilities of students at different ages create ceiling effects for expected changes in attitudes and behaviors? Evaluation research needs to address program effectiveness and impact across ages, taking into account that different content and methods of teaching are used with students of different ages. These issues demonstrate the need for basic developmental theories and research to intersect with and inform the development and evaluation of programs as discussed in chapters in this volume by Wilkenfeld et al., and Metzger and Smetana. The current evidence from high-school research suggests that the effectiveness of service learning in producing commitment to current and future political and civic engagement rests on empowering students by giving them responsibility and voice in guided and reflective experiences over some substantial period of time.

Service Learning and Critical Pedagogy

Critics of service-learning experiences, as indicated above, say that such programs teach students to accept the status quo of structural inequalities and to see the world as divided into the *haves* and the *have-nots*. Hart (2006) and Butin (2003) critique mainstream service learning as a functional or technical way of engaging students in perpetuating structural and power inequalities, reinforcing a deficit model regarding those who receive services, and losing the inherently reciprocal nature of service in which both students and those served gain. Hart (2006) contends that the combination of service learning and critical pedagogy can develop into a new *liberatory pedagogy* that sensitizes students to power inequities and gives them intellectual skills and factual knowledge to uncover problems, think of solutions, and work toward enacting them at a service-learning site.

Butin (2003) argues that because service learning has received federal support (the Citizen Service Act) and become mainstream, it is urgent to combine it with critical pedagogy in order that it continues to meet its goal of developing abilities for mature citizenship. He believes that federal support for service learning has created expectations that such programs be efficient, sustainable, and accountable, evaluated in the same way as other educational curricula. Using these standards, their effectiveness would be based only on their impact on individual student outcomes, such as enhanced social or politicial tolerance. Butin contends that evaluating service learning only in terms of efficiency, sustainability, and accountability disconnects it from one of its major goals, which is to build the critical analytic capacities necessary for active citizenship in a democratic society. The functional evaluation criteria take attention away from the goal of promoting student analyses of the role of their service-learning projects in maintaining society's power structures.

The shortcomings of service-learning evaluations are that they do not present evidence of the interventions offering a meaningful short- or long-term benefit to communities as a whole or solutions to existing systemic inequities that contribute to clients' poor circumstances. A clearer articulation of service-learning goals and methods in terms of critical and reflective pedagogies including procedures to address the reciprocal nature of service can only aid the development of this field.

Participatory Democratic Education and School Climate

Some interventions place the power to create a working democracy jointly in the students' and teachers' hands. They are designed to promote participatory school citizenship through democratizing authority and power structures, fostering strong bonds of community and relationships, and developing courses focused on civic, societal, and moral issues.

One such program is the Just Community approach, of which the Scarsdale Alternative School is one long-standing example (Power, Higgins, & Kohlberg, 1989; Power & Higgins-D'Alessandro, 2008). It has been in existence for over 30 years. A recent survey of its graduates, now between the ages of 20 and 45 years, found that the majority were either civic leaders or politically or civically active. This exemplifies citizenship education's often stated long-term goal of mature, engaged citizenship. In addition, most alumni reported that they continue to rely on what they learned in the process of creating a working democracy with teachers, such as valuing others' perspectives and developing the skills of empathic listening, leadership, teamwork, and negotiation (Vozzola, Higgins-D'Alessandro, Rosen, & Horan, 2009).

When students and teachers democratically decide upon rules and create enforcement strategies (fairness committees, constructive punishments), the resulting school climate is positive and strong. When rationales for upholding rules are explicitly discussed, both understanding and compliance increase dramatically, forming the basis of a positive school climate (Power, Higgins, & Kohlberg, 1989). Power et al. found substantial improvement in school climate using qualitative methodologies.

Frequently, civic education programs include a school climate survey as one of their assessment measures. When researchers use survey methods to assess school climate, the question arises about what is being measured—the average of respondents' perceptions or some real characteristic of the school as a whole (Higgins-D'Alessandro & Guo, 2009). Many researchers aggregate individual perceptions (Cohen, 2006) or use both aggregate and individual measures (Torney-Purta & Wilkenfeld, 2009). Higgins-D'Alessandro and Guo describe a method for assessing school climate more directly by asking students and teachers to be informants about what they see as true in their school, rather than reporting as individuals about their feelings about being in the school.

Whole school reform efforts that also seek to improve school climate often fail to include an assessment of the importance of student voice or power in the school. Everyday experience with *participatory* democracy at school may be necessary to achieve the goal of civic engagement for students (Torney-Purta, 2002; Power & Higgins-D'Alessandro, 2008). Furthermore, a large study of Chicago high-school students found little evidence that creating a school culture supportive of academic learning and social relationships affected student commitment to civic or political engagement (Kahne & Sporte, 2008). In fact, Kahne and Sporte were pessimistic about the ability of whole school reform efforts to promote civic growth unless it was explicitly endorsed as a goal of reform.

Since many educators and scholars are convinced of the power of school climate to influence a wide range of student political and civic attitudes and behaviors, it is important that both those planning interventions and evaluators consider the role of school climate in citizenship education. This could mean incorporating improved climate as an explicit program goal, setting a minimal climate standard to be evaluated as part of program implementation, or examining climate as a mediator between program elements and citizenship outcomes. Kahne and Sporte's (2008) study is the clearest example of a citizenship intervention evaluation that paid attention to the role of school climate. Some of the secondary analyses of the IEA Civic Education Study's data have demonstrated the value of students' belief about the power of their participation in decision making at school in relation to several civic outcomes (for example, Torney-Purta et al., 2008). The conditions under which school climate interacts with other factors to affect citizenship education interventions deserve more attention from researchers and evaluators.

OUT-OF-SCHOOL INTERVENTIONS TO PROMOTE CIVIC ENGAGEMENT

Scholars as well as practitioners contend that moving beyond service learning programs to immerse youth in community problem solving promotes the development of youth cognitive and social capabilities as well as enhancing civic understanding and the willingness to work for social justice. For instance, Watts, Williams, and Jagers (2003) reported that urban youth developed strategies that made community institutions more responsive to their needs. Working for social justice enfranchised those youth.

Generation Y is the youth-led activist program of a larger program, *Youth Action,* which focuses on educational justice and equal rights for minority youth. They recruit Hispanic, African American, and Arab American youth from working-class neighborhoods; the project began shortly after the attack of September 11, 2001, and is supported by a grassroots parent organization. Its purpose is to engage young people in social change and promote self-development. A four-month qualitative study with observations and interviews using grounded theory revealed that the program increased youth civic knowledge, promoted problem-solving and citizenship skills, and enhanced self-efficacy (Larson & Hansen, 2005).

These out-of-school civic and political youth engagement activities may be most accurately considered nonformal educational activities. The examples of nonformal programs discussed in a special issue of *New Directions for Evaluation* (Norland & Somers, 2005) are performing arts and conservancy programs. However, these civic and political engagement interventions fit the description, and evaluation strategies offered there are appropriate. The five defining characteristics of nonformal education are as follows:

1. Attendance is usually voluntary.
2. Leaders do not stay long, creating inconsistent leadership.
3. Staff members vary in their abilities, their command of teaching techniques, their content expertise, and their group management skills.
4. Programs within an organization vary even though they share similar goals.
5. The purpose of these programs is not only educational, but also social, recreational, or service-oriented.

According to Wiltz (2005), nonformal settings most often see evaluators as collaborators who accept the goal of program improvement, thus making participatory evaluations most appropriate.

Recommendations for introducing evaluation to nonformal civic engagement settings could be applied to school-based citizenship interventions. Pre-evaluation activities, such as cementing support from the director or principal, having discussions with stakeholders, and providing education about evaluation, are essential in order to prepare both schools and nonformal settings for evaluation and to help staff make use of evaluation findings (Wiltz, 2005; Clavijo, Fleming, Hoermann, Toal, & Johnson, 2005). Additionally, stakeholders' expectations about the length of time and the intensity of implementation necessary for the impact of a citizenship-building program to be evident are often unrealistic and could be addressed in pre-evaluation activities (Sridharan, Campbell, & Zinzow, 2006).

The Potential of Electronic Media to Enhance Political and Civic Engagement

Multimedia forums, such as blogs, personal communication spaces, online polling, and use of mass e-mailing, twitter, and so forth, for political campaigning are new arenas for political discussion and activism (Blumler & Gurevitch, 2001; Papacharissi, 2004, Bennett et al., this volume; Haste, this volume). The electronic media are becoming an increasingly important component of citizenship education, and appropriate evaluation models need to be developed.

Murphy (2004) calls on educators in rhetoric and in communication to join participatory democratic approaches to teaching civic participation in order to facilitate both students' competencies and skills of citizenship and to engender awareness and understanding of the ways in which different forms and types of media shape political and social issues. Citizenship education research could usefully delve deeper into students' understanding about the power of the media and their skills in decoding political media messages (Torney-Purta & Wilkenfeld, 2009).

CIVIC EDUCATION PROGRAMS' EFFECTS ON PARENTS

Just as it is important that parents actively support academic achievement by being involved with children's homework, it is equally important that parents support citizenship education by actively engaging their children in political and civic discussions and activities. Two studies (McDevitt & Chaffee, 2000; McDevitt & Kiousis, 2006) assessed the effects that *KidsVoting USA* had on parents' political discussions with their children. The school curriculum involved having middle-school children and parents watch and discuss news programs together during an election campaign. Lower SES families, both children and parents, benefited the most; they gained more knowledge and showed more sustained attention to news events. In the larger study (McDevitt & Kiousis, 2006), the intervention effects were stronger at follow-up, indicating that civic engagement programs can develop *self-perpetuating habits* of attention to news and the motivation for ongoing political conversations with family members. Evaluations of civic interventions too rarely assess their impact on families, which is important to understand how interventions create the conditions that will sustain their benefits over time and into adulthood.

CONCLUSIONS

Although there are strong programs and some rigorous evaluations in this field, the effectiveness of the full range of programs has not been evaluated. It is not even clear on what bases programs should be judged as being of quality and effective. It is also important for evaluators to optimize both the validity and transferability of concepts and constructs. To do so, this means:

1. Developing constructs and measures that are robust indicators of key influences on outcomes and of commonly assessed outcomes themselves

2. Identifying particular aspects of intervention contexts and experiences that promote desired short- and long-term outcomes
3. Elucidating key processes of citizenship development interventions such as ways to foster strategic problem-solving abilities, critical analysis of issues, leadership skills, ability to participate in issue discussions, perspective-taking, and empathy (see McLeod et al., this volume; Beaumont, this volume)

It would be very useful for the field for evaluators to identify minimal levels of cognitive and social skills needed for youth to successfully participate in civic and political engagement activities and to thrive in the complex environments created by such interventions both in- and outside of schools.

EVALUATION IN THE FIELD OF CITIZENSHIP EDUCATION

This section focuses on specific issues that arise in the evaluation of citizenship education interventions (see also Campbell-Patton & Patton, this volume). Ways in which evaluation can contribute substantively to the field of civic education and engagement practices as well as some specific challenges in civics and citizenship education evaluations are discussed as illustrative of steps toward becoming a transdisciplinary science. The final section introduces the feasibility of schools and youth organizations building their own evaluation capacity.

An Overview of Evaluation Strategies

Jacobs's (2003) definition of evaluation is concise and yet broad enough to encompass both quantitative and qualitative methods. An evaluation is "a set of systematically planned and executed activities designed to determine the merit of a program, intervention, or policy or to describe aspects of its operation" (p. 63, 2003). She proposed a five-tier approach that has some similarities with the comprehensive approach of Rossi and Freeman (1993) previously discussed. The five tiers are: Tier 1—needs assessment; Tier 2—monitoring and accountability; Tier 3—quality review and program clarification to help assess the likelihood of a program achieving its outcomes; Tier 4—achievement of outcomes; and Tier 5—establishing impact.

Actual evaluations may consider more than one tier, especially if they are multilevel or multimethod, or both (Natasi & Hitchcock, 2009). Multilevel evaluations assess group (classroom, service-learning experience), organization (school, out-of-school program), and community effects as well as individual effects. Multimethod is the employment of several quantitative strategies or the use of quantitative and qualitative methods to address the same set of research questions. One example is using a combination of the following procedures to address questions of the influences of school and classroom climates on the effectiveness of a citizenship intervention—giving paper-and-pencil measures to students, conducting classroom observations, using structured interviews with teachers, and holding more wide-ranging ethnographic interviews with various community stakeholders.

Many evaluation professionals as well as policy-makers also think that evaluation should:

- Be incorporated into a program
- Be iterative over the development, implementation, and maintenance of a program
- Involve and educate a program's stakeholders and use their input about program goals to inform design and methods
- Build capacity of a program for self-evaluation after the professionals leave
- Adapt to the context of a program, its political and fiscal realities, and where it is on its own life course from development to maintenance or expansion
- Meet standards of scientific rigor
- Have productive utility, that is, provide results and information that are useful for program development or change, for understanding students' developmental strengths and needs, and for developing standards of practice

In 1978, Patton argued that this last characteristic, usefulness, could even trump scientific rigor, and he called for utilization-focused evaluation. Jacobs (2003) and others contend that by focusing on defining the most appropriate evaluation type for a specific program at a particular time, reasonably high standards of both utility and scientific rigor can be satisfied.

To create a useful research base for informing social and educational policies in this relatively new field of citizenship education, multilevel and multimethod evaluations that include and also go beyond individual schools or programs to the levels of school districts, states, and organizations are required (Natasi & Hitchcock, 2009). Multilevel and multimethod evaluation research also creates the strongest conditions for developing and testing theories regarding the processes through which effective programs impact outcomes. When these are combined with rigorous research designs, such as RCTs or certain kinds of quasi-experimental designs (West, 2009), evaluation research will be able to make important theoretical as well as practical contributions to the field of citizenship education.

How Evaluation Can Contribute Substantively to the Field of Citizenship Education

Evaluation has always been an interdisciplinary field, and some propose it should be transdisciplinary (Preskill & Donaldson, 2008). This means that the content of its work is based in a discipline, such as education or psychology, and that it can develop and contribute basic as well as applied knowledge. Tackling issues in substantive areas such as citizenship education and civic and political engagement enhances evaluators' knowledge about how to best design and conduct evaluations in general (Preskill & Donaldson, 2008), and those evaluations in turn will contribute new substantive insights and ideas to the fields of citizenship education and development.

Thus, it is important that scholars and practitioners discuss, debate, and reflect creatively on their programs and interventions, as well as examine their goals and how their means are related to the developmental tasks and needs of students and other stakeholders. They should also demand that evaluators understand their interventions' goals and means. Suchman (1967) noted that many evaluations have null findings because of *theory failure*; that is, the evaluation theory, research questions, and methods do not address what is actually occurring in a program (Jacobs, 2003).

This section highlights issues that those designing interventions and evaluators should agree upon as the first step of a citizenship education evaluation. The overall framework of this section takes the perspective of quantitative evaluation research; however, it is relevant to qualitative evaluation methods as well. Addressing the issues detailed in the next sections will help to ensure that evaluations are aligned with the theories and goals of civic education and citizenship or political engagement programs and interventions. As more citizenship education evaluations are conducted, their cumulative effect has the potential to build the transdisciplinary field of citizenship education evaluation, to provide useful information for enhancing the effectiveness of civic and citizenship interventions, and to build a strong research base for social and educational policies.

Partnering in the development of evaluation theory and design. Partnerships between those who design interventions and evaluators can range from formal agreements, in which the evaluator is external to the project but sufficiently informed to develop an objective plan, to close partnerships, in which the evaluator and intervention stakeholders plan the evaluation as a critical aspect of the intervention. In the middle ground, partnerships are defined by the intervention stakeholders and the evaluator, each confined to their separate roles while engaging in ongoing discussions and agreeing on key issues. A recent document put out by the U.S. Department of Education (*Mobilizing for Evidence-Based Character Education*, 2007) represents this middle ground. Working as partners can be difficult because there are fairly strong negative stereotypes, sometimes due to bad past experiences, about the fairness and usefulness of evaluation research. This is compounded by the fact that evaluators are often not skilled in taking the perspectives of practitioners and stakeholders, using language they can understand (see Donaldson, Gooler, & Scriven, 2002), or understanding the program's underlying value assumptions.

Education for citizenship, in particular, is grounded in values as determined by specific curricula and interventions, as well as by school administrators and teachers (see Levine & Higgins-D'Alessandro, this volume). Evaluators must understand not only the value assumptions of the interventions to be studied but also the assumptions they bring to the evaluation. It is important for program specialists and evaluators to discuss the ways in which the underlying values of a preliminary evaluation theory or model fit or conflict with the underlying values of the civic education or engagement program. This is routinely a part of qualitative evaluations but it is sometimes neglected when quantitative evaluation approaches are taken.

Discussing the theory specifying how a program works to effect specific goals can clarify program assumptions and align them with evaluation design and methods. The evaluator also uses theories and basic research in human development, social psychology, and citizenship education to inform the development of a program theory. The evaluator should help those who design interventions and stakeholders to articulate a program's goals within the social and political contexts in which the intervention will be nested. Finally, informed decisions need to be made regarding what and how many types of evaluation strategies should be employed.

The most informative evaluations include an assessment of implementation (commonly referred to as process or implementation fidelity evaluations) as well as an evaluation of outcomes. An implementation evaluation examines the content of materials and activities as well as the pedagogy by which students are taught civics knowledge (and how it is related to civic engagement experiences, such as service learning). This information indicates individual or group level mechanisms or processes (discussed in the following paragraphs) and also allows the interpretation of results from the outcome evaluation to inform basic theories of teaching, learning, and human development. An implementation evaluation prepares the evaluation team working with the intervention team to decide upon an appropriate evaluation design, measures, and methods to capture the complexity of the intervention and its results at different levels or in different domains (e.g., social justice attitudes, commitments to voting, and so forth).

Developing theories of practice and evaluation. Citizenship education practitioners and evaluators need to understand how an intervention's impact will be augmented or weakened by other daily or ongoing learning experiences of the young people who participate in it. It is useful to look across the school to find opportunities for student leadership and governance as well as to assess other programs such as conflict resolution, peer mediation, and service learning that may be related to civic education program components. It is also important to define spaces and contexts other than schools in which these interventions occur—after school, nonformal settings, camps, shopping malls, neighborhood streets, clubs, sports, and religious institutions. Thinking beyond programs to the whole school curriculum and school structure will give insights into understudied patterns and paths that influence student political and civic attitudes and behaviors. Thinking beyond the school setting will test the usefulness of citizenship education principles and goals in nonformal settings.

A well-conceived intervention theory should also describe the roles of teachers and other stakeholders and the skills they are expected to employ in implementing a program. In citizenship education, the development and levels of teachers' skills and how they use them to effectively teach and engage students in civic or political activities should be better covered in evaluation studies. Finally, a challenging issue for evaluators is to assess the value added by a specific program, which means separating the effects of a program from the effects of a child's ongoing development and from the effects of other experiences that foster goals similar to those of the program.

Examining mechanisms and processes. Many view one of the most important challenges of citizenship evaluation as identifying the mechanisms for effective civic education and engagement, rather than just focusing on outcomes. Ideas about what the mechanisms are and how they create the paths and patterns of a program's influence on outcomes and broader impacts should be tested as part of the program theory. It is important to know the extent to which mechanisms are useful across different programs, and ages, cultural groups, and identities of young people as well as across settings and over time. In other words, how does an intervention promote individual cognitive, attentive, and affective processes and skills, as well as develop positive civic attitudes or behaviors?

An excellent example of testing a model that hypothesized interactive mechanisms of interpersonal political discussion with family and peers to explain a program's effectiveness is the research on *Kids Voting USA* (McDevitt & Kiousis, 2004; Pasek, Feldman, Romer, & Jamieson, 2008). McDevitt and Kiousis tested a model of deliberative democracy; that is, that *Kids Voting USA* would create enduring habits of news media use and discussion that, in turn, would foster positive attitudes of future political participation. In a follow-up study, Pasek et al. (2008) found that both political attentiveness as measured by continued use of news media in ongoing familial and peer discussions and a sense of internal efficacy mediated attitudes regarding political participation.

Intervention timing, time lines, and the timing of feedback. The timing of interventions is an important consideration. Although adolescence is commonly accepted as the critical time for committing oneself to political and civic positions, research shows that by age 14, young adolescents' political attitudes are highly similar to those of adults in their cultures (Torney-Purta, Lehmann, Oswald, & Schulz, 2001), suggesting that middle school may be key. Astuto and Ruck (this volume) propose attention to preschool and elementary programs. Whatever the age of the student, evaluations should focus on how well the civic and political concepts used in a program match children's competencies or tap into developmental tasks that they face in their civic and social lives.

Evaluators must also recognize that civic and political engagement activities have their own timelines. In civics courses the teacher may alter the sequence of study to match current events (e.g., an upcoming election) and adjust the focus or difficulty of lessons. In contrast, once a civic or political service-learning project has been launched, its time line is set—students go into the community on a regular weekly schedule, regardless of their individual readiness for these experiences. Civic or political service learning demands that students learn skills in real time in order to function usefully in their communities. This is an uninvestigated area in which individual differences are likely determinative of overall program outcomes and impact, and speaks again to the importance of including levels of student competencies as mechanisms in program theory models.

Having students use online diaries or chat rooms for their daily individual reflections could maximize an evaluation's value, providing real-time information about student functioning and skills, especially those needed to effectively participate in service-learning programs, which would be helpful to students, teachers, site mentors, and evaluators (Lehtonen, 2006). Such strategies are also methodologically useful, as they cut down on the biases inherent in retrospective self-reports.

Examining individual variability. Good evaluations isolate the impact of pre-existing individual differences from the impact of citizenship education; however, existing civic knowledge and citizenship or political education programs do not always take account of them. It seems clear that students' cognitive abilities such as critical reasoning and moral understanding levels, emotional regulation, executive functioning, and social skills may create either floor or ceiling effects for the impact a program has on different students. In addition, taking seriously the conceptualization and measurement of neighborhood and community effects has also not been done in evaluation research in this field (Hart, Atkins, Markey, & Youniss, 2004). Hart (this volume) has conducted research on the effects of the population density of youth in a community, graphically illustrating that wider social conditions hinder the best efforts of schools, community centers, and youth organizations to help youth become politically aware and civically active. Torney-Purta and Wilkenfeld (2009) have shown that the socioeconomic makeup of a school is related to students' civic-related achievement over and above the socioeconomic status of any individual student. Both these studies suggest that evaluations should examine the extent to which the school, neighborhood, and community composition influence the effectiveness of citizenship education programs above and beyond using these contexts as demographic characteristics attached to individuals. They also demonstrate the multi-leveled complex nature of what too often are seen as variables to control, rather than as dynamic and changeable influences to be analyzed in order to better understand outcomes (Fox et al., this volume).

Operationalizing concepts and measuring constructs. This section gives two kinds of examples illustrating the difficulty in measurement development to assess concepts related to civic knowledge and to citizenship or political engagement. Concepts of citizenship, civic engagement, and civic responsibility are multifaceted and they are understood differently by different generations. Moreover, many of these complex concepts are best described using a range of indicators, some of which may be attitudinal, others behavioral, and yet others assessing beliefs or concepts.

Many key concepts in citizenship education and engagement have not been well delineated. An important first step in identifying the range of relevant concepts has been taken by Flanagan, Syvertsen, and Stout (2007), who systematically identified more than a dozen broad conceptual categories. Matching existing instruments to their broad categories would reveal many holes in our current thinking about what should be evaluated and the paucity of instruments available. There is a need for the development of valid and reliable instruments of different kinds—paper-and-pencil measures, observational tools, structured interviews, and questions suitable for use in focus groups (Torney-Purta, Amadeo, & Andolina, this volume). Practically speaking, the instruments used in citizenship education evaluation are often developed for specific studies, and if used by others, they are adapted, often extensively.

We must address issues of measurement validity at the same time as new instruments are assessed for reliability across different ages or areas of the country and world. Methods such as focus groups can be used to enhance initial or face validity of an instrument during its development. Data from school records such as grades, standardized test scores, and disciplinary records, or participation in clubs and after-school activities may be helpful for establishing external validity. However, privacy policies often limit the availability of this information. The development of good measures is critical to establishing civic education and engagement as a field of study.

Different definitions for different generations. The definition of good citizenship is multifaceted and changes meaning across different generations (Andolina, Jenkins, Keeter, & Zukin, 2002). Evaluators need to be sensitive to the definitions employed in civics curricula or citizenship engagement interventions as well as to the definitions understood by students participating in them. These implicit definitions may or may not be similar to those imposed by students when they respond. Andolina et al.'s (2002) research illustrates this issue and offers some solutions. They sought to find out about youth's views of civic engagement in part by using focus groups. These revealed that for youth, civic engagement meant helping one's friends and family. Thus, for evaluators to accurately assess the goals of programs in civic engagement, they must ensure that their measures make clear distinctions. For instance, Andolina et al. suggest that activities should be assessed separately as prosocial, political, or civic, and also that the beneficiaries of each of the three activities—one's family, friends, or community be assessed separately, as well.

Construct validity issues. The following examples serve to illustrate the difficulties of establishing construct validity (Kane, 2006). Often, surveys use very few items to reflect each of several concepts being assessed. This raises the issue of whether such groups of items adequately assess the constructs they are supposed to measure; this is the core construct validity question. As an example, assume the content of all items comprising a measure is negatively worded. In citizenship education, as in most developmental and social psychological fields, the rejection of a negative statement is not the same thing as affirming or committing to a positive statement about the same subject. Reporting that one's neighborhood is not violent is different than reporting that one feels safe there. Strong evaluative and research studies acknowledge this and related problems (Pasek et al., 2008; Flanagan, Syvertsen, & Stout, 2007).

Another example is that researchers often combine items into scales to assess constructs. In citizenship education evaluation it is often necessary to use different kinds of items or different measures, or both, to tap into different aspects of one construct. For instance, a researcher may want to assess how a program affected students' beliefs, attitudes, and behaviors toward the homeless. Measures of these facets of the construct may have different underlying assumptions and use different response rubrics or scoring systems. Often, different scale scores are transformed into a common scale score, such as a Z score.

Kahne and Sporte's (2008) evaluation effectively used Rasch scaling to address some of the problems of scaling; it is a more sensitive strategy than simple conversion to a standard score. Rasch modeling uses probabilities to create one hierarchical scale based on the likelihood that items are endorsed by respondents and the likelihood that any one respondent endorses each item in a group of items (see Bond & Fox, 2001). In this example, Kahne and Sporte (2008) showed that service-learning indicators did not fit with classroom-based indicators of civic learning opportunities. Given this result, they tested two models with service learning both separate and combined with classroom opportunities in order to more accurately identify the effective mechanisms of each experience. The IEA Civic Education Study also relied on Rasch models to produce 20 scales. In that study, it was possible with this methodology to distinguish a civic content-based knowledge scale and a civic skills-based measure. Although these scales were highly correlated, they showed different patterns of associations with characteristics of civic education (Torney-Purta et al., 2001).

Data collection procedures. Traditionally, evaluations of school-based programs have relied heavily on paper-and-pencil measures, classroom or group observations, focus groups, and interviews with key stakeholders, including students. Program materials are reviewed and, through various methods, teachers describe their teaching techniques and strategies for engaging children and youth. None of these methods captures or evaluates the experiences of civic and political engagement in real time.

For both school-based and nonformal civic engagement interventions, valuable insights can be gleaned from observing interactions in real time, and using interactive online diaries and other twenty-first century information technology tools to track teacher or staff decision making and insights in context as they happen. Intensive, online diaries also help document a program's evolution (Cohen, Leviton, Isaacson, Tallia, & Crabtree, 2006). Other suggestions for creative data collection approaches for citizenship education and engagement projects include incorporating mini pre-post knowledge self-assessments into activities, having student focus groups discuss the program's development and give feedback about the measures, using Post-it sticky note mini surveys after each activity, and having students engage in a talk-aloud exercise, reporting what they are doing, seeing, and feeling, while engaged in an activity (Hudley, 2006).

CONCLUSIONS

The purpose of the previous sections was to introduce some ideas and provide references across a range of issues pertinent to evaluations of civic education and citizenship or political engagement programs. They illustrate that evaluation expertise must be combined with content expertise to optimize evaluations. By combining content and evaluation expertise, Preskill and

Donaldson (2008) contend that a transdisciplinary field will result, with the capacity to contribute to basic understanding and program development in citizenship education and engagement.

The final section of the chapter discusses ways to build evaluation capacity and work with evaluators to strengthen citizenship education and civic or political engagement program theories and practices.

BUILDING EVALUATION CAPACITY

Evaluation capacity building (ECB) is defined as intentional efforts to create and sustain specific organizational procedures and processes involved in the collection of data. This includes management information systems that can make high-quality evaluation routine, continuous, and useful (Stockdill, Baizerman, & Campton, 2002). In ECB, the evaluator educates administrators, teachers, and/or community agency and youth organization staff in evaluation techniques and helps the school, school district, state, or organization to put in place the necessary data collection and information systems. The evaluator also partners with as well as teaches the intervention project director and staff to take on the responsibilities of evaluation. Preskill and Russ-Eft (2004) produced a volume for trainers of ECB that offers 13 different approaches including both quantitative and qualitative designs.

Building evaluation capacity involves enhancing cultural awareness, sensitivity, and competence within an organization to be able to develop a program theory and plan with focused questions, identify stakeholders with whom to collaborate, and finally to develop an evaluation model and design. In addition, evaluators work with stakeholders so they become familiar with and can use the ideas of validity and reliability, credibility, and usefulness. School or organizational personnel learn data collection procedures and basic data analytic techniques appropriate for the kind of data and information their organization systematically and routinely collects. Lastly, evaluators teach school or organizational staff how to produce clearly written reports that address the research questions chosen for that round of evaluation.

Miller, Kobayashi, and Noble (2006) contrast building evaluation capacity within schools and community organizations with *insourcing*, a mixture of an internally conducted and an external evaluation. The goal of insourcing is to optimize the partnership between evaluators and program staff by having evaluators provide clear structures and means to carry out the evaluation while the program staff agree to learn enough about evaluation research to appreciate and understand its main ideas and to make a commitment to promote and sustain it, which often includes seeking funding. They give an example of how *Youth Outcome Network* used insourcing. This network keeps evaluation costs relatively low by having schools, districts, or youth organizations share data collection protocols, outcome toolkits, and report templates. The network makes comparative information available from its databases so that organizations can construct their own comparison groups.

Because evaluation is still relatively new in the field of citizenship education, school-based service learning, and out-of-school youth organizations, evaluators have real power and responsibilities regardless of the kind of evaluation undertaken. The choice of which evaluation theory and method to use for any particular civic education and engagement program is a double-edged sword. It can provide useful or distorted feedback to the program, fairly or unfairly evaluate its outcomes, help understand or cloud the processes by which it is effective or ineffective. Evaluators can help practitioners articulate their goals and program theories, advise about how to create and sustain an evaluative environment, and assess reasonable short- and longer-term outcomes, impact, and effectiveness. Guidelines for assessing evaluator competencies and ideas for professional development (Braverman & Arnold, 2008; Ghere, King, Stevahn, & Minnema, 2006; Monroe et al., 2005) signal that the field is flourishing and that standards are developing that can be used to hold evaluators accountable. It will benefit theorists, practitioners, and policy-makers in citizenship education and political or civic engagement to continue to develop their understanding of the ways in which evaluation research can make substantive contributions to their fields.

CHAPTER SUMMARY

Citizenship is multifaceted and changes meaning across different generations; thus theories and practices of citizenship education also must be dynamic, reflecting changes in attitude, content, strategies, and processes of delivery, as well as in their often tacit value, learning, and developmental assumptions. Evaluation theories should align with program value assumptions, theories, and goals. This is best accomplished when evaluators themselves are also experts in citizenship education—that is, when they are able to practice evaluation as a transdisciplinary science.

More specifically, evaluators must be aware of how their value assumptions align with those of an intervention. They must understand and develop program theories that delineate the mechanisms and processes through which a program effects change and impacts outcomes. They must be able to understand and use the changing definitions of citizenship and of civic and political engagement when developing program theories with intervention partners and creating new measures or adapting existing ones. Evaluators also need to have a good background in one or more basic areas of relevant research such as human development, applied psychology, social psychology, or educational research.

The spaces for civic engagement are expanding into after-school, youth-organized activities; religious institutions; and neighborhoods; as well as expanding within schools, especially in defining service learning as civic or political engagement rather than personal helping. With the upsurge in service learning and out-of-school youth programs that promote community involvement and civic and political awareness, evaluations should be designed to examine the influence of multiple levels of settings and multiple contexts. Evaluation research should also be informed by all stakeholders and assess an intervention's influence on them; this especially includes teachers but also administrators, and mentors as well as students, youth leaders, youth peers, and others. Evaluations should use multiple or mixed methods and triangulate results from different kinds of measures to optimize validity and credibility.

Citizenship education evaluation has the potential to become a truly transdisciplinary science. It need not be limited to analyzing the effectiveness of civics and citizenship engagement programs, but can do so in ways that also inform what should be included in them and what mechanisms and processes must be present for these programs to be successful. Cumulative knowledge from evaluations should help to define sustainable infrastructures and alert stakeholders to power differentials and barriers that compromise a program's implementation at the local, state, or national level.

Since policy-makers and funders as well as the public expect that educational and social service programs will be evaluated, it is important for civic education and engagement practitioners and evaluators to work together. They can develop plans for building evaluation capacity within interventions and institutions or train staff. Good arguments from both quantitative and qualitative orientations can be made for increasing the knowledge and understanding of all stakeholders, but especially for those teaching and for those receiving service as well as those giving service. Additionally, it is critical that educational and organizational leaders be informed and committed to building basic evaluation capacity or a culture that appreciates and values evaluation.

Implementation issues and dosage effects of citizenship education with its range of curricula and activities pose a real challenge. Likewise, measurement remains an issue in this field, compounded by the conflation of fine-grained theoretical distinctions of constructs with the use of much less well-differentiated and often short measures, whether given in surveys, as observational ratings, or incorporated into qualitative coding schemes.

Evaluations should pay more attention to time lines and sequences of study in formative and implementation evaluations in order to provide the most useful feedback to practitioners about gaps between curricular content and civic experiential learning opportunities, about the levels of knowledge and skills of teachers, mentors, and guides, and about the developmental levels, knowledge base, and capacities of children, adolescents, and youth. Sensitivity to timing and sequence should also inform modeling of outcomes and interpretations of qualitative interviews and observations. While some evaluations have focused on the role of various components, thus far, none has attempted to model skill learning in real time. Since democratic participatory skills as well as knowledge are tied with the desired outcomes of future voting, civic involvement, volunteering, and sustained political interest, it seems important to understand how long it takes for children and adolescents to learn such skills and for practitioners to learn about the conditions and settings that optimize student learning and development.

Whether short or longer term, student outcomes should include: acquiring knowledge about citizenship and democracy; developing the interest to attend to civic and political matters; cultivating civic and political attitudes; sustaining a sense of being politically and civically competent and efficacious; and having high-level democratic, deliberative, problem-solving, and leadership skills that express their cognitive, moral reasoning and social emotional competencies. Equally important, teacher outcomes should include some assessment of their cognitive, moral, and social competencies as well as their levels of expertise as subject teachers and as citizenship educators. Finally, the roles of schools and other organizations, including their climate and culture, relationships between teachers or facilitators and children or youth, child or youth peer relationships, and the civic and political learning and engagement activities themselves should be examined in depth to aid in understanding the processes and mechanisms that are involved in young people becoming informed and active citizens.

REFERENCES

Althof, W., & Berkowitz, M. (2006). Moral education and character education: Their relationship and roles in citizen education. *Journal of Moral Education, 35(4)*, 495–518.

Alviar-Martin, T., Usher, E. L., Randall, J., & Engelhard, G. (2008). Teaching civic topics in four societies: Examining national context and teacher confidence. *The Journal of Educational Research, 101(3)*, 177–187.

Andolina, M., Jenkins, K., Keeter, S., & Zukin, C. (2002). Searching for the meaning of youth civic engagement: Notes from the field. *Applied Developmental Science, 6, 4*, 189–195.

Baldi, S., Perie, M., Skidmore, D., Greenberg, E., & Hahn, C. (2001). *What democracy means to ninth-graders: U.S. results from the International IEA Civic Education Study.* Washington, DC: National Center for Educational Statistics, U.S. Department of Education.

Blumler, J., & Gurevitch, M. (2001). The new media and our political communication discontents: Democratizing cyberspace. *Information Communication and Society, 4, 1,* 1–13.

Bond, T., & Fox, C. (2007). *Applying the Rasch model: Fundamental measurement in the human sciences.* Mahwah, NJ: Lawrence Erlbaum Associates, Inc.

Boyte, H. (2003). Civic education and the new American patriotism post-9/11. *Cambridge Journal of Education, 33, 1,* 85–100.

Branson, M.S. (in preparation). Civic education and prosocial behavior. In A. Higgins-D'Alessandro, M. Corrigan, & P. M. Brown (Eds.), *Prosocial education: The second side of the educational coin.*

Braverman, M. T., & Arnold, M. E. (2008). An evaluator's balancing act: Making decisions about methodological rigor. *New Directions for Evaluation, 120,* 71–86.

Bush, V. (1945). *Science, the endless frontier.* A report to the president by Vannevar Bush, director of the Office of Scientific Research and Development. Washington, DC: U.S. Government Printing Office.

Butin, D. (2003). Of what use is it? Multiple conceptualizations of service learning within education. *Teachers College Record, 105(9),* 1674–1692.

Christensen, L., Nielsen, J. E., Rogers, C. M., & Volkov, B. (2005). Creative data collection in nonformal settings. *New Directions for Evaluation, 108,* 73–80.

Clavijo, K., Fleming, M. L., Hoermann, E. F., Toal, S. A., & Johnson, K. (2005). Evaluation use in nonformal education settings. *New Directions for Evaluation, 108,* 57–72.

Cohen, D. J., Leviton, L. C., Isaacson, N., Tallia, A. F., & Crabtree, B. F. (2006). Online diaries for qualitative evaluation: Gaining real-time insights. *American Journal of Evaluation, 27, 2,* 163–184.

Cohen, J. (2006). Social, emotional, ethical, and academic education: Creating a climate for learning, participation in democracy, and well-being. *Harvard Educational Review, 76, 2,* 201–237.

Coleman, R., Lieber, P., Mendelson, A. L., & Kurpius, D. D. (2008). Public life and the Internet: If you build a better website, will citizens become engaged? *New Media & Society, 10,* 179–201.

Donaldson, S., Gooler, L., & Scriven, M. (2002). Strategies for managing evaluation anxiety: Toward a psychology of program evaluation. *American Journal of Evaluation, 23(3),* 261–273.

Dudley, R., & Gitelson, A. (2002). Political literacy, civic education, and civic engagement: A return to political socialization? *Applied Developmental Science, 6(4),* 175–182.

Flanagan, C., Jonsson, B., Botcheva, L., Csapo, B., Bowes, J., Macek, P., Averina, I., & Sheblanova, E. (1999). In M. Yates & J. Youniss (Eds.), *Adolescents and the "social contract": Developmental roots of citizenship in seven countries.* New York: Cambridge University Press, 135–155.

Flanagan, C., Syvertsen, A., Gill, S., Gallay, L., & Cumsille, P. (2009). Ethnic awareness, prejudice, and civic commitments in four ethnic groups of American adolescents. *Journal of Youth and Adolescence, 38,* 500–518.

Flanagan, C. A., Cumsille, P., Gill, S., & Gallay, L. (2007). School and community climates and civic commitments: Patterns of ethnic minority and majority students. *Journal of Educational Psychology, 99(2),* 421–431.

Flanagan, C. A., Syvertsen, A. K., & Stout, M. D. (2007). *Civic measurement models: Tapping adolescents' civic engagement* (CIRCLE Working Paper 55). Medford, MA: CIRCLE.

Ghere, G., King, J. A., Stevahn, L., & Minnema, J. (2006). A professional development unit for reflecting on program evaluator competencies. *American Journal of Evaluation, 27, 1,* 108–123.

Gonzales, M., Riedel, E., Avery, P., & Sullivan, J. (2001). Rights and obligations in civic education: A content analysis of the National Standards for Civics and Government. *Theory and Research in Social Education, 29(1),* 109–128.

Hart, S. (2006). Breaking literacy boundaries through critical service-learning: Education for the silenced and marginalized. *Mentoring & Tutoring, 14(1),* 17–32.

Hart, D., Atkins, R., Markey, P., & Youniss, J. (2004). Youth bulges in communities: The effects of age structure on adolescent civic knowledge and participation. *Psychological Science, 15(9),* 591–597.

Hart, D., Atkins, R., & Matsuba, M. K. (2008). The association of neighborhood poverty with personality change in childhood. *Journal of Personality and Social Psychology, 94(6),* 1048–1061.

Hart, D., Donnelly, T. M., Youniss, J., & Atkins, R. (2007). High school community service as a predictor of adult voting and volunteering. *American Educational Research Journal, 44,* 197–218.

Higgins-D'Alessandro, A., Choe, J., Guo, P., & Elgendy, S. (2009, April 15). *School culture and student academic behavior as mediating the effects of a school reform intervention on student attitudes and teacher practices: Evaluation of PCEP project.* Paper presented at the annual conference of the American Educational Research Association, Denver, CO.

Higgins-D'Alessandro, A., & Guo, P. (2009, July 2–4). *School culture: Can it be adequately operationalized as a school level variable?* Paper presented at the annual conference of the Association for Moral Education, Utrecht, Netherlands.

Hudley, C. (2006). Who is watching the watchers? Challenge of observing peer interactions on elementary school playgrounds. *New Directions for Evaluation, 110,* 73–86.

Jacobs, F. (2003). Child and family program evaluation: Learning to enjoy complexity. *Applied Developmental Science, 7(2),* 62–75.

Junn, J. (1999). Participation in liberal democracy: The political assimilation of immigrants and ethnic minorities in the United States. *American Behavioral Scientist, 42(9),* 1417–1438.

Joint Committee on Standards for Educational Evaluation (1994). *The Program Evaluation Standards* (2nd ed.). Newbury Park, CA: Sage Publications.

Kahne, J., & Middaugh, E. (2008, February). *Democracy for some: The civic opportunity gap in high school* (CIRCLE Working Paper 59). Medford, MA: CIRCLE.

Kahne, J., & Sporte, S. (2008). Developing citizens: The impact of civic learning opportunities on students' commitment to civic participation. *American Educational Research Journal, 45,* 738–766.

Kane, M. T. (2006). Validation. In R. L. Brennan (Ed.), *Educational measurement* (4th ed., pp. 17–64). Westport, CT: Praeger.

Larson, R., & Hansen, D. (2005). The development of strategic thinking: Learning to impact human systems in a youth activism program. *Human Development, 48,* 327–349.

Lee, S., Olszewski-Kubilius, P., Donahue, R., & Weimholt, K. (2007). The effects of a service-learning program on the development of civic attitudes and behaviors among academically talented adolescents. *Journal for the Education of the Gifted, 31(2),* 165–197.

Lehtonen, M. (2006). Deliberative democracy, participation, and OECD peer reviews of environmental policies. *American Journal of Evaluation, 27(2),* 185–200.

Lochman, J. E., Boxmeyer, C., Powell, N., Roth, D. L., & Windle, M. (2006). Masked intervention effects: Analytic methods for addressing low dosage interventions. *New Directions for Evaluation, 110,* 19–32.

Lutkus, A., Weiss, A., Campbell, J., Mazzeo, J., & Lazer, S. (1999). *NAEP 1998 Civics Report Card for the Nation.* Washington DC: U.S. Department of Education.

McDevitt, M., & Chaffee, S. (2000). Closing gaps in political communication and knowledge: Effects of a school intervention. *Communication Research, 27,* 259–292.

McDevitt, M., & Kiousis, S. (2004). *Education for deliberative democracy: The long-term influence of Kids Voting USA* (CIRCLE Working Paper 22). Medford, MA. CIRCLE

McDevitt, M., & Kiousis, S. (2006). Deliberative learning: An evaluative approach to interactive civic education. *Communication Education, 55(3),* 247–264.

Miller, T. I., Kobayashi, M. M., & Noble, P. M. (2006). Insourcing, not capacity building, a better model. *American Journal of Evaluation, 27, 1,* 83–94.

Molas-Gallart, J., & Davies, A. (2006). Toward theory-led evaluation: The experience of European science, technology, and innovation polices. *American Journal of Evaluation, 27(1),* 64–82.

Monroe, M. C., Fleming, M. L., Bowman, R. A., Zimmer, J. F., Marcinkowski, T., Washburn, J., & Mitchell, N. J. (2005). Evaluators as educators: Articulating program theory and building evaluation capacity. *New Directions for Evaluation, 108,* 57–72.

Morgan, W., & Streb, M. (2001). Building citizenship: How student voice in service-learning develops civic values. *Social Science Quarterly, 82,* 154–169.

Mowbray, C., Lewandowski, L., Holter, M., & Bybee, D. (2006). The clubhouse as an empowering setting. *Health & Social Work, 31(3),* 167–179.

Murphy, T. (2004). Deliberative civic education and civil society: A consideration of ideals and actualities in democracy and communication education. *Communication Education, 53(1),* 74–91.

Natasi, B. M., & Hitchcock, J. (2009). Challenges of evaluating multilevel interventions. *American Journal of Community Psychology, 43,* 360–376.

Niemi, R. G., & Junn, J. (1998). *Civic education: What makes students learn.* New Haven, CT: Yale University Press.

Norland, E., & Somers, C. (2005, Winter). Evaluating nonformal education programs and settings. *New Directions for Evaluation, 108.*

Papacharissi, Z. (2004). Democracy online: Civility, politeness, and the democratic potential of online political discussion groups. *New Media & Society, 6(2),* 259–283.

Pasek, J., Feldman, L., Romer, D., & Jamieson, K. (2008). Schools as incubators of democratic participation: Building long-term political efficacy with civic education. *Applied Developmental Science, 12(2)*, 26–37.

Patton, M. (2002). Two decades of developments in qualitative inquiry. *Qualitative Social Work, 1(3)*, 261–283.

Power, F. C., Higgins, A., & Kohlberg, L. (1989). *Lawrence Kohlberg's approach to moral education*. New York: Columbia University Press.

Power, F. C., & Higgins-D'Alessandro, A. (2008). The Just Community approach to moral education and the moral atmosphere of the school. In L. P. Nucci & D. Narvaez (Eds.), *Handbook of moral and character education* (pp. 230–247). New York: Routledge.

Preskill, H., & Donaldson, S. (2008). Improving the evidence base for career development programs: Making use of the evaluation profession and positive psychology movement. *Advances in Developing Human Resources, 10*, 104–121.

Preskill, H., & Russ-Eft, D. (2004). *Building evaluation capacity: 72 activities for teaching and training*. Thousand Oaks, CA: Sage Publications.

Print, M., & Coleman, D. (2003). Towards understanding of social capital and citizenship education. *Cambridge Journal of Education, 33(1)*, 123–149.

Rossi, P., & Freeman, H. (1993). *Evaluation: A systematic approach* (5th ed.). Newbury Park, CA: Sage Publications.

Rossi, P., & Wright, J. (1984). Evaluation research: An assessment. *Annual Review of Sociology, 10*, 331–352.

Rossi, P. H., Lipsey, M. W., & Freeman, H. E. (2004). *Evaluation: A systematic approach* (7th ed.). Thousand Oaks, CA: Sage Publications.

Shadish, W. R., & Cook, T. D. (2009). The renaissance of field experimentation in evaluating interventions. *Annual Review of Psychology, 60*, 607–629.

Shah, D., Cho, J., Eveland, W., & Kwak, N. (2005). Information and expression in a digital age: Modeling Internet effects on civic participation. *Communication Research, 32(5)*, 531–565.

Sherrod, L., Flanagan, C., & Youniss, J. (2002). Dimensions of citizenship and opportunities for youth development: The what, why, when, where, and who of citizenship development. *Applied Developmental Science, 6(4)*, 264–272.

Sridharan, S., Campbell, B., & Zinzow, H. (2006). Developing a stakeholder-driven anticipated timeline of impact for evaluation of social programs. *American Journal of Evaluation, 27(2)*, 148–162.

Stern, D. (2009). Expanding policy options for educating teenagers. *The Future of Children, America's High Schools, 19(1)*, 211–239.

Stockdill, S. H., Bazerman, M., & Campton, D. W. (2002) Toward a definition of the ECB process: A conversation with the ECB literature. *New Directions for Evaluation, 93*, 7–25.

Torney-Purta, J. (1998). Evaluating programs designed to teach international content and skills. *International Negotiation, 3*, 77–99.

Torney-Purta, J. (2002). The school's role in developing civic engagement: A study of adolescents in twenty-eight countries. *Applied Developmental Science, 6(4)*, 203–212.

Torney-Purta, J., Amadeo, J., & Richardson, W. (2007). Civic service among youth in Chile, Denmark, England and the United States: A psychological perspective. In A. McBride & M. Sherraden (Eds.), *Civic service worldwide: Impact and inquiries* (pp. 95–132). Armonk, NY: M. E. Sharpe.

Torney-Purta, J., Barber, C., & Wilkenfeld, B. (2007). Latino adolescents' civic development in the United States: Research results from the IEA Civic Education Study. *Journal of Youth and Adolescence, 36*, 111–125.

Torney-Purta, J., Lehmann, R., Oswald, H., & Schulz, W. (2001) *Citizenship and education in twenty-eight countries: Civic knowledge and engagement at age fourteen.* Amsterdam: IEA. Retrieved from http://www.terpconnect.umd.edu/~iea

Torney-Purta, J., & Wilkenfeld, B. (2009). *Paths to 21st century competencies through civic education classrooms: An analysis of survey results from ninth graders.* Chicago, IL: American Bar Association Division for Public Education. Retrieved from http://www.civicyouth.org

Torney-Purta, J., Wilkenfeld, B., & Barber, C. (2008). How adolescents in 27 countries understand, support and practice human rights. *Journal of Social Issues, 64(4)*, 857–880.

U.S. Department of Education (2007). *Mobilizing for evidence-based character education.* Ed Pubs. Education Publications Center, U.S. Department of Education, P.O. Box 1398, Jessup, MD, or edpubs@inet.ed.gov

Vozzola, E. C., Higgins-D'Alessandro, A., Rosen, J., & Horan, J. (2009). The Scarsdale Alternative School: Perspectives of alumni 5 to 25 years later on their Just Community experiences. Paper presented at the annual conference of the Association for Moral Education. Utrecht, The Netherlands, July 2.

Watts, R., Williams, N., & Jagers, R. (2003). Sociopolitical development. *American Journal of Community Psychology, 31(1–2)*, 185–194.

Watts, R. J., Armstrong, M., Cartman, O., & Guessous, D. (2008). *Findings on a theory of youth sociopolitical development*. Paper presented at the Annual Meeting of the American Educational Research Association, New York.

West, S. G. (2009). Alternatives to randomized experiments. *Current Directions in Psychological Science, 18(5)*, 299–304.

Westheimer, J., & Kahne, J. (2000, January 26). Service learning required—But what exactly do students learn? *Education Week, 42*.

Westheimer, J., & Kahne, J. (2004). What kind of citizen? The politics of educating for democracy. *American Educational Research Journal, 41(2)*, 237–269.

Wilkenfeld, B. (2009). *Does context matter? How the family, peer group, school, and neighborhood contexts relate to adolescents' civic engagement.* (CIRCLE Working Paper, No. 64). Medford, MA: CIRCLE. Retrieved from http;//www.civicyouth.org

Wiltz, L. K. (2005). I need a bigger suitcase: The evaluator role in nonformal education. *New Directions for Evaluation, 108*, 13–28.

Youniss, J., McLellan, J., & Yates, M. (1997). What we know about engendering civic identity. *American Behavioral Scientist, 40(5)*, 620–631.

CHAPTER 22

Conceptualizing and Evaluating the Complexities of Youth Civic Engagement

CHARMAGNE CAMPBELL-PATTON
World Savvy

MICHAEL QUINN PATTON
Utilization-Focused Evaluation

THE WORLD BANK'S *World Development Report 2007: Development and the Next Generation* was the first WDR to focus entirely on youth. This report identified youth civic service as a "promising but unproven" intervention for positive youth development worldwide (p. 184). The document generated substantial interest among youth development and civic engagement professionals about how to move youth service from "promising but unproven" to the *proven successful* category. *Proven* approaches can attract both substantial resources and political support. In May 2008, the not-for-profit organization *Innovations in Civic Participation* partnered with the Children and Youth unit of The World Bank to host a conference on the question of what evidence would be needed to prove the effectiveness of youth civic engagement programs.

Presentations by World Bank staff at that conference made it clear that the standard of evidence for proof of success would be randomized controlled trials (RCTs). The only publication on evaluation available from the Children and Youth unit on "Evaluating Youth Interventions" (2007) at that time insisted on randomized controlled trials. That guidance publication highlighted the conclusion of the World Development Report: "... *Few solid evaluations of youth programs in developing countries unambiguously identify the causality from policy to program to effect* ... many [youth] programs fall into the promising but unproven camp" (p. 2; emphasis in the original).

This means that the criterion for designation as "proven successful" requires "unambiguous" causal attribution. How does one establish unambiguous causal attribution? The dominant answer from The World Bank was through randomized controlled trials. For example, economist Gertler (2007), an economist at the University of California, Berkeley, conducted a World Bank evaluation workshop on impact evaluation for youth programs that focused on randomized controlled trials as the evidentiary gold standard, a perspective consistent with a wider emphasis on evidence-based policy both domestically and internationally (Evaluation Gap Working Group, 2006; Boruch, 2007; Julnes & Rog, 2007; What Works Clearinghouse, 2006).

This chapter will argue that the RCT "gold standard" is not only inappropriate for evaluating many youth civic engagement initiatives, but can do harm. This is especially the case for complex youth civic engagement initiatives that are based on principles of youth ownership, local adaptation, and cultural responsiveness. This chapter will examine briefly the limitations of RCTs, particularly in the case of youth civic engagement, and offer evaluation alternatives based on complexity science and on an evaluation approach that is especially appropriate for youth civic engagement programs: developmental evaluation. The chapter will also offer examples of how developmental evaluation can be used to evaluate the impact of youth civic engagement initiatives, drawing on several real-world examples.

THE GOLD STANDARD DEBATE

The question of what constitutes *the methodological "gold standard"* remains contested for programs of all kinds, including evaluation of youth engagement programs. The standards and guiding principles of the evaluation profession manifest a consensus that evaluators need to know and use a variety of methods in order to be responsive to the nuances of particular evaluation questions and the idiosyncrasies of specific stakeholder needs (Joint Committee, 1994; AEA Task Force, 1995). There is some contradiction in the assertion that one question is more important than others (the causal attribution question) and one design is superior to all other designs in answering that question (randomized controlled trials). This debate is not merely an academic argument among evaluation methodologists. Evaluation practitioners are deeply affected, as are users of evaluation—policy-makers, program staff, managers, and funders.

In 2003, when the U.S. Department of Education's Institute of Education Sciences first published criteria making RCTs the gold standard for educational evidence of impact, the American Evaluation Association (AEA) took the unprecedented step of submitting a formal statement of concern opposing such a narrow and rigid view of evaluation. In particular the elected leadership of AEA opposed designating randomized controlled trials as the methodological gold standard. The AEA position argued that making RCTs the gold standard "manifests fundamental misunderstandings about first, the types of studies capable of determining causality, second, the methods capable of achieving scientific rigor, and third, the types of studies that support policy and program decisions" (2003, p. 1).

In 2007, the European Evaluation Society (EES) adopted a statement on "the importance of a methodologically diverse approach to impact evaluation—specifically with respect to development aid and development interventions." As context, the EES noted that this statement was prepared in response to strong pressure from some interests advocating for "scientific" and "rigorous" impact of development aid, where this is defined as primarily RCTs. This debate has the potential to influence the future direction of evaluation—not only with respect to international development programs but potentially in other areas such as youth civic engagement as well. EES was concerned about the fact that one perspective on evaluation was being strongly advocated:

> [That the] best or only rigorous and scientific way of doing so is through randomised controlled trials (RCTs). In contrast, the EES supports multi-method approaches to IE [impact evaluation] and does not consider any single method such as RCTs as first choice or as the "gold standard." (EES, 2007, p. 1)

In 2007, a Network of Networks on Impact Evaluation (NONIE) was established by international evaluation offices representing more than 100 United Nations, World Bank, and other development organizations, plus representatives from developing countries and various regional and global organizations. That group drafted a document providing guidance for conducting impact evaluations in developing countries that emphasizes the importance of methodological diversity and appropriateness in support of rigor, and warned against designating any single design as a gold standard.

Reinforcing these concerns, in 2008 the World Bank Children and Youth Unit and Innovations in Civic Participation (ICP) co-hosted a meeting that brought together an international group of youth service practitioners, policy-makers, and evaluation experts to consider standards of evidence for impact evaluations of youth service programs. After three days of thoughtful discussion, the group concluded:

> There is not one universal way to conduct impact evaluations. With varying benefits and challenges, experimental and quasi-experimental designs all provide techniques for evaluating the impact of an intervention. Evaluations must be designed individually and it is important to take into account the context, resources, and program design in determining the combination of evaluation approaches to be used. (World Bank & ICP, 2009, iii)

What has emerged from the debate is a recommendation of an alternative evaluation gold standard: *methodological appropriateness*. Methodological appropriateness means matching the evaluation design to the evaluation situation, taking into account the priority questions and needs of primary intended users, the costs and benefits of alternative designs, the decisions that are to be made, the level of evidence necessary to support those decisions, ethical considerations, and utility. No design should be lauded as a "gold standard" without regard to context and situation. For an extended discussion of the "gold standard" debate in evaluation, including the implications of methodological appropriateness as an alternative, see Patton (2008, Chap. 12).

In the remainder of this chapter, we examine the implications of methodological appropriateness as *the standard* for evaluating youth civic engagement initiatives and apply that standard in a real-world example.

EVALUABILITY ASSESSMENT FOR YOUTH CIVIC ENGAGEMENT INITIATIVES

While the "gold standard" debate appears to be about methods, it is actually about much more than methods. It is about how initiatives, interventions, and programs are conceptualized. This is sometimes called the *IT* question in evaluation. When it is said that something works or doesn't work, what is the *IT* that works or doesn't work? Answering this question involves conceptualizing *the theory of change* embodied in a youth civic engagement initiative or program. The idea that evaluators should be involved in conceptualizing and testing theories of change emerged in the 1970s as part of a more general concern about assessing a program's *readiness for evaluation*. The notion was basically this: Before undertaking an evaluation, the program should be clearly conceptualized as some identifiable set of activities that are expected to lead to some identifiable outcomes. The linkage between those activities and outcomes should be both logical and testable. This process is sometimes called evaluability assessment: "Evaluability assessment is a systematic process for describing the structure of a program and for analyzing the plausibility and feasibility of achieving objectives; their suitability for in-depth evaluation; and their acceptance to program managers, policymakers, and program operators" (Smith, 2005).

One primary purpose of an evaluability assessment for youth civic engagement programs is usually the delineation of a program's theory. This means specifying the underlying logic (cause and effect relationships) of the program, including what resources and activities are expected to produce what results. What resources will be available for working with young people? What activities will participating youth undertake? What will be the outcomes for the young people as well as others in the community with whom they may engage? An evaluability assessment is also expected to gather various stakeholders' perspectives on the program theory and assess their interest in evaluation. What do the young people think? How do program staff, parents, teachers, community members, policy-makers, and funders understand and perceive the youth civic engagement program? Also assessed is the program's capacity to undertake an evaluation, including staff knowledge of evaluation and availability of funds to support evaluation. Finally, an evaluability assessment should explore program readiness for rigorous evaluation, including whether the program's theory is sufficiently well conceptualized and measures of outcomes adequately validated to permit a meaningful summative evaluation.

The knowledge base for the program would also be made explicit, for example, the extent to which a program is grounded in research and knowledge about *the craft of youth civic engagement* (Roholt, Hildreth & Baizerman, 2008). Consider, for example, four different approaches to youth civic engagement: civic education, service learning, social organizing, and youth development. Civic education engages youth to increase their knowledge about society with the hope that this will extend to thoughtful participation. Service learning aims to develop youth's sense of social responsibility. Social organizing engages young people in actual advocacy for social change. Youth development approaches aim to build the competence, confidence, character, and connections of young people. These different approaches emphasize different outcomes and, therefore, invite different evaluation questions (Roholt, Hildreth & Baizerman, 2008, p. 74).

Youth civic engagement activities vary widely in their activities and intended outcomes, so it is important that these programs state their objectives clearly, preferably in the format of a theory of change, in order to provide a framework for evaluators to determine the extent to which the program activities are meeting their objectives. As an example, we can look at two youth civic engagement programs that undertake a similar activity with different objectives. Both *Un Techo Para Mi Pais* in Chile and *YouthBuild* in the United States engage youth in the activity of building homes in high-need communities. Through *Un Techo Para Mi Pais*, the dual program objectives are to alleviate poverty in the communities served and to expand the social awareness of Latin American youth by offering volunteer opportunities working to improve the lives and livelihoods of the poor. Through the *YouthBuild* program, a similar activity (building houses) is intended to "unleash the potential of unemployed youth to transform their lives" and "build tangible community assets to improve local neighborhoods." Thus rather than raising awareness about poverty among volunteers, *YouthBuild* focuses on helping volunteers out of poverty through skill development and experience.

While the activities youth are engaged in may be similar in these two programs, the theories of change are quite different, as are the intended outcomes. On the one hand, *Un Techo Para Mi Pais* is focusing on the theory that youth from privileged backgrounds will gain a better understanding of poverty and development issues by volunteering in these communities, and the communities will benefit from their actions. On the other hand, *YouthBuild* is focused on empowering members within impoverished communities to become engaged in improving their communities, through which they gain valuable skills for future employment.

An evaluability assessment would examine what research and knowledge the program designers used to inform their program models. *Un Techo Para Mi Pais* brings relatively privileged youth into poor communities to perform service, while *YouthBuild* provides opportunities for unemployed or disadvantaged youth to perform service in their own or other high-need communities. What literature and research informs these two approaches? In what ways do these two programs apply shared values and fundamental principles in the field of youth civic engagement? An evaluator, working with program designers, would examine the program's theory of change and help program managers to design a program model that can be evaluated based on the program's theory of change. It is important that all stakeholders involved in the design, implementation, and evaluation of each program understand the program's underlying theory of change.

In effect, evaluability assessment puts evaluators in the business of facilitating an explicit statement of the design of the program in order for it to be evaluated. For already existing programs, this often means redesigning the program because the original program model is insufficiently specified to be evaluated. As evaluators become involved in working with program people to more clearly specify the program's model (or theory), it frequently becomes clear that evaluation should be an *up-front activity*, not just a back-end activity. That is, traditional planning models laid out some series of steps in which planning comes first, then implementation of the program, and then evaluation, making evaluation something done at the end. But to get a program plan or design that could actually be evaluated means involving evaluators—and evaluative thinking—from the beginning. Evaluative thinking, then, becomes part of the program design process including conceptualizing the program's theory of change. In other words, how will what the program does lead to the desired results?

What is especially important about this for our purposes is that the very process of conceptualizing the program's theory of change can have an impact on how the program is implemented, understood, talked about, and *improved*. This means that evaluators have first to be astute at conceptualizing program and policy theories of change and, second, skilled at working with program people, policy-makers, and funders to facilitate their articulation of their implicit theories of change.

ALTERNATIVE YOUTH CIVIC ENGAGEMENT THEORIES OF CHANGE

Let us consider two opposing theories of development and change. The first approach is a top-down model that conceptualizes the challenge of development as disseminating around the world proven and standardized "best practices." Proven best practices are those that have been validated by randomized controlled trials. This approach to change draws on pharmaceutical and agricultural metaphors, conceptualizing effective social interventions to be the equivalent of vaccinations or drugs in the health arena, or new varieties of plants in the agricultural arena. This is the framework of change that undergirds the World Development Report that distinguishes "promising but unproven practices" from "proven practices" and is in search of the latter for worldwide dissemination.

The second approach detailed above, in contrast, conceptualizes social change as a bottom-up process of adaptation in which an idea and intervention like a civic engagement program must be adapted and attuned to local culture, priority concerns, history, capacity, and politics. The second approach eschews standardized practices and universal or decontextualized "best practices." Instead, guided by shared values and fundamental principles, initiatives are customized collaboratively with local partners to create an approach that is appropriate to the local setting and sensitive to local needs, concerns, priorities, and hopes. The second approach is driven by adaptation and innovation on the ground.

Given the participatory nature of youth civic engagement programs, practitioners tend to prefer this second approach because it necessitates that the programs be designed and adapted with regard to local circumstances. While the program may be informed by similar programs in other locations, no single youth civic engagement program can be implemented exactly the same in two different locations. This is particularly true in the context of developing countries, where differences between communities, power structures, and resources (personal as well as financial) are likely to be even more significant than in the developed world.

For example, Student Partnerships Worldwide (SPW) is a youth service organization that works to place young people at the forefront of development. SPW mobilizes young people by recruiting and training 18- to 28-year-olds to serve as Volunteer Peer Educators, who live full-time in rural communities for 6 to 12 months and lead health, environmental and education programs. SPW currently conducts programs in India, Nepal, Sierra Leone, South Africa, Tanzania, Uganda, Zambia, and Zimbabwe.

While the theory of change that informs the program model used in each of these countries is the same, each program is adapted in partnership with local organizations to ensure that the program is appropriate to the local setting and sensitive to local needs, concerns, and priorities. Were SPW to implement exactly the same program in each location, it is unlikely that they would achieve the same level of success because they would not be able to target their work to address local development issues or adapt their education program to take into account the local culture. This is particularly important for their reproductive health education program, given how sensitive this topic can be and how significantly sexual norms vary across Africa and South Asia. The implication of local program adaptation as an implementation strategy is that evaluations must also be adapted to fit the specific program context.

Moreover, the contrasting top-down and bottom-up approaches to change also involve fundamentally different evaluation designs. When change is conceptualized as top-down dissemination of best practices, RCTs are appropriate and the critical program implementation issues are standardization and fidelity. Typical evaluation questions include: How closely must implementation of a program in new localities follow an original blueprint? How much can implementation vary from the original ideal and still be considered the same program? These questions point to one of the central issues in implementation: *adaptation versus fidelity as a premier evaluation criterion of excellence.*

Consider the case of JUMP Math, an approach to teaching developed by mathematician John Mighton in 1998. Although originally conceived as an after-school supplement for inner-city students struggling with math, by 2003, JUMP programs ran in 12 Toronto inner-city elementary schools involving more than 1,600 students. It has evolved into a classroom curriculum with a complete package of materials intended to cover all elementary school grades. The program has been adopted in schools throughout North America and other regions of the world. With such widespread adoption, there will be variations in implementation. For teachers and students to realize the full benefits of the approach, those who are supporting dissemination of the program want *high-fidelity implementation*. This is true for any model that gets identified as a "best practice" or "evidence-based" model, or a model validated by a review process like the U.S. Department of Education *What Works Clearinghouse*. To evaluate fidelity is to assess adherence to the core blueprint specifications of how a model program is supposed to be implemented. Models that aim at widespread dissemination strive for careful replication, and the degree to which that replication is attained is a primary implementation evaluation question. In that sense, once the model has been proven, the evaluation design is relatively simple. Indeed, evaluation criteria and outcomes to be measured are part of the specification of best practices. Of course, before a program like JUMP becomes designated as a proven-practice curriculum, it goes through several years of development and formative evaluation. So, even when a top-down approach to change is taken, a new program should not start out being evaluated by a summative RCT design. The purpose of formative evaluation is to improve the program and work out implementation issues so that the program is ready for summative evaluation.

SIMPLE VERSUS COMPLEX MODELS

As we consider alternative approaches to change, it is useful to distinguish simple from complex approaches. A *simple* problem is how to bake a cake following a recipe. A recipe has clear cause and effect relationships and can be mastered through repetition and developing basic skills. The steps in baking a cake can be standardized and a recipe written with sufficient detail that even someone who has never baked has a high probability of success. Best practices for programs are like recipes in that they provide clear and high-fidelity directions since the processes that have worked to produce desired outcomes in the past are generalized as highly likely to work again in the future. Assembly lines in factories have this recipe quality as do standardized school curricula. Part of the attraction of the 12-Step program of Alcoholics Anonymous is its simple and standardized formulation.

In contrast, the adaptive management approach emphasizes and attends to the uncertainty and unpredictability of social change and innovation processes. Evaluating social innovations is a *complex problem* (Westley, Zimmerman, & Patton, 2006). Parenting is *complex*. There are no clear books or recipes to follow to guarantee success. Clearly, there are many experts in parenting and many expert books available to parents. But none can be treated like a cookbook for a cake. In the case of the cake, the intervention is mechanical. The flour does not suddenly decide to change its mind. On the other hand, children, as we all know, have minds of their own. Hence, our interventions are always in relationship with them. There are very few stand-alone parenting tasks. Almost always, the parents and child interact to create outcomes. *Any highly individualized program has elements of complexity.* The outcomes will vary for different participants based on their differing needs, experiences, situations, and desires.

Like parenting, youth civic engagement is a complex process that cannot be achieved by following a simple recipe. As noted previously, youth civic engagement programs can take a number of different forms and there is no agreement about a single model that will always and everywhere achieve the best results. There is general agreement, however, that each civic engagement program must take into account the specific needs, goals, and desires of the youth as well as the community.

Simple formulations invite linear logic models that link inputs to activities to outputs to outcomes like a formula or recipe; the evaluation measures and design can, likewise, be standardized. Complex problems and situations invite adaptation and individualization. Evaluation, in such cases, requires a design that is flexible, emergent, and dynamic, mirroring the emergent, dynamic, and uncertain nature of the intervention or innovation being evaluated. This is what is meant by the "gold standard" of methodological appropriateness: matching the evaluation design to the nature and characteristics of the intervention.

Zimmerman (2001) generated a matrix of two dimensions that helps distinguish simple, complicated, and complex situations. One dimension scales the degree of certainty in the cause-effect relationship. Programs and interventions are close to certainty when cause and effect linkages in the logic model are highly predictable, as in the relationship between immunization and preventing disease. At the other end of the certainty continuum are innovative programs where the outcomes are unpredictable; a youth civic engagement initiative, we suggest, would typically involve considerable uncertainty about the attainment of desired outcomes. Extrapolating from past experience is problematic because, like rearing a child, each community of youth is unique. This point deserves emphasis. The characteristics of a particular community, its unique cultural, social, economic, and political issues, and the youth and adults therein are core considerations in any civic engagement work. For example, service-learning programs can look a lot like charity when done in middle-class communities, whereas they can have a more political action component when the students in a poor community engage in service or even activism that promotes their own community's welfare. These differences affect both program designs and evaluations.

The vertical axis of the matrix captures the degree of agreement among various stakeholders about a program's needed inputs, goals, processes, outcomes, measures, and likely long-term impacts. High levels of agreement make situations fairly simple; high degrees of values conflict foment complexity.

- Simple interventions are defined by high agreement and high causal certainty; immunization to prevent disease fits this zone on the matrix.
- Socially complicated situations are defined by fairly high predictability of outcomes, but great values conflict among stakeholders; abortion is an example.
- Technically complicated situations are defined by high agreement among stakeholders but low causal certainty; everyone wants children

to learn to read but there are ferocious disagreements about which reading approach produces the best result (Schemo, 2007).

- Complex situations are characterized by high values conflict and high uncertainty; what to do about global warming would fall in the complexity zone of the matrix.

Let us now examine the evaluation implications of these different ways of understanding a program or intervention by looking at a specific youth civic engagement model.

A YOUTH CIVIC ENGAGEMENT EXAMPLE: INNOVATIONS IN CIVIC PARTICIPATION

Innovations in Civic Participation (ICP), based in Washington, DC, has begun to put together a set of principles and values that inform youth civic engagement initiatives that provide opportunities for youth service. This set of principles and values was developed by ICP after an extensive review of existing youth civic engagement programs and, where available, evaluations of these programs. It was also informed by in-depth discussions with practitioners of youth civic engagement programs, researchers, and evaluators.

Key elements of an effective youth service program in ICP's approach are (1) quality local leadership and (2) coordination by a central dedicated entity. Both of these elements are essential for (3) democratic input to create and (4) diverse opportunities for youth leadership. Right away, it is clear that this approach is not a recipe. The key elements are principles and values that will have to be given meaning in a local context. ICP's underlying theory of change is therefore based on adaptive management and co-creating a program in partnership with local people, including local young people. They are not the ingredients in a recipe that can be precisely specified and mixed in precise and predetermined amounts. The ICP approach further specifies that an effective initiative must (5) use local resources effectively and be of (6) manageable size to support (7) flexibility and creativity, while also manifesting (8) accountability to standards. Again, these have the flavor of guiding principles that must be defined and interpreted in context as opposed to a standardized model amenable to high-fidelity implementation. ICP's approach goes on to specify that all eight of the above elements should be integrated elements and stay focused on (9) valuable and meaningful youth projects that include (10) fulfilling service and (11) recognition for youth involved. Adding to the complexity is that these eleven elements interact dynamically so that as one element changes, the others are affected as in any system that acts *as a whole,* such that a change in one part reverberates through the system to affect other parts. Figure 22.1 takes the ICP

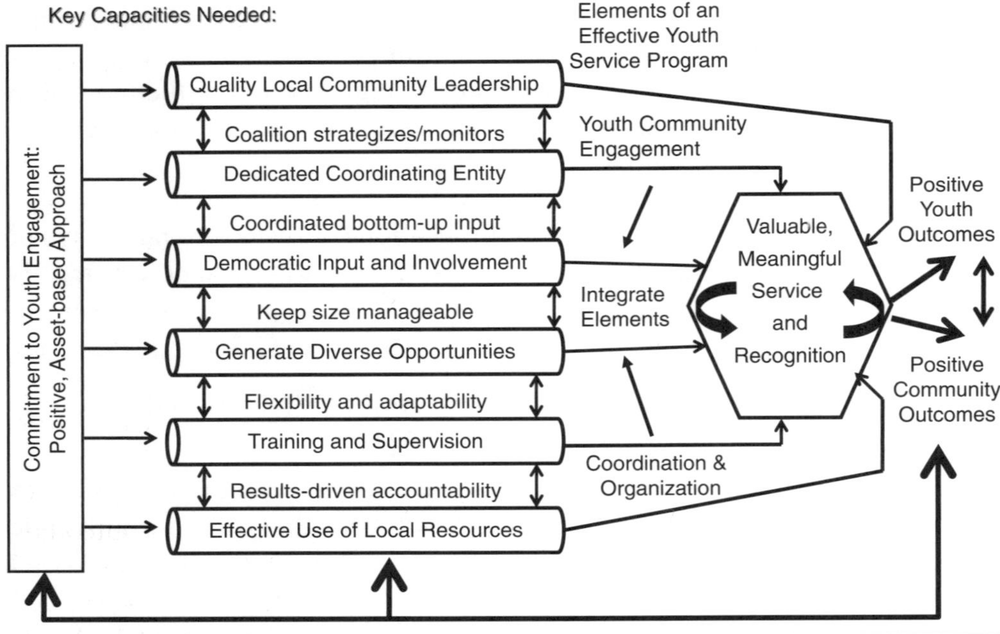

Figure 22.1 Youth Civic Engagement Model

principles and values and conceptualizes ICP's approach to youth service as a complex, dynamic system intervention aimed at positive youth and community outcomes.

In this model, the precondition for youth civic engagement is a commitment to a positive, asset-based approach in which the capabilities of young people are emphasized. The civic engagement intervention (the *IT*, or evaluand, for evaluation) is conceptualized as interactions among the eleven ICP principles and values identified earlier. The youth community engagement principles identified in the six *pipelines of engagement* are quality local leadership, a dedicated coordinating entity, democratic input and involvement, diverse opportunities for youth, training and supervision, and effective use of local resources. The five key elements of coordination and organization are: a coalition that strategizes and monitors, coordinated bottom-up input, keeping size manageable, flexibility and adaptability, and results-driven accountability. The model depicts ongoing interactions and mutual reinforcement among these key elements all aimed at valuable, meaningful, and fulfilling youth service and recognition for the youth involved. Because of the bottom-up nature of the approach, the precise youth and community outcomes have to be identified and owned by the local leadership and young people involved in the initiative. Finally, the model depicts a feedback loop from positive youth and community outcomes back to the original commitment to youth civic engagement, indicating that as positive outcomes are attained, commitment is strengthened and deepened (and vice versa: Lack of outcomes would diminish commitment).

This complex, dynamic systems conceptualization of youth civic engagement stands in stark contrast to the more typical linear logic model that evaluators have become used to conceptualizing. Figure 22.2 presents a generic linear logic model for youth civic engagement. This is a classic education model that begins with recruitment of young people, which leads to their participation in an initiative. Knowledge and skills are attained through participation, leading to attitude and behavior change, and ultimately to positive community outcomes. The advantage of this classic logic model for evaluation purposes is that it focuses attention on outcomes. What knowledge and skills are acquired? What attitudes are changed? What behaviors are developed and sustained? What community outcomes are attained? The focus on outcomes reinforces the search for a standardized "best practice" intervention that can produce those outcomes reliably and validly. The classic counterfactual question is also highlighted: What would have happened in the absence of the intervention? Asking that question leads to a randomized controlled trial as the evaluation design of choice. The focus of such an evaluation is to answer the simple question: Did it work?

In contrast, the complex, dynamic ICP approach makes the process part of the outcome (Figure 22.1). The process is aimed at building the long-term capacity for and commitment to youth civic engagement, and both capacity and commitment depend on the bottom-up, authentic involvement of local leadership and youth. The ICP systems model balances attention to

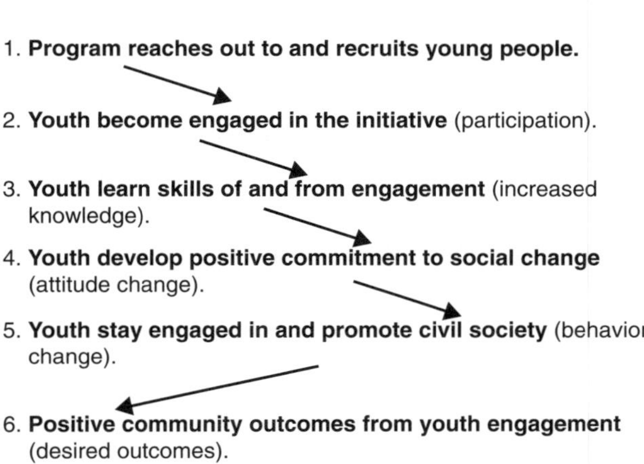

Figure 22.2 Traditional Linear Logic Model for Youth Civic Engagement

both processes and outcomes, and depicts their interactions as inherently dynamic. Implications for evaluation include the following:

1. The model's processes must be documented and their interactions tracked. What is the quality and engagement of local leadership? What diverse opportunities for youth are generated? What changes occur as the initiative creatively adapts as the program is repeated?
2. Youth and community outcomes must be generated locally, as part of the bottom-up engagement process, and these outcomes are subject to change and development as the engagement process unfolds.
3. Given the preceding implications, the evaluation cannot be simply a pre-post design focused on standardized and predetermined outcomes attainment because the outcomes are emergent and dynamic as the engagement process unfolds.
4. No standardized recipe will be implemented or emerge because each locality, and the leaders and young people in that locality, will design a process that fits their situation. Adherence to principles and values can be evaluated (e.g., to what extent is there democratic input throughout the process?) but part of the purpose of the evaluation is to support monitoring and interpretation of how various principles and values are applied in the adaptive management and development process.
5. The evaluation question changes from the simple "Did *IT* work?" to more complex evaluation questions: What elements work for which youth in what ways and in what context? How do the civic engagement elements and dimensions interact with different young people in particular contexts to produce what variations in outcomes?
6. In contrast to simple linear logic models, which show causation flowing in only one direction, from intervention to outcomes, complex dynamic models include attention to system dynamics in which feedback loops come into play.

This last point deserves elaboration. Figure 22.3 displays a sustainable dynamic system for youth service. In the first step, a program offers meaningful youth engagement. This engagement leads (in the theory of change) to positive youth outcomes that then lead to positive community outcomes #2 to #3). As those outcomes are realized, the meaningfulness of youth engagement is also enhanced (as shown in the feedback loops from community outcomes back to positive youth outcomes and back to further engagement). Positive reinforcement and rewards contribute to sustainability. In the dynamic model, following the arrows in Figure 22.3 clockwise, positive outcomes lead to recognition and appreciation of youth, which deepens youth engagement and enhances outcomes (again depicted in feedback loops that

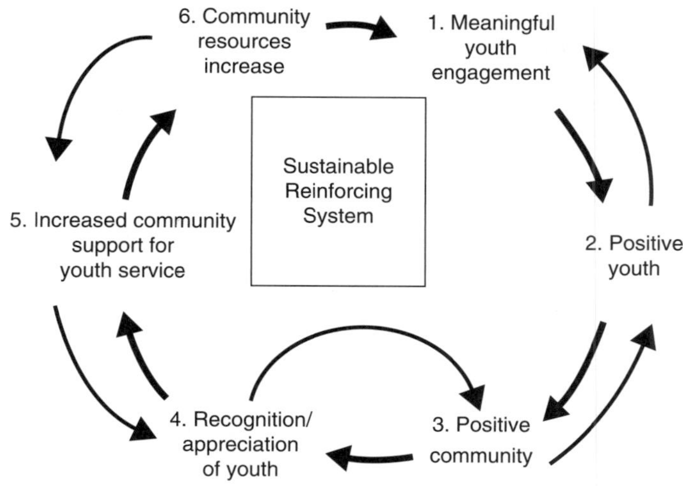

Figure 22.3 A Sustainable Reinforcing System for Youth Service

go counterclockwise). Attaining outcomes increases community support for youth engagement (#5 in the systems dynamics model in Figure 22.3), which feeds back to increase recognition and appreciation of youth. Increased community support results in more community resources for youth engagement. These dynamics, in interaction and combination (#5 to # 6), generate additional resources for youth civic engagement and attract more leadership, which produce still more meaningful opportunities for youth service. The evaluation challenge is to inquire into and document these complex system dynamics and interactions, which will be different in different contexts. The clockwise arrows show the direction of primary youth engagement actions and outcomes while the feedback loops (counterclockwise) show how positive actions produce positive feedback, making the system of interactions both dynamic and sustainable.

COMPLEX, DYNAMIC SYSTEMS MAPS TO UNDERSTAND YOUTH CIVIC ENGAGEMENT OUTCOMES

Another important theory of change issue is whether outcomes are understood to be individualized or standardized. Traditional linear logic models of the kind depicted in Figure 22.2 lead to standardized, operationalized outcomes and therefore evaluation pre-post instruments that measure the attainment of those standardized outcomes. In contrast, the ICP approach assumes that different young people will experience and attain different outcomes depending on their situations. Figure 22.4 illustrates how individualized outcomes depend on and emerge from a young person's relationships.

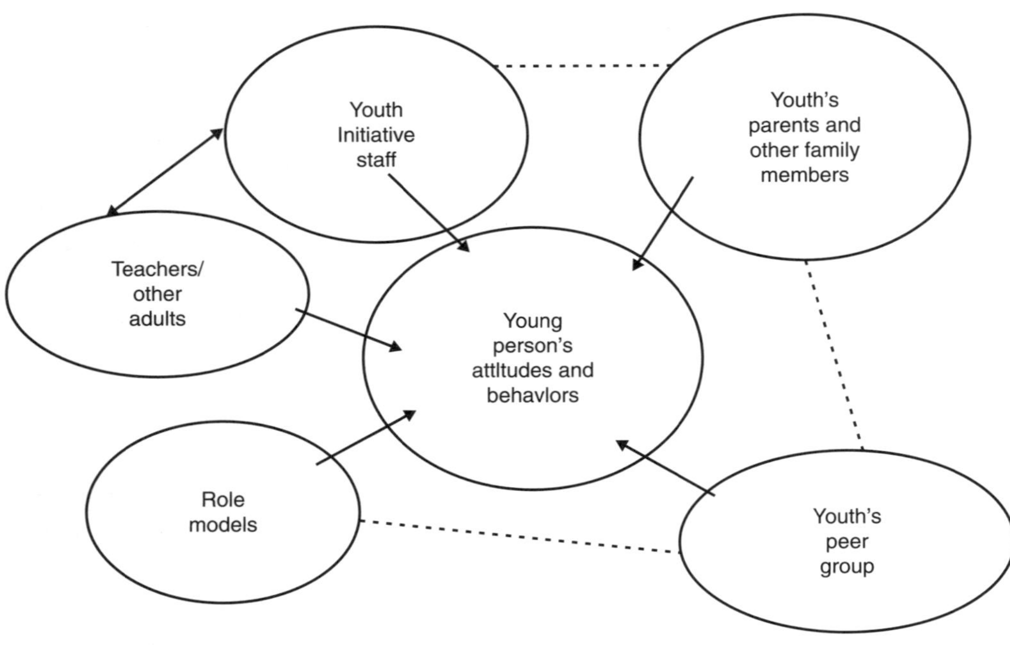

Figure 22.4 Systems Web Showing Possible Influences on a Young Person's Civic Engagement

It is a generic systems map of important interpersonal relationships and raises evaluation questions about the effects of those relationships in connection with youth engagement outcomes. For example, what relationships in a young person's life influence that youth's attitudes and behaviors? The narrowly focused, linear model in Figure 22.2 focuses entirely on a program's effects and ignores the rest of the young person's world. When we ask about that larger world, we are inquiring into the multitude of relationships and connections that may influence both the nature of a young person's civic engagement and the outcomes of that engagement. Figure 22.4 is a rough sketch (map) of possible system connections and influences. We know, for example, that teenagers are heavily influenced by their peer group. The traditional linear, narrowly focused logic model, targets the individual teenager. A systems perspective that considers the influence of a young person's peer group might ask how to influence the knowledge, attitudes, and behaviors of the entire peer group. This would involve changing the subsystem (the peer group) of which the individual young person is a part.

Figure 22.4 also invites evaluation inquiry into the relative influence of the young person's parents and other family members, or teachers and other adults, as well as the relationship to the staff of the civic engagement program. In effect, this systems perspective reminds us that the behavior of a young person will be affected by a number of relationships and not just participation in the civic engagement program with designated leaders. In working with such a model with program staff, the conceptual elaboration of the theory of change includes specifying which direction arrows run (one way or both ways, showing mutual influence), which influences are strong (heavy solid lines) versus weak (dotted lines), and which influences are more dominant (larger circles versus smaller circles). This conceptualization then guides the evaluation data collection, which will have to include multiple methods such as case studies to capture variations in participants' individualized experiences and outcomes.

Systems thinking can involve looking at system relationships operating at different levels. While Figure 22.4 focuses on the set of interpersonal relationships a young person has, Figure 22.5 invites a look at the program and organizational systems that affect youth civic engagement outcomes. This systems map depicts possible institutional influences affecting teenagers' attitudes and behaviors. The narrowly focused, linear logic model in Figure 22.2 treats the program's impact in isolation from other institutional and societal factors. To be sure, that is the model that is most familiar to funders, and often required by them, so community-based youth programs may have to include such a model to satisfy funders. But, in working together on what most accurately captures and reflects program realities, they might move toward the systems web in Figure 22.5, which shows the youth civic engagement program as one potentially strong influence on

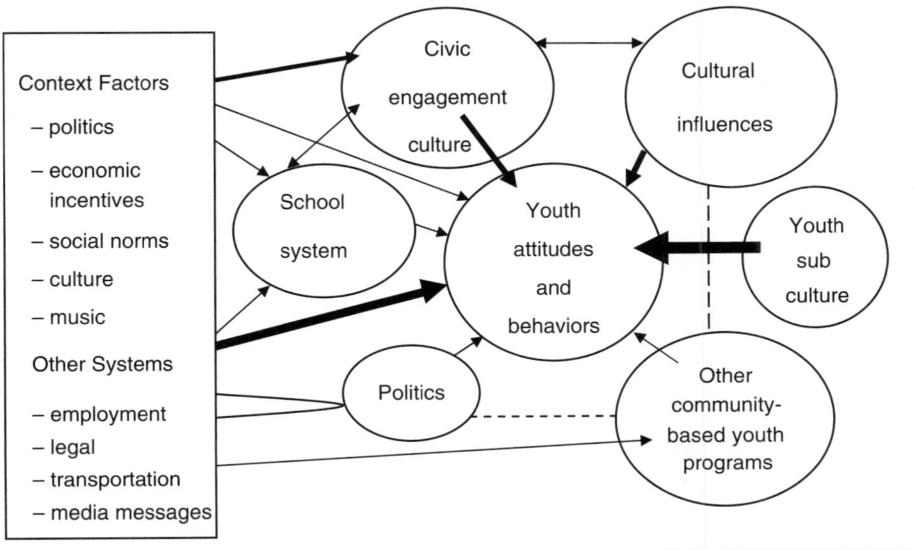

Figure 22.5 Systems Web Showing Possible Institutional Influences Affecting Youth Civic Engagement Outcomes

participating teenagers but also takes into account the important influences of the youth culture, the school system, and other community-based youth programs. Moreover, the participating young person may be affected by other systems: the legal system (laws governing what young people can do), the transportation system (which affects how the teenager gets to the program's activities and where opportunities can be offered), and the pervasive influences of the media (television, movies, music) that affect teenagers' attitudes and behaviors. The systems diagram in Figure 22.5 also includes larger contextual factors like the political environment; economic incentives that can affect a teenagers' participation in youth service; and social norms and larger cultural influences that affect how society responds to civic engagement by young people.

Constructing such a systems map with a civic engagement initiative may lead the program to consider a more collaborative effort in which various institutional partners come together to work toward the desired youth and community outcomes. The system diagrams suggest that a civic engagement or youth service program by itself, focusing only on the teenager and only on its own delivery of knowledge to the teenager, is less likely to achieve the desired outcome than a model that takes into account the influences of other people in the teenager's system (the teenager's world) and collaborates with other institutions that can have an effect upon the attainment of desired outcomes.

INTERDEPENDENT AND INDIVIDUALIZED OUTCOMES

Youth civic engagement initiatives may target multiple outcomes like life skills, employment skills, increased educational attainment (a high-school diploma), and prevention of risky behaviors as well as civic engagement. Such outcomes are interdependent rather than isolated and autonomous. A systems approach to evaluating multiple outcomes directs the evaluation to look at *the relationship among outcomes* rather than treating them simply as distinct and separate entities with each measured in isolation as separate indicators.

The precise nature of the interdependence among multiple outcomes will vary by young person, which directs us again to the challenge of individualized outcomes in both theory of change formulations and evaluation. Consider the example of Youth Star Cambodia, a youth service program founded by Eva Mysliwiec that matches Cambodian university students with rural communities that want and can benefit from the knowledge and skills of that student. The young people volunteer for a year of service. As the program states:

> Some volunteers will work to promote sustainable livelihoods. Other volunteers will help villagers improve their health and well-being. Still others will strengthen business entrepreneurship skills in communities. (Youth Star Cambodia, 2008)

In describing this new program at the May 2008 conference on evaluating youth service organized by Innovations in Civic Participation and the Children and Youth unit of The World Bank, Mysliwiec emphasized the importance of a good match between the youth volunteer and the community. With fewer than 100 participants at the time of her presentation, she communicated the hard work involved in making the initial match and supporting youth volunteers during their service. Community projects vary and the outcomes young people experience vary. The program is highly individualized and personalized.

Mysliwiec's presentation was followed by a panel that included advice on how to evaluate the program. The Senior Monitoring and Evaluation Specialist for The World Bank was emphatic that the program should aim toward conducting a randomized controlled trial, lauding RCTs as the gold standard. But the program design requires careful matching of volunteers to communities. Randomization would undermine the program design, increasing the risk of poor matches between communities and volunteers. Moreover, given the size and nature of the program, a control group is not appropriate. Control groups only work where there is a standardized intervention for comparison with the control. The rigidity and standardization of an evaluation using a randomized controlled trial design would likely do major harm to the program. For example, it might hamper the recruitment of talented local staff who could modify the program to suit the context. Rather, the substantial natural variation within the program as it is offered in different settings gives ample opportunities for evaluating individualized outcomes for both volunteers and communities. That is the *appropriate* focus of an evaluation, one that would meet the standard of methodological appropriateness discussed earlier. A systems approach to evaluating the Youth Star Cambodia program offers intriguing possibilities for both learning and accountability, especially if framed as a developmental evaluation (discussed in the following section). Basically, this would mean picking a diversified sample of different villages with different youth service volunteers and conducting case studies of what happens in each village and what happens to each young person serving as a volunteer in that village. These diverse case studies could then be analyzed for patterns and the impacts assessed using engagement criteria and outcomes appropriate to the unique nature of each village. In essence, such a diversified and individualized program will produce diversified and individual outcomes, which makes case studies especially appropriate (Patton, 2002; Beaumont, this volume; Torney-Purta, Amadeo, & Andolina, this volume).

The preceding figures and examples have provided only a brief overview of the possibilities for incorporating systems perspectives in evaluation of youth civic engagement programs (Williams & Iman, 2006). In the case of youth civic engagement, this means looking at the entire system in which the youth civic engagement program operates and how it impacts not only the participants or the community individually, but also the complex interactions and interconnections between the different participants, beneficiaries, and stakeholders.

DEVELOPMENTAL EVALUATION

Developmental Evaluation is an approach to evaluation built on the understandings that have emerged from studies of complex adaptive systems, especially innovative initiatives where outcomes are emergent, individualized, and interdependent rather than predetermined and fixed (Patton, 2008, 2010; Westley, Zimmerman, & Patton, 2006). Innovative initiatives are characterized by a state of continuous development and adaptation, and they often unfold within dynamic and unpredictable conditions. Developmental evaluation supports such innovative initiatives by bringing data to bear to inform and guide emergent choices. In this section, we will look at developmental evaluation as a major alternative for conceptualizing what evaluation can contribute to youth civic engagement initiatives, an approach informed by insights from the characteristics of complex, dynamic systems.

Developmental evaluation supports program and organizational development to guide adaptation to emergent and dynamic realities on the ground in real time. Developmental evaluation differs from typical program improvement evaluation (making a program better) in that it involves changing the program model itself as part of innovation and response to changed conditions and understandings. Developmental evaluation doesn't render overall judgments of effectiveness (traditional summative evaluation) because the program never becomes a fixed, static, and stable intervention. However, what is lost in standardization is more than compensated for by the gains in resilience and adaptability. This is an especially critical point for youth civic engagement programs if one thinks about ever-changing political dynamics within communities, including changes in participating young people, for example, in their political efficacy and their relationship to their community if they have a civic victory, and changes in the community's stereotypes about teenagers when teens engage in community improvement projects. These impacts are dynamic and interacting. Developmental evaluation of youth civic engagement initiatives supports social innovation and adaptive management. Evaluation processes include asking evaluative questions, applying evaluation logic, and gathering real-time data to guide program, product, and organizational development. The evaluator is often part of a development team whose members collaborate to conceptualize, design, and test new approaches in a long-term, ongoing process of continuous improvement, adaptation, and intentional change. The evaluator's primary function in the team is to infuse team discussions with evaluative questions, data, and thinking to facilitate data-based reflection and decision making in the developmental process. Table 22.1 summarizes major differences between traditional evaluations and complexity-based developmental evaluation.

Developmental evaluation is an alternative to formative and summative evaluation, the most common distinctions in evaluation discussed earlier in this chapter. (Summative evaluations are conducted after completion of the program for the benefit of some external audience or decision-maker to determine whether to continue, expand, or disseminate the program. Formative evaluations serve the purpose of getting ready for summative evaluation by helping work through implementation problems and get the program sufficiently stabilized to be ready for a summative assessment.) The World Development Report that labeled youth service as a "promising but unproven practice" is in search of summative evaluations that can prove how desired youth outcomes can be attained.

Table 22.1
A Comparison of Two Approaches to Evaluation

Traditional Evaluations	Complexity-Based, Developmental Evaluations
Render definitive judgments of success or failure.	Provide feedback, generate learning, support direction, or affirm changes in direction.
Measure success against predetermined goals.	Develop new measures and monitoring mechanisms as goals emerge and evolve.
Position the evaluator outside to ensure independence and objectivity.	Position evaluation as an internal, team function integrated into action and ongoing interpretive processes with external evaluation support and feedback.
Design the evaluation based on linear cause-effect logic models.	Design the evaluation to capture system dynamics, interdependencies, and emergent interconnections.
Aim to produce generalizable findings across time and space.	Aim to produce context-specific understandings that inform ongoing innovation.
Accountability focused on and directed to external authorities and funders.	Accountability centered on the innovators' deep sense of fundamental values and commitments—and learning.
Accountability to control and locate blame for failures.	Learn to respond to lack of control and stay in touch with what's unfolding.
Evaluator determines the design based on the evaluator's perspective about what is important. The evaluator controls the evaluation.	Collaboration of evaluator with those engaged in the change effort to design an evaluation process that matches philosophically and organizationally.
Evaluation often engenders fear of failure.	Evaluation supports hunger for learning.

But suppose an innovative youth civic engagement intervention is using the ICP bottom-up approach and is being implemented in a highly dynamic environment where those involved are engaged in ongoing trial-and-error experimentation, figuring out what works, learning lessons, adapting to changed circumstances, working with new participants—*and they never expect to arrive at a fixed, static, and stable model*. They are adapting principles and values rather than following a recipe. They are interested in and committed to ongoing development. Developmental evaluation supports this kind of ongoing change in a program, adapting it to changed circumstances, and altering tactics based on emergent conditions and youth responses and feedback. It includes the possibility of actively involving the young people themselves in the evaluation in a participatory evaluation approach (Flores, 2007; Delgado, 2005; Flores, 2003).

The evaluation of Student Partnership Worldwide's (SPW) *Integrated Approach Youth Programs* in Africa is an example of an evaluation with strong youth participation in all aspects of programming, including monitoring and evaluation at the highest technical level. SPW is an international development organization mobilizing young people in eight countries across sub-Saharan Africa and South Asia by recruiting and training 18- to 28-year-olds to serve as Volunteer Peer Educators (VPEs). The VPEs live in rural communities for 6 to 12 months and lead health, environmental, and education programs. SPW currently has almost 1,000 volunteers who are estimated to reach approximately 400,000 youth. The monitoring and evaluation (M&E) efforts focus on capturing both intended outcomes of the programs and unintended outcomes. The organization measures the outcomes of the youth involved but also the influences on support groups such as teachers and parents, line ministries and departments, opinion and pressure groups, and the general community. A variety of methods are used including closed-ended questionnaires; focus groups with volunteers, teachers, and other community members; structured surveys among the former volunteers; and process monitoring. SPW staff believe that the full-time, high-level participation of young people improves the reliability of evaluation measurements and the long-term presence of the young people in the communities supports careful evaluation. In addition, the program involves former volunteers to help with regular monitoring and feedback. Evaluation also includes long-term case studies. The SPW evaluation was one of the featured participatory evaluations at the World Bank/ICP conference (discussed at the beginning of this chapter) because of its emphasis on including youth in every aspect of the evaluation process (World Bank and ICP, 2009, p. 18). SPW has articulated and follows participatory principles of youth civic engagement, but it adapts to the emergent and dynamic complexities of each community.

EVALUATING INNOVATION

Complexity science offers insight into the changed role that evaluation can usefully play in highly innovative and dynamic circumstances. Studying how living systems organize, adapt, evolve, and transform challenges the largely mechanistic models of most programs—and most evaluations. Complexity science reveals that the real world is not a machine. Complex systems like young civic engagement systems are too dynamic, emergent, and, yes, complex, to be reduced to simple cause-effect recipes. Social innovators are often driven not by concrete goals but by possibilities, which are often ill-defined possibilities expressed as values, hopes, and visions. In the early days of innovation, when ideas about possibilities are just being formed, the innovative process can actually be damaged by forcing too much concreteness and specificity.

The Youth Star Cambodia program discussed earlier offers an illustrative example. The program is still in development and engages in ongoing adaptation, so it would be especially inappropriate to force the program prematurely into identifying and measuring standardized outcomes that could well interfere with the emergent, developmental process of learning and adaptation. Instead, as suggested earlier, a series of case studies of what youth volunteers are doing in diverse communities would be more appropriate. The case studies would capture individualized outcomes and identify patterns of youth engagement. Because the size of the program is fewer than 100 youth volunteers, case studies are manageable. These would include interviews with the volunteers and people in the participating villages during site visits to the villages. It is to be expected that some youth engagement projects would be more successful than others. The developmental evaluation feedback emerges from comparing more successful with less successful projects to identify lessons about patterns of success (and patterns of failure). The insights that come from examining these patterns and engaging in thoughtful reflect practice (What worked? What didn't work? Why?) become the basis for ongoing development. Unexpected outcomes can be captured and documented. Intended outcomes can be described and placed in context of the specific youth volunteer and village where the project occurred. The process is learning-oriented and developmental for the program.

This contrasts with how traditional evaluators typically approach these situations. Evaluators are trained to insist that hoped-for changes and visions be specified as clear, specific, and measurable goals, and the process for attaining those goals must be mapped in a linear logic model. That is typically all the evaluator has to offer, the only conceptual tool in the evaluator's toolkit. We saw this in the response of The World Bank evaluation specialist to the Cambodia Youth Star program. The only design in his toolkit was a randomized controlled trial. It was as if he hadn't even heard the program description. This is a classic case of *when all you have is a hammer, everything looks like a nail.* It is the opposite of methodological appropriateness and responsiveness in evaluation. In contrast, developmental evaluation offers an opportunity to conceptualize an initiative as a complex, dynamic system with individualized and interdependent outcomes as illustrated earlier with the ICP example.

COMPLEXITY AND ACCOUNTABILITY

Complexity-based developmental evaluation shifts the locus and focus of accountability. Traditionally, accountability has focused on and been directed to external authorities and funders. But for values-focused, principles-driven civic engagement, the highest form of accountability is internal. Are we walking the talk? Are we being true to our values and vision? Are we dealing with reality? Are we connecting the here-and-now reality with our vision? And how would we know? What are we observing that's different, that's emerging? What are we learning? These become internalized questions, asked continuously, because those involved want to know.

Asking such questions and engaging the answers, as uncertain as they may be, is not easy. It takes courage to face the possibility that one is deluding oneself. When this works, each individual's sense of internal and personal accountability connects with the group's sense of collective responsibility and ultimately connects broader questions of institutional and societal accountability.

POLICY IMPLICATIONS

Public policy now includes requirements and guidelines for evaluation. Most of these requirements are based on simple rather than complex understandings of programs and apply a one-size-fits-all approach to evaluation evidence. For example, as noted earlier, the *What Works Clearinghouse*, established in 2002 by the U.S. Department of Education's Institute of Education Sciences to provide educators, policy-makers, researchers, and the public with a central and trusted source of scientific evidence of what works in education, has adopted randomized controlled experimentation as its gold standard. Such designs are inappropriate under conditions of complexity. Likewise, the Office of Management and Budget (OMB) requires federal agencies to use the Program Assessment Rating Tool (PART) to help budget examiners and federal managers measure the effectiveness of government programs. PART evidence requirements portray a simple (as opposed to complex) view of how interventions work, and PART evidence guidelines are based on standardized and static notions of program design and causal inference. In the international arena, as discussed here, The World Bank favors an equally narrow and rigid conception of evaluation evidence based on experimental designs with an emphasis on simple counterfactuals.

Evaluation policy needs to include options for acknowledging and dealing with complexity. The theme of the 2008 annual conference of the American Evaluation Association was *Evaluation Policy and Evaluation Practice*. The tenor of the plenary presentations, panels, and papers called for evaluation policy being informed by evaluation practice, and evaluation practice being grounded in evaluation policy, where both policy and practice recognize diverse approaches to evaluation, diverse stakeholder needs, and diverse types of interventions, including those that are complex and implemented under conditions of complexity. This will mean new, more appropriate, and more flexible evaluation policies and guidelines for many governmental agencies, international organizations, and others involved in funding and implementing youth civic engagement initiatives.

CONCLUSION: WHERE METHOD AND THEORY INTERSECT

If methodological appropriateness is the standard for judging evaluation designs, what is the criterion for determining appropriateness? The issue is basically one of matching. Just as the Youth Star Cambodia program attempts to match the skills and interests of youth volunteers with the needs and help needed in a particular community, methodological appropriateness is a matter of matching an evaluation approach to the characteristics and stage of development of a program. We have argued in this chapter that the evaluation methods and design should match the program's theory of change. Standardized interventions with predetermined and standardized outcomes can be implemented with randomized controlled trials. Individualized, customized, and innovative interventions developed collaboratively with local partners and young people require an evaluation an evaluation approach that is flexible, responsive, and attuned to the dynamics of complex adaptive systems. Developmental evaluation, as described in this chapter, is the appropriate approach for such youth civic engagement initiatives.

REFERENCES

American Evaluation Association (AEA). (2003). *Scientifically based evaluation methods*. Retrieved from http://www.eval.org/doestatement.htm

American Evaluation Association Task Force on Guiding Principles for Evaluators. (1995). Guiding principles for evaluators. *New Directions for Program Evaluation*, *66*, 19–34.

Boruch, R. (2007). Encouraging the flight of error: Ethical standards, evidence standards, and randomized trials. Informing federal policies on evaluation methodology: Building the evidence base for method choice in government sponsored evaluation. *New Directions for Program Evaluation, 113*, 55–73.

Children & Youth Unit. (2007). Evaluating youth interventions. *Youth development notes, II (5)*, 1–4.

Delgado, M. (2005). *Designs and methods for youth-led research*. Thousand Oaks, CA: Sage Publications.

European Evaluation Society (EES). (2007). *The importance of a methodologically diverse approach to impact evaluation*. Retrieved from http://www.europeanevaluation.org/news?newsId=1969406

Evaluation Gap Working Group. (2006). *When will we ever learn? Improving lives through impact evaluation*. Washington, DC: Center for Global Development. Retrieved from http://www.cgdev.org/section/initiatives/_active/evalgap

Flores, K. S. (Ed.). (2003, August). *Youth participatory evaluation: A field in the making. New Directions for Evaluation, No. 98*. San Francisco, CA: Jossey-Bass.

Flores, K. S. (2007). *Youth participatory evaluation: Strategies for engaging young people*. San Francisco, CA: Jossey-Bass.

Gertler, P. (2007, November 7–8). *The value of evaluation*. Workshop presentation for The World Bank, Washington, DC.

Joint Committee on Standards for Educational Evaluation. (1994). *The program evaluation standards*. Thousand Oaks, CA: Sage Publications. Retrieved from http://www.wmich.edu/evalctr/jc/

Julnes, G., & Rog, D. (Eds.). (2007, April). *Informing federal policies on evaluation methodology: Building the evidence base for method choice in government sponsored evaluation. New Directions for Evaluation, No. 113*. San Francisco, CA: Jossey-Bass.

Patton, M. Q. (2002). *Qualitative Research and Evaluation Methods* (3rd ed.). Thousand Oaks, CA: Sage Publications.

Patton, M. Q. (2008). *Utilization-focused evaluation* (4th ed.). Thousand Oaks, CA: Sage Publications.

Patton, M. Q. (2010). *Developmental evaluation: Applying complexity concepts to enhance innovation and use*. New York: Guilford.

Roholt, R. V., Hildreth, R. W., & Baizerman, M. (Eds.). (2008). *Becoming citizens: Deepening the craft of youth civic engagement*. New York: The Haworth Press.

Schemo, D. J. (2007, March 9). War over teaching reading. *New York Times*. Retrieved from http://www.nytimes.com/2007/03/09/education/09reading.html?ex=1174708800&en=2cbb6a85da135c47&ei=5070

Smith, M. F. (2005). Evaluability assessment. In S. Mathison (Ed.), *Encyclopedia of evaluation* (pp. 136–139). Thousand Oaks, CA: Sage Publications.

Westley, F., Zimmerman, B., & Patton, M. Q. (2006). *Getting to maybe: How the world is changed*. Toronto, Canada: Random House Canada.

What Works Clearinghouse. (2006). *Evidence standards for reviewing studies*. Washington, DC: U.S. Department of Education's Institute of Education Sciences. Retrieved from http://www.whatworks.ed.gov/whoweare/overview.html

Williams, B., & Iman, I. (2006). *Systems concepts in evaluation: An expert anthology*. AEA Monograph. Point Reynes, CA: EdgePress.

World Bank, The. (2007). Exercising citizenship. *World Development Report 2007: Development and the next generation* (pp. 160–186). Washington, DC: The World Bank.

World Bank, The, & Innovations in Civic Participation (ICP). (2009). *Measuring the impact of youth voluntary service programs: Summary and conclusions of the international experts' meeting*. Washington, DC: The World Bank.

Youth Star Cambodia. (2008). *Program Description*. Retrieved from http://www.youthstarcambodia.org/template1.aspx?PageName=31&l=1

Zimmerman, B. (2001). Agreement and certainty matrix. In B. Zimmerman, C. Lindberg, & P. Plsek (Eds.), *Edgeware: Insights from complexity science for health care leaders* (pp. 136–143). Irving, TX: VHA, Inc.

CHAPTER 23

Critical Youth Engagement: Participatory Action Research and Organizing

MADELINE FOX
City University of New York

KAVITHA MEDIRATTA
Brown University

JESSICA RUGLIS
Johns Hopkins University

BRETT STOUDT
City University of New York

SEEMA SHAH
International Baccalaureate

MICHELLE FINE
City University of New York

THIS CHAPTER EXPLORES *critical youth engagement*: how young people—especially those from low-income and immigrant communities—understand conditions of social inequity and negotiate these stresses psychologically and politically. Further, it examines the conditions under which they decide to take up civic engagement by confronting structural injustice and human rights violations collectively. We witness critical youth engagement among low-income urban youth through a youth participatory action research (YPAR) and youth organizing approach. The second half of the chapter describes and explores this methodology. We also consider what critical youth engagement and YPAR means for social research, especially for research on youth civic engagement across populations of youth from any background. We hope that our chapter provides a wide-angle research agenda that can capture the theoretical and empirical wingspan of critical youth engagement projects on youth, adults, institutions, social movements, and youth policy, over time.

Toward a Critical Youth Engagement

In New York City, an observer is quickly struck by the uneven distribution of *human security* across the city. Indeed a palpable sense of human insecurity characterizes low-income communities as fundamental contingencies are called into question: Will I graduate from high school if I don't pass these high-stakes exams? Will my house be foreclosed? Will gentrification make us homeless? Will my mother go to prison, my dad be deported, or foster care remove me? Will those who are important to me stay healthy, or alive? Will I get into college as an undocumented student? Do we have to move when my brother comes out of prison because he can't live in public housing? Yet, as compelling as pains of insecurity are young people's desires to mobilize for social change (Fine & Ruglis, 2009).

Our work with youth organizers and youth researchers stands in substantial contrast to much of traditional thinking about youth and civic engagement. When we consult the literatures on civic engagement, we find that youth who attend urban schools, youth of color, immigrant youth, and young people living in poverty typically score *lower* on civic engagement measures than their White, suburban peers (Flanagan, Cumsille, Gill, & Gallay, 2007; Lutkus, Weiss, Campbell, Mazzeo, & Lazer, 1999; Sherrod, 2005). While there is some variation in the research, (e.g., Flanagan, 2004; Marcelo, Lopez, & Kirby, 2007; Smetana, Campione-Barr, & Metzger, 2006), we find ourselves in substantial agreement with Rubin's (2007) analysis of general trends in the civic engagement literatures. She writes:

> Multiple studies suggest that differences in civic achievement of US students appear to be linked to racial and socioeconomic backgrounds of students being tested.... For example students in "high poverty" schools score lower on these measures than students in "low poverty" schools, African American and Latino students score lower than their White and multiracial peers. (Baldi et al., 2001; Niemi and Junn, 1998) and parents' educational attainment is noticeably correlated with student performance. (p. 452)

See also Torney-Purta, Barber, & Wilkenfeld, 2007 for similar findings.

We find the empirical pattern of a *gap* in civic engagement to be quite problematic. Without careful theorizing about the lack of access, resources and opportunities to engage, the problematic indicators of engagement, and the relative lack of trust in civic institutions, it is understandable that young people of color and youth living in poverty appear more disengaged than their more privileged peers (Haste & Hogan, 2006). However, the existing literature on civic engagement often confuses and therefore misrepresents *lack of access* to civic engagement opportunities as *lack of motive*. Across race and class, young people enjoy extremely uneven opportunities to participate in civic life. Relative to their more privileged counterparts, poor and working-class youth of color and immigrants are far less likely to enjoy opportunities for meaningful involvement in civic activities and far more likely to have familial responsibilities that keep them from full participation. Low-income urban youth have fewer opportunities to build consistent and trusting relations with educators and to participate in enrichment programs and after-school activities (Kahne & Middaugh, 2008). Thus, the severely uneven distribution of familial responsibilities, the lopsided landscape of opportunities for civic engagement, and the heavy weight of human insecurity in the lives of poor and working-class youth systematically confound the findings of diminished levels of engagement. Further, what gets defined as an *engagement* activity is contoured by asymmetries in class, race, and gender.

CRITICAL YOUTH ENGAGEMENT: A CONCEPTUAL AND POLITICAL FRAMEWORK

We conceptualize *critical youth engagement* as the intellectual, political, emotional, and bodily space shared by three overlapping areas of social justice work with youth: youth leadership, youth organizing, and youth participatory action research (YPAR). See Figure 23.1.

Projects of critical youth engagement link social inquiry to collective action for youth justice, and embody five threshold commitments, which call for the recognition that:

1. *Youth carry knowledge and expertise* about conditions of their everyday lives shaped in contexts of oppression, colonization, and resistance.
2. Youth and adults can engage together in *serious inquiry into the histories and contemporary conditions of injustice and struggle.*
3. It is crucial to examine cross-sector *circuits of dispossession and pools of resistance* as they intersect across time, space, communities, and bodies.
4. *Research should be linked to organizing and action.*
5. Effective research teams include *youth leaders and adult allies.*

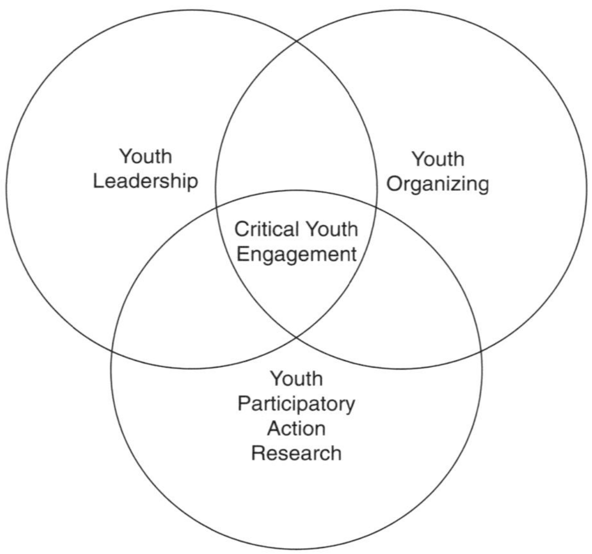

Figure 23.1 Critical Youth Engagement

In order to better understand this framework of critical youth engagement, we will first profile four exemplar YPAR/youth organizing projects.

GROUNDING OUR WORK IN THE PRACTICE OF YPAR AND YOUTH ORGANIZING

Our chapter explores the key elements of *critical youth engagement* through a close look at one youth participatory action research project and three youth organizing campaigns, respectively: Polling for Justice (PFJ) in New York City; Sistas and Brothas United (SBU) of the Northwest Bronx Community and Clergy Coalition in the Bronx, New York; South Central Youth Empowered Thru Action (SC-YEA) of the Community Coalition in Los Angeles; and Youth United for Change (YUC) in Philadelphia.

Situated primarily in low-income communities, these projects were built by diverse collectives of young people and adult allies. Committed to the blending of rigorous research, popular education, and organizing, these projects are cultivated in educational or political spaces, or both, where young people teach and learn the skills of democracy, social inquiry, and political action (see Sherrod, 2005). Dedicated to collective action, youth are in conversation with policy-makers, youth organizers, researchers, and practitioners within and across the fields of education, health, and criminal justice. All four projects sit at the intersection of youth organizing and youth-led research. They offer a spectrum of practices for examining young people's critical beliefs and actions, and organizing sites that mobilize social action.

Polling for Justice (PFJ)

Recruited from youth organizations, schools, and via word of mouth, youth researchers in Polling for Justice started meeting in February 2008, as part of a PAR project to document and create policy action around youth experiences with health, education, and criminal justice. Drawn from public and private high schools all over New York City, these young people are diverse by race, ethnicity, socioeconomic background, educational level, religion, sexuality, gender, disability, and immigration status. The 40 youth, ages 14 to 21, are academically diverse and represent a range of educational experiences: from push-outs to Advanced Placement classes, from detention rooms to student leadership.

Nicole[1] started coming to the meetings because her friends were coming. However, after several months of being involved as a Polling for Justice youth researcher, her motivations shifted. Nicole talked about why she likes being a researcher:

> Mostly [it's] about hearing about other people's issues, and like, your issues similar to theirs and to realize it's not only you that have problems, it's other people. It's just different problems. It's mainly that. And just being around people that want to try to change stuff.

The research activities of Polling for Justice are familiar: Youth and adult allies spend their time writing, reading, discussing issues, building research skills, designing surveys, piloting items, and performing data collection and analysis. PFJ youth researchers make a considerable commitment to the work, spending at least two hours each week on the research project. In the beginning, we collaborated to determine our areas of inquiry, our research questions, and to think forward toward possible actions. The project takes participation, action, and research seriously. With a series of standardized measures of health, education, well-being, and even more newly constructed items, the adult and youth researchers who constitute the research team set out to document the experiences of a broad cross-section of high-school-age youth with education, health, safety, and juvenile justice in New York City; to understand further the particular experiences of subpopulations of young people—particularly across gender, neighborhood, race or ethnicity, sexual orientation, disability, and immigration status; and to provide relevant data to NYC youth organizing campaigns for safe schools and college access, and against high-stakes testing and police harassment of youth of color. An attempt is made to bubble up new issues that are circulating in the everyday lives of youth of color but haven't reached the policy screens. In the tradition

[1] At request of youth researchers in the Polling for Justice project, names have been changed to protect confidentiality.

of C. W. Mills (1959/2000) of encouraging *private troubles* to become *public issues*, some of our most significant findings have resulted.

For example, as the Polling for Justice research collective discussed what we wanted to know, the conversation turned to urban youths' relations with police. In one discussion on police treatment of young people in the streets, anger at the police was close to the surface. With a strong sense of outrage, youth told researchers stories of being arbitrarily stopped, humiliated, disrespected, and sometimes arrested. One African American, 16-year-old male complicated the discussion by saying that police treated him fairly well. His comment was supported by another young person, and the debate boiled.

ROBERT: I don't know, cops treat me just fine. Not all cops are bad. I pretty much trust the police. (People on the outskirts of the discussion audibly snickered.)

CHERISSE: Please—I don't know what part of the city you live in, but I don't know anyone who is trusting the police.

SARAH: No, I agree with him. Cops have the power to stop a situation, like to arrest someone, and that's why they can make you feel safer.

CHERISSE: The cops might have the power to arrest or whatever, but they're never there when you need them.

TIMOTHY: Or, they're always after the wrong people.

This conversation percolated in focus groups and informal meetings across the city. In response to these varied perspectives on policing and over-policing, the research team intentionally crafted a series of items to assess young people's contacts with police (positive, negative, mixed) and to document the consequences, whether the contact was in school or out of school. Nearly half of the over 1,000 students surveyed reported negative experiences with police in the last six months, and most of those students reported two or more incidents. Looking more closely, we see that disparities in negative policing experiences exist for youth occupying nearly all categories of socially liminal spaces: Black (including African American and African Caribbean) as well as multiracial youth experience a greater likelihood of negative experiences with police than other racial categories; boys more than girls; LGBT youth more than those who identify as straight; and young people in the Bronx more than any other borough of the city. The project continues to track the educational, economic, trust, mental health, and criminal justice implications of adolescent engagement with police. The project has interviewed lawyers, judges, and police about these activities; and formed alliances with youth and researchers along the Northeast corridor in order to track police harassment as a threat to the public health and well-being of youth of color.

Some of the PFJ youth researchers are also actively involved in a youth rights campaign to require city officials to publicly report the number of police-student incidents that take place inside New York City public schools. Polling for Justice survey data will complement the official Department of Education—New York City Police Department (DOE-NYPD) data and produce findings to use in ongoing campaigns to interrupt the school-to-prison pipeline (Browne, 2003; Meiners, 2007). While this example illuminates the shared influence of research-action policy on issues of safety and violence, concerns about education, criminal justice, and health were expressed and interrogated in equally complex ways.

Sistas and Brothas United (SBU)

Young people's desire to take control of their lives propelled the creation of Sistas and Brothas United in the Bronx, New York City, in 1999. As the youth organizing arm of the Northwest Bronx Community and Clergy Coalition (NWBCCC), some of the youth had participated in community rallies alongside their parents in campaigns for safer streets, affordable housing, and better elementary schools. In forming SBU, young people wanted to confront an alarming situation in their high schools: Only a third of students in the area met math standards, barely a fifth met English standards, and more than half were likely to drop out of school. These youth hoped that SBU would provide a structure through which they could "identify and address issues affecting youths' lives and win changes."

Jorman[2] stumbled upon SBU in a moment of boredom. His friend brought him to the organization on a day when youth were discussing an upcoming meeting with school safety officials. Jorman recalls telling the group:

> You [can] not just meet with people in charge, and everybody there basically told me, yes we can. We in fact have a meeting scheduled in a day and that's what we're preparing for. And I was like, wow. So then that's when I wanted to do this. . . . I never thought, like residents, you know, regular community people [could] just go and actually meet with politicians. I thought, we were us and they were them and that's the way it was. Until I came here.

Initially, SBU operated out of one of the NWBCCC's offices as a committee staffed informally by an NWBCCC housing organizer. As the number of young people at meetings grew, SBU developed into a distinct youth action group, with its own office and staff of two full-time organizers. SBU created its own decision-making structure with a youth organizing committee and board of directors, composed entirely of youth. Youth also participated on

[2] Names of youth from Sisters and Brothers United, Youth United for Change, and South Central Youth Empowered thru Action are used with permission.

the NWBCCC board of directors, helping to define the direction and strategy for the overall organization.

Within a few years, the organization's membership had grown to more than 60 core members, with a larger group of 200 young people who regularly turned out for community events. Youth were involved in multiple campaigns to address problems in their schools. They led tours to introduce new principals and teachers to their Bronx neighborhoods. They met with district officials to negotiate facility improvements (such as repairing broken escalators and bathrooms) so that students could get to class on time. And they created forums for teachers and students to discuss how to improve communication and academic counseling in their schools.

As SBU grappled with how to embed the vision and principles of youth leadership into the daily life of schools, youth began to look at creating their own school. In an unusual alliance with adult educators, youth designed and won district leaders' approval for a new small high school called the Leadership Institute. According to Antoine Powell, an SBU member who was involved in the youth-led design process:

> Our goal was to design a school in which SBU's three central themes of leadership, social justice and community action would be incorporated into the school environment. We not only want our members to become familiar with these concepts, we want them have these characteristics instilled in their character so they can apply them in the future. In the Leadership Institute, a leader is a person who is not only able to identify a situation in their community that may be detrimental, but also possesses the power to unite the members of his or her community to work towards fixing the issue at hand. (Carlo et al., 2005, p. 62)

As the local work expanded, SBU began developing relationships with other youth organizations in the city. In 2004, SBU helped found a new citywide coalition, the Urban Youth Collaborative (UYC), through which young people could take action at a citywide level and connect to other youth organizations and youth activists. Allying with researchers and policy analysts at the Annenberg Institute for School Reform, SBU and UYC leaders built citywide campaigns to improve student access to academic support and college advising through the creation of student success centers. They also organized to reduce the police presence in their schools and to expand the opportunities for student voice in school decision making.

Youth United for Change (YUC)

In contrast with SBU, Youth United for Change (YUC) began in 1993 as a youth leadership project within a social service organization in north Philadelphia, Pennsylvania. Rebecca Rathje, a youth worker in a drug prevention program, wanted to create a program where young people could provide their perspectives on school and community issues. Rathje's initial project focused on helping youth create a media project to share their ideas to reduce the dropout rate in their school. But when youth went to a school board meeting to present their ideas, board members could barely disguise their lack of interest (in fact, the board president left the room during the youths' presentation). Angry and dismayed at the experience, Rebecca and the youth turned to another youth organization, Youth Force, in New York City, for advice. With mentoring and training from Youth Force and a local organizing group, the Eastern Philadelphia (now Pennsylvania) Organizing Project (EPOP), YUC reinvented itself as a youth-led organizing group.

YUC organizes high-school students through youth-led, school-based chapters at local high schools, with support from an adult organizer. Currently, five such chapters exist in high schools where the school principal has agreed to the organization's activities on the campus. YUC leaders meet weekly in these chapters to define and carry out school improvement campaigns. Similar to SBU's approach, YUC's organizing campaigns proceed through a cycle of:

- Recruitment through classroom presentations and passing out flyers to students in the lunchroom and outside of school before and after the school day
- Group meetings after school to discuss issues of concern to youth
- Outreach to assess the scope of the issue and its resonance with the larger student body through school-wide surveys and listening campaigns, often with support from teachers who facilitate access to classrooms for YUC organizers
- Research to gather information on reform alternatives and to define a strategy for engaging school officials
- Presenting reform recommendations to school and district officials

YUC chapters have won agreements with principals to implement new math curricula and improve student access to guidance counselors. They also have won commitments from district leadership to improve buildings and to provide new resources for libraries and new computers for classrooms. When asked why she is involved in the organization, Rasheeda, a high-school junior, says, "[Being involved] makes you feel better about yourself, like that you are trying to make a change in the school and it lets you know that you can do it."

Youth leaders of the different chapters gather once a month for YUC-wide meetings at which they discuss crosscutting issues and potential campaigns, and lend support to each other's efforts. Leadership development training is integrated into these meetings and is also provided in intensive weekend retreats and a weeklong summer institute. Facilitated by adult organizers and YUC alumni, training sessions focus on education reform strategies, but they also examine political and economic issues, including workshops on the role of the International Monetary Fund and World Bank policies in promoting economic disparities, and the history of the labor movement. Like SBU, YUC has initiated or participated in district-level campaigns—to fight attempts to privatize the Philadelphia public schools, and to demand structural and policy reforms to improve the quality of education in north Philadelphia neighborhoods. These campaigns have brought visibility to YUC leaders as a force to be contended with in the city's political landscape. In 2005, for example, YUC's exposure of test-taking improprieties in a local high school resulted in the Philadelphia School District creating new standards for testing and limiting the instructional time devoted solely to test preparation.

In 2002, after almost 10 years of local organizing, YUC initiated a campaign to restructure two large high schools into campuses of small schools. By this time, participation in YUC had grown to more than 1,000 membership-card carrying YUC youth leaders. YUC envisioned the creation of small autonomous schools on the campus, each with no more than 400 students, as means of substantially transforming school quality. With funds and advice from the Cross City Campaign for School Reform, YUC youth organizers and leaders traveled to Oakland, Chicago, Rhode Island, and New York City to learn about different small school models. They reviewed literature on the effectiveness of small schools, surveyed their peers to gather design ideas, and wrote a proposal to create four new small high schools focused on themes related to college access and career preparation. Joining with another youth organization—the Philadelphia Student Union—as well as adult groups, such as EPOP, Cross City, and Research for Action, YUC succeeded in winning district support for the youths' proposal in 2005. YUC is now actively monitoring the implementation of the redesign, as well as building community engagement in the schools.

South Central Youth Empowered thru Action (SC-YEA)

In this project, the experience of Marcus McKinney, a former gang member who got involved with Los Angeles's South Central Youth Empowered thru Action while in high school, is instructive. He eventually went on to become a staff member at SC-YEA. He reflected on how getting involved with SC-YEA helped him redirect his intellectual and leadership abilities into something more productive:

> [Before SC-YEA], I was part of a gang out here—I grew up around them and kind of idolized them. That is why I was reluctant to join initially, I thought

> it was not for me. . . . Even though I was a gang member I did not fit the stereotype, I was always interested in school. . . . They knew I should be doing something more productive. [SC-YEA] has helped me in that.

Training the next generation of leaders for social justice organizing was the impetus for the creation of South Central Youth Empowered thru Action. Initiated in the aftermath of the Rodney King riots in Los Angeles, SC-YEA drew its inspiration from the Civil Rights and Black Power Movements, promoting a vision of "Black and Brown Unity" for south Los Angeles.

SC-YEA formed in 1993 as the youth leadership and mobilization arm of the Community Coalition. Early work focused on criminal justice campaigns—mobilizing against the three strikes policy for minor felony offenses. In 1996, SC-YEA began organizing youth in local high schools as a complement to its statewide work. The first issue SC-YEA took on was the overcrowded and rundown conditions of school facilities. Armed with disposable cameras, youth documented the dilapidated conditions of their schools. With support from the Community Coalition, SC-YEA developed a list of repairs needed—using surveys and forums with youth to gather data and discuss their ideas—and created a multimedia proposal for a needs-based process of distributing school facilities funds. Together, adults and youth mobilized parent and community support for a school bond act. When the bond act passed, the organization successfully pressured the superintendent and school board to repair south L.A. schools.

As SC-YEA became more deeply involved in schools, organizers and youth began to notice data on local schools, which showed that more than 60% of south L.A. high-school students were dropping off of school rolls before reaching their senior year. SC-YEA released a report denouncing what they called the "disappearance" rate, which they said cut off young people's options for the future. Worse yet, SC-YEA argued, even if students remained in school, a majority would not have the necessary coursework to gain entry into a state university. In 1999, they wrote, "Only 12 percent of students graduating from South LA high schools went on to attend California's public four-year colleges."

In December 2000, SC-YEA launched a campaign to win a policy of mandatory access to college preparatory curricula in all Los Angeles high schools, because as one SC-YEA member explained, "Some people are taking cosmetology when they should be taking math analysis or trigonometry." To build district support for their proposal, SC-YEA worked with a broad coalition of youth groups, community organizations, and researchers from UCLA's Institute for Democracy, Education, and Access (IDEA) and Education Trust-West, as well as education reform groups. The coalition held rallies and press events, and met one-on-one with district leaders. Five years later, in 2005, the L.A. Unified School District passed a new district policy mandating college preparation for all (Hayasaki, 2005). With its allies, SC-YEA is now in the process of monitoring the implementation of a college preparatory curriculum policy to hold the district leadership accountable for allocating resources, both teachers and materials, to the areas that are most in need.

CRITICAL YOUTH ENGAGEMENT CORE COMMITMENTS

With the stories of these four youth organizing/YPAR projects in mind, we now detail the five threshold commitments to critical youth engagement: (1) youth carry knowledge, (2) critical analysis toward critical consciousness, (3) youth leadership in partnership with adults, (4) intersectionality, and (5) collective action for social change.

YOUNG PEOPLE AS SOURCES OF KNOWLEDGE AND POWER

In critical youth engagement projects, youth are not small adults in need of being filled up with the political wisdom of their elders. They are not lacking a real understanding of injustice or in need of remediation. Youth participatory action research and organizing are grounded in the recognition that youth hold important knowledge about their social conditions and about social change. This stance draws on deep tradition within community organizing about the right of disenfranchised members of society to participate in public life and to contribute their knowledge to the public sphere. Horton and Freire (1990) argue:

> The more people participate in the process of their own education, the more the people participate in the process of defining what kind of production to produce, and for what and why, the more the people participate in the development of their selves. The more the people become themselves, the better the democracy. The less people are asked about what they want, about their expectations, the less democracy we have. (pp. 145–146)

Challenging traditional epistemologies in which expertise is equated with university-based researchers, or elders, in sites of critical youth engagement, multigenerational collectives of elders, adults, and youth gather together to pool experience, knowledge, expertise, and lines of social inquiry. Decisions about research questions, methodological approaches, and interpretations of the data are made across generations. While organizing campaigns or activist research designs may be planned by a core group of highly involved youth leaders, the focus is always on expanding that leadership circle to bring new youth into the process and to ensure that the issues tackled and the solutions proposed resonate with a broader constituency of young people. Before tackling an issue, youth organizing groups typically survey their peers or conduct focus groups to ensure that their activism is responding to the concerns most salient to young people themselves. Surveys collected by SBU, SC-YEA, and YUC provided both ideas and evidence for campaigns to improve school counseling, facilities, and access to rigorous curriculum.

A Critical Analysis to Facilitate Critical Consciousness of History, Privilege, and Power

At the heart of critical youth engagement are spaces designed for critical community education with youth, to harvest what Freire refers to as "critical consciousness" (Horton & Freire, 1990). By inviting youth to unpack the historic and current role of structural forces such as racism, sexism, homophobia, and classism, which perpetuate inequality, and by understanding the history of social justice movements as key to this analysis, youth develop what Watts, Williams, and Jagers call a "systematic perspective on their life circumstances and current events" (2003, p. 188).

Among youth organizing groups, connections to the history of youth-led social movements in the United States are common. When youth join SC-YEA, for example, they participate in an eight-session Leadership Academy as a foundation for the educational and political work they do in their local high-school organizing committees. Youth read about the civil rights, women's, and Chicano movements, with an eye toward finding the common threads between historical struggles and their own experiences. SC-YEA youth learn to plan, research, study, mobilize phone banks, and use media and grassroots theater to effectively move campaigns forward. Critical analysis develops in tandem with a range of skills required to carry out the work of organizing, such as crafting agendas, facilitating meetings, public speaking, and mentoring peers (Watts et al., 2003). This kind of *liberation behavior* builds confidence in the youth as they confront oppression and see the impact of their own power (Watts et al., 2003; also discussed in Wilkenfeld et al., this volume).

Youth Leadership in Partnership with Adults

Youth voice and youth empowerment are at the core of critical youth engagement. Youth organizing places a heavy emphasis on youth leadership. Young people take the lead in generating ideas, facilitating meetings, and making decisions. At the same time, adults are not absent. Adults actively guide and educate young people but do so in a spirit of mutual inquiry, collaboration, and problem solving. Adults act as important allies to young people as they grapple with making informed decisions about research and social action. Adult organizers are guided by a core principle that they are not authorized to lead meetings, to speak for youth, or to represent the organization in public meetings of any kind. Instead, adult organizers' roles are to help young people identify and evaluate relevant information, share knowledge and insights, role-play and rehearse, and listen and challenge. Emphasizing youth leadership, in partnership with adults, frames youth themselves as assets and actors, contributing to growth and change in adults, institutions, systems, communities, and society (Zeller-Berkman, 2007).

Intersectionality: Analyzing and Organizing Across Sectors of Everyday Life

Critical youth engagement is grounded in the recognition that discrete *sectors* of public life—health, criminal justice, education, housing, immigration status, economics—are not separated but woven in the lives and communities of these youth. Drawing from critical race theory, Crenshaw (1995) describes critical youth engagement as focused on *structural* intersectionality, or "the diverse structures that shape one's experiences intersect to create one's social reality," and *political* intersectionality, or "the ways that those who occupy multiple subordinate identities, . . . may find themselves caught between the sometimes conflicting agendas of two political constituencies to which they belong" (Crenshaw, 1995), or are "overlooked by these movements entirely" (Cole, 2008, p. 444).

Young people study and organize *within and across* sectors of everyday life to demand college access, resist over-policing, and agitate for good schools. They take seriously the argument described by Collins (2000):

> Intersectionality refers to particular forms of intersecting oppressions, for example, intersections of race and gender, or of sexuality and nation. Intersectional paradigms remind us that oppression cannot be reduced to one fundamental type and that all oppressions work together in producing injustice. (p. 18)

Seeing, naming, and understanding the raced, classed, gendered, homophobic, and xenophobic policies (and milieu) that shape the life worlds of youth living in cities simultaneously creates the conditions necessary for a critical imagining of an alternative future.

Collective Action for Social Change

By analyzing problems historically and structurally, through an intersectional lens, young people and adult allies are primed to develop strategies for collective action that bear witness, challenge, and seek to change those conditions. In organizing, young people often meet with public officials to negotiate and make demands for change. In an effort to sway public policy, they are likely to sign petitions, stage protests, or hold public actions that put pressure on school administrators or public officials to shift policies. In SBU, a practice of *stepping up-stepping back* means that a youth member can attend a classroom presentation by SBU youth leaders one day, attend an education committee meeting the next, and testify before the school board the following week. SBU leaders are encouraged to see themselves as an integral part of the struggle to improve conditions in their communities. This sense of collective efficacy, of what they can accomplish together, is reinforced in the expectation that everyone present must contribute to the effort. The notion of collective efficacy—the perception of mutual trust and willingness to help community members in need—is even more powerful when we consider its positive effects on health and student academic achievement.

CRITICAL YOUTH ENGAGEMENT AS RESEARCH METHOD: PARTICIPATORY DESIGN AND METHODS IN POLLING FOR JUSTICE

To appreciate how critical youth engagement shapes research methods, we will focus on the participatory design, methods, and analysis of Polling for Justice, a project that has been conceptualized and implemented by all of the authors and many young (and older) collaborators. The three youth organizing projects described earlier also utilize participatory action research methods, although they use these methods within the broader conceptual frame of youth-led campaign development and action. In this second half of the paper, we focus on PFJ to provide a deep look at research methodology as an element of critical youth engagement. While we have spent the first half of the piece addressing the similarities of youth organizing and youth research, it is important to note that the methodologies for organizing and research are, on the ground, quite distinct. We focus here on PFJ as a participatory youth research project linked to youth organizing.

The PFJ researchers set out to study, theoretically and empirically, what we call *circuits of dispossession* (Fine & Ruglis, 2009) and *pools of youth resistance* in New York City, the ways in which social policies, institutions, and practices systematically deny youth of color key human rights across sectors (education, criminal justice, and health care), and the ways in which youth mobilize to resist, negotiate, and challenge collectively these very forms of dispossession. Living with rapid gentrification; intense police surveillance in communities of color; privatization of schooling, under the guise of choice; deportation of massive numbers of immigrants; shrinkage of the supportive public sphere; and expansion of the *disciplining* public sphere, we sought to investigate how urban youth experience, respond to, and organize against the profoundly uneven opportunities for development across the five boroughs of New York City in three sectors: education, health care, and criminal justice. PFJ is explicitly designed to gather and funnel social science evidence into organizing campaigns for youth justice—violence against girls and women, police harassment, college access, high-stakes testing, and access to comprehensive sexuality education, to name just a few. Through PFJ, we can see how critical youth engagement influences participatory action research design, method, analysis, and productions.

Youth as Holders of Knowledge: Challenging Traditional Notions of Expertise

In 2008, at our first gathering, more than 40 youth arrived, recruited from activist organizations, public schools, detention centers, LGBT youth groups, foster care, undocumented youth seeking college, and elite students from private schools, and they were joined by educators, representatives of the NYC department of adolescent health, immigrant family organizers, lawyers, youth workers, psychologists, Planned Parenthood researchers, geographers, and psychology and education doctoral students, in the basement of the Graduate Center of the City University of New York (CUNY).

We posed a single, simple challenge to the group: We would like to collectively design a large-scale, citywide research project, creating a youth survey of standardized and homegrown items and conducting a series of focus groups, to document youth experiences across various public sectors of the city. We explained that the youth and adults were recruited because of their distinct experience, knowledge, and expertise. The young people and adults then formed groups to pool their knowledge about prisons and their impact on youth, and about foster care, immigration and deportation, homeless shelters, peer relationships, access to health education, worries about feeling safe, and concern for communities. Once groups were formed, jackets and hats came off and the groups began their work. We created a graffiti wall where youth could jot down the questions they would want to ask of other NYC teens.

We organized groups across certain experiences of urban youth: In one corner was a young man whose father was in prison, a girl worried her mother would be deported, and a ninth grader fearful about gentrification, and they were designing questions about the real homeland security. In another corner, youth were reviewing standardized health items, such as the Youth Risk Behavior Survey (YRBS) and the National Longitudinal Study of Adolescent Health (AddHealth) about sexuality, reproduction, health, and nutrition. Angry about these surveillance systems asking questions that are "none of your business" and equally concerned with "risky" health behaviors without accounting for questions and issues of access, resources, opportunity (educational or otherwise), and cultural differences, we worked to understand why it would be important to track the relation of unsafe sex practices with type, quality, and access to comprehensive sexuality education (versus abstinence only, or none at all), or violence in a relationship, or dropping out of school. But these work groups also helped to stimulate critical discussions on the meaning of *health*; societal fears of and judgments about adolescence; cultural influences on health; reified and racist perceptions of *urban* youth and youth of color; and about how health behaviors cannot be divorced from opportunity structures and the social, economic, and political contexts into which one is embedded.

Down the hall, yet another group was talking about where they felt safe: At home? On the streets? In school? And a fourth group discussed youth experience with the criminal justice system. Together, they created a long checklist of contacts with police. What grew out of this was the most politically mobilized set of questions contained within the survey. In fact, nearly all of the criminal justice survey questions were developed by the youth. It became overwhelmingly evident that existing measures of youth experiences with policing in New York City failed to capture their realities.

Nesting the Research within an Analysis of Historic and Contemporary Injustice

Our work was designed as a contact zone (Torre, 2005) among youth from varied communities and ethnicities; and between young people and adults—advocates, practitioners, and researchers from the education, criminal justice, and public health fields. Within our research team, questions of privilege, power, and oppression are interrogated in community; youth experience leads the inquiry and adult skills surround and support; expertise is democratized and the *right to research* is assumed fundamental (Appadurai, 2004). This isn't always smooth, but creating spaces—for experience, analysis, theory, and design to be explored—happens in the prepared spaces of our Youth Research Camps.

Research camps are a method for building the democratic capacity of a research collective that both contains and interrogates difference and power. We begin our first session with exercises designed to strip away misconceptions about what constitutes scientific inquiry and who can engage in social research, democratizing notions of knowledge and expertise. We design scavenger hunts to reveal the different insights that researchers import—for instance, how the least formally educated members of our collectives (e.g., students in special education classes) often can read between the lines. We develop exercises and activities in the traditions of critical pedagogy and popular education to extract and honor multiple perspectives, and not just one designated right answer. Acknowledging many forms of intelligence is sometimes resisted by students who have been "at the top" of their schools, or privileged, or professionals who believe it is their job to teach the youth what they do not know. We spend much time helping young people explore themselves as intersectional: defined at once by culture, neighborhood, gender, class, adolescence, their interest in books and music, politics, sexuality, gender, language, humor, how people treat them, how they resist, and how they embody their worlds.

We read psychological theory, critical race theory and methods, and newspaper articles, and listen to music to *hear* how youth are represented, and to search for voices of dissent, challenge, and resistance; we "take" standardized scales and try out new survey questions; we learn to conduct interviews and role-play focus groups; we watch films and create questions; we spend time writing and discussing issues on the streets, and in their schools and homes; meeting other youth researchers from other regions; building research skills like designing the survey, piloting items, and collecting and analyzing qualitative and quantitative data; and presenting findings across NYC and at professional meetings.

We sponsored *seminars* for youth researchers and doctoral students called Statistics for the People. This is a statistical collective where everyone takes a set of questions and investigates the topic using our growing data. The collective is trained to approach their questions inductively using the philosophy and techniques of Tukey's (1977) exploratory data analysis. And all participating researchers—both youth and adult—take on the responsibility to *train* the next generation of youth researchers on the next project that grows out of the Institute for Participatory Action Research and Design at the Graduate Center of CUNY.

Over 18 months, Polling for Justice organized a series of multigenerational research camps focused, at the beginning, on building research expertise; sharing readings on the issues, histories of injustice, and political struggles of resistance; refining our research questions; specifying the design and sample; exploring intersectional analyses of qualitative and quantitative data; and generating provocative ideas for products, actions, scholarly papers, testimony, white papers, and performances.

INTERSECTIONALITY AS AN ELEMENT OF DESIGN, METHODS, AND ANALYSIS

Drawing from Crenshaw, Anzaldua, Du Bois, and Cole, in our research camps we explore *structural intersectionality*—the ways in which miseducation or police harassment, for instance, may trigger consequences for health disparities, days lost from school, and push-out or criminal justice involvement (or both). As a multigenerational research collective, we also explore each of our own *political intersectionalities*, the ways in which political categories such as race, ethnicity, gender, sexuality, (dis)ability, and class live in our bodies and communities, affecting how people see us, the institutions with which we find ourselves engaged, and how we see ourselves.

Several months after these groups met, following shared readings, histories, and a teenaged sense of intersectionality, the Polling for Justice Research Collective completed a 45-minute to one-hour survey, disseminated broadly across the city, on the streets and the Internet. Snowball samples were launched for geographic, ethnic, and social class diversity, with nodes starting in distinct public and private schools, youth organizing groups, community health clinics, a participatory action research collective of girls going through bat mitzvah, LGBT, and homeless youth groups. We completed data collection, with an N of 1,000, and with more than half the youth identifying as Black, Latino, Asian, or Multiple ethnicities. Because we are testing theories of critical consciousness and youth engagement, as well as documenting the landscape of opportunities for youth development across education, health care, and criminal justice, the survey includes items from national standardized instruments about education (NCES and the Consortium on Chicago School Reform) and health (YRBSS, AddHealth), items from Jost's systems justification scales, psychological well-being, and discrimination items, and Flanagan's measures of civic engagement, along with homegrown questions about relations with police, hunger, sex, drugs, safety, and understanding of injustice.

Intersectionality has deeply influenced our thinking about epistemology, design, methods, and analysis. Consider, for instance, our analyses of youth-police relations. As noted above, the focus on police as an environmental stressor emerged entirely from the youth. In our early discussions and research camps, among the youth researchers and in varied focus groups, the conversations about everyday life would often turn to confrontations with police. Both criticism of and support for police boiled over in focus groups and informal meetings across the city, filled with dissent, agitation, disagreement, and ambivalence. It was clear that we would need to dedicate a section of the survey to youth relations with police.

The researchers designed, piloted, and finalized a series of items to assess young peoples' varied contacts with police: positive—Have you been helped by a police officer? or Have you been given a second chance from a police officer?; and negative—Have you been called names, touched, stopped, frisked, ticketed, and so forth, by a police officer? (both in school and out of school).

Our preliminary evidence (Figure 23.2), suggests that across the sample, negative police contact is an unfortunately common experience in the lives of many NYC youth. Slightly less than half (48%) of the youth who responded to our survey reported, in the last six months, having at least one negative encounter with police; 21% reported three or more negative encounters.

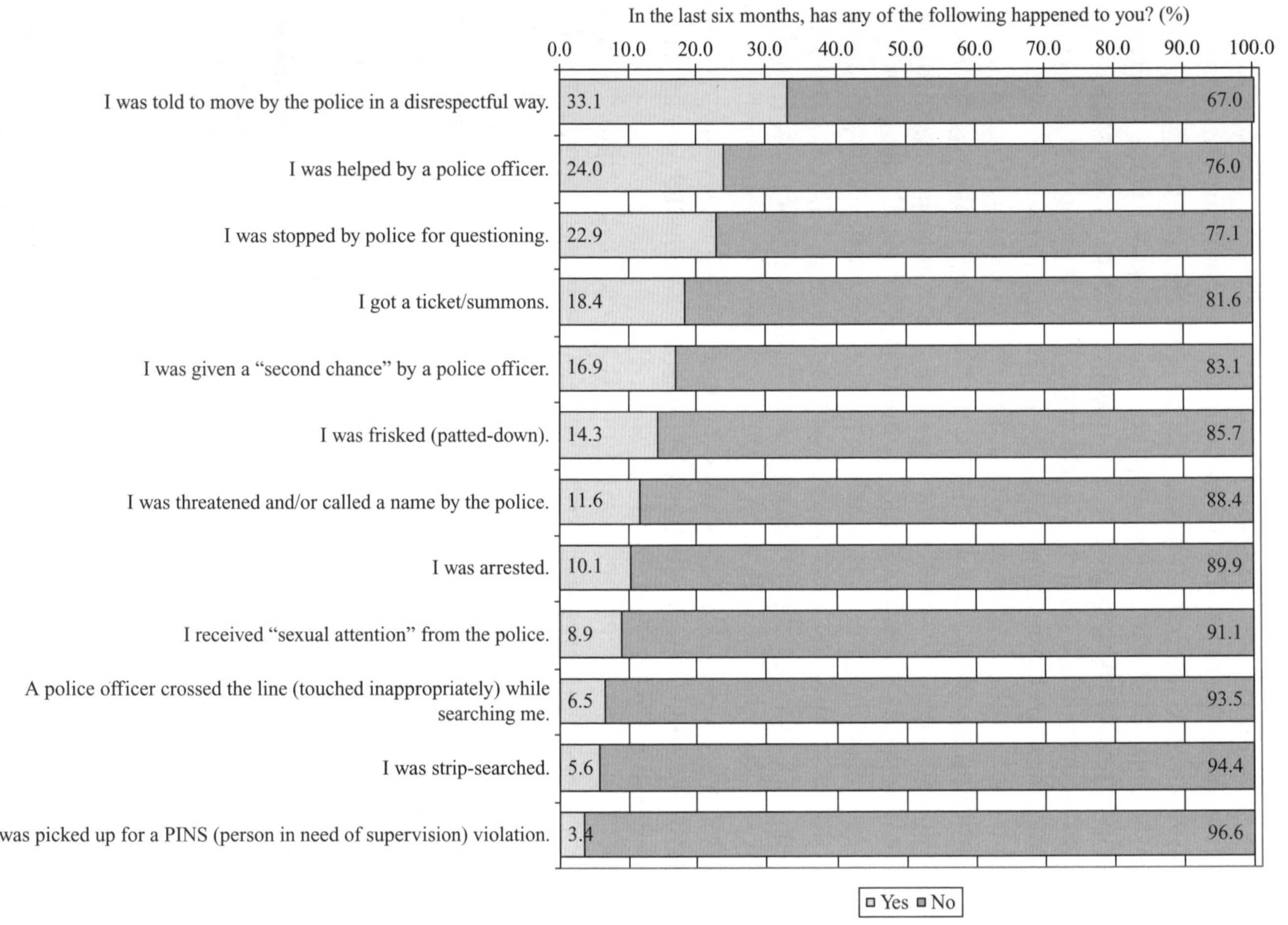

Figure 23.2 Youth Interaction with the Police

Marking the full complexity, 34% of the youth reported having at least one positive interaction with police in the last six months. When focusing our attention to what happens in school, we found that 14% of the youth experienced negative interactions with police and only 6% experienced positive interactions within the last six months.

With a commitment to analyses by gender, borough, sexuality, race or ethnicity, and social class, we learned that males, youth who are Black or multiracial, those from the Bronx, as well as youth who identify as gay, lesbian, or bisexual are more likely to report negative encounters with police in the last six months than other demographic groups in their age cohort.

To explore questions of structural intersectionality, we are investigating the educational and mental health consequences of negative police interactions (see also Ruglis, 2009). A cursory look reveals that a substantial majority of students who have dropped out or been pushed out of school report higher levels of trouble with police; the same is true for those who have been suspended or expelled. Regardless of the causal sequence, we can see the shape of the problem, raising questions about the role of the NYPD in New York City public schools.

We are also interested in documenting the intersection of negative police contact and youth mental health. We have learned that negative contact with police appears to be associated, in the aggregate, with elevated depression scores (based on the CES-D, Radloff, 1977). Taking intersectionality one step deeper, we are beginning to see racialized patterns in the mental health consequences of negative police contact. Blacks (including African Americans and African Caribbeans) and multiracial youth are quite likely to experience negative contact with police, but Blacks and multiethnic youth show the lowest rates of depression in relationship to the contact. While further analyses are needed, our concern is that in the African American community, negative contacts with police have become routine.

Intersectional analyses allow us to speak to the policy implications of heavy police surveillance, in terms of criminal justice, but also education, mental health, and youths' sense of trust in adults. These analyses allow us to map which groups of youth in which communities are most vulnerable to the surveillance and to the adverse consequences.

Youth Leadership and Adult Allies

These questions of youth-police interactions originated with the concerns of young people. At the start of the project, it was this issue that youth most wanted to discuss, and it has emerged significantly as the area in which our data are most provocative. When the preliminary evidence began to take shape, the adult researchers were outraged by the evidence of sustained patterns of negative interactions between police and young people, while the youth researchers were relatively nonplussed. The youth led the adults in the consideration of this provocative evidence. Our investigation brought us upon unexpected lines of inquiry, for example, a more nuanced understanding of how police policy impacts youth experience.

We mentioned the patterns of police youth interactions to a judge in the South Bronx, who seemed unsurprised and said, simply, as if it were obvious, "overtime." When pressed, she elaborated, telling us that police pick up groups of youth after school and book them.

Judge L. explained to the young people that police get "overtime" for picking up groups of youth after school and booking them. Even if they find nothing, usually there is some evidence of "resistance" or a joint or a box cutter that will ultimately justify the stop. Students then lose time from school and develop a record. All of which has been confirmed in our data. The interview with the judge led us on the path to investigate Operation Clean Halls, whereby police have the right to patrol in the hallways of public housing and anyone caught in the halls who "should not be there" or doesn't have appropriate ID can be picked up and charged with trespassing. We, adults and youth, are unbraiding the policy and institutional strands of dispossession and in so doing, we are rewinding the causal tale of how so many youth of color end up entangled in the juvenile justice system, following the lead of the youth, with the skills of adult researchers, lawyers, and advocates.

At the Intersection of Social Theory, Youth Experience, Research, and Action

We have presented these data in a variety of venues and have gotten calls and e-mails about interest in collaboration, from lawyers and researchers (and the Hong Kong Police Research Division), seeking to replicate the study. Six teams of researchers from Washington, DC, Baltimore, Philadelphia, Newark, and NYC are exploring a five-city study of police harassment as a public health threat to the development of urban youth. Further, we are preparing an amicus brief on the frequency, geography, racialized distribution, and consequence of police harassment of urban youth as a risk factor in public health and education for use by lawyers, educators, and youth who end up in court. In addition, youth will be crafting youth documents (flyers, web sites, performances) on youth-police relations.

And finally, we are moving these data into performance. Youth researchers are being trained in Playback Theatre, a form of improvisational theatre, to prepare for a performance of the material at a variety of professional and youth organizing events. We have been deeply influenced by not only W.E.B.

Du Bois's scholarship, but also by something else of his that is little known—his pageant form. In 1913, W.E.B. Du Bois produced a pageant called "The Star of Ethiopia" (DuBois, 1915a). It was "a great human festival" with a cast of 1,000 African Americans using procession, story, and extravagant costumes to tell a productive history of African Americans. The pageant form was designed to "teach the colored people themselves of their history and their rich emotional life" (Du Bois, 1915b, p. 230). The stage was a corrective on the long history of the reality that "any mention of Negro blood or Negro life in America for a century has been occasion for . . . a dirty allusion, a nasty comment or a pessimistic forecast" (Du Bois, 1924, p. 56). Du Bois used pageantry, performance, and circus theater in order to explore alternative possibilities about African American history and reality and inject them into the public imagination. Building on the DuBoisian legacy of pageants, the Polling for Justice project plans an artistic performance of our mixed methods data in order to spark new visions of, and for, adolescent engagement and ignite our audiences to participate with us in re-envisioning adolescent experience. A theatre/dance/mural/musical production, "Who Cares? Youth Desire and Outrage," is a provocative representation of the Polling for Justice research study.

CRITICAL YOUTH ENGAGEMENT, ORGANIZING, AND PARTICIPATORY ACTION RESEARCH: IMPLICATIONS FOR METHODOLOGY

Synthesizing the research, organizing campaigns, and conceptual frameworks introduced in this chapter, in conclusion we now consider a *theory of method for critical youth engagement*, a research agenda that might capture the wide net of outcomes propelled by critical youth engagement projects. How might research be organized theoretically and methodologically to capture the psychological, social, academic, educational, and civic consequences of projects like Polling for Justice, Sistas and Brothas United, Youth United for Change, and South Central Youth Empowered thru Action? How might we assess the impact on youth over time and also on the adults, institutions, policy changes, and mobilization of social movements?

While research on youth organizing and YPAR is relatively embryonic, what exists is predominantly positive. Preliminary evidence suggests that at the level of individual and collective developmental outcomes, academic persistence, civic engagement, and educational aspirations over time, youth organizing and YPAR offer significant opportunities for civic engagement that bear substantial fruit in terms of varied outcomes of academic, psychological, and social well-being (see Cammarota & Fine, 2008, for ethnographic accounts of YPAR projects; see also Gambone et al., 2004).

Research by the Annenberg Institute provides further evidence of how young people experience their involvement in organizing and what outcomes this form of engagement produces. In a survey of 124 core leaders involved in SBU, SC-YEA, and YUC, researchers found that organizing provided a platform for engaging students in political and civic activity, and this engagement encouraged long-term plans among youth for sustained political and civic involvement. Youth in the Annenberg study reported *higher levels of political engagement* than their counterparts in a national survey by the Center for Information & Research on Civic Learning and Engagement (Mediratta, Shah, & McAlister, 2009). Sixty percent of youth involved in organizing, for example, stated they had participated in community problem-solving within the past year, while only 19% of the national sample had done so. In addition, more than half of the organizing sample reported planning to learn more about politics and stay involved in activism in the future, and close to 40% reported planning to pursue a job in organizing.

We found that involvement in organizing was positively associated with a sense of *agency and youth civic and political engagement*. Involvement in organizing significantly predicted *school motivation*, above and beyond the effects of gender, age, and grades. Overall, 80% of youth in the organizing sample planned to *pursue a college education*, and 49% said they *expected to obtain a graduate or professional* degree beyond college. Compared to national rates of 39% of African American youth and 33% for Latino youth who expected to pursue graduate work, these research findings are very encouraging (Ingels & Dalton, 2004).

There is, however, much more we need to learn if we are to understand how urban youth and adults engage, and yearn to engage, in civic and community problems. Reflecting on the work of PFJ, SBU, YUC, and SC-YEA, we conclude with a sketch of a research framework inspired to broaden our ideas about the empirical outcomes activated by critical youth engagement projects. Table 23.1 is a research and organizing matrix that embodies the central commitments of *critical youth engagement* and invites a broad panoramic documentation of and inquiry into the wide reach of such projects. As the Annenberg research suggests, and the case studies in Cammarota and Fine (2008) describe, powerful youth organizing and Youth Participatory Action Research projects have consequences well beyond the participating youth. Outcomes can be documented in young people, over time, and also in the adults, in approaches to organizing, program governance, and decision making; in institutional arrangements; in the ways that science is conducted; in how social movements are organized; and in the democratic, participatory reformation of public policy.

Across the top of the chart are our preliminary notions of key elements of critical youth engagement that may be found at the intersection

Table 23.1

A Research Matrix for Analyzing Critical Youth Engagement:
Documenting Access and Outcomes for Youth, Adult Allies, Program Governance/Dynamics, and Policy Change

		Elements of Critical Youth Engagement				
		To what extent do these strategies of research/organizing cultivate, support, and rely upon **youth knowledge,** experience, and wisdom?	To what extent do these projects undertake critical inquiry **of historic struggles for human rights**?	How does the project study structural intersectionality and political intersectionality?	To what extent is there evidence of **youth leadership in collaboration with adult allies**?	What forms of **action/ activism** are foundational to, or grow out of the project?
Levels of Documented Impact	Mapping a racial topography of access and opportunity					
	Documenting Individual level outcomes—youth *and* adult development					
	Documenting youth outcomes over time[a]					
	Program level changes[b]					
	Policy changes provoked or inspired by youth organizing/youth research					
	Shifts in youth alliances and networks with other youth and adults[c]					
	Transformations in how universities see themselves[d]					

[a] e.g., pursuit of education, sustained engagement in social change efforts, involvement with the next generation, sense of responsibility and agency for advancing social change, jobs in fields of policy-making/social change.

[b] e.g., governance, power dynamics, effects on adult allies.

[c] e.g., across organizations, generations, and communities.

[d] e.g., as resources and participants in reimagining public life for the next generation.

of youth leadership, youth participatory action research, and youth organizing projects. These elements are offered to provoke a radical image of civic engagement opportunities rather than a five-point checklist. Along the side are levels of analysis that might be part of the research to understand the broad reach and complex consequences of critical youth engagement on youth, adults, institutions, social movements, and social policy. We offer the table to signify possibilities for rich research projects that could be designed to assess the differential impact of youth research and youth activism, or the value of studying history and critical analysis of contemporary conditions. We could imagine quasi-experimental designs, across cities, with surveys and ethnographies documenting varied outcomes of YPAR and youth organizing on policy, program, youth, and adults, over time.

Youth organizing and YPAR projects bear substantial consequences that ripple out into waves of democratic engagement and participation, across generations, across sectors, and across time. There is an electricity of collective inquiry and action that spirals out from the center of these projects. It is an electricity that encourages youth to know that they have a *right to research* (Appadurai, 2004) and an obligation to speak back and give back, and that adults may be counted on as allies. Such ambitious work deserves an equally ambitious research design to capture the breadth and complexity of critical youth engagement.

Across communities and institutions, we have found YPAR and youth organizing to be strategic initiatives in which critical inquiry and youth leadership feed educational policy-making. Simultaneously undertaking research and activism, the projects described in this chapter are pitched to address key policy concerns about school size, policing of urban youth, high-stakes accountability, college access, and school culture. Fueled by the urgency and specificity of policy reform, each project is grounded in a vision of educational justice as youth develop very specific skills of inquiry, organizing, and civic engagement. Indeed, with a new Special Interest Group (SIG) at the American Educational Research Association, a stream of new books and volumes that address organizing and youth PAR (Cammarota & Fine, 2008; Ginwright, 2009; Mediratta, Shah, & McAlister, 2009; Anyon, 2005; Fine, 2009), ironically (or predictably), at a moment of national crisis, the field of critical youth engagement is flourishing. In these very difficult times, we witness—in the United States and abroad—collectives of youth researchers and organizers collaborating with adult allies, speaking out for human rights and educational justice for all youth, and most particularly those who are low income, youth of color, immigrant youth, indigenous youth, LGBT youth, and youth with disabilities. We are humbled, and hopeful, that critical youth engagement marks a significant turn in academic and applied projects once designed *for* youth—now designed and led *by* youth.

REFERENCES

Anyon, J. (2005). *Radical possibilities: Public policy, urban education and a new social movement*. New York and London: Routledge.

Appadurai, A. (2004). Capacity to aspire: Culture and the terms of recognition. In R. Vijayendra and M. Walton (Eds.), *Culture and public action* (pp. 59–84). Stanford: Stanford University Press.

Baldi, S., Perie, M., Skidmore, D., Greenberg, E., & Hahn, C. (2001). What democracy means to ninth graders: U.S. results from the international IEA Civic Education Study. Washington DC: NCES, U.S. Department of Education.

Browne, J. (2003). *Derailed! The schoolhouse to jailhouse track*. Washington, DC: Advancement Project.

Cammarota, J., & Fine, M. (2008). *Revolutionizing education*. New York: Routledge.

Carlo, F., Powell, A., Vasquez, L., Daniels, S., Smith, C., with Mediratta, K., & Zimmer, A. (2005). Youth take the lead on high school reform issues: Sistas and Brothas United. *Rethinking Schools, 19(4)*, 62.

Cole, E. R. (2008). Coalitions as a model for intersectionality: From practice to theory. *Sex Roles, 59*, 443–453.

Collins, P. H. (2000). *Black feminist thought: Knowledge, consciousness, and the politics of empowerment* (2nd ed.). New York: Routledge.

Crenshaw, K. W. (1995). Mapping the margins: Intersectionality, identity politics, and violence against women of color. In K. W. Crenshaw, N. Gotanda, G. Peller, & K. Thomas (Eds.), *Critical race theory: The key writings that formed the movement* (pp. 357–384). New York: New Press.

Du Bois, W. E. B. (1915a). Star of Ethiopia. *The Crisis, 11*.

Du Bois, W. E. B. (1915b). A pageant. *The Crisis, 11*.

Du Bois, W. E. B. (1924). The Negro and the American stage. *The Crisis, 28*.

Fine, M. (Ed.). (2009). Postcards from metro America: Reflections on youth participation critical research for urban justice. *Urban Review, 41(1)* [special issue].

Fine, M., & Ruglis, J. (2009). Circuits and consequences of dispossession: The racialized realignment of the public sphere for U.S. youth. *Transforming Anthropology, 17(1)*, 20–33.

Flanagan, C. (2004). Volunteerism, leadership, political socialization, and civic engagement. In R. M. Lerner & L. Steinberg (Eds.), *Handbook of adolescent psychology* (pp. 721–745). Hoboken, NJ: John Wiley & Sons, Inc.

Flanagan, C., Cumsille, P., Gill, S., & Gallay, L. (2007). School and community climates and civic commitments: Patterns for ethnic minority and majority students. *Journal of Educational Psychology, 99(2)*, 421–431.

Gambone, M. A., Yu, H. C., Lewis-Charp, H., Sipe, C. L., & Lacoe, J. (2004). A comparative analysis of community development strategies (CIRCLE Working Paper 23). Medford, MA: CIRCLE (The Center for Information and Research on Civic Learning and Engagement).

Ginwright, S. (2009). *Black youth rising: Race, agency and radical healing in urban America.* New York: Teachers College Press.

Haste, H., & Hogan, A. (2006). Beyond conventional civic participation, beyond the moral-political divide: Young people and contemporary debates about citizenship. *Journal of Moral Education, 35(4)*, 473–493.

Hayasaki, E. (2005, June 15). College prep idea approved in L.A. *Los Angeles Times,* p. 1, sec. B.

Horton, M., & Freire, P. (1990). *We make the road by walking* (B. Bell, J. Gaventa, & J. Peters, Eds., pp. 145–146). Philadelphia: Temple University Press.

Ingels, S. J., & Dalton, B. W. (2004). *Trends among high school seniors 1972–2004* (NCES 2008–320). Washington, DC: National Center for Educational Statistics.

Kahne, J., & Middaugh, E. (2008). Democracy for some: The civic opportunity gap in high school (CIRCLE Working Paper 59). Medford, MA: CIRCLE (The Center for Information and Research on Civic Learning and Engagement).

Lutkus, A., Weiss, A., Campbell, J., Mazzeo, J., & Lazer, S. (1999). *NAEP 1998 civics report card for the nation*. NCES, U.S. Department of Education.

Marcelo, K., Lopez, M., & Kirby, E. (2007). *Fact sheet: Civic engagement among minority youth*. Medford, MA: CIRCLE (The Center for Information & Research on Civic Learning & Engagement).

Mediratta, K., Shah, S., & McAlister, S. (2009). *Community organizing for stronger schools: Strategies and successes*. Cambridge: Harvard Education Press.

Meiners, E. (2007). *Right to be hostile: Schools, prisons, and the making of public enemies.* New York: Routledge.

Mills, C. W. (1959/2000). *The Sociological Imagination*. Oxford, UK: Oxford University Press.

Niemi, R., & Junn, J. (1998). *Civic education: What makes students learn.* New Haven, CT: Yale University Press.

Radloff, L. S. (1977). The CES-D Scale: A self-report depression scale for research in the general population. *Applied Psychological Measurement*, *1*, 385–401.

Rubin, B. (2007). There's still not justice: Youth civic identity development amid distinct school and community contexts. *Teachers College Record*, *109(2)*, 449–481.

Ruglis, J. (2009). *Death of a Dropout: (Re)Theorizing School Dropout and Schooling as a Social Determinant of Health* (Doctoral dissertation). New York: City University of New York.

Shah, S., & Mediratta, K. (2008). Negotiating Reform: Young people's leadership in the educational arena. *New Directions for Youth Development*, *117*.

Sherrod, L. (2005). Ensuring liberty by promoting youth development. *Human Development*, *48*, 376–381.

Smetana, J. G., Campione-Barr, N., & Metzger, A. (2006). Adolescent development in interpersonal and societal contexts. *Annual Review of Psychology*, *57*, 255–284.

South Central Youth Empowered thru Action. (1999). *Check the facts*. Los Angeles, CA: Community Coalition for Substance Abuse Prevention and Treatment.

Torney-Purta, J., Barber, C., & Wilkenfeld, B. (2007). Latino adolescents' civic development in the United States: Research results from the IEA Civic Education Study. *Journal of Youth and Adolescence*, *36*, 111–125.

Torre, M. E. (2005). The alchemy of integrated spaces: Youth participation in research collectives of difference. In L. Weis & M. Fine (Eds.), *Beyond silenced voices* (pp. 251–266). Albany: State University of New York Press.

Tukey, J. W. (1977). *Exploratory data analysis*. Reading, MA: Addison-Wesley.

Watts, R. J., Williams, N. C., & Jagers, R. J. (2003). Sociopolitical development. *American Journal of Community Psychology, 31(1/2)*, 185–193.

Zeller-Berkman, S. (2007). Peering in: A look into reflective practices in youth participatory action research. *Children, Youth and Environments, 17(2)*, 315–328.

CHAPTER 24

Informed Social Reflection: Its Development and Importance for Adolescents' Civic Engagement

ROBERT L. SELMAN AND JANET KWOK
Harvard University

And you can also commit injustice by doing nothing.

Marcus Aurelius, *Meditations*

In seventeenth-century England, political philosopher Thomas Hobbes cautioned in *Leviathan* that without a strong central government, humanity's infinite greed would erupt in "the war of all against all" (1994). Four-hundred years later, Neo-conservative op-ed writer David Brooks of the *New York Times* concludes from the research on evolutionary psychology (Hauser, 2006; Haidt, 2001) and the most recent findings from social-cognitive neuroscience (Zelazo, Chandler, & Crone, 2010) that cultural chaos and tribal violence are the inevitable result of "what humans beings do without a strong order-imposing state" (2007). Both conclusions dismiss the reflective capacities of human nature as powerless before the giants of culture and biology. These grim forecasts are unsurprising given their contexts: Hobbes was in the midst of the English Civil War, while Brooks was attempting to make sense of the brutality of the Iraq War. Unlike Hobbes, however, Brooks ascribed the source of man's unrest to an urge more atavistic than avarice: "We're tribal and divide the world into in-groups and out-groups." The failed utopian living experiments of the 1960s and 1970s, he claimed, emphasize the futility of attempting to live in harmony and to defy "the nature of our [socially oriented] neurons and the lessons of evolutionary biology."

While the enhancement of human capacity for reflection has served as a pillar of educational practice from kindergarten through college (Yoshikawa & Shinn, 2008; Faust, 2009), it has had a tepid reputation in the social sciences and public opinion for quite some time—and the outlook is far from sanguine. Among the challenges that reflection faces is the perception that it ought to act as a crystal ball in which what we say we will do will materialize as what we actually do; if we cannot seriously expect any person to commit to this responsibility, how can we insist the same of human thought? Yet, as much as a defeatist attitude may appeal to our pessimism, it provides no solutions for how we must continue to live. Even Hobbes did not write about his troubled times without proposing a solution; he detailed the need for a social contract and a singularly powerful ruler. Despite Brooks's dismissal of experimentation in communes and collectives as foolhardy efforts to elude our destructive impulses, he neglects that these endeavors flowered in the midst of the Vietnam War. While these experiments might be failures in that they did not endure, the impetus and boldness in pursuing them is a reminder that in spite of all evidence to the contrary, a number of individuals believed in humanity's capacity for living in peace, and chose to act upon this belief through challenging and extending contemporary notions of community.

Decades later, researchers are asking the same questions, but with a more acute sense of our species' limitations. Given human nature's complexity, we, as researchers in search of answers, need to start with reasonable and manageable questions: How do adolescents make meaningful choices in their lives, for instance, when they are given the opportunity to take a stand or participate in proactive civic engagement, confront ethical dilemmas in everyday social situations, or consider the implications of civic and ethical choices made in historical events for their own choices? Yet, neither past research on these topics (Adelson, 1971; Haste, this volume; Metzger & Smetana, this volume) nor attempts to design sound empirical measures to assess adolescents' interpretations of these experiences (e.g., Loevinger, 1966, 1978) are new. Some earlier scientific explorers in this general area of psychology, like Loevinger, have used theoretical perspectives grounded in empirical measures to build a developmental model of individual worldviews. Others, through cognitively oriented developmental theory, have deduced the ontogeny of each of one or more of these disciplines, domains, or similar constructs, led by Kohlberg's stage theory of justice as emerging moral reasoning structures (Kohlberg, 1979), and followed by other disciplinary domains, for example, faith development (Fowler, 1981), religious development (Oser, Scarlett, & Bucher, 2006), and historical understanding (Kuhn & Franklin, 2008; Seixas, 1996).

Building on this past work, this chapter describes a newly defined and interdisciplinary construct we argue is necessary for understanding the conditions that promote or hinder youth civic engagement. *Informed social reflection* integrates three psychological domains that can be examined from the combined perspectives of developmental and cultural or contextual psychological theory: civic orientation, ethical awareness, and historical understanding.[1] There are several reasons why this construct fulfills a need in contemporary psychological theory, research, and practice. First, it helps to clarify an important tension in psychological science: the debate about whether moral actions are primarily driven by cognitions or emotions (Fischer & Bidell, 2006). Second, it addresses a related fault line in educational science and practice: the degree to which one can or should teach civic engagement and moral conduct in terms of either or both understanding the issues and acting as an ethical citizen (Sherrod, 2005; Haste, 2005; Kahne & Westheimer, 2006; Torney-Purta, 2009). Third, the construct of informed social reflection integrates the ontogeny of civic orientation, ethical awareness, and historical understanding in ways that have currency in both psychological research and educational practice; it suggests measures that can speak to both the individual's developing competencies and the impact of classroom climate on teaching and learning in the humanities and social studies (Schaps, Battistich, & Solomon, 2004; Lowenstein, in press). In addition, it also acknowledges that students' awareness of historical perspectives such as collective cultural narratives (Salomon, 2004a, 2004b; Fuxman, 2007) and individual autobiographies (Lightfoot, 2008) play a central role in the ontogeny of civic thought and action.

This construct, informed social reflection, can be examined in a way that takes into account both the contextual support available to adolescents and their own rapidly expanding cognitive capacity. Furthermore, the construct can be measured in a way that is sensitive to the impact of programs designed to improve the quality of its use (Selman & Barr, in press). Although it is challenging to include all these elements in one construct, we find that the integration of this array allows researchers to deepen their

---

[1] The conceptualization of the ideas about informed social reflection we express in this chapter have been well informed by intense discussions and collaborative work undertaken by a team of investigators working to formulate methods to assess the impact of the Facing History educational model on students whose teachers participated in a professional development and subsequently implemented the approach it espouses (Facing History, 2010). In particular, Melinda Fine, New York University, Ethan Lowenstein, Eastern Michigan University, and Dennis Barr, Facing History and Ourselves, worked with the first author as a group of co-investigators to conceptualize and design methods that could capture the integrative practice embedded in the Facing History theory of change and the integration of knowledge currently in the field. Various conceptualizations of ways to integrate civic, historical, and ethical reflection are under consideration by members of that group. This chapter represents the authors' current thinking, which has benefited immeasurably from this partnership; however, all faults in this conceptualization are ours alone.

understanding in a way that would not be possible with a more limited scope. In theory today, it is easy to preach interdisciplinarity but hard to practice it. Measurement capacity is one road toward practice. In education today, we are often willing to compromise by superimposing the marginal content subject-matter of civic and ethical education over the warp of history or literacy, rather than truly weaving them together. In social science today, we often end up with a patchwork quilt of motley multiplicity rather than a Persian rug of well-integrated domains and disciplines—the latter process takes time.

Fundamental to our own exploration is the integration of empirical research with educational *practice,* particularly educational programs that promote thoughtful deliberation and discussion in classrooms. Here, in this paper, our practice focus is on Facing History and Ourselves (1994), a mature multidisciplinary student and teacher development program with which we have partnered for many years.[2] With respect to our own research on adolescent social development, we have sought to apply a developmental perspective embedded in a contextual framework to measure adolescent students' informed social reflection: their civic competencies, their historical understanding, and their ethical awareness. With respect to research on the nexus of psychological development and school and classroom climate, we are interested in new avenues to understand and to measure how classroom structures and school climates support or hinder teachers in their efforts to promote students' desire and capacity to apply reflective competencies to ethical and civic engagement (Jones, Brown, & Aber, under review; Schaps et al., 2004).

By developing theory-driven methods to assess how young people understand their social and societal choices within their own peer groups and classrooms, we can see ways in which students' civic, historical, and ethical interpretations of the social world interweave and enrich (or encumber) each other. The work we report here has developed over more than 30 years, guided by the lure of the knowledge developmental social and psychological scientists can obtain when they leave behind the confinement of their carefully controlled laboratories and venture into the unruly thicket of practice in search of theoretical and empirical inspiration (Selman & Dray, 2006).

[2] But we will also allude to others' approaches, both those implemented in the recent past, such as the Just Community Schools movement (Power, Higgins, & Kohlberg, 1989), as well as the present, for instance, Voices Reading and Social Development (Selman, 2003), an elementary-grade approach that makes the moral lessons in children's literature an integral part of the literacy block; and the Developmental Studies Center's Caring School Community (Schaps, Battistich, & Solomon, 2004), which emphasizes that learning best occurs when schools are strong communities with purposeful deliberative processes.

We begin this chapter with a general framework for the integration of practice and theory as it directs research on the ontogeny of civic, ethical, and historical consciousness. In the section that follows, we explore how our earlier assessment of the impact of one learning organization, the Facing History and Ourselves program (hereafter, Facing History), inspired research using this theory. The third section describes how the theory has evolved over time through exchange with and inspiration from practice, first as a vehicle for the understanding of how adolescents make civic and ethical choices, and then through the translation of such findings into tools for both educational evaluation of program impact *and* for the assessment of students' social learning and development.

A FRAMEWORK FOR THE INTEGRATION OF PSYCHOLOGICAL RESEARCH AND EDUCATIONAL PRACTICE

Our current approach to the measurement of adolescents' ethical and civic competencies has evolved from earlier practice-driven research in program evaluation (Schultz, Barr, & Selman, 2001) that made use of quasi-experimental methods, including assigning teachers, schools, and students matched on relevant factors to intervention and control groups, and also from theory-driven research on the growth of youth social awareness and their ethical and social choices (Selman, 2003).[3] To illustrate this theory-driven measurement strategy, consider the following three incidents that commonly occur in middle and high schools. We will use them to illustrate the way middle- and high-school students think about the choices they and others make in social situations of modest to severe duress.

1. At recess, a student sees a group of his friends teasing a boy who is often mocked and picked on for his eccentric behavior. They are making fun of the way he speaks and making jokes at his expense. The student who sees this wonders what to do.
2. Midway through the school year, a student, recently arrived from another country, joins the class. She wears a headscarf every day as part of her religion. The teacher who thinks that she could be teased for wearing the headscarf decides to ask her about it after class to try to be helpful. Students in the class wonder why the teacher has taken this step.

[3] In 2005, Facing History, with the support of the Richard and Susan Smith Foundation, implemented another evaluation, described in *The Facing History and Ourselves National Professional Development and Evaluation Project: Continuing a Tradition of Research on The Foundations of Democratic Education* (2010).

3. Some students have written racist slurs on one of the walls of the auditorium. The principal responds by banning the use of the auditorium for after-school activities. Members of the student government debate having a "student-only" meeting at lunch to talk about what to do.

The first incident taps into students' awareness of the ethics of social relationships, while the second allows for the examination of the degree to which students appreciate the complex historical and cultural dynamics that underlie the ethnic and religious differences they regularly experience. The third incident, a threat to a school's civic climate and to its students' civil rights, presents students with an opportunity to deepen their understanding of the importance of participation in the school community. While each scenario draws most obviously upon one particular competency in the student and one primary categorical domain within the academic disciplines, all three vignettes actually require a capacity for ethical awareness, civic orientation, and historical understanding. These prompts might be compared to a funnel into which knowledge and experience in each of these three domains are poured to mix and unite as *informed social reflection*.[4] This informed social reflection, in turn, can have a reciprocal exchange with active engagement with people and social institutions. While the use of incidents or dilemma discussion in categorical psychological research (Turiel, 2010; Rest, 1986; Lind, 2006) or historical understanding (Kuhn & Franklin, 2008) is certainly not new, we believe the way we interpret students' responses to these situations represents a next step toward what the aim and purpose of adolescent civic engagement might be.

Like others, we also believe that students who are taught to think critically and reflectively about history, civic issues, and ethics—through the pedagogical tools of course work and the teacher's capacity to foster a safe and vibrant classroom climate—will be better equipped to deal with analogous incidents, both in school and in society (Torney-Purta, Lehmann, Oswald, & Schulz, 2001). Figure 24.1 provides an integrative view of the three student competencies we perceive as in need of a seamless integration if we are to more fully understand the meaning of informed social reflection and apply it to civic engagement. Taken together, this Venn diagram captures the adolescent competencies that we believe need to be assessed in concordance with one another, both in research and in practice.

In practice, these competencies are essential to the core pedagogical aims of programs such as Facing History, Voices Reading and Social Development,

[4] Figure 24.2, which is explained in greater detail elsewhere in this chapter, provides a sense of why a funnel metaphor is appropriate for describing how the constituent parts of informed social reflection interact.

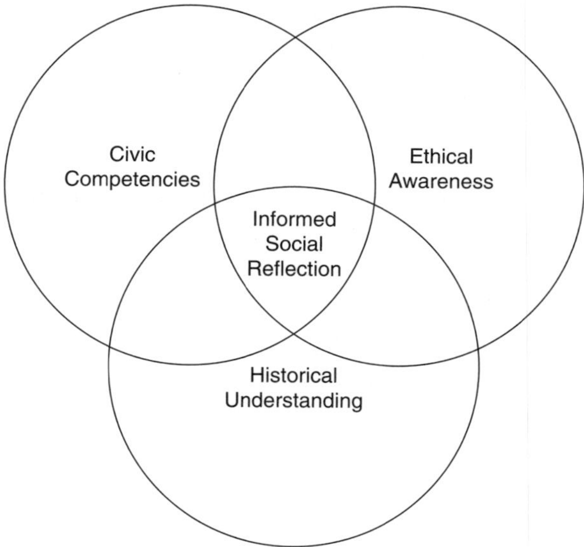

Figure 24.1 Primary Components of Informed Social Reflection

Caring School Community, and the Just Community Approach, but they also represent another method of conceptualizing the individuals' management of relationships among the self and the other over the developmental arc of time, within or without the structure of an ethical or civic education program (Selman & Feigenberg, 2010). As Piaget argued, it is this mutual mixing of social perspectives that provides the awareness of others' perspectives, and the crucial awakening of choosing to place those alongside, not behind, or below, one's own (Lightfoot, 2008). The harmony created through balancing these competencies and their interactions—how our own perspectives are shaped and how we let others' perspectives join the discussion—is the foundation for building civic engagement.

What kinds of educational programs promote the skills to integrate these domains and what kind of evidence is needed to demonstrate to educational decision makers the importance, both of the programs and the skills? We often hear that what one can measure, one can improve. Yet, valid psychological measures grounded in the structure of how developmental psychological theory and empirical evidence operationally define *student improvement* are still sorely needed in social science and in education (Solomon, Watson, & Battistich, 2001). In order to consider student outcomes in programs with similar goals to promote civic and ethical awareness, we propose both finding and recording students' responses to incidents like those mentioned in the preceding section, wherever they occur—through observations, ethnographies, interviews, and surveys. In order for incidents such as these to be useful as *meaning-oriented* evaluation tools—that is, as measures that require the interpretation of students' responses to assess the development of students' informed social reflection—they also need to be seen as authentic and engaging by students and teachers alike.

In order to dramatize this process, consider the nexus of research and practice as seen through the telescopic lens of our 15-year partnership with Facing History. Facing History is an international nonprofit educational organization founded in 1976 by two eighth-grade social studies teachers in a Massachusetts public school (Strom, 1980; Strom, Sleeper & Johnson, 1992). Today, it provides professional development to middle- and high-school educators both in the United States and internationally. Most of the educators who participate are history teachers, but social studies, literature, and service-learning instructors, as well as school principals also take part in the program. The Facing History and Ourselves mission statement is:

> . . . to engage students of diverse backgrounds in an examination of racism and prejudice, as well as equity and social justice, in order to promote the development of a more humane and informed citizenry. By studying the historical development and lessons of the Holocaust and other examples of genocide, students make the essential connection between history and the moral choices they confront in their own lives.

Melinda Fine, a civic learning specialist and a member of the Facing History and Ourselves Board, characterizes the unique contribution of the Facing History approach to the integration of historical, ethical, and civic education as follows:

> Through a carefully crafted "scope and sequence," students begin their study by exploring themes relevant to adolescents' lives and peer relationships, such as identity, belonging, exclusion, conformity, and resistance. Early in the course, they acquire a "civic vocabulary" that helps them think about why human beings do what we do—what drives our need to belong and to divide ourselves into groups; what enables or constrains our decision to ostracize or to include; to obey or to speak out; to act or to stand by. These questions guide students' subsequent study of particular historical periods, informing their understanding of why individuals and groups chose to act (or not act) as they did. As students' historical inquiry deepens and a fuller constellation of factors are introduced and explored, they continue to weave back and forth between historical particularities and human universals—between "history" and "ourselves." This rich interplay helps students "own" their study in a very personal way: reflecting on their own behaviors and beliefs, students gradually come to interpret, judge, and ultimately draw important civic lessons from history itself. (Fine, 2006, p. 3)

Teachers trained in the Facing History pedagogy ask students to put themselves in the shoes of others, both throughout history and in their own lives, facing dilemmas similar to those presented above. Students learn that throughout history, the choices individuals make in response to situations such as these can fall into categories termed bystanding, resisting (also called upstanding), or joining (perpetrating). When students stand by, they do nothing to stop the harm unfolding. When they upstand, they attempt to stop the hurtful behavior. When they join the perpetrators, they surrender or escalate to negative actions. Within the scope of the program, students consider how the issues at stake in these familiar situations are relevant to significant historical events. As Ethan Lowenstein, a teacher educator and social studies researcher notes (2003):

> It is essential to students' capacity to make informed choices about civic and ethical engagement that they understand several elements of interpreting past events. Students should gain an understanding of how decisions in the past led to patterns in society today [see, for example, Lee & Shemilt, 2007], possess an historical consciousness of how individual, group, and national identities are formed [e.g., Seixas, 2004], and develop some comfort with diverse perspectives through the critical and collaborative examination of historical accounts. (Parker, 2003)

This expanded historical knowledge base allows students to be more thoughtful participants in discussions and deliberations on contemporary social and political issues. Bystanding in a class or school or neighborhood can be extrapolated to the bystanding that occurred collectively and individually in historical cases. Bear in mind, however, Barton and Levstik's (2004) reminder: "How the past led to the present is useful as a basis for contemporary decision making when it acknowledges the degree of free will both of people in the past and of ourselves" (p. 75). Students also wrestle with the extent to which they are truly free to act according to an idealized view of the best responses to contemporary and historical situations.

As described earlier, the Facing History pedagogy we draw upon for theoretical and empirical inspiration includes the expectation that students will make connections between the historical events and eras they study and their reactions to events in their own lives. The curriculum emphasizes case studies about historical periods when individuals and group members in civil society find themselves in tense and challenging situations with difficult choices to make; these choices tend to define the actors' chosen roles in the context of events: victim, bystander, perpetrator, upstander, or resister. The program's original resource book for educators (which is still the integral or core program material), *Facing History and Ourselves: Holocaust and Human Behavior*, asserts: "Our students must learn that the world they live in did not just happen. It is the result of choices made by countless individuals and groups" (Facing History and Ourselves, 1994, *xiv*).

One classic pedagogical debate that classroom-based civic and ethical education programs must grapple with is whether and when the program should concentrate on influencing students' actions directly or on providing students with the capacity and motivation to engage in informed reflection that increases the likelihood they will be engaged members of society. This discussion is essentially a question about a program's *theory of change*. The second strategy is often perhaps the more realistic and appropriate school and classroom option, given that students do not make decisions isolated from their backgrounds or the particular situations they are facing. If, however, informed social reflection provides a crucial communicative connection between action and the underlying reasoning, we arrive at another question: What does this kind of communicative expression look like?

Attempts to assess a program's effectiveness in instilling informed social reflection in the context of these core debates raise a significant challenge. For instance, while a program might seek to inculcate an awareness of psychological or cultural differences among ethnic, religious, and other identity groups, which is an important part of the pedagogy, it is important not to confuse the promotion of this sensitivity to identity group difference with a simplistic relativistic ethical framework (Barr, 2005). Is it possible to establish whether adolescent choices are less or more adequate ethically, regardless of the identity or group background of the students? This is what Kohlberg (1979) and Rawls, by implication (1971), suggest, although philosophers with a communitarian orientation do not necessarily agree (Sandel, 1998).

To construct measures that address both of these aspects of adolescent decision making—the content of their choices and the quality of their justifications—requires a theoretical framework that can account for responses understood as both qualitatively different in cultural (and other diverse) orientations and measurably distinct (quantitatively) in their adequacy (for better or worse) of informed social reflection. That is, we need to be able to assess how imaginative and well-informed students' awareness of individual and group differences are in correspondence with the depth, connectivity, and knowledge behind their reflective capacity to communicate. In addition, such measurement needs to clarify the degree to which it is measuring the competence of deep reflection, and the degree to which it is measuring the competence of communicative expressions. Nevertheless, as scholars and educators, we cannot be burdened by the inability—or refusal—to say what ethical choices are more or less adequate, with all due respect for the particularities of cultural and contextual variation notwithstanding.

The outcome study of Facing History, which we began in 1996, suggested promising results but also hinted at the limits of any attempts to provide ethical education to children (Schultz et al., 2001). While eighth-grade students who had taken a Facing History class showed gains in interpersonal relationship awareness and decreases in racist attitudes and self-reported fighting behavior relative to the matched control group, their civic awareness was not significantly greater than those of their peers who had not received the program. This is not surprising. Eighth-grade students are at a developmental phase where, motivationally speaking, they apply their new social-cognitive skills—based on a growing awareness of the importance of mutual social reflection—to their social lives and peer relations. But these middle-school years may very well be a time when their social awareness both undergoes significant growth and becomes habituated with respect to their theories about how the social world works (Martin, Sokol, & Elfers, 2008), so it is important not to wait. Educators need to demonstrate to students what is interesting (and of self-interest) about civic issues in the broader society.

REFLECTIONS ON ADOLESCENT INFORMED SOCIAL REFLECTION: THE CASE OF SOCIAL INCLUSION AND EXCLUSION AMONG PEERS IN SCHOOL

Let us go back a bit further in time to seek a way to better understand this possibility. In April of 1992, several high-school students who had taken the Facing History module in the ninth grade had been invited to participate in a conference with Elie Wiesel, the Nobel Prize winning essayist and Holocaust survivor, where they had the opportunity to discuss the role of hatred in the world. An essay by Eve Shalen, a public school student in a Chicago suburb, on her personal experience with the painful experience of exclusion and the powerful lure of being accepted captured the imagination of the audience. Here is her (abridged) story:

> My eighth grade consisted of 28 students most of whom knew each other from the age of five or six. Although we grew up together, we still had class outcasts. From second grade on, a small elite group spent a large portion of their time harassing two or three of the others. I was one of those two or three, though I don't know why.... The harassment was subtle. It came in the form of muffled giggles when I talked, and rolled eyes when I turned around. If I was out in the playground and approached a group of people, they often fell silent. Sometimes someone would not see me coming and I would catch the tail end of a joke at my expense.
>
> There was another girl in our class who was perhaps even more rejected than I. One day during lunch... one of the popular girls in the class came up to me to show me something she said I wouldn't want to miss. We walked to a corner of the playground where a group of three or four sat. One of them read aloud from a small book, which I was told was the girl's diary. I sat down and, laughing till my sides hurt, heard my voice finally blend with the others. (Facing History and Ourselves, 1994, p. 29–30)

Nearly 15 years ago, while pondering the design of the study just mentioned to evaluate its impact, the Facing History program's leaders and a group of affiliated co-investigators were inspired by the words of this ninth grader. Eve's essay encouraged us to pursue a line of research and practice focused on how adolescents make social choices in two time frames. While Eve made a snap judgment at one particular moment, she also wrote an essay showing reflective judgments she developed over a longer period of time.

Using Eve Shalen's story as a paradigm for how adolescents can make meaning of past events, in this case a personal one, our analysis focused on various ways in which the dynamics of social inclusion and exclusion play out among adolescents (Killen, McGlothlin, & Lee-Kim, 2002)—in the classrooms and corridors as well as during the recess and lunchtime periods. Practitioners and researchers alike valued Eve's story for both its expression of quintessential feelings of adolescence and its illumination of the way in which context influences adolescents' responses. Translating a critical incident like the one Eve described into a methodological vehicle for applied research, however, requires a research process involving several steps, and the tyranny of time excluded it from the initial 1996 evaluation study.

Instead, we decided to use Eve's essay as an essential and authentic thread running through our ongoing research program to study social and ethical development during adolescence (Barr, 2005; Feigenberg, 2007; Feigenberg, Steel King, Barr, & Selman, 2008; Selman & Feigenberg, 2010; Selman & Barr, in press). Eve's dramatization of how she made her decision became part of a research method we called the *In-Group Assessment* (Feigenberg et al., 2008). This measure asks adolescents to consider choices that can be made when one stands in different roles in incidents of peer social exclusion as a means of gaining insight into how they view interpersonal relationships and social exclusion. The method is notable in that it sought to evaluate, within an integrated theoretical framework, both the strategies that adolescents would take in such hypothetical situations and the justifications for their actions.

Two fundamental questions framed the basic research:

1. How do adolescents understand the difficult civic, social, and ethical choices they commonly confront in situations of interpersonal, group, or intergroup conflict, including the explicit strategies that they can draw upon when they make their choices, and the conscious justifications they can give for their actions?
2. What can systematic attention to the variations in the classroom and school context, climate, and culture in which these choices are made contribute to our understanding of how adolescents interpret the social behavior of others and reflect on their own?

The questions above provide guidelines for how we might adapt the events in Eve's essay (and in the three critical incidents we previously described) to think about the development of civic engagement. If we design questions to determine the individual's level of informed social reflection (awareness of how social perspectives are taken into account through the integration of civic, historical, and ethical understanding) and the degree to which this awareness is coordinated with that individual's perceptions and interpretations of the social context (the reading of "contextually" and "culturally" significant meaning), we can achieve a more nuanced picture of how such components interact and ultimately converge to form a pattern of adolescent engagement in social and civic life. This is a topic we will return to when we discuss how interpretations of events from the past, present, and future are informed by social climates such as those found in schools and classrooms.

These questions could then be integrated with questions drawn from one of Facing History's pedagogical aims, ensuring that students understand how choices depend on how one chooses to define one's role—victim, bystander, perpetrator, or resister—and the extent to which these roles determine the conduct and character of people in the past and in ourselves. By examining students' responses as witness or bystander to social exclusion, as well as suggestions about what Eve could do, a dual-prompt approach would invite comparisons of strategies and justifications from two vantage points (or roles). Samples of students' responses from the 8th to 12th grades were collected (Feigenberg et al., 2008; Steel King, 2007; Feigenberg, 2007).

Under both conditions, witness-observer and invitation to join the perpetrators, we coded the students' responses in two steps. First, we classified the strategies the participants in our study believed were available to Eve in dealing with the choices she faced in both roles as observer and invitee. Next, we coded the justifications participants gave for the strategies they said they thought they would suggest Eve use in each role. We found we could reliably code for the students' responses for three types of strategies that Facing History emphasizes in its pedagogy: upstanding-resisting, joining the perpetrators or perpetrating the exclusion, and the bane of Marcus Aurelius, bystanding.

We then coded for four orientations that covered most of the justification they gave for the strategies chosen. We characterized these four interpretative orientations as:

1. Personal safety oriented, where actions are guided by self-or-other-defense or protection (where safety refers to a focus in individual self-protection, rather than building a safe and caring climate within which self and others can relate)
2. Rule oriented, where actions are guided by an adherence to conventions and order

3. Respect and care oriented, where actions are aimed toward the cultivation of equitable treatment or kindness or where actions are directed toward harmonious social relationships
4. Prosocial transformative orientated, which most saliently focuses on the justifications for actions that promote or ensure the sustainability of better group circumstances and may include an awareness of how actions in the moment are informed either by the sociohistorical past of the group and/or its future

The three-by-four matrix in Table 24.1 provides an integrated view of responses that suggests how each type of strategy and each justification orientation can or might pair up with one another. Although prosocial

Table 24.1
Adolescent Social Reflections: Strategies and Justifications with Anchor Responses

	Safety	Conventional	Relational	Transformational
Upstand	Eve could have told the girls she thought it was wrong to be doing what they were doing. At least she would be helping to protect someone else.	I think the best way would be to tell the girls that it was wrong to steal a diary and then read it. It was personal property.	The best way to go would be to say no and help the person in trouble, because isn't that what you would want someone to do for you.	Convince them not to mock her is the best choice because she could maybe change someone from bad to good. But they have to understand it's better for them in the long run.
Perpetrate	Eve could have gone and joined in because then she wouldn't be picked on.	The best thing to do would be to make fun of the girl because that is what everyone does.	I would accept the offer to join in to fit more in.	I think if she first went along with them she would have then been able to later on stop the mocking of the other girl or anybody else.
Bystand	Eve should say no because then she wouldn't get in any trouble.	Eve could have made an excuse and left. It is wrong to pick on people.	Say "I can't, I'm too busy now," and walk away would be best because you would leave another chance for you to hang out with girls.	Probably declining would be better. Then maybe she wouldn't have the friends but she would know how to be a good strong person. In the long run that's more important.

transforming justifications do not appear in our data with perpetrator strategies, and are not likely to be made for perpetrating, they do appear for *perpetuating*, where some students believe that attacking perpetrators with their own strategies is necessary for social change (Feigenberg et al., 2008). For instance, one might attempt to intervene on behalf of a victim of social exclusion through redirecting the ostracism at the perpetrators with the justification that it will ultimately reduce victimization all around.

How did the adolescents in our study understand the types of strategies available to Eve, and what kinds of justifications did they give for them? From the vantage point of Eve as a witness to the victim's exclusion, many adolescents recommended active resistance to the perpetrators. From Eve's vantage point, when invited to participate in mocking the girl, however, they were far less likely to propose this upstanding posture. This is not surprising, since Eve herself tells us she joined the perpetrators. However, the practical implications, both for measurement and for the program, are important.

Adolescents who chose to bystand—neither supporting nor participating in perpetration—tended to emphasize social norms and rules in their justifications. Put differently, attention to norms and rules did not increase the likelihood that a student would choose to upstand or intervene. Students who were more likely to recommend direct support for the victim (choosing to upstand), however, were also more likely to perceive their social environment as one that was amenable to prosocial change and future improvement (as indicated by their justifications for upstanding).

When we compared the strategies given by students from each of the different schools, we were surprised to find that, on average, students in some of the schools in the sample were more likely than students in other schools with similar demographic characteristics to favor defending the victim, as opposed to remaining uninvolved, even when invited to join in the teasing. There were also clear school-level differences in the proportion of students who supported their choices based on socially transforming justifications, although it is important to note that the number of such justifications coded in this orientation was modest across all the schools. But in some schools, they were greater than in others.

In all schools, however, a prosocial and transformative orientation was still a minority stance. In hindsight, we wished we had collected more detailed data on the contextual factors in all the schools that might have shed light on students' choices. In fact, this finding suggests that it is essential to take school context into account when trying to understand students' informed social reflections. In particular, research that taps into the students' background and the culture or climate of the school could help to clarify possible reasons for the variation we saw in our results (Torney-Purta, 2009; Coll & Vasquez Garcia, 1995; LaRusso & Selman, 2003; Serpell, 2002).

Lacking the quantitative evidence to illuminate the impact that differences in social climate might have on students, we relied on some qualitative, in-depth interview data that we did collect on the strategies they saw as available to Eve, and their justifications for selecting one over the others (Feigenberg, 2007; Selman & Feigenberg, 2010). We also explored how they aspire to and do handle issues similar to Eve's in their own school. This method can provide some insight into the psychosocial maturity of the study participants as embedded in their own context and expressed in an evolving conversation. After all, students do not live in a vacuum. Decisions are, unsurprisingly, a product of not only their cognitive development, but also the contexts in which those decisions are made. In the next section, we discuss these interactions and how they both challenge and inform practice and research.

HOW PRACTICE-INSPIRED RESEARCH EVIDENCE IS INCORPORATED INTO A THEORY OF INFORMED SOCIAL REFLECTION

Theorizing about how students would act in hypothetical contexts is one-dimensional if students' regular or particular contexts—that is, their day-to-day school environment—are neglected. Considering students' background and the culture or climate of their schools is essential in clarifying how students make their decisions in difficult social situations embedded in school (Coll & Vasquez Garcia, 1995; Serpell, 2002; Torney-Purta, 2009). For instance, it is insufficient to evaluate a student's actions without knowing the student's reasons, and these are not necessarily evident through observation or even self-report (Selman & Feigenberg, 2010). To illustrate this point, we will compare interviews with two girls from very different backgrounds who were interviewed about Eve's situation, and their own: Ann, an upper middle-class ninth grader in a school located within a resource-rich community, and Danielle, a student in the eleventh grade who lives in a low-income community with high crime rates and weapons inspections at her high school's entrance.[5]

In considering the implications of being asked to join in, Ann suggested, as the way to deal with exclusion, a choice that we coded as an upstand strategy: "tell [the bullies] what they were doing was wrong." In contrast, Danielle recommended a mix of bystand and perpetuation-perpetrate: "you got to do what's best for yourself, join in if that's what you have to do." Ann justified her choice with a response we interpreted as a Prosocial Transformational orientation: "If enough people are willing to do something right about a problem, the problem would not exist anymore"; and Danielle relied

[5] For more about these girls, see Selman and Feigenberg (2010).

primarily on a Safety (or self-protective) justification: "The most important thing is to protect yourself. You know how girls are, bitchy, and in this community you gotta know how to deal with them." Do these responses provide evidence that Danielle and Ann differ in their ability to understand the different kinds of strategies or justifications in our analytic framework? Far from it—consider context, such as the girls' schools, or even culture, and the differences between how girls from distinct social backgrounds make sense of how the world operates.

While longitudinal evidence would be more compelling, nevertheless, the fact that prosocial-transformative accounts emerge in children's repertoire of expressed justifications slightly later chronologically than the other types of justifications (Steel King, 2007) could be used to interpret the transformational justification used by Ann as more developmentally advanced. However, it is important to consider that Ann's response is embedded within a social or school context that probably supports, or at least does not present obvious hurdles to, the tendency to express the sense of self-empowerment and social transformation implied by that type of orientation. Ann's primary day-to-day concerns are less likely to be focused on her own psychological or physical safety, as may very well be the case for Danielle.

In other words, Danielle operates within a school climate that, for whatever reasons, if it were measured, could be marked by—at worst—disorder, aggression, violence, lack of safety, and disconnection among teachers and students. At best, it might be characterized by regulations and policy that impose a strict order, strong unyielding authoritarian hierarchy, and unelaborated, arbitrary enforcement of rules. Ann's school, on the other hand, also for reasons beyond our evidence, might be marked at the least by a sense of fairness and respect for students and for student-teacher relationships, and at best, an authentic concern for mutual well-being. Ann's use of a transformational justification can just as reasonably be interpreted as reflecting the supportive context in which she lives, which Schaps and colleagues (2004) refer to as the provision of opportunities for influence (voice) and self-direction (choice), as well as by an interpretation focused solely on her developmental level of social awareness. We do not know the extent of either girl's repertoire of potential strategies, but we do know their expressed social reflections are contextualized within their school's (and by implication and social science evidence, their community's and their culture's) climate.

To understand how powerfully the burden of history and context is expressed through something like school climate, consider the example of contemporary Chinese adolescents whose parents endured the Cultural Revolution. The years between 1966 and 1976 were characterized by widespread chaos and societal collapse triggered by the Chinese Communist Party's efforts to break from the past and embrace a modern, industrialized vision of China. The ideology was strongly anti-intellectual and destructive: Chinese youth recruited to eradicate bourgeois influence were encouraged to use violence, resulting in teachers being publicly humiliated by their students, while neighbors and family members accused each other to preempt their own persecution (Mitter, 2008).

Those who came of age in the aftermath of a suspicious and fearful time understandably instilled in their children the necessity of avoiding self-disclosure, having witnessed their families being betrayed by even the most trusted confidants (Fong, 2004). To further compound this interpersonal tension, the education system in China became examination-based and thus intensely competitive as a result of test scores becoming the only factor in determining where one would be educated, and ultimately, what standard of living one could attain (Fong, 2004). Under these circumstances, Zhao has found troubling revelations from her ongoing investigation of how Chinese adolescents and their parents experience and understand the meaning and importance of adolescent friendship (Zhao, 2007). Some of the youth reported that they could not remain friends with those who transferred to better ranked schools due to jealousy, while others lamented that their parents often discouraged friendships with lower ranked students. What would these adolescents do if confronted with a situation of social injustice similar to Eve's case: Would they bystand, intervene, or join in the ostracism? It would be unsurprising if the students were advised by their parents to remain uninvolved. Since communities everywhere must grapple with the civic legacy of the past, historical understanding is essential to creating informed social reflection.

The comparison of the two girls, as well as the experiences of a generation of contemporary Chinese youth, demonstrate how both the individual's developmental capacity and the social structure's level of support need to be jointly considered to inform our interpretation of the choices adolescents see as available and the choices they might make under different circumstances (LaRusso & Selman, 2003). A developmental analysis at the level of each individual—here that of the adolescent student—can inform our analysis of the competencies that underlie Ann and Danielle's interpretations of choices available to them and their justifications for the choices they selected. However, we cannot understand or interpret the meaning of the variety of responses given in the interviews solely by turning a single developmental lens upon individuals' competencies alone. We cannot even adequately interpret the meaning of their expression of ideas. We need another kind of developmental lens to examine the quality of support or to suppress the various contexts and settings imposed upon individuals. This is the need and the purpose of the dual lenses, a bifocal developmental analysis of individual and setting qualities and competencies as described in Figure 24.2.

Social Developmental Factors (Individual level of analysis) The individual's **capacity** for the reflective **coordination** on social perspectives, i.e., of different "social" points of view (p.o.v)	**Social Contextual Factors (Group/context level of analysis)** The developmental organization of the (interpreted) social context (e.g, the school) within which the individual functions
0 Undifferentiated Perspective (Unaware of or dismissive of different p.o.v)	**0 Egocentric Defined Relationships** (Contexts marked by disorder, aggression/violence, lack of safety, disconnection)
1 First Person Perspective/One-Way Strategies (One-way—either mine or yours—understanding of p.o.v)	**1 Unilateral Relationships/Interactions** (Contexts marked by order, hierarchy, and strict enforcement of rules)
2 Second Person Perspective (Effort to understand the other's p.o.v and the self's p.o.v from other's perspective)	**2 Reciprocal Relationships/Interactions** (Environments marked by equality, fairness/justice, and respect for others)
3 Third Person Perspective (Consideration and effort toward coordination of both points of view, understanding of mutuality of views)	**3 Mutual Defined Relationships** (Contexts marked by concern for mutual well-being, equity, freedom of expression [voice], and civic participation [choice])

Qualities of Social Reflection of ethical, civic, and historical evidence and experience
(from dismissive-uninformed to engaged, informed, "meta-reflective")

Possible Psychological Orientations toward Civic and Ethical Engagement (Upstand/Resist—Bystand/Ignore—Perpetrate/Retaliate)

Self-Protection Oriented/ Survival-Based; Power Oriented/Rule-Based; Respect and Care Oriented/ Empathic Fairness-Based; Future Oriented/ Prosocial-Transformative Based

Figure 24.2 The Interdependence of Individual and Contextual Developmental Factors in the Quality of Informed Social Reflection

It is significant for both theory and practice that by early adolescence (roughly between 10 and 15 years of age), but probably not much earlier, individuals have developed the competencies to understand each type of social strategy and justification used in our analysis (see also Flanagan & Tucker, 1999; Kohlberg, 1979; Martin et al., 2008; Selman & Adalbjarnardottir, 2000). While at times a concern with personal safety will determine their actions, at other times the promotion of systemic social change will be their motivation, whether it occurs on a small scale, as in a class or school, or on a large scale, as in society. A supportive school environment can be the crucial element in what kinds of social, ethical, and civic conduct are seen and interpretations are heard: Giving students the sense that they are valuable and respected members of the community produces an array of positive effects ranging from increased academic motivation to a rise in altruistic behaviors and a decreased likelihood of participating in risky behaviors like substance use and violent behavior (Schaps, 2007). Sometimes they will think that following rules is preferable, and sometimes caring for others is the guiding concern. There are probably times when some or all these motivations are in play simultaneously. Students' capacities to choose between these terms of engagement need to be attuned to the context in which they express them.

Paradoxically, as portrayed in Figure 24.2, while both the individual and contextual (setting level) inputs (upper right and left side of the figure respectively) can be organized hierarchically, the outputs, the interpretations the students express (bottom center) cannot. Their interpretations are an amalgam, determined not only by the habits of *self and social reflection* that, for example, Ann and Danielle have developed, but also bound to and *informed by* the social context in which these interpretations are made. This, however, is far from the end of the story. In the conclusion to her essay, Eve demonstrated the experience of greater self-awareness than we typically encounter in the early adolescents we interview:

> Looking back, I wonder how I could have participated in mocking this girl when I knew perfectly well what it felt like to be mocked myself. I would like to say that if I were in that situation today I would react differently, but I can't honestly be sure. Often being accepted by others is more satisfying that being accepted by oneself, even though the satisfaction does not last. Too often our actions are determined by the moment. (Facing History and Ourselves, 1994)

Eve's comments suggest that through reflection on this past event in her life, she is able to see beyond the context of her immediate situation, even as she is aware of the impact it had on her actions in that moment.

When Eve says, "I would like to say . . . ," she is reflecting on both her own thoughts about the past and speculating about her possible actions in the future. These *imagined* actions are based on what she has learned in the past about herself and concluded about human nature. When a comment demonstrates an awareness of what the self has learned in reflection on the past about oneself, we call it an autobiographical statement: It is an instance of—as well as a form of—self-understanding. When a comment applies to the awareness of the thoughts expressed and actions taken and lived *long ago and far away* by those removed from the self—by individuals or groups—in that society's time and place, we call it historical understanding. More specifically, it is a sophisticated form of understanding of human agency that requires historical perspective-taking (Hartmann & Haselhorn, 2008; Carretero & Voss, 1994).

Theoretically speaking, Eve suggests an important type of critical and informed ethical reflection, one that goes beyond the four types of orientations we most commonly found to different degrees in the repertoire of the adolescents in our research. Our interpretation of Eve's final comments is that she has refined her capacity to apply insights gleaned from the evidence from past actions to project her choices, her conduct, and her justifications into the multiple possibilities of the future. Figure 24.3 provides a *flexible interpretation* of Eve's final comments as it aligns with each of the four justification orientations that emerged from our empirical studies, flexible in the sense that each comment is not necessarily aligned precisely with each code, but approximates its essence. This process of differentiation across orientations that Eve is able to express, here of Eve's perspective *then* and her perspective *now* ("when I knew perfectly well what it felt like to be mocked myself") and of hierarchical integration ("Often being accepted by others is more satisfying than being accepted by oneself, even though the satisfaction does not last. Too often our actions are determined by the moment."), is the classical hallmark of an emergent developmental capacity (Werner, 1948).

Imagining the future in this sense, however, expresses as much a form of *reflection on engagement* with others as it suggests a cognitive-developmental capacity or competence. In a recent theoretical paper, Martin et al. (2008)

Figure 24.3 An Application of Metareflective Sociality on the Orientations of Four Types of Justifications

describe the development of *metareflective sociality*, as the emerging capacity to reflect on the range of strategic social opportunities and their justifications *in situ,* without value judgments. This form of awareness goes beyond the four justification orientations laid out in the figures and in Table 24.1. Not only does this "[metareflective] level of 'informed social reflection'" better integrate all of the four types of orientations we found in our research, this awareness requires students to understand the orientations of people in a range of different contexts. Nurturing this level of consciousness is an unassailable developmental aim of education (Kolhberg & Mayer, 1972). Teachers who see their craft as a moral enterprise aspire to this goal (Lowenstein, 2003), and we collectively hold this forth as a capacity of mind, which students might eventually reach with sufficient reflection on actual engagement.

THE EVOLUTION OF TOOLS TO ASSESS PROGRAMS THAT PROMOTE INFORMED SOCIAL REFLECTION

Though they are excellent points of departure, interviews with individual students cannot provide an adequately complete picture of whether or why students in general have successfully developed informed social reflection. Assuming a capacity to imagine the widest possible range of social strategies and justifications, how well do students on average understand and justify their social choices? To answer this question, researchers must find the balance between measuring the degree to which students—on average—value choices, such as upstanding, while at the same time acknowledging the forces that may prevent or promote their implementation. This requires a method that is true to both developmental and contextual factors and yet can be applied to large samples. This means it needs to be both relatively easy to score and highly reliable, on the one hand, and able to ascertain the range of possible meaning behind students' choices, on the other. It is challenging to translate a complex theoretical framework into a simple assessment measure. To demonstrate one way this can be done, we now return to the three critical incidents we portrayed at the beginning of this chapter.

FROM EVE TO A STRATEGY FOR PROGRAM EVALUATION

To compare the research process we just described to code the Eve Shalen vignette with ways we might translate those findings into practical tools for evaluation research, we return to the first of the three critical incidents we described earlier in portraying the construct of Informed Social Reflection (portrayed in Figure 24.4).

At recess, a student sees a group of his friends teasing a boy who is often mocked and picked on for his eccentric behavior. They are making fun of the way he speaks and making jokes at his expense. The student who sees this wonders what to do.

1. Below are several choices other students gave to this situation. Please rate each response on a scale from "Would not recommend at all" to "Strongly recommend." You can give responses the same rating if you wish. Then select the one you would recommend to the student, and give a brief reason why.

	Would Not Recommend at All	Do Not Recommend	Recommend	Strongly Recommend
a. Teasing is hurting the new boy. (*Safety oriented*)	□	□	□	□
b. There is a school rule against this behavior. (*Rules oriented*)	□	□	□	□
c. Saying something now might help other students feel that they can speak out in these situations. (*Prosocial future oriented*)	□	□	□	□
d. The new boy should know he has support and is not alone (*Relational*)	□	□	□	□

2. Now choose which one of these four reasons you think is the best? (Check only one):
   a □ b □ c □ d □
3. Why do you think that reason is the best?________________________________
4. How often does this kind of situation happen in your school? (Check only one)
   Very rarely □ Rarely □ Often □ Very often □
5. If you saw this situation in your school, how would you rate each of the following actions you might take? Once again, you may give the same rating to different actions:

Actions: Check one for each row (You may check the same rating more than once)	Very bad	Bad	Good	Very good
a. Just stay out of it. (*Bystander*)	□	□	□	□
b. Tell the students to stop making fun of the new boy. (*Upstander*)	□	□	□	□
c. Go over and join in making fun of the new boy. (*Perpetrator or Perpetuator*)	□	□	□	□

6. Which one of these three actions would you be most likely to take?
   a □ b □ c □
7. Please explain why:
____
8. What else would you do in this situation and why?
____
____

Figure 24.4 Translating a Critical Incident: Item Responses Created from Eve Shalen's Essay

We have designed this mixture of closed-ended and open-ended responses to be both cost effective and sensitive to the theoretical ideas and empirical evidence described in this chapter. Each of the four "Item Responses" in questions 1 and 5 are *anchors* (Boyatzis, 1998) drawn from evidence gathered during the practice-inspired research phase to represent the primary categories we found at that time. (See Table 24.1.) Question 4 orients to issues of school climate. Questions 3, 7, and 8 are open ended but limited in scope. They provide a brief opportunity to probe more deeply into the participant's reflective processes and to make a connection between a recommended action and the rationale behind it. This measurement strategy asks students to rate, rank, and reflect/respond upon their choices; it combines the closed ended independent rating of each of four individual items, the ranking or selection of one of those items from the set of four empirically derived items (multiple choice), and the written response to provide a reason for (reflection on) the choice they select. [6]

It is worth noting several distinctive characteristics of this methodology. First, as mentioned and perhaps, most important, the responses to the prompt "What would you recommend?" are drawn from the anchor responses in the interview data. Second, and this too is crucial, the participants do not immediately choose which response they would recommend, but instead, first rate (i.e., judge, evaluate) each response separately and autonomously. Next, the method employs both this item rating and a multiple-choice selection process. The prototypical justifications are rated in the hypothetical situation (question 1), and the prototypical choices are rated in incidents familiar to the student who is taking the measure (question 5). In both cases, participants are asked to briefly describe why they recommended an option, and there are opportunities to provide responses to questions both about strategies to recommend and justifications for strategies recommended. Their application to a range of situations also allows us to apply the same

[6] The antecedent work upon which this methodology is built is a questionnaire we developed to assess students' interpersonal competencies, which we designated and validated as the Risk and Relationship Questionnaire (Schultz, Selman, and LaRusso, 2003). The application and adjustment of this measure to the methodology we describe here and to the measurement of Informed Social Reflection was undertaken in the context of a study supported by the first author and by Facing History and Ourselves to have the impact of its program on students evaluated. This measure, designated as Adolescent Informed Social Choices, is currently undergoing a validation process that looks promising enough to allow us a feeling of comfort in providing an early description of its design in this chapter. The authors of the measure as currently being validated are Robert L. Selman, Luba Falk Feigenberg, Dennis J. Barr, and Andres Molano, as well as the Facing History organization, which has generously provided us with data to which the analytic tool can be applied. Many other practitioners, scholars, and researchers have helped us in the design of this instrument, including but not limited to Angela Bermudez, Melinda Fine, Ethan Lowenstein, Lauren Merkle, and Abbey Mann.

theoretical lenses and empirically based methodology to incidents and situations focused more centrally on civic participation (critical incident 2) and historical understanding (critical incident 3, for example).[7]

Just as Eve Shalen was an inspiration from within the Facing History program's study of ethical choices in interpersonal situations, we can trace the origins of the study of civic choices to another innovative educational practice, the Just Community school programs, a movement begun in the 1980s (Kohlberg, 1985). Whereas Facing History focuses on the teacher in the classroom, in Just Community schools, students, teachers, and school leaders participate in collaborative decision making on issues that concern all aspects of school life, from disciplinary issues to what behavioral norms they want to adopt. In the past, the focus of the Just Community School approach was on its impact on ethical development, framed in the theoretical framework of Kohlberg's stage theory of moral development (Kohlberg, 1985; Higgins, 1991; Power, 1981). More recently, Oser has claimed that Just Community pedagogy also aligns with civic participation. He notes, "Still, what happens in a Just Community meeting does not only concern justice, but also political issues, and politicians often do not use moral justifications for creating a just balance, but rather refer to situations of power use, majority vote or equity application" (Oser, in press).

Oser's evaluation of several schools that programmatically used the Just Communities system (in press) found that despite having to work harder to maintain the system, teachers who participated reported feeling more supported by their colleagues and superiors, and also perceived more trust between teachers and students, as well as among students. But what gains did the students make? A battery such as the one we are developing, empirically grounded in how students think about engaging in these issues, both hypothetically and in their own lives, has potential for application to large-scale studies where developmental and contextual difference between intervention and control groups can signal how students are thinking about civic choices in context. (Appendix A provides an example of the item responses that have been theoretically generated as anchors for the incident focused on racist graffiti found in the auditorium, a particularly civic-oriented incident. These, too, will need to be validated in the field.)

When applied to the evaluation of programs and their impact as well as the assessment of individuals, this measurement strategy allows us to keep one eye on developmental influences and the other on contextual influences.

[7] In the case of Facing History—since the program focuses on the ability students have to make meaning of events in history and their connection to their own lives—assessment tools such as these will need to use materials that connect knowledge about history and knowledge about self and society today. Equally important, they need to be familiar to most students and historically authentic to their teachers.

For instance, in the hypothetical case of the auditorium vandalism presented earlier, it is impossible to know the degree to which any one student's responses is influenced by that student's individual capacities for civic reasoning and the degree to which the student has engaged with civic experiences and participation in schools. Ironically, when applied to cross-school comparisons, or to program evaluations of initiatives such as Facing History or the Just Community Schools, a whole school approach (using random assignment of students to intervention and control by school), we can begin to separate (and ultimately integrate) these different factors. We say ironically because experimental evaluations are designed to hold constant just those contextual factors, for example, teacher variability, student background, school climate, and so on, which otherwise are the greatest concern for programs that are pedagogically progressive and focus on the promotion of personal and shared meaning about self and society.

A MORALITY TALE ABOUT CIVIC AND MORAL EDUCATION

It is important to stress, then, both theoretically and practically speaking, we do not claim, or suggest, that each individual student will or should act as an upstander or in a prosocial-transformative orientation at any given moment, and certainly not all of the time. However, we do want students to be able to imagine the possibility of a full range of choices and to understand a full range of justifications for each of their possible choices, and ultimately, to be able to demonstrate their informed social reflections. If this expanded awareness enables more students to express the kind of perspective Eve shared in her essay, we believe this would be a very positive result. It would indicate an alignment of the student outcome evidence with the program's theory of change, and an alignment of the program's practice with a theory of social development in context.

And if we can begin to understand how certain types of climates and contexts influence students' willingness to engage in imagining a full range of civic and ethical choices, and giving appropriate strategies and justifications, that too is a very positive result. It may be, for example, that they are engaged in a class that is supportive of deliberation and reflection and characterized by respectful relationships, but this set of strategies may not work for them in their next classroom, or in the corridor, or in their walk home from school.

As teachers, researchers, and program designers, of course, we hope that students can be influenced to favor strategies that stand up for victims of discrimination or injustice. Valuing or even seriously considering the idea of becoming involved to support the victim in a situation of social exclusion or injustice might seem like the more moral or sophisticated response. However, the contextual part of this psychological theory asks practitioners and researchers to look beyond the strategy an individual recommends when faced with difficult choices. While it is important to know the justification a student gives for either helping the victim or joining the perpetrators, it also is important to remember that the justifications students offer for actions are embedded both in the individuals' conceptual and communicative competence and in their interpretation of their contexts and communities, including the school or classroom they attend.

Given the tension between an individual's capacity for choosing a more mature interpersonal or ethical or civic strategy and the power of the environment within which an individual operates to influence her choices, in the school context, the program should target—and the measure should assess—progress toward informed *and* reflective civic engagement. The *quality* of students' civic engagement can be defined as the convergence of a student's level of social reflective capacity (as informed by the domains we argue are primary, as in Figure 24.1, and the methods we describe to assess them in Figure 24.4), and by their perceived range of available social strategies and justifications (as organized in Table 24.1 and Figure 24.2). This is not synonymous with simply monitoring students' orientation toward upstanding. Informed and reflective civic or ethical engagement involves actions, including upstanding, that are done within the context of purposeful reflection on how this upstanding is placed within past and future orientations. We all have an individual past (biography) and a cultural past (history), and social science has clearly demonstrated how each of these pasts influences our current and future actions. We ought to teach our students and ourselves how this happens.

A program that can demonstrate that it informs civic participation in this way is worthwhile. If our measures can capture that impact, then we have successfully brought together the theory of development in context behind the assessment model and the theory of change behind the practice.

Some Final Words: The Art and Science of Being a Citizen

> Man will become better when you show him what he is like.
>
> Anton Chekov

Would Hobbes find our faith in adolescents' capacity for informed social reflection foolhardy? In spite of the serious atrocities that can be perpetrated among members of our species, it is the human network that gives youth its greatest opportunity to embark on a developmental trajectory that leads to becoming healthy adults who will contribute to the community. Schools are a natural place to nurture this kind of growth, populated by peers who share experiences and by adults who direct their learning; but schools are not supportive without active attempts to create that kind of environment.

Schools that "deliberately emphasize not only the importance of learning, but also the other qualities that are essential to our society" such as "fairness, concern for others, and responsibility" encourage students to make a connection between these goals and how they can become integrated into their daily lives (Schaps, 2007, p. 75).

Giving students the responsibility for participation in creating the norms and values of the community or school provides both bonding to the group and a sense of psychological agency. Consider again the hypothetical school incidents presented earlier in this chapter: How students choose to approach threats to fellow students and to the bonds of their school community reveals how they perceive their roles beyond the school, both in their adolescent present, and in their adult future. Taking youth civic engagement seriously, however, is far from an initiative that ends with graduation: It is "as important to maintaining democracy as are wars in non-democratic countries such as Iraq, as is working through the United Nations to promote democracy worldwide, and as are other macro-political venues that countries such as the U.S. pursue to ensure our democracy" (Sherrod, 2005, p. 380). Becoming a valued member within the school community is a crucial step toward growing into a strong thread in the vibrant tapestry that extends far beyond the boundaries of the school, city, state, and country.

We prescribe the promotion of *informed social reflection* as an antidote to making decisions without meditating on how we arrive—or arrived—at them. Eve Shalen's meditations on her actions are powerful because she is able to access the different levels of justifications to be able to express or communicate her regret for her actions as well as her awareness of what led her to them. Is Eve as unusual as we suggest? Fortunately, probably not! But, we need hard evidence to supplement anecdotes and single case studies suggesting that in schools and classroom climates (such as those that value trust and self-exploration) led by committed, skilled, and reflective educators, many students can achieve this way of looking at their social world (Bermudez, McKeown, Barr, & Selman, 2003). We are dynamic creatures and our choices can be refined through the process of reflecting on what we want our future actions to be. Although we may not be able to do what is right at all times, our efforts to approach it are noble and worthy of the species. We owe it to each other to think about ourselves, in the past, in the moment, and beyond.

REFERENCES

Adelson, J. (1971). The political imagination of the young adolescent. *Daedalus, 100(4)*, 1013–1050.

Barr, D. J. (2005). Early adolescents' reflection on social justice: Facing History and Ourselves in practice and assessment. *Intercultural Education, 16(2)*, 145–160.

Barton, K. C., & Levstik, L. S. (2004). *Teaching history for the common good*. Mahwah, NJ: Lawrence Erlbaum.

Bermudez, A., McKeown, C., Barr, D., & Selman, R. L., (2003). Caught in the middle: Ethnographic document of eighth grade classroom discussion of identity, gender and society. *The promotion of social awareness in students and a sense of community in classrooms.* Retrieved from http://my.gse.harvard.edu/course/gse-h370/2009/fall

Boyatzis, R. E. (1998). *Transforming qualitative information: Thematic analysis and code development.* Thousand Oaks, CA: Sage Publications.

Brooks, D. (2007, February 18). Human nature redux. *The New York Times.* Retrieved September 11, 2009, from http://select.nytimes.com/2007/02/18/opinion/18brooks.html

Carretero, M., & Voss, J. V. (Eds.). (1994). *Cognitive and instructional processes in history and the social sciences.* Hillsdale, NJ: Lawrence Erlbaum Associates.

Christiansen, E. J., & Evans, W. P. (2005). Adolescent victimization: Testing models of resiliency by gender. *The Journal of Early Adolescence, 25(3),* 298–316.

Coll, C T.G., & Vasquez Garcia, H. A. (1995). Developmental processes and their influence on interethnic and interracial relations. In W. Hawley & A. Jackson (Eds.), *Toward a common destiny: Improving race and ethnic relations in America* (pp. 103–130). San Francisco, CA: Jossey-Bass.

Facing History and Ourselves. (1994). *Facing History and Ourselves resource book: Holocaust and human behavior.* Brookline, MA: Facing History and Ourselves National Foundation, Inc.

Facing History and Ourselves. (2010). *The Facing History National Professional Development and Evaluation Project: Continuing a Tradition of Research on the Foundations of Democratic Education.* Brookline, MA: Facing History and Ourselves National Foundation, Inc.

Faust, D. (2009). The university's crisis of purpose. *The New York Times.* Retrieved November 15, 2009, from http://www.nytimes.com/2009/09/06/books/review/Faust-t.html?_r=1&pagewanted=2&ref=review

Feigenberg, L. F. (2007). Context matters: The influence of school climate on early adolescents' behavior and social development. *Dissertation Abstract International, 68B(6).* Retrieved September 27, 2009, from ProQuest Dissertations & Theses. (AAT 3271680)

Feigenberg, L. F., Steel King, M., Barr, D. J., & Selman, R. L. (2008). Belonging to and exclusion from the peer group in schools: Influences on adolescents' moral choices. *Journal of Moral Education, 37(2),* 165–184.

Fine, M. (2006). Facing history and civic learning. In Facing History and Ourselves National Foundation (Ed.), *Pedagogy Brief.*

Fischer, K. W., & Biddell, T. R. (2006). Dynamic development of action and thought. In R. M. Lerner (Ed.), *Handbook of child psychology, Vol. 1: Theoretical models of human development* (6th ed., pp. 313–399). Hoboken, NJ: John Wiley & Sons, Inc.

Flanagan, C., & Tucker, C. (1999). Adolescents' explanations for political issues: Concordance with their views of self and society. *Developmental Psychology, 35(5),* 1198–1209.

Fong, V. (2004). *Only hope: Coming of age under China's one-child policy*. Stanford, CA: Stanford University Press.

Fowler, J. W. (1981). *Stages of faith: The psychology of human development and the quest for meaning*. San Francisco, CA: Harper & Row.

Fuxman, S. (2007). *Collective narratives and political understandings in intractable conflicts: A prelude to peace education in the Israeli/Palestinian context* (Unpublished doctoral qualifying paper). Harvard Graduate School of Education, Cambridge, MA.

Haidt, J. (2001). The emotional dog and its rational tail: A social intuitionist approach to moral judgement. *Psychological Review, 108*, 814–834.

Hartmann, U., & Hasselhorn, M. (2008). Historical perspective taking: A standardized measure for an aspect of students' historical thinking. *Learning and Individual Differences, 18*, 264–270.

Haste, H. (2005). Moral responsibility and citizenship education. In D. Wallace (Ed.), *Education, arts, and morality: Creative journeys* (pp. 143–168). New York: Kluwer Academic/Plenum Publishers.

Hauser, M. D. (2006). *Moral minds: How nature designed our universal sense of right and wrong*. New York: Harper Collins.

Higgins, A. (1991). The Just Community approach to moral education: Evolution of the idea and recent findings. In W. M. Kurtines & J. L. Gewirtz (Eds.), *Handbook of moral behavior and development, Vol. 3: Application* (pp. 11–141). Hillsdale, NJ: Lawrence Erlbaum Associates.

Hobbes, T. (1994). *Leviathan: With selected variants from the Latin edition of 1668* (Edwin Curley, Ed.). Indianapolis: Hackett Publishing Company.

Jones, S. M., Brown, J. L., & Aber, J. L. (under review). The longitudinal impact of a universal school-based social-emotional and literacy intervention: An experiment in translational developmental research.

Kahne, J., & Westheimer, J. (2006). The limits of political efficacy: Educating citizens for a democratic society. *Political Science and Politics, 39(2)*, 289–296.

Killen, M., McGlothlin, H., & Lee-Kim, J. (2002) Between individuals and culture: Individuals' evaluations of exclusion from social groups. In H. Keller, Y. H. Poortinga, & A. Scholmerich (Eds.), *Between biology and culture* (pp. 159–190). Cambridge, England: Cambridge University Press.

Kohlberg, L. (1979). *The meaning and measurement of moral development* (Heinz Werner Lecture Series, Vol. 13). Worcester, MA: Clark University Press.

Kohlberg, L. (1985). The Just Community approach to moral education in theory and practice. In M. W. Berkowitz & F. Oser (Eds.), *Moral education: Theory and application* (pp. 27–87). Hillsdale, NJ: Lawrence Erlbaum Associates.

Kohlberg, L., & Mayer, R. (1972). Development as the aim of education. *Harvard Educational Review, 42*, 449–496.

Kuhn, D., & Franklin, S. (2008). The second decade: What develops (and how)? In W. Damon & R. M. Lerner (Eds.), *Child and adolescent development: An advanced course.* Hoboken, NJ: John Wiley & Sons, Inc.

LaRusso, M. D., & Selman, R. L. (2003). The influence of school atmosphere and development on adolescents' perceptions of risks and prevention: Cynicism versus skepticism. In D. Romer (Ed.), *Reducing adolescent risk* (pp. 113–122). San Francisco, CA: Sage Publications.

Lee, P., & Shemilt, D. (2007). New alchemy or fatal attraction? History and citizenship. *Teaching History, 129*, 14–19.

Lightfoot, C. (2008). The refractoriness of history. *Human Development, 51(5–6)*, 326–331.

Lind, G. (2006). The moral judgment test: Comments on Villegas de Posada's critique. *Psychological Reports, 98(2)*, 580–584.

Loevinger, J. (1966). The meaning and measurement of ego development. *American Psychologist, 21(3)*, 195–206.

Loevinger, J. (1978). *Scientific ways in the study of ego development* (Heinz Werner Lecture Series, Vol. 12). Worcester, MA: Clark University Press.

Lowenstein, E. A. (2003). Teachers transformed? Exploring the influence of "Facing History and Ourselves" on teachers' beliefs about citizenship and civics education. *Dissertation Abstract International, 63A(11)*. Retrieved September 27, 2009, from ProQuest Dissertations & Theses. (AAT 3071162)

Lowenstein, E. (in press). Navigating teaching tensions in civic learning. *Learning and Teaching: The International Journal of Higher Education in the Social Sciences.*

Martin, J., Sokol, B., & Elfers, T. (2008). Taking and coordinating perspectives: From prereflective interactivity, through reflective intersubjectivity, to metareflective sociality. *Human Development, 51*, 294–324.

Mitter, R. (2008). *Modern China: A very short introduction.* New York: Oxford University Press.

Oser, F. (in press). The Just Community approach to political thinking: Towards a new model of civic education in schools. In M. Martens, U.Hartmann, M. Sauer, & M. Hasselhorn (Eds.), *Interpersonal understanding in historical context* (pp. 1–18). Rotterdam: Sense Publishers.

Oser, F., Scarlett, G., & Bucher, A. (2006, March). Religious and spiritual development throughout the life span. In W. Damon & R. M. Lerner (Eds.), *Handbook of Child Psychology* (6th ed., Vol. 1, pp. 942–998). Hoboken, NJ: John Wiley & Sons, Inc.

Parker, W. C. (2003). *Teaching democracy: Unity and diversity in public life.* New York: Teachers College Press.

Power, F. C. (1981). Moral education through the development of the moral atmosphere of the school. *The Journal of Educational Thought, 15(1)*, 4–19.

Power, F. C., Higgins, A., & Kohlberg, L. (1989). *Lawrence Kohlberg's approach to moral education.* New York: Columbia University Press.

Rawls, J. (1971). *A theory of justice.* Cambridge, MA: Belknap Press of Harvard University Press.

Rest, J. R. (1986). Moral research methodology. In S. Modgil & C. Modgil (Eds.), *Lawrence Kohlberg: Consensus and controversy* (pp. 455–470.) Philadelphia: Falmer Press.

Salomon, G. (2004a). A narrative-based view of coexistence education. *Journal of Social Issues, 60(2)*, 273–287.

Salomon, G. (2004b). Does peace education make a difference in the context of an intractable conflict? *Peace and Conflict: Journal of Peace Psychology, 10(3)*, 257–274.

Sandel, M. (1998). *Liberalism and the limits of justice* (2nd ed.). New York: Cambridge University Press.

Schaps, E. (2007). Community in school: The heart of the matter. In P. D. Houston, A. M. Blankstein, & R. W. Cole (Eds.), *Spirituality in educational leadership* (pp. 73–87). Thousand Oaks, CA: Corwin Press.

Schaps, E., Battistich, V., & Solomon, D. (2004). Community in school as key to student growth: Findings from the child development project. In J. E. Zins, R. P. Weissberg, M. C. Wang, & H. J. Walberg (Eds.), *Building academic success on social and emotional learning: What does the research say?* New York: Teachers College Press.

Schultz, L. H., Barr, D. J., & Selman, R. L. (2001). The value of a developmental approach to evaluating character development programmes: An outcome study of Facing History and Ourselves. *Journal of Moral Education, 30(1)*, 3–27.

Seixas, P. (1996). Conceptualizing the growth of historical understanding. In D. Olson & N. Torrance (Eds.), *Handbook of education and human development: New models of learning, teaching, and schooling* (pp. 765–783). Oxford, UK: Blackwell Publishing.

Seixas, P. (2004). *Theorizing historical consciousness.* Toronto: University of Toronto Press.

Selman, R. L. (2003). *The promotion of social awareness: Powerful lessons from the partnership of developmental theory and classroom practice.* New York: Russell Sage Foundation.

Selman, R. L., & Adalbjarnardottir, S. (2000). A developmental method to analyze the personal meaning adolescents make of risk and relationship: The case of "drinking." *Applied Developmental Science, 4(1)*, 47–65.

Selman, R. L., & Barr, D. (in press). Can the history of human rights help adolescents develop greater interpersonal understanding? In M. Martens, U. Hartmann, M. Sauer, & M. Hasselhorn (Eds.), *Interpersonal understanding in historical context* (pp. 19–42). Rotterdam: Sense Publishers.

Selman, R. L., & Dray, A. J. (2006). Risk and prevention. In K. A. Renninger & I. E. Sigel (Eds.), *Handbook of child psychology, Vol. 4: Child psychology in practice* (6th ed., pp. 378–419). Hoboken, NJ: John Wiley & Sons, Inc.

Selman, R. L., & Feigenberg, L. F. (2010). Between neurons and neighborhoods: Innovative methods to assess the development and depth of adolescent social awareness. In P. D. Zelazo, M. Chandler, & E. Crone (Eds.), *Developmental social cognitive neuroscience* (pp. 227–250). New York: Taylor & Francis Group, LLC.

Serpell, R. (2002). The embeddedness of human development within sociocultural context. *Social Development, 11(2)*, 290–295.

Sherrod, L. (2005). Ensuring liberty by promoting youth development. *Human Development, 48*, 376–381.

Solomon, D., Watson, M. S., & Battistich, V. (2001). Teaching and schooling effects on moral/pro-social development. In V. Richardson (Ed.), *Handbook of research on teaching* (4th ed., pp. 566–603). Washington, DC: American Educational Research Association.

Steel King, M. (2007). Ethnic variation in interpersonal styles: Investigation developmental and cultural themes in African American, White, and Latino students' social competence. *Dissertation Abstract International, 68B(6)*. Retrieved September 27, 2009, from ProQuest Dissertations & Theses. (AAT 3271689)

Strom, M. (1980). Facing history and ourselves: Holocaust and human behavior. In R. L. Mosher (Ed.), *Moral education: A first generation of research and development* (pp. 216–233). New York: Praeger.

Strom, M., Sleeper, M., & Johnson, M. (1992). Facing history and ourselves: A synthesis of history and ethics in effective history education. In A. Garrod (Ed.), *Learning for life: Moral education theory and practice*. Westport, CT: Praeger.

Torney-Purta, J. (2009). International psychological research that matters for policy and practice. *American Psychologist, 64(8)*, 822–837.

Torney-Purta, J., Lehmann, R., Oswald, H., & Schulz, W. (2001). *Citizenship and education in twenty-eight countries: Civic knowledge and engagement at age fourteen.* Amsterdam: IEA. Retrieved from http://www.terpconnect.umd.edu/~iea

Turiel, E. (2010). The role of moral epistemology and psychology for neuroscience. In P. D. Zelazo, M. Chandler, & E. Crone (Eds.), *Developmental social cognitive neuroscience* (pp. 313–331). USA: Taylor & Francis Group, LLC.

Werner, H. (1948). *Comparative psychology of mental development* (2nd ed.). Chicago: Follet.

Yoshikawa, H., & Shinn, M. (2008). Improving youth-serving social settings: Intervention goals and strategies for schools, youth programs, and communities. In M. Shinn & H. Yoshikawa (Eds.), *Toward positive youth development: Transforming schools and community programs* (pp. 350–363). New York: Oxford University Press.

Zelazo, P. D., Chandler, M., & Crone, E. (Eds.). (2010). *Developmental social cognitive neuroscience.* New York: Taylor & Francis Group, LLC.

Zhao, X. (2007). *Friendship in cultural context: A qualitative study of how urban Chinese adolescents and their parents understand the meaning of friendship.* Unpublished manuscript, Harvard University, Cambridge, MA.

APPENDIX A

ASSESSING INFORMED SOCIAL REFLECTION: A CIVIC-ORIENTED SCENARIO

Some students have written racist slurs on one of the walls of the auditorium. The principal responds by banning the use of the auditorium for after-school activities.

1. Members of the student government suggest having a student-only meeting at lunch to talk about what to do. Please rate each reason on a scale from "Would not recommend at all" to "Strongly recommend" as a good reason. You can give responses to the same rating if you wish. Then select the one you would recommend to the student government, and give a brief reason why.

Reasons	Would Not Recommend At All	Do Not Recommend	Recommend	Strongly Recommend
a. It will help students understand that racist attitudes affect everyone. *(Prosocial future oriented)*	☐	☐	☐	☐
b. They need to make the school safer. *(Safety oriented)*	☐	☐	☐	☐
c. It will show support for the group who was disrespected by the slur. *(Relational orientation)*	☐	☐	☐	☐
d. They think it is unfair to punish everyone for the actions of a couple of students. *(Rules oriented)*	☐	☐	☐	☐

2. Which one of these reasons do you think is best? (Check only one):

   a ☐ b ☐ c ☐ d ☐

3. Why do you think this is the best reason?

4. How common is it in your school for students to try and solve problems like this together? **(Check only one)**

   Very rare ☐ Rare ☐ Common ☐ Very common ☐

5. If this were your school, how good is each of the following actions that students might take?

Actions: Check one for each row (You may check the same rating more than once)	Very Bad	Bad	Good	Very Good
a. Tell the principal that the students themselves will take matters into their own hands and deal with whoever did it. *(Perpetuation/Perpetration)*	☐	☐	☐	☐
b. Organize a meeting to discuss racism in the school. *(Upstanding)*	☐	☐	☐	☐
c. Just let the principal deal with it. *(Bystanding)*	☐	☐	☐	☐

6. If this were your school, which one of these three actions would you recommend students should take?

   a ☐ b ☐ c ☐ d ☐

Please explain why:

___

Author Index

Subject Index